Children's
Literature
Review

Guide to Gale Literary Criticism Series

When you need to review criticism of literary works, these are the Gale series to use:

If the author's death date is:

You should turn to:

After Dec. 31, 1959
(or author is still living)

CONTEMPORARY LITERARY CRITICISM

for example: Jorge Luis Borges, Anthony Burgess,
William Faulkner, Mary Gordon,
Ernest Hemingway, Iris Murdoch

1900 through 1959

TWENTIETH-CENTURY LITERARY CRITICISM

for example: Willa Cather, F. Scott Fitzgerald,
Henry James, Mark Twain, Virginia Woolf

1800 through 1899

NINETEENTH-CENTURY LITERATURE CRITICISM

for example: Fedor Dostoevski, Nathaniel Hawthorne,
George Sand, William Wordsworth

1400 through 1799

LITERATURE CRITICISM FROM 1400 TO 1800
(excluding Shakespeare)

for example: Anne Bradstreet, Daniel Defoe,
Alexander Pope, François Rabelais,
Jonathan Swift, Phillis Wheatley

SHAKESPEAREAN CRITICISM

Shakespeare's plays and poetry

Antiquity through 1399

CLASSICAL AND MEDIEVAL LITERATURE CRITICISM

for example: Dante, Homer, Plato, Sophocles, Vergil,
the Beowulf Poet

Gale also publishes related criticism series:

CHILDREN'S LITERATURE REVIEW

This series covers authors of all eras who have written for
the preschool through high school audience.

SHORT STORY CRITICISM

This series covers the major short fiction writers of all nationalities
and periods of literary history.

ISSN 0362-4145

volume 23

Children's Literature Review

Excerpts from Reviews,
Criticism, and Commentary
on Books for Children
and Young People

Gerard J. Senick
Editor

Sharon R. Gunton
Associate Editor

 Gale Research Inc. • *DETROIT* • *LONDON*

STAFF

Gerard J. Senick, *Editor*

Sharon R. Gunton, *Associate Editor*

Jeanne A. Gough, *Permissions & Production Manager*
Linda M. Pugliese, *Production Supervisor*
Maureen A. Puhl, Jennifer VanSickle, *Editorial Associates*
Donna Craft, Paul Lewon, Lorna Mabunda, Camille Robinson, *Editorial Assistants*

Victoria B. Cariappa, *Research Manager*
H. Nelson Fields, Judy L. Gale, Maureen Richards, *Editorial Associates*
Jennifer Brostrom, Paula Cutcher, Alan Hedblad, Robin Lupa, Mary Beth McElmeel, *Editorial Assistants*

Sandra C. Davis, *Permissions Supervisor (Text)*
Josephine M. Keene, Kimberly F. Smilay, *Permissions Associates*
Maria Franklin, Michele M. Lonoconus, Shalice Shah, Nancy Sheridan,
Denise M. Singleton, Rebecca A. Stanko, *Permissions Assistants*

Patricia A. Seefelt, *Permissions Supervisor (Pictures)*
Margaret A. Chamberlain, *Permissions Associate*
Pamela A. Hayes, Keith Reed, *Permissions Assistants*

Mary Beth Trimper, *Production Manager*
Evi Seoud, *Assistant Production Manager*

Arthur Chartow, *Art Director*
C. J. Jonik, *Keyliner*

Laura Bryant, *Production Supervisor*
Louise Gagné, *Internal Production Associate*
Yolanda Y. Latham, *Internal Production Assistant*

The paper used in this publication meets the minimum requirements of American National Standard for Information Sciences—Permanence Paper for Printed Library Materials, ANSI Z39.48-1984. ∞™

Contents

Preface

As children's literature has evolved into both a respected branch of creative writing and a successful industry, literary criticism has documented and influenced each stage of its growth. Critics have recorded the literary development of individual authors as well as the trends and controversies that resulted from changes in values and attitudes, especially as they concerned children. While defining a philosophy of children's literature, critics developed a scholarship that balances an appreciation of children and an awareness of their needs with standards for literary quality much like those required by critics of adult literature. *Children's Literature Review (CLR)* is designed to provide a permanent, accessible record of this ongoing scholarship. Those responsible for bringing children and books together can now make informed choices when selecting reading materials for the young.

Scope of the Series

Each volume of *CLR* contains excerpts from published criticism on the works of authors and illustrators who create books for children from preschool through high school. The author list for each volume is international in scope and represents the variety of genres covered by children's literature—picture books, fiction, nonfiction, poetry, folklore, and drama. The works of approximately twenty authors of all eras are represented in each volume. Although earlier volumes of *CLR* emphasized critical material published after 1960, successive volumes have expanded their coverage to encompass criticism written before 1960. Since many of the authors included in *CLR* are living and continue to write, it is necessary to update their entries periodically. Thus, future volumes will supplement the entries of selected authors covered in earlier volumes as well as include criticism on the works of authors new to the series.

Organization of the Book

An author section consists of the following elements: author heading, author portrait, author introduction, excerpts of criticism (each followed by a bibliographical citation), and illustrations, when available.

- The **author heading** consists of the author's name followed by birth and death dates. The portion of the name outside the parentheses denotes the form under which the author is most frequently published. If the majority of the author's works for children were written under a pseudonym, the pseudonym will be listed in the author heading and the real name given on the first line of the author introduction. Also located at the beginning of the introduction are any other pseudonyms used by the author in writing for children and any name variations, including transliterated forms for authors whose languages use nonroman alphabets. Uncertainty as to a birth or death date is indicated by question marks.

- An **author portrait** is included when available.

- The **author introduction** contains information designed to introduce an author to *CLR* users by presenting an overview of the author's themes and styles, occasional biographical facts that relate to the author's literary career or critical responses to the author's works, and information about major awards and prizes the author has received. Where applicable, introductions conclude with references to additional entries in biographical and critical reference series published by Gale Research Inc. These sources include past volumes of *CLR* as well as *Authors & Artists for Young Adults, Contemporary Authors, Contemporary Literary Criticism, Dictionary of Literary Biography, Nineteenth-Century Literature Criticism, Short Story Criticism, Something about the Author, Something about the Author Autobiography Series, Twentieth-Century Literary Criticism,* and *Yesterday's Authors of Books for Children.*

- **Criticism** is located in three sections: **author's commentary** and **general commentary** (when available) and within individual **title entries,** which are preceded by **title entry headings.** Criticism is arranged chronologically within each section. Titles by authors being profiled are highlighted in boldface type within the text for easier access by readers.

The **author's commentary** presents background material written by the author or by an interviewer. This commentary may cover a specific work or several works. Author's commentary on more than one work appears after the author introduction, while commentary on an individual book follows the title entry heading.

The **general commentary** consists of critical excerpts that consider more than one work by the author or illustrator being profiled. General commentary is preceded by the critic's name in boldface type or, in the case of unsigned criticism, by the title of the journal. Occasionally, *CLR* features entries that emphasize general criticism on the overall career of an author or illustrator. When appropriate, a selection of reviews is included to supplement the general commentary.

Title entry headings precede the criticism on a title and cite publication information on the work being reviewed. Title headings list the title of the work as it appeared in its first English-language edition. The first English-language publication date of each work is listed in parentheses following the title. Differing U.S. and British titles follow the publication date within the parentheses.

Title entries consist of critical excerpts on the author's individual works, arranged chronologically by publication date. The entries generally contain two to six reviews per title, depending on the stature of the book and the amount of criticism it has generated. The editors select titles that reflect the entire scope of the author's literary contribution, covering each genre and subject. An effort is made to reprint criticism that represents the full range of each title's reception—from the year of its initial publication to current assessments. Thus, the reader is provided with a record of the author's critical history. Publication information (such as publisher names and book prices) and parenthetical numerical references (such as footnotes or page and line references to specific editions of works) have been deleted at the editor's discretion to provide smoother reading of the text.

Entries on authors who are also illustrators will occasionally feature commentary on selected works illustrated but not written by the author being profiled. These works are strongly associated with the illustrator and have received critical acclaim for their art. By including critical comment on works of this type, the editors wish to provide a more complete representation of the author's total career. Criticism on these works has been chosen to stress artistic, rather than literary, contributions. Title entry headings for works illustrated by the author being profiled are arranged chronologically within the entry by date of publication and include notes identifying the author of the illustrated work. In order to provide easier access for users, all titles illustrated by the subject of the entry will be boldfaced.

CLR also includes entries on prominent illustrators who have contributed to the field of children's literature. These entries are designed to represent the development of the illustrator as an artist rather than as a literary stylist. The illustrator's section is organized like that of an author, with two exceptions: the introduction presents an overview of the illustrator's styles and techniques rather than outlining his or her literary background, and the commentary written by the illustrator on his or her works is called illustrator's commentary rather than author's commentary. Title entry headings are followed by explanatory notes identifying the author of the illustrated work. All titles of books containing illustrations by the artist being profiled as well as individual illustrations from these books are highlighted in boldface type.

• Selected excerpts are preceded by **explanatory notes,** which provide information on the critic or work of criticism to enhance the reader's understanding of the excerpt.

• A complete **bibliographical citation** designed to facilitate the location of the original book or article follows each piece of criticism.

• Numerous **illustrations** are featured in *CLR*. For entries on illustrators, an effort has been made to include illustrations that reflect the characteristics discussed in the criticism. Entries on major authors who do not illustrate their own works may also include photographs and other illustrative material pertinent to the authors' careers.

Other Features

• An **acknowledgments,** which immediately follows the preface, lists the sources from which material has been reprinted in the volume. It does not, however, list every book or periodical consulted for the volume.

• The **cumulative index to authors** lists authors who have appeared in *CLR* and includes cross-references to *Authors & Artists for Young Adults, Contemporary Authors, Contemporary Literary Criticism, Dictionary of Literary Biography, Nineteenth-Century Literature Criticism, Short Story Criticism, Something about the Author, Something about the Author Autobiography Series, Twentieth-Century Literary Criticism,* and *Yesterday's Authors of Books for Children.*

- The **cumulative nationality index** lists authors alphabetically under their respective nationalities. Author names are followed by the volume number(s) in which they appear. Authors who have changed citizenship or whose current citizenship is not reflected in biographical sources appear under both their original nationality and that of their current residence.

- The **cumulative title index** lists titles covered in *CLR* followed by the volume and page number where criticism begins.

New Features

Beginning with Volume 23, the CLR series will include two new features, a major works section and a section heading to introduce criticism on individual titles.

- Author introductions now list a group of **representative titles** for which the author or illustrator being profiled is best known. This section, which begins with the words "major works include," follows the genre line of the author introduction.

- Just as *CLR* includes section headings for author's commentary and general commentary, a heading for **title commentary** now appears before the first title entry.

A Note to the Reader

When writing papers, students who quote directly from any volume in the Literature Criticism Series may use the following general forms to footnote reprinted criticism. The first example pertains to material drawn from periodicals, the second to material reprinted from books.

[1]T. S. Eliot, "John Donne," *The Nation and the Athenaeum,* 33 (9 June 1923), 321-32; excerpted and reprinted in *Literature Criticism from 1400 to 1800,* Vol. 10, ed. James E. Person, Jr. (Detroit: Gale Research, 1989), pp. 28-9.

[1]Henry Brooke, *Leslie Brooke and Johnny Crow* (Frederick Warne, 1982); excerpted and reprinted in *Children's Literature Review,* Vol. 20, ed. Gerard J. Senick (Detroit: Gale Research, 1990), p. 47.

Suggestions Are Welcome

In response to various suggestions, several features have been added to *CLR* since the series began, including author entries on retellers of traditional literature as well as those who have been the first to record oral tales and other folklore; entries on prominent illustrators featuring commentary on their styles and techniques; entries on authors whose works are considered controversial or have been challenged; occasional entries devoted to criticism on a single work by a major author; explanatory notes that provide information on the critic or work of criticism to enhance the usefulness of the excerpt; more extensive illustrative material, such as holographs of manuscript pages and photographs of people and places pertinent to the authors' careers; a cumulative nationality index for easy access to authors by nationality; and occasional guest essays written specifically for *CLR* by prominent critics on subjects of their choice.

Readers who wish to suggest authors to appear in future volumes, or who have other suggestions, are cordially invited to write the editor.

Acknowledgments

The editors wish to thank the copyright holders of the excerpted criticism included in this volume, the permissions managers of many book and magazine publishing companies for assisting us in securing reprint rights, and Anthony Bogucki for assistance with copyright research. We are also grateful to the staffs of the Detroit Public Library, the Library of Congress, the University of Detroit Library, Wayne State University Purdy/Kresge Library Complex, and the University of Michigan Libraries for making their resources available to us. Following is a list of the copyright holders who have granted us permission to reprint material in this volume of *CLR*. Every effort has been made to trace copyright, but if omissions have been made, please let us know.

THE EXCERPTS IN *CLR*, VOLUME 23, WERE REPRINTED FROM THE FOLLOWING PERIODICALS:

Adolescence, v. XXII, Fall, 1987. Reprinted by permission of the publisher.—*The ALAN Review*, v. 9, Spring, 1982; v. 11, Fall, 1983; v. 13, Fall, 1985. All reprinted by permission of the publisher.—*America*, v. 115, November 5, 1966. All rights reserved. Reprinted with permission of America Press, Inc., 106 West 56th Street, New York, NY 10019.—*Appraisal: Children's Science Books*, v. 5, Winter, 1972; v. 8, Fall, 1975; v. 12, Spring, 1979. Copyright © 1972, 1975, 1979 by the Children's Science Book Review Committee. All reprinted by permission of the publisher.—*Appraisal: Science Books for Young People*, v. 17, Fall, 1984; v. 18, Spring, 1985; v. 19, Spring, 1986; v. 20, Spring, 1987; v. 20, Summer, 1987; v. 20, Winter, 1987; v. 21, Fall, 1988. Copyright © 1984, 1985, 1986, 1987, 1988 by the Children's Science Book Review Committee. All reprinted by permission of the publisher.—*Best Sellers*, v. 33, November 15, 1973; v. 41, May, 1981. Copyright 1973, 1981 by the University of Scranton. Both reprinted by permission of the publisher./ v. 35, July, 1975. Copyright © 1975 Helen Dwight Reid Educational Foundation. Reprinted by permission of the publisher.—*Bookbird*, v. XII, September 15, 1974; v. XIII, June 15, 1976; v. XIV, December 15, 1976; n. 1, March 15, 1980. All reprinted by permission of the publisher.—*Booklist*, v. 74, October 15, 1977; v. 75, September 1, 1978; v. 75, October 1, 1978; v. 75, October 15, 1978; v. 75, November 15, 1978; v. 77, May 1, 1981; v. 78, December 1, 1981; v. 78, June 1, 1982; v. 78, August, 1982; v. 79, March 15, 1983; v. 80, October 1, 1983; v. 80, June 1, 1984; v. 81, September 1, 1984; v. 81, February 15, 1985; v. 82, September 15, 1985; v. 82, October 15, 1985; v. 82, November 1, 1985; v. 82, March 1, 1986; v. 82, April 1, 1986; v. 83, September 1, 1986; v. 83, December 1, 1986; v. 83, January 1, 1987; v. 83, June 1, 1987; v. 84, September 1, 1987; v. 84, November 1, 1987; v. 84, December 1, 1987; v. 84, December 15, 1987; v. 84, February 15, 1988; v. 85, November 1, 1988; v. 85, August, 1989; v. 86, September 15, 1989; v. 86, December 1, 1989; v. 86, May 1, 1990. Copyright © 1977, 1978, 1981, 1982, 1983, 1984, 1985, 1986, 1987, 1988, 1989, 1990 by the American Library Association. All reprinted by permission of the publisher.—*The Booklist*, v. 71, December 15, 1974; v. 72, September 1, 1975. Copyright © 1974, 1975 by the American Library Association. Both reprinted by permission of the publisher.—*Book Week—New York Herald Tribune*, October 17, 1965; October 31, 1965. © 1965, *The Washington Post*. Both reprinted by permission of the publisher.—*Book Week—The Washington Post*, October 30, 1966; June 18, 1967. © 1966, 1967, *The Washington Post*. Both reprinted by permission of the publisher.—*Book Window*, v. 5, Spring, 1978 for a review of "Power of Three" by E.A.A.; v. 6, Winter, 1978 for a review of "Leopard" by J. McC. © 1978 S.C.B.A. and the respective contributors. Both reprinted by permission of the publisher.—*Book World—The Washington Post*, July 10, 1979; May 9, 1982; April 19, 1983; May 13, 1984; May 10, 1987; July 12, 1987; August 9, 1987. © 1979, 1982, 1983, 1984, 1987, *The Washington Post*. All reprinted by permission of the publisher.—*Books for Keeps*, n. 43, March, 1987; n. 58, September, 1989. © School Bookshop Association 1987, 1989. Both reprinted by permission of the publisher.—*Books for Your Children*, v. 3, Summer, 1968; v. 16, Summer, 1981; v. 16, Autumn/Winter, 1981. © *Books for Your Children* 1968, 1981. All reprinted by permission of the publisher.—*British Book News Children's Books*, Winter, 1987. © The British Council, 1987. Reprinted by permission of the publisher.—*Bulletin of the Center for Children's Books*, v. 27, September, 1973; v. 27, March, 1974; v. 28, November, 1974; v. 29, December, 1975; v. 29, February, 1976; v. 30, December, 1976; v. 30, March, 1977; v. 31, November, 1977; v. 31, February, 1978; v. 32, March, 1979; v. 33, April, 1980; v. 34, November, 1980; v. 34, April, 1981; v. 34, July-August, 1981; v. 35, February, 1982; v. 35, April, 1982; v. 36, September, 1982; v. 36, April, 1983; v. 37, February, 1984; v. 38, September, 1984; v. 39, December, 1985; v. 39, May, 1986; v. 40, October, 1986; v. 40, February, 1987; v. 40, March, 1987; v. 40, May, 1987; v. 40, June, 1987; v. 42, October, 1988; v. 42, November, 1988; v. 42, January, 1989; v. 42, February, 1989; v. 42, April, 1989; v. 43, November, 1989; v. 43, December, 1989. Copyright © 1973, 1974, 1975, 1976, 1977, 1978, 1979, 1980, 1981, 1982, 1983, 1984, 1985, 1986, 1987, 1988, 1989 by The University of Chicago. All reprinted by permission of The University of Chicago Press.—*The Canadian Forum*, v. LI, June, 1971.—*Canadian Geographical Journal*, v. LXXXIII, August, 1971. Reprinted by permission of the publisher.—*Catholic Library World*, v. 50, May-June, 1979. Reprinted by permission of the publisher.—*Chicago Tribune*, December 27, 1953 for "Science of Flight" by John Lewellen. Copyrighted 1953, renewed 1981, Chicago Tribune Company. All rights reserved. Reprinted by permission of the Literary Estate of John Lewellen./ June 17, 1956 for a review of "The House of Four Seasons" by Polly Goodwin. © copyrighted 1956, renewed 1984, Chicago Tribune Company. All rights reserved. Reprinted by permission of the author.—Chicago Tribune—*Books*, Part 4, November 2,

THE EXCERPTS IN *CLR*, VOLUME 23, WERE REPRINTED FROM THE FOLLOWING BOOKS:

and Patterns in Contemporary Children's Literature. American Library Association, 1981. Copyright © 1981 by the American Library Association. All rights reserved. Reprinted by permission of the publisher.—Fisher, Margery. From ***The Bright Face of Danger.*** The Horn Book, Inc., 1986, Hodder and Stoughton, 1986. Copyright © 1986 by Margery Fisher. All rights reserved. Reprinted by permission of The Horn Book, Inc. and Hodder and Stoughton Limited.—Fisher, Margery. From ***Who's Who in Children's Books: A Treasure of the Familiar Characters of Childhood.*** Weidenfeld & Nicolson, 1975. Copyright © 1975 by Margery Fisher. All rights reserved. Reprinted by permission of the publisher.—Fryatt, Norma R. From "Picture Books Today," in ***Newbery and Caldecott Medal Books: 1956-1965.*** Horn Book, 1965. Copyright © 1965 by The Horn Book, Inc. All rights reserved. Reprinted by permission of the publisher, 14 Beacon St., Boston, MA 02108.—Green, Roger Lancelyn. From ***Tellers of Tales.*** Revised edition. Franklin Watts, Inc., 1965, Kaye and Ward, 1969. Copyright 1946, 1953, 1956, © 1965 by Edmund Ward (Publishers) Ltd. Reprinted by permission of Kaye & Ward Ltd.—Helbig, Alethea K., and Agnes Regan Perkins. From ***Dictionary of American Children's Fiction, 1960-1984: Recent Books of Recognized Merit.*** Greenwood Press, 1986. Copyright © 1986 by Alethea K. Helbig and Agnes Regan Perkins.—Hinton, S. E. and William Walsh. From an interview in ***From Writers to Students: The Pleasures and Pains of Writing.*** Edited by M. Jerry Weiss. International Reading Association, 1979. Copyright 1979 by the International Reading Association, Inc. Reprinted by permission of the publisher.—Hogarth, Grace Allen. From "The Artist and His Editor," in ***Illustrators of Children's Books: 1957-1966.*** Lee Kingman, Joanna Foster, Ruth Giles Lontoft, eds. Horn Book, 1968. Copyright © 1968 by The Horn Book, Inc. Reprinted by permission of the publisher, 14 Beacon St., Boston, MA 02108.—Holtze, Sally Holmes. From ***Presenting Norma Fox Mazer.*** Twayne, 1987. Copyright 1987 by Twayne Publishers. All rights reserved. Reprinted with the permission of Twayne Publishers, a division of G. K. Hall & Co., Boston.—Hopkins, Lee Bennett. From ***Books Are By People.*** Citation Press, 1969. Copyright © 1969 by Scholastic Magazines, Inc.—From a review of "Rumble Fish," in ***Human—and Anti-Human—Values in Children's Books.*** Edited by The CIBC Racism and Sexism Resource Center for Educators. The Racism and Sexism Resource Center for Educators, 1976. Copyright © 1976 by the Council on Interracial Books for Children, Inc. All rights reserved. Reprinted by permission of the publisher.—Lacy, Lyn Allen. From ***Art and Design in Children's Picture Books.*** American Library Association, 1986. Copyright © 1986 by the American Library Association. All rights reserved. Reprinted by permission of the publisher.—Landsberg, Michele. From ***Reading for the Love of It: Best Books for Young Readers.*** Prentice Hall Press, 1987. Copyright © 1986, 1987, by Psammead Associates Ltd. All rights reserved. Published in Canada as ***Michele Landsberg's Guide to Children's Books.*** Penguin Books, 1986. Copyright © Michele Landsberg. Used by permission of Prentice Hall Press/A Division of Simon & Schuster, Inc., New York, NY 10023. In Canada by Penguin Books Canada Limited.—McCrosson, Doris Ross. From ***Walter de la Mare.*** Twayne, 1966. Copyright 1966 by Twayne Publishers. All rights reserved. Reprinted by permission of Twayne Publishers, Inc., a division of G. K. Hall & Co., Boston.—Morley, Christopher. From ***Shandygaff: A Number of Most Agreeable Inquirendoes upon Life and Letters, Interspersed with Short Stories and Skitts, the Whole Most Diverting to the Reader.*** Doubleday, Page & Company, 1918. Copyright 1918, renewed 1946 by Christopher Morley. Reprinted by permission of HarperCollins Publishers, Inc.—Moss, Elaine. From ***Picture Books for Young People 9-13.*** Revised edition. The Thimble Press, 1985. Copyright © 1981, 1985 Elaine Moss. Reprinted by permission of the publisher.—Nesbitt, Elizabeth. From "A Rightful Heritage: 1890-1920," in ***A Critical History of Children's Literature.*** By Cornelia Meigs and others, edited by Cornelia Meigs. Revised edition. Macmillan, 1969. Copyright 1953, © 1969 by Macmillan Publishing Company. Renewed © 1981 by Charles H. Eaton. All rights reserved. Reprinted with permission of the publisher.—Peterson, Linda Kauffman. From "The Caldecott Medal and Honor Books, 1938-1981," in ***Newbery and Caldecott Medal and Honor Books: An Annotated Bibliography.*** By Linda Kauffman Peterson and Marilyn Leathers Solt. G. K. Hall & Co., 1982. © 1982 by Marilyn Solt and Linda Peterson. Reprinted by permission of Linda Kauffman Peterson.—Sebesta, Sam Leaton and William J. Iverson. From ***Literature for Thursday's Child.*** Science Research Associates, 1975. © 1975, Science Research Associates, Inc. All rights reserved. Reprinted by permission of the authors.—Smith, Lillian H. From ***The Unreluctant Years: A Critical Approach to Children's Literature.*** American Library Association, 1953. Copyright 1953, renewed 1981, by the American Library Association. All rights reserved. Reprinted by permission of the publisher.—Stott, Jon C. From ***Children's Literature from A to Z: A Guide for Parents and Teachers.*** McGraw-Hill Book Company, 1984. Copyright © 1984 by McGraw-Hill, Inc. All rights reserved. Reproduced with permission.—Sutherland, Zena, and May Hill Arbuthnot. From ***Children and Books.*** Seventh edition. Scott, Foresman, 1986. Copyright © 1986, 1981, 1977, 1972, 1964, 1957, 1947 Scott, Foresman and Company. All rights reserved. Reprinted by permission of the publisher.—Townsend, John Rowe. From ***Written for Children: An Outline of English-Language Children's Literature.*** Third revised edition. J. B. Lippincott, 1987, Penguin Books, 1987. Copyright © 1965, 1974, 1983, 1987 by John Rowe Townsend.

PERMISSION TO REPRODUCE ILLUSTRATIONS APPEARING IN *CLR*, VOLUME 23, WAS RECEIVED FROM THE FOLLOWING SOURCES:

Illustration by Barbara Cooney from ***Chanticleer and the Fox,*** by Geoffrey Chaucer. Adapted by Barbara Cooney. Thomas Y. Crowell Company, 1958. Copyright © 1958 HarperCollins Publishers. Reprinted by permission of HarperCollins Publishers./ Illustration by Barbara Cooney from ***The Little Juggler,*** adapted from an old French legend by Barbara Cooney. Hastings House, Publishers, 1961. Copyright © 1961 by Barbara Cooney Porter. Reprinted by permission of Eagle Publishing Corp./ Illustration by Barbara Cooney from ***Miss Rumphius,*** by Barbara Cooney. Puffin Books, 1985. Copyright © Barbara Cooney Porter, 1982. Reprinted by permission of Puffin Books, a division of

Children's Literature Review

W(ilbert) V(ere) Awdry

1911-

English author of picture books.

Major works include *The Three Railway Engines* (1945), *Thomas the Tank Engine* (1946), *Railway Map of the Island of Sodor* (1958; revised edition, 1971), *Enterprising Engines* (1968).

The following entry presents criticism of the Railway Series.

A popular author for preschool and early elementary grade readers who is also a vicar in the Church of England, Awdry has been lauded as an English institution for creating the Railway Series, approximately thirty-five picture books in which he develops an entire folklore and typography and celebrates the age of the steam engine. Praised as an especially inventive depicter of character and locale, he is recognized for originating the island of Sodor, a fictional setting in the Irish Sea which lies between the Isle of Man and the Lancashire coast and is characteristically inhabited by colorful, anthropomorphic trains and buses with distinctive personalities and universal attitudes and behaviors; Awdry also includes a few human characters in his series, notably Sir Topham Harry, the benevolent father figure who runs the railway and is called both the Fat Director and the Fat Controller, and the Thin Clergyman, modeled on Awdry himself. Awdry is perhaps best known as the creator of Thomas the Tank Engine, a little train who reforms after his impatience and playfulness cause a series of accidents, becomes a Very Useful Engine, and receives his own branch line as a reward. Throughout the series, Awdry introduces young readers to several other characters, engines and buses in a variety of hues who learn their lessons after instances of pride, insolence, laziness, and irresponsibility. Presenting children with small homilies based around the choice to obey or disobey, Awdry underscores his works with positive values and hopefulness; despite their headstrong behavior, his characters are always forgiven and are rewarded with such benefits as praise and a new coat of paint. The series is illustrated by several artists, most notably C. Reginald Dalby and Gunvor and Peter Edwards, whose pictures are credited with helping to define the personality of the works.

Introduced to trains by his father, a clergyman and amateur railwayman, Awdry developed his idea for steam engines with personality when he lived in a vicarage near the Great Western Railway. When his son Christopher fell ill at the age of three, Awdry amused him by telling him stories about trains that could express themselves; these stories became the basis for his first book, *The Three Railway Engines*. The success of the book prompted Awdry to continue the series, volumes of which have achieved bestseller status and cumulatively have sold millions of copies. When the initial works appeared, steam engines were still much in operation; however, by the 1950s, the books began to reflect negatively the advent of diesel engines and buses. Designed to be read aloud to children, the Railway

Series is often directed to the nostalgic feelings of adults and is often noted for its resistance to modernization and bureaucracy. The series also represents values which some observers view as conservative, such as patriotism and utalitarianism. In addition, Awdry outlines a definite social hierarchy in his works, one in which the female coaches respond passively to the male engines that pull them; critics, in fact, often comment on the parallels between Sodor and Great Britain. However, the Railway Series continues to be a consistent favorite among both English children and adults and has recently become the subject of an industry: although Awdry retired in 1972, the popularity of the original books and the success of both Britt Allcroft's television series "Shining Time Station" and the new Sodor stories written by Christopher Awdry have prompted books, tapes, clothing, train sets, bedding, and other items with a Railway Series theme; international distribution of the television show and some of the spinoff books is also introducing Awdry to a larger audience. Often praised for the authenticity of his books for children, all of which are based on real events which he discovers in his research, Awdry is also the author and editor of several well-received works on railways for adults.

(See also *Contemporary Authors,* Vol. 103.)

Diana Gardner

[The Railway Series] began twenty-three years ago and is now known in nearly every home in Britain. Almost 3,000,000 copies have been sold, and this at a time when steam locomotives are certainly on the way out. What is the secret of the series?

One can only answer, after browsing through the books and reading what the Rev. Awdry himself has said, that the magic lies in the deep love felt by the author for these puffing companions of his early childhood—lying in bed at night he could hear the locomotives pulling up the steep incline at Box, in Somerset, a few hundred yards from his home—coupled with the affection for them inspired by the enthusiasm of his father who was a keen amateur railway-man. When his own son went down with measles, the Rev. Awdry entertained him with stories about locomotives as characters, as people—until his wife prevailed upon him to write the stories down and take them to a publisher.

From those days the series . . . has developed into an entire folklore. Some people even believe that the Island of Sodor and its railways and topographical details actually exist! If the Rev. Awdry makes a mistake, shoals of letters pour in, putting him right. Even letters from grown-ups.

Perhaps other reasons for the attraction of the escapades of these railway engines and the sense that the reader is somehow involved in them, lies in the fact that each tale is based on a real event about which the Rev. Awdry has heard; and that the behaviour of the engines is like real boys and girls; covetous and mean, *and* magnanimous; stupid or humorous; forgiving, unforgiving—everything is there. And also that, over all presides the Fat Controller, in top hat and tailcoat, who sees that the system *works*, and that the passengers get there on time and that justice is done. A very reliable Father-figure!

And, of course, that every page carries a delicious, gay, colourful illustration full of those down-to-earth details which children love, of the goings-on of the little, sturdy railway engines.

> *Diana Gardner, "The Railway Series," in* Books for Your Children, *Vol. 3, No. 4, Summer, 1968, p. 8.*

The Times Literary Supplement

Devotees of Mr Awdry's engines will be delighted by the reappearance of Thomas, Percy and Toby in No 26 of the series [*Tramway Engines*]. The jaundiced parent may boggle at the way in which machines subject to a rigid system of control involving rails, signals, points and, above all, a driver, so frequently act in an apparently autonomous manner. One of Mr Awdry's favourite themes is pride leading, via disobedience, to disaster—appropriate for people since the time of Adam and Eve, but not for such circumscribed mechanisms as railway engines. Such considerations make not a scrap of difference to the fascination these books exercise over the anthropomorphic young.

> *A review of "Tramway Engines," in* The Times Literary Supplement, *No. 3692, December 8, 1972, p. 1495.*

Margery Fisher

The four stories in the book mainly concerned with Thomas [*Thomas the Tank Engine*] are fair examples of the art-less-artful technique which has kept the Railway Series in the best-seller lists for many years. Since 1945, when the Revd Awdry introduced his first engines, he has built up a whole topography of the island of Sodor and Man and has developed a railway system into which he has fitted a host of splendidly convincing characters. There is Duke, who is proud of being named after the Duke of Sodor and is frequently heard to observe 'That would never have suited His Grace'. There is Bud, a cocky American engine who 'doesn't care a dime for a few spills'. There is Oliver the Western Engine, who boasts 'What do I care for trouble. I just push it aside', but who is sorry for being conceited after his rebellious trucks have caused a crash.

As time went on the books included more specialized vehicles like coy Mavis the diesel engine at the quarry, Toad the loyal brakevan and Toby, the sturdy tram-engine with his cow-catcher and side-plates. There are carriages and trucks with personality like Henrietta, who complains that she has seen better days and finds a branch line demeaning. There is the belligerent red bus called Bulgy by the engines, who tells them: 'Come the Revolution, railways'll be ripped up. Cars 'nd coaches 'll trample their remains'; pride goes before a fall and Bulgy, taking a short cut to prove he can carry passengers faster than the trains, is jammed under a low bridge and ends his days in a poultry-field. The author himself makes an appearance now and then among the few human characters given a name, as an advisory and interested Thin Clergyman.

The humanizing of locomotives is no new thing in children's books and half the credit for the success of the engine stories must go to Gunvor Edwards, who has taken every chance to differentiate character by emphasizing the salient points of certain types of engine and coach, never altering shape or construction except by the subtle addition of 'features' at the front. To him also goes half the credit for the amusing and wholly believable presentation of the Fat Controller, the epitome of all self-important large frogs in small ponds.

But the Railway Series does not depend on visual effects alone. By ingeniously combining ordinary speech with onomatopoeic words (chuff, peep, agh, shooh and so on) and exact terminology, settings and action, this clever writer gives his engines 'voices' and behaviour which sharply denote personality. (pp. 343-44)

> *Margery Fisher, in a review of "Thomas the Tank Engine," in* Who's Who in Children's Books: A Treasury of the Familiar Characters of Childhood, *Holt, Rinehart and Winston, 1975, pp. 343-44.*

John Churcher

One of the great literary events of post-war austerity was a new train book from the Reverend W. Awdry. The Railway Series is not to everyone's taste. There are adults who read it then, who even now wince with boredom at the prospect of Gordon the Big Engine refusing to pull, James at the mercy of demonic trucks, or that haunting vignette of withdrawal and return—of neurasthenic seizure and

Jungian transfiguration with blue paint—Henry the green Engine, walled-up inside the tunnel.

Under the supervision of my daughter, who is three, I have received lately a splendid second chance to come to grips with the live text. *The Three Railway Engines* assuredly remains a classic. In this context it would be churlish to mention that the new tunnel cut beside the unhappy Henry on page 48 has already appeared in every picture since page 36. Aficionados who, like myself, have read at least a portion of it, every night for the past three months, will have been rather struck by the way the book cunningly projects the characters and situations of public school life on to a collection of pre-Beeching railway rolling stock. The shed is the dormitory; Edward, the anxious new boy; Gordon, a boastful bully.

Presiding over this often endearing world, where the reward for all effort is a fresh coat of paint, we witness in the Fat Director (after nationalisation he became a mere Controller, though he lost no weight) a human power figure of almost Kafkaesque proportions. Rather than simply fulfilling the duties of an ersatz head master, the man is aware of no obvious limits conferred on his power whatever. As an apparent representative of the British upper middle classes, and recalling the ad hoc manner in which Dickens once organised railway rescue operations, the Fat Director, when Henry will go no further, orders the frustrated passengers down on to the tracks. Here, at his command, they attempt first to pull, and then equally unavailingly to push the naughty engine out of his tunnel.

"Everyone pushed except the Fat Director, 'My Doctor has forbidden me to push', he said".

Is this self-appointed commissar a director of railways? One might assume so; for he certainly spends a great deal of time hobnobbing with the engines. Yet the Director of a railway could scarcely justify his use of customers as unpaid labour. In the absence of any textual definition, the power of the Fat Director issues solely from the charisma associated with his class; he is what our Chinese comrades on the ant-hill recognise as a Paper Tiger.

In 1945, when *The Three Railway Engines* first appeared, the world of the Fat Director, as the earlier flaming shell of the Hindenburg had done, remained in some respects momentarily and uncannily intact. The collapse of those assumptions which supported it lay eleven years into the future. Since my own journeyings along Awdry's railroad ended in the early fifties, I had supposed that though the world had changed the genteel whimsy of Awdry's evident industry would have stayed remote from the considerations of the nineteen-sixties and 'seventies.

I had intended to divert my daughter's monomania not to what I took to be late imitations, but to those books in the canon which I remembered myself. Unfortunately at all times many of Awdry's works are out of print. In these circumstances, encountering from necessity a book called *Oliver the Western Engine* proved an arresting experience. A chief pleasure of the earliest works had resided in the illustrations; indeed much of the series' power to fascinate is invested in the emotive lines of the engines' 'faces'. Coming up for air in this Lower Binfield of British Rail, I was at first merely appalled by the coarseness of the later drawings. Yet, as devotees may have noticed, the text of *Oliver the Western Engine* contains even greater sur-

Awdry with a model of Thomas the Tank Engine.

prises. The very Preface, bristling with crack-brained donnishness about tyrannous publishers, was a poor augury. As cousins not seen for twenty years will change, and though Awdry idiosyncratically retains steam engines, the ethos of Oliver is that of its publication date; 1969. The whimsy remains: but now the Fat Director is unquestionably a director of railways. Like that of a retired colonel, his world has shrunk to a 'lately re-opened branch line'. Time, which stripped him of his omnipotence, has made of him a kind of genial conservation crank; a tweedy old fogey, whose scarcely suppressed strain of blimpish fascism is, in this antique backwater, allowed a little harmless rein. As oiks from the town, in say Bunteresque school books, trucks were always troublesome, in *Oliver* their menace is felt so keenly that, with the Fat Director's winking connivance, they are smashed to shreds. Occurring in an Awdry book of twenty years ago, such violence would have stood out like an ink-stain. By the same token a suggestion that political fanaticism might one day colour these gentle stories would then have been received as a morbid joke; yet buses which once played no part in the Series, now emerge as rabid revolutionaries.

"Come the Revolution", they growl in their double-decker scarlet, and "railways'll be ripped up. Cars'nd coaches'll trample their remains".

Such a progression into violent imagery is oddly quite common among aging writers. Compare for instance the dashing Wyndham Lewis who wrote 'Tarr' with the blind titan who conjured, out of the darkness of Notting Hill, the evil fantasies of 'Malign Fiesta'. Only, for some reason, rather than that of any English writer, Awdry's development curiously calls to mind the literary career of the great French reactionary and anarchist, Louis-Ferdinand Celine. The shift from the delicate dreamlike atmosphere of **'The Three Railway Engines'** to the jovial rantings of *Oliver* mirrors in miniature Celine's realistic trance through the 'Journey to the End of the Night' to the crazy staccato outbursts of venomous humour which we find in a late work, like 'North'. Had Celine survived into a world of nuclear holocaust he would certainly have relished it, and indeed gone on writing with gusto. In the same manner, one can well imagine Awdry's steam engines, pulling and pushing in the midst of the Apocalypse; ferrying under the guidance of a fat directing Charon ('Everyone was dead, except the Fat Director . . . '), the teeming souls to their final terminus. (pp. 267-69)

> *John Churcher, "Journey to the End of the Tunnel," in* The Junior Bookshelf, *Vol. 41, No. 5, October, 1977, pp. 267-69.*

Brian Sibley

The sign on the door reads STATION MASTER, and the house, in Stroud, is one of those sensible, four-square houses such as a station master might easily have lived in—if only the railway line were nearer. Inside the station master's office, an agreeable clutter abounds: railway books, magazines, maps and timetables, tottering piles of cuttings and correspondence. For this is the home of the Revd W. Awdry, co-author of *A Guide to the Steam Railways of Great Britain,* but better known as the Thomas the Tank Engine man.

At 74, the Reverend Wilbert Vere Awdry has lived over half his life being labelled an eccentric. His eccentricity, such as it is, is that he has an abiding affection for the lost joys of the age of steam, and has celebrated that age in a highly successful series of children's books about railway engines with faces on their smokeboxes and endearingly human characteristics.

A lean, slightly hunched figure, with a mane of silver hair and beetling brows that lour over NHS spectacle frames, he puffs—engine-like—on a battered pipe and theorises about the personalities of trains. 'The steam engine,' he explains, 'is an extrovert. Unless he's standing in a siding with his fire drawn, he's always got something to say. He likes people to know how he's getting on. There's the goods engine, always complaining of being badly treated; then there's the express engine, bustling about saying "Come on! Come on!" followed by a train of calm, unflappable coaches, saying like dutiful wives "Yes dear, of *course!* Yes dear, of *course!*", while all along you know they're thinking about much more important things, like when they're going to get a new coat of paint!'

Giving a self-mocking chuckle—lest you take him *too* seriously—he stokes his pipe with fresh tobacco and gets up a new head of steam.

There was a time, before he became quite such an institution, when journalists used to call him 'The Puff-Puff Par-

son'—an epithet which rather annoyed him, since he has never seen anything particularly odd about a vicar liking trains. After all, it was his father—also a clergyman—who began his passion for railways by taking him, at the age of four, on walks along the line that ran through the Hampshire village where they lived.

Later, the family moved to Box, in Wiltshire, to a vicarage that stood just 200 yards from the Great Western Railway's main line from Paddington to Bath and Bristol. 'In bed, at night,' he recalls, gazing dreamily into the middle distance through the thickening cloud of tobacco smoke, 'I would listen to the trains, and it needed little imagination to hear, in the sounds they made, the engines talking to each other . . . From that time, there developed in my mind the idea that steam engines had personality, and could express it.'

It was these childhood memories which were to surface in 1943 when Mr Awdry, by then an ordained curate in the Church of England, began telling stories for his own son, Christopher. 'Once upon a time there was a little engine called Edward,' began the first of these, told to the three-year-old Christopher when he was confined to a darkened room with measles. 'Edward had not been out for a long time; he began to feel sad.' Eventually, 'as a form of self-defence' against a child who grew to know the stories better than the teller of the tales, Mr Awdry scribbled them down on the backs of old circulars.

He wasn't the first to give anthropomorphic life to railway engines, but there was something unique about the characters in his stories, or at least so it seemed to Mrs Awdry. It was through her prompting that the by now dirty scraps of paper containing the stories ended up on the desk of the publisher Edmund Ward. Maybe it was their economy of style which appealed to him, or their lack of condescension, or the fact that they were based on the exploits of *real* steam locomotives; in any event, he decided to publish. In 1945, ***The Three Railway Engines*** appeared in its now familiar oblong format with a brightly coloured picture facing each page of text.

The book's success brought a request for a sequel, and the following year saw the arrival of Thomas the Tank Engine—a fussy little character, full of his own importance, who rushed about cheeking all the big engines, but who sincerely wanted to become a Really Useful Engine. Soon a new book was appearing every year; there were to be 26 of them in all, containing over a hundred stories, and featuring such characters as James the Red Engine, Henry the Green Engine, Gordon the Big Engine and Percy the Small Engine, all of whom were answerable to the strict, but kindly, Fat Controller who ran the railway. (p. 13)

In 1965, [Awdry] retired (or, as he puts it, 'went into private practice'), and continued writing until the demand for new stories became too much and, in 1972, he wrote his last book, ***Tramway Engines.*** But 12 years on, the enormously popular television series based on his books—and the staggering merchandising industry which it spawned—pushed him back into the limelight once more.

Today, genuinely rather bemused by all the attention he receives, he is compiling a gazetteer of the railways on the Island of Sodor; while Christopher Awdry, now grown up with a son of his own, has begun writing new titles for the Railway Series.

The Revd W. Awdry has few illusions about himself: he knows that, despite a lifetime's service in the Church, it is as the Thomas the Tank Engine man that he will always be remembered. But he doesn't mind too much; after all, it has earned him the affection of thousands of children from whom he receives scrawly letters of thanks and wobbly drawings of Thomas and his friends.

Besides, his little stories contain at least something of his philosophy: 'This is God's world; you can obey him or disobey him. The engines, like us humans, go their own way and, inevitably, come to a sticky end.' He pauses thoughtfully and knocks out the dottle from his pipe. 'The point is, they are punished but they are never scrapped.'

In the world inhabited by Mr Awdry's characters, there is always redemption and forgiveness, another opportunity to try harder to become a Really Useful Engine. In the real world, where humanity—like British Rail—is forever claiming (but never quite proving) that it is 'getting there', that is a reassuring philosophy. (pp. 13-14)

> Brian Sibley, "A Runaway Success," in The Listener, Vol. 114, No. 2960, May 15, 1986, pp. 13-14.

Bruce Carrington and Martyn Denscombe

The world depicted in [The Reverend W. Awdry's] stories is quaint and, arguably, quintessentially English; the sentiments conveyed are conservative and straight-laced. In this article, we attempt to explain the continuing (and indeed increasing) popularity of these anachronistic stories.

Thomas the Tank Engine, the central character in the series, has continued to captivate young and old alike since the appearance of the first book in 1945. Although the twenty-sixth (and final) volume in the original series was published in 1972, Thomas's popularity has subsequently been maintained. . . . Following the introduction of Britt Allcroft's television programmes based on the series, Thomas and his friends have been elevated to the status of superstars. There can be little doubt that television has done much to enhance Thomas's standing with children, especially of preschool and infant school age. There is now a flourishing "Thomas the Tank Engine industry" in the United Kingdom. As well as the original books published by Kaye & Ward, Ladybird also publishes books and tapes. Furthermore few shoppers could have failed to notice the appearance of Thomas and friends on all kinds of toys, clothes, and bedding aimed at younger children. . . . There are also the ubiquitous train sets. . . . (pp. 45-6)

This recent growth popularity is interesting because it stands in contrast to the new wave of children's favourites. Compared with He Man and She Ra, Zoids, Transformers, Space Lego, etc., based on futuristic or fantasy worlds far removed from reality, the Railway Series is all rather mundane and parochial. The anthropomorphic trains, buses, and other vehicles largely belong to the years following World War II, the nationalization of the railways and the introduction of diesel locomotives. We hope to show that although the settings for Awdry's stories are decidedly anachronistic, the values and beliefs which they articulate are, nevertheless, contemporaneous. There is, in fact, a large measure of congruence between the ideology of Thomas the Tank Engine and that of the New Right.

The setting for the Railway Series is the mythical island of Sodor, which lies between the Isle of Man and the Cumbrian coast. The railway system on Sodor is run almost single-handedly by the autocratic Sir Topham Hatt, otherwise known as the Fat Controller. He carries the burden of responsibility for the day-to-day running of the entire railway, including timetabling, safety, rolling stock, and the "pastoral care" of the locomotives *qua* persons. This burden he takes seriously because the railway system on the island of Sodor is more than just a preservation society for steam locomotives and rolling stock discarded in the wake of progress on the (sic) "Other Railway" (i.e., British Rail). Rather, it is a working railway in direct competition with Sodor's bus system. A bridge between Sodor and the mainland at Barrow-on-Furness allows British Rail diesels to run on the Island and also enables the famous engines of the halcyon days of steam, such as "The Flying Scotsman" and "City of Truro," to make guest appearances in the books.

Although Awdry's anthropomorphism is likely to appeal to children aged between two and six years, an average reader of nine would find the text too demanding. The Railway Series is written for adults to read to children. In view of this, it is not surprising to find that the subject-matter is often aimed directly at adults, for whom the series may invoke feelings of nostalgia. There are occasions, however, when Awdry's remarks are likely to leave all but the railway cognoscenti baffled. What can many adults today, let alone five year olds, make of extracts like the following from *Main Line Engines?*

> "One of your crank-pins broke, Edward," said his Driver at last.
>
> "We've taken your side-rods off. Now you're a 'single' like an old fashioned engine. Can you get these people home? They must start back tonight."

(This particular passage is especially incongruous when one considers that almost all "singles" had been withdrawn from active service by 1920!).

Any explanation of the continuing popularity of Awdry's books which fails to take account of the high quality of their illustrations will necessarily be lacking. The bold, colourful drawings of C. Reginald Dalby warrant particular recognition. His characterisations in the first 11 books in the Series (1945-56) set the scene. . . .

The models in the TV version of Thomas the Tank Engine and Friends capture Dalby's simplicity of style.

In so far as the Railway Series can be shown to embody elements of both traditional and radical conservatism, one might ask: is it merely coincidental that the rise to superstardom of Thomas the Tank Engine and his friends has taken place at this, rather than an earlier juncture, in Britain's postwar history? In common with Thatcherism, Awdry's stories emphasise the importance of individual responsibility, discipline, order, and respect for authority. The Series also celebrates the work ethic, enterprise, utilitarianism, patriotism, and meritocratic values. Moreover, along with traditional forms of conservatism, his work may be read as a polemic against modernisation, technological change, and bureaucracy. Certainly, the series presents a romantic vision of the way things were in the "good old days." Life on the well-ordered Island of Sodor, where everyone (irrespective of their position in society) has a use, place, and purpose, contrasts sharply with conflict-ridden contemporary Britain with its spiralling unemployment, uncertainty, and alienation.

Under the benevolent dictatorship of the Fat Controller, the engines recognise that they have "to do as they are told." But, as befits the British way of life, even the Fat Controller knows the limits of his power. In *Toby the Tram Engine,* we find him in dispute with an overzealous policeman who insists that, because Thomas's track runs along a public road for some distance, regulations oblige Thomas to fit cow-catchers and side-plates. Though the Fat Controller argues that Thomas is not a "Danger to the Public," he eventually concedes that he has to obey the law of the land:

> The policeman was on the platform at the other end. The Fat Controller spoke to him at once, and a crowd gathered to listen. Other policemen came to see what was happening and the Fat Controller argued with them too; but it was no good.
> "The Law is the Law," they said, "and we can't change it."
> The Fat Controller felt exhausted. He mopped his face.
> "I'm sorry Driver," he said, "it's no use arguing with policemen. We will have to make those cow-catcher things for Thomas, I suppose."
>
> (pp. 46-9)

The social hierarchy beneath the Fat Controller is based upon the status of the various locomotives and on a structure that puts engines above carriages, and carriages above trucks. Size is the major determinant of an engine's status. (Gordon, Henry, James, and Edward have tenders and, apart from Edward, *assume* a higher position in the railway society.) But the question of age and lineage complicates the hierarchy somewhat. The famous historic locomotives, "The Flying Scotsman" and "City of Truro," provide role models or "significant others" for the engines of Sodor. Duck, for example, an ex-Great Western Railway pannier tank, is singularly impressed with the record-breaking G.W.R. "City of Truro" visits the island, attracting considerable attention from the press and an adoring public. Gordon, himself an express engine but with L.N.E.R. (London North-Eastern Railway) antecedents, when confronted by Duck's expressions of idolatry, is predictably jealous of the visitor whose achievements he tries to emulate. In an action arguably analogous to racial stereotyping, Gordon makes these disparaging remarks about "City of Truro" to his Swindon stable-mate Duck: "Never trust domeless engines, they're not respectable." On another occasion, when Gordon is suffering from boiler-ache and an apparent ontological crisis brought about by the demise of steampower, the Fat Controller arranges for "The Flying Scotsman" to visit him and bolster his flagging spirits.

In contrast to the standardised stock of the Other Railway, eclecticism is the order of the day on Sodor. Some engines, like Duck and Oliver, retain the regional liveries of their G.W.R. prototypes, while others (e.g., Gordon, Edward, Douglas, Donald, Percy) appear in a flamboyant array of colours which have no foundation in historical reality. The engines (together with the rolling-stock and trucks) represent a wide range of human behaviour, attitudes, and personality traits, and no doubt children readi-

ly identify with their idiosyncrasies, feelings, predicaments, and dilemmas. For example, whereas Percy enjoys his creature comforts and leisure, he is mindful of the fact that work *qua* public service must always come first. In *Troublesome Engines* when the track is flooded by a sudden downpour, he doesn't retire to a 'nice dry engine shed' but recalls his 'promise' to convey a group of children (on a Sunday School outing) home. Upon his return, he's elated when the vicar and children cheer him, and the Fat Controller announces: "You're a really useful engine." Elsewhere, the Fat Controller recognises Thomas' diligence and enterprise (in rescuing James after a crash) by rewarding him with his "own line."

In the same way that enterprise, utility, modesty, and altruism are rewarded, indolence, insubordination, pride, and caprice are often vigorously proscribed. In *Duck and the Diesel Engine,* for example, Diesel arrogantly disregards Duck's advice about handling "cheeky" and "troublesome" trucks. "We diesels," he exclaims, "don't need to learn, we know everything . . . we are revolutionary." Predictably, he is later brought down to size when his clumsy shunting techniques result in a goods train blocking the line. Diesel scuttles away to his shed to sulk, but only after both Duck and the trucks have openly ridiculed his behaviour. Elsewhere, when Henry, Gordon, and James refuse to undertake shunting duties (claiming that such work is demeaning for engines with tenders) the Fat Controller simply remarks: "We'll see about that; engines on My Railway do as they are told." The engines are then confined to a shed as a punishment for their insubordination.

An unquestioning acceptance of hierarchy and authority is a dominant characteristic of life on Sodor. Notwithstanding this, authority has to be exercised in an appropriate manner: that is, firmly and with justice and humanity. Thus in *The Little Old Engine* the reader is informed that "Peter Sam never bumped trucks unless they misbehaved" but that Sir Handel "bumped them even if they were good; so they didn't like him and played tricks whenever they could."

Everyone on Sodor has (and is taught to know) their place in a clearly delineated hierarchy extending from the Fat Controller at the top through to the trucks at the bottom. The engines, in particular, employ various strategies to maintain the marginal position of the trucks. The images presented of this group bear a strong resemblance to ruling class images of the "lower orders" in Victorian society or right-wing populist images of the "underclass" in Britain today.

The safety record on the Island's railway leaves much to be desired, and the trucks are continually scapegoated for the many accidents which occur. Not surprisingly, the engines are keen to maintain the social distance which exists between them and recalcitrant and potentially subversive trucks. When Diesel alleges that Duck had undermined his authority with the trucks, Henry exclaims: "Nonsense, Duck would never do that. We have our differences, but we would never talk about them to the trucks." These status differences *within* a "social class" (such as the engines) are a constant source of comment and friction. As Gordon remarks to Thomas,

> We tender engines have a position to keep up. You

haven't a tender and that makes a difference. It doesn't matter where *you* go, but *we* are *important,* and for the Fat Controller to make us shunt trucks, fetch coaches and go on some of those dirty sidings it's—it's—well, it's not the proper thing.

Between the tender engines and tank engines on the one hand, and trucks, on the other, is an intermediate stratum: the coaches. The "female" coaches (i.e., Clarabel, Annie, Henrietta) are passive and compliant and, unlike the trucks, offer no resistance to the "male" engines which pull them. On Sodor, women too have their place, but make no attempt to disturb the status quo.

In this railway society, the symbolic significance of names is especially important. Not only do they serve to demarcate gender divisions (between the engines and carriages) or social class divisions (between the engines and trucks) but they signify an important distinction between Sodor and the (sic) "Other Railway." With standardisation, nationalisation, and the advent of the characterless and ubiquitous diesel, individuality becomes anathema. Numbers (denoting a locomotive's class and type) rather than names are the symbols of the new era of bureaucracy. Thus, when British Rail Diesel 7101 comes to Sodor from the mainland the other engines nickname him Bear. "This," says 7101, "is nicer than just a number. Having a name means you really belong."

Because of the constant harping-back to the past, diesel locomotives are regarded with a degree of ambivalence and even disdain on the island. There are frequent "moral pan-

ics" about them. The arrival of a Metropolitan-Vickers diesel at Tidmouth Docks, for example, prompts a pair of tank engines (whose livelihood is presumably threatened by the newcomer) to refer to "him" as the "Diseasal." In other stories, diesels are described by steam engines as "ulgy," "smelly," "noisy," and even as "murderers."

Other forms of transport are also parodied, though less aggressively than diesels. Thomas the Tank Engine's race with Bertie the Bus is an up-to-date version of the "Hare and the Tortoise" fable. Predictably, despite his poorer acceleration, Thomas beats his competitor. Elsewhere, Awdry recounts the sad demise of Bulgy the Bus in *Oliver the Western Engine.* Bulgy, a red double-decker, attracts an increasing number of passengers from Sodor Railways, though by deceit rather than honest competition. Of course, in this magical world, the "revolution" predicted so confidently by Bulgy that, "railways will be ripped up and cars'nd coaches will trample their remains," never occurs. Bulgy, taking a shortcut (to better the trains' journey-time) crashes into a low-level bridge. He spends the rest of his days condemned—as a hen house!

Whereas some conservatives, sexists, and railway buffs will no doubt continue to commend the Railway Series to their children, others will read between the lines and argue that there are grounds for doubting Thomas! (pp. 49-53)

Bruce Carrington and Martyn Denscombe, "Doubting Thomas: Reading between the Lines," in Children's literature in education, *Vol. 18, No. 1, Spring, 1987, pp. 45-53.*

Cecil Bødker

1927-

Danish author of fiction.

Major works include *The Leopard* (1978), *Silas and the Black Mare* (1978), *Silas and Ben-Godik* (1978), *Silas and the Runaway Mare* (1978).

One of Denmark's most respected authors for readers in the middle grades through high school, Bødker is praised for creating distinctive, often surreal adventure stories which feature young heroes who triumph over life-threatening situations through courage, cunning, and the strength of their personalities. Celebrated for her vivid characterizations, for her effective use of suspense and fast-paced action, and for the beauty and clarity of her prose style, she is best known in the English-speaking world for her trilogy about Silas, a resourceful, independent, and often audacious young boy who is the protagonist of *Silas and the Black Mare, Silas and Ben-Godik,* and *Silas and the Runaway Coach,* picaresque adventures set in an indeterminate past which combine reality and fantasy in the folktale tradition. Silas's wanderings in a desolate and poverty-stricken unnamed setting bring him into contact with treacherous, greedy adults, almost all of whom want to harm him in some way; most notable among these characters is the Horse Crone, an evil knife-grinder who appears in the latter two stories. Encountering a dark and hostile world in which the inhabitants operate out of suspicion and desperation, Silas meets thieves, kidnappers, and other villains whom he outwits through luck and skill as well as some tactics which observers consider either amoral or defensible as part of his method of survival. At the end of the third volume, Silas, who has grown into adolescence, begins to develop a sense of compassion and also decides to learn to read; Bødker has also written an additional book about Silas which has not yet been translated into English in which he starts a family. Bødker brings broad humor, evocative detail, and a keen sense of the grotesque to her trilogy, which is compared to the works of such writers as Franz Kafka and Jerzy Kosinski.

In 1969, Bødker and her husband were invited to live in a small Ethiopian village so that she could write about the Ethiopian lifestyle for the children of that country, who at that time did not have a literature of their own. This experience resulted in the publication of *The Leopard,* a young adult novel written for use in East African secondary schools which was also Bødker's first book to be published in the United States. Set in a rural village in central Ethiopia, the novel describes how the shepherd boy Tibeso discovers that a calf stolen from the herd he was tending was taken by a wicked blacksmith and not by the leopard feared by his village; after being abducted by the blacksmith, Tibeso escapes by creating decoys and disguises for himself and finally helps to arrange an ambush in which the villain is killed by the leopard. Acknowledged as an gripping story which creates an exciting atmosphere with a minimum of words, *The Leopard* is also noted for its authentic depiction of and social commentary on Ethiopian life. Bødker is also the author of *Mary of Nazareth* (1989),

an expansion of the gospels of Matthew and Luke for early and middle graders which describes Mary's experiences from the Annunciation through the twelfth year of her Son's life. In addition to being a writer for children and young adults, Bødker is also a well known poet, playwright, and author of novels, short stories, and radio scripts for adults. Very few of her works have been translated into English; even Bødker's poetry, called visionary by Danish critics, has yet to appear. She has won numerous international awards for her literature for both audiences: among the honors she has received for her juvenile books is the only prize ever bestowed by the Danish Academy for a children's book, an honor she received in 1967 for *Silas og den sorte hoppe* (*Silas and the Black Mare*); this work also received the Børnebogspris, the prize for the best Danish book for children and youth, in 1968. In 1973, *Leoparden* (*The Leopard*) received the Gouden Griffel or Golden Plaque as part of the Het Kinderboek van het jar, an award for the best children's book of the year in the Netherlands; it also received the Mildred L. Batchelder Award in 1977. *Silas and Ben-Godik* was named a *Boston Globe/Horn Book* honor book for fiction in 1979. For her body of work, Bødker received the Drachmann Prize for her poetry, prose, and children's books in 1973, was named a highly commended author by the International

Board on Books for Young People (IBBY) in 1974, and won the Hans Christian Andersen Award in 1976.

(See also *Contemporary Literary Criticism,* Vol. 21; *Something about the Author,* Vol. 14; *Contemporary Authors New Revision Series,* Vol. 13; and *Contemporary Authors,* Vols. 73-76.)

AUTHOR'S COMMENTARY

[*The following excerpt is from Bødker's Hans Christian Andersen Award acceptance speech, originally delivered at the award ceremonies during the fifteenth Congress of IBBY held from 28 September to 2 October 1976.*]

Since children are not conscious of style or critical in their attitudes—as adults are, or can be—we must take great care in creating books for them. Children are open-minded and receptive, and therefore, from an early age they must be provided with reading experiences of the standard they deserve, that is the best possible.

Unfortunately the gift for writing, given to me at birth, didn't include the ability to support my writing with my own person. My books are stronger than I am, and on the whole, they have had to get along without me from the day I have submitted the manuscripts. Physically and emotionally I cannot live up to the public appearances that are expected of an author. I have had to learn to live with this, but it has often been humilating to have to admit my own shortcomings. I am always having to disappoint people. For an author whose reputation is being built on stories about dynamic boys like Silas and Tavs, who can cope with almost any situation, it is perhaps especially painful—almost like having to admit that wishful thinking is what moves me to write about them.

I have sometimes asked myself if this is, indeed, the case. I wonder if my predilection for Silas is rooted in my own feeling of inadequacy.

At the same time I feel that Silas also stems from something else in me, that he is the sum total of my four great-grandfathers.

The first was a member of the clergy and a stern man.

The second was an inventor of things like a typewriter and carbon paper.

The third was a pirate, a privateer to be exact.

The fourth was a foundling with no knowledge of his family history.

If the four of them were blended into one person, wouldn't the result be a Silas?

Certainly, I didn't turn out to be a Silas, but it seems to me that I should have. Silas is very much a part of me now for I have just submitted a new manuscript about his exploits. It will be the fourth book about him. (pp. 3-4)

In the fourth book, Silas establishes a family of his own but he does it in an unorthodox manner. By behaving according to his own instincts and ideas, he inevitably acts at cross purposes with the society in which he lives.

Usually I feel that I know Silas just as well as I know the real people around me; even so, I cannot always foresee what he is going to do in a given situation. Frequently I am the one to get him into difficulty, it is almost always Silas who gets himself out of it again, and sometimes I do not quite approve of how he does it. I almost dread the thought of what will happen to him as he grows older, uncompromising and headstrong as he is now at the age of fifteen. What will become of him when he is an old man? Will he succeed in continuing to behave according to his own convictions? Or will his surroundings prove to be the stronger so that he ends his days a disappointed, cranky old eccentric, rejected by and rejecting his fellow human beings?

I do not know myself. In any case, the possibility of his leading a varied and eventful life is inherent in him and, as a matter of course, he will develop as he gains experience.

Many children have written to tell me how much they like Silas, that they want me to write more about him and that they are eager to learn what is going to happen next. (p. 4)

My true expression of gratitude to IBBY for having honored my books with this Medal must be in the form of more books of the quality that you and the children deserve, not only in the immediate future but for as long as I am able to write.

So, this is just to thank you for the time being.

I try to work towards this end.

Now I have come so far that I am being rewarded for it, not only by IBBY with the Hans Christian Andersen Medal, but also by the children for whom the books have been created. They write to me asking for more. An author can hardly ask for more. (pp. 4-5)

Cecil Bødker, "Acceptance Speech—1976 H. C. Andersen Author's Medal," in Bookbird, *Vol. XIV, No. 4, December 15, 1976, pp. 3-5.*

GENERAL COMMENTARY

Bookbird

Mrs. Bødker's first juvenile, **Silas and the Black Mare,** won the only prize for children's literature ever given by The Danish Academy. About this book The Danish Academy said,

> . . . the book is a perfect work without an aesthetic blemish written by a poet who plays magically on her instrument. [*Berlingske Tidende,* November 19, 1967]

And a critic [Preben Ramløv] wrote:

> It is as if The Danish Academy competition has released a new side of her talent, an until now hidden warmth, a burlesque sense of humour and a sense for grotesque situations, sometimes quite Rabelaisian in character . . . Her style is brilliant . . . and her books can be read with equal pleasure by adults and children, and particularly by them together. [*Kristeligt Dagblad,* March 3, 1970]

(p. 9)

A sequel to the first book, **Silas and Foot-Godik** [published in translation as **Silas and Ben-Godik**], appeared in 1968, and a Swedish critic [Gunilla Ambjörnsson] wrote;

> From her two books about Silas, Cecil Bødker must be considered among the most important authors for children. The second story about Silas is just as fascinating as the first and has just as exceptional artistic qualities . . . one of those unusual books that functions on several levels and captures adults in the same degree as it does children. [*Bokrevy,* 1970]

In 1969, Cecil Bødker and her husband were invited to Ethiopia where they lived for four months in a small village about three hundred miles south of Addis Ababa. The purpose of this invitation was to acquaint Cecil Bødker so well with Ethiopian children and their milieu that she could then write for them, and her books could then be translated into their own language; in other words, for her to contribute to the development of an Ethiopian children's literature. **The Leopard,** her first book about Ethiopia, was published in 1970:

> One must continue to be grateful that Cecil Bødker entered and won the Danish Academy competition; otherwise she might never have begun to write for children. She does so better and better in each book . . . The plot described might sound like a plain thriller, but Bødker is a poet. Tibeso is an African boy. He doesn't react like an European boy. [*Berlingske Tidende,* November 30, 1970]

> The foreign milieu, especially the landscape, is depicted with unbelievable intensity. Nature is so much a part of the people's existence that it seems to have a soul . . . Superstition plays a big role in the lives of the people in this book. Fear of the unknown is described masterfully in the chapter where Tibeso is left to his destiny alone in the deserted village. His anxiety is so crushing that the reader can hardly bear it . . . Cecil Bødker has demonstrated that a book of high literary quality can surpass 'thrillers' in excitement and dramatics, and at the same time leave the reader with an impression of real, living people. [*Aarhus Stiftstidende,* October 23, 1970]

(p. 10)

[**Silas and the Runaway Coach**], published in 1972, was again about the adventurous, quick-witted and independent boy Silas. [Critic Anne Marie Glistryp wrote]:

> In **Silas Rescues a Four-In-Hand** [translation of Norwegian title], Cecil Bødker has created yet another piece of valuable literature for children. Elementary excitement and subtle humour make this book easily accessible and tempting reading. It is written in exceptionally beautiful and clear language. Praiseworthy, too, are the bright and well-formulated dialogues for they enliven the story. [*Politiken,* November 11, 1972]

About the authorship in general Preben Ramløv—a distinguished author and critic in his own right—has said,

> The (stories) move rapidly, the plot is of uppermost importance, descriptions are exact and always help to carry the action forward, and the reflections are so marvelous and earth-bound that children recognize themselves in them . . .

> Occasionally one says about a woman who can make anything grow that she has a green thumb. The same can be said about Cecil Bødker's relationship to the situations in which she places (her characters). One, two, three—a situation develops so that the reader bubbles with satisfaction and hurries on, eager to learn what she can make out of *that.*

> . . . Looking at this author's production of prose and poetry, one is profoundly astonished, how rich and how varied it is. [*Berlingske Tidende,* January 20, 1971]

(p. 11)

"Cecil Bødker (Denmark—Author)," in Bookbird, *Vol. XII, No. 3, September 15, 1974, pp. 9-13.*

Lucia Binder

[Cecil Bødker's] popularity can be traced back to her subject matters as well as her style of presentation.

Research in reading has repeatedly shown that young readers between the ages of 12 and 14—the reading public addressed by Cecil Bødker's juvenile books—look first of all for suspense, action and atmosphere. In Cecil Bødker's books they find all three of these elements.

The setting of her first book, **Silas and the Black Mare,** is the circus, but the story is far removed from the romantic stereotypes which so often characterize books about circus people. The life lead by Silas after his flight from the circus is also anything but romantic. The author depicts the light as well as the dark aspects of life. The boy Silas has to fight against hardships and financial need, but also against the injustice which is being done to him. That he thereby has to do things which are "not right", according to middle-class concepts, is a natural consequence.

It is a general characteristic of Cecil Bødker's human portrayals that there are no black-white depictions. Her narratives always remain grounded in reality and show how an unmerciful environment can produce unscrupulous people.

Besides the very lively action which can be found in most of Cecil Bødker's books, her unsparing candor and the unrestrained desire for freedom and independence of her characters have no doubt also contributed to their popularity among young readers. Her outstanding ability to understand young people, their behaviour and their problems comes from the fact that she had contact with a great many other young people in her childhood—five brothers and their friends—and that she now has four teenage daughters.

Some critics have characterized her works—particularly the "Silas" books—as anti-authoritarian. This is not true, however. They merely dispense with the teaching of all lessons and morals and attempt to come to grips with the world in a very realistic way.

Even the early **Timmerlis,** which appeared in 1969, suggests the realism of Bødker's children's books. It contains a series of simple, realistic environmental stories of daily life, unsentimental, humorous in parts and very candid.

In spite of the excitement which arises out of her action-packed novels, Cecil Bødker also weaves atmospheric passages and nature descriptions into her works, which fascinate because of their unusualness and accuracy of aim. Such passages are particularly captivating in books such as *The Leopard* which were influenced by the writer's travels in Ethiopia. Cecil Bødker succeeds not only in painting vivid pictures with few words, but inserts these passages in such a way that the continuity of the plot is not impeded (otherwise young readers would be likely to "page over" these), but help to carry it forward. They hint at coming developments, which the reader has already half-guessed, whereby the question, if what one has assumed will actually happen, even heightens the suspense. (pp. 4-5)

Lucia Binder, "Cecil Bødker—Author Medalist," in Bookbird, *Vol. XIII, No. 2, June 15, 1976, pp. 4-6.*

Tordis Orjasaeter

[*The following excerpt is from a speech which was originally delivered at the 1978 IBBY Congress. The theme of the last day of the Congress was "The Handicapped in Literature."*]

[In] the fantastic books about the boy Silas by the Danish writer Cecil Bødker, human handicaps are used symbolically to make the story even more dramatic. In these books we meet the blind girl Maria with her gapingly empty eye sockets. Silas, who is never afraid, is struck with horror at the sight of her empty eye sockets; his horror makes him evil and he scorns her for her handicap. Maria tries to commit that which is the gravest and most final sin in the Silas books: She tries to kill Silas, the vital essence of life. But in her blindness she fails.

Cecil Bødker's tale is brutal, blindness is grotesque and ominous, threatening. But even so, *the impression* it makes *is not* brutal. Is it because Ben-Godik, the boy with a club foot, and Silas's best friend, is described the way he is—sensitively—and yet without sentimentality? He just is. Or is it because we become aware that the blind girl Maria is wicked only as long as she is the victim of other people's wickedness and becomes good when she meets goodness? She is not blind because she is wicked, blindness is not the result of cruelty—as in some fairy-tales. She is wicked because of other people's wickedness. That is quite another matter and psychologically true. (p. 6)

Tordis Orjasaeter, "The Handicapped in Literature," in Bookbird, *No. 1, March 15, 1980, pp. 3-6.*

TITLE COMMENTARY

The Leopard (1975)

For *The leopard* the Danish writer has used a visitor's knowledge of Ethiopia, and her interest in the country and her sharp reactions to it are evident in the way she builds up the background of her story. It is clear, too, that in describing Tibeso's adventure she has gone far towards understanding the way such a boy might have felt and behaved. This book was written for secondary school use in East Africa and, like Catherall's stories, it relies on constant changes of scene and event to compel attention. It is

a book I would not hesitate to recommend to English readers from twelve or so, for the story is well organised and swift and the atmosphere of mountain village, busy town and river-bank is definite and fascinating. Tibeso leaves home to ask advice from a local "big man" about a marauding leopard which has snatched a calf from the herd he was tending. He finds another "leopard", just as dangerous, the local blacksmith, whose depredations could well be revealed by reason of a clue which the observant boy has noticed. After the blacksmith has snatched him Tibeso fears for his life, but he is brave and has the slippery tricks of a boy at his disposal, and after more than one escape and recapture he helps to ambush the villain and witnesses his terrible death. The author has used lightly idiomatic speech and has relied for excitement mainly on a swift alternation of moments of action with moments of doubt and speculation as the boy reviews each situation. (pp. 2362-63)

Margery Fisher, in a review of "The Leopard," in Growing Point, *Vol. 12, No. 9, April, 1974, pp. 2362-63.*

Danish author Cecil Bodker wrote this originally for East African children. Thus the Ethiopian village background is taken for granted and the boy shepherd Tibeso is free to plunge immediately into an adventure—a leopard hunt in which he soon becomes the hunted when he is naive enough to identify a cattle thief and murderer to his face. Tibeso keeps one step ahead of this murdering blacksmith by a combination of manly courage and boyish tricks. Some of his stratagems, like leaving a clay pot-and-straw dummy of himself on the roof while he escapes into the night, work with folk tale efficiency and though Tibeso, dressed as a girl, eventually joins forces with a band of Arab traders who are also pursuing the blacksmith, his enemy is eventually finished off by the big leopard, forgotten since the first chapter, which reappears symbolically to wreak justice. At times Tibeso's inability, or unwillingness, to get help from adults is more frightening than the blacksmith himself (though of course trusting a grownup was what got him into trouble in the first place). But even when his isolation seems more foreign than the ghost villages, straw houses and donkey caravans, it keeps the reader eager for the next stage of the chase.

A review of "The Leopard," in Kirkus Reviews, *Vol. XLIII, No. 3, February 1, 1975, p. 121.*

There is more to *The Leopard* than its title would indicate. On one level, this is a gripping and suspenseful story about the occasionally exasperating adventures of a shepherd-boy, Tibeso, in a rural village in central Ethiopia. The underlying theme that gives the story its continuity is Tibeso's courageous fight for survival when his discovery "that a disguised blacksmith, not a leopard, is responsible for a great many missing cattle in the area" imperils his life. For older children, *The Leopard* is a book that anyone, even adults, would find very enjoyable and informative.

But the book has another dimension. It depicts graphically and, except for a few minor details, authentically, life in a small rural Ethiopian village. (There is, for instance, a knife-throwing sequence that makes a caravan trader resemble a character in a "spaghetti western.") The book offers a lot of relevant social commentary along the way.

Among other things, Bodker succinctly describes the predominant economic and social role women play. Likewise, the male chauvanism prevalent in the rural society is tersely depicted (and this is a good topic for classroom discussion). For example, in one episode Tibeso is forced, by tactical imperatives, to dress as a girl. He is mortified: "Never had he imagined that such a shame would come to him." The author, a Dane who spent three months in the region from which the book's setting is derived, is to be commended for having captured so well the texture of life in that area.

The Leopard will be invaluable to all those wishing to know more about village life in Ethiopia. Bodker's style is clear and her handling of suspense surprisingly unobtrusive.

> *Taye Brooks Zerihoun, in a review of "The Leopard," in* Interracial Books for Children Bulletin, *Vol. 6, No. 2, 1975, p. 3.*

The boy's escape, and the blacksmith's ultimate downfall are full of adventure, with many chases, apprehensions, and disguises, though there are too many coincidences. Bødker successfully weaves details of life in an Ethiopian village into a readable and well-written tale of survival, but this type of foreign adventure usually has a very small readership.

> *Judy Johnson, in a review of "The Leopard," in* School Library Journal, *Vol. 21, No. 8, April, 1975, p. 49.*

The author seems single minded, telling this tale of an Ethiopian boy cowherd living in dread of a fearsome leopard and a ruthless human cattle thief, murderer and child-stealer, who pursues and terrifies him day and night till the end. Skilfully constructed, swiftly told, the end is poetic justice—leopard and villain kill each other. But perhaps, as R. L. Stevenson said, "It is what he leaves in the inkpot that is significant." Is [Bødker] really protesting against the shabby treatment of Ethiopian children? Schools are not mentioned; kindness is not apparent; children are not valued as children; mothers of stolen girls lament only the loss of drudges and their "bride-price". The atmosphere is of grey materialism, suspicion, superstition and evil. Has an ancient stronghold of Coptic Christianity become a spiritual desert? Tobeso's only gain is the leopard's ear which makes him a folk hero. The author's reward is the Hans Christian Andersen award of 1975 and the Batchelder award of 1977. These honours say more than any critic can say about this book.

> *J. McC., in a review of "Leopard," in* Book Window, *Vol. 6, No. 1, Winter, 1978, p. 31.*

Silas and the Black Mare (1978)

[The time period for the setting of **Silas and the Black Mare** is not] distinct, although the brilliant illustrations by Julek Heller hint at Brueghel. The society is that of peasants and the only representative of a wider world is the pedlar. Against these earth-bound, prejudiced, brutalized creatures born of poverty and ignorance shines Silas, a very small boy who owns nothing but his wits, an abundance of self-confidence, and a way with horses. Silas is much too big a creation to be squandered on one book. As

he rides off, not into the sunset, at the close of this high-spirited frolic of a book, it is clear that more adventures lie ahead to be chronicled in the same blend of realism and lyricism. Cecil Bødker, . . . likes the byways of history and topography, but can sustain a major mainstream character, one who owes something to Tyl Eulenspiegel but who bids fair to win a small place among the immortals in his own right.

> *Marcus Crouch, "Rule of the Boy Kings," in* The Times Literary Supplement, *No. 3979, July 7, 1978, p. 767.*

This fresh, hearty Danish import is the first of a series about Silas, a resourceful and quick-thinking innocent, who runs away from an abusive sword swallower and soon wins a beautiful black mare from a horse trader who takes the loss of the wager with exceptionally bad grace. From the first-page moment when Silas drifts down the river into the horse trader's view, he commands a wary curiosity; and he continues to astound and to be astounded throughout his subsequent encounters—with a girl who has no eyes, her fierce mother, a treacherous farmer who steals the mare, a cowardly peddler, a friendly lame cowherd Silas' age, and a delightfully drawn otter hunter who sees through all the others and plays his own sly games with them. The story ends with the full cast assembled for an auction of the mare on the one street of a mean, impoverished village; Bødker pulls off this climactic scene as adeptly as Silas does the recovery of his mount. The whole, highly original story is related with a degree of shrewd humor and an absence of moralizing interference that are still hard to come by in children's books.

> *A review of "Silas and the Black Mare," in* Kirkus Reviews, *Vol. XLVI, No. 14, July 15, 1978, p. 749.*

The story takes place in a mysterious fairytale setting somewhere in the past. Silas appears from nowhere, drifting downriver, to become for a short while deeply involved with the horsedealer Bartolin, from whom he wins the black mare by a riding wager the dealer refuses to acknowledge, and a small oppressed peasant community, grasping to a man, save for an old woodcarver, Joanna and her lame son, Ben-Gulik the cowherd, who befriends Silas, and the otterhunter who loves Joanna. The values of this small group are humane; they take pride in their skills, Silas in his riding and strange other-worldly flute music, Gulik in his secret woodcarving. They support each other in a kind of unacknowledged brotherhood when the rich pedlar, and Silas' mother the tightrope dancer, with Philip, the bullying sword-swallower, also converge on the village. The other characters are brutal and treacherous. Even the pathetic blind girl Maria is tainted, and at the end when the two boys set out together, Silas taunts her unkindly in revenge, though the cripple, who can put himself in her place, reproves him. There are no blacks and whites: one is also persuaded to see the viewpoint of and sympathise with even the nastiest characters. The tension and menace build up remarkably in this world of fear and suspicion, until Silas recaptures his black mare and escapes. At such a level of writing, one looks forward eagerly to the sequels. (pp. 263-64)

> *M. Hobbs, in a review of "Silas and the Black*

Mare," in The Junior Bookshelf, *Vol. 42, No. 5, October, 1978, pp. 263-64.*

Reminiscent of Heironymus Bosch paintings and the adult novels of Jerzy Kosinski, this almost surrealistic tale set in a timeless European landscape follows young Silas who runs away from his traveling circus family. . . . While the cruelty and avarice of the villagers Silas encounters are unremitting (almost all want to cheat him, beat him, or kidnap him), Silas himself is no bargain either. He survives only by putting his own needs first; for example, when he finds himself trapped in a fisherman's hut, he shocks his host into providing a bed for the night by suggesting the man sell his blind daughter as a side-show attraction ("All she would have to do is go around in the crowd looking for her eyes. . . . Everyone can see that she's lost them, so they'll put money in the holes to comfort her.") Bødker's writing, even in translation, is spare and clean, harshly appropriate to the country and people described. It is a bizarre and hostile story illuminated only rarely by glimmers of love or caring, but readers who felt an affinity with Julia Cunningham's *Dorp Dead* (Pantheon, 1965) will recognize and appreciate this novel's bleak power.

> *Whitney Rogge, in a review of "Silas and the Black Mare," in* School Library Journal, *Vol. 25, No. 3, November, 1978, p. 56.*

Silas and the Black Mare is an even grimmer reminder that adult cruelty to children is perennial, and that, in earlier centuries, it was even more pervasive and brutal. Cecil Bødker is a Dane with a reputation for Kafkaesque fiction which the present book does nothing to diminish. It chronicles the travels of a lone boy through a harsh and desolate countryside some time in the distant past. Every encounter the child has with an adult is treacherous and problematic, and the boy's eventual survival is something of an improbable deliverance. (p. 626)

> *John Naughton, "Gangs and Fans," in* The Listener, *Vol. 100, No. 2585, November 9, 1978, pp. 625-26.*

Silas and Ben-Godik; Silas and the Runaway Coach (1978)

The harsh environment in the first book hasn't improved any in these two additions. Again poverty is rife and adults too often not to be trusted: in **Silas and Ben-Godik** the boys tangle first with an allegedly deaf old woman involved in silver smuggling, and then with a bizarrely evil Horse Crone who steals his mare and nearly causes him to lose his life to the ruthless silver smugglers. In **Silas and the Runaway Coach** the Horse Crone reappears in a new but no less troublemaking situation—and again makes off with Silas' novel mare. In this last story, however, Silas finds himself under the benevolent wing of a wealthy merchant whose runaway coach he managed to halt. The primary theme here is Silas' steadfast maintenance of his precious independence while staying with the merchant, teaching his son to think for himself, and deciding to learn to read. Bødker's characters, whether good or evil, are memorable, and Silas in particular continues to awe with his cool self-possession and wise-beyond-years abilities to deal with people—both these traits believable in light of

his circus years described in the **Black Mare** book. More first-rate picaresque adventure.

> *Denise M. Wilms, in a review of "Silas and Ben-Godik" and "Silas and the Runaway Coach," in* Booklist, *Vol. 75, No. 6, November 15, 1978, p. 542.*

In **Silas and the Black Mare,** Bodker projected her resourceful young hero's memorable encounters with penetrating, uncompromising shrewdness; in these subsequent volumes she settles for merely *using* similar treacherous and bizarre figures to spice and propel Silas' adventures. Nevertheless her strong, stinking, conniving Horse Crone—who steals a little boy and hitches him to her knife-sharpening wagon, steals Silas' mare (though he tracks her down and retrieves it), and tries to do Silas in on more than one occasion—is a most imposing villain; and Silas' further adventures, particularly in the latter volume, are corking, invigorating ones. . . . By now the once-amoral Silas has developed a compassionate sense of humanity, and he is forever rescuing unsavory victims (even the Horse Crone, and a dancing bear more than once) from angry crowds and cohorts; but his kind deeds are undertaken with such dash and defiance of risk that there's no question of going soft. Silas continues to speak out refreshingly, to outwit opponents and readers, to maintain his wary independence and keen exuberance—well into a crackerjack series that shows no sign of lagging.

> *A review of "Silas and Ben-Godik" and "Silas and the Runaway Coach," in* Kirkus Reviews, *Vol. XLVI, No. 24, December 15, 1978, p. 1356.*

[In **Silas and Ben-Godik**] Silas, the young ex-circus performer, along with the lame cowherd Ben-Godik, travels from town to town exploring the country. Lured by the prospect of adventure rather than by any specific destination, the two soon find their itinerary determined by the unwitting involvement with a bizarre cast of shifty characters conditioned by greed, hunger, and poverty to disregard conventional morality in a search for immediate gratification. . . . The desolate setting against which the characters move is as evocative as an Ingmar Bergman landscape: It is at once a backdrop for the actors and an explanation for their deeds. The contrast between the provincial villagers and the quick-witted Silas not only heightens the suspense but also provides an earthy, humorous note. Smoothly translated and filled with action, the book lends itself to reading aloud; however, the story can be better appreciated as a sequel to **Silas and the Black Mare** than as a separate entity.

> *Mary M. Burns, in a review of "Silas and Ben-Godik," in* The Horn Book Magazine, *Vol. LV, No. 1, February, 1979, p. 58.*

Hairbreadth escapes from the deaf landlady who fronts for smugglers, a knife-grinding crone after contraband silver, and a performing bear rampaging through a town market keep the plot of **Silas and Ben-Godik** rolling. . . . In the following book, Silas, footloose as Huck Finn and with the bluntness and spunk of Pippi Longstocking, stops a . . . **Runaway Coach** team to save a merchant's family . . . In both adventures, Silas contends with disbelief that the mare is his and uses his flute time and again to escape tight corners. Frequent references to earlier books in the series distract readers. The foreign locale and folktale quality will limit the American audience, but the author's broad humor (sometimes bordering on the grotesque), earthy detail, and riveting descriptions make these deserving of space in collections.

> *Pat Harrington, in a review of "Silas and Ben-Godik" and "Silas and the Runaway Coach," in* School Library Journal, *Vol. 25, No. 8, April, 1979, p. 53.*

These two Bodker novels can easily stand on their own as good literature, yet when one knows that they are part of a series, the reader will probably devour all of them and still want to read more. Through Silas, Bodker has created one of the most delightful boys in all of children's literature. He has such a zest and love of and for life! In addition to Silas is a complete cast of vividly memorable characters of all types. If for no other reason, Bodker's works should be read for her character portrayal. These two works are filled with the fast paced adventure, suspense and drama which young readers crave in their books. (pp. 447-48)

> *J. N., in a review of "Silas and Ben-Godik" and "Silas and the Runaway Coach," in* Catholic Library World, *Vol. 50, No. 10, May-June, 1979, pp. 447-48.*

Mary of Nazareth (1989)

A readable narrative and [Bengt Arne Runnerström's] intriguing paintings tell the story of Mary, beginning with the bewildering message from a stranger that she will give birth to a "a holy child," to her witnessing Jesus' coming of age in the temple. The story ends somewhat abruptly; Jesus begins to learn his father's trade while Joseph muses that his son will become a fine carpenter. Incisive storytelling brings the human drama of this familiar story to the fore. Detailed watercolors present with historical and cultural accuracy a panoramic view of marketplaces, the village surrounding the temple, the countryside, and much more. The pictures also present intimate interiors of domestic and temple life and emotional portraits of the characters. Readers may be convinced that this is the story as it might have happened and that these are the times as they really were. A helpful map introduces this unique version of the traditional story.

> *Susan Hepler, in a review of "Mary of Nazareth," in* School Library Journal, *Vol. 35, No. 14, October, 1989, p. 40.*

A realistic expansion of the account in Matthew and Luke of Mary's experiences from the Annunciation to Jesus' 12th year, by a Danish Andersen medalist.

With careful attention to biblical clues, Bodker presents real people responding with dignity to an unexpected supernatural event. When Ann sees that Mary is trembling after the visitation, she asks, "Did he hurt you?" and explains to her husband that Mary is ill. The neighbors gossip; Mary goes away for a while, to visit her aunt Elizabeth, who is carrying John the Baptist; the meeting of these two women confirms the miraculous nature of the coming event. Bodker makes some interestingly plausible and logical additions: Mary's parents are also in Bethlehem to be taxed, as descendants of David; Joseph works as a shipbuilder in Egypt. The carefully authentic illustrations show dark, Middle Eastern faces, often expressing emotion with subtlety; many of the scenes are nicely evocative of ancient Israel, although there are also clumsy passages in the art, which is uneven in quality.

A memorable, reverent, unusual, and unusually detailed approach to this beloved story.

> *A review of "Mary of Nazareth," in* Kirkus Reviews, *Vol. LVII, No. 20, October 15, 1989, p. 1526.*

Mary, the mother of Jesus, takes on distinctly human proportions in this story that incorporates what is known from New Testament sources and adds its own embellishments. She appears as a proper, well-reared young woman, vastly troubled by the revelation that she will bear a son. After all, she is betrothed to Joseph, who will likely reject her since he knows he is not the father of the child she carries. But there is clearly a higher power at work as Mary, her family, and Joseph are all given signs that Mary's pregnancy is indeed the will of God and that her child, shown born in a stable and worshipped by shepherds and kings, is the Son of God. These events, as well as others detailing Mary's role in Jesus' childhood, are seen from a slightly altered perspective, one that conjures up a remarkably real sense of what everyday life in Mary's time might have been like. The watercolor paintings firmly ground the setting in the Middle East. Mary is no blue-eyed blond—just the opposite, in fact, with a sensual (but by no means licentious) dimension in her dress and demeanor. Evocatively drawn and compellingly told.

> *Denise Wilms, in a review of "Mary of Nazareth," in* Booklist, *Vol. 86, No. 7, December 1, 1989, p. 740.*

Barbara Cooney

1917-

American author and illustrator of picture books, retellings, fiction, and nonfiction, and illustrator.

Major works include *Chanticleer and the Fox* (1958), *The Little Juggler: Adapted from an Old French Legend* (1961; new edition, 1982), *Ox-Cart Man* (written by Donald Hall, 1979), *Miss Rumphius* (1982), *Island Boy* (1988).

A writer and artist who is acclaimed for providing elementary grade readers with fifty years of outstanding works, Cooney is often praised for her diversity and for the thorough research and attention to detail to which the authenticity of her books is attributed. A prolific illustrator who has contributed pictures to over one hundred titles, Cooney is also recognized for the approximately fifteen books for which she is both author and illustrator. These works, which often reflect Cooney's affection for New England, especially her home state of Maine, and her international travels, are often acknowledged for their insightful and elegant depictions of lifestyle and the connectedness of generations and for the strong sense of place with which she underscores them. The creator of books in several genres, she is best known for her retellings of European tales, including two from the Brothers Grimm and one from Geoffrey Chaucer, and for her picture book biographies with American settings. Cooney is often noted as a writer who brings freshness, wit, and accessibility to her retellings and vigor and dignity to her own tales. As an illustrator, she is well regarded for her development of the scratchboard technique and the craft of color separation as well as for the variety of formats and mediums with which she composes her pictures. Cooney is characterized artistically by colorful paintings which often incorporate medieval and folk-art details, and she is often celebrated for her evocation of both landscapes and interiors. Attempting to fit her mediums to the spirit of her texts, Cooney initially employed line drawings highlighted with areas of color but more recently has experimented with wash, charcoal, acrylics, and collage.

Cooney began her career as an illustrator of works by such writers as Homer, Edward Lear, Louisa May Alcott, Felix Salten, Rumer Godden, Walter de la Mare, Margaret Wise Brown, Lee Kingman, and John Bierhorst; when she deleted a portion of Sarah Orne Jewett's text to create the picture book *A White Heron: A Story of Maine* (1963), she received a mixed reception. Her first works as both author and artist are fictional stories set in Maine: a fantastic tale about a shipwrecked sailor, a family story about identical twins who switch places, and a summer mystery adventure. With *Chanticleer and the Fox,* a picture book in which she retells one of Chaucer's *Canterbury Tales,* Cooney created a work that is often considered a classic. A fable about how a handsome rooster nearly loses his life through the flattery of a sly fox, *Chanticleer* is lauded both for its contemporary flavor and for the beauty of its illustrations, line drawings in a five-color wash. Cooney received her first Caldecott Medal in 1959 for *Chanticleer,* an award which she won again in 1980 for *Ox-Cart Man.*

A picture book about a nineteenth-century New Hampshire farmer who makes the long journey from his inland home to a coastal market, Cooney illustrates Donald Hall's story with art which evokes early American primitive wood paintings. She is also especially lauded for writing and illustrating two life stories in picture book form: the first, *Miss Rumphius,* addresses the theme of bequeathing beauty as a legacy as it describes how young Alice Rumphius promises her grandfather that she will make the world more beautiful when she grows up. After traveling the world and coming to Maine to live by the ocean, she fulfills her promise by scattering five bushels of lupine seed around the countryside. With *Island Boy,* Cooney creates a hymn to self-reliance and the continuity of life by describing the life and death of a nineteenth-century man on a remote island; loosely based on the story of Matthias Tibbetts, who settled on an uninhabited Maine island in the last century, the story is noted for sensitively presenting death to the picture book audience. In addition to her original stories and retellings, Cooney is the author and illustrator of several nonfiction and concept books, including a history of the Nativity, an alphabet book of Southern Colonial games, and an adaptation of Noah Webster's popular Blue-Backed speller that teachers children about phonics. In addition to her Caldecott Medals and several other awards for her illustrations, Cooney received an American Book Award in 1983 for *Miss Rumphius* as well as two awards for her body of work: the Silver Medallion from the University of Southern Mississippi in 1975 and a medal from Smith College in 1976. In 1989, the Children's and Young Adults' Services Section of the Maine Library Association created the Lupine Award in honor of Cooney and *Miss Rumphius.*

(See also *Something about the Author,* Vols. 6, 59; *Contemporary Authors New Revision Series,* Vol. 3; and *Contemporary Authors,* Vols. 5-6, rev. ed.)

AUTHOR'S COMMENTARY

The first twenty years of my life I spent growing up. The next twenty years I was busy getting married and having children, staying home and taking care of my family, and decorating books. I drew what was near at hand—children—over and over again. Children—and animals. It sometimes seemed that the number of jobs offered was in direct proportion to the quality of the fur I drew.

In those years, landscape in my pictures was usually incidental. I saw the world in color but I had to work in black-and-white—not from choice but because that is most economical for publishers. I used to yearn for color, but without much luck. One editor told me I had no color sense whatsoever. The little color I was now and then allowed was always in the form of overlays, which, for me, are awkward, certainly tiresome, and, worst of all, unspontaneous.

Besides, I did not have confidence in my ability to capture the moods of landscapes. There was one exception, though; for a book called *Peter's Long Walk* by Lee Kingman I put my heart and soul into trying to capture a certain time, place, and mood: early spring in New England. I spent days in the woods with a sketch book and a fishing rod, and sometimes one of the children and a picnic. These pictures are awkward, not particularly wonderful, but my heart was in them.

It was not until I was in my forties, in the fifth decade of my life, that the sense of place, the *spirit* of place, became of paramount importance to me. It was then that I began my travels, that I discovered, through photography, the quality of light, and that that I gradually became able to paint the mood of places.

Earlier, while working on Chaucer's story of *Chanticleer and the Fox,* I had stayed home and studied the middle ages through books and old manuscripts and pictures in museums. But when I began to work on the story of *The Little Juggler,* also set in the medieval period, I went to France to see what it was like, to see the places where the little juggler might have wandered. In the book, I showed actual scenes of Tours and Normandy. I was still restricted by black-and-white and overlays, but my travels had begun. And what unconsciously happened was that my characters began to be no longer isolated from their backgrounds. More and more they become part of the landscape, part of their environment. Perhaps a certain humility was born. . . .

Soon after, something else happened. Some of our publishers began issuing familiar tales translated into foreign languages—such as *Winnie Ille Pu, Winnie the Pooh* in Latin. When my editor suggested I work on a project of this sort, Mother Goose in French, I happily packed up my children and sailed for France.

We rented a house on Lake Annecy, in the French Alps; I had Mother Hubbard keep her bones in an armoire like the ones where we kept our clothes in that house, and I sent Jack and Jill up the hill to fetch some edelweiss. I drew the castles and farmhouses we visited and the bakery where we got the croissants for our breakfast.

I had such a good time makeing **Mother Goose in French** that I decided to do **Mother Goose in Spanish.** The Spanish Mother Goose, unlike the French one, is in acrylics, because of their strong and brilliant quality. I think of Spain as strong, often harsh, masculine, and of France as softer, more pastel, more feminine.

In Spain, little Tommy Tittlemouse, now Tomasino Tinito, lived in his little house raising rice for paella in the Albufera marshes. I drew the Plaza Mayor of a sleepy little town baking in the noonday sun, and people sitting in their doorways in the cool of the evening, the women doing needlework with their backs to the road as they do in Spain.

I have done three different ABC books. For the one commissioned by Colonial Williamsburg, the setting is, of course, tidewater Virginia. During every season of the year, I went up and down the James River searching for my locations. F was for fishing, G was for girls and geese, H for hunting, and so on.

Unlike Mother Goose and ABC books, there is only one place that Greek myths can take place; and I have been lucky enough to do three of these stories in picture-book form. Lucky, because in museums and in going through art books, I came to realize that no matter how glorious Greek art is, the vases and statues tell us little about what the land itself is like. So began my trips to Greece.

In **Dionysos and the Pirates,** pirates stole across a genuinely wine-dark sea, landing on the island of Naxos to kidnap Dionysos. For the story of Hermes stealing the cattle of Apollo, I climbed to the cave in the mountains behind Corinth where Hermes was said to have been born, and also, one dawn, to the top of Mt. Olimpos, the place called the Lap of the Gods.

In the story of Demeter and Persephone, the earth splits open, and Hades, Lord of the underworld, seizing Persephone, carries her off to his underground kingdom. There are several places in Greece that are said to be the actual entrance to the underworld. Three I visited. But the place at Ermione seemed the nicest, and that is the one I show in the book. When Persephone was restored to her mother, she returned to Ermione; in that picture I showed the fig trees putting out their leaves, the fruit trees blossoming, and the field once again covered with spring flowers.

It was during the years that I was doing these Greek myths that I fell in love with photography. What had been just a tool for me now became a new form of art, a new way to make pictures; but more important, it gave me an awareness of the quality of light which has influenced my work as an illustrator. Photography is, after all, "painting with light."

Years ago, when I began illustrating, fairy tales were unfashionable. Today they are almost too much in fashion. True, they are a mighty good vehicle, and I myself have contributed to the glut. But I have done only one Grimm tale since being to Hesse in Germany, where the brothers Grimm lived and collected their tales. It was particularly green when I was there because it was raining all the time, and I painted one of those typical wet, dismal days in *Little Brother and Little Sister,* when the children ran away from home. The King in the story lived in the castle that is said to be the one where Sleeping Beauty slept. Today it is a very nice castle hotel—except in the middle of the day when busloads of tourists arrive, mostly older women in suits and important hats, or, when raining, under umbrellas and plastic kerchiefs, and cherishing, I think, dreams of a handsome prince.

In the castle scenes in *Little Brother and Little Sister,* I also show a horse-chestnut tree with a bench around it which stands in the courtyard of the Grimms' own house in Steinan, and also, one end of the house itself.

I have visited, and recorded in picture books, France, Spain, Mexico, Tidewater Virginia, Greece, Hesse, and other lands. But imaginary worlds are places also. In the pictures for Elinor Horowitz's *When the Sky is Like Lace,* I show a place where many odd and wonderful things happen. This is definitely a real place—but I don't know where it is.

After travelling to many places, both physically and in my head, I finally came home again. I built a house on the coast of Maine, and there, years after *Peter's Long Walk,* I finally painted New England in full color. The pictures for Donald Hall's *Ox-Cart Man* were the first I did in the new house. They show the passage of the seasons in the New Hampshire hills.

After that book came *Miss Rumphius,* which is so much my heart that I cannot see it clearly. It is many places, and all of them are part of me: my grandmother's house in Brooklyn where I was born, the library in the town of Pepperell, Massachusetts where I raised my children, the greenhouse at Smith College where I went to school, and also, the island in the Molluccas, the place by the sea, *that* room, the fields of flowers in the fog. They are all part of me—and I am part of them.

My latest book, *The Spirit Child;* is translated from the Aztec by John Bierhorst. It has a Mexican background. The text was written in 1583 by the monk Fray Bernardino Sahagun and is one of the first books printed in this hemisphere. Until now it has never been translated from the original Nahuatl, the Aztec language. (pp. 152-53)

It is the story of the Nativity. In it are the volcanoes, which the Aztecs believed to be the entrances to Hell before Jesus was born. And when Jesus was born, three suns

From Chanticleer and the Fox, *written by Geoffrey Chaucer. Illustrated by Barbara Cooney.*

shone over Tenochtitlan, the capitol of Mexico. Mary went to Bethlehem on foot. There was no donkey for her to ride, for prior to the coming of the Spaniards, the only domestic animals the Aztecs had were dogs and turkeys, and in 1583, when the text was written, the Indians were forbidden to ride the horses, mules, and donkeys introduced by the Spaniards on pain of death.

In conclusion, I would like to quote from a book on Chineses painting—*The Tao of Painting,* by Mai Mai Sze: ". . . the literal aim of painting [was the magic that] happened when skill with brush could transmit the spirit to silk or paper." This is what I am trying to do. (p. 153.)

> *Barbara Cooney, "The Spirit Place," in* Children's Literature Association Quarterly, *Vol. 9, No. 4, Winter, 1984-85, pp. 152-53.*

GENERAL COMMENTARY

Anna Newton Porter

My claims to distinction are few and frail. But that my daughter-in-law should love and trust me enough to ask me to write this sketch of her is surely one of them. When I told her I was neither an artist nor an intelligent critic, she said, "But you know about *me.*" So I Shall try my best. . . .

Barbara's nervous energy is enormous and her capacity for the sensuous enjoyment of life is inexhaustible. She is many people—a conscientious wife for a busy doctor; a fiercely loving mother, enjoying—and spoiling—her babies with passionate devotion; an ambitious and excellent cook; an ardent gardener, and a serious dedicated artist. (p. 315)

There is no separation of her creative life from her everyday domestic activity. That is perhaps because she lives as creatively as she works. The children who run and dance across her pages run and dance across her life.

Barbara is very serious about her work. A "deadline" is a sacred thing, even if she has to wait until everyone has gone to bed to get on with her pictures. If she likes a book, she lives in it while she is illustrating it. When she did *Little Women* she even wore a bun. (p. 317)

When she did *Grandfather Whiskers M.D.,* a cage of mice stood near her work-table to the delight of her children. *Chanticleer* meant a pen of chickens loaned by a neighbor. But more than that, it meant the Middle Ages and with scrupulous and loving care she studied the period of Chaucer until it came alive for her. Indeed, I think there is something a bit medieval in much of her work, a perception of the beauty of humble flowers or tiny, peering animal faces which the illuminators of old missals felt. Dürer expressed the same feeling in the delicate foregrounds of many of his etchings and in his water colors of common weeds and grasses. I have noticed that when Barbara takes a walk in the woods she seldom returns with great armfuls of ferns or branches. She will show you, perhaps, some strange mosses or gray-green lichens or the pale untimely bloom of witch hazel.

I asked her once which of her books she liked the best—she has illustrated fifty! She thought a bit and said, "Well, *Christmas in the Barn* and *Where Have You Been?* by

Margaret Wise Brown, *American Folk Songs for Children* by Ruth Crawford Seeger, *Grandfather Whiskers M. D.* by Nellie M. Leonard, *Peter's Long Walk* by Lee Kingman, and *Chanticleer.*"

Peter's Long Walk, the story of a very small boy's adventure, gave her an opportunity to draw the country scenes around [her home in Pepperell, Massachusetts] to the surprise and delight of her neighbors. Like all good artists, she gives meaning and poetry to ordinary things. But if she never touched a brush again, she would still bring color and meaning and humor into her everyday living and into the lives of those she loves, for she lives so ardently. (pp. 317-18)

She, somehow, makes dreams come true.

I think no one but Barbara would contemplate taking four children with her and [her husband] Talbot to Washington so that they can see her receive the Caldecott Medal. It is as if she were giving them part of the credit for her achievement. Perhaps they deserve it. For she has always used them as models for her book children and through loving them has learned to love and understand all childhood. (p. 319)

> *Anna Newton Porter, "Barbara Cooney," in* The Horn Book Magazine, *Vol. XXXV, No. 4, August, 1959, pp. 315-19.*

Marcia Brown

Who presumes to re-illustrate the verses of Edward Lear is up against formidable competition from Mr. Lear himself. Lear has never really been out of fashion with children. Several artists have recently challenged his drawings with their own or have tried to draw humor in a similar vein. (p. 21)

With gentle satire and great delicacy Barbara Cooney has recreated the woeful little tragedy of Cock Robin [in *The Courtship, Merry Marriage, and Feast of Cock Robin and Jenny Wren, to which Is Added the Doleful Death of Cock Robin*]. The satire never bursts out of the miniature frame of the story. In an unassuming but very skillful way she has been extremely successful in her illustrations for Lear. Her drawings seem extensions of his, so completely has she caught their quality. (pp. 21-2)

> *Marcia Brown, "One Wonders," in* Illustrators of Children's Books: 1957-1966, *Lee Kingman, Joanna Foster, Ruth Giles Lontoft, eds., The Horn Book, Inc., 1968, pp. 2-27.*

Grace Allen Hogarth

When Barbara Cooney cut the text of *A White Heron* so that it could become a picture book, she made a work of art that I am certain Sarah Orne Jewett would have loved. But the book was received with a storm of protest. . . . Is the material wrong, or right, for a picture book? In the case of *A White Heron* I feel that the editor, Elizabeth Riley of Thomas Y. Crowell, made a decision which has increased the author's audience and given her a new stature. (pp. 40-1)

The development of [the] craft of color separation by American artists from the mid-thirties to the present day is a fascinating chapter in printing and publishing history. As the artist's skill developed, the printer's skill also improved until it was possible to produce an almost flawless result in, for example, *A White Heron* with Barbara Cooney's illustrations. Her earlier color separations had, for the most part, been simply line drawings with areas of solid color, as in *Chanticleer and the Fox* and *The Little Juggler.* Her separations for *A White Heron,* however, were given a wash effect which she obtained by tying chamois leather over her brush. The printer faithfully reproduced each delicately shaded separation by using a screen in the making of his plates. Barbara Cooney is a master in this craft. . . . (pp. 47-8)

> *Grace Allen Hogarth, "The Artist and His Editor," in* Illustrators of Children's Books: 1957-1966, *Lee Kingman, Joanna Foster, Ruth Giles Lontoft, eds., The Horn Book, Inc., 1968, pp. 36-53.*

Lee Bennett Hopkins

To date Miss Cooney has illustrated over 60 books. Her work is a tremendously important part of her life, for it is interrelated with her life. Her books are gay, entertaining, and simple, yet complex. Is it any wonder that children young and old enjoy books by Barbara Cooney? (pp. 42-3)

> *Lee Bennett Hopkins, "Barbara Cooney," in his* Books Are by People, *Citation Press, 1969, pp. 41-3.*

Constance Reed McClellan

Perhaps because of her wide reputation, her prolificacy, her varied accomplishments, and her success as an illustrator, artist, and winner of Caldecott Medals, many people, even her friends, stand in awe of Barbara Cooney. I am a friend, but I am not awed—I am *amazed.* Amazed at her stamina, her stick-to-it-iveness, her strength, and her ability to tackle something new, again and again. (p. 384)

In the last two decades Barbara Cooney has moved on in her illustrating, taking broad leaps and jumps from her early scratch-board technique and her drawings of mice and ponies. New assignments have meant new places to be visited, new languages to be studied: a summer in France, a crash course at Berlitz. There were also trips to Ireland, Spain, Greece, Bali, Germany, and Mexico, and to India to see a daughter and a first grandchild. She is an inveterate traveler, reader, and student.

And she pursued a new art—photography. Before long came a Nikon camera, photography courses, her own darkroom, and a Cooney book of photographs for the Bicentennial.

The growth continued: illustrating in new formats, mediums, and techniques; a book of games for Colonial Williamsburg; a poster map for Smith College and a cover for the alumnae magazine; illustrations for Homeric legends and for Mother Goose in French and Spanish—along with chalk talks, television appearances, and a long tour of duty as a town library trustee. She did it all. Amazing Barbara. (p. 385)

Barbara has been lucky. Her keen mind combined with inherited and learned talents, a fine liberal arts education, and family stability all provide the most advantageous

background; but the success, the fame, and the satisfaction could not have been achieved without her self-discipline, her drive, and her motivation for independence.

As Barbara Cooney goes along in her sexagenarian years—what next? Nothing would surprise me—still another language to be learned, a new art medium, a canoe trip down the Amazon? She does not appear to be slowing down at all but, instead, just looking for another challenge, another pinnacle. She is a very exciting woman, an inspiration to young illustrators and to women everywhere. Amazing Barbara. (pp. 386-87)

> *Constance Reed McClellan, "Barbara Cooney," in* The Horn Book Magazine, *Vol. LVI, No. 4, August, 1980, pp. 383-87.*

Julia Smith

In this interview for *Instructor* readers, Barbara Cooney reveals secrets to be found on the open pages of her picture books. Knowing how this artist's life is intimately bound up in her stories will increase both teachers' and students' delight in the magic of picture books.

Like the Lupine Lady [Miss Rumphius], Barbara Cooney lives in a house overlooking the sea. Her house is large, however, and full of sunlight. Barbara Cooney is little, but not so very old. Spry and spirited, she is comfortable in jeans and flip-flops, with her silvery hair braided atop her head.

Barbara Cooney's resemblance to the Lupine Lady is not coincidental. *Miss Rumphius* is a mixture of many parts of Cooney's life, and of the artist herself. Scattered throughout the book, we find things dear to Cooney—an embroidered shawl, a favorite armchair, a picture of her grandson. And the story, though not precisely autobiographical, begins with a scene in Brooklyn, New York, where Cooney was born. Alice Rumphius's grandfather is an artist and carves cigar store Indians just as Barbara Cooney's great-grandfather once did. Alice helps her grandfather paint the skies on some of his paintings, just as Cooney's grandmother once did for her father.

As we accompany Miss Rumphius in her search for a way to make the world more beautiful, we see her as a librarian (Cooney has been a library trustee for 18 years); touring a conservatory that bears a striking resemblance to one at Smith College (Cooney's alma mater); and traveling to faraway places (travel is one of Cooney's delights). The pastoral scenes are a patchwork of favorite buildings and places in New England where Cooney has lived for much of her life.

The inspiration for *Miss Rumphius* came when Cooney was building her house in Maine and asked one of the carpenters why there were so many of the lovely lupines growing all around. He told her of Hilda, the real-life Lupine Lady, who planted all the flowers. The story began to grow in Cooney's mind until, one day, she plunked herself down on the sofa and wrote it from beginning to end. "I had something in my head," she says, "and I just had to get it out." *Miss Rumphius,* the artist feels, was a major development in her art. "Because," says Cooney, "she has *real* soul."

Miss Rumphius is the story of an artist's challenge. Wanting to add to the beauty of the world, an artist must search for the right means of adding to the beauty that already surrounds us. Miss Rumphius finds her answer and challenges the artist in all of us to find ours. (p. 94)

Cooney has published over 100 books, establishing a reputation for delicate, folk-art charm, meticulous research, and attention to detail. She began to travel widely, collecting images, ideas, and snatches of reality from which to create her illustrations. "It is my pleasure in life to go to the source."

In creating the art for poet Donald Hall's **Ox-Cart Man** Cooney returned to the early American tradition of painting on wood. "I've spent most of my life in New England. That's why I was able to evoke the life of a farmer and his family and the bustle of the marketplace. I have observed the people and the places." For her rendition of 19th-century rural New England, her portrayal of the cyclical nature of life, Cooney won her second Caldecott Award in 1980.

Cooney's latest book, **Spirit Child, A Story of the Nativity,** was translated from the Aztec by scholar John Bierhorst. Cooney's illustrations are full of details and symbols gleaned from a trip to Mexico. The adobe buildings, growing maize, and draped attire are all typical of Aztec country. Cooney's angels are styled after those depicted in Mexican churches. And such symbols as squash blossoms for fertility, and marigolds for death, are spread throughout the book. These details are Cooney's hallmark. However, she claims, they are for her own satisfaction. Readers don't generally know these things, and they are not important to the magic of the story. In fact, the deep colors in *Spirit Child* are alone enough to evoke the religious fervor and intensity of love and wonder that are intrinsic to the Nativity story.

Looking back at her growth as an artist, Cooney notes the development of her characters. At first, she says, the people all resembled her own children. And they didn't show much "soul." Cooney scorns illustrations where the people seem to be made of dough. "I think the heart of the soul is what you're trying to get into."

Cooney's characters are often born right on the page. "Sometimes, they just arrive," she says. "Then, as they are transferred from pen to paper, they become little people." Cooney says she is often surprised by her own work as personalities seem to develop almost independently of her brush.

Barbara Cooney begins to illustrate a book with page one. Books, she says, are like movies in which the eye moves from frame to frame in a progression. The illustrator must keep that progression in mind, keeping the eye always interested and content.

Cooney starts with a "dummy" of the book, or a rough, rather messy, version. Later, after getting the dummy okayed by the book's editor, she begins the painstaking work on the final illustrations, working carefully to get just the right colors, just the perfect tone.

The jacket comes last. "It's like a can of tomatoes," states Cooney. "You can't put a tomato on the label until you know you have a tomato in the can." (pp. 94-6)

Barbara Cooney doesn't write for anyone in particular. Rather, she paints and writes simply for her own enjoy-

ment, hoping that others will find the same joy she finds in her sometimes tender, sometimes bold, illustrations. And she is rewarded. Cooney has received letters from young and old. Many adolescents trying to find their way in life write that **Miss Rumphius** has helped them with its quiet wisdom. And older women write, thanking Cooney for her affirmation of their lives—for the message that by planting flowers, raising children, teaching school, or any of a multitude of things they can "make the world more beautiful."

Cooney is trying, through her picture books, to show people that there is magic in the world if only we open our eyes to it. "To me, the world is a magic place," smiles Cooney, "and that's what I'd like to point out. It's like when you are traveling with a friend who says 'Hey, look at that beautiful thing!' You might have missed it if your friend hadn't pointed it out." (p. 96)

> *Julia Smith, "Barbara Cooney's Award-Winning Picture Books . . . 'Make the World More Beautiful'," in* Instructor, *Vol. XCIV, No. 7, March, 1985, pp. 94-6.*

Lyn Ellen Lacy

The same red, ocher, and black that [Nicholes] Mordvin-

From The Little Juggler, *adapted and illustrated by Barbara Cooney.*

off used so somberly combine quite cheerfully with brilliant cobalt blue, vivid green, and rich red-brown in varying harmonious combinations by Barbara Cooney in the first of her two Award winners, the 1959 *Chanticleer and the Fox.* Once again an alternating system was devised for book design, this time with black-and-red illustrations interspersed with five-color pages. In fact *Chanticleer* exhibits the most artful of all such systems discussed here and also has some of the best total page design among all the Caldecotts. Double-page spreads sensitively accommodate informal text placement, and color is used to best advantage as a point of interest and as a balancing element in itself, especially when only red is used with black for moments of danger in the story. Cooney's crisp style is reminiscent of decorative folk art that includes the right amount of detail in costumes, household, and plants. In addition, all these elements were researched and are correct for a fourteenth-century English setting of a story that is an adaptation of Chaucer's "The Nun's Priest's Tale" from *The Canterbury Tales.* The necessary formality of text makes *Chanticleer* usually more successful with an older picture-book audience. It is interesting, though, that this morality tale dating back to Aesop is often given a modern-day interpretation by even the youngest children, who often see it as a kidnapping or child-molesting fable. (pp. 100-01)

Barbara Cooney's second Caldecott Award-winning title was the 1980 *Ox-Cart Man* with text by Donald Hall. Executed in an early-American primitive technique resembilng painting on wood and in similar style to that of nineteenth-century painter Edward Hicks, *Ox-Cart Man* is a staid and simple cyclical tale given an unusual spark of life by appropriately formal yet imaginative page layouts, delightful richness in coloration, and a pleasantly surprising use of light and dark in a series of three illustrations. Most of the book pictures New Hampshire pastoral and Portsmouth marketplace settings with a keen eye for authentic detail of time and place and always in the flat shapes and blunt colors of primitive style, even for October leaves fallen to the ground or May blossoms on the apple trees. When a wonderfully red sunset appears just as the Ox-Cart Man approaches home from the market, it is something of a surprise. It dramatically transforms sky and hills by implying depth and contour, and after a dozen illustrations it is the first to demonstrate interest in a source of illumination. A turn of the page, and one has the welcoming home scene in warmth of the kitchen with exquisite modeling and highlighting of figures gathered around softening firelight. . . . Another turn of the page, and one finds a barn scene in which the Ox-Cart Man carves a yoke while the winter sun casts across the floor and walls a long low shadow that is stunningly unique for such a work in early-American primitive style. Fire and red sky are repeated in a later illustration, but neither gives off the light or indeed offers the pleasurable surprise that Cooney's pictures of sunset, hearth, and barn offer in *Ox-Cart Man.* (p. 104)

> *Lyn Ellen Lacy, "Light and Dark: 'The Little House', 'Where the Wild Things Are', and 'Jumanji',' " in her* Art and Design in Children's Picture Books, *American Library Association, 1986, pp. 104-43.*

Zena Sutherland and May Hill Arbuthot

Children were delighted by Barbara Cooney's black-and-white pictures for those two fine animal stories—Rutherford Montgomery's *Kildee House* and Barbara Reynolds' *Pepper.* But in color she did not come into her own until she made the pictures for Lee Kingman's *Peter's Long Walk.* They are in muted colors and interpret tenderly a child's sad homecoming which turns out cheerfully. She went on to win the Caldecott Medal for her scratchboard illustrations for *Chanticleer and the Fox* adapted from Chaucer's "The Nun's Priest's Tale" in *The Canterbury Tales.* Every detail is historically accurate, but what the children love are those pages in bright clear reds, greens, and blues, alive with action. She prefers working in full color, using acrylic paints, but has also used pen and ink for *Cock Robin,* wash for the delicate pictures in Sarah Orne Jewett's *A White Heron,* and charcoal for her pictures in the Grimms' *Snow White and Rose Red.* Her illustrations for *Ox-Cart Man* by Donald Hall and *When the Sky Is Like Lace* by Elinor Horwitz exemplify both her artistic diversity and the research that results in authentic detail. (pp. 148-49)

> *Zena Sutherland and May Hill Arbuthnot, "Barbara Cooney," in their* Children and Books, *seventh edition, Scott, Foresman and Company, 1986, pp. 148-49.*

TITLE COMMENTARY

King of Wreck Island (1941)

A fantastic tale of a hermit whose dory capsized on Wreck Island when he was only a boy, leaving him stranded until seventy years later when the bay froze solid. Moses Pennypacker tells Randy of his life on the island with the seals, scavenger gulls, thieving crows, and eagles, chickadees, woodchucks, moles, etc., and finally persuades the boy to become Prince of Wreck Island and return with him before the ice melts. A shipwreck story that will delight fourth and fifth graders, humorously told. Both story and black and white illustrations by the author send forth a breath of Maine, with its stormy coast, its shipping, and its interesting characters.

> *Sonja Wennerblad, in a review of "King of Wreck Island," in* Library Journal, *Vol. 66, No. 14, August, 1941, p. 677.*

Somewhere on the Maine coast, perhaps near Wiscasset, lies a small island so ringed round with ledges that it is impossible for a boat to make a landing. This is Wreck Island. One severe winter, however, the Bay froze over and a mysterious old man walked ashore into Blueberryville where the Pebbles family lived. All this is but introduction to the marvelous tale he told Randy Pebbles. . . . The pictures for this joyous and amusing story are as perfect as its Maine village life.

> *Alice M. Jordan, in a review of "King of Wreck Island," in* The Horn Book Magazine, *Vol. XVII, No. 5, September-October, 1941, p. 368.*

The Kellyhorns (1942)

Very complicated plot, including twins brought up apart who meet and change places, various match-making schemes, and two mysteries. Grown characters are better realized than are the children, but writing is skilful enough to make whole plausible and to give tang of the Maine woods.

> *Evelyn W. Turpin, in a review of "The Kelly-horns," in* Library Journal, *Vol. 67, No. 20, August, 1942, p. 685.*

These adventures of Pam and Penny make a tale of identical twins, separated as babies and meeting at twelve—up in coastal New England, where all this time they have been near each other without knowing it. So far this is familiar, but there is a different twist. Their mother had died when they were born; her sister Ivory took one twin, while the other stayed with Puppa. The reason why they had not met was that Aunt Ivory had been Puppa's first sweetheart. So when the girls do meet, and decide that their two households must be condensed into one, some finesse in matchmaking is called for. Pam and Penny change names, live in each others houses, and get a preliminary view of the situation. It is necessary to believe that they could carry this through, and to be prepared to accept more and more calls on the imagination as the story proceeds. For the exuberance of plot that showed in *The King of Wreck Island* now burgeons in several sensations. Aunt Ivory, resenting this management of her affairs, disappears; the parents of the twins' cousin turn out to be circus people, and when at last Aunt Ivory—whose five white cats disappeared with her—comes to light, it is in a circus, cats and all. As she has, on the night of her reappearance, substituted for the lion tamer with almost fatal results, and as her former suitor saves her life, all ends as the twins had planned.

It is a bustling story with more sensations than it needs—it could do without a trial for arson, comic as it is—but Miss Cooney shows vigor and humor worth watching.

> *May Lamberton Becker, in a review of "The Kellyhorns," in* New York Herald Tribune Books, *August 16, 1942, p. 7.*

This book introduces a new author of talent, one who gives color and life to such Maine matters as the seasons, fairs and village dances, and especially to the people. It is all as merry as the wedding bell for which the twins wished so ardently and, if to adult eyes it seems a little incredible, it comes as close as one could wish to a little girl's dream of adventure.

> *Ellen Lewis Buell, "On a Maine Island," in* The New York Times Book Review, *August 23, 1942, p. 9.*

Captain Pottle's House (1943)

When Cherry Dean went to Maine to spend the summer with Great-Aunt Freddy she got the hearty welcome she had expected. But something was wrong, as Cousin John, home on sick-leave from the Navy, and Cherry were quick to see. Who was the cross old Mr. Critchlow who had bought the old house and kept Great-Aunt Freddy on as housekeeper? Why did he make her so miserable and why didn't he like grown-ups *or* children? And how was he connected with Mrs. Pottle, widow of the captain of the Three Sisters, wrecked years before?

Cherry and Sailor John do some effective snooping in cautious Maine style around the waterfront and village stores and church socials and when they have the answer they're not quite sure what to do with the obstinate Mr. Critchlow and the loyal Mrs. Pottle. But they set things right, even though they have to interrupt a wedding to do it.

There is just enough mystery in this new book by the author of *The Kellyhorns* to snare the interest of 8 to 11 year old readers while they follow Cherry through a story which has the tang of a Maine breeze, the smell of good Maine cooking and other delightful experiences of a country summer.

> *Ellen Lewis Buell, "Mystery in Maine," in* The New York Times Book Review, *October 17, 1943, p. 8.*

Chanticleer and the Fox (1958)

AUTHOR'S COMMENTARY

[*The following excerpt is from Cooney's Caldecott Medal acceptance speech, which was originally delivered in 1959.*]

[You] must know that the honor you have given me is the pinnacle of my life as an illustrator. And I thank you with all my heart. (p. 199)

The question most generally asked me since the Caldecott Award was announced is how did I happen to do this book, what inspired me. That question is a little embarrassing because the answer is so simple. I just happened to want to draw chickens. Quite truthfully, I have not always drawn pictures simply because I loved my subject matter. When you have a large and lovely and impractical old house with a furnace the size of the boiler on the *Queen Mary* and children growing up and needing education, sometimes, shameful as it may seem, you work for money. On the other hand, when I am working with material that I love, I do work in a sort of passionate frenzy and then I am a proper unbusinesslike artist. Sometimes books that I have loved doing have not received so much attention as some of the more routine books. Then I feel the way a mother must feel when no one dances with her daughter. But tonight—if you can stand a mixed metaphor—*Chanticleer* is belle of the ball. And nobody could be happier than I that you have chosen a book that I loved working on.

To answer more exactly this question about what inspired me, I have tried to pinpoint the event that started the ball rolling. For years I have admired the work of Chinese and Japanese artists, in particular, their landscapes and their birds. But I think that the actual day that *Chanticleer* was conceived was three years ago one autumn day. I had been out in the woods picking witch hazel and was on my way home to cook supper. As I came out of the woods I passed a little barn that I had often passed before. But never at that time of day nor when the barn door was wide open. At that hour the sun was getting low and it shone right into the doorway. The inside of the barn was like a golden stage set. At that time of year the loft was full of hay, gold hay. And pecking around the floor of the barn was a most gorgeous and impractical flock of fancy chickens—gold chickens, rust-colored chickens, black ones, white ones, speckled ones and laced ones, some with crests on their heads, some with feathered legs, others with iridescent tails, and all with vermilion-colored wattles and combs. I don't know how their egg production was but they were beautiful. I think *that* was the beginning of this book.

Then I started casting around for a vehicle for my chickens. One day when I was in bed with the grippe—I do seem to get my best ideas when I'm slightly feverish—I was reading *The Canterbury Tales.* And there, in "The Nun's Priest's Tale," was my story. Besides chickens, I had a fourteenth century setting, a farm and children, animals and growing things. What more could I ask?

Of course, the story of Chanticleer and the Fox antedates Chaucer, but I liked the pictures he conjured up in my mind and the way in which he told the story. Chaucer had a great time poking fun at human foibles, but at the same time he understood and loved people. For, of course, Chanticleer and Partlet and the other hens are people. Partlet is a bossy little woman who winds her husband around her finger. And Chanticleer is a rather puffed-up man who does not realize that he is being pushed around. I tried to convey in my pictures what Chaucer conveys in his words: that people—in this case, chickens—can be beautiful and lovable even when they are being ridiculous.

There is another reason too for *Chanticleer and the Fox,* and that is, I do think Chaucer is possible for children. (pp. 199-201)

I believe that children in this country need a more robust literary diet than they are getting. *Huckleberry Finn* is a classic now, but I wonder how many editors today would allow the scene in which Huck's father has the "d. t.'s"—very graphic "d. t.'s" too—and chases Huck around the cabin with a clasp-knife. In my experience, which is limited compared to that of many of you, I find that children are not harmed by such scenes and that they will digest only as much as they are ready for. On the other hand, they have a greater capacity for accepting the world as it is than seems generally supposed. It does not hurt them to read about good and evil, love and hate, life and death. Nor do I think they should read only about things that they understand. " . . . a man's reach should exceed his grasp." So should a child's. For myself, I will never talk down to—or *draw* down to—children. Much of what I put into my pictures will not be understood. How many children will know that the magpie sitting in my pollarded willow in *Chanticleer and the Fox* is an evil omen? How many children will realize that every flower and grass in the book grew in Chaucer's time in England? How many children will know or care? Maybe not a single one. Still I keep piling it on. Detail after detail. Whom am I pleasing—besides myself? I don't know. Yet if I put enough in my pictures, there may be something for everyone. Not all will be understood, but some will be understood now and maybe more later. That is good enough for me. (pp. 201-02)

Barbara Cooney, "Caldecott Award Acceptance," in Newbery and Caldecott Medal Books: 1956-1965, *edited by Lee Kingman, The Horn Book, Incorporated, 1965, pp. 199-202.*

A volume, destined by its design and superb illustrations to be a modern classic, frames a fable from the famed 14th century *Canterbury Tales.* . . .

To illustrate the fable, which she has adapted with a sure touch, Mrs. Cooney spent months studying rare books and illuminated manuscripts in the Morgan library, the Fogg museum, the Cloisters, and many libraries. As a result, the vigor and beauty of medieval farm life flow thru the artist's skilled brush to create memorable pictures. Many children will love and recognize this book as a treasure. Many adult collectors will claim it for their own.

M. B. K., in a review of "Chanticleer and the Fox," in Chicago Tribune—Books, *Part 4, November 2, 1958, p. 11.*

The famous fable of the flattering fox and his victim is well known to many children in La Fontaine's brief version where a crow is the dupe and his loss merely the bit of cheese he drops when he begins to sing. Chaucer's account in the Nun's Priest's tale, the source used for the text of *Chanticleer and the Fox,* in an outstanding new picture book, is far more amusing. In careful detail and with mock seriousness we learn of Chanticleer's home in a poor widow's yard "fenced all around with sticks," of his pride and beauty (legs and toes of azure, feathers of jet and burnished gold) and of his seven wives, especially the favorite Demoiselle Partlet who had "the prettiest neck" and was "polite, discreet, debonair"! Though warned by a dream at which Partlet scoffs, Chanticleer listens to the wily fox when he appears, closes his eyes and sings, standing on tiptoe. Instantly seized he uses his wits, quite as good as those of the fox, to free himself, and the tale ends with two morals—not to close your eyes when you should watch, not to prattle when you should hold your peace.

Barbara Cooney, by quoting the most delightful parts of the tale, has given young children a happy foretaste of Chaucer rather than the simplified, flavorless outline usual in adaptations. Moreover, she has made handsome pictures using fourteenth-century motifs for landscapes and figures mingled with more modern elements. Her color work is bold enough not to be overwhelmed by her forceful use of black and white. In six double-page spreads with highlights in white and black shadows, emerald, gentian blue, bright red and ochre—pure clear colors—are beautifully balanced. The pictures in black, white and red are equally effective, except where pages in full color and those in two colors face each other, and even this is triumphantly surmounted in the magnificent portrait of Chanticleer. Here is no "expression of affable imbecility" such as Marchette Chute noted in beast portraits of Chaucer's day, but a shrewd, self-confident, glorious creature, one we are sure would have delighted his famous creator. A book for all ages to cherish.

Margaret Sherwood Libby, in a review of "Chanticleer and the Fox," in The New York Times Book Review, *November 2, 1958, p. 2.*

I like Barbara Cooney's *Chanticleer and the Fox* because

From Miss Rumphius, *written and illustrated by Barbara Cooney.*

it has succeeded in becoming a good, illustrated book. It has been well designed, in a manner appropriate to the period of the story's origin, and yet it has a subtle sense of reality. The arrangement of the house, barnyard with its woven sapling fence, trim pig house, and frugally pruned shade trees leave the reader with a strong desire to wander into the pictures. It would be good to toss the thrifty hens some corn, push an affectionate hand deep into the sheep's wool nap, or watch the pigs greedily nuzzling up every last crumb from the wooden trough. But there is nothing quaint, or contrived, or facile in the drawings. With sparing detail they have been honestly drawn to "illustrate" the simple story.

To lure, coax, or lead the reader to take part in such a story is an art; but to have combined art and artistry in such an ancient and repeatedly published tale as that of Chanticleer is an achievement. It has the look of having appeared now for the first time. For all its old world charm, the setting satisfies the demands of truth, and the characters take on life, although the pictures are built to a rather set pattern of the medieval tapestry.

Printed in five powerful and controlled flat colors, these pictures take their place on the pages, relate to the type matter, and are neither overpowered by the type nor steal the show. (p. 386)

Aldren A. Watson, in a review of "Chanticleer and the Fox," in The Horn Book Magazine, *Vol. XXXVI, No. 5, October, 1960, pp. 386-87.*

Barbara Cooney has perfected herself in the use of scratchboard. Her pictures for ***Chanticleer and the Fox*** are scrupulously drawn to achieve that crispness which the medium permits. She uses gay primary colors, also sharp and pure, in this retelling of one of Chaucer's *Canterbury Tales.* There is liveliness, from the parade of farmyard animals to Chanticleer strutting and his seven hens settling on their roosts. As you turn these pages, note the many ways in which seven hens can be arranged. In a dramatic night-dark scene, Fox enters. No color here. As he turns a smiling, beguiling face to Chanticleer, color again comes in to suggest bright sunlight and fair omens. But blackness returns as Fox shows his true purpose and makes off to the dark wood with Chanticleer by the throat! The dramatic possibilities in the tale are exploited gently but firmly, even turning the limitations of color printing into advantages.

Hours spent at the Cloisters and at the New York Public and Morgan Libraries have been repaid in the satisfaction of having the details correct: the costumes right for the period and every flower and grass just those that grew in England in Chaucer's time. The artist has placed the strawberry plant in the initial O of the first page as it might be seen in an illuminated book of the 14th century. There are other small delights for the eye in the clump of blue flag beside the woven fence, some mice playing with a spice pink far down in one corner. Generous white space sets off these details, and thought has been given to the book design as a whole, particularly shown in the calligraphy on the title page and in that beautifully plain copyright page—often a necessary but awkward hurdle in picture books!

Chanticleer and the Fox is retold with clarity, freshness and dedication to the task. (p. 274)

> *Norma R. Fryatt, "Picture Books Today," in* Newbery and Caldecott Medal Books: 1956-1965, *The Horn Book, Incorporated, 1965, pp. 270-80.*

Most notable of Barbara Cooney's illustrations are those that appear in *Chanticleer and the Fox.* Her work in this book and in others is recognized by her attention to minute detail. Each setting is authentically and faithfully presented, even to the carefully delineated thatch-roofed cottage and the variety of flowers that appear in the countryside scenes. . . . The delicacy of the lines and the meticulous attention to detail highlight the medieval flavor of this fable, yet it is as fresh and contemporary as one would want it to be. Barbara Cooney also expresses a sophisticated wit in her drawings for this adaptation of *The Canterbury Tales,* a spirit that prevails throughout her other picture books, also. (pp. 82-3)

> *Patricia Cianciolo, "The Artist's Media and Techniques," in her* Illustrations in Children's Books, *second edition, Wm. C. Brown Company Publishers, 1976, pp. 58-93.*

Barbara Cooney has interpreted this moralistic fable in wholesome, solid shapes of red, blue, green, and ochre. The design of the book—the physical relationship of the text to the illustrations and the design of the objects within the illustrations—reflects much thought and skill. Carefully selected vegetation, common to the setting, complements the compositions, adding authenticity and interest to the visual presentation.

The black and ochre of the patterned plumage of the hens and the rooster produce a dramatic design, yet the black and white illustrations, with a touch of red, are equally interesting. The careful placement of the color on the page—the red tongue and eye of the fox or the ruby beaks of the ducks and dangling cherries—serves to emphasize and entice movement of the eye in the desired direction. Cooney has created a visual experience of disciplined style and composition, which is reflective of the traditional origins of the tale itself. (p. 314)

> *Linda Kauffman Peterson, "The Caldecott Medal and Honor Books, 1938-1981," in* Newbery and Caldecott Medal and Honor Books: An Annotated Bibliography, *by Linda Kauffman Peterson and Marilyn Leathers Solt, G. K. Hall & Co., 1982, pp. 235-378.*

The American Speller: An Adaptation of Noah Webster's Blue-Backed Speller (1960)

Noah Webster's speller was, one hundred years ago, almost as much a part of the American home as the Bible. Here in an adapted version, with quaint illustrations by the author, is this compendium of sounds, letters, and meaning. Letters, individually, or in common combination are introduced and used in illustrative context. By the time the child has absorbed this text—and he should eagerly—he will be familiar with not only the vagaries of English spelling and phonetics, but with the appealing wit of Noah Webster, a plain talking American who managed to look everywhere at once with the freshness of a child's eye.

> *A review of "The American Speller," in* Virginia Kirkus' Service, *Vol. XXVIII, No. 19, October 1, 1960, p. 866.*

What a joy! Here is a book that fairly calls out to be owned, cherished and pored over. [At] first glance it seems to be all pictures, hundreds of them (actually only 131), black and white with just enough red to make the pages gleam. Pictures of an old schoolhouse, of squirrels, of pets, of castles and Laplanders, small scenes and wider views, each one illustrating one of the quaint sentences on its page. For there is a text. At first we did not notice it for joy in the pictures. A blue letter at the top of each page is the consonant, vowel or other sound for which sentences printed in black are given as examples with the particular sound picked out in blue again. Noah Webster carefully assembled these examples to illustrate his spelling rules in his original Blue-Backed Speller which sold over a hundred million copies, and of which this is an adaptation. What a way to stretch a child's mind . . . "the buffalo has an aversion to fire and to red colors," "never pester the little boys," "the little ants make hillocks," "Hannibal crossed the Alps in the rigor of winter" (the underlined sounds are in blue). No baby stuff there, but a wide variety of stimulating remarks.

The study part of the book is thoughtfully arranged. All the basic sounds are there, first the consonants from B to Z, then the vowels both long and short, then special consonants, silent letters, vowels followed by r, consonant blends, words ending in le, words with ci, si and ti, and words ending in e. . . .

Whether modern children, offered this famous old book in an edition that would have entranced the children of long ago too, will learn phonics, the essential sounds of our language, from it or simply look at the gay, carefully drawn decorative pictures, we hope with Barbara Cooney that they will find "the words of Noah Webster sticking to their ribs like good roast beef."

> *Margaret Sherwood Libby, in a review of "The American Speller," in* New York Herald Tribune Book Review, *November 13, 1960, p. 3.*

Many people looking at early children's books see pictures in their minds, but it takes a Barbara Cooney not only to see the pictures in the lines of an old spelling book but to make and share them. The result here is a most engaging picture book with many illustrations in red, black, and white. The very conglomeration and understatement of Noah Webster's sentences add amusement as the reader grows aware of the sounds of consonants and vowels and letter combinations which are printed in blue to contrast with the black type. This may be very useful for children learning to read and spell; it certainly calls attention to fine-sounding words not on any elementary school vocabulary list; and as a picture book it is truly distinguished for its beauty, originality, and humor.

> *Ruth Hill Viguers, in a review of "The American Speller, an Adaptation of Noah Webster's Blue-Backed Speller," in* The Horn Book Magazine, *Vol. XXXVII, No. 1, February, 1961, p. 43.*

The Little Juggler (1961)

Barbara Cooney calls this retelling of the old legend of the juggler of Notre Dame "my contribution to Christmas, 1961," and it, in turn, should contribute much true Christmas spirit and joy. The story is of the little orphaned juggler who, having no other gift to bring to Mary and the Child, whose statue stood in the little chapel, entertained them with his tumbling. The telling of the story is dignified and tender, as are the drawings, which are touched with humor as well. In preparation for work on the book Miss Cooney went to Paris to see the thirteenth-century manuscript of the legend and traveled throughout France to sketch places where the little juggler may have plied his skill. The result is a beautiful book rich in medieval background. Alternating with the black-and-white illustrations are pictures in which bright colors are added to the black: clear Christmas red and green and the luminous blue of stained glass. A Christmas gift to delight all the family.

> *Ruth Hill Viguers, in a review of "The Little Juggler," in* The Horn Book Magazine, *Vol. XXXVII, No. 6, December, 1961, p. 545.*

The story is told in simple, dignified, faintly archaic English and is well illustrated with the delicate, formalized precision of a medieval missal. It would be hard to find a story in subject and spirit more appropriate to Christmas.

> *"Nursery Corner," in* The Times Literary Supplement, *No. 3118, December 1, 1961, p. xxvi.*

This is a delightful book that enshrines something old and rich and good and deep. Miss Cooney has taken an old French legend and retold it with simplicity and delicacy and with a sure understanding of its meaning, while her illustrations have the care and precision that comes from observation, feeling, and close sympathy with the text. Indeed her illustrations are almost more articulate than the text and make a very large contribution to the distinction of the whole, but text and illustrations belong to each other and depend upon each other. One can linger long here and be satisfied to the full on every page by the happy combination of text and picture. The book is one of universal appeal, and very appropriate for the Christmas season, as the author intended it to be. The whole production is in excellent taste.

> *A review of "The Little Juggler," in* The Junior Bookshelf, *Vol. 26, No. 1, January, 1962, p. 13.*

The Courtship, Merry Marriage, and Feast of Cock Robin and Jenny Wren, to which Is Added the Doleful Death of Cock Robin (1965)

A captivating picture book, worthy to be placed on the shelf beside those of Caldecott and Leslie Brooke, is this new one by Barbara Cooney. . . . She gives modern children exactly the sort of robustly whimsical scenes of animal behavior that are cherished in the work of these earlier great illustrators, and visual comments on human nature as witty and sly as La Fontaine's verbal ones.

The texts used are the famous old rhymes about Cock Robin and Jenny Wren, given in their entirety, with the death of the bridegroom, Robin, at the wedding feast described as an accident due to Sparrow's poor aim when he tried to shoot the rioting Cuckoo. This and the very ceremonious funeral offer the kind of sorrow and comfort that find response in tender-hearted young readers.

The gay use of red, yellow and brown does not overshadow the skilful pen-and-ink drawings that give each bird a distinct personality—from the fluffy flower-girl chick to the menacing highwayman Cuckoo with smoking gun, enveloping cloak and great slouch hat. Modest Jenny in her russet gown is very fetching both in her pert wedding veil and her mourning costume, and so is Linnet, her bridesmaid, with floppy hat and pink ribbons, and the gleaming, elegant Goldfinch. All—even Parson Rook, poor Sparrow in his deerstalker hat, bold Kite and Bullfinch (an Al Smith sort of a bird with cigar and bowler hat)—are vivid, imaginative creations, giving a long-loved tale new opportunity to enchant.

> *Margaret Sherwood Libby, "New Feathers on Old Birds," in* Book Week—New York Herald Tribune, *October 17, 1965, p. 37.*

Within the limits of its modest conception, Miss Cooney's version of *The Courtship, Merry Marriage and Feast of Cock Robin and Jenny Wren, To Which Is Added the Doleful Death of Cock Robin* is a genuine *tour de force.* These animated and charmingly imagined pictures focus to marvelous effect on the minute details of the action. There is an amusingly jaded *joie de vivre* combined with a nice subtlety of discrimination in the characterization of Cock Robin and his seedy crew. Jenny Wren is the perfect portrait of the well-rounded, "getting on" type, who thought she'd never be asked; her simultaneous wedding and widowhood is all the more affecting for her air of I-knew-it-couldn't-be-true. Though artful, prankish and contemporary in mood and manner, these pictures never stray beyond the poetic logic of the verse. (pp. 39-40)

> *Maurice Sendak, "Mother Goose's Garnishings," in* Book Week—New York Herald Tribune, *October 31, 1965, pp. 39-40.*

The old nursery-rhyme telling of the courtship and marriage of Cock Robin is not so well-known as the one about his death. Together they make a story both merry and sad that has as much appeal to young children today as it has had for generations. The format and page design are beautiful and the illustrations exactly right: they complement and interpret the story with humorous nuances, flowing with the text and never overwhelming it. Added to the black, white, and gray drawings are soft yellow, brown, and red—the only colors needed. A beautiful little book, as distinguished as it is modest.

> *Ruth Hill Viguers, in a review of "The Court-ship, Merry Marriage, and Feast of Cock Robin and Jenny Wren, to which Is Added the Doleful Death of Cock Robin," in* The Horn Book Magazine, *Vol. XLI, No. 6, December, 1965, p. 620.*

Snow-White and Rose-Red (1966)

Barbara Cooney has done a fine job of retelling this fairy tale and given it very appealing black-and-white pictures with various shades of pink wash. The well-spaced print and attractive format will appeal especially to the slow or reluctant readers as well as the younger ones who will want to pore over the delicious pictures.

> *Book Review Consultants, in a review of "Snow-White and Rose-Red," in* Library Journal, *Vol. 91, No. 18, October 15, 1966, p. 5216.*

Barbara Cooney's **Snow-White and Rose-Red** is an exemplary, if unadventurous, job of illustrating the Grimm Brothers' fairy tale. Done in only two colors, red and black, the drawings are quietly illuminating. What a wonderful leer of avarice lights the face of her surly dwarf; what an ideal prince springs forth from the enchanted bear! Miss Cooney is just old-fashioned enough not to try to upstage the text.

> *Selma G. Lanes, in a review of "Snow-White and Rose-Red," in* Book Week—The Washington Post, *October 30, 1966, p. 24.*

Barbara Cooney has adapted this wonderful old tale without spoiling its warmth and magic. Her illustrations are tenderly realistic, showing details of forest and home life, and pointing up the individual characteristics of the humans, the friendly bear and the bad-tempered dwarf.

> *Ethna Sheehan, in a review of "Snow-White and Rose-Red," in* America, *Vol. 115, No. 19, November 5, 1966, p. 551.*

Christmas (1967)

After recounting the Nativity as it appears in the Gospels, Miss Cooney introduces the observance of the event thus: "Long before the birth of Jesus there were midwinter festivals," signal that this is to be a historical and not a doctrinaire Christmas. The Northern Yule season is credited with the ceremony of the Yule log and the appearance of Odin as precursor to St. Nicholas; to the Roman Saturnalia is attributed the practice of ceasing activity, feasting and exchanging gifts in December. "Finally, five hundred years after Jesus was born, the Church decided to celebrate Jesus' birthday in December. In this way, many of the merry pagan customs become part of the Christmas festival." Brief mention of the manner of celebrating in different countries (including the U. S.) and some legendary references conclude. Without approaching irreverence, this is an informed, sensible presentation and a supplement to the many legendary recreations.

> *A review of "Christmas," in* Kirkus Service, *Vol. XXXV, No. 20, October 15, 1967, p. 1276.*

This book written and illustrated by the American Caldecott award winning artist Barbara Cooney is in a class alone, it is excellent. The author has achieved a perfect balance between the religious meaning of Christmas and the present giving, between ancient customs and modern revelry. The story of the Nativity is told with the gentle simplicity that appeals to all. The very young will enjoy the delightful pictures whilst more sophisticated children will be amused by the descriptions of Christmas celebrations of long ago.

Barbara Cooney's delightful book is indeed worthy of its subject.

> *A review of "Christmas," in* The Junior Bookshelf, *Vol. 33, No. 2, April, 1969, p. 105.*

A Little Prayer (1967)

Not by exact definition a Christmas book, but a lovely old French prayer so full of wonder and joy—a joy mirrored in Barbara Cooney's lovely illustrations—that it seems inevitable that it will join the host of carols and poems that celebrate Christ's birthday.

> *A review of "A Little Prayer," in* Publishers Weekly, *Vol. 192, No. 19, November 6, 1967, p. 51.*

A beautiful old French prayer, "Little Jesus of the Crib," is illustrated in the typical Barbara Cooney style of colorful, satisfyingly detailed miniatures. Although the format is that of a small (5½" x 5") picture book, interest in this artist's illustrations and, especially, in the prayer, will extend beyond the intended audience of small children.

> *Marian Herr Scott, in a review "A Little Prayer," in* School Library Journal, *Vol. 14, No. 4, December, 1967, p. 62.*

For an old Provencal prayer the artist has drawn, in the expressive lines and clear colors familiar from **The Little Juggler** and **Chanticleer and the Fox,** all the many creatures mentioned in its cadenced lines. Prayerfully sought are "The cheerfulness of the pigeon, / The impulsiveness of the cock, / The discretion of the snail, / The meekness of the lamb." From "Little Jesus of the crib" to "Jesus, hear us. With your loving kindness / bless us and keep us from harm," the whole is expressed with a deep religious faith and the charm of a true poem.

> *Virginia Haviland, in a review of "A Little Prayer," in* The Horn Book Magazine, *Vol. XLIV, No. 1, February, 1968, p. 73.*

A Garland of Games and Other Diversions: An Alphabet Book (1969)

An alphabet of southern colonial pastimes that you'll run your fingers over first (the flecks of oil paint are that palpable), grin at (such cheerful, airy scenes) then examine for the sly detail. Altogether from A—"A wicked Archer with cruel Arrow / Shot and killed a little sparrow"—to V—"Across the field and over by the pond / I found a Valentine from one of whom I'm fond"—and beyond, it's one of Miss Cooney's most beguiling gambols. And one of the most artfully designed—a succession of sturdy paintings that somehow float on the page.

> *A review of "A Garland of Games and Other Diversions," in* Kirkus Reviews, *Vol. XXXVII, No. 9, May 1, 1969, p. 499.*

It is curious that while many commissioned works of music or art are wholly successful, a made-to-order book, particularly one for children, usually seems contrived. In the recent book produced for Colonial Williamsburg, the verses and the idea behind them appear deliberately devised. A rhymed couplet for each letter describes an activity; but many of the second lines limp to a weak conclusion. "Oranges and lemons, say the bells of St. Clemens. / Choose whom you wish, boys, girls, men and women" and "Across the field and over by the pond / I found a Valentine from one of whom I'm fond." The inviting illustrations in lovely, fresh colors show children at play, indoors and out, alone and in groups. The figures and scenes, although conscientiously authentic, have charm and spontaneity.

> *Ethel L. Heins, in a review of "A Garland of Games and Other Diversions: An Alphabet Book," in* The Horn Book Magazine, *Vol. XLV, No. 5, October, 1969, p. 525.*

The games children played, indoors and outdoors, winter and summer, are the subject of this imaginative alphabet book. The setting is Colonial America; the medium, a couplet for each letter detailed in bright and carefree color illustrations. Authenticity prevails throughout, in the dress, landscape, family associations, social relationships, and the playtime or cultural activities depicted; an atmosphere of peace and tranquility is conveyed. . . . Happy listening and viewing for pre-readers; a bonus of factual information.

> *Lena Dame, in a review of "A Garland of Games & Other Diversions," in* School Library Journal, *Vol. 16, No. 4, December, 1969, p. 40.*

Ox-Cart Man (1979)

[Ox-Cart Man *was written by Donald Hall.*]

AUTHOR'S COMMENTARY

[The following excerpt is from Cooney's Caldecott Medal acceptance speech, which was originally delivered in 1980.]

There are a few standard questions that I am always asked. The most popular is: How come you're an artist? My great-grandfather was an artist. He was a German immigrant and lived . . . in Manhattan. . . . For a living he made cigar-store Indians. He also painted pictures by the yard. My grandmother, when she was little, sometimes helped him "putting in the skies." In my mind's eye I see that little girl, named Philppina Krippendorf, painting away, making yards and yards of fluffy clouds and sunsets and storms with lightning and rainbows. When the paint was dry, my great-grandfather would go snip, snip and have a dozen or more pictures to sell.

Next in line was my mother. She was an enthusiastic painter of oils and watercolors. She was also very generous. I could mess with her paints and brushes all I wanted. On one condition: that I kept my brushes clean. The only art lesson my mother gave me was how to wash my brushes. Otherwise, she left me alone. I was no more talented, however, than any other child. I started out ruining the wallpaper with crayons, like everybody else, and making eggs with arms and legs. Most children start this way, and most children have the souls of artists. Some of these children stubbornly keep on being children even when they have grown up. Some of these stubborn children get to be artists. So my answer to Question Number One is that I became an artist because I had access to materials and pictures, a minimum of instruction, and a stubborn nature.

Question Number Two then follows: But how come you're an illustrator?

The answer is that I love stories. Lots of artists have loved stories. The sculptors and vase-painters of ancient Greece were forever illustrating Homer. The Byzantine and Romanesque and Gothic artists spent their lives illustrating the Bible. Stories from the Ramayana were the basis for much of the great art in the Orient. Like all these artists, I love illustrating a good story.

"Okay," they say. And then they ask Question Number Three: But how come you decided to make picture books for *children?*

I can answer that quickly. First, in the world of illustration, the picture-book field is far and away the most exciting. And second, I am *not* making picture books for children. I am making them for *people*.

Okay. End of question-and-answer period.

I often go to great lengths to get authentic backgrounds for my illustrations. I climbed Mount Olympus to see how things up there looked to Zeus. I went down into the cave where Hermes was born. I slept in Sleeping Beauty's castle. But to illustrate **Ox-Cart Man,** all I had to do was step outside my back door. (It was a lot cheaper too.)

Ox-Cart Man is the story of a New Hampshire farmer who lived in the last century. The story begins in October, when Ox-Cart Man hitches up his ox, loads up his cart with all the things he and his family have been making and growing all year long, and makes the long trip from the inland hills to Portsmouth Market on the coast. There he sells everything, including the ox, buys a few things, and starts the long trek home. Then the cycle of working and growing begins again.

Even though the story took place, as I said, just outside my back door, I still had to do some preliminary research. First of all, I had to establish *exactly* when the story could have happened. "When" is very important to an illustrator becuase the sets (the landscape and architecture) must be accurate; so must the costumes, the props, the hairdos, everything.

To begin, I tackled the road that the Ox-Cart Man would have followed. This, I found out, would have been one of the early New Hampshire turnpikes, one which opened to traffic in 1803. This was a toll road. The Ox-Cart Man would have paid one and a half cents a mile for his two-wheeled cart. He paid by the axle, as we still do on the

New Hampshire turnpikes. Going to the big markets along the seaboard were great events for New England farmers. Along the road were plenty of wayside inns where they could get hay for their horses and oxen and food for themselves. There were toddy irons in the fire and toddies in the tummy and a good night's sleep for everyone at the end of the day. Every year thousands of carts and wagons passed this way until the railroads arrived in 1847 and commerce took to the rails.

Next, I investigated Portsmouth and Portsmouth Market to ascertain what buildings would have been there between 1803 and 1847. The main difficulty here was that Portsmouth buildings, including the Market, had a bad habit of periodically burning down. It was a puzzle trying to figure out what was where and when.

What finally determined the date was the Ox-Cart Man's beard. I wanted him to have a lovely red beard like Leon's [the carpenter who worked on Cooney's home]. The story, therefore, had to happen between 1803 and 1847, when the turnpikes were busy, at a time when the brick market building in Portsmouth was standing, and when beards were in fashion. Thus, the date of 1832 was settled upon. After that it was downhill sledding all the way. (pp. 379-82)

Although **Ox-Cart Man** ends with the beautiful month of May, the month of hope, it starts with October, another beautiful month, the month of fulfillment. In conclusion, I want to read to you a few words from *The New-England Almanack* of 1810. Under the heading "October" it says:

> What pleasure exceeds that of the farmer?
> Now he exultingly beholds the fair fruits of his labor. He picks his apples; he gathers his corn; he digs his potatoes, and dances round the cider mill with a delight that kings and emperors cannot enjoy with all their pompous parade and tinsel splendor.

So, thank you very much, everybody. Tomorrow I am going back to New England to dance around my cider mill. (p. 382)

Barbara Cooney, "Caldecott Medal Acceptance," in The Horn Book Magazine, *Vol. LVI, No. 4, August, 1980, pp. 378-82.*

It's not been a brilliant season for picture books, but the best are astonishing. Donald Hall's **Ox-Cart Man** with illustrations by Barbara Cooney would be remarkable in any season. The text is deliberately simple and precise: An early 19th-century farmer packs his cart and drives to Portsmouth Market, N. H., in the fall. He sells all he has, including the ox and the cart, and walks home. As the seasons change, he and his family work hard until it's time for him to take their produce to market again.

It's the pictures that knock you out. Barbara Cooney has evoked early 19th-century primitive folk art, painting on wood. Her figures are carefully drawn and a little stiff, her colors clear, her scenes breathtaking in their detail of the human and natural worlds: the farm carpeted with October leaves, the long road over the hills to the town, the bustling market, the shops, the cold journey home beneath a wintry sunset, the barnyard in March, sheepshearing in

April, the blooming apple trees of May. This is the kind of picture book that you can return to again and again, for as pretty as it is, it's better than pretty: it's true in a way that moves children and grown-ups alike.

Harold C. K. Rice, in a review of "Ox-Cart Man," in The New York Times Book Review, *November 11, 1979, p. 51.*

Like a pastoral symphony translated into picture book format, the stunning combination of text and illustrations recreates the mood of nineteenth-century rural New England. Economical and straightforward, the narrative achieves a poetic tone through the use of alliteration and repetition. . . . As an appropriate contrast, the full-color illustrations, suggesting early American paintings on wood, depict the countryside through which [the Ox-Cart Man] travels, the jostle of the marketplace, and the homely warmth of family life. The various phenomena of the New England landscape—the vibrant foliage of autumn, the lurid sunsets of winter, the delicate abundance of an orchard in spring—evoke the pattern of a lifestyle geared to the rhythm of the seasonal cycle. Quiet but not static, the book celebrates the peacefulness of a time now past but one which is still, nevertheless, an irrefutable part of the American consciousness. (pp. 44-5)

Mary M. Burns, in a review of "Ox-Cart Man," in The Horn Book Magazine, *Vol. LVI, No. 1, February, 1980, pp. 44-5.*

The **Ox-Cart Man** text is little more than a poet's sonorous list of farm commodities. . . . The farmer's cross-country jaunt and his cartload of wares provide material for the illustrator; however a text needs more engaging content.

Barbara Cooney's pictures are sometimes decorative in concept, compact in design, and varied in the use of shape, color, and contrast. In the faraway scenes, she usually flattens each object and makes toylike, static motifs that are essentially lyrical. Trim, little houses on smoothly curving hillsides are embellished with crisp, tidy details and the result is Hallmark-card-pretty, but nonetheless effective.

On the other hand, Cooney uses a "zoom lens" perspective on some pages, bringing large objects into the foreground, and here she has difficulty maintaining a consistent sensibility and style. She hasn't decided whether she wants an ornamental design, a cartoon stereotype, or a sculptural effect that utilizes shading and perspective drawing. For example, one composition contains a flat, even-colored house on the left, and on the right a cart with boards drawn and shaded to give a sense of depth and dimension. In another illustration (a scene where the farmer is buying things in town) the approach is to create light and dark areas in the folds of a woman's skirt and shawl, but this style is not duplicated in any of the garments on four other persons. This discontinuity from page to page and within several pages is visually disturbing. The eye confronts an irregular array of techniques, and this unevenness undermines an otherwise lyrical presentation. (pp. 582-83)

Donnarae MacCann and Olga Richard, in a review of "Ox-Cart Man," in Wilson Library Bulletin, *Vol. 54, No. 9, May, 1980, pp. 582-83.*

Ox-Cart Man which won the Caldecott medal, annoyed me. It describes a year in the life of a New Englander and his family. The pictures are in the style of American Primitive paintings, and the text is a simple statement of the things that the family made and sold in the market. Again, this should be delightful; Laura Ingalls Wilder can charm us with details like this of pioneer survival. But this book has the details without any of her spirit. There is fine opportunity to be witty or wry or in any other way human in books like this; we have always enjoyed *Grandfather Ben* by Eva Scherbarth for all these qualities. But this book just takes the whole thing too seriously. One can't help feeling that the medal was awarded by one lot of solemn adults to another as a celebration of some empty myth.

> *Ruth Hawthorn, "Pre-School Pictures," in The Times Literary Supplement, No. 4042, September 19, 1980, p. 1029.*

Barbara Cooney won her second Caldecott Medal for her drawings for this very original book. We may not always be happy about the awards made by our American cousins, but there should not be much argument about this one. This book is a winner. (p. 283)

[The] most basic of stories is told in deceptively simple words. In her lovely lithographs Barbara Cooney weds the text to pictures in the nineteenth-century American tradition, very clean, direct drawing of everyday scenes and objects which reveal the beauty of ordinariness. Notice how subtly she varies the shape of her pictures to give variety and to maintain interest as the pages turn. It all looks so easy, but there are many lessons here for young, and for some established, artists. Excellent in draughtsmanship, the designs are equally fine in colour, and especially in the control of colour from page to page. Here is a whole way of life set down and preserved in all its integrity and beauty. (p. 284)

> *Marcus Crouch, in a review of "Ox-Cart Man," in The Junior Bookshelf, Vol. 44, No. 6, December, 1980, pp. 283-84.*

Plenty of space surrounds the text of the pages, giving the book a rich look and contributing to the unrushed, calm tempo of the text. Subtle differences in the spacing between the lines of the text facilitate the flow of reading, while the illustrations harmoniously mimic the characters' quiet, complacent acceptance of their Early American lifestyle.

Barbara Cooney's intentionally primitive style captures well the atmosphere of this 1980 Medal Book. In a style reminiscent of tole paintings on wood, the shapes, buildings, and landscapes communicate the simple existence of

From Island Boy, *written and illustrated by Barbara Cooney.*

nineteenth-century New England families. Even the winter scene of the collection of maple sap, though reminiscent of Brueghel's painting *Winter / Return of the Hunters,* retains an air of simple wholesomeness.

The changing seasons and accompanying color schemes add variety to the book, as does the changing format of the illustrations. Horizontal spreads accentuate the Ox-Cart Man's journey to and from the marketplace, while the final illustration, within its smaller rectangular frame, symbolizes the end of the story, but not necessarily the end of the cycle of life.

An appreciation by children of the artistic style of the book and its story will be judged with the passage of time. The style undoubtedly holds appeal for adults in word and picture—an appeal which could easily be transferred to younger audiences with the proper approach and guidance. (p. 371)

> *Linda Kauffman Peterson, "The Caldecott Medal and Honor Books, 1938-1981," in* Newbery and Caldecott Medal and Honor Books: An Annotated Bibliography, *by Linda Kauffman Peterson and Marilyn Leathers Solt, G. K. Hall & Co., 1982, pp. 235-378.*

Little Brother and Little Sister (1982)

Though this isn't Cooney's best work, it's still an oasis in the desert. While the dramatic possibilities of some of the drawings are undercut by cuteness, most are handsome, and the story of love, loyalty and enchantment is one that has not been overworked.

> *Ann Haskell, "Something Easy to Read," in* The New York Times Book Review, *April 25, 1982, p. 42.*

[In] the right hands, some Grimm retellings are welcome. That is the case, I think, with Barbara Cooney's **Little Brother and Little Sister.** In the first place, this particular story is less well-known than some of the others, and in the second place, the telling here seems both faithful and pleasingly readable. A brother and sister, to escape their evil stepmother, flee into a deep forest where Brother drinks from an enchanted stream and is changed into a fawn. Sister takes him with her to an abandoned cottage where they live simply until one day years later the King comes to the forest to hunt, sees the fawn's golden collar, and is led to the cottage where he finds Sister, falls in love with her, and makes her his queen. The fawn lives with them at the castle, and all is well until the Queen bears a son. Then the evil stepmother comes and by trickery kills her, putting her own daughter in her place. The Queen, now a spirit, comes three times in the night to visit her baby and the fawn, and on the third night is discovered and brought back to life by an embrace from the King, after which everyone gets what he deserves and the fawn becomes Brother once again.

The tale is full of undertones and resonances, and Cooney, wisely avoiding bravura, lets it have its way. Her watercolor paintings are simple and direct, with clear colors and a very nice immediacy to them. The texture of the paper is everywhere allowed to show itself, with the result that you can almost feel the sure sweep of the brush laying in

grass, sky, wood, and stone, while details of forest growth, costumes, and faces—these last nicely varied—are added with admirable skill and invention. I happen to think watercolor of this type is the most difficult of all mediums; you have to get it right the first time, or begin again from scratch. Barbara Cooney knows how to do it right, and has made for this story a handsome setting that never overwhelms it.

> *Natalie Babbitt, "Fairy Tales and Far-Flung Places," in* Book World—The Washington Post, *May 9, 1982, p. 16.*

Barbara Cooney's clear, neat watercolors portray the forest as verdant and sheltering, not threatening. Her King is a strong and kindly man with a distinct likeness to Francis I. Even the ghostly Queen is attractive, though transparent; and the settings are so clean and peaceful, so down-to-earth and simple, that the darker elements in the story are not disturbing. This tale deserves to be better known, and Barbara Cooney's familiar style should guarantee it a wide audience. (pp. 94-5)

> *Patricia Dooley, in a review of "Little Brother and Little Sister," in* School Library Journal, *Vol. 28, No. 10, August, 1982, pp. 94-5.*

Miss Rumphius (1982)

With the publication of this book Cooney will have to make room for more awards to join those given to **Ox-Cart Man** and many more of over 100 books graced by her art. Like the exquisite paintings illustrating the life of Miss Rumphius, the story flows in a style representing the art that conceals art: betraying no strain. The narrator explains that Miss Rumphius was once little Alice, now her great-aunt who lives on a hill overlooking the sea in New England. As a child, Alice had promised her grandfather to do something to make the world beautiful and she intends to, when she has sailed the seas and visited far-off places. What she experiences is gloriously shown in the pictures, and so is her gift to the world, the lupines Miss Rumphius causes to grow by scattering their seeds so that they make all the town and its surroundings a heavenly garden.

> *A review of "Miss Rumphius," in* Publishers Weekly, *Vol. 222, No. 2, July 9, 1982, p. 49.*

This low-key tale of aspiration and idealism, of obligations to oneself and to the world at large, is perfectly accompanied by paintings that sound either a quaint-but-real old-fashioned, or a calm, unchanging pastoral, note. Pictures of Miss Rumphius as a librarian (in a shirtwaist), in the South Pacific (with a parasol), or astride a camel show her to be cheerful, competent and composed. She moves in settings that time or distance make exotic; but Cooney's clear, detailed scenes are as neat and precise as an old woman's memories. And her lupines *are* lovely, even if one feels that the rugged shores of Maine really didn't need to be made more beautiful.

> *Patricia Dooley, in a review of "Miss Rumphius," in* School Library Journal, *Vol. 29, No. 1, September, 1982, p. 106.*

The simple story is accompanied by glowing pictures reflecting the comfort of Alice's girlhood and the serenity of her seaside home. Entrancing landscapes sweep generously across the pages in contrast to quiet interiors enclosing the well-loved furniture and bric-a-brac of Alice's past. Particularly well designed for the attention span of young readers, the text frequently shares space with other delightfully detailed smaller illustrations, most of which are washed in the purples, pinks, and blues of the lupines themselves, thus creating an attractive pictorial unity. A strong feeling for Alice's independent spirit shines throughout the book yet is tempered, at the same time, by the peace and beauty of the landscapes.

Ethel R. Twichell, in a review of "Miss Rumphius," in The Horn Book Magazine, *Vol. LVIII, No. 6, December, 1982, p. 639.*

This tale of a life of work, adventure, and fulfilment of ambition is nicely told and illustrated by the author. The words alone paint pictures in the mind, but the beautifully detailed illustrations are enchanting and children will love to discover something new each time they open the book. The picture of Miss Rumphius, the librarian, is a good example, with the child at a table in the reading room off the main library not noticed perhaps at first. The description of her work in the library—'dusting books and keeping them from getting mixed up'—is well within the experience of the helper in the book corner of the classroom. Miss Rumphius, cautioned as a child by her grandfather to make the world more beautiful, has done just that, and the book leaves us wondering how *we* might fulfil the challenge.

A book to be read aloud to five-to seven-year-olds, and one which children will look at and try to read.

Maisie Roberts, in a review of "Miss Rumphius," in The School Librarian, *Vol. 31, No. 2, June, 1983, p. 127.*

Island Boy (1988)

Cooney's ongoing fascination with family ties and elder / younger relationships and her keen awareness of the interdependence of all people and their living styles are newly expressed in *Island Boy.* She steers her lyrical, lengthy illustrated story with confidence through four generations on a New England coastal island. Pa, Ma, and their 12 children settle the island. When he's ready, young Matthais sails with his uncle's schooner, first as cabin boy and 15 years later, as master. Finally acting on the pull of island memories, Matthais returns and soon marries Hannah, a school mistress from Boston. Matthais stays on Tibbetts Island after their three girls grow up and leave, and after Hannah's death. One year, his daughter Annie and her son join Matthais, until Matthais' accidental death. The text is occasionally poetic, with satisfyingly repetitive references to the astrakhan tree and the wild bird, for example, which underscore the book's continuity. Cooney's palette ranges from the clear greens and blues of the island and the water to the browns she employs effectively for domestic interiors and city street scenes. Her humans have individual characteristics. An endpaper map and a well-designed title page introduce this resolutely beautiful account of the interconnectedness of generations and lifestyles. Cooney's flawless transitions between the genera-

tions and between third-person points of view always maintain a child's perspective. *Island Boy* is certain to be a favorite for family sharing, as well as a must for school and public libraries. Teachers will love it; buy extra copies. (pp. 116-17)

Ginny Moore Kruse, in a review of "Island Boy," in School Library Journal, *Vol. 35, No. 2, October, 1988, pp. 116-17.*

Cooney brings a rich texture to her beautifully shaped and cadenced story. Matthias, the youngest of 12 lively children, is the last to leave home (he spends years sailing the coast, trading commodities like bricks for the growing communities) and the only one to return. Unhackneyed incidents beautifully illuminate his character and surroundings: though told it can't be done, as a boy he tames a gull (called Toad: too young to fly, it hops) that gets seasick when taken fishing; when "the hens ain't laying," he gets eggs for the family from the plentiful sea birds. In old age, Matthias isn't tempted to sell his valuable property to the rich folks "from away," although he does sell them vegetables. And when his dory goes down in rough seas, his family and neighbors (new and old) can truly say, "A good man . . . A good life."

Cooney's serene illustrations for this tribute to self-reliance and an ideal American life are as lovely as the ones for *Miss Rumphius,* and as evocative of their setting as those in *Ox-Cart Man.* Who could fail to love this clean world where luminous water meets luminous sky, where each delicately rendered detail is vibrant with its own reality and essential to an elegant composition? Outstanding.

A review of "Island Boy," in Kirkus Reviews, *Vol. LVI, No. 19, October 1, 1988, p. 1467.*

Island Boy is an invitation to our budding rocket scientists and corporate moguls to consider and vicariously enjoy another sort of successful life. For them, Ms. Cooney has created a book in which every word and picture fits her story and its themes. Her matter-of-fact prose indulges in the emotional only as much as her salty characters might. Her illustrations are almost primitive, focusing on scenes that could have attracted Grandma Moses—but Ms. Cooney's work is Grandma Moses slightly retouched by Mary Cassatt. And here is the harshness of a homesteading existence nicely balanced by ample evidence of the pleasure Matthais takes in a life close to the earth and sea. Even proud possessors of toy-crammed closets will be able to appreciate the love this island boy has for his spare home.

The author also shuns the fantastic in order to engage children in the life of her characters. When Matthais's pet sea gull flies off, it does not return later to perform a rescue at sea; it doesn't even visit. Such absolute leave-taking is rare in literature for 5-year-olds; so is Matthais's death at the end of the book.

Along the way, Matthais takes his own leave of the island, working first as a very young cabin boy and then as master of the ship. Such is the nature of progress that Matthais's parents and 11 siblings abandon their island to pursue easier livelihoods elsewhere. But steadfast Matthais wants nothing more than to return to the way of life he enjoyed as a child and to offer it as a gift to his wife and three daughters. His daughters choose not to remain on the island, and when his grandson asserts that *he* will spend *his* life there, Matthais admonishes him to see the world beyond the bay, to "know where your heart lies."

Like Donald Hall's *Ox-Cart Man,* which Barbara Cooney illustrated, and her own *Miss Rumphius, Island Boy* speaks clearly to a child's sense of values, never shouting or preaching. It is a book for children too young or too restless to sit through the pages of Laura Ingalls Wilder. It is also a treasure for all island dwellers, visitors and rusticators who will savor this glimpse of the true spirit and history of all the islands and shores that have become our coveted, strife-free, romantic summer places. One closes the book convinced of the goodness of the life described, and hoping that there may be Tibbettses living and toiling there still.

> *Rebecca Lazear Okrent, in a review of "Island Boy," in* The New York Times Book Review, *December 4, 1988, p. 40.*

Island Boy is a hymn to nineteenth-century rural life on the coast of Maine. Its theme is bold and unsentimental—life goes on, people are born and die, but the sea and human aspirations are the same in every age. The variations on this theme are played out mostly in the life of a boy named Matthias Tibbetts, with echoes in the lives of his father, his wife, his daughter, and his grandson, young Matthias. The characters in this book age and succumb to death, and hardship is not ignored nor prettified. But the

yearnings of the island boy to travel, and then to return home, are detailed in prose compelling for its homespun simplicity.

In a picture close to the end of the book, old Matthias and his grandson play checkers while his daughter does dishes. On the edge of the page, a satisfied cat comes proudly by with a mouse in its jaws. Domestic bliss and the harsh facts of the natural world belong together in this picture; the warm shades of green of the lampshade and the woodbox are carried over to the next page, in the colors of the stormy sea that swamps the dory and drowns old Matthias.

It is such precise emotional coloring in simple scenes that gives the Cooney paintings their strength. Not since McCloskey's *Time of Wonder* has a picture book revealed the moods of the Maine coast so accurately. The sea and the sky are different colors on every page; the sand is a startling, perfect gray; the red astrakhan tree under which Matthias is buried has grown, during the book, to a tired, fulsome arch. The endpapers show a coastline of three dozen islands; the implication is that full lives are lived everywhere, in the shadow and light of a harsh and beautiful world. Kudos to Barbara Cooney.

> *Gregory Maguire, in a review of "Island Boy," in* The Five Owls, *Vol. III, No. 3, January-February, 1989, p. 40.*

Barthe DeClements

1920-

American author of fiction.

Major works include *Nothing's Fair in Fifth Grade* (1981), *Seventeen and In-Between* (1984), *Sixth Grade Can Really Kill You* (1985), *Double Trouble* (with Christopher Greimes, 1987).

A popular writer of contemporary realistic fiction for readers in middle and upper elementary school and high school, DeClements is noted as an especially insightful and empathetic observer of children and their problems. Often praised for her skill with characterization and dialogue in works both humorous and serious, she is acknowledged for appealing to young readers through her honesty, optimism, and accurate depiction of home and school life. DeClements's books reflect her two chief interests, literature and counseling: a teacher of creative writing and psychology at the elementary, junior high, and high school levels, she is also an educational psychologist who has worked as a high school counselor. In her works, DeClements presents situations that require her young, characteristically female protagonists to make personal choices that bring them closer to maturity. For example, in her trilogy *Nothing's Fair in Fifth Grade, How Do You Lose Those Ninth Grade Blues?* (1983), and *Seventeen and In-Between,* she describes how Elsie Edwards changes from an overweight ten-year-old with a domineering mother and a lack of self-confidence into a slender, assured young adult who is able to forgive her mother and to begin to love her. DeClements has also written a prequel to her series, *The Fourth Grade Wizards* (1988), in which she includes some of the characters from the Elsie Edwards trilogy, and has begun a new trilogy with *Five Finger Discount* (1989), the story of how ten-year-old Jerry Johnson, whose father has been imprisoned for car theft and who has himself been involved with stealing, realizes through his friendship with a minister's daughter that he can change his own behavior if not that of his father.

In addition to her stories with purely realistic settings, DeClements has written two novels that blend the natural and the supernatural: *Double Trouble,* coauthored with her son, which features ninth grade twins who communicate through ESP and have powers of astral projection, and *No Place for Me* (1987), in which Aunt Maggie, a witch, shows her niece how to take charge of herself. Throughout her works, DeClements is credited for her sympathy toward characters with a variety of problems, which include coming to terms with being learning disabled, with the death of a mother, with alcoholic or sexually abusive parents, or with adult figures who are uncaring or antagonistic. DeClements, who writes her fast-paced books in unembellished prose, is sometimes discredited by critics as a stylist and creator of plot as well as for creating overly positive endings. However, her consistent popularity with children and young people affirms that she speaks clearly to them. DeClements has received several child-selected awards for her books.

(See also *Something about the Author,* Vol. 35 and *Contemporary Authors,* Vol. 105.)

GENERAL COMMENTARY

Kemie Nix

Although Barthe De Clements has written novels featuring high school students, her forte is writing about upper-elementary students. She has a rare and compassionate understanding of the peculiar perspective of pre-adolescents. She is a natural champion of underdogs—which pre-adolescent readers both sense and are.

> Kemie Nix, "A Trio to Tickle the Funny Bone," in The Christian Science Monitor, November 1, 1985, p. B4.

TITLE COMMENTARY

Nothing's Fair in Fifth Grade (1981)

The new girl in school is so fat that "[h]er chins rippled down her neck," is annoyingly infallible in math class and steals classmates' lunch money to spend on candy. She couldn't really be a human with feelings—or could she? It's hard to tell, since nothing's fair in fifth grade, anyway. The class-reject topic is a catchy one, the author's attitude is engaging, but the writing (although conversational and current) just misses having that lilt that carries readers. The problem is related to the plot, which is too strictly episodic and too singularly focused on whether the gross Elsie will find the acceptance she deserves. Characters (children, parents, teachers) are drawn lovingly and respectfully, but haven't the depth to command interest. The book is fun and worthwhile to read, but its weaknesses make it average in a very competitive genre.

> *Liza Bliss, in a review of "Nothing's Fair in Fifth Grade," in* School Library Journal, *Vol. 27, No. 8, April, 1981, p. 125.*

A frightening hitchhiking incident, a pajama party, and difficulty with fractions provide ballast for a humorous tale that rocks with fifth-grade truth. Though Elsie's problems with her mother are not resolved, her own sense of self is reinstated, and DeClements subtly probes the favorite lament—"it's not fair."

> *Barbara Elleman, in a review of "Nothing's Fair in Fifth Grade: A Novel," in* Booklist, *Vol. 77, No. 17, May 1, 1981, p. 1194.*

The theme is not unusual, but it's competently handled; relationships and characterization (particularly of Elsie and her mother) are nicely tied to motivation and plot development in a good but not outstanding first novel by a school counselor.

> *Zena Sutherland, in a review of "Nothing's Fair in Fifth Grade," in* Bulletin of the Center for Children's Books, *Vol. 34, No. 11, July-August, 1981, p. 210.*

How Do You Lose Those Ninth Grade Blues? (1983)

Formerly fat ninth-grader Elsie Edwards now has more trouble shedding her insecurities than her extra pounds. Her problems stem from a broken home, as well as her conviction that she is basically unlovable. Her lack of self worth generates trouble as she unsuccessfully tries to convince herself that handsome Craddoc Shaw really likes her. The premise here is a good one, but it is tarnished by one-dimensional characters who can be easily labeled (understanding boyfriend, mean mom, etc.) when they should be developed. Still, this is a recognizable if slight slice of early-teen-age life that should find an audience among junor high school students. **Ninth Grade Blues** continues the story of Elsie Edwards begun in **Nothing's Fair in Fifth Grade.**

> *Ilene Cooper, in a review of "How Do You Lose Those Ninth Grade Blues?" in* Booklist, *Vol. 80, No. 3, October 1, 1983, p. 261.*

A disappointing sequel to the author's popular first novel. DeClements seems uncomfortable with her young adult characters and, to make them "realistic," incorporates too much slang—a great deal of it dated Valley-girl talk. While attempting some insight into adolescent behavior and insecurity, this doesn't measure up to Conford's best

or to Perl's *Hey, Remember Fat Glenda?* (Houghton, 1981).

> *Anne Connor, in a review of "How Do You Lose Those Ninth Grade Blues?" in* School Library Journal, *Vol. 30, No. 4, December, 1983, p. 72.*

In a sequel to **Nothing's Fair in Fifth Grade** in which Jenifer wrote about her unhappily fat friend Elsie, Elsie is the narrator. . . . This isn't strong on plot, or highly original in the situation it explores, but DeClements does a fine job of analyzing and developing the complex emotions of an adolescent, the relationships are perceptively drawn, and the dialogue is natural.

> *Zena Sutherland, in a review of "How Do You Lose Those Ninth Grade Blues?" in* Bulletin of the Center for Children's Books, *Vol. 37, No. 6, February, 1984, p. 105.*

Seventeen and In-Between (1984)

In this sequel to **Nothing's Fair in Fifth Grade,** Elsie, the fat rejected child of the earlier book, is the central character and narrator. Now slender, self-assured and socially successful, she is nonetheless beset with problems: Should she become sexually intimate with Craddoc (her boyfriend of three years)? Should she tell the school principal her suspicion that sports star Rick has broken into the computer records and changed his failing grade? Can she establish a positive relationship with her previously hostile mother? Why do the letters from her old friend Jack mean more to her than Craddoc's letters? How Elsie deals with these problems makes an adequate teen novel despite the somewhat flat characterization, predictable plot and pedestrian writing. DeClements spends a lot of time rehashing incidents from the previous books which slow down the pace of this one considerably. Young fans of **Nothing's Fair in Fifth Grade** and **How Do You Lose Those Ninth Grade Blues?** will want to read this sequel, but its subject matter is more relevant to older readers to whom the style will probably seem juvenile. Better coming-of-age novels such as Cynthia Voigt's *Dicey's Song* (Atheneum, 1982) and Katherine Paterson's *Jacob Have I Loved* (Harper, 1980) might be compared to this, but that would be similar to comparing filet mignon to a fast food hamburger.

> *Louise L. Sherman, in a review of "Seventeen and In-Between," in* School Library Journal, *Vol. 31, No. 3, November, 1984, p. 130.*

This is a better-than-average teen dilemma novel, written with grace and insight. The reader wants to know Elsie better, and wants to hear more about her struggle to forgive her mother for years of neglect. That early psychic harm seems to cast a residue over the story as seemingly stable relationships flounder, and Elsie's compassion is repeatedly triggered and exercised. Teachers and librarians looking for likely titles for a bibliography on Child Abuse will want to make note of all of the Elsie books so far.

> *Judith N. Mitchell, in a review of "Seventeen and In-Between," in* Voice of Youth Advocates, *Vol. 7, No. 6, February, 1985, p. 324.*

Elsie is a strong character, though still unsure in some aspects of her life, but the reader quickly becomes confident that she is on her way to making the right decisions. These form the plot of the novel. . . .

Although there is some suspense in the novel and the action is generally believable, DeClements's skill in characterization surpasses her talent in plot development. Elsie genuinely comes alive for the reader, and even the minor characters have depth and are credible. Dialogue is natural, and the use of letters between Elsie and Jack add a realistic note to Elsie's ruminations about the meaning of life and her character.

> *Marjorie Kaiser, in a review of "Seventeen & In-Between," in* The ALAN Review, *Vol. 13, No. 1, Fall, 1985, p. 27.*

Sixth Grade Can Really Kill You (1985)

Helen dreads the first day in sixth grade. Good in math and gifted on the pitcher's mound, she is a nonreader diagnosed as a behavior problem. Against the slice-of-life background of a skating party, pierced ears and overnights at friend Louise's, Helen loses the battle with the printed word. Mid-year, she transfers to the other sixth grade class, where the teacher lets her choose whether or not to study in the special ed classroom. Despite the label "retard," she decides to get the special help. Hard work results in progress. Given her caring parents, sympathetic principal and wholesome friends, the motivation for Helen's pranks and booby traps is obscure. DeClements fails to relate Helen's deliquency to her frustration or anger. In addition, since help is just down the hall, it is unrealistic for Helen to suffer for half the year before trying the special ed room. Still, cameo appearances by Jenny and Elsie from *Nothing's Fair in Fifth Grade* will attract readers to this less successful problem novel. Like Gilson's *Do Bananas Chew Gum?* (Lothrop, 1980), *Sixth Grade . . .* illuminates the bleak world of the learning disabled while it entertains. (pp. 82-3)

> *Pat Herrington, in a review of "Sixth Grade Can Really Kill You," in* School Library Journal, *Vol. 32, No. 3, November, 1985, pp. 82-3.*

DeClements gives an accurate portrayal of what life is like for the learning disabled child. Here the problem is complicated by Helen's mother who refuses special classes, insisting she can help Helen herself. A sympathetic teacher saves the day. Although bibliotherapeutic in nature, this is also a good read, and Helen at her worst will undoubtedly provoke laughter as well as sympathy.

> *Ilene Cooper, in a review of "6th Grade Can Really Kill You," in* Booklist, *Vol. 82, No. 5, November 1, 1985, p. 403.*

Some of the characters from earlier DeClements books will be familiar to her readers, in a story that amply compensates for its uneven pace by the natural quality of the relationships and the dialogue in the classroom environment and by the insight gained through the first person treatment of a learning disability. . . . A serious subject is not handled so seriously that the story is marred.

> *A review of "6th Grade Can Really Kill You,"*

in Bulletin of the Center for Children's Books, *Vol. 39, No. 4, December, 1985, p. 65.*

I Never Asked You to Understand Me (1986)

A fictional look at an alternative school, the kinds of troubles that bring young people to it and the education it offers.

Cooperation High includes samples of every problem: drug dealer Larry, on probation; sweet, handsome TJ—who has left home to live a responsible life, when he's not smoking pot; Stacy, whose father molests her and beats her mother; and the narrator, Didi. While her mother dies of cancer, Didi suffers terminal misunderstandings with her high school, whose punitive, unsympathetic staff fails to discover the reason for the sudden changes in behavior of a model student. Lacking home support—her cold, unimaginative father is preoccupied with his own problems—Didi lands unprotesting at permissive CHS where she finds caring teachers, no academic challenge, and self-styled rejects who form their own society to replace the failed adult world.

DeClements, counselor in such a school, paints a grim view of the tragedy that can fill young lives. Trying to get it all in, plot is contrived around message; when Didi and Stacy are both able to find alternative living arrangements and end the story on a note of hope, the sudden change is jarringly simplistic. Still, a well-written problem novel with authentic, believable characters. Teens will recognize themselves.

> *A review of "I Never Asked You to Understand Me," in* Kirkus Reviews, *Vol. LIV, No. 13, July 1, 1986, p. 1020.*

Discerning readers will realize early on that Stacy's problems stem from her father's sexual abuse. This is as much Stacy's story as Didi's, and readers learn very little about Didi, despite the fact that the story is told from her point of view. They do not have the chance to see her work her way through her mother's death. Moreover, most of Didi's relationships—with her father (shadowy at best), with TJ, with the priggish housekeeper Monica—are left hanging and never develop. In a few instances, however, DeClements captures minor characters well—her portrayal of a counselor at the "normal" high school is stingingly accurate. There are numerous references to drug and alcohol use, as well as some mild sexual encounters, the combination of which tends to overshadow an already weak plot. Written in a biting vernacular, the language is occasionally crude, and while DeClements offers a brilliant slice-of-life setting, the story goes nowhere. A better choice for dealing with parental death is Roni Schotter's *A Matter of Time* (Ace, 1981).

> *Kathleen Brachmann, in a review of "I Never Asked You to Understand Me," in* School Library Journal, *Vol. 33, No. 2, October, 1986, p. 189.*

Double Trouble (with Christopher Greimes, 1987)

Following the death of their parents in a car accident, twins Faith and Phillip are separated, Faith sent to an aunt, Phillip to foster parents. The twins are psychic, involved with such phenomena as astral projection; quickly, both find themselves in trouble. Faith suspects that her well-liked social-studies teacher is actually a cruel person hiding a dangerous secret—and he knows she suspects. Phillip, after admitting his ability to project, is dragged to his foster parents' religious meetings in an attempt to "rid him of the devil." After some edge-of-the-seat adventures, all turns out even better than expected.

An engrossing story, but, unfortunately, never believable. It's told as a series of letters between Faith and Phillip, yet in order to fill the reader in on certain salient information, the twins often write about things there's no reason to mention or make awkward references to people they know; and their letters rarely sound like the narration of ninth-graders. Furthermore, although the twins appear to have impressive powers, they rarely try to contact each other, relying almost entirely on their letters. The mystery involving Faith's social studies teacher is trite and unrealistic (a teacher who regularly carries to school a cane that in reality is a gun), especially in comparison to Phillip's more compelling problems. Nevertheless, readers with an interest in ESP may find the story enthralling.

> *A review of "Double Trouble," in* Kirkus Reviews, *Vol. LV, No. 10, May 15, 1987, p. 793.*

The story is told entirely through letters between Phillip and Faith, a device that skillfully heightens the tension. The authors give almost a blueprint for astral projection, which may disturb some adults, and the depiction of Phillip's foster parents as strange religious fundamentalists might also offend (though their religion is more cultlike than mainstream). These special problems notwithstanding, the book should prove popular thanks to clever plotting, keen characterizations, and touches of the occult.

> *Ilene Cooper, in a review of "Double Trouble," in* Booklist, *Vol. 83, No. 19, June 1, 1987, p. 1521.*

An interesting and believable depiction of ESP and out-of-body experiences, this is less successful as a problem novel. Almost without exception, the adult characters are unfriendly or hostile, the misery of the twins is unrelieved, the parallel stories are too neatly symmetrical, and the resolution is a little too pat. Some may be offended by the language that occasionally (although realistically) crops up. An additional purchase to meet junior high interest in ESP.

> *Barbara Hutcheson, in a review of "Double Trouble," in* School Library Journal, *Vol. 33, No. 11, August, 1987, p. 92.*

No Place for Me (1987)

Copper Jones' mother is in an alcohol treatment center, and her stepfather arranges to have her stay with her Aunt Dorothy. From the beginning, Aunt Dorothy makes it clear that Copper is not really a member of the family. Copper is shipped out, eventually living with Aunt Maggie, who practices witchcraft. Maggie is the most completely drawn adult character in the book, and her developing relationship with Copper is the best part of the story. Maggie is calm in the face of Copper's lies and de-

ception, and tells her that she can change whenever she wants to. The Tarot cards have told Maggie that a trusting relationship will come in time, and she is content to wait. She guides Copper in using her own mind to change her dreams, and, ultimately, her self-image. The end of the story sees their relationship growing and working smoothly. Running through the story is Copper's delicate relationship with her alcoholic mother. DeClements does a good job of showing the insecurity and fears faced by children of alcoholics. Copper is left with no panacea, but she does realize that she can take charge of her life and make changes in herself when she wants to. DeClements' usual fast pace is evident here, and the sensitive treatment of serious problems give the story special appeal.

> *Candy Colborn, in a review of "No Place for Me," in* School Library Journal, *Vol. 34, No. 3, November, 1987, p. 104.*

DeClements carefully blends the supernatural with everyday life; Maggie's witchcraft is more philosophical than supernatural, and teaches Copper that there are other ways to cope. The portrayals of family situations are humorous. Copper is a fully realized character; tough, but bright and perceptive, she will win sympathy and admiration from readers. (p. 66)

> *A review of "No Place for Me," in* Publishers Weekly, *Vol. 232, No. 24, December 11, 1987, pp. 65-6.*

The book is at its best when slyly depicting Copper's various relatives. The characterizations are keen though understated, and readers will appreciate the subtlety. However, the story loses some of its finesse when Copper arrives at Maggie's. The townspeople seem perfectly comfortable with Maggie's recognized witchiness (there's a whole coven in the surrounding environs). Readers who have been hooked will read on to the end, but the detour into New Age philosophy that Maggie espouses may pull some up short. (pp. 704-05)

> *Ilene Cooper, in a review of "No Place for Me," in* Booklist, *Vol. 84, No. 8, December 15, 1987, pp. 704-05.*

The Fourth Grade Wizards (1988)

A prequel to the author's popular **Nothing's Fair in Fifth Grade,** etc., this one focuses on quiet Marianne, whose mother has died in a plane crash. Both Marianne and Jack (see the other books) want to be "Wizards," students extended special privileges, but Jack must learn to behave, and Marianne has to bring up her grades. The school story—more subdued than is usual from this author—is meshed with Marianne's adjustment to her mother's death, her move to a new home, getting a puppy (a wolf-dog hybrid) and growing to love Dad's new girlfriend. This is a resolutely ordinary story, told in forthrightly commonplace prose without a hint of nuance or complexity. Middle-graders love DeClements' books, perhaps for their easy-reading plainness and unsophisticated humor, but also for the author's unmistakable respect for her audience and its concerns. Her perceptions are not deep or unusual, but they honestly reflect common denominators that any kid will recognize: classroom pranks, moving from gold to brown in the SRA box, the heartache of searching for a lost pet.

Roger Sutton, in a review of "The Fourth Grade Wizards," in Bulletin of the Center for Children's Books, *Vol. 42, No. 2, October, 1988, p. 31.*

Encouraged by a sympathetic teacher and the smart-aleck class cutup, Jack, Marianne works through her loneliness and feelings of abandonment; moves to a new home; gets a puppy; and is happily anticipating the addition of a perfect stepmother at the novel's end. An expert at creating believable classroom situations and realistic dialogue between students, DeClements is less successful with adult characters. These are one-dimensional, stock figures, especially Marianne's father, who seems to sleepwalk through life, oblivious to his only child's very understandable problems and unhappiness. In addition, the humor and realism of the school situation trivialize the sober theme of what a parent's sudden death can do to a nine year old. In O'Neal's *A Formal Feeling* (Viking, 1982) and Girion's *A Tangle of Roots* (Putnam, 1985), both for slightly older children, the feelings engendered by similar tragic events are explored and developed without such abrupt mood shifts. This prequel to **Nothing's Fair in Fifth Grade** and **Sixth Grade Can Really Kill You** will appeal to middle-grade readers seeking another fast-paced, undemanding school story. Those looking for depth of characterization and descriptions of children in crisis will be better served elsewhere.

Martha Rosen, in a review of "The Fourth Grade Wizards," in School Library Journal, *Vol. 35, No. 2, October, 1988, p. 143.*

What do children really think of "happily ever after"? Do they believe that a lonely young girl whose mother has died, who is doing poorly in school, who lives in a shabby apartment she hates, will by the end of a book have a whole new life? Does it seem likely that she will move to a lovely cottage with enough acreage to keep a half-wolf puppy as a companion, and will find a woman who is loving stepmother material living next door, *and* will become a leader in her class, a "wizard" who is allowed special privileges?

That, in fact, is the plot of Barthe DeClements's novel **The Fourth Grade Wizards,** and it is, actually, an appealing one, told with great warmth. . . .

For most children, losing a parent is the most appalling thing they can imagine happening to them. But this isn't a book about assimilating that never-to-be-forgotten pain into a life forever changed by death. Instead, it is a modern-day fairy tale in which all of Marianne's wishes come true. The characters are painted in dramatic images of good and bad. The new neighbors in the apartment building Marianne and her father move into after her mother's death are greedy, conniving sorts. The new neighbor after they leave the apartment house is a sympathetic social worker who just happens to be available matrimonially—and who owns her own horse.

It seems too simplistic on one level. But on another level—one that children often inhabit—it can be very important to find comforting solutions to storybook problems. Tying all the loose ends together can ease their fears about the ambiguous way in which their own problems get resolved.

In fairy tales the hero and heroine have had so many magical adventures that children (and adults) think "happily ever after" simply means that nothing worth hearing about ever happens again. But when characters have problems children can identify with, neat endings can offer free reign for their imaginations, a chance to envision what it would feel like to be happy once again after a great sorrow, or to be the fourth-grade heroes and heroines they've always wanted to be. That may be why Ms. DeClements's books, which include **Nothing's Fair in Fifth Grade** and **Sixth Grade Can Really Kill You,** are so popular with children. . . .

An author like Beverly Cleary, on the other hand, who writes for the same age group—middle-grade readers—rarely solves her characters' problems for them. That great pest Ramona learns how to live with her troubles at the end of a Cleary book by arriving at a greater sense of herself and her place in the world.

My guess is that children need a little bit of both approaches—happy endings and more truthful, less than happy ones—to make it through childhood.

Gloria Jacobs, "Wishes Come True," in The New York Times Book Review, *November 13, 1988, p. 44.*

Five Finger Discount (1989)

Another solid effort from a favorite writer for middle-grade readers, who here initiates a trilogy about two PK's: a preacher's kid and a prisoner's kid.

Jerry Johnson's father is serving time in Washington State's Monroe Reformatory for his part in a car-theft ring. When the resulting economic circumstances force Jerry, ten, and his waitress mother to move to a new neighborhood, Jerry faces not only the usual trauma of a new school but the fear that his father's situation will become known—not to mention his own about how he'll respond to the temptations offered by material goods beyond his reach. When his problems are exacerbated by a classmate's attempt at blackmail, Jerry at first tries to tough it out on his own. Eventually, though, he accepts the help of Grace Elliot, daughter of the local minister, whose family has its own problems. Their growing friendship helps Jerry to face his father's return on parole, understanding that, while he may not be able to change his father's behavior, he can change his own.

Well-drawn characters and a hopeful, yet realistic, story. Though her style is not distinguished, DeClements understands these children well and describes them sympathetically. A promising start for a new series. (pp. 290-91)

A review of "Five-Finger Discount," in Kirkus Reviews, *Vol. LVII, No. 4, February 15, 1989, pp. 290-91.*

DeClements is an earnest, direct writer whose prose has little nuance, but whose perspective is clear, honest, and in absolute empathy with her audience. In this latest—first in a projected trilogy—fifth-grader Jerry is worried that his new schoolmates will find out his dad is in prison for auto theft. . . . Friendship and classroom dynamics are dead on, and Jerry's ongoing encounter with a blackmailing bully will bring many nods of cynical recognition. Characterization is simplistic, particularly as the author seems to tell readers that you can tell a "mean" person from a "good" person just by looking at them. Jerry's dad is more subtly drawn: fresh out on parole, he attempts to steal a pair of shoes, and then becomes saddened to learn that Jerry has done the same thing for his Mom's Christmas present. It is interesting that DeClements' books have achieved enormous popularity despite their almost absolute lack of humor, usually a prerequisite for preteen approval.

> *Roger Sutton, in a review of "Five-Finger Discount," in* Bulletin of the Center for Children's Books, *Vol. 42, No. 8, April, 1989, p. 192.*

This novel is unlikely to achieve the popularity of other DeClements books such as ***Nothing's Fair in Fifth Grade,*** but it is a credible story with enough action to keep many children reading. . . . Well-rounded characterizations and believable dialogue, along with realistic portrayals of family relationships and friendships, elevate this above the typical problem novel. Values are presented smoothly within the context of the story.

> *Ronald A. Van De Voorde, in a review of "Five-Finger Discount," in* School Library Journal, *Vol. 35, No. 8, April, 1989, p. 101.*

Walter de la Mare

1873-1956

(Also wrote as Walter Ramal) English author of poetry, fiction, short stories, retellings, and plays, and anthologist.

Major works include *Songs of Childhood* (1902; revised edition, 1916), *The Three Mulla-Mulgars* (1910; also published as *The Three Royal Monkeys,* 1935), *Peacock Pie: A Book of Rhymes and Poems* (1913), *Come Hither: A Collection of Rhymes and Poems for the Young of All Ages* (1923; revised edition, 1928), *Collected Rhymes and Verses* (1944), *Collected Stories for Children* (1947).

The following entry emphasizes general criticism of de la Mare's career. It also includes a selection of reviews to supplement the general criticism.

Acknowledged as a major English lyric poet of the twentieth century, de la Mare is often considered perhaps the greatest writer of adult literature to have contributed to the field of children's literature. He is lauded as a poetic genius with a unique voice whose vision of childhood is the central focus of his total body of work. A prolific creator of books for both children and adults, de la Mare was acclaimed for such adult works as the poetry collection *The Listeners and Other Poems* (1902) and the novel *Memoirs of a Midget* (1921), received regular comparisons with such poets as William Blake and William Butler Yeats, and was often regarded as one of England's most influential writers as well as perhaps its most anthologized. However, recent critics characterize him as a minor poet whose only lasting work is his juvenile literature, especially his poetry. In this area, de la Mare is considered to have written as an inspired child, a writer of mature technique who combines his own early memories with his understanding of children to create books which attempt to determine the essence of childhood while describing the beauty of the natural world. De la Mare perceived childhood as a time of fleeting intuition into the eternal, a transient period characterized by innocence, imagination, depth of emotion, and closeness to spiritual truth. Relaying his mystical visions in highly literary language notable for its sound and movement, de la Mare ultimately assures young readers that life, although filled with terror, mystery, and pain, is essentially a beautiful experience. Investing his poetry with studies of both the natural and the supernatural, de la Mare addresses such subjects as fairies, sleep and dreams, England, death, animals, and grownups in poems noted for their delicacy and, in many cases, their humor.

De la Mare is often praised for setting a new standard in poetry for children by presenting his readers with works which are authentic poetic compositions rather than verse. With his first book for the young, *Songs of Childhood,* de la Mare is credited with revolutionizing children's poetry through his individualistic tone and a virtuosic style which includes a variety of meters and lengths. *Peacock Pie,* however, is usually considered the work which solidified de la Mare's reputation as a poet for children, a reputation further enhanced by such books as *Down-Adown-Derry: A Book of Fairy Poems* (1922) and *Bells and Grass: A Book*

of Rhymes (1941). Influenced as a poet by mythology, traditional ballads and nursery rhymes, and the language of the Bible, de la Mare continues to reflect this background in his prose works. He is especially well regarded as the creator of *The Three Mulla–Mulgars,* his sole novel. An epic allegorical fantasy, the book describes the odyssey of three simian brothers, exiled princes who search for their father through lands both magical and dangerous. Acknowledged as both a masterpiece which describes humanity's strivings with lyricism and insight and a difficult work filled with strange names and symbols, *The Three Mulla–Mulgars* is often mentioned as a precursor of such classics of modern British fantasy as J. R. R. Tolkien's *Ring* trilogy and Richard Adams's *Watership Down.* De la Mare also wrote several volumes of short stories noted for their characterization and wit and retellings of traditional tales and the Old Testament which expand on their original sources. In addition, he is well known for compiling three anthologies of which *Come Hither,* a collection of songs, ballads, and poetry which includes an extensive introduction and copious notes by de la Mare, is the most popular. Among contemporary authors and scholars of children's literature, de la Mare is also respected for his quote from the introduction to *Bells and Grass* in which he states that "only the rarest kind of best of anything can be good enough for the young," a sentiment which has become a guiding principle of the field. Poet Eleanor Farjeon has written that "the name of Walter de la Mare will dwell, beyond the power of axe or storm to destroy, as long as English poetry is green." In addition to many awards for his adult literature, de la Mare won the Carnegie Medal in 1947 for *Collected Stories for Children* while *A Penny a Day* received the Lewis Carroll Shelf Award in 1962.

(See also *Twentieth Century Literary Criticism* Vol. 4; *Something about the Author,* Vol. 16; *Contemporary Authors,* Vol. 110; and *Dictionary of Literary Biography,* Vol. 19.)

AUTHOR'S COMMENTARY

As this small volume [*Bells and Grass*] will be the last collection of its kind that I shall make, I should like to explain in a few words how it came into being—notwithstanding the days in which we are now living.

About a year ago I was looking through a jackdaw jumble of old papers and old letters—the contents of a packing case, a Tate sugar-box, which had been left undisturbed since 1924. A bonfire merrily blazing away under the blue skies of early May soon disposed of most of this hoard. But among a few old manuscripts in the box I came across a commonplace book, bound in black leather. It had been completely forgotten; yet at a glimpse it at once came welling up into memory again. About twenty pages of it had been crammed, top to bottom, with pencil scribblings, many of them dated 1905, the remainder of a date not later, I think, than 1906. Some of these were marked "Copied." A few are still incompletely readable even by the writer of them!

Three years before this, owing to the kindness of Andrew Lang and of Charles Longman, my first book of rhymes had appeared, *Songs of Childhood.* First snowdrop of the year, first primrose, first cuckoo-call and returning swallows, first memories, first love—all such firsts may carry with them a thrill or delight or edge or sweetness, and perhaps even a magic, of their own. So, however faulty it may be, however far short it may have fallen of hope or wish or intention—so may a first book. There is a peculiar joy in seeing what has been all but a secret source of interest and pleasure out in the open, so to speak. Some of the rhymes in that collection had been written during the last years of Queen Victoria, and had then been shared solely with my mother. Moreover I hid myself behind a pen-name. Charming—with its pale-blue cloth, parchment spine, gilded Longman *Ship,* and Dickie Doyle frontispiece—charming though the little volume was in outward appearance, its welcome hardly resembled that bestowed on hot cakes. But there it actually was, in print.

Eleven years afterwards, in 1913, another collection of rhymes, called *Peacock Pie,* was published. Needless to say, this title for it was not in the least intended to suggest a delicacy. Indeed, I had never so much as tasted a peacock pie, although I had frequently feasted my eyes on one in the windows of Mr. Pimm's restaurant in Cheapside—the bird itself, or rather its lovely but vacant plumage, seated in splendour upon the pastry's moulded upper-

crust. No. The book contained a piece called **"The Mad Prince"**; and that begins:

"Who said, 'Peacock Pie?'"

Hence the spectacular title.

The rhymes, then, in this forgotten old commonplace book were "made up" more than thirty-five years ago. It is a rather odd experience to read again anything written in the distant past which has long ago passed out of recollection—even if it be only an old letter to butcher, baker, or candlestickmaker. It is like chancing on a half-forgotten photograph—as I also did that morning: the photograph of a moon-faced boy in a surplice. It may be a happy experience; it may be a saddening one; it may be a mingling of both.

Now, as with the contents of the two volumes I have mentioned, many of these rhymes . . . had had the young in mind. Or, to put this in another way, they had been written by and through that self within which, in however small a degree, there still lurked *some*thing that might merit so precious a tribute as that of being described as young. It was the self that still delighted—and no less than it had in childhood perhaps—in the old folk-tales and fairy-tales, in the old nursery rhymes and jingles, in early memories, and in whatever else goes with being young; whether merry or sad, grave or gay or tender.

How old, then, are the young? And how young is it possible for the old in years to remain—without, that is, being merely immature, undergrown, or silly? Is this in fact a question of age, of mere time? I doubt if it is. Even one's body seems in certain respects to be independent of the mechanical hands of a clock, and of an earth spinning on in space, as we are told, through its four strange and lovely seasons, in its annual revolution round the sun. We know very little what we mean by Time. I have seen a baby apparently of only twenty-four hours' experience in this world that yet was not only the minute image of, but also looked even older than its grandmother. I have seen grandmothers with eyes as guileless and youthful as a frank and happy seven-year-old's; and, clearly, with hearts to match. The body ages: that is certain. No old ewe, whatever its inclinations may be, can gambol, leap, and pirouette like a lamb. Every seven years, it is said, as with an umbrella that has been repaired—new ferrule, new stick, new handle, new ribs, new silk or alpaca—the body itself is renewed. Yet it continues to age and at last wears out.

None the less, handle to ferrule, we ourselves remain much the same umbrella. The self within is still the self within, however much knowledge and experience, and whatever treasures of memory it may have acquired. It is still the silkworm in its cocoon, whatever the quality of the silk may be. As the years go by, we put away childish things. We have to. And yet what we love and delight in when we are young we may continue to love and delight in when we are old; and not much less ardently, perhaps. So with all that is meant by heart, feelings, mind, the fancy, and the imagination.

However that may be, I confess that on reading over again the scribblings in my old manuscript book, the time intervening seemed to have vanished away like smoke—like the smoke of my bonfire that day in May. And in spite of all their far too evident defects and deficiencies, I found myself sharing the self in them as if they and it were of yesterday.

Not only this, but I began again. I began, as fancy led, to scribble yet more rhymes. The bee, the wind, the wild bird—without them, flowers would be few and fruit would be scanty. Like a plant, the mind and the imagination may lie in wait, as it were, for dew and rain and sunshine, for the bird of the air—impulses. And even a weed may bloom and seed. The new rhymes that came, however faultily, however far short of the aim, were written, too, with precisely the same hope as the old had been.

I know well that only the rarest kind of best in anything can be good enough for the young. I *know* too that in later life it is just (if only just) possible now and again to recover fleetingly the intense delight, the untellable joy and happiness and fear and grief and pain of our early years, of an all but forgotten childhood. I have, in a flash, in a momentary glimpse, seen again a horse, an oak, a daisy, just as I saw them in those early years, as if with that heart, with those senses. It was a revelation. But only such poets as William Blake and Vaughan and Traherne have been able to communicate, as if by means of a language within a language, this strange, scarcely earthly rapture, vision, being, grace. I know also that the young can be very patient with even the much less good; and may find *some* good in everything—in the simplest of stories, in a mere jingle. May they then be no less patient and hospitable to what is here.

A last word may be said about the rhymes themselves. As with those in the earlier books, some of them tell of actual and personal memories. Most of them, whether fanciful or not, are concerned with the imagined and the imaginary. The "I" in a rhyme is not necessarily "me." . . . Imaginary children of differing sorts and ages (though all of the same parentage) are speaking in **"Nicoletta,"** in **"The Voice,"** in **"The Feather,"** in **"The Shadow,"** in **"Somewhere."** (pp. 5-10)

To write anything solely to please someone else is rather dangerous; and particularly if it happens to be in rhyme. To write for one's own delight and out of the sheer impulse and desire to do so is less dangerous, though one may of course keep such things to oneself! To hope to please others with what has been so written is a wildish aspiration, but an aspiration which it should not be too difficult even to condone. It may not be *too* difficult, perhaps, even when the writer is distinctly "old" in birthdays, and when those "others"—whatever *their* age in birthdays may be—were not only born young, but young will always remain. (p. 10)

Walter de la Mare, in an introduction to his Bells and Grass, *The Viking Press, 1942, pp. 5-10.*

The Times Literary Supplement

[The] poetry in these two little volumes [**Peacock Pie: A Book of Rhymes** and **Songs of Childhood**] is, perhaps, the purest poetry for children that has ever been made; Blake and Stevenson not forgotten. Mr. de la Mare does not write down to children. He makes for them his very subtlest and most cunning music; but so pure is it that while we, who can tell how it is done, are gloating over the art of it, children . . . are delighting in a glorification—say,

rather, a revelation—of their own ideas and dreams and doings.

I looked out of window, in the white moon light,
The leaves were like snow in the wood—

> "Listen, O listen,
> Music is falling;
> Tiny lanterns clash and glisten;
> Voices are calling;
> Far, far the blue air shakes;
> Hov'ring and winging,
> Float we in light and shadow,
> Singing—singing."

The child that has learned to enjoy that is equipped to enjoy the most "æthereal" poetry in *Prometheus Unbound.*

> In the black furrow of a field
> I saw an old witch-hare this night;
> And she cocked a lissome ear,
> And she eyed the moon so bright,
> And she nibbled o' the green;
> And I whispered "Whsst! witch-hare,"
> Away like a ghostie o'er the field
> She fled, and left the moonlight there.

Children may not realize how fine an achievement are those last five words; but the sound of that picture, if we may so express it, must surely pass, as beauty, into their lives.

And here we are, sheltering ourselves behind children, when what we really want to talk about is our own, grown-up, critical enjoyment of these delicious things! Yet who is going to "review" such intimately dear treasures as these? There is only one good way of recommending them, and that is to quote them.

"Pearl, Dew, and Silver," in The Times Literary Supplement, *No. 778, December 14, 1916, p. 604.*

The Saturday Review, London

Mr. Walter de la Mare is the Shepherd of Faërie. With a shining crook he leads from fold to fold. For not alone do his poems [in **Peacock Pie** and **Songs of Childhood**] brim with the music, colour, magic that children love, but they are tiny pastorals as well, reflecting not less the beauties of "reality", sunrise and sunset, moonshine and starshine, dew and frost, trees and flowers, than the radiant insubstantiality of the elves themselves. The melodies flow sweetly as from a river reed or "green corn pipe". As with him of whom Milton sang, this poet "sees, Or dreams he sees the fairies". And it is his special gift to speed envisagement straight from the imagination to the imagination, and to give us—children all—part in his visions of the small immortals. There is but to watch in the hour

> "When the last colours of the day
> Have from their burning ebbed away";

or when

> "Ere yet the dawn with firelight fills
> The night-dew of the bramble cap".

Thence onward we may see and dream, dream and see, until each illusion is merged in light and sound of day. For Mr. de la Mare will have nothing lost. In his vision illusion and reality play at hide-and-seek; illusion gilds reality as in **"Silver"**, reality conserves illusion as in **"Sleepy-head"**. The calling by fairies' voices, the singing in distant woods, are not solely dream stuff, after all! . . .

In these two books the faërie empire is restored, or, more correctly, a cobwebbed door is opened to old enchanted spaces of the mind. Once, as Chaucer sings, the land was "fulfilled of faërie". But then the "limitoures", in dread of an anti-sacerdotal power, drove back the tiny shades into the poet-brain, where, as dimensionless, they only bred. Their power, perhaps, yet not their charm, was so destroyed. Let Shakespeare or another open the door a crack, or Mr. de la Mare or another fling it wide, and in a twinkling they are around us, "black, grey, green, white", piping upon a wren's quill, "chattering like grasshoppers", and dancing their "thistledown dance". . . .

This mastery of the faërie atmosphere never fails. By it all faded fancies stir and shine. Loveliness and "silver stillness" are in the vision of **"The Sleeping Beauty"**: the ordered music of vowels, the cunningly directed service of consonants, the potent magic of sibilation, enhance the envisagement of the **"Prince of Sleep"**. . . .

Here, as elsewhere, is seen Mr. de la Mare's use for the sibilant. Again, it "hisseth swetely" in English ears. Moreover, do not silver, sleep, shine, sheen, sleek own its domination, and are not they words that, through the subtle sympathy of sound with meaning hold spells for enchantment? It is a charm for sleep. The child is soothed to rest by utterance of the long, slurring "s-s-s-sh" that resembles the sound of the wind in the trees, or of the swaying of ripe corn, or of the smooth rush of far-off water. One is not sure that the reciting of, say, **"Silver"**, would not ensure sleep as certainly as the ancient plan of pouring water rhythmically from one vessel into the other. . . .

This poet, be it noted, is completely master of his elfin tool—the very Puck of the alphabet. Far from allowing it to run amok, as did more than once great Coleridge himself, to the killing of his music, he puts it through the prettiest of paces. . . .

In the pieces the merely gay, and the false, Faërie throng and jostle each other. "Crier Hobgoblin" has made "the fairy Oyes", and, like bees that swarm, they come tumbling forth: Ride-by-Nights, Peak the Changeling, Follets the Haunters, Ogres, Giants, Dwarfs. There are beautiful and tender imaginings also, and the jolliest rhymes for children of babes and beasts and birds. Only, from covers to covers, the most captious critic may hardly find a poem that is not a joy to meet and to keep.

> *"A Shepherd of Faërie," in* The Saturday Review, *London, Vol. CXXIII, No. 3202, March 10, 1917, p. 232.*

Conrad Aiken

[Walter de la Mare's] *Peacock Pie* consists of lyrics ostensibly for children; in reality it contains some of the most delightful work he has done. It is doubtful whether any other living American or English poet can weave simple melody as deftly as Mr. de la Mare, melody both as regards words and ideas. If after a century has passed one may recall Leigh Hunt's categories of imagination and fancy as the two springs of the poetic, it would be no vio-

lence to say that Mr. de la Mare's power over us is rather in fancy than in imagination. It is delicate, elusive, impalpable; over the simplest lyrics hangs an overtone of magic. And now and again, as in the **"Song of the Mad Prince,"** this magic reaches a grave intensity which strikes well to the marrow of things. Mr. de la Mare is not an innovator, and his scope is not great; but within his scope he has no superior. (p. 152)

> *Conrad Aiken, "Three English Poets," in* The Dial, *Chicago, Vol. 63, August 30, 1917, pp. 150-52.*

Susan Buchan

It is curious but true that, while we all start life by being children, and have had, even the dullest of us, a love of adventure, a rapacity in acquiring new experience, and above all a consciousness of a mysterious world around us, which moves along somehow on parallel lines with that of grown-up people, of whose tyrannical ways we are so annihilatingly aware, only once or so in every generation arises some one who can write, not only about children, as Mr. Kenneth Grahame has done with such beauty and complete understanding, but for children—write, as it were, as one child to another.

The mantle of the two great master-children, Robert Louis Stevenson and "Lewis Carroll," has fallen in our generation on Mr. Walter de la Mare. . . . Mr. de la Mare wears the mantle of the masters with a difference. "Lewis Carroll" and Robert Louis had in all their unlikeness one point in common: they were both enchantingly able to express the delightful pedestrianism of childhood. . . .

This daily life of childhood is fully understood by Mr. de la Mare, as we see in the poem—

> "I know a little cupboard
> With a teeny tiny key,
> And there's a jar of Lollipops
> For me, me, me.
> I have a small fat grandmamma,
> With a very slippery knee . . .
> And she's keeper of the cupboard
> With the key, key, key"—

and in the *cri du cœur* of all children who have ever been taken marketing by their parents and guardians:—

> "I can't abear a Butcher,
> I can't abide his meat,
> The ugliest shop of all is his,
> The ugliest in the street;
> Bakers' are warm, cobblers' dark,
> Chemists' burn watery lights:
> But oh, the sawdust butcher's shop,
> That ugliest of sights!"

But he speaks most clearly to the child's other side: to the mood in which bed, meals, lessons, all the scaffolding of existence, are slipped through and left behind: the dimensions of the world alter: probability and possibility, those two spectres which haunt ceaselessly all grown-up people to the paralysing of interesting effort, are chased away: and, free in mind, you step into a wood or meadow where Robin Goodfellow may await you at every turn, and where no elf is too small or giant too large to slip into your mirage. . . .

Another avenue of Mr. de la Mare to the childish mind is his feeling for magic in animals. . . .

> "The old Pig said to the little pigs,
> 'In the forest is truffles and mast;
> Follow me, then, all ye little pigs,
> Follow me fast!'"

will go straight to childhood's heart. . . .

In **"The Thief to Robin's Castle"** we have a child's story in ballad form, a thing rare in the literature of childhood. What could be more wholly romantic than the opening lines? . . . (p. 200)

To each of us there comes at times a sensation that words cannot express, a waft of magic, a feeling that we have once known of something which is just beyond our everyday consciousness. We know that scent, notes of music, the virgin freshness of an early morning, a sunset colour, can revive it for an instant. The nearest we ever got to it was in that dream we children vainly hoped to recapture each night when sleep came, but which was almost too shadowy in its loveliness even for a dream. In **"Will Ever"** we seem very near to it. We breathe the true rarefied atmosphere of magic again, and hear the piping of the spirit ditties of no tone. (pp. 200-01)

To those of us who are looking in secret dread to see whether the war pressure, the air raids, and worse, the rumours of raids, are filling our children's heads with unchildlike thoughts and fears—or at any rate with nothing but echoes of "base mechanic happenings"—these poems come as a help and a comfort. This procession of witches, knights, thieves, and goblins winds round the walls of our mind with the brilliant completeness of a Benozzo Gozzoli fresco, and can wile us all back for a time to lost fairylands. (p. 201)

> *Susan Buchan, "Walter de la Mare for Children," in* The Spectator, *Vol. 121, No. 4704, August 24, 1918, pp. 200-01.*

Christopher Morley

Once a year or so one is permitted to find some book which brings a real tingle to that ribbon of the spinal marrow which responds to the vibrations of literature. . . . [In] 1913 I read **Peacock Pie** and **Songs of Childhood,** by Walter de la Mare.

Peacock Pie having now been published in this country it is seasonable to kindle an altar fire for this most fanciful and delightful of present-day poets. . . . He has the knack of "words set in delightful proportion"; and **Peacock Pie** is the most authentic knapsack of fairy gold since the *Child's Garden of Verses.*

I am tempted to think that Mr. de la Mare is the kind of poet more likely to grow in England than America. The gracious and fine-spun fabric of his verse, so delicate in music, so quaint and haunting in imaginative simplicity, is the gift of a land and life where rewards and fairies are not wholly passed away. Emily Dickinson and Vachel Lindsay are among our contributors to the songs of gramarye: but one has only to open *The Congo* side by side with **Peacock Pie** to see how the seductions of ragtime and the clashing crockery of the Poetry Society's dinners are coarsening the fibres of Mr. Lindsay's marvellous talent

as compared with the dainty horns of elfin that echo in Mr. de la Mare. (pp. 271-72)

To say that Mr. de la Mare's verse is distilled in fairyland suggests perhaps a delicate and absent-minded figure, at a loss in the hurly burly of this world; the kind of poet who loses his rubbers in the subway, drops his glasses in the trolley car, and is found wandering blithely in Central Park while the Women's Athenaeum of the Tenderloin is waiting four hundred strong for him to lecture. But Mr. de la Mare is the more modern figure who might readily (I hope I speak without offense) be mistaken for a New York stock broker, or a member of the Boston Chamber of Commerce. Perhaps he even belongs to the newer order of poets who do not wear rubbers.

One's first thought (if one begins at the beginning, but who reads a book of poetry that way?) is that **Peacock Pie** is a collection of poems for children. But it is not that, any more than *The Masses* is a paper for the proletariat. Before you have gone very far you will find that the imaginary child you set out with has been magicked into a changeling. The wee folk have been at work and bewitched the pudding—the pie rather. The fire dies on the hearth, the candle channels in its socket, but still you read on. Some of the poems bring you the cauld grue of Thrawn Janet. When at last you go up to bed, it will be with the shuddering sigh of one thrilled through and through with the sad little beauties of the world. You will want to put out a bowl of fresh milk on the doorstep to appease the banshee—did you not know that the janitor of your Belshazzar Court would get it in the morning?

One of the secrets of Mr. de la Mare's singular charm is his utter simplicity, linked with a delicately tripping music that intrigues the memory unawares and plays high jinks with you forever after. Who can read **"Off the Ground"** and not strum the dainty jig over and over in his head whenever he takes a bath, whenever he shaves, whenever the moon is young? (pp. 273-74)

The sensible man's quarrel with the proponents of free verse is not that they write such good prose; not that they espouse the natural rhythms of the rain, the brook, the wind-grieved tree; this is all to the best, even if as old as Solomon. It is that they affect to disdain the superlative harmonies of artificed and ordered rhythms; that knowing not a spondee from a tribrach they vapour about prosody, of which they know nothing, and imagine to be new what antedates the Upanishads. The haunting beauty of Mr. de la Mare's delicate art springs from an ear of superlative tenderness and sophistication. The daintiest alternation of iambus and trochee is joined to the serpent's cunning in swiftly tripping dactyls. Probably this artifice is greatly unconscious, the meed of the trained musician; but let no singer think to upraise his voice before the Lord ere he master the axioms of prosody. (p. 275)

One may well despair of conveying in a few rough paragraphs the gist of this quaint, fanciful, brooding charm. There is something fey about much of the book: it peers behind the curtains of twilight and sees strange things. In its love of children, its inspired simplicity, its sparkle of whim and Æsopian brevity, I know nothing finer. . . .

Peacock Pie is immortal diet indeed, as Sir Walter said of his scrip of joy. Annealed as we are, I think it will discompose the most callous. It is a sweet feverfew for the heats of the spirit. It is full of outlets of sky. (p. 276)

> *Christopher Morley, "Peacock Pie'," in his* Shandygaff: A Number of Most Agreeable Inquirendoes upon Life and Letters, Interspersed with Short Stories and Skits, the Whole Most Diverting to the Reader, *1918. Reprint by Scholarly Press, Inc., 1971, pp. 271-77.*

Edmund Gosse, C. B.

Mr. Walter de la Mare's earliest volume, called ***Songs of Childhood,*** did not attract much attention, partly because of its quietness, but more because it was entirely out of key with the poetry fashionable at the end of the nineteenth century. In ethical respects extremely unlike the verse of Mr. Thomas Hardy, that of Mr. de la Mare, especially in its earlier manifestations, has this in common with it, that it examines with scrupulous care little phenomena of Nature, and of Nature acting upon the soul, which had appeared too insignificant to attract the attention of other recent poets. But the ***Songs of Childhood*** also exemplified a quality which is essential to Mr. de la Mare, the delicate splendour of his fancy, as in **"Tartary"** and in **"The Isle of Lone,"** exhibited often with a recklessness which is on the border of incoherency, but is preserved by a happy instinct from passing outside the bounds of what poetry permits itself. The authors of past time with whom Mr. de la Mare has most in common are Blake (in the *Songs of Innocence*), Coleridge (in "Kubla Khan"), and Christina Rossetti (in *Goblin Market*). He has not borrowed from these magicians, but his enchantments are of the same order as theirs. (p. 312)

> *Edmund Gosse, "The Fairy in the Garden," in his* Books on the Table, *Charles Scribner's Sons, 1921, pp. 309-17.*

Padraic Colum

Down-Adown-Derry is a collection of Mr. de la Mare's fairy poems—some are new, some are from ***The Listeners,*** some are from ***Peacock Pie,*** and some are from ***The Veil.*** . . . [One] would like to believe that there are some imaginative enough to make ***Down-Adown-Derry*** as much of a classic as *A Child's Garden of Verses.*

Between *A Child's Garden of Verses* and ***Down-Adown-Derry*** there is as much difference as between a hobby-horse and a live bird. Most children will get on better with the hobby-horse. They will remember Leary the lamplighter passing by when their memory of "The courts of the lord Pthamasar where the sweet birds of Psuthys are" will have faded. So it will be for most children. But for the rare imaginative child ***Down-Adown-Derry*** will have a great appeal. One might be sorry for the child who absorbs these glamorous poems—Will not **"Cumberland"** and **"The Little Green Orchard"** and **"Truants"** take the magic out of many poems he or she will read afterwards!

These fairy poems are full of the elfin, and they are steeped in a tradition too. Walter de la Mare has heard the horns of Elfland, but he has heard them from a definite spot—from the English countryside, with its fields and lanes and villages, with its houses full of dear and familiar things, where there are maids and men who know of Loblie-by-the-fire and the Rides-by-nights, and witches and changelings, and the witch's great grandchildren. To the child who is imaginative enough to take possession of it he gives a double garden. . . . ***Down-Adown-Derry*** has both quaintness and sorcery, and much of the rare mood of entrancement that is in ***The Listeners.***

One cannot write at length about this book without repeating everything that has been said about Walter de la Mare's poetry: in it he gives us, whether we are adults or children, lovely, whimsical and enchanting poetry. (pp. 261-62)

> *Padraic Colum, "The Later de la Mare," in* The New Republic, *Vol. XXVI, No. 399, July 26, 1922, pp. 261-62.*

F. L. Lucas

The new thing in Mr. de la Mare is [the] remarriage of classical simplicity and restraint with the romantic quest for questing's sake of the strange and mysterious. Thus his epitaphs, his laments, breathe the still, small perfectness of the graves of Carameicus or the pages of the *Anthology:* and yet in the new mythology which he has created, filling again dead waste and woodland with those bright, lurking eyes, gracious or sinister, that the Greek felt always ambushed there, there lives, too, the teeming grotesqueness, the haunting mystery, the laughing exaggeration of the Middle Ages.

Thus not only might the charming lines of Gavin Douglas on *Æneid VI.:*

> All is bot gaistis and elriche fantasies,
> Of brouneis and bogillis full this buke,

stand on the title-page of ***Down-Adown-Derry*** as of several of its predecessors (most indeed, of the poems are old friends from earlier collections); but to their beauty of nimble fantasy there is nothing nearer than Dunbar on the Giant Fyn:

> He wald apon his tais stand
> And tak the sternis doune with his hand
> And set them in a gold garland
> Above his wyfis hair.

Not, indeed, since Thomas the Rhymer has there been such a poet of Faerie. . . . The strange thing is that Mr. de la Mare's lightness of touch keeps ever fresh his repetitions of gaunt houses with something lurking behind their blank and glassy gaze, of the rank, sequestered beauty of gardens in decay, of doors that never open to the knocker or open only on a void. Always this Lilliputian delicacy, like the gift of Melampus, who could hear the growing grass and the whisper of the worm—now watching the shadow that a bubble casts, or hearkening at the fireside to "the tiny crooning" of the flames, or seeing in **"Remembrance"** how

> The sky was like a waterdrop
> In shadow of a thorn,
> Clear, tranquil, beautiful,
> Forlorn,—

now dancing in its fairy-ring to the music of a metrical inventiveness unequalled since Swinburne. Although Mr. de la Mare gets his effects not so much, like Swinburne, by devising regular new metrical schemes as by loosening the bonds of the familiar forms. It is his careful irregularity and variation of length with monosyllabic and quadrisyllabic feet that restores to verse arrangements, almost decrepit, a youth and spring in his hands, as different from their usual jog-trot as a living creature from the mechanical duck of the *encyclopédiste.* (pp. 356-57)

F. L. Lucas, "The Poetry of Walter de la Mare," in New Statesman, *Vol. XX, No. 506, December 23, 1922, pp. 356-57.*

John Middleton Murry

Mr de la Mare is a poet of the great theme [of the opposition of the real and the ideal] who is distinguished chiefly by his faculty of pressing invention and fancy to the service of his need. He has named his other kingdom with many names; it is Arabia,

> 'Where the Princes ride at noon
> 'Mid the verdurous vales and thickets
> Under the ghost of the moon.'

It is Tartary; it is Alulvan. Queen Djenira reigns there, and when she sleeps, she walks through

> 'The courts of the lord Pthamasar,
> Where the sweet birds of Psuthys are.'

Or again it is Thule of the old legend, upon which the poet beautifully calls:—

> 'If thou art sweet as they are sad
> Who on the shore of Time's salt sea
> Watch on the dim horizon fade
> Ships bearing love and night to thee . . . '

Within its shifting frontiers are comprised all the dim, debatable lands that lie between the Never-Never country of nursery rhyme and the more solid fields to which the city mind turns for its paradise, the terrestrial happiness which only a shake of the gods' dice-box has denied:—

> 'Had the gods loved me I had lain
> Where darnel is and thorn,
> And the wild night-bird's nightlong strain
> Trembles in boughs forlorn.
>
> Nay, but they loved me not; and I
> Must needs a stranger be
> Whose every exiled day gone by
> Aches with their memory.'

That, surely, is a kingdom of solid earth. And yet we wonder. Is it not also rather a symbol and projection of the poet's desiderium, his longingness (to use his own word), than an earthly kingdom from which fate has exiled him? We do not wonder long. The peace that comes from the satisfaction of this haunting desire is not to be found in any actual countryside. Nature has no medicinable balm for this unease. (pp. 125-26)

The loveliness of earth comes to the poet with the perpetual shadow of regret; and even the memory of it dissolves into nothingness. . . .

Life haunted by death, beauty by decay. What remedy will avail against this malady of mankind? Nothing but the courage of a dream. (p. 127)

But how to keep the courage of that dream—there is the question. The poet belongs to his age; it is not possible for him to elude it. The shadowless asphodel is haunted by the shadows of the earthly flowers that have died. When the delight of fancy and invention has begun to fade where shall the poet place his other kingdom? What if Arabia and Tartary and Thule and Alulvan cease to delight, and Queen Djenira dream no more? Not all the princes of Arabia, with their splendours and their music, can lull the poet's mind into forgetfulness that he seeks not only a symbol, but a satisfaction for his longing. There comes a time when he knows that the delight of discovering a new name is not the delight of discovered peace. The urgent, incessant question begins to dominate; the pattern in the carpet to appear.

The other kingdom is the kingdom of peace, the country where the soul can rest. And now the poet no more makes a triumphant deduction of immortality from mortality, of the eternal from the temporal. He declares his need, but the haven where it will be satisfied is one which no earthly ship will find:—

> 'Where blooms the flower when her petals fade,
> Where sleepeth echo by earth's music made,
> Where all things transient to changeless win,
> There waits the peace thy spirit dwelleth in.'

And so, by nuances almost imperceptible of emotion and expression, we pass from this undiscoverable country to the clear, comfortless conclusion of what we must consider on this and on other grounds to be Mr de la Mare's finest poem. In a sense **The Tryst** marks the end of his poetical journey. The curve is complete. The dream is only a dream. (pp. 127-29)

On the path of that curve all Mr de la Mare's memorable poetic achievements—and they are many—will be found. On it, too, will be found the greater part of those rhymes for children which, to the casual glance, seem to be eccentric to it. For, as we have said, Arabia is on the same continent as the Never-Never land of the nursery rhyme; they march with one another. They were created to satisfy the same impulse. In the magic kingdom of childhood 'the shadowless asphodel' seemed really to exist, in a realm where all perfections and splendours and beauties persisted without change; and one might truly regard Mr de la Mare's 'grown-up' poetry as an effort to recapture the simple certainty of that childhood belief, or to express the regret at the shadows that have encroached upon it. Therefore, his rhymes for children take a definite place in his poetry as a whole, and are also essentially different from other rhymes of the kind; they are the natural, inevitable expression of the poet's deepest feeling. How natural and inevitable can be seen, if not from the tenor of this exposition, from the final verse of the exquisite poem **Dreams**:—

> 'What can a tired heart say,
> Which the wise of the world have made dumb?
> Save to the lonely dreams of a child,
> "Return again, come!" '

To recognise that the dream is a dream, yet to refuse to put it away, this is the vital act of comprehension which animates the enduring part of the poetry of the present age. It is a reflection of our devastating experience and our shadowy faith; for even while we know that the dream is a dream, having no counterpart in the reality without us, it cannot be wholly surrendered because we live by its enchantment. For to live is to make ourselves of a certain quality; to fashion ourselves to a certain temper; and if the dream is impotent to reshape the stubborn world beyond us, its power to work upon our own souls is undiminished. (pp. 129-30)

> *John Middleton Murry, "The Poetry of Walter de la Mare," in his* Countries of the Mind: Essays in Literary Criticism, *E. P. Dutton & Company, 1922, pp. 121-36.*

The Times Literary Supplement

The merit of Mr. De La Mare's collection [***Come Hither***], though we advance no claim to infallibility for his choices, is that, with utmost diversity in the parts and in spite of a pardonable but regrettable prolixity in the handling of them, it achieves artistic unity. Every piece he takes affects us newly because he takes it and because he places it as he does. . . .

This thing that Mr. De La Mare has created is a thing of delight for us all, and a thing which it greatly interests us not only to enjoy but also to understand. Here all the time and for all time is the magical aroma of poetry, and the poetry is children's poetry and the children are English children. There is a bond of sympathy between the three. What is it? Longing to tell us, and knowing that he can only tell us indirectly, Mr. De La Mare begins and ends his collection with the same piece, **"This is the Key"**; anonymous he calls it, but if he did not write it himself, who did?

Putting first the key into our hands, he next (in a section called "Morning and May") gives us **"A New Year Carol"**:—

> Here we bring new water
> from the well so clear,
> For to worship God with,
> this happy New Year,

and then Montgomerie's

> Hay, nou the day dauis,

which he translates in a parallel column. Next, with cunningly calculated surprise, he puts Isaac Watts:—

> Tis the voice of a sluggard; I heard him complain—

having read which, we are ready for
Hearke, hearke the Larke at Heaven's gate sings, and for

> Awake, awake! the morn will never rise

Till she can dress her beauty at your eyes!

How deftly the key turns in the oiled wards! Four pages have brought us straight to the heart of the mystery.

So the series goes on, with an alternating and developing ravishment, like that of a movement in music, drawing to itself all the riches of nursery rhyme, folk-song, and "poet's poetry," and gradually leading us to perceive that the nursery rhyme and the folk-song are a standard of perfection and that the question we have to ask of the poet's poem is whether it comes up to them.

> Lavender's blue, dilly dilly, lavender's green,
> When I am king, dilly dilly, you shall be queen.

We call lines like this artless, but the truth about them is

that they satisfy all the canons. Words and rhythm, gay thoughts and pretty feelings, all trip along together in tenderest *insouciance*. One conscious touch, one hint of seriousness or solemnity, would destroy their texture like a fingermark on a butterfly's wing. (p. 799)

Mr. De La Mare, deeply impregnated as he is with the spirit of worship which presides over these mysteries and persistencies, has given us a new image of our national gift and our national achievement. Looking through his eyes, we see that the poetry of England is a poetry which need not forget the nursery where it was born, since it is strong enough to live in the pure and hospitable impulses of the inquiring child. (p. 800)

> *"The Child Among His Blisses," in* The Times Literary Supplement, *No. 1141, November 29, 1923, pp. 799-800.*

J. B. Priestley

[Mr. de la Mare's] work is one of the most individual productions this century has given us, every scrap of it being stamped with its author's personality and taking its place in the de la Mare canon. If Mr. de la Mare were to wander into half a dozen literary forms that so far have not known him, if he were to bid farewell to poetry and fiction and do nothing but essays, criticism, and even history, the new work would promptly link up with the old and take on a quality different from that of any other essays, criticism, or history, so marked is his individuality. Nevertheless, he remains to criticism an elusive figure, whose outline and gestures are not easily fixed in the memory—a shadowy Pied Piper.

One fairly common misconception must be brushed aside before we can begin to examine Mr. de la Mare, and that is the notion that he is primarily a creator of pretty fancies for the children. Because he has occasionally produced a volume for children, many persons regard him merely as the latest and most delicate of nursery poets, an artist for the Christmas Tree. Nor is this notion, except in its crudest form, confined to the uncritical, for even at this late hour there is a tendency on the part of many critics to treat Mr. de la Mare as if he were not an artist with a unique vision, a man of strange delights and sorrows, but a rather gentlemanly conjurer they had engaged for their children's party. There is, of course, an element of truth in this view, but at the moment it is hardly worth while disengaging it, though, as we shall presently see, this element of truth happens to be of supreme importance. Regarded as a general view this popular misconception is so preposterous that if we go to the other extreme, if we argue that Mr. de la Mare is a writer that no child should be suffered to approach, we shall not be further from the truth. . . . [An] account of Mr. de la Mare as an unwholesome decadent is manifestly absurd, but on the whole it is probably less absurd than the more popular opinion of him as a pretty-pretty children's poet. Yet we can use his work for children as a kind of jumping-off place in our pursuit of him.

We can begin with the large and very successful anthology of poetry that Mr. de la Mare has brought out recently, ***Come Hither,*** "a collection of rhymes and poems for the young of all ages." This very personal and delightful anthology has a curious introduction, in which very characteristically the author, by the use of quaint anagrams, makes a kind of story out of his account of Nature and Poetry; and it also contains an enormous number of rambling notes and quotations from all manner of curious old books. And this happy volume makes it clear that when he set out to please the "young of all ages," he also set to please himself and brought together all the poetry he loved, whether it was something by Shakespeare or Milton, or an old jingle of nursery rhyme. There is about this anthology, though it contains some of the most solemn and moving passages in our literature, something of the golden spacious air of childhood, something a thousand leagues removed from the atmosphere of most anthologies of this kind, and one realizes that this is not merely the result of good taste, a sense of what is fitting, and so on, but of something much rarer, an imagination of an unusual kind, one that is infinitely wider and more sensitive than a child's, and yet, in one sense, still is a child's imagination. It has been said that a keen remembrance of childhood, the ability of a man to see again at will the world as he saw it when a child, is a test and sign of genius. But imagination, it is clear, includes the ability to recapture former states of mind, whether they belong to childhood; youth or later life, and the childhood theory of genius is obviously much too wide. It is probably true to say that geniuses of the first rank, the Homers and Shakespeares and Dantes, feed imaginatively on all their experience and are no more dependent on childhood than they are on any other period of their life; they are for ever gorging on existence, and as they age, their vision widens, or at least changes. But there is a lesser order of geniuses who create worlds for themselves that have a distinct life of their own, but are obviously different, running obliquely, from the actual world we know, and it appears to me that such writers (Dickens is the type) build up their little universes from their childish impressions and carry forward with them into manhood their early imaginings and memories. What they do not understand and cannot enter into imaginatively during their youth they never do understand, not, at least, for the purposes of their art. (pp. 32-5)

It is only when they are compared with the very greatest, the demi-gods of creative literature, that such writers are found to be faulty, for the very intensity of their imagining lifts them high above the great mass of authors. Their work has a personal vision and a curiously fascinating "glamourie" that delights the more imaginative reader. Nor must they themselves be supposed to be "childish" (in the looser sense of the term) merely because the world of their imagination was put together during childhood, for they may have, and often do have, the deepest feelings to express, the most subtle emotions to convey, and their work may be quickened with the touch of a sublime philosophy. The world they show us may not enlarge its limitations, may present the same colours, surfaces and shapes, but as time goes on and their vision widens, this world becomes more and more symbolical, just as in the childhood of a race men people the earth and the heavens with images of beauty and dread, the gods, demi-gods, demons, and fairies, and these figures persist and retain their ancient lineaments while the race that imagined them ages and changes, making ever-increasing demands upon the spirit, until such figures symbolize a whole universe of complicated values: the tale, in its outline, remains the same, but interpretation succeeds interpretation and its significance ever deepens. Now Mr. de la Mare, in his finest and most characteristic work, shows himself to be a writer who belongs to this order. The world he prefers to move in is one that has been pieced together by the imagination of childhood, made up of his childish memories of life and books, nursery rhymes, fairy tales, ballads, and quaint memorable passages from strange old volumes. Behind this, using it as so many symbols, is a subtle personality, a spirit capable of unusual exaltation and despair. There is nothing conscious and deliberate, I fancy, in all this; his mind instinctively seeks these forms in which to express itself; his imagination, when it is fully creative, instinctively avoids the world of common experience and runs back to this other world it created long ago. . . . Mr. de la Mare could not casually wave away his fairies and witches and ghosts and Arabias and Melmillos and Princess Seraphitas, not because they are really anything more than exquisite images and symbols, but because they are part of a world to which his imagination instinctively turns, in which it probably actually lives, not so much a beautifully embroidered coat that his Muse wears for a season, but her actual form and presence. . . . One of the most beautiful and significant of Mr. de la Mare's earlier poems, ***Keep Innocency,*** puts before us the paradox of innocent childhood's love of what seems to its elders terrible and cruel, such as warfare. . . . And we may say that there is a central core in Mr. de la Mare's imagination that has "kept innocency," though his spirit should walk the awful borderlands and proclaim its despair; a man has *felt* the world he shows us, but a child's eyes have *seen* it, lit with strange stars or bright with unknown birds. (pp. 37-41)

[The world of Mr. de la Mare's poetry], as we have seen, is one that has largely been made up of the impressions of childhood. Nursery rhyme, ballad, fairy tale, quaint memories have run together and formed a world that is filled with curious symbolism, romantic images, and a haunting elusive music that is like nothing so much as the exquisite stammer of some elfin-hearted girl. And nothing less than music and strange imagery that hangs upon one miraculous adjective could express what the poet has in his heart. . . . [Such] a poet would make more and more use of the idea of exile itself, and an examination of the poetry only confirms the opinion. . . . It is, after all, but a step from the exile from childhood to the exile from Paradise. Mr. de la Mare's delight in the world (and some of his loveliest poems are expressions of that delight, and what is perhaps his very finest poem, ***Farewell*** is noble praise of it) only leads him away from life, that is, not the whole cosmic process, but the battle between belly and worm that stirs the surface of this planet; and every lovely thing only increases his desire to glimpse:

Pure daybreak lighten again on Eden's tree.

and when he wishes to praise music, as so many poets have done, it is characteristic of his most constant mood that he should praise it because it remakes the world or lifts the shades of the prison-house for an hour:

When music sounds, gone is the earth I know,
And all her lovely things even lovelier grow. . . .

He will put his songs into the mouths of those who are "simple happy mad," because such Fools, carolling on the blasted heaths of life, are still as children, have kept innocency. . . . [Pity,] a boundless noble charity, is probably the dominant note of his work. Whatever it is that he has lost and now regrets, whether it is childhood, platonic pre-existence, eternity, Paradise, that the flash of a bird's wing or the glimpse of a burning face recalls for a moment, it is not merely for the saved or the sensitive; if he is an exile, then so are all men, and so his pity is universal. And his greatest weakness . . . is his failure to express certain ideas in the concrete imagery that poetry demands, his tendency to find refuge in vague and woolly abstractions; and this weakness is easily understood when we realize that a poetic imagination like his is clearly limited and is unable to grapple with ideas that belong entirely to maturity. . . . [He] remains one of that most lovable order of artists who never lose sight of their childhood, but re-live it continually in their work and contrive to find expression for their maturity in its memories and impressions, its romantic vision of the world; the artists whose limitations and weaknesses are plain for any passing fool to see, but whose genius, and they are never without it, never mere men of talent, delights both philosophers and children; the artists who remember Eden. (pp. 51-4)

J. B. Priestley, "Mr. de la Mare," in his Figures in Modern Literature, *1924. Reprint by Books for Libraries Press, 1970, pp. 31-54.*

R. L. Mégroz

Walter de la Mare's poetry of childhood is to be found in the prose of *Henry Brocken* and *The Three Mulla-Mulgars* and in much of his verse besides that of the *Songs of Childhood* and *Peacock Pie*. Confronted with it, a critic is unable to find any parallel in literature. Its contents are too rich, varied, complex. (p. 50)

The particular virtue of De la Mare as a poet of childhood is that he can remain himself, the artist, the thinker of primitive phantasy, the epicure in pleasing imagery and wistful inconsequence. The reader does not feel [as in *A Child's Garden of Verses*] that

"He has grown up and gone away,
And it is but a child of air
That lingers in the garden there,"

but that the child in him is the child in us. (p. 53)

[The] wonders of Tartary, the towers and groves of Arroar, and all the other marvellous things the poet sings about as if he knows that we have heard of them before, appeal to the primitive simplicity of mind which we had well-nigh lost, and which belongs to the age of gold. In the mood of *Songs of Childhood* and *Peacock Pie* the poet can say almost anything that springs up into his consciousness; we believe. Look again at the first stanza of **"Tartary."** You could not possibly foretell those "great fishes," after tigers and peacocks, and certainly the genius of the language which makes "slant" a pleasing rhyme with "haunt" and "flaunt" took hold of the poet's pen to give us the delight of seeing the fishes' fins also, "athwart the sun." Every stray impression is food to the poet's imagination, as it was to another famous Cockney—Keats. . . . (pp. 54-5)

Another element in this type of poetry is the inventiveness as distinguished from the imaginative creation. With many exceptions, delightful as they all are, the *Songs of Childhood,* the unique book of rhymes entitled *A Child's Day,* and those in *Peacock Pie* and *Down-a-Down Derry* are more inventive than creative, and therefore they are

not the finest poetry of Mr. de la Mare, although the rarity of such work done so perfectly will alone give them an important place. This peculiar kind of cataloguing of unexpected objects and incidents is just what appeals to the child, as undoubtedly it appealed to our primitive ancestors who listened to the storyteller of the tribe weaving his romances. The difference between the mythology of the child and the mythology of the savage is merely in the atmosphere. The inventive manner is the same. What child would not enjoy the truly marvellous natural history in *A Child's Day?* (pp. 55-6)

No writer has made finer use of the catalogue than De la Mare. In *The Three Mulla-Mulgars* there are gorgeous heaps of things all glittering in bright names. And the author's inventive dexterity finds ample scope in the making of new words belonging to this monkey world. (pp. 56-7)

All primitive epic poetry discloses the same delight in names and objects, and detail.

Already in *Songs of Childhood,* however, may be found the nostalgia, the sickness of the soul for a home which is not here, and when we have read **"Alulvan,"** a poem of broad daylight,

"Yet soft along Alulvan's walks
The ghost at noonday stalks,"

a shadow is crossing the clear joy of childhood; the imagination is beginning to ruffle its impatient pinions; suddenly Alulvan and Arroar and even Tartary are not as they seem. We are aware of mankind's hunger for an unattained heaven, a paradise of peace and beauty. (pp. 57-8)

The poems of childhood do not disillusion. Their wistfulness is never sophisticated, rarely reflective, retrospective. The child lives absorbed in the moment. So the eeriness, or the humour, too, is always consistent with the mood of the poem. **"The Hare"** is a piece of witchery which appeals to the immortally infantile and poetic in us:

"In the black furrow of a field
I saw an old witch-hare this night;
And she cocked a lissome ear,
And she eyed the moon so bright,
And she nibbled of the green;
And I whispered 'Wh-s-st! witch-hare,'
Away like a ghostie o'er the field
She fled, and left the moonlight there."

Is that not perfect? But it is not easily written; there is nothing of the exuberant verbal facility and perhaps felicity of Swinburne's roundels on babies. The very difficulty of the composition contributes to the just effect, because it reveals the artistic and childish seriousness as one. The lovely song, **"I met at Eve the Prince of Sleep"** is genuine child poetry. . . . (p. 59)

Although not all children could appreciate [its] subtleties . . . , the colour and music, the rich tapestry of image and the melodious sweetness of the song respond to the essentially childish desire for sensuous beauty. (p. 60)

The child's absorption in the business of gaining sensory experience is the counterpart of its continual dreaming and myth-making. Its eager perception of new sights and sounds was never expressed before with such *élan* as in *Peacock Pie*. . . . (p. 61)

There is the child's playfulness. A kind of serio-comic pathetic fallacy! Such work comes from a first-hand knowledge of children. (pp. 61-2)

The poet himself has enough humour to satisfy the big demand of the child. "**The Bandog**" is surely one of the most pathetically comic poems ever written. (p. 62)

And has the child's metaphysical curiosity ever been answered so justly as in "**Mrs. Earth. . . .**"

[This type of the poet's work] is never merely that abominable make-believe, children's verse; it is never less than good English poetry.

When De la Mare looks at instead of living in childhood, he is artist enough to avoid the sentimental manner which spoilt *A Child's Garden of Verses,* and he writes, as only he can write, poetry in which dream and memory are intermingled. (p. 63)

There is a riot of lovely phantasy, of sly fun, of poetic vision, in [*The Three Mulla-Mulgars*]. There is also a sympathy, almost tenderness, arising from the quality of vision, which gives to Nod, Thumb, and Thimble, the three adventurous brothers, and to Seelem, their father, and Mutta, their mother, distinct and half-human characters. (p. 73)

Packed as the story is with the perils and triumphs of adventure, the physical adventure of travel in strange regions, a spiritual epic runs all through it, culminating in the arrival of the travellers in Tishnar. The author has been enabled here, "to observe all, by ranging at an altitude above all." The vision is . . . a vision of the whole of life.

When we first have our eyes fully opened to the profundity of the satire behind the fairy tale is when Nod, lost and parted awhile from his distressed brothers, falls into the hands of an "Oomgar," or man. It becomes obvious then that the poet has drawn the universe of monkeys to a perfectly self-consistent scale of intelligence and incident and aspiration, so that when little Nod, who owns "the Wonder-Stone of Tishnar" and is a nizza-neela, or one who has magic in him, is brought into contact with Andy Battle, the stranded, exiled sailor, the significance of human life on the earth is illuminated as only W. H. Hudson in *Green Mansions* has illuminated it before. . . . The beauty and the wisdom of *The Three Mulla-Mulgars* are qualities displayed by the child at its serious play. The monkey universe is but the sphere of mankind's infantile poetic thought. Every detail in the story fits into the primitive picture with so unobtrusive a justice that when little Nod is caught by Battle, the reader is suddenly surprised at the width as well as the shallowness of the gap between man and nature. Nod, Thumb, and Thimble had seemed so familiar: they had seemed the child in any one of us. (pp. 75-6)

The long process of the growth of language is reflected in miniature when children invent words to serve the emotional need of the passing moment; and when poets adapt old words to new uses or, more rarely, coin a new one with success, a similar act of creation takes place. Certainly here again De la Mare reveals himself as an artist of quite extraordinary skill. In using words to express child-like moods he is supreme in English poetry. In the whole

sphere of the evocative use of words of course the author of "daffodils that take the winds of March with beauty" remains supreme. No other poet has to his credit so many imperishable creations of sound and sense, born of the momentary embrace of passion and thought. But De la Mare's work is a rich field for the student of word-evolution. So constant is his faculty, not perhaps of lending a new shade of significance to the lexical meaning of words, although he does this also, but of using words for their atmosphere and for the music that is in them, that this might almost be regarded as the main characteristic of his style. A scrupulous selection of the phrase is evident in his prose as well as his verse. He does not always succeed in his eager search for the inevitable word, and sometimes he will indulge in a capricious avoidance of a wholesome, honest term in order to give us an unnecessary archaism like *eftsoones,* or an unfortunate coinage like *wonderly.* Far more frequently, however, especially in **Songs of Childhood** and **Peacock Pie,** his archaisms and experiments are carried off with a happy verve which is irresistible, while in his "grown-up" poetry and prose one constantly finds a beautiful but neglected word like "scrutiny" flourishing anew in his hands, so that he is probably the best living maker of the English language. (pp. 206-07)

[The diction of **Henry Brocken** and **The Three Mulla-Mulgars** is] . . . at once precise logically and charged with a dream atmosphere. The **Songs of Childhood** and **Peacock Pie** are marked by the author's not always successful employment of words for a quaint effect. If any one but De la Mare had made such free use of *dreariment, lissomely, wis, loveful, faërie, shin-shining, knick-knackerie, eftsoones, lonesome, tightsome, waesome,* and *glamourie,* the result would probably have been insupportable. Even where this eccentric diction is used with the least effect of inappropriateness, the success of the piece is not due to such words. Just as the rhythm of many of the child poems recalls that of the old border ballads, so does the vocabulary. But the essence of the old ballad, whether fantastic, humorous, or passionate, is not in the diction, which was perfectly natural. The use of *leggen bones, mimbling-mambling, jimp, hie, shoon, lanthorn, ghostie,* and *gnomie* does not explain the success of **Peacock Pie** and **Songs of Childhood.** The least eccentric in diction are frequently the finest of De la Mare's child poems. "**The Silver Penny**" is a remarkable reincarnation of the old ballad. So is "**The Pilgrim**"; and "**The Englishman**" would be if it were not also charged with so much of the imaginative glamour of *The Ancient Mariner.* In this class of work the poet is at his best, whether humorous or fantastic, when the Scottish ballad and Percy's *Reliques* alike are but a dim background. "**The Bandog**," "**Mima**," "**Alas, Alack!**" the tremendously jolly farmers in "**Off the Ground**," the wizardry (or is it witchery?) of "**I met at Eve the Prince of Sleep**," "**The Hare**," "**I saw Three Witches**," owe nothing of value to archaisms. That the poet's archaisms often please must be attributed to his skill in reviving the old ballad language and imbuing it with the modern love of children and childish thought. (pp. 235-36)

[Evidences] abound that he often felt the lack of verse measures. His prose constantly leaps into little metrical trills, and occasionally begins forming a metrical paragraph in the manner of Sir Thomas Browne's. The first time I read *The Three Mulla-Mulgars* such incipient prosodic movements would echo in my mind for many days: they obviously were more than prose. (pp. 242-43)

Indeed it is almost a certainty that the author of *Henry Brocken* and *The Three Mulla-Mulgars* gained more than he lost by using prose instead of verse. When he does use verse in his narrative these songs have something of the divine fitness of the sudden songs in Shakespeare's comedies. (p. 244)

The danger confronting De la Mare as a creative artist in literature arises from a tremendous energy of poetic thought incompletely subdued to that shaping power of the creative imagination. The soil of his mind is so fertile that the methodical gardener is hard pressed in his task of preserving the outline of the landscape he intended to impose upon that luxuriant wildness. From a cause opposite to that of the intellectual effeminacy of the decadent writer, his style continually tends in the direction of the disintegration which M. Bourget unerringly marked as the main symptom of literary decadence. A decadent style, he wrote, is that in which the book disintegrates . . . to make room for the independence of the page; in which the page disintegrates to make room for the independence of the sentence, and the sentence for the independence of the word. Certainly that is a fair description of the change which came over French poetry with the passing of the Parnassians and the arrival of the symbolists. It is also to some extent an account of what was happening to English literature in the 'nineties, when De la Mare was mastering his craft. *Henry Brocken,* containing scenes and chapters of a wonderful beauty, has the same fault as *The Memoirs of a Midget:* its completed whole does not exceed in beauty the sum of the beauty of the parts. . . . This is why, if *The Memoirs* is the most mature and the richest in content of all our author's books, it must as a work of art rank second to *The Three Mulla-Mulgars,* which, by no addition, subtraction, or alteration conceivable (to at least one reader) could be brought nearer to triumphant and perfect fulfilment of rich diversity in eternal unity. (pp. 271-73)

> *R. L. Mégroz, in his* Walter de la Mare: A Biographical and Critical Study, *Hodder and Stoughton, 1924, 303 p.*

P. C. Kennedy

Mr. de la Mare suffers, like Mr. Thomas Hardy, from a cult, from a legend of infallibility, so that everything he does exercises a sort of hypnotic influence on the public, and is welcomed and admired without any reference to its merits. These two writers, Mr. Hardy and Mr. de la Mare, have always displayed a noble indifference to popularity; they have gone their own ways, truckling to no habit, creed, convention or expectation; and the public, recognising the magnificence of those who despise its judgments, has responded with idolatry. But idolatry, however comforting and inspiring it may be to the idolaters, is grossly unfair to the idols. We recognise that a good deal of the work of the greatest—a good deal of Wordsworth, a good deal of Byron, a noticeable proportion even of Shakespeare—is æsthetically worthless: we have no right to refuse the tribute of the same discrimination to Mr. Hardy or Mr. de la Mare. Mr. de la Mare is a poet, a great poet. It does not follow that all his verse is excellent. It certainly does not follow that he is a master of prose. It is an inter-

esting speculation what would have been made of *Broomsticks* if it had been published as by John Jones.

We are told by the publishers that these stories are for children. It is a high claim, which I can find little in the stories themselves to justify. If there is one thing which a writer for children must not be, it is arch: and Mr. de la Mare is quite dreadfully arch.

Much less important, but not negligible in a book designed for children, is the question of grammar. Mr. de la Mare (and I confess this flabbergasts me) has not even taken the trouble to write with the correctness which would be exacted from a boy or girl in the fourth form. He says: "Being an only child, his mother treasured him beyond words"; and "strangers in outlandish guise whom he suspected at once must be princes and noblemen from foreign climes"; and "She advanced into the room, and, with her own hand, lay before him on the oak table beside his silver platter, first the nibbled apple, next the golden ball, and last the silken cord"; and "The ass whom you tell me is hearkening at the moment to all that passes between us."

To turn to a brighter side of the picture—here is a passage, typical of many, which I should think worthy of Mr. de la Mare if my admiration of him did not considerably exceed that manifested by most of his admirers:

> How crisscross a thing is the heart of man. Solely because this lord loved his daughter so dearly, if ever she so much as sighed for change and adventure, like some plodding beast of burden he would set his feet together and refuse to budge an inch. Beneath his louring brows he would gaze at the brightness of her unringleted hair as if mere looking could keep that gold secure; as if earth were innocent of moth and rust and change and chance, and had never so much as hearkened after the restless footfall of Time.

That is not magical writing; but it has rhythm in it, and character, and situation. The story in which it occurs, *The Lovely Myfanwy,* is a good story; so is *Broomsticks* itself, and there are beautiful moments in *Lucy.* Altogether, this would be a remarkable book if it had been written by John Jones. But it wasn't. It was written by a man of genius, a man with one of the rarest and loftiest and most sensitive minds of our time; and to pretend to find every page of it, or even the general effect of it, worthy of him, is not compliment but depreciation. If you want to measure how far short it falls of what a book about fairies and for children, a book of dreams and moralities, should be, take down your Hans Andersen. Set the worst page of Hans Andersen against the best page of Mr. de la Mare! It may be said that this is a cruelly hard comparison, since Hans Andersen is the greatest of all story-tellers, as indisputably as Shakespeare is the greatest of dramatists or Homer of epic poets. Nevertheless I insist on making the comparison; it is the measure of my reverence for Mr. de la Mare—and of my conviction that his genius is here on the wrong tack.

> *P. C. Kennedy, in a review of "Broomsticks and Other Tales," in* New Statesman, *Vol. XXVI, No. 659, December 12, 1925, p. 273.*

Forrest Reid

[*Songs of Childhood*] still seems to me a marvellous first book, filled with a romantic beauty, innocent and happy even in its more pensive moments. Moreover, its beauty has proved lasting, and we can, I think, find in it the first hints and stirrings of a great deal that has followed. It is too easy to call it fantastic, for when all is said one of its rarest qualities is its truth. We can, in fact, just as if we were criticizing a short story, say that the child in these poems lives. It is this living child, yielding to that streak of a darker curiosity so characteristic of him, who stands stockstill, rooted in his path, while he stares in fascination at the rats running over John Mouldy in his cellar—appalled, delighted.

> I spied John Mouldy in his cellar,
> Deep down twenty steps of stone;
> In the dusk he sat a-smiling,
> Smiling there alone.
>
> He read no book, he snuffed no candle;
> The rats ran in, the rats ran out;
> And far and near, the drip of water
> Went whispering about.
>
> The dusk was still, with dew a-falling,
> I saw the Dog Star bleak and grim,
> I saw a slim brown rat of Norway
> Creep over him.

It is horrible and it is beautiful, and the beauty is like a flickering zigzag play of lightning by which we see the horror. There is a stark intensity in its realism. Nothing could be more gruesome than the whispering water unless it be that slim brown rat of Norway. And then, suddenly, with the first two lines of the third stanza, the cold pure beauty of the sky at nightfall arches above us.

John Mouldy comes closer to the mature work of Mr. de la Mare than anything else in the volume. It is all his, while a few of the other poems betray to a slight extent the influence of his reading. (pp. 38-40)

There are poems which are hardly more than strains of music. . . . —there are poems which are hardly more than nursery nonsense. . . . —there are poems which are pure fantasy, such as **Dame Hickory** and **I Saw Three Witches:** but most of the poems have a story in them. (p. 41)

Imagination is the power by which we grasp reality. An imaginative man is less a dreamer than a seer. It is when the imagination weakens that we sink into dream. That is why Blake, in whom the imagination is all-powerful, is never dreamy, but always definite and sure; and that is why the children in these poems are so living to us that we know what they look like, know their names and their ages, the colour of their eyes and hair, even their clothes. We know that the child in **The Buckle** is a nimble, elfin, little creature; we know that Jane is plump and often rather hot, and that she usually carries her hat swinging by its brim instead of wearing it properly on her head. We know that the slimmer, taller, more sophisticated Elaine is flaxen-haired, delicate-skinned, and wears a cool-tinted muslin dress and long black stockings that never get into wrinkles. And I protest this is not fanciful, not made up for the occasion. If, as Coleridge says, 'the power of poetry is, by a single word perhaps, to instil that energy into the mind which compels the imagination to produce the picture,' then already, in these earliest poems, we find this power constantly in evidence. The very names contribute their

share to the illusion, their fitness is not due to happy chance.

> When slim Sophia mounts her horse
> And paces down the avenue. . . .

—call the girl by any other name—Priscilla, Miranda, Jemima, Rebecca—and the picture will be different. Even the metre in which the poem is written moves with a curiously liquid tune that follows the measured pacing of the horse.

But it is the more fantastic poems whose charm is so individual. Here we have, what is always to remain characteristic of the author, the clearest, most exact and detailed painting of earthly beauty, mingled with an unearthly and spiritual beauty. The vision is closely akin to the absorbed, penetrating, wonder-working vision of childhood, though there is something added which comes from experience. But beauty and vision are as yet untinged by mysticism, are almost exclusively a matter of light and colour and atmosphere. (pp. 43-5)

In these poems, of course, we find only the dawn of Mr. de la Mare's genius. Much will be added, much will be developed; but this first clear youthful note possesses its own appropriate beauty. The writer outgrew his book, became dissatisfied with it, attempted to bring it into closer harmony with his later work, or perhaps one should say with his later technique. The attempt was interesting and not very happy. One gets from it an odd impression that he has lost touch with this beginner, is not trying to help him in *his* way, but wants to make him different: in fact it is almost like a case of imperfect sympathy. Some of the poems are dropped, some expanded, some altered nearly out of recognition. A few new ones are added—the delightful **Funeral** among them, which should not be, as it is in the **Collected Poems,** dated 1901, since in mood and form it belongs clearly to the **Peacock Pie** group. (p. 48)

Is Mr. de la Mare's [**The Three Mulla-Mulgars**] . . . not for the nursery? That . . . is a matter for each nursery to decide. . . . [Much] of the enchantment of Mr. de la Mare's tale is produced by the beauty of the writing. True, any intelligent child will enjoy the adventures; but only a rather rare little mortal will grasp all the older reader grasps. (p. 111)

[There] can be no doubt that, taking it merely as a story, **The Mulla-Mulgars** is among the most amusing and exciting ever offered to intelligent boys and girls. Its strangeness is no handicap so far as they are concerned: what may have proved a handicap, what certainly could not have *helped* it, is the number of difficult and invented words in the opening chapter. It is unfortunate that these words should be scattered so much more thickly over the first pages than over the rest of the book. The less persevering young reader may very well be discouraged by 'Exxzwixxia', 'Azmamogreel', 'Oggewibbies', 'Garniereze': how can he tell he has only to break through this somewhat prickly hedge to find himself in the most thrilling and variegated world of wonder and adventure!

But not in fairyland: the book is not in the ordinary sense a fairy tale, though there is magic in it, and Nod, the hero, is the youngest of three brothers. The brothers are monkeys, princes born in exile, and the story tells of their perilous journey in search of their Uncle Assasimmon's kingdom, which lies far away in the beautiful Valleys of Tishnar. . . . They can talk; all the animals in the book can talk; and this gift of speech brings them very close to humans. Does it bring them too close for reality? The question would only be pertinent if the story were a realistic animal story, which it isn't; and Thumb, Thimble, and Nod are alive and convincing. A love of beasts fills the book. . . . Mr. de la Mare writes of animals as he writes of children. . . . (pp. 113-14)

What is so refreshing about **The Mulla-Mulgars** is this natural understanding. The monkeys' thoughts, we feel, even when they are very like our own rather better thoughts, are still monkey thoughts. Nod is perhaps more than three-quarters way between beast and human; the difference between him and a pleasant but unusually grave little boy is slight; still it is there and is maintained consistently. He is an exceptional monkey of course, a small super-monkey, not only a prince but a Nizzaneela, which means a pet, one dear to the gods and specially guarded by them: in the Bible the infant Samuel is a Nizza-neela. . . . The adventure of [Nod's meeting with Andy Battle] and of their friendship is the beautiful centre of the book. So finely conceived and written is it, so true to both man and beast, that we reluctantly accept it as but an episode in this odyssey, and watch Nod making his preparations for departure. There are dangers of every kind, natural and supernatural; there are enemies strong and crafty and very hungry; the track itself at times is nearly impassable, and that winter of continuous ice and frost and snow is maybe the greatest danger of all.

It is strange that this radiant, iridescent, winter beauty should haunt a tale of the tropics; but its dazzling whiteness of moon-fire and glittering frost gives the entire book a colour scheme definite as that of an actual picture, and diametrically opposed to the no less definite colour scheme of **The Return.** The air, too, is thinner, colder, more bracing than the air we breathe in **The Return:** it is difficult to explain how it is created, but the effect none the less sharply impresses itself upon us that the whole thing is written an octave higher. A mysterious music sounds through it, always high up in the treble clef—clear, insistent, unearthly—a music of strings and harps. It is a story of copious incident and adventure, but it is kept from first to last on the plane of poetry. The element of wonder in it is not the irresponsible wonder-working of the old nursery tales; it is more imaginative, more real. There is a vast difference between the wicked troll of Asbjörnsen or Grimm and Mr. de la Mare's Immanâla. This dire creation, half ghostly, half reptilian, as she writhes in her tight cloak—tall, slender, undulating, with her grey flattened head, her long neck, her colourless glassy eyes, her faint gigglings and whimperings—is the very incarnation of fear, cruelty, and treachery. Similarly Tishnar, bright starry spirit of the hills—pure, shining, yet softened with compassion—bears no resemblance to any queen of fairyland. She is not a creation of fancy; she is the divine protectress, the spiritual guardian, the mother goddess. She is at once the universal mother and all 'that which cannot be thought about in words, or told, or expressed'. . . . Tishnar is the goddess not of midnight fears and spectres but of poetry, of the kind of poetry, above all, we find in this book. (pp. 116-19)

The book breaks off somewhat abruptly, but with the half-promise of a sequel—a sequel which will never now be

written. It never, I think, could have been written; for our travellers are home, and that is the end. A description of their home would be an anti-climax, and would moreover deprive the reader of the pleasure of imagining it for himself. And all through, the book is written so that he can if he likes view in it his own earthly pilgrimage. I do not mean that there is the least suggestion of allegory: I do not believe the author had any other thought than of his monkeys' adventures while he was writing it. Still, its beauty relates it to the main body of Mr. de la Mare's work: behind earth's loveliness hovers a dream of the absolute: a divine discontent awakens in it and is comforted. (pp. 124-25)

The Listeners unquestionably places Mr. de la Mare among the greatest poets of childhood and dreamland. (p. 148)

In **The Listeners** and **Peacock Pie** we never pass beyond the boundaries of a world the poet has by now made peculiarly his own:

> What can a tired heart say,
> Which the wise of the world have made dumb?
> Save to the lonely dreams of a child,
> 'Return again, come!'

—and much of the substance of these books is composed of 'the lonely dreams of a child'.

Much of the substance of **The Listeners,** I should say, for the mood of **Peacock Pie** is altogether lighter, gayer. . . . (pp. 149-50)

[It] is as if the author deliberately had arranged his palette as a painter does, using in **Peacock Pie** only cool, clear, delicate tints, while the colour of **The Listeners** is rich and sombre. (pp. 151-52)

[**Peacock Pie**] contains a good many things addressed directly to the nursery. They are of a different kind, some of these things, from the earlier rhymes for children. Behind even the lightest and slightest of the **Songs of Childhood** there can be detected an impulse that relates them to Mr. de la Mare's serious poetry; but in **Peacock Pie** this is not always so, the nursery pieces are in fact subject to an odd variation of tone. There are rhymes, like **The Huntsmen,** which are good, jolly rhymes and nothing more; but there are others, which also set out to be just good, jolly rhymes, and yet have somehow become poetry. (p. 159)

Peacock Pie has for sub-title 'a book of rhymes', as if therein lay an implicit avowal of its less serious intention: and yet some of it is serious poetry, and not all of it is even poetry of childhood. Things like **The Song of Shadows,** or **The Song of the Mad Prince,** are closely akin to the most beautiful lyrics in **Motley** and **The Veil.** (p. 160)

For the purpose of this essay I re-read the entire work in poetry and prose, and, though I was approaching nothing for the first time, my impression was of a constant freshness and variety, a constant element of surprise. Things recur: themes—treated with a difference; a certain favourite physical type; certain humours and idiosyncrasies; a few favourite images and landscapes. But image and picture at least are the symbols every poet uses, and they have this symbolic value in the prose and verse of Mr. de la Mare. (pp. 245-46)

The landscape is always spiritualized, becomes a changeless, eternal landscape of the soul. There are old churchyards, and old gardens, with green sunken walks and trees spreading mossy and lichened boughs above them. There are dark old houses, with the wind sighing through their key-holes, and perhaps, from an upper casement, a face looking 'out of sorcery'. There are the burning fires of frost and stars, and black ice-bound winter pools, and frozen snow marked by the rabbit's 'tell-tale footprints'. There are birds hovering within vision, yet singing out of a molten glory of Paradise.

In this poetry, this prose, the unseen world is more constantly present than it is in the work of any other English poet perhaps, except Blake. . . . Beneath everything there is that human undertone, a fineness of spirit, an attitude of mind composed of tenderness and kindness and understanding. It is too frequently overlooked in the eagerness to do justice to the glamour of a more supernatural beauty, but without it there could not be that moral and spiritual beauty which springs as much from the heart as from the imagination, and which seems to me, in the case of Mr. de la Mare, to be the rarest, the most endearing and precious gift of all. (pp. 246-47)

> *Forrest Reid, in his* Walter de la Mare: A Critical Study, *Henry Holt and Company, 1929, 256 p.*

Charles Williams

In Mr. de la Mare's poems there is a state of removed ecstasy; it is as though death had become, not a gate to experience, but itself a rich experience, a summing-up and transcending of all present beauty and richness. It is removed in two senses; first, it is—as it must be in poetry—not something to be looked forward to in time and with the natural mind, but to be felt here and with the 'holy imagination' which Blake perceived to be the Saviour of men; it is therefore something more removed than a promise, being a state which exists already within us, but into which we have not entered. And secondly, it is a state which is beyond, and beyond in the sense of including, those other experiences of fear and mistake and terror. These, which are separate poems, are elements of the whole; transforming these into beauty, Mr. de la Mare has persuaded us of an inclusive ecstasy.

In this most passionate verse there is one thing perhaps lacking, and yet it seems ungracious to speak of it. If it is spoken of at all, it must be not in complaint or regret but merely as a warning to some readers. Not even Mr. de la Mare can give us everything, and the thing he has not condescended to give us is philosophy. This statement implies no pride on his part, but it does imply that this beauty will not of itself shape itself in metaphysical thought, or anyhow not in rationalized metaphysical thought. The emotion is too intense, it seems, to do so, yet some such modification might be a relief. It is, normally, when the intensity of emotion no longer exists that we turn to thought, or perhaps the turning is itself a natural lowering of the emotion. Normally, but not necessarily; certain great and passionate minds have had intellect as well as feeling enlarged and influenced. But that hardly happens here—though such a phrase should be modified with all the 'perhapses' possible. For it is, by whatever road he has reached it,

from *beyond* thought that this communication comes, and thought in itself could never find the way to know it.

That Mr. de la Mare could have dealt with metaphysics if he had chosen is suggested by at any rate two or three of the earlier poems, as, for example, *Poor Jim Jay,* a metaphysical fairy-tale.

> Do diddle di do,
> Poor Jim Jay
> Got stuck fast
> In Yesterday . . .
> We pulled and we pulled
> From seven till twelve,
> Jim, too frightened
> To help himself.
> But all in vain.
> The clock struck one,
> And there was Jim
> A little bit gone.
> At half-past five
> You scarce could see
> A glimpse of his flapping
> Handkerchee . . .

This is an extreme example, because here the subject of the poem is very much less a simple fact than is usual with Mr. de la Mare. It seems ridiculous to say of a poet who has been admired so generally for his fantastic or faery poems that he is in those poems always concerned with facts, and yet it seems to be true. For in poetry (it is the first rule in the book) we need not concern ourselves with the question whether a fact is a fact in the phenomenal world or not. A poem which begins

> There were two Fairies, Gimmul and Mel,

deals as much with a fact as that other which begins

> Thick in its glass
> The physic stands.

A reader has of course the right to say he is not interested in one set of facts, as he has to refuse to be concerned with, say, electricity, economics, or biology, and then there can be no further discussion. But if there is to be, we must accept all a poet's facts, and it is then that we discover the extreme simplicity and yet the multitudinousness of Mr. de la Mare's approaches to them. In a quatrain which appears to one reader as an immortal simplicity of English verse, he has said—

> It's a very odd thing
> As odd as can be
> That whatever Miss T. eats
> Turns into Miss T.

This stands with such other simplicities as Donne's

> I wonder, by my troth, what thou and I
> Did till we loved;

or the anonymous

> When Molly smiles beneath her cow
> I feel my heart I can't tell how.

It is the astonishing *fact* that holds all three poets in amazed entrancement. The surprise is not, in Mr. de la Mare, the thing that is always most immediately communicated by his verse; he has many ways of approach, but it is always the central fact that he concerns himself with, in the moods of lyric verse, or the statements of narrative. His goblins and fairies, moons and queens, Arabia and England, are accompaniments and definitions. But, with those few exceptions which show us he could have dealt with philosophy if he had chosen, this fact is one of the emotions with which in ordinary life we are most generally acquainted—sorrow and hope and ardour and anger and their like; and others—more rare and more intense than they—terror, and the desire for rest, and ecstasy. In some of 'the old wisdoms' of which Mr. Yeats has spoken, ecstasy was to be experienced in the magical trance, and, so far as Mr. de la Mare can be called a 'magical' poet, it is because he throws us half into a trance with his incantations.

In the poem which closes **Peacock Pie** he achieves one of the most remarkable effects in modern verse.

"The Song of Finis"

At the edge of All the Ages
A Knight sate on his steed,
His armour red and thin with rust,
His soul from sorrow freed;
And he lifted up his visor
From a face of skin and bone,
And his horse turned head and whinnied
As the twain stood there alone.

No bird above that steep of time
Sang of a livelong quest;
No wind breathed,
Rest:
'Lone for an end!' cried Knight to steed,
Loosed an eager rein—
Charged with his challenge into Space:
And quiet did quiet remain.

'And quiet did quiet remain.' We are—to put it clumsily—*there* even to experience that quiet, and yet we are *not* there; nothing is there. The single image has vanished into space; we are, for a moment, in a state beyond images, and therefore beyond intellect. Poetry has many ways of doing this, but it rarely does it so simply and finally as here. And yet that quiet, if it is not broken by, is at any rate achieved after, other states as rare and as rarely communicated. There is, for example, in one or two poems, even of these earlier ones, something inexplicably sinister; as in **Jemima** or **The Mocking Fairy**. It may be a merely personal temperament that finds those two poems—the first slightly, the second altogether—terrifying. In this world of facts what dreadful fact expresses something of itself in the poem about Mrs. Gill [**The Mocking-Fairy**]? (pp. 85-90)

Why is that Fairy so dreadful? 'Quiet did quiet remain.' Was Mrs. Gill dead? and did the Fairy know it? Obviously; but the mere indirectness of the communicated fact increases the terror. And what joy of non-human malice lay behind that mockery?

So in **Jemima**—the child whose father and mother always call her 'Meg', though her name is Jemima:

Only my sister, jealous of
The strands of my bright hair,
'Jemima-mima-mima'
Calls, mocking, up the stair.

It is childish malice and childish mockery, but the childishness does not lessen the mockery and malice, and the

cry pursues us up the stair into the higher towers of this house of verse.

These earlier poems deal with facts, of the world of phenomena or the world of fairy and romance. They deal with them directly, they deck them with actual or fantastic details, they wake in the reader either a surprised and delightful recognition—as in the poem about Miss T.—which is kin to ecstasy, or a surrender to some rare emotion. In some of them there is an intense expectation; something is just about to happen—and it might seem an unfair limitation of Mr. de la Mare's genius if we complained that nothing ever does happen. It has not happened *in* the poems; it has happened *to* the poems. (pp. 90-1)

Charles Williams, "Walter de la Mare," in his Poetry at Present, *Oxford at the Clarendon Press, 1930, pp. 82-95.*

G. K. Chesterton

[One] of the first facts which a good poetical critic will realize, is one which the poet of necessity realizes: the limitation of language, and especially the poverty and clumsiness of the language of praise. There is hardly any praise of poets that does not sound as if they were all the same sort of poets, and this is true even when the praise is intended to say precisely the opposite. Thus the habit of calling somebody "unique" has become universal, and we may insist that a man is original, and still leave the impression that originality is about as rare as original sin.

But this difficulty applies in a special way to Mr. Walter de la Mare and his poetry, because the common poetical terms of praise for that poetry are also applied to a totally different sort of poetry. He stands very close, in time and place and appearance, to a group of writers, most of them good writers and some of them great writers, from whom he is really quite free and distinct. Only the epithets applied to him are also applied to them. When we say that he is a dreamy and fantastic poet, an interpreter of elfland, a singer of strange rhymes that have a witchery and wild charm for children, and the rest, we are driven to use a number of terms that have now become a little trite, perhaps, as applied to other talented persons who are utterly different. The fountains, the foundations, the primary principles of imagination and the view of life, are really quite different in a man like Mr. de la Mare from all that they are let us say, in a man like Sir James Barrie or a man like Mr. A. A. Milne. This, I need hardly say, has nothing to do with depreciating these authors, but only with appreciating each author for his own sake. Yet there is a sort of tangle of tradition, and a recognized traffic in certain subjects, which may well confuse a modern reader about all this sort of literature of fancy. For instance; we might start by saying that the tradition of *Treasure Island* and its pirates was continued in *Peter Pan* and its pirates. We might say that the elvish children of *Peter Pan* were continued in the elvish children of *When We Were Very Young*. And then we might imagine vaguely that all this sort of thing, the bottle of rum and the crocodile's dinner and the king's breakfast, were all somehow stuffed or stirred up together in a hotch-potch called **Peacock Pie**. But this is to miss the whole point about the poet, and especially where he is rather more than a poet. It would be easy to link him up with the tradition of Treasure Island;

for he has himself written a very fascinating fantasia about Desert Islands. But the association would be an error, for he has not really laid up for himself treasure in the same sort of treasure islands. There is really a sort of dynasty, a Scottish dynasty, of Stevenson and Barrie. But it descended on the infantile side to Scots like Kenneth Grahame and on the manly, or at least boyish side to Scots like John Buchan. It has nothing to do with Walter de la Mare; because his philosophy is different. One way of putting it would be to say that, poetic as are the fairy-tales of the Scots, they are the fairy-tales of the Sceptics. The fairy-tales of de la Mare are not those of the Sceptic but of the Mystic. Take the primary idea with which all the best work for imaginative infancy, as supplied by Stevenson and Barrie, really began. It began with an idea which is called, "make-believe". That is, strictly speaking, it is written by men who do not believe; and even written for children who do not believe; children who quite logically and legitimately make believe. but de la Mare's world is not merely a world of illusion; it is in quite another sense a world of imagination. It is a real world of which the reality can only be represented to us by images. De la Mare does not, in the material sense, believe that there is an ogre who crawls round houses and is turned back by the influence of the Holy Child; any more than Barrie believes that there is an immortal little boy who plays physically in Kensington Gardens. But de la Mare does believe that there is a devouring evil that is always warring with innocence and happiness; and Barrie does not believe that innocence and happiness go on having an uninterrupted legal occupation of Kensington Gardens. Stories of the school of *Peter Pan* are radiant and refreshing dreams; but they are dreams. They are the dreams of somebody taking refuge from real life in an inner life of the imagination; but not necessarily of somebody believing that there is also a larger universal life corresponding to that imagination. The first is a fabulist but the second is a symbolist; as if we were to compare the talking animals of La Fontaine with the typical animals of Blake. Blake (though certainly mad in a quiet way) probably did not believe that golden lions and tigers walked about on the hills of Albion; and La Fontaine did not believe that garrulous lions engaged in chatty conversation with foxes. But Blake did believe that certain tremendous truths, only to be shown under the types of golden lions, were really true; and , what is most important of all, were not only within him, but beyond him. So the conversation of Mr. Milne's funny little pigs and bears is as delightful as La Fontaine, and only deceptive in the same sense as La Fontaine. That is to say, it is not false, because it is fictitious; or what was called fabulous. But the rhymes of the Mad Prince, though they would be called fantastic, are not merely fabulous. The Mad Prince, like the Mad Poet, in the person of poor Blake, is, after all, something essentially different from The Mad Hatter. There are hollow undertones in his queer questions, about green grass for graves, which do really re-echo from things deep and secret as the grave.

Many who remember the apparently nonsensical nursery rhymes which figure among Walter de la Mare's verses for children may imagine that I am drawing a fine distinction; but it is not a distinction of degree but of direction. The parrot and the monkey who attended the dwarfs on the Isle of Lone, may seem quite as disconnected from normal natural history as the owl and the pussy-cat who went to sea. But there remains a real distinction, outside all natural history, between unnatural history and supernatural history. Mr. de la Mare's parrots and monkeys are as symbolical as the strange beasts in the Book of Apocalypse. Only they are symbolical in a sense that means something better than the allegorical. Symbolism is superior to allegory, in so far that the symbol exactly fits; and there is therefore no superfluous explanation that needs to pass through ordinary language, or need be, or indeed can be, translated into other words. If a parrot only means speech, or a monkey only means mischief (as he generally does) then nothing beyond pictorial elegance is gained by not dealing directly with mischief, or speaking plainly about speech. And the mere allegory never gets beyond a pictorial elegance, adorning what might well be unadorned. But the great mystic can sometimes present to us a purple parrot or a sea-green monkey, in exactly such a manner as to suggest submerged or mysterious ideas, and even truths, that could not possibly be conveyed by any other creature of any other colour. The meaning fits the symbol and the symbol the meaning; and we cannot separate them from each other, as we can in the analysis of allegory. And there is a side of spiritual life, so to speak, which might well be represented by sea-green monkeys, whose colouring is not merely arbitrary colouring like that of the mysterious monsters in that admirable but purely nonsensical rhyme about the Jumblies, whose heads were green and whose hands were blue. The colour scheme here is pleasing, but it is no disrespect to the great Mr. Lear of the *Nonsense Rhymes,* to say that his cosmic philosophy would not have been convulsed even if their hands had been green and their heads had been blue. Walter de la Mare's nonsense is never nonsensical in that sense. If his monkey is sea-green, it is for some reason as deep and significant as the sea; even though he cannot express it in any other way except by patient and uncomplaining greenness. And he would never mention even a green weed, a dock or nettle in a ditch, without meaning it to bear the same witness in the same way.

It is the first paradox about him that we can find the evidence of his faith in his consciousness of evil. It is the second paradox that we can find the spiritual springs of much of his poetry in his prose. If we turn, for instance, to that very powerful and even terrible short story called **"Seaton's Aunt,"** we find we are dealing directly with the diabolic. It does so in a sense quite impossible in all the merely romantic or merely ironic masters of that nonsense that is admittedly illusion. There was no nonsense about Seaton's Aunt. There was no illusion about her concentrated and paralysing malignity; but it was a malignity that had an extension beyond this world. She was a witch; and the realization that witches can occasionally exist is a part of Realism, and a test for anyone claiming a sense of Reality. For we do not especially want them to exist; but they do. Now the wonderland of the other charmers of childhood consists entirely of things that we want to exist, or they want to exist. Whether they are of the older English or Victorian school of Lewis Carroll and Lear, or of the later Scottish school of Stevenson and Barrie, their whole aim is to create a sort of cosmos within the cosmos, which shall be free from evil; a crystal sphere in which there shall be no cracks or flaws or clouds of evil. *Peter Pan* is a wonderful evocation of the happy daydreams of childhood. There is plenty of fighting and ferocity; because fighting and ferocity are among the very happiest dreams of a really innocent and Christian childhood. But Captain Hook the

Pirate is not really wicked; he is only ferocious; which, after all, it is his simple duty as an honest and industrious pirate to be. But there are rhymes, even nursery rhymes, of Walter de la Mare in which the shiver is a real shiver, not only of the spine but of the spirit. They have an atmosphere which is not merely thrilling, but also chilling. They lay a finger that is not of the flesh on a nerve that is not of the body; in their special way of suggesting the chill of change or death or antiquity. To do this was against the whole purpose and origin of the fairyland of the later Victorians. Like all literature, it cannot really be understood without reference to history; and, like all history, it cannot really be understood without reference to religion. As scepticism gradually dried up the conventional religion of the English, and even of the Scotch, poetic and humane spirits turned more and more to the construction of an inner world of fancy, that should be both a refuge and a substitute. . . . And it is the irony of the case that these men, who were rationalists and realists about the real world, were for that very reason resolved to be radiant optimists when once they were inside the city of dreams which was their city of refuge. The pessimists insisted on having happy dreams; the sceptics insisted on having omnipotent drugs. But the mystic does not deal in dreams but in visions; that is, in things seen and not seeming. The mystic does not desire drugs but the drinking of that wine that wakes the dead; different in nature from any opiate that soothes the living.

In short, we may say that the early twentieth century presented two movements towards the fanciful or fantastical, and away from the merely rational or material: a centripetal movement and a centrifugal movement. The one spiritual spiral worked inwards, towards the secret subjective dreams of man; the other worked outwards towards the spiritual powers or truths that seemed beyond the reach of man. The new world made by the first was the great, glowing, iridescent bubble of the Barrie daydream; the world revealed by the second was that world of strange skies, at the ends of the earth and the corners of the sea, that appears in the far-off flashes of the de la Mare imagination. We might say shortly that Stevenson and Barrie could produce grisly buccaneers dripping with gore without frightening the children; whereas de la Mare could produce pollarded willows or whitewashed barns with an imminent risk of frightening the children, and even the grownup people. But it is only fair to say that there is a subtlety only possible to the first method, as well as a subtlety possible to the second. It is, as has been already suggested, the subtlety of an irony which at once accepts and discounts illusion. It is the whole point of the best work of Barrie, for instance, that somebody is deceiving himself, but also that somebody is looking on at somebody who is deceiving himself; and if they are both deceiving themselves, so much the better for the third person who is looking on from a third angle. Much of this sort of work is like a world of mirrors reflected in mirrors; the reduplication of reflection; the shadow of a shade. To name but one instance: a fairy-tale palace is itself only a fancy; but the court scene in *A Kiss for Cinderella* is not merely the fairy-tale fancy, but a child's fancy about the fancy. This sort of intensive imaginative delicacy is in theory a thing of infinite possibilities; and this does belong to the merely subjective school of symbolism. But what I have called the truly symbolic school of symbolism does still belong altogether to another and, I cannot but think, a larger world.

It is all that world of the powers and mysteries beyond mankind, which even the sceptic would consent to cover with the celebrated label: "Important, If True". Perhaps as good an example as can be found is in that truly extraordinary sketch by de la Mare called **"The Tree"**. I can imagine multitudes of quite intelligent people being totally unable to make head or tail of it. It is concerned with a fruit merchant and his brother, who was an artist, and with a Tree, which is talked of in a manner utterly indescribable; as if it were not only more important than anything, but were outside the world. Now Barrie might have dealt admirably with a theme like that; and probably made the human comedy clearer. But the difference is precisely this. Even the reader who cannot understand anything else about de la Mare's story does definitely understand this: that somehow the fruit merchant was wrong, and the artist was right; and, above all, the Tree was right. Now if Barrie had told the tale, he would have taken a gentle pride in leaving us in doubt on that very point; of suggesting that the sceptic might be the sane man, and the Tree might be a delusion. But the Tree is not a delusion. (pp. 47-53)

G. K. Chesterton, "Walter de la Mare," in The Fortnightly Review, *Vol. 138, No., July 1, 1932, pp. 47-53.*

Thomas J. Hardy

Perhaps the first thing to strike the reader coming fresh to De la Mare's work is the preponderance in it of the child-element. Many of his poems are of course written expressly for children—for 'tinies'. *Songs of Childhood, Peacock Pie, Down-a-Down Derry* and that engaging epic of the nursery, *The Child's Day*. . . . How far such pieces appeal to the 'tinies' I am not sure. A friend of mine tells me he has read them aloud to his Sunday School with marked appreciation, but I suspect the novelty of the performance may have had something to do with its success. As a rule children are as hard to please with the attempt to portray their thoughts as a woman is with her photograph—and for the same reason, namely that naïveté and beauty are both idealisations and elude the stereotype. But whatever may be their effect on children, I am very sure that for us grown-ups these enchanted bye-paths open into our lost paradise. They are means, not an end. Their magic is transitional. They are agents in our transformation. By the mere lure of them we quit the blind-alleys of maturity for 'the renaissance of wonder'. (pp. 183-85)

Thomas J. Hardy, " 'A Faerie Way of Writing'," in his Books on the Shelf, *Philip Allan & Co. Ltd., 1934, pp. 182-203.*

Edward Wagenknecht

[*The Three Mulla-Mulgars* is a] glorious adventure story. . . . Ostensibly written for the amusement of de la Mare's four children, it is really an epic of courage, a song of loyalty and love; its mood is that of the noble sonnet on "Virtue":

Yet, yet: O breast how cold! O hope how far!
Grant my son's ashes lie where these men's are!

The three mulla-mulgars are monkeys, royal monkeys, born in exile, who are called upon to undertake the unspeakably perilous journey to the Kingdom of Assasimmon in the glorious vale of Tishnar. De la Mare is closer to Blake here than anywhere else in his work; he has created his own mythology. The book plunges us into forest depths, terrifies us with immense heights, and dazzles our eyes in the snow fields. It is neither an allegory nor a sermon, but it is a serious picture of human life in the guise of a wonder-tale. In the Andy Battle episode love bridges even the seemingly impassable gulf between man and beast. (p. 242)

> Edward Wagenknecht, "News of Tishnar," in College English, *Vol. 3, No. 3, December, 1941, pp. 239-50.*

Margery Bianco

[*An English author of fiction and nonfiction for children best known as the author of* The Velveteen Rabbit *and other stories of nursery toys, Bianco is the mother of illustrator Pamela Bianco, who drew the pictures which inspired de la Mare to create the rhymes for* Flora *(1919).*]

Looking back over the years since *Songs of Childhood* and *Peacock Pie* first became widely known, one can only now begin to realize how great has been Walter de la Mare's influence upon the whole field of imaginative literature for children, and the full significance of his contribution. Poetry of and for childhood there had always been, but never poetry like this. He brought not only beauty but something rarer and even more vital, the perception of beauty. His poetry is intensely visual. He is concerned with the living quality of things, their shapes and colors, their texture. When he speaks of a tree, a bird, a flower, it is as though one were seeing it—really seeing it—for the first time, through the eyes of one who is sensitive to beauty in whatever form, even under the guise of what is called ugliness.

To speak of "the eyes of a child" may sound hackneyed and sentimental, but that is because most adults have forgotten what that clear and unspoiled vision is really like. A child does see an object clearly because he is looking at it for the first time and he sees it with all the elements of wonder and miracle. De la Mare is among those happy few who can recapture, or perhaps have never wholly lost, the keenness of that vision, which is of the spirit as much as of the physical eye. In *Maria-Fly* he describes the almost unbearable wonder with which a small child looks, for the first time consciously, at a house-fly. Something extraordinary has happened to her, she wants to share, instantly, the wonder that she feels, and all she can explain is that she has just seen a fly, *really* seen it. But no one understands, and in her failure to express just what she means by "seeing" one feels the whole tragic gulf that lies between child and adult. (pp. 142-43)

Beauty and the transience of beauty is the essence of de la Mare's poetry. His cry is always for the grasping, even for a fleeting moment, of that which can never be held. . . .

[In] *Flora,* where a little girl's need to set down on paper the pictures that grew in her mind moved a great poet to some of his loveliest and most poignant verse. . . . (p. 143)

Yet never was a poet who has done more to hold that clear

flame of beauty in a shaken world, and never perhaps has our need of it been more urgent.

Imagination is only another word for the interpretation of life. It is through imagination that a child makes his most significant contacts with the world about him, that he learns tolerance, pity, understanding and the love for all created things. The generation that has grown up with *Peacock Pie* and *Down-Adown-Derry,* and *Flora,* with all this treasury of wise, gay and lovely verse, has a richer gift than it may know. Poor Miss 7 on her hospital bed, the old grizzled cobbler, Miss Loo and old Susan and flustered Dame Hickory, all the old and tired, the dumb, the foolish and bewildered, become living figures in memory. Many a child afraid of the dark may well go to bed comforted remembering little Ann in the old house and her wistful visionary playmate. Lucky are those who still possess *Songs of Childhood* in its original form. Many of the poems from it have been reprinted in *Down-Adown-Derry,* but this particular one, with many others as lovely, is not among them, including **"The Pedlar,"** most haunting of all in sheer beauty.

There have been repeated efforts to draw a line, in imaginative literature, between the child's range and the adult's. Actually no such line exists; children certainly have always disregarded it. It will be a good thing when we cease once and for all to puzzle whether a certain book is "for children" or "about children," and leave the young to choose for themselves. *Crossings* has been spoken of as a touchstone, but it is as much a touchstone for adults as for children—perhaps more. If you do not respond to its magic you have either traveled many leagues from the enchanted land, or will never qualify to enter it. Many of De la Mare's stories take place in two worlds at once. Reality and unreality interpenetrate, but this is confusing only to those who feel that unreality—or that which takes place in the imagination—should be kept always in a properly labeled compartment. For reality is not only a matter of what one can see and touch. It is perhaps this two-world consciousness, a dislike of mental boundaries in any form, which influences De la Mare to leave so many of his stories, in a sense, unfinished. He creates a situation but the explanation of it is left hanging—he has told his tale and it is for the reader, if he cares, to find the key. Often there appears no key, or we seem to grasp at something which at the same time eludes us. Is there any key to *The Almond Tree,* to the story about the grandmother and the children and the chest in the attic, or are there instead a dozen keys of which we are puzzled to take our choice? Can one find any reason except in the writer's artistry for the mounting terror one feels in *Seaton's Aunt*—a tale beside which Henry James' *Turn of the Screw* becomes pallid and artificial. There needs no resort to the supernatural in *Seaton's Aunt.* Perhaps her malignity was entirely in Seaton's own mind; perhaps she was no more than an eccentric but really benevolent old lady. Here again the reader must decide for himself.

A great many of de la Mare's tales have this queer undersurface quality of reaching out in unsuspected directions. *The Three Mulla-Mulgars* is something more than a beautiful and moving fantasy; it has dimensions outside the story itself. I think I am right in saying that Walter de la Mare has always had a particular personal affection for this story, more than justified by the delight children take in it and the vividness with which, once read, it remains always in memory. Perhaps he has, too, a special affection for monkeys, of all creatures most intriguing in their near-human quality, for we have the three old apes in *The Isle of Lone,* shambling and pathetic, "bemused by dwarfish wine," and the wonderful story of Jaspar the monkey in *The Lord Fish.* (pp. 144-45)

The word "anthology" has always a cold and uninviting sound, rather like "herbarium." It has been left for Walter de la Mare to give us for the first time an anthology which is a living work in itself, not just a collection of poems, thanks to his notes and the introduction in story form which is a key to the whole meaning and function of poetry. Mr. Nathum's Room is the starting point from which we must all set out on that journey of the mind which has no ending; it exists not as a point in space, but in spiritual experience. . . .

[So] many of de la Mare's tales deal with those curious "extensions of reality" which occur more frequently to the child than to the adult and which the child's mind accepts more readily and without question, so that they seem a natural part of life and only by the later light of acquired reasoning appear in any way strange. Many of us have had at one time or another some such experience, which in retrospect we are contented to class as dream, but who can say where dream ends and reality begins? This is the debatable region to which De la Mare returns again and again, and not the least of his gifts to childhood is his insistence upon the respect at least, if not understanding, due to the child's imaginative dream-life and its importance to the full growth of the mind. There is no privacy deeper or more precious than that in which the spirit finds its inner nourishment, and it is this that De la Mare defends. In nearly all that he writes there is this reading between the lines, plain for all who may wish to see it, and there are many of his tales which those who think they understand children would do well to consider. (p. 146)

Margery Bianco, "de la Mare," in The Horn Book Magazine, *Vol. XVIII, No. 3, May-June, 1942, pp. 141-47.*

Eleanor Graham

In both [Walter de la Mare's] poetry and his prose the same rare gifts shine out: his sense of words and of music, love of beauty, humour, and an imagination richly fertile and so powerful that he seems able to step right into the skin of another being. Most of his stories and, I think, all of his verse have a perfection of form, a crystalline quality as though they had lain a long time in his mind before being set down on paper.

It is worth looking back for a moment to what De la Mare said in the Preface to *Come Hither.* Using Miss Taroone as his mouthpiece, he reminds the reader that what he sees with his eyes remains with him always. He further advised young Simon to keep his senses, heart and courage, and to go where he was called—and so the boy came to *The Other Worlde.*

It is surely from the richness of that *Other Worlde,* the world of his mind, that Mr. De la Mare draws the dreams and visions which have become the stories and verses which have been collected together in [*Collected Stories for Children* and *Collected Rhymes and Verses*]. (p. 59)

As I read and brooded on his stories, it seemed to me that in them the author has given children of the present and of generations to come, a great treasure house to explore, one stores with "all Time's delight, green dusk for dreams, moss for a pillow." I found myself breathing as though sweet country airs were actually in my nostrils. . . .

There are secret places in his treasure house, rooms he has furnished cunningly to rouse the curious, to kindle imaginations—perhaps to provoke young readers to dream tales of their own. (p. 60)

All his stories start from ideas pleasantly familiar to most children, but Mr. De la Mare's poetic mind they develop sometimes very strangely—even unpleasantly for the impressionable reader though she is who will generally get most out of them. It seemed to me that a chill is likely to fall for instance on the affectionate child when she reads of the lovely Myfanwy, faced with her beloved and dotingly jealous father, bewitched into the shape of a common, braying, long-eared donkey; and to me there was an eeriness about the three little chimney sweeps who fell asleep and could not be awakened; who were not dead, but were put in a glass case in a Museum. Again, there is a shudder in the vivid picture of the Giants' kitchen with Dick tied to a stool and a score or more of giant mice—half as large again as English rats—thin and hungry, scrabbling round him in search of food, and jumping up at him.

Alternately reading and brooding, I found myself often pondering on the mind and personality of the man who conceived these stories. How far did he of set purpose write for children? (pp. 61-2)

[Are] his stories spun out of imagination for his own pleasure in their creation, as day dreams? They have the vivid colours of actual experience: that is what makes them so real, so haunting. No detail is lacking. Man, fish, fly, fairy or ghostly apparition comes clear and living from his pen. The pages glow with jewels of descriptive writing and the reader is transported into the very beating heart of the life he is describing. To hold back, to refuse to yield to his magic is not merely to lose the stories, but to miss a whole world of experiences. The reader must travel with him in spirit. Yet I doubt if all children will be able to take them.

It is very clear that all Mr. De la Mare writes is inspired by his poetic genius. The same force of imagination illumines both his stories and his verse; the same feeling for words, the same intense laying hold of living experience, of the light and colour and flow of the blood in one precious, pulsing moment. His verses are alive as palpably as a sparrow held in a child's hand. His sense of music and mystery is unfailing.

Children, even those making their first excursions into the world of poetry, should find the *Collected Rhymes and Verses* a perfect browsing ground. It contains so rich a choice of subject, mood and feeling; and a variety and originality of rhythms, rhymes and metres, as will delight young and old alike. De la Mare is easy to read. He leaves few traps for the untutored and the unwary. He knows just how to make the rhythm guide the reader, defining the beat so delicately yet so strongly that it takes care of the sense. He makes his words dance and sing, run like the wind, or pace slow in funereal gloom. He writes of familiar country things, or of ghostly happenings, or of his own fanciful fairyland. Sometimes he points a moral. He is merry. He is mysterious. But whatever he has to say, is expressed with the same lovely perfection. (pp. 62-3)

[Much] of his verse gives [the] feeling of having been long worked over before being committed to print, as the old rhymes were polished into shape by generations of mothers, singing them to their children. I often feel that—

> "I had a little nut tree,
> Nothing would it bear
> But a silver nutmeg
> And a golden pear."

might have been distilled right from De la Mare's own heart.

It is this originality of treatments, his experimenting carried out so skillfully and agilely and with such incomparable grace, which makes Walter De la Mare's verse such a glorious revelation to the novice, quite regardless of age. It keeps him on his toes. He is obliged to keep mind and senses alert to catch each change of mood and tone. Probably all poetry, except perhaps the most abstruse, should be read aloud. Certainly something vital from Walter De la Mare's poetry will be lost if it not heard as well as read. Best of all, let it be read aloud in a quiet place so that the music may ring and the words say all the poet meant them to. (p. 65)

Eleanor Graham, "The Riddle of Walter de la Mare: An Appreciation of His Work for Children," in The Junior Bookshelf, *Vol. 12, No. 2, July, 1948, pp. 59-65.*

Henry Charles Duffin

More than once in these last years I have read over again the bulk of de la Mare's poetry, and have found there an almost unparalleled beauty and wonder, mystery, revelation and assuagement of soul beyond anything that can be got except from the greatest of poets and musicians. (p. ix)

He is a supreme poet: his utterly delightful prose stories represent surplus creative energy; their light is of the same kind, but it is a reflected light, like that which makes the moon the modest partner of the sun. And not quite the same kind of light either. As a poet de la Mare is essentially a visionary: in prose he walks on earth, though in byways unknown to most of us. (pp. ix-x)

De la Mare is not, to any large extent, a children's poet, except in the way that *The Tempest* is a play for children. In the two-volume Collected Edition of 1942 and 1944, one volume is called **Collected Rhymes and Verses,** and it comprises the contents of those separate volumes which, de la Mare says, "were intended for children". Yet three out of four even of these "rhymes and verses" are poems in a fully adult sense: giving delight to children, indeed, just as *The Tempest* does, but moving the sensitive and experienced reader to tears, to dream, to an understanding of life and of what lies behind life. And still it remains true that not only in these poems but in the confessedly more serious productions of the companion volume, **Collected Poems,** de la Mare writes "as a child", in the sense of that wisest of all wise sayings, that which declares that to enter the Kingdom of God a man must "become as a child". The mind at work behind de la Mare's poetry has, for its creative qualities, just those which Jesus must have intended to be covered by His phrase: first, simplicity; then, hu-

mility, faith and love; clear-eyed wonder; fresh, direct, untroubled vision, unobscured by sin or doubt, free from the long years' accumulation of inhibition and reservation; complete surrender to the light of coming knowledge—delighted acceptance of miracle. Outside his study, too, in his normal human responses to life, de la Mare exhibits a preference for irrational explanations of phenomena which disconcerts the more commonplace mind of his interlocutor. Hermann Keyserling, who had some claim to be considered a "profound thinker", suggested that "the non-rational faculties of the soul will in the future contribute most to progress".

Lyric poetry is the voice of God. But the voice speaks, in different poets, with varying degrees of authenticity. The degree of authenticity corresponds not so much with the greatness of the poet (greatness depends on many factors beside this one) as with the nature of the contact the poet is able to make with the underlying reality, with the spiritual beauty and truth which are the tangible substance of reality. De la Mare belongs to a very small band of poets whose contact is peculiarly close and vital because it partakes of the directness, the immediacy, of mysticism. In very many of his poems, constituting probably more than half of his total output, de la Mare makes us aware of a life, a world, an experience, which are instantly recognized as not only different from anything the common day has to offer, but more real, partaking more of the eternal, in the same way as the mystic's knowledge of God. And it is especially to be noted that de la Mare not only communicates to us the fact that he has had this mystical (or, if you like, quasi-mystical) experience, but enables us to enter upon it (or something parallel to it) ourselves: this he does through his supreme gift of poetic form, which promotes in the mind an awareness by which it participates in the poet's comprehension of the uttermost nature of things. (pp. 6-8)

There is, of course, poetry *for* children, and there is poetry *about* children. Of de la Mare as a writer of poetry for children I have said something, and shall not say much more, except that he seems to me to enjoy an unchallengeable supremacy in this kind, if we take, as the two criteria of excellence, first, aptness to children's taste, and second, high poetic quality. There are nine-and-twenty ways of writing verse for children: one of the best is the frolicsome doggerel of the nursery rhymes, but this art has been lost with other simplicities—when we try to recapture it we are as likely as not to arrive at something "ruthless", like the rhymes of Harry Graham. Lear and Lewis Carroll revel in their own cleverness and wit, and achieve poetry for children by a fortunate accident; Blake sees the child through his own mystic absorption, Wordsworth studies him with almost painful seriousness, Stevenson observes him humorously; A. A. Milne and Eleanor Farjeon join in the children's games, guiding and suggesting like a jolly elder brother or a charming teacher; Allingham and Rose Fyleman write out of sheer delight in children's fancies, Longfellow and Jean Ingelow out of a tender parental love, Swinburne out of a sensuous joy in the exquisiteness of a child's body. All these ways are "right", and what each way has produced for the delectation of young and old is beyond praise. But there is yet another way, and it is de la Mare's. He alone has written as an inspired child: rather perhaps as if the genius of an inspired poet should take possession of the personality of a delightful child.

With all a great man's matured wealth of experience, he has been able to keep the priceless gift of a child's feeling for life.

Apart from an occasional hint of "the wisdom I lost as a child" (*In a Library*) there is no question of endowing children with any of those powers of insight which Wordsworth apostrophized in the Immortality Ode, so bringing upon himself the blandly devastating criticism of Coleridge. What de la Mare does is to keep, side by side with his man's sense of power, the child's sense of humility. O Man! he exclaims—thy dreams, thy passions, hopes, desires!—all but the riddles and fancies of a child's fond universe. More than this, to "keep innocency" is the sovereign antidote for the mortal disease of cynicism. Life is full of terrors, but the child hears only a fine music, and the man who can keep the illusion through life keeps his head high and his soul unsullied. . . . And even though sooner or later life trample him down, he shall fall unconquered, because he has kept unto his "last content" the pure bright vision of a world that evil cannot make ugly. (pp. 127-29)

Parents of young children have been known to deny to de la Mare an understanding of the child mind on the ground that he allows the thief at Robin's Castle to carry away Robin's two beauteous little children in his bag along with the rest of the plunder. They see a similar obtuseness in Stevenson, who wrote a poem for children about all the wicked shadows going tramp, tramp, tramp with the black night overhead. But if these poems are read in the spirit in which they were written, with the glowing and enchanted unreality of the one, the arch humour of the other, no child of normal sensitiveness gets anything but joy out of them. That de la Mare comprehends a child's night-fears, and sympathizes with them (but without morbidity) is shown in the poem *Hark!*—"My little Charles is afraid of the dark". He demonstrates over and over again that he has done what many parents and educators of the young fail to do—has got inside the child-mind, seen with the eyes of a child, felt with its feelings, thought its childish thoughts. (pp. 129-30)

The question will always arise whether poetry written for or about children is likely to be enjoyed, or even ought to be enjoyed, by children. With writers like Stevenson, Blake, Swinburne and de la Mare the question may be answered by asking another—do adults enjoy the poetry which these writers wrote for adults? The answer to that question is that some do and some do not, and the answer to the other question is that those children enjoy the child-poetry who are like the adults who enjoy the adult-poetry. None of these poets writes for the ordinary man or the ordinary child. They write what they must write, and have not condescended. Their child-poetry, like the rest of their poetry, is written in the language of poetry, which is a foreign language. Mr. A. A. Milne leaps to the mind as a writer with a different aim. He tells little stories in metre; and the dainty metres are handled with such ease that the child does not know that what he is hearing is "poetry" at all—as of course it is not. He thinks he is hearing—as indeed he is—an amusing story told in sentences that are strangely charming, alluringly pretty and dancing; but he has not to rise above himself to any understanding of "poetry". De la Mare always makes this demand, and in *Peacock Pie* the demand is heightened as the book proceeds. The first section, *Up and Down*, consists chiefly of simple

poems for children but many are touched with beauty, and at any moment imagination may be invoked. . . . Twice, in *Old Shellover* and *Miss T.,* the poet passes far over the heads of his little readers, to the lasting joy of his larger ones. Nothing, at first blush, could seem more innocent, childish, than the duologue between Shellover and Creep. Yet do but think of that night-enchanted garden, bejewelled with dew and gazed upon by the rising moon; given over to the lowliest forms of life, snail and slug and old Sallie Worm; the higher beings, alien and tyrannous, man and thrush, withdrawn to distant lands of sleep, so that all is stillness and shimmering beauty, broken only by the tenuous drawl of the wakeful molluscs: do but project yourself in spirit into that brilliant dream-like scene, and you will know by direct experience what the primitive creation was like. This, through the magic of a rhythmic lift, is wonder and poetry. So inspiration deepens, through such miracles as *The Thief at Robin's Castle, Nicholas Nye, The Pigs and the Charcoal Burner, The Changeling, Silver,* to that last section, out of the reach of any child, to be achieved by long devotion to beauty, to poetry, to life—the section of the marvellous songs, ending with the *Mad Prince* and *The Song of Finis.* Setting aside these two great poems, what happy children are those who shall find among their rhymes such starry stanzas as these to set them dreaming:

> Twilight came; silence came;
> The planet of Evening's silver flame;
> By darkening paths I wandered through
> Thickets trembling with drops of dew.
>
> But the music is lost and the words are gone
> Of the song I sang as I sat alone;
> Ages and ages have fallen on me—
> On the wood and the pool and the elder tree.

But who shall chronicle or adequately praise all the verses de la Mare has written to give delight to children: the swift enchanting tales, the poems about animals and birds, fairies and fancies? No less delightful, and of more permanent value as throwing a more penetrating light on life—a search-light as against a Chinese lantern—are the poems written for adults about children. These are on the whole the work of later years, just as the best of the other kind are to be found in the earlier books. (pp. 132-34)

[All] the poetry that de la Mare has written for and about children is instinct with love. . . . (p. 137)

There is a special rapprochement between de la Mare and the childmind. There is in him a "lost child" who has never ceased to regard life as something to play with—and is prepared to justify the attitude before High Heaven (*A Dull Boy*). Assessing (in his seventh decade) the brighter and more obscure elements in his vision, he calls them "Two gardens for two children—in one mind". The general opinion is with St. Paul, that there comes a time when it is good to "put away childish things", to assume a protective coat of worldly wisdom and cynicism; but I have said enough to show that I believe close contact with the ultimate life of spirit is only to be preserved by those who, like de la Mare, can keep, with the matured mind of an adult, the simple heart of a child. (pp. 140-41)

Henry Charles Duffin, in his Walter de la Mare: A Study of His Poetry, *Sidgwick and Jackson Limited, 1949, 209 p.*

Frank Eyre

Walter de la Mare's contribution . . . stands head and shoulders above that of any of his contemporaries. His **Poems for Children, Peacock Pie,** and other collections set a new standard in poetry for children. They contained in fact almost the first poetry, as distinct from verse, to have been written for children, and their lesson, which is implicit in everything de la Mare has written, that children can enjoy the best we can give them, is even now not fully appreciated. . . . Walter de la Mare's most enduring contribution to children's literature may well prove to be his wonderful anthology **Come Hither,** which must have introduced more children (and adults) to the delights of real poetry than anything else of its kind. (p. 64)

Frank Eyre, "Fiction for Children," in his 20th Century Children's Books, *Longmans, Green and Co.,* 1952, pp. 50-64.

Kenneth Hopkins

It is more than fifty years since the quiet, consistent, and magical voice of Walter de la Mare was first heard in English poetry, and throughout those years he has given us poetry that epitomizes the mystery and the evocative loveliness of the written word; an essence of poetry, it may seem, that has not been obviously affected by the violent changes of the contemporary world. Yet to say this—even to say he is a great lyric poet, with Campion, Blake, Shelley, Landor, Bridges—is insufficient. Walter de la Mare cannot be labelled in a sentence. The range and quantity of his work, in verse and prose, is considerable, its uniform excellence is remarkable, for he has never written a book, a paragraph, or a word which was not the best he could do. No poet of our time has commanded a purer or more spontaneous initial inspiration, and none has brought to the aid of inspiration so cautious and deliberate a craftsmanship. 'Second thoughts in everything are best, but in rhyme third and fourth don't come amiss', says Byron. De la Mare has achieved the marriage of craftsmanship with inspiration without damaging either. Nowhere in his work is there any element of the careless or the facile. The delicate art may be conscious, but the unaltering integrity is inherent, conditioning, and informing every chapter, every line. (p. 7)

In the years 1904-10, between the publication of **Henry Brocken** and **The Return,** de la Mare reached maturity as a writer of prose. In 1910 appeared two very different works, **The Three Mulla-Mulgars** and **The Return:** different, but with this much in common: both were stamped with a genius of which **Henry Brocken** had given only the promise.

The Three Mulla-Mulgars—later renamed (I think unfortunately) **The Three Royal Monkeys**—is a story for children: not young children, but children from, say, ten to fourteen. The adult reader ought not to overlook it on this account, for it contains some of de la Mare's most delicate writing. (pp. 13-14)

Into [his] comparatively uncomplicated plot the author introduces the subtlest under- and overtones of characterization and description. His three heroes, and especially the youngest, Nod, are (we feel) truly monkeys: they behave, react, think, and speak as monkeys should, with that small extra something which naturally would be added in

royal blood. A comparison here with *The Jungle Book* is inevitable, but Kipling's animals although more realistic are somehow less credible. 'Look well, O Wolves!' is theatrically effective, but under scrutiny it does not appear true. . . . Absorbing and at times exciting as the story is, it is in the writing itself that **The Three Mulla-Mulgars** is most rewarding; like **Henry Brocken** before it, but more maturely, it gives us a remarkable exercise in sustained poetic prose. (p. 14)

These early prose works all show, in different ways, the mark of a writer with great gifts not yet fully under control; we feel in **Henry Brocken** that the narrative takes the writer along paths of its own choosing, rather than those he intends; some of the early stories are exercises, trials of strength: and why not? For only so can a writer develop and come to perfection. **The Three Mulla-Mulgars** in another way reveals this conflict between the writer and his writing, for it is a work without a distinct purpose. If it is a children's story—and certainly the author read it to his children—then why is so much of it in manner and content beyond the immediate appreciation of children? On the other hand, if it is not a children's story, what is it? What comment did it evoke from the young listeners who heard it first? (p. 16)

One warning must be given before the reader embarks upon the **Collected Rhymes and Verses.** Do not suppose this title to mean a volume of amusing and unimportant trifles not strong enough for the companion **Collected Poems;** for **Collected Rhymes** contains some of de la Mare's finest, and most characteristic, work.

Walter de la Mare is the supreme English lyric poet of our time and one of the great masters of the short lyric in English, as truly a master as were Campion, Herrick, Herbert, Landor, and Bridges before him; a master, moreover, in the same tradition that was theirs, of saying the perfect thing in perfect form and language. (pp. 26-7)

His utterance is sometimes deceptively quiet, deceptively undemonstrative. The effect is often cumulative; line by line, stanza by stanza—even in a twenty-line poem—the essential development proceeds unsuspected but inevitable. (p. 27)

[He] is never afraid of the conventional or 'poetic' word or phrase if that best suits his need; but he is able by mingling the familiar with the unexpected to heighten the value of both. 'The poet is to deal with the commonplace', says George Saintsbury, 'and make it *not common*'. This de la Mare does. (pp. 28-9)

While he is evoking with delicate skill an apparently familiar landscape of the poetic world, another image appears behind it more remote, less known to humanity and at times charged with fear. The first image may be miniature, graceful, well known, the other is cold and giant like, drawn from impersonal worlds, where a single human consciousness is no more than a momentary affair. In many of the earlier lyrics we may feel this second world appears only as a hint or a question. . . .

I do not suggest, of course, that the sentiment is always commonplace; for a hundred lyrics with a conventional theme one might find another hundred with an original and 'de la Marian' inspiration, for de la Mare looks at the world with inquiring and unprejudiced eyes and he sees things—as a poet should—for the 'first time' no matter how many poets have seen them before him. That is why his titles at first reading seem unadventurous enough: **'Evening', 'Dawn', 'Age', 'The Dreamer', 'A Child Asleep', 'Winter Dusk'**, subjects rubbed by a hundred rhymsters, battered a thousand times'. It makes no difference, for these subjects are the stuff of human life and experience and he comes to them—despite his vast reading in the world's poetry—with the innocence of a child. To him they are new, and the poems he makes from them are new. Even his occasional 'echoes' indicate merely an affinity, natural and unconscious, with Poe, or Burns, or Landor, or Shakespeare. There is no 'world of Walter de la Mare', peopled with fairies and children; he is squarely in the same world as the rest of us, but he sees deeper and further into its implications and even of the tangible and visible he sees more, or 'sees it more abundantly'. (p. 29)

Animals, flowers, the seasons, the single uncomplicated emotions of fear, hunger, desire, these are his themes often enough; and always to what we have heard before he will add the twist, or bring the extra insight, which stamps even the shortest of his poems with the unmistakable signature of its author. For de la Mare is a poet working within a conventional tradition whose genius is not for flamboyant disregard of the rules, but for triumphant conformity with them. He has not been obscure because he has not been a leader in the 'new' and the revolutionary. It is not easy to find new things to say in poetry, or to say the old things freshly. But genius can be flexible enough to accommodate itself to tradition. (p. 31)

[Like] all the great poets, de la Mare can be lived with; taken in short passages, he gives refreshment; in extended reading he gives counsel and comfort. Before all else, he is to be read for pleasure; and few living poets can give greater pleasure. He is to be read for the marvel of technique to be found in his verse and the variety of his music. He shows almost every excellence of which the four-line stanza in English is capable—and what a wealth of excellence that is. (pp. 32-3)

[Readers] will always look to him first for the short lyrics which—any time in the past fifty years—have graced periodicals, anthologies, and, more recently, radio programmes. Some of these poems are among the most widely known of our time, their opening lines familiar to all who care for poetry: 'Here lies a most beautiful lady', ' "Bunches of grapes", says Timothy', ' "Is there anybody there?" said the Traveller', 'Who said, "Peacock Pie"?', 'What lovely things thy hand hath made'—and many more. The poetry of our time does not always enter easily into the consciousness of millions; these poems do so because they have a simplicity, a universality, which captures the reader at the outset and never lets him go. (p. 37)

Kenneth Hopkins, in his Walter de la Mare, *Longmans, Green & Co., 1953, 44 p.*

Lillian H. Smith

There are many ways of writing in verse for children but, for the purpose of this inquiry, the only way that is relevant is the way of *poetry.* That thought immediately brings to our minds Walter de la Mare's *Songs of Childhood,* and his other books for children to which he has given such enticing titles: *Peacock Pie, Down-adown-derry, Bells and Grass.* (p. 110)

It is [his] capacity to see "the rarest charm of familiarity in strangeness," the beauty of this earth in its relation to spiritual beauty, separated one from the other only by a veil of gossamer thinness, that is, I think, Walter de la Mare's quality. His poetry is compounded of imagination, vision, and dream, into which beauty breaks through when we least expect it. His mastery of flexible and subtle rhythms is so deft that it is, perhaps, hardly realized. Yet it sweeps us into the mood of the poem almost unaware. No one can read

> Ann, Ann!
> Come! quick as you can!

without feeling the urgency and excitement of the revelation about to be made. Nor can one miss the listening expectancy of

> Someone is always sitting there
> In the little green orchard;

and the clop, clop, rhythm of an old donkey's hoofs can be heard in

> Nicholas Nye was lean and grey
> Lame of leg and old.

Perhaps the most subtle of all de la Mare's rhythms is found in **"The Listeners"**; a rhythm which Forrest Reid calls "syncopated":

> Is there anybody there? said the Traveller,
> Knocking on the moonlit door.

and we stand, hesitating, in the moonlight, at one with the strange eerie mood the poem has evoked in the first line.

There has been discovered no process of analysis by which a poem can be taken apart to show why it is poetry or why it is not. It is something intensely felt or it is nothing. But it is possible to study the devices a poet uses to obtain the effect he achieves even though the devices are inherent in his poetic gift. Walter de la Mare says that it is "one of every poet's loveliest devices with words—to let the music of his verse accord with its meaning"; and that "loveliest device" is his in greatest measure. (pp. 111-12)

Reading his poems for children we find ourselves asking how it is possible to reach to the other side of dream, and name the magical spell that is de la Mare's own. We are at a loss for the identifying word, but we are conscious of having discovered a touchstone by which we can estimate how closely verses written for children approach poetry. The influence of de la Mare's poetry on children themselves is that of an awakening of minds, hearts, and imaginations to wonder, to a sense of beauty unseen, but waiting only on the awareness of all the senses to reveal itself. (p. 112)

Walter de la Mare makes no concessions to the popular idea that poetry for children should be simplified or watered down. He imposes no age levels. Instead, he trusts wholly to their intuitive response to wonder and beauty. (pp. 112-13)

Lillian H. Smith, "Poetry," in her The unreluctant Years: A Critical Approach to Children's Literature, *American Library Association, 1953, pp. 96-113.*

V. Sackville-West

Invited, as I have been, to express in nine hundred words my idea of Mr. de la Mare as a poet of childhood, I find that I can do it in nine:

He is the natural inheritor of the nursery rhyme.

Having said that, how can I fill up the 891 words remaining to me? Perhaps by analysing the essence of the nursery rhyme, though that might come near to brushing off the down on a butterfly's wing.

The nursery rhyme, as I see it, is made up of three ingredients:

(1) Memorability—which involves an elementary verse-form of rhythm, rhyme, and metre. First-cousin to ballads, in this respect.

(2) Fantasy, absurdity, and realism all combined. Example: it is fantastic and absurd to imagine a cow jumping over the moon or a fork running off with a spoon, yet all these objects (cow, moon, fork, spoon) have a realistic familiarity which invests the situation with sufficient plausibility around the nursery table. Let us take two verses from Mr. de la Mare:

> 'Bunches of grapes,' says Timothy:
> 'Pomegranates pink,' says Elaine:
> 'A junket of cream and a cranberry tart
> For me,' says Jane.
> 'Chariots of gold,' says Timothy:
> 'Silvery wings,' says Elaine:
> 'A bumpity ride in a waggon of hay
> For me,' says Jane.

Or the adorable Miss T. who is at one and the same time a very real person and a person out of Mother Goose's rhymebook. . . .

(3) The element of nonsense, and incongruity, always at the heart of much pure poetry. George Moore remarked that Shakespeare never soiled his songs with thinking; a profound and suggestive remark, well worth consideration. 'Never soiled his songs with thinking.' George Moore might have pushed his argument further, to its logical conclusion in Lewis Carroll,

> Twas brillig, and the slithy toves
> Did gyre and gimble in the wabe;
> All mimsy were the borogoves,
> And the mome raths outgrabe,

words of ridiculous nonsense, but which still convey some impression of a poem, even as a nursery rhyme does; or some of the *Songs of Childhood* or *Peacock Pie* poems of Mr. de la Mare. He possesses this peculiar genius for writing songs unsoiled by thinking; songs to please the ear, jingle with poetry stirred into it; songs that any child and any adult will remember, since he has the rare gift of capturing our early days when we learnt nursery rhymes at our mother's foot.

V. Sackville-West, "De la Mare: Poet of Childhood," in Books: The Journal of the National Book League, *No. 301, April-May, 1956, p. 79.*

Alfred Noyes

In de la Mare's poems there is, indeed, a very clear statement—of something lost in life but remembered with infi-
nite longing. This, too, is perhaps the secret of the magic and music in his poems for children. It is quite unnecessary to depreciate Stevenson in order to appreciate [the] exquisite flowers in the child's garden of Walter de la Mare. . . . Indeed the "breath of the bogey" on the stair is perhaps more nearly what a child feels than the sometimes almost macabre touch of a ghostly hand in some of de la Mare's work, where his imagination is more akin to that of Coleridge in "Christabel" or "Kubla Khan," or to the weird suggestions in that eerie poem "Dead Maid's Pool," by that greatly under-valued poet Sydney Dobell:

> Ash-tree, ash-tree,
> Bending o'er the water—
> Ash-tree, ash-tree,
> Hadst thou a daughter?

De la Mare's work is indeed not so much that of a man putting himself in the place of a child. It is rather the work of a child's heart surviving in a man beset by all manner of unearthly apprehensions, apprehensions that constantly bring him word of those things in heaven and earth that are undreamed of in our philosophy. (pp. 72-3)

Alfred Noyes, "The Poetry of Walter de la Mare," in Contemporary Review, *Vol. 190, No. 1088, August, 1956, pp. 70-3.*

M. S. Crouch

No other poet of this or any other age has looked so intensely on the world as if each moment were the last; none has been so profoundly convinced that "Beauty vanishes; beauty passes." How strange then that he should have been the poet of childhood, pre-eminently the poet of, and for, those who are seeing the beauty of the world for the first time. (p. 187)

The work of few writers has been as compact as Walter de la Mare's, so much of a piece, that it is impossible to distinguish between prentice work, work of maturity, and work of old age. He developed; he did not change. Similarly one cannot successfully distinguish between his work for children and for adults. Many hints for the understanding of his children's books lie in the adult verse and novels and in these infinitely wise and rewarding anthologies which are perhaps his most individual contribution to literature. Least of all is it possible to consider his children's books as on a lower plane than his work for adults. Is *Peacock Pie* a lesser achievement than *Motley?* or *The Three Mulla-Mulgars* less profound than *The Return?* Absurd! He poured infinite riches of mind and spirit into the children's stories and poems.

He was incomparably the finest poet to give his best work to children. His verse has the utmost rhythmic and melodic variety and ingenuity. Its patterns are subtle, but not difficult, springing from the quality of the words and the thought. It is possible to read at length in *Peacock Pie* or *Bells and Grass* without a hint of tediousness or monotony, for each poem is different in form and content. Writing, as he must have done, to placate his daemon rather than to please any particular child, he was not troubled with theoretical problems of what is suitable for children. He has delighted generations of children, therefore, with poems which are far beyond their intellectual range as well as others which are as simple as they are exquisite in word and form. He is very memorable, because he so successfully matches word and thought; his are for most children the first poems other than nursery rhymes which are got by heart, and this without tears. He has, too, a genius for the same queer logic and inevitability as the nursery rhyme. **"Three Jolly Gentlemen"** and **"Blindman's Inn"** are of the same family as "Jack and Jill." Above all, he writes "straight," without condescension or sentimentality, with strength and with sweetness. (pp. 187-88)

[In] the original stories there is an actuality, an exactness of observation and description, which makes them live and linger obstinately in the reader's mind. It is characteristic that he mates so closely the incredible and the homely. Dick, who also climbs the beanstalk and lives most dangerously among giants, is a Gloucester lad to the life. John's adventures as a fish wrapped in green moss are credible because he, with his love of fishing and his susceptibility to beauty in distress, is so real. And the three little Warwickshire sweeps are of the very stuff of reality and their adventures read like a page of history, far-off, sad, but convincing. De la Mare's detail is meticulous, precise. He builds his story in leisurely fashion (although he knows the value of swift climax), dwelling lovingly on each scene and character, setting the stage and introducing the actors with due care. The stories, for this reason, are best read to children. A child reader may well become bogged down in detail which, in an adult's voice, can be vividly alive and enthralling.

His romantic masterpiece, **The Three Mulla-Mulgars**, is also difficult for children to read themselves, for its strange names and its complex symbolism. It is, for all that, a very great children's book, a great adventure-story, superbly told. The remote scene, the exciting incidents, the odd and lovable characters, above all the melancholy atmosphere, haunt the mind after a reading. Children may well fail to understand the meaning of the story; they are likely to absorb it unconsciously as they consider the modest heroism of little Nod on his great quest.

It is characteristic of de la Mare that he shares the riches of his mind so generously with the reader. . . . Surely no anthology conveys the delight of literature so surely as **Come hither**, which shows that good writing has no frontiers and no limitation of subject. It is gay, thoughtful, light, provocative; full of that grave enthusiasm which is so much more infectious than ecstacy. (pp. 189-90)

[Walter de la Mare's] place in literature is assured. In children's literature it is indeed unique. If his are not the greatest of all children's books he is unquestionably the greatest writer to have dedicated his finest powers to children. Nowadays the tendency is to cater primarily for the "backward" reader; we all court the cretinous and the moronic. But surely, however much the cult of the C-Stream prevails, there will never lack readers who can share little Nod's wondrous vision, or follow John across the great wall into the Lord Fish's domain, or linger like ghosts "in the darkening air" when the subtle, haunting music of de la Mare's verse calls them "home once more." (p. 191)

M. S. Crouch, "Farewell to Walter de la Mare," in The Junior Bookshelf, *Vol. 20, No. 4, October, 1956, pp. 187-91.*

Harry Behn

Blake had begun it, when I was a child. Years later, but

years ago, something touched me like a magnet and turned all my molecules one way. That was the day my ambition to be an engineer ended. The day I read **The Listeners.** My head still hums like Mel's hive. I trot along with practical folk somehow, useful at mending an old pot or whistling a tune. If only they knew! the world I most comfortably inhabit is Mr. Nahum's. I don't have to open Walter de la Mare's books any more to hear his music. It has naturalized itself. I need only stand still in the woods, and listen. (pp. 235-36)

Harry Behn, "The Books of Walter de la Mare," in The Horn Book Magazine, *Vol. XXXIII, No. 3, June, 1957, pp. 235-36.*

Eileen H. Colwell

Of all poets and storytellers, Walter de la Mare has given me the deepest joy. After the strange and profound fantasy of **The Three Royal Monkeys**, two short stories are my favorites, perhaps because I have shared them so often with children.

The first is the lovely tale of **"The Three Sleeping Boys of Warwickshire,"** three little chimney sweeps whose sooty bodies are separated from their dream-shapes by the greed of Old Nollykins. For fifty-three years the boys sleep on until one April morning they are awakened by a girl's kiss on their "stone-cold mouths" and, their dream-shapes home at last, they leap out into the glory of Spring. So wonderfully is the ecstasy of Spring and its new life conveyed that I can never finish the story without a lift of the heart.

My second choice is **"The Old Lion,"** the story of the friendship between the sailor, Mr. Bumps, and Jasper, the little monkey he buys in "a village of black men." So perceptive is Walter de la Mare's understanding of Jasper's loneliness and dignity in his alien captivity that as we watch Jasper we too feel a "peculiar coldness" stealing through our blood. When Mr. Bumps has to leave Jasper on the African shore, a stranger to his own people also, we feel as grieved as the sailor himself. A haunting and moving story.

These two stories contain for me the very essence of Walter de la Mare's genius, beauty, wisdom, passionate concern for all unhappiness, and his consummate literary skill. (pp. 236-37)

Eileen H. Colwell, "The Books of Walter de la Mare," in The Horn Book Magazine, *Vol. XXXIII, No. 3, June, 1957, pp. 236-37.*

David McCord

Every reader worth his salt is conscious of at least two or three contemporary writers whose names are magic. Walter de la Mare is a magic name to me. I think of him always as a poet—not simply as one of the purist lyric poets that England has produced but as a poet in the larger sense of attitude. (p. 5)

With Walter de la Mare the strange aberration of otherworldliness, the magic of wake and dream, his "marvelous music and a matchless sense" are constant in everything he has written or touched. His prose is poetry. His voice is one of the few totally original voices of our time. His obvious limitations—and all first-rate artists have limitations, just as all second-rate artists fail to recognize their limitations—gave him the strength to produce a unified body of work that is worth exploring at any point. But his ultimate worth, it seems to me, will be predicated on his sense of human compassion rather than on his sense of the elfin, the mysterious, the thridding instead of the threading of words. Anyone who could say, as he does in **"Winged Chariot,"** "And saddest of all earth's clocks is Others growing old," can be trusted with metaphor and all the symbols of his craft. (pp. 5, 32)

> *David McCord, "Flowers in a Secret Garden," in* The New York Times Book Review, *September 29, 1957, pp. 5, 32.*

John Ciardi

There is no anthology like [**Come Hither**] in English, and none that does better by the pure oaten-pipe of English poetry. There are no hard-knocking poems in this collection, and one will search a long way through these melodies for a good thumping spondee. Although there are over 500 poems here. there is not one complete poem by John Donne, for example, though three fragments of Donne poems occur in the notes. Walter de la Mare, that is to say, was tuned primarily to one voice of English poetry and only one. And in the exclusion of all else lies the particular strength and flavor of this collection. When the reader's mood is for the trilled note, this is the book to reach for, and bless it for being there. There is nothing in English, moreover, quite as charmingly learned and provocative as de la Mare's comments on these poems in his final section of notes, **"About and Roundabout."** If there is a child in the family, or if one has himself been a child at some time, this is certainly one of the books that needs to be built into what used to be called "the family" before the demon ad man came up with "togetherness." (pp. 42-3)

> *John Ciardi, "Two Voices of Poetry," in* The Saturday Review, *New York, Vol. 40, November 9, 1957, pp. 42-3.*

Elizabeth Bishop

[**Come Hither: A Collection of Rhymes and Poems for the Young of All Ages**] is the best anthology I know of. . . . It is a marvellous book for children, but not at all a "children's book"; de la Mare maintains a little of his air of mystery even as to whom his readers are to be. . . . Auden has said that he learned more from it "than I have from most books of overt criticism". I don't believe in forcing poetry on anyone, even a child, but if one knows a child at all interested in the subject, this is the perfect birthday book. One can't expect a little Auden every time, but at least, as he also said about the possible effects on children of reading de la Mare's own verse, "he will not have a tin ear." It is a fine book to memorize from. . . . (pp. 50-1)

The introduction is a de la Mare-ish allegorical account of how he discovered poetry as a boy,—or perhaps it is not allegorical but the literal truth. This is the one part of the book that might seem a bit dated to an adult reader; but by means of dream-like landscapes, old ladies in lost farmhouses, mysterious tower rooms crammed with old trunks and books, in his own way de la Mare is explaining how the anthology was made up, and also letting fall some wise thoughts on the writing of verse in general. In the tower room the boy finds books filled with copied-out poems and sets to work re-copying them for himself. (p. 51)

Later on in the notes he tells the story of the mediaeval traveller who made a complete circuit of the world without knowing it, and came back to where he'd started from. To illustrate this story the book begins and ends with the same poem: *This is the Key of the Kingdom:* a gentle hint to turn back and read it through again. He also points out that "many of the customs, beliefs, lore they [ballads] refer to may be found scattered up and down throughout the world." Since his vision of both time and poetry seems to be cyclical, he is implying, I think, by the story of the copying, that simple repetition of poetry, copying or memorizing, is a good way of learning to understand it, possibly a good way of learning to write it. Isn't the best we can do, he seems to be saying, in the way of originality, but a copying and re-copying, with some slight variations of our own?

The book proper consists of songs and ballads, folk-poetry, and frankly romantic poems, all chosen for melodiousness as well as romance. (pp. 51-2)

De la Mare has some practical things to say about meters (which he used so beautifully himself), and even suggests how to read certain of the poems; but he never speaks directly of any of the usual concerns of the critics; for one, let's say, "imagery". Instead, the old woman of the introduction tells the boy: "learn the common names of everything you see . . . and especially those that please you most to remember: then give them names also of your own making and choosing—if you can." And wouldn't that be imagery? He loves "little articles", home-made objects whose value increases with age, Robinson Crusoe's lists of his belongings, homely employments, charms and herbs. As a result he naturally chose for his book many of what Randall Jarrell once called "thing-y" poems, and never the pompous, abstract, or formal.

After the poems come the notes, and the book is well worth buying for them alone. It is a Luna Park of stray and straying information. He quotes journals, letters, samplers, gravestones, and his friends; then throws in a few recipes. He discusses the calendar, that "anomalous litter of relics". He is against rigid rules of spelling, and cruelty to animals and children. Would you like to know the name of Noah's dog? Or the derivation of "cat's-cradle"? Or read the world's earliest poem? They are all here, and de la Mare's transparent delight in what he is telling provokes immediate replies, which is probably just what he intended. (p. 53)

Besides the hundreds of better-known and loved poems he chose, surely it is of this kind of random poetry that Walter de la Mare can make child readers, or us, aware; the kind to which he lent his fine ear with such loving attention. As the boy in the tower room copies his poems, "an indescribable despair and anxiety—almost terror even—seized upon me at the rushing thought of my own *ignorance;* of how little I knew, of how unimportant I was . . ." Then daylight comes, he puts down his pen and goes to the window: "I was but just awake: so too was the world itself, and ever is." And in reading this book we can often recapture what children and other races perhaps still share: de la Mare's lyrical confidence. (p. 54)

> *Elizabeth Bishop, "I Was But Just Awake," in*

Poetry, *Vol. XCIII, No. I, October, 1958, pp. 50-4.*

Marcia Dalphin

Fresh from the reading of [*The Three Mulla Mulgars*], no praise seems to me too extravagant. All compact of poetry, of the magic of strange, beautiful words: dramatic to a degree, employing every art of suspense, yet never falsely or cheaply: instinct with high qualities of loyalty and courage: full of a tenderness that never degenerates into sentimentality: constantly surprising the reader with its touches of a sly and pawky humor: how one wishes that every one might have his imagination kindled by it!

No one should miss the experience of sharing this book with some sensitive child. And be sure that any one who has read and loved it as a child will have it in his heart forever. I know a young scientist, now studying for his doctorate, who says that he "remembers with particular delight Nod's wonderstone, and with real desolation the burning of the hut." And whenever I read the story I find myself hearing his delighted chuckles in places where as we read it aloud some combination of word sounds or some turn of the plot took his fancy.

It is impossible in a few paragraphs to do any justice to this wonderful story of the three royal monkeys' search for the valleys of Tishnar. One might better hand it to a friend and say, "Read it for yourself and see what a poet can do when he turns his hand to prose, and what a father can do when he is writing a story under the peculiar stimulation that must come from reading it chapter by chapter to his children at bedtime." Or read him that page which tells of Nod and his brothers toiling up a dizzy mountain ledge on Arakkaboa and suddenly come to the end of the path that drops away into nothingness around a corner of the cliff. And as they stand there aghast, hoping to devise some means by which little Nod at least may turn back in safety, suddenly comes on Thumb's head a touch light as thistledown and he looks up into the hairy face of a Mountain Mulgar dangling at the end of a long living rope of his fellows, up which they may climb ladderwise to safety. Or bid him turn to those delightful chapters that tell of Nod's capture by Andy Battle and of the friendship that grew up between the sailor and the little wanderer. Will he not have always clearly etched in his memory a picture of Andy and Nod in their little space of firelight surrounded on all sides by darkness and enemies, the sailor thrumming on his old lute while Nod dances a Mulgar jig on the log beside him? Through the frosty night of Munza echoes thinly the chorus:

He sits 'neath the Cross in the cankering snow,
And waits for his sorrowful end,
Yeo ho!
And waits for his sorrowful end.

(pp. 138-39)

Marcia Dalphin, "I Give You the End of a Golden String," in A Horn Book Sampler: On Children's Books and Reading, *edited by Norma R. Fryatt, The Horn Book, 1959, pp. 133-39.*

William Walsh

[Walter de la Mare] was a minor poet. This is not quite the platitude it ought to be. Naturally one discounts the amiable plaudits uttered at his death which seek to inflate his importance as a poet. . . . The death of a minor poet is an occasion for reflecting how hard, in our brutal times, is the part of the true minor talent. Circumstances like ours, so inimical to the development of artistic capacity, require even from the major writer dedication, originality, force and stamina. If we leave Lawrence aside as a great natural genius of surpassing powers, who must have been a great writer in this or any age, we can hardly estimate the immensity of effort exacted from the major modern writer by the conditions of our time. We cannot guess what it must have cost Eliot to have re-established his connection with an older tradition or Yeats to have created a whole new idiom. These circumstances are peculiarly severe on the minor poet who may like de la Mare have the devotion and the integrity but not the great creative span. The minor writer desperately needs the support of a thriving tradition. Given the stability of a background and the solidity of a ground underfoot, given the soil and air, he may go on to nourish his own gifts with some prospect of success. But when de la Mare began writing in the early nineteen hundreds . . . there was available nothing but the residue of a decayed Romanticism, the bent of which was towards a cloistered and decorative poetry, not only remote from anything like 'a criticism of life' but even far from life itself. How then did he, with no more than a modicum of the creative power of the major writer and with a markedly less positive sensibility than a writer like Edward Thomas, succeed, as he did succeed, in achieving out of the clichés of Romanticism a distinctively personal tone and a recognisably individual vision?

The answer seems to be that what I have called the bent of Romanticism accorded well with a bias of the poet's nature which was set against the lucid and waking world and towards a universe of dream and enchantment, where the most vivid life is a period of drowsy consciousness between sleep and sleep.

Very old are we men;
Our dreams are tales
Told in dim Eden
By Eve's nightingales;
We wake and whisper awhile,
But, the day gone by,
Silence and sleep like fields
Of amaranth lie.

Validity is given to this minor Keatsian mood, a certain definition and authenticity are communicated to it, by the poet's successful identification with the consciousness of the child, since this is an order of feeling which has a sanction in the life of the child. I say identification with the consciousness of the child. But really it is one sort of child, the sensitive, introspective child, lonely and a bit odd, contemplative and shy. One can picture him, the chief *persona* of de la Mare's poems, stalky and pale, with thin bones and fine hair, inclined to lassitude, occasionally shaken with the tremors of curious fears, inhabiting with a subdued happiness a private world and resenting the intrusion of bumbling and uncomprehending adults. It is this child, 'perplexed and still' like the Traveller in *The Listeners,* as he faces a massive and indifferent universe whose experience is the substance of de la Mare's poetry. It is the combination of a child's feeling, the experience of immaturity, with a sophisticated and highly literary language, the vocabulary of maturity, which gives to de la Mare's poetry its low-toned but unmistakable individuality. (pp. 174-76)

The actuality, the state of being to which the best poems of de la Mare correspond, is the mind of the young child, say between five and nine. It is this short space of life that the poet explores with address and realises inwardly and subtly, and it is this particular kind of awareness which he adopts as a means—not of examining—that is for de la Mare too ratiocinative a word—hardly of looking at— but rather of glancing obliquely at his own experience. As I shall point out, it is a method attended by its own dangers. In this miniature cosmos size or the lack of it is very important. The child himself is small; the de la Mare child like the bird in his poem *A Robin* is:

> Changeling and solitary,
> Secret and sharp and small.

The things he cares for are diminutive—notice the many poems of de la Mare devoted to tiny subjects, *The Bottle, The Spark, The Robin, The Snowdrop, The Snowflake, The Owl, The Moth, The Linnet, Fenny Wren* ('A tiny, inch-long, eager, ardent, Feathered mouse'). Beyond a certain point of size, indeed, things cease to engage the child's attention and recede into a vague and neutral background. The first stanza of *The Scribe* illustrates this concern with the tiny and the sharply detailed.

> What lovely things
> Thy hand hath made:
> The smooth-plumed bird
> In its emerald shade,
> The seed of the grass,
> The speck of stone
> Which the wayfaring ant
> Stirs—and hastes on!

The beginning of *The Bottle* shows the recession from the small particular thing to the vague and inscrutable

> Of green and hexagonal glass,
> With sharp, fluted sides—
> Vaguely transparent these walls,
> Wherein motionless hides
> A simple so potent it can
> To oblivion lull. . . .

A sharp figure on a vague ground is a classical description of perception; but in the perception of the young child the figure is uncannily sharp, the ground mistily vague. And since the child must have a strong bond of interested attachment towards what is to hold his attention, the ground can never be merely vague or just neutral. For the child a merely neutral universe becomes actively indifferent and so oppressive and even terrifying. . . . Even time, which we think of as a colourless medium for events, utterly neutral and impersonal, has for the child a hint of menace, a sort of personal vindictiveness. It consumes itself away when he is happy and drags itself out when he is wretched. (pp. 177-78)

In a world where the known is little, the familiar comfortingly small, and where the indifferent and the alien are immense and hostile, the young child is powerfully influenced to retreat into his own small, lit space, and especially into the comfort of the day-dream which suspends the rough operations of an intimidating reality.

> Isled in the midnight air,

> Musked with the dark's faint bloom,
> Out into glooming and secret haunts
> The flame cries, 'Come!'

Here again is a quality which fits smoothly the poet's daylight-shunning temperament. It is clear that this could be a dangerous and retrogressive habit. It is one thing to recreate this childish tendency with delicacy and conviction, as the poet often does. It is another for the adult to take it over as a permanent device for evading the disagreeable. There is no doubt that in many poems de la Mare makes no bones about which of the two, the sleeping or the waking consciousness, he prefers.

> Two worlds they have—a globe forgot,
> Wheeling from dark to light;
> And all the enchanted realm of dream
> That burgeons out of night.

Poetry of this sort is no more than an inducement to a self-indulgent reverie, an opiate for the active intelligence and all the more insidious for the skill with which the invitation is offered. (pp. 178-79)

More effective are those poems in which the poet preserves sufficient of his own identity to allow him to hold the object some distance away, if only at arm's length. Then we are aware of the poet not only as participant but also as observer. It is a curious thing that what in most poets is a sign of failure—the reader's impression that the poet is writing *about* his experience, describing it instead of presenting it—is for de la Mare a condition of success. The reason is the nature of the experience the poet addresses himself to, which, with no gap left between him and it, with a too complete identification of the two, is liable to betray him into an indolent and self-deceiving fantasy. (On the other hand, when de la Mare stepped out of the guise of the articulate child and wrote as an adult of purely adult themes, he could be guilty of the lurid and garish *In the Dock* or the prim whimsy of *Mercutio*.)

But when he wrote with, or from, the awareness of the sensitive child and yet kept in reserve a measure of adult detachment, de la Mare composed many poems remarkable for fineness of discernment and remarkable also, within his chosen range, for virtuosity of theme. In these poems the language is sparer, the movement nimbler, the curve of the dreamy line more delicately modulated. *Martha* is a good example of the poet in his double rôle of participant and observer: he is both one of the spellbound audience and also the casually interested adult passing by. . . . He had an unusual gift for evoking the stillness and the hush in which the children are suspended as in an element in this poem. D. H. Lawrence spoke of 'Walter de la Mare's perfect appreciation of life at still moments'. *The Sleeper* beautifully suggests how a child realises the intense and positive quality of silence as Ann comes into the house to find her mother asleep in a chair. . . . In *Myself,* another poem which evokes the quality of silence, he shows a different facet of his apprehension of the child mind. The poem figures with astonishing finesse one of those disturbing 'metaphysical' gropings of the young child. In *Myself* it is the child's strange capacity to be aware of himself, and simultaneously aware of himself as another, an *alter ego*. . . . In this poem we note a subdued melancholy, a tone appropriate to the child's feeling of affectionate, and almost detached, pity for himself. The same combination of pity and 'metaphysical' speculation occurs in the famous *Fare Well,* except that now the pity is more prominent, but the speculation is there working to brace and control the feeling. The first lines might have been composed as de la Mare's version of the child's question, What is it like, what will it be like when I'm not there?—

When I lie where shades of darkness
Shall no more assail my eyes,
Nor the rain make lamentation
When the wind sighs;
How will fare the world whose wonder
Was the very proof of me?

But what after all dignifies this poetry which some would want to dismiss as a poetry of the nursery? It seems to be this, that beneath the murmur of childish voices we hear a more ancient and wiser tongue, the language of myth and fairytale, dream and symbol. And why do we feel that these poems have a touch of universal truth? It is because under de la Mare's falling and lapsing rhythms we are aware of another rhythm, a faint and profound harmony, the rhythm of a regress to the womb, the sound of the timid soul in flight back to its origins. Walter de la Mare made his poetry out of what may be a radical failing but is certainly a permanent fact of human life. (pp. 180-82)

William Walsh, "The Writer and the Child: Mark Twain, Henry James, D. H. Lawrence and Walter de la Mare," in his The Use of Imagination: Educational Thought and the Literary Mind, *Chatto & Windus Ltd., 1959, pp. 137-82.*

Leonard Clark

Walter de la Mare is the greatest writer of English lyrical poetry (particularly for children) of the first half of this century. It is tendentious and futile to label this poetry as being merely 'minor' or 'Georgian' or 'romantic'. And it is patronising and insulting to say of this poetry that it is little more than 'accomplished'. Yet this is what some recent critics, who have lost their sense of wonder, have said of it because it does not measure up to what *they* say poetry ought to be. . . .

For the facts are . . . that Walter de la Mare was a consistent and resolute writer, a master of the English language both in prose and poetry, and one who has delighted—and will continue to delight—generations of readers of diverse gifts, beliefs and social class. He possessed an unusual talent—an individual vision, and this talent is unsurpassed in power and significance by any English poet within the field he made peculiarly his own. His poetry had no period limitations. Time which did not over-praise him in his own day, will not belittle him when it comes to the final reckoning. (p. 10)

Walter de la Mare wrote steadily for sixty years, seeking to perfect his craftsmanship and to develop that rare talent to the full; he succeeded in doing so in a score or so of poems and in a dozen or so of tales. These wear the bloom of immortality. How many writers ever do as much, for all the books they write? His imagination was unique, particularly in his own day, though of the same cast as Coleridge's and Poe's; he was blessed with foreknowledge and an uncanny understanding of children and their world; he knew by heart as well as by intellect what are the salient characteristics of childhood. Neither was he led astray by the more paradisal aspects of childhood, by the 'trailing clouds of glory'. He saw it, as D. H. Lawrence did, and Wordsworth did not, as a whole thing, divine, elemental, wayward, unfathomable. (p. 14)

[Until] he died in 1956, loved and honoured the world over, childhood was one of his major themes. To the end of his days he strove to bring home to his readers its characteristics of innocence, delight, imagination and deep feeling. And he made no distinction of quality whether he wrote for adults or children. (p. 19)

[Walter de la Mare's] unity with children was as the touch of dewdrop is to rosebud. He was, in fact, a practical mystic, who discovered very early in his life that it was the ugliness of the world which was always threatening to destroy his 'intimations of immortality.' Walter de la Mare was a true and unswerving man who accepted life and came to terms with it. . . . Until the day of his death he remained a bubbling spring of charmed English water. Many have drunk of that spring, deeply or in sips, but few have done so and not been affected in some measure by its power and enchantment. (pp. 23-4)

The secrets of Walter de la Mare's craftsmanship [as a poet] are quaint fancy, vowel melody, and cunning rhythm, all combining to give haunting overtones, strangeness and spellbinding dreams. The strongest influences upon his poetry were Shakespeare (most of de la Mare's fairies come from Shakespeare's England), Christina Rossetti and, to a lesser degree, Robert Louis Stevenson. But it must always be remembered how steeped he was in the knowledge and the spirit of traditional poetry, nursery rhymes, and the Bible. (pp. 29-30)

[It] is *Peacock Pie* which is de la Mare's masterpiece and finest memorial as far as his poetry for children is concerned. . . . [It presents a childhood world] which, full of fantasy and fun, is yet drenched in moonlight—romantic, brooding, questioning. Ghostly horsemen ride over the hill, and not so ghostly ones up to bed, 'someone' knocks at a small door, 'Whatever Miss T. eats, Turns into Miss T.', there is a cupboard of lollypops and Banbury cakes, and the boys and girls who dance, or float, through these pages are called Tim, Ann, Jemima, Bess, Henry, Jack, Dick and Lucy. These de la Mare children keep dogs and chickens, hate butchers, enjoy stories of the ship of Rio with a crew of ninety-nine monkeys, of the Watch trudging to and fro all through the night, of the old woman who went blackberry picking and met a fairy, of the thief who came to Robin's castle, of old farmer Turvey who danced farmers Bates and Giles off the ground. (pp. 33-4)

Peacock Pie also contains widows, sweeps, lonely spinsters, soldiers, sailors, old houses, and a new range of animals, including lion, bear, mole, donkey, pig, cat, and rat—all playing their part in a kind of enchanted children's zoo. Of course, there are witches and fairies with a few changelings into the bargain, and odd names such as Gimmul, Mel, Melmillo. The terrain seems to be an offshoot of a delightfully mad and inconsequential England, with English trees, and the English seasons, lit always by a wandering full moon, washed by great seas, and humming with sighing winds. Not all children will be able to enter this peacock territory, though many, the more imaginative ones, will do so easily and willingly. For all the changes in the social climate since de la Mare baked his extraordinary pie, the ingredients for children remain the same. Some of the wit and humour will not be obvious to a few, but how many will be able to resist the stories, the beasts, the strange grown-ups, the other children, and the 'othere worlde'? There cannot be many books of poetry with so many poems which have stood up so well to the test of time—*Some One, The Ship of Rio, Miss T., The Cupboard, The Window, Full Moon, The Quartette, Off The Ground, Nicholas Nye, Five Eyes, Silver, The Song of the Mad Prince*—to make but one selection. Children's debt to de la Mare can never be fully paid because he showed them, as no one had ever shown them before in quite the same way, how to see beauty and wonder in the most unlikely places. . . . It is a wonder which remains wonderful because its patina has the property of being able to stay bright for ever. Shakespeare's fairies in *A Midsummer Night's Dream* and the spirits from *The Tempest* would quickly recognise themselves in *Peacock Pie.* (pp. 34-6)

Most of de la Mare's poems for children, or about children, were included by him in *Collected Rhymes and Verses*. . . . —over three hundred of them. Three hundred poems. What a contribution to the poetry of childhood! Who has matched it in range and quality? Who has written finer poems about fairies, witches, winter, snow, dreamland, the moon? But it is necessary to study the earlier books in order to see how *Collected Rhymes and Verses* came into being.

Now what does all this amount to? How important *is* Walter de la Mare as a writer of poetry for children? Is he unique? What chances has he of survival? And if he survives into history, will he, two hundred and fifty years hence, be called 'minor', then?

Walter de la Mare was a poet who believed in the beauty and everlastingness of the human spirit. And he saw these flashes of eternity—as Traherne, Vaughan and Wordsworth had seen them before him—at their loveliest and strongest in childhood. His poetry has, in the first place, quality of a very high and individual order, and in the second, it concerns itself with that cosmos which is essentially the cosmos of childhood. Lear and Carroll were witty poets, Wordsworth was in deadly earnest, Blake saw children as a mystic enjoys heaven, Stevenson's children were wistful or gay, Allingham's, fanciful, Christina Rossetti held hers in her arms. But Walter de la Mare wrote as if he were a child himself, as if he were *revealing* his own childhood, though with the mature gifts of the authentic poet. His children are true to childhood. They are certainly not *all* children. But they are de la Mare children. And they are alive. He was ensnared by the boy who was the fatherless de la Mare. And that child was modest, withdrawn, in sensitive touch with terrors and splendours, never corrupted by the world, fanciful, constant. The de la Mare child has fears and uncertainties but unusual joys and pleasures. He dwells with common things but is never far in spirit from the supernatural. He is at one and the same time in an England of fields and seas, and in a Nowhere of dreams and sleep. This child is a complex being, very imaginative and always listening. De la Mare's verses and rhymes give delight because they go to the hearts of children, to the essence of childhood. As Lillian H. Smith wrote in *The Unreluctant Years:* 'It is this capacity to see

"the rarest charm of familiarity in strangeness," the beauty of this earth in its relation to spiritual beauty, separated one from the other only by a veil of gossamer compounded of imagination, vision, and dream, into which beauty breaks through when we least expect it. His mastery of flexible and subtle rhythms is so deft that it is, perhaps, hardly realised.'

No other English poet has possessed *all* these gifts, and as childhood more and more re-inherits its birthright, so will de la Mare be seen to be the rarest of them all because he trusted childhood's intuitive response. His genius was not so much in knowing by instinct, experience and observation, as in his ability to put all these into words which conveyed what he knew and felt, and yet had a divintiy of their own. (pp. 43-5)

Walter de la Mare was a writer whose voice was so personal and whose style so wonderfully matched that voice, they cannot accurately be torn apart. But the craftsmanship is there as well as the shining quality and unearthly loveliness; the glow of the fire as well as the fire itself. His poems, more so than his stories, are a part of the canon of children's literature, and will remain so. These poems see beauty on earth, are aware that beauty vanishes, but that its recognition, however minute, is sufficient to give a glimpse through a few cracks in Time into eternity. These poems are 'shoots of everlastingness'. And yet Walter de la Mare's full stature has yet to be acknowledged, even in his own country, and this perhaps, because he so often wrote of lonely mysteries. He was, too, a pioneer born into an age when writing for children was at a low ebb. Nevertheless it would be a mistake to think that he was only a poet who thought in terms of beauty. He was too forthright a character for that. Neither would it be proper to isolate what he wrote for children from the main body of his work. He wrote intuitively as if he were a child with a child's vision and willingness to believe, and for those who, besides children, retain in their spirits some of the genuine characteristics of children. We turn to Walter de la Mare, English poet and storyteller, for delight, innocence, perfect harmony of sound and colour, enormous variety of rhythms and poetic structure. We soar with him on the wings of imagination, so that on each cloud we see a child. He has also his distant echoes and inexplicable shadows. But, above all, he had a devotion to his art which was never obscured and which, in the end, is recognised as being purely religious, because it rejoiced in all creation, and hallowed its Creator. (pp. 75-6)

Leonard Clark, in his Walter de la Mare, *The Bodley Head, 1960, 82 p.*

Margery Fisher

Tolkein's [*The Hobbit* and *The Lord of the Rings* trilogy] is an intensely active, bardic work. It grew out of family story-telling over many years and it is communicated very directly to the reader. With Walter de la Mare we have a country described by a poet, where appearances matter as much as events, sometimes more. Here we have come back to the land of traditional fairy-tale, but we are seeing it through a magnifying glass. Take *Dick and the Beanstalk* for example. What a beanstalk it is—not *a* beanstalk but *the* beanstalk. When Dick came upon it, that rimy afternoon in Gloucestershire, he was bound to recognize it. How sharply visualized every detail is in this brilliant tale. . . . The barn where Grackle, the young giant, lies hidden, the giants' kitchen where Dick is nearly caught, the ogre's widow, the hills Dick sees in the distance, the very hair and hide of his pony—everything is precisely and superbly described.

This is a cheerful story, because Dick is a cheerful lad who does not worry about a little danger. In most of de la Mare's work there is an undercurrent of sadness, mystery and fear. He knows what is involved in a glance into the fairy world, however brief. His apparitions have nothing to do with the gauzy and inept creatures our children see on birthday-cards. It seems hardly right to call de la Mare's beings *fairies,* even using the word in its oldest sense. Perhaps the being in *Miss Jemima* is the nearest to a fairy:

> '. . . on the other side of the flat gravestone a face appeared. I mean it didn't rise up. It simply came into the air. A very small face, more oval than round, its gold-coloured hair over its wild greenish eyes falling on either side of its head in a curous zig-zag way . . .'

At least it is an extraordinarily evocative and mysterious picture. (pp. 87-8)

How could his beings fail to be unique, when he sees everything as freshly as a child would? One of his stories, *Maria-Fly,* illustrates not only the nature of a child but also of the poetic impulse. Maria, alone in a room, suddenly sees a fly. It seems to her as though she had never seen one before. She tries to communicate her vision, to the cook, to her father, to the gardener. Each one answers after his kind, each utterly fails to understand her. She goes on trying to explain:

> 'I—have—just—seen—a—fly. It had wings like as you see oil on water, and a red face with straight silver eyes, and it wasn't buzzing or nothing, but it was scraping with its front legs over its wings, then rubbing them like corkscrews. Then it took its head off and on, and then it began again—but I don't mean all that. I mean I sawn the fly—saw it, I mean.'

It is all there—the vision, the effort to communicate, the picture that comes to us. Maria, too, was a poet.

Even in this short, artless story, there is a feeling of precariousness, of one world dissolving into another. The fairy world of de la Mare is precise in detail but hazy in outline, a country unmapped and largely uninhabited. Even in a story like *The Three Sleeping Boys,* the harsh world of hunger and cold and soot, which is a version of historical fact, merges without effort into a silvery dreamland where the boys are at peace. In that incomparable piece of myth-making, *The Three Royal Monkeys,* the characters are the animals of the African plain and jungle, their names fancifully modified, and the country is, on the face of it, equally recognizable. But this, too, is a magic land, the land where the traveller must seek the fabulous stone called Kiph, the land of de la Mare's poems. Here all is strange and remote. An ancient hare makes magic; Nod, youngest of the monkey princes, is at once child, pongo and fairy; there is poetic hyperbole in the descriptions of fearful mountain passes and the beautiful gardens of Tishnar. Homely, prosaic details are fused with other-worldly beauty. . . . (p. 90)

Best of all de la Mare's stories is *The Lord Fish,* perhaps the most perfect example of imaginative prose, in fairy-tale idiom, of the present century. Here is the English countryside, tree, river, cottage, great house and all, but with the light of enchantment hanging over it. Here lives John, who tries to help his needy, hard-working mother, but who is led astray time and again by his passion for fishing. One day he leaps a stone wall, finds a mer-maiden in a stone tower, undergoes a transmogrification, and at last returns home with a princess for wife and a box of jewels. These are the bare bones of the story. How is it at once actual and magical, simple and full of overtones? Not with what happens, certainly, but with word after word a spell is woven round ordinary events. . . . The changing of John when he rubs himself with the green ointment is almost clinically described, yet there is magic in it too. . . . There is the Lord Fish who catches John, with grey glassy eyes and a cod-like chin and a hand that was 'little else but skin and bone'; there is the little maid with grey-green plaits and an ageless face who saves him; there is the larder where he hangs, with its glass jars of dried roots and lily-bulbs and various herbs for flavouring fish, and the great leaden casket stamped with an A for Almanara. All these things are precise and clear, but round them is an atmosphere of mystery, of other-worldliness. True, the village has a name; but the house has not, and the steward is only the Lord Fish; in short, behind the meticulous detail, the setting remains truly anonymous as it is anonymous in the tales of Grimm and Perrault. (pp. 92-3)

[The landscape of de la Mare's stories in *Collected Stories for Children*], as of other magic worlds, is to be visualized by each reader in his own way. For as he reads he will see in his mind's eye patterns and colours, scenes from real life, fragments from pictures half-remembered. Each of us makes a particular picture for each fairytale scene, so that illustrations do not represent the story to us. They decorate it, and help to send our imaginations off on a voyage which has no goal and no limit in time or space. De la Mare's stories reconcile the poet's skill and insight with the instinctive marvelling of a primitive mind. This is the true land of fairy-tale. (p. 93)

> *Margery Fisher, "The Land of Faerie: Traditional Fairy-Tales and Modern Variants," in her* Intent Upon Reading: A Critical Appraisal of Modern Fiction for Children, *Brockhampton Press, 1961, pp. 69-96.*

W. H. Auden

As a revelation of the wonders of the English Language, de la Mare's poems for children are unrivaled. (The only ones which do not seem to me quite to come off are those in which he tries to be humorous. A gift, like Hilaire Belloc's for the comic-satiric is not his; he lacks, perhaps, both the worldliness and the cruelty which the genre calls for.) They include what, for the adult, are among his greatest "pure" lyrics, e.g., *Old Shellover* and *The Song of the Mad Prince,* and their rhythms are as subtle as they are varied. Like all good poems, of course, they do more than train the ear. They also teach sensory attention and courage. Unlike a lot of second-rate verse for children, de la Mare's descriptions of birds, beasts, and natural phenomena are always sharp and accurate, and he never prettifies experience or attempts to conceal from the young that terror and nightmare are as essential characteristics of human existence as love and sweet dreams.

There is another respect in which, as all writers of good books for them know, children differ from grown-ups; they have a far greater tolerance for didactic instruction, whether in facts or morals. . . . Without ever being tiresome, de la Mare is not afraid to instruct the young. What could be more practically useful than his mnemonic rhyme *Stars,* or more educative, morally as well as musically, than *Hi!* ?

> Hi! handsome hunting man
> Fire your little gun.
> Bang! Now the animal
> Is dead and dumb and done.
> Nevermore to peep again, creep again, leap again,
> Eat or sleep or drink again. Oh, what fun!
>
> (pp. 389-90)

W. H. Auden, "Walter de la Mare," in his Forewords and Afterwords, *edited by Edward Mendelson, Random House, Inc., 1973, pp. 384-94.*

Leland Jacobs

Walter de la Mare is the poet's poet of childhood. His lines dance and gambol; his images of fairies and beasts and witches and farmers and kings and children are always masterfully sketched. His cadences are sparkling and sure. And he mixes perceptions of the realities of everyday living with the fanciful so deftly that his verses are always different from anything else one has ever read. . . .

Every good anthology of poetry includes some of de la Mare's poems. Indeed, were they not to be found, one would wonder if the anthologist knew his craft. One of the poems most widely quoted is **"Alas, Alack!"** It is a poem in the spirit of Mother Goose: the content is slight but earthy (a talking fish in the frying pan mourns his fate); the mood is light and folksy; the style is direct, stripped of all superfluity. From the opening admonition to Ann, "Come quick as you can," through the closing lines, in which the fish "turned to his sizzling" in the frying pan, the tempo is swift, verbs ("talked," "moaned," "sank") are virile, and the bizarre situation created, while sufficiently open for the reader to use his imagination, is graphic and credible.

Another of de la Mare's most widely quoted poems is **"Some One."** This poem epitomizes one of the strongest threads running through his lines for children—that of posing an unanswered query, of leaving the reader or listener wondering and pondering. In **"Some One,"** although the question of who was knocking at the "wee, small door" is never answered, there is no ambiguity in the actions ("I listened, I opened, I looked to left and right") or the sounds (the busy beetle "tap-tapping in the wall," "the screech-owl's call," the cricket's "whistling") presented in the poem. Children are sure to want to guess, and hear again, and guess some more about who was at the door. . . .

Walter de la Mare also wrote of the everyday happenings of childhood. An everyday experience that always seems to fascinate young children is having one's hair cut. The barber is almost a magical wonder, as the poet tells us so well in **"The Barber's."** (p. 100)

In poems such as **"The Cupboard," "Chicken," "The Huntsmen," "Tired Tim,"** which express the reality of

childhood, there is always found an extraordinary facility to illumine the daily experience with sensitive, fresh insights. For example: In **"The Cupboard,"** notice the "dark as dark can be" shelf from which the much desired lollypops and banberry cakes come when the child has been good. What a precise picture, too, the poet creates of the "small, fat grandmamma," "with a very slippery knee." . . .

For older boys and girls, de la Mare's deft character sketches of three quite different children in **"Bunches of Grapes"** should lead to considerable discussion and speculation. . . .

Here is Timothy, an imaginative, gentle boy; Elaine, a dainty, dreamy girl; and Jane, a robust, busy child who gets great joy from everyday, ordinary things. The selection of the children's names seems to go right along with their comments on foods, flowers, and rides. . . .

The poem invites going on: What vegetables, what games, what books might well be the choices of each of these children? From just the phrases which each child says, it is possible to develop much of what they would look like, how they would behave.

De la Mare's poems of fanciful folk are not from the traditional fairy realm. They are creatures of far more robust doings than could be accomplished by gossamer wings and delicate fay movements. **"Tillie"**—really "Old Tillie Turveycombe"—who, when she yawned, swallowed a magic fern seed and thenceforth has been floating around on the wind, is splendidly homely nonsense.

Throughout de la Mare's poems in **Songs of Childhood, Peacock Pie, Come Hither, Down-Adown-Derry, Poems for Children,** and **Bells and Grass,** one notes certain poetic qualities that make his work distinctive: his keen ear for what is melodious, his neatly varied rhythms, his sensitive creation of mood and feeling, his unique subject matter whether it be things ordinary or extraordinary.

Walter de la Mare once wrote that "only the rarest kind of best in anything can be good enough for the young." His own poetry for children is an apt illustration of that "rarest kind of best." (p. 108)

Leland Jacobs, "Walter de la Mare," in Instructor, *Vol. LXXIII, No. 5, January, 1964, pp. 100, 108.*

Roger Lancelyn Green

[The] strange, homely tales of wonder [in **Broomsticks, and Other Tales** and **The Lord Fish, and Other Tales**] captivate a limited audience—and are frequently foisted on children by adults who have fallen under their very real spell. It *is* a spell, however, and one of selective magic, catching some readers away into the true lands of enchantment, and boring others to distraction. In his proper field, however, de la Mare was one of the greatest poets of the first part of this century, and perhaps the only great poet of childhood since Blake. [His] are definitely 'poems' and not 'verses' such as Mrs Hart, Stevenson and Milne had written; though some were no more than beautiful, happy jingles, the majority aimed higher and achieve the perfect bridge between the child's delighted awareness of rhythm and rhyme growing through Nonsense verse and versified nursery lore and the great verse narratives like 'Horatius' and 'The Pied Piper of Hamlyn', and the first intoxicating draught of Keats or Milton, William Morris or Tennyson. (p. 270)

Roger Lancelyn Green, "New Wonderlands," in his Tellers of Tales, revised edition, 1965. Reprint by Kaye & Ward, Ltd., 1969, pp. 269-79.

Doris Ross McCrosson

Since the publication in 1902 of *Songs of Childhood* . . . , de la Mare's reputation has rested principally on his poetry. What anthology of recent British poetry has not included **"The Listeners"**? What school child has not, at one time or another, intoned " 'Is there anybody there?' said the Traveller . . . " and has not wondered who, really, is the Traveller? Happily, some have gone on to read more of de la Mare's poetry to find that, in the poet's view, we are all Travellers and all Listeners.

So often, however, have the words "childlike" and "faerie" been applied to de la Mare's poetry that all but the most careful readers are likely to think of the poet as having a rather fey and delightful, but a little too precious, imagination; that his poetry is not about the real world at all. Nothing, of course, can be further from the truth. For de la Mare was aware that in the very innocence of childhood can be found the later evil. . . . [To] claim that de la Mare's poetry is realistic in the accepted sense of the word would be to do a disservice to a poet who, I think, may well rank in time to come, at least in certain respects, with Yeats. There is, of course, no place here to go into a detailed comparison of the two poets; but Yeats, although unquestionably the greater poet, appeals today to a certain extent because of his complexity. As T. S. Eliot and a score of others have reminded us, modern poetry is complex because the age is complex. But perhaps in this idea lies the explanation for de la Mare's apparent simplicity: he is not reflecting this age or any other specific time. He is not topical—a word which, paradoxically, can be applied to Yeats; he is not Romantic, Victorian, Georgian; he is not even metaphysical although W. H. Auden suggests that in his later work there are suggestions of metaphysical wit. De la Mare's finest poetry—and a great deal of it is fine—is above, or beyond, topicality.

Perhaps the real difficulty in the term "childlike" is that it connotes "childish" to a great many people who probably also confuse sentiment with sentimentality. If one agrees with de la Mare's conception that the "childlike" imagination is opposed to that of "boyhood" . . . , one must agree that de la Mare's own imagination is childlike; that is to say, it is "intuitive, inductive" rather than "logical, deductive." It is true, also, that de la Mare wrote a good many poems about and for children: a rough estimate of the number of poems in his collection of children's poems, *Rhymes and Verses* shows approximately six hundred poems. But they are not by any means poems exclusively for children; and, if one thinks of children as having the sensibilities that the "Run, Dick, Run," authors seem to think they have, these poems are not for children at all. . . .

[What] is childlike in de la Mare is that same awareness and perception that one finds in William Blake and Emily Dickinson, both of whom he resembles more than superficially. They also illustrate my feeling that de la Mare's poems are not topical: they do not reflect this age any more than they do any other historical period. As W. H. Auden recently pointed out, in de la Mare's poetry there are no machines and no modern buildings. One could easily go further: there is no concern with politics or history, or with creeds or with religion itself; neither is he a philosopher, for he has no specific answers to the epistemological and teleological questions all philosophers must somehow answer.

If these are none of Walter de la Mare's concerns, then what is his poetry about? It is about nothing more or less than the human condition. *Who are we? What are we? Whence? Whither? Why?*—these are the major themes not only of his poetry but also of his fiction. To define these questions, let alone to attempt to answer them, is to make even the most inarticulate among us, in a sense, poets. Adequately to define them is what de la Mare did. He did not, however, propose any answers: there is no progression (or retreat, some might call it), as in Eliot's poetry; there is no reaching for certainties, as in Yeats's. In a sense, de la Mare is more nearly like Aldous Huxley, who continued to grope intellectually although he seemed certain that there were no answers. De la Mare continued to explore, but his was an emotional, intuitive search and therefore more sure. In other words, although Huxley mistrusted intellectualism, he was unable to escape from it and thus became disillusioned; de la Mare, although he too mistrusted the intellect, still was able to retain the belief that life is somehow meaningful. He knew he did not know the answers; he knew he could never know them; but he did not despair. Nor did he think life is a cosmic joke because he knew that someone or something would have had to have played it, and his poetry shows he was uncertain even about the existence of a someone or something:

Starven with cares, like tares in wheat,
Wildered with knowledge, chilled with doubt,
The timeless self in vain must beat
Against its walls to hasten out
Whither the living waters fount . . .
(from **"Dreams,"** *The Fleeting*)

It is the "timeless self," then, about which de la Mare was concerned. But notice, this "self" *must* beat against its walls *in vain*. This conception, central in all of his work, removes him forever from any consideration as "childlike" or "faerie" in the usual senses of those terms. This conception also explains his preoccupation with death, dreams, the supernatural, children, and nature. (pp. 47-51)

Among Walter de la Mare's best poems are those he wrote for and about children. (p. 63)

[Never] once to my knowledge does de la Mare patronize or, for that matter, idealize children. They are from his point of view neither miniature, and therefore rather dull, adults—nor sage philosophers and seers blessed. And his interest in childhood was not the result of an escape mechanism; or, if it were, it is not apparent in his work. His poems reflect his fascination and delight in children and, even more apparently, his knowledge of them. He seems to know almost instinctively what appeals to them, as well as what they are really like.

What child is not delighted by rhythmic sound: " 'Grill me some bones,' said the Cobbler"; "Whsst, and away and over the green, / Scampered a shape that was never seen"; "Old Tillie Turveycombe / Sat to sew"; "Far away in Nanga-noon / Lived an old and grey Baboon"; "Slowly, silently, now the moon / Walks the night in her silver shoon." The sounds enchant. But it is not for the sounds only that de la Mare's rhymes and verses captivate children. They can be as grizzly and terrible as any child could wish; an understated horror, however, enhances their terror. "At the Keyhole," of which " 'Grill me some bones,' said the Cobbler," is the first line, is an outstanding example of this technique. Another even more subtle one is **"I Can't Abear"**:

> I can't abear a Butcher,
> I can't abide his meat,
> The ugliest shop of all is his,
> The ugliest in the street;
> Bakers' are warm, cobblers' dark
> Chemists' burn watery lights;
> But oh, the sawdust butcher's shop,
> That ugliest of sights!

In such a poem the speaker does not need to tell what the sights are. Any child hearing or reading **"I Can't Abear"** can imagine them—that is, any child who has ever seen anything other than pre-packaged, supermarket meat.

But although de la Mare sometimes assumes the point of view of a child, he also comments upon a child's fascination with bloodshed and death. **"Dry August Burned"** is such a comment. In it a small child has seen a newly-shot hare lying on the kitchen table, and she "wept out her heart to see it there." Soon, the sound of soldiers on their way to maneuvers in a field nearby interrupts her weeping. She runs out-of-doors to watch them pass,

> And then—the wonder and the tumult gone—
> Stood nibbling a green leaf, alone,
> Her dark eyes, dreaming. . . . She turned, and ran,
> Elf-like, into the house again.

and into the kitchen where she finds her mother. The devastating conclusion to the poem comes as the child, "her tear-stained cheek now flushed with red," looks for the rabbit and asks her mother, "Please, may I go and see it skinned?"

Of course, **"Dry August Burned"** is about more than one child, and the situation can be generalized to have far greater significance than that of a child discovering the fascination of death. The initial impact worn off: "Mother, then what happens?" is the child's normal response. The poem also shows that de la Mare's vision of childhood was not by any means sentimentalized or unrealistic: his appraisal was shrewd.

His genius for seeing and for discovering nature as a child does is apparent in so many of his rhymes that it is difficult to select one or two for purposes of illustration. "Before I melt / Come, look at me!" cries a newly-fallen snowflake who then goes on to boast,

> Of a great forest
> In one night
> I make a wilderness
> Of white.

The power of the snowflake established, reality reasserts itself as the snowflake admits, "Breathe, and I vanish / Instantly." It is just a short step in the imagination of a child

from the fate of the snowflake to the fate of all things in a child's world—including himself. Children do not articulate these feelings because they do not have the words with which to do so. If one asked a child who has just breathed upon a snowflake what he is thinking, one could not possibly expect to have him say, "Oh, I am thinking of the transience of all things lovely, including myself." But one knows that in some preternatural way that this is the knowledge that the child has gained from the experience. (pp. 64-6)

A child's mind is uncluttered; it is occupied with the elemental things to which it attends with unwavering, though brief, concentration. Truly Blakean, de la Mare knew what it was to "see a world in a grain of sand" and knew that this is the way children see. But, although a child's imagination can see "eternity in an hour," it can also see without comprehension the realities of existence—among which one must include death. (p. 68)

De la Mare also sees children from an adult point of view and especially later in life the tone of his poetry is tinged with nostalgia. . . . (p. 70)

Relatively few, however, are the poems which look somewhat wistfully and longingly at that lost paradise, that "pre-Edenic" peace that childhood was, or that an aging adult might think it was. To emphasize them would be a disservice to the great bulk of his rhymes and verses for children, many of which have already become classics:

> Ann, Ann!
> Come! quick as you can!
> There's a fish that *talks*
> In the frying-pan.

This one poem is enough to endear de la Mare to all children. (p. 71)

Doris Ross McCrosson, in her Walter de la Mare, *Twayne Publishers, Inc., 1966, 170 p.*

Elizabeth Nesbitt

Among the loveliest of all the quest books is Walter de la Mare's *The Three Mulla-Mulgars*. . . . There should be little need to stress the shining quality and unearthly beauty of De la Mare's style, with its power of underlining the story with the saving grace of great compassion for the fears and sorrows, the elusive hopes of mankind, and equally with the faith-reviving perception of man's eternal striving and potential greatness.

This is a story of the search of three royal monkeys for the vale of Tishnar, the symbol of all things lovely and hoped for. Once read, it haunts the memory, and one returns to it again and again, each time hoping for new insight into its ineffable secret. It has moments of fear and awe and great drama, but its most lasting impression is of a great capacity for love and tenderness. He who reads is enriched by the sharing of this capacity, especially in the feeling aroused for Nod, the tiny monkey to whom, because there is magic in him, is given the Wonderstone, the talisman for their journey. He is so pitiably anxious, so often sad and lonely and weary, so oppressed by the weight of his burden—and yet so indomitable in the discharge of his responsibility. It is impossible to overpraise this book—it is impossible to praise it adequately. (p. 347)

It is impossible to form any transition from other poetry of and for childhood to that of Walter de la Mare. His poetry simply exists in itself, independent of significances and trends and time. There had been others, and would be others, who write for childhood with a sure touch, but none with his penetrating and illuminating insight. There had been others who wrote of the beauty of this world, but none with his sense of the transience of beauty, and at the same time his perception that the evanescent beauty of this world affords a glimpse into a greater and eternal beauty. There had been others who invoked the supernatural, but none in his varied keys—weird, grotesque, mysterious, enchanted. There had been others who were fascinated by sleep and dreams, but none with his feeling of lovely mystery. There were others who had mastery over words and form, but none greater than his. He loves England as Chaucer loved it, as a "land all possessed of faërie," as Shakespeare and Kipling loved it. (pp. 380-81) . . .

The name of De la Mare is now famous, but a first reading of the **Songs** must have been an unforgettable and not to be repeated experience. It is easy to trace here similarities to William Blake, to the Pre-Raphaelites, to Keats, but there is something more, something indefinably De la Mare. There is his rich, rare power of imagination, which can imbue the eerie, the grotesque, even the gruesome, with a strange beauty; which can give to nursery rhymes an exquisite charm; which can, through perception of the significance of finite beauty, give a momentary glimpse into the infinite. There is in this book the secret life of childhood, the enchantment of the land of faerie, the spirit of England, that "land so witchery sweet." There is in it the liquid loveliness of his lullabies. . . . To the fullest extent the second collection [**Peacock Pie**] fulfills the promise of the first. There are nursery rhymes, strongly individualized by the De la Mare touch; verses with rare and unique nonsensical conception; fairy tales that seem to belong to the beginning of time; the strange and haunting mystery of **"The Little Green Orchard"** and of **"Some One"**; the twilight spell of **"Dream-Song"**; the soft, gleaming patina of **"Silver."** His exquisite melody, his extraordinary facility in varied rhythm, lend to his poems, even those which at first sight seem to be mere objective stories, a haunting sense of ultimate significance. It is just this combination of penetrating and illuminating vision made apprehensible by music of word and line that gives to De la Mare's poetry such distinct and unique loveliness.

A Child's Day is the writing of a man whose tender understanding of the importance and meaning of childhood is so finely expressed in **Early One Morning in the Spring,** and in the introduction to his anthology **Come Hither.** This long narrative poem surrounds the child with a love that is completely without sentimentality. Simply and objectively, but with moving charm and revealing imaginative quality, it draws a picture of a small child's day; a day of routine experiences, made exciting and novel by touches of nonsense and humor; a day of wonder and dreams and half-seen visions, caught in some of De la Mare's loveliest songs. (pp. 381-82)

[His] perceptiveness of the vision of a child gives to the poetry of De la Mare an unequaled supremacy in inspiration and high poetic quality, in understanding and interpretation, in abundance of mood and emotion, in diverse but always extraordinary imaginative quality, in pervasive, poignant beauty. (p. 383)

Elizabeth Nesbitt "A Rightful Heritage: 1890-1920," in A Critical History of Children's Literature, *by Cornelia Meigs and others, edited by Cornelia Meigs, revised edition, Macmillan Publishing Company, 1969, pp. 275-392.*

Eleanor Cameron

A fantastical world, most particularly, it seems to me—such as the one Alice discovered underground and beyond the looking glass—must give the reader a sense of endlessly flowing imaginative vigor on the part of its creator. Once one is aware of any thinness or paleness, any wavering in the clarity of detail which can only have resulted from lack of knowledge or of vision, immediately one's disbelief ceases to be suspended, the whole edifice disintegrates, together with the thoughts and feelings which had pervaded it, and all is lost. What is so remarkable in the work of such writers as Swift in *Gulliver's Travels,* as Tolkien in *The Hobbit* (and even more overwhelmingly in *The Lord of the Rings*) and de la Mare in **The Three Royal Monkeys,** is exactly this feeling that the author seems never to be telling all he knows.

The Three Royal Monkeys has been called de la Mare's prose masterpiece, one of the most poetical tales ever written for children. Here is another created world complete with landscape, inhabitants, language and beliefs. Where it must lie, precisely, is hard to tell, for the towering Munza forests, with their Ephelantoes, Skeetoes, Coccadrilloes, Jaccatrays, Babbaboomas, Zevveras and all kinds of Mulgars (monkeys), from Mulla-Mulgars (royal monkeys) to Munza-Mulgars, Gunga-Mulgars and the dread, flesh-eating Minimuls, seem now Indian, now African. Tolkien speaks of cream and honey and clover and cockscomb and pines and bracken. But de la Mare puts before us a flora of evening-blooming Immamoosa, of Gelica, Exxwixxia, Samarak, Manga, Nano and Ukka trees. Little Nod stores Ukka nuts against the Witzaweelwülla, the White Winter, and makes Sudd loaves, Manaka cake, Manga cheese, and Subbub, a kind of drink. The boundaries of this world seem to be the dark forests of the Munza on the one hand and the shining Land of Tishnar with its Ummuz groves on the other, toward which Nod and his brothers travel in intense and wasting cold through the forests of the Telateuti and up over the terrible mountains of the Arrakaboa.

None of these Munza names have we ever heard before, nor are they to be found in any dictionary. Yet all are hauntingly familiar: known names, perhaps, syllabled through monkey lips, some shortened like Nano, some coughed like Ukka, some lengthened like Babbabooma, others softened like Zevvera and some comically changed like Ephelanto. But the wealth of flora and fauna, named and visualized, is only a part of de la Mare's marvel of place, for something *felt* pervades it, which is almost impossible to analyze—and this is exactly de la Mare's power as a poet. He has somehow made belief haunt his country of the mind, the animals' belief in things sensed but rarely seen: Noomas, shadows, a word which comes from Noomanossi—darkness, change, and the unreturning; Meermuts, shadows of lesser light lost in Tishnar's radiance; and Tishnar itself, a very ancient word in Munza meaning that which cannot be thought about, or spoken in words—the wonder of sea and wind and stars and the endless unknown. We are seeing this created world through a monkey's eyes, not just an ordinary monkey, but little Nod . . . , who was royal and who was filled with an unspeakable longing. It was said of him that he had the color of Tishnar in his eyes, and we do most hauntingly hear the phantom music of Tishnar pervading the book, as though de la Mare had held Nod's Wonderstone as he wrote, rubbing it occasionally with his thumb, samaweeza: left to right, which was the only way the magic worked. (pp. 197-99)

> Eleanor Cameron, "Writing Itself," in her The Green and Burning Tree: On the Writing and Enjoyment of Children's Books, Atlantic-Little, Brown, 1969, pp. 137-230.

Joan Aiken

I can date some of my first reading quite accurately because of two major events that happened in my life early on. At the age of about three and a half I had diphtheria, and then when I was nearly five my family moved from the house I was born, in Rye, to the house where my mother and my stepfather still live. So from the circumstances in which I first read some books, or they were read to me, I can tell how old I was at the time. (p. 30)

[My] favourite books were those with a mysterious déja vu atmosphere to them. I had all the proper things read to me and I loved Peter Rabbit and the Just So Stories and Mother Goose and Struwelpeter—but four in particular had a really powerful effect. One of them was Pinocchio. . . . (p. 32)

Anyway that was at age two. The next two books that made a mark, when I was between three and four, having my diphtheria, were both by de la Mare: Peacock Pie and the Three Mulla Mulgars. In Peacock Pie the poem that unquestionably had the most impact was 'Someone came knocking at my wee, small door'. I knew masses of those Peacock Pie poems by heart before I could read them myself, but that one, with its unanswered question, its mysterious location and its marvellous Heath Robinson illustration, lent a kind of dark aura to everything else in the book. . . . (p. 33)

My younger brother, a sensitive child, could hardly bear that poem when it was later read to him, and had a phobia about beetles for years. There are lots of other poems almost equally potent in Peacock Pie—'Grill me some bones, Susie' and 'Old Shellover' and 'Miss T' and the mocking fairy in the garden. I doubt if a better collection of children's poems will ever be written. After that we went on to the Three Mulla Mulgars which is a unique work of genius. (pp. 33-4)

The Three Mulla Mulgars embodies absolutely all the qualities that so appealed to me then. To begin with it is set in some mysterious, removed region of forest and mountain with its own flora and fauna—ollaconda trees, mullabruks, jaccatrays, skeetos. . . . But that was by no means all, for the father of the three heroes had himself come from yet another, even more beautiful, luminous, Eden-like lost country, and he set off almost before the story opened to return to it, so that the heroes have to follow after him on a pilgrimage that takes the whole book.

In fact it is never disclosed whether they find their father or not—part of de la Mare's genius is that he leaves so many things unexplained. For instance the strange winter, a sort of supernatural Fimbulwinter, which descended, it seemed for ever, on what had apparently before that been a tropical region. Reading the book again in one's teens one guessed that this was a dead season like that caused by Persephone's absence. The story has all the classic features of myth; talking beasts, witch-hares, loreleilike water maidens on the underground river that the three travellers have to navigate, who try to seduce them from their quest, as well as its own—I'll have to call it religion; the divine, omnipresent Tishnar, and the frighteningly beautiful, leopardlike Nemesis-character Immanala, who though temporarily defeated by Nod the hero was, one realized, immortal and would always return. The language of the book is hauntingly beautiful. I can remember from when I was three, my elder brother and sister reciting like a sort of incantation:

> The Queen of the Mountains is in the forest. With fingers of frost. And shoulders of snow. And feet of ice. Colder and colder, pigs my brothers, colder and colder, colder and colder.

And the details are all marvellously telling and thought out. (p. 34)

> Joan Aiken, "A Thread of Mystery," in Children's literature in education, No. 2, July, 1970, pp. 30-47.

Keith Clark

One of the most important factors behind the success of any writer for children is the ability to re-create the essence of childhood with sympathy and understanding. Although this ability can be seen in many great children's writers, no one children's writer had such a complete understanding of his readers as did Walter de la Mare—the popularity of his books, and the regularity with which his poems appear, even in modern anthologies, illustrates this well. (pp. 89-90)

[Although The Three Mulla-Mulgars] was a considerable success—and has since become accepted as a classic book for children—de la Mare did not really become established amongst the front ranks of the army of children's writers until the publication in 1913 of the collection of poems with that tempting, magical title—Peacock Pie.

Peacock Pie is, without doubt, a masterpiece. Few other poets could manage to combine fantasy, humour and pathos so well, and in so many varied situations. The poems, whether they are about witches, fairies, veteran soldiers forced to beg for food, lonely women, or ships with ninety-nine monkeys for the crew, are all written in a manner that makes them compulsive reading, and with a rhythm (and often humour) that makes them positively itch to be recited. . . . (pp. 90-1)

Many of the characters and situations are portrayed so vividly that one finds oneself forgetting they are fictional and starting to associate oneself—or someone one knows—with the poem. Who has not at some time thought like the child in The Window?

> Behind the blind I sit and watch
> The people passing—passing by,

And not a single one can see
My tiny watching eye
They cannot see my little room,
All yellowed with the shaded sun,
They do not even know I'm here
Nor'll guess when I am gone.

(p. 91)

De la Mare wrote prolifically—short stories, novels, lectures, appreciations, essays, anthologies, forewords, even a play. Although he will always be remembered as one of the great twentieth century English poets (on his 80th birthday *The Times* wrote that the love of English poetry will have faded away if ever his name was forgotten) it is for children that he left his richest heritage—and for those adults fortunate not to have had all their imagination drained by the pressures and responsibilities of adulthood. . . . His world is made up of people of simplicity and innocence, in fact people that one can feel actually exist—even those that encounter witches, fairies and the forces of evil. His poems, which have introduced thousands of children to the pleasures to be found in verse, are like the traditional ballads—they yearn to be recited, perhaps even sung, rather than be confined to the printed page. Meanwhile his stories have all the qualities of the most well-known, most loved, fairy tales.

His imagination, sensitivity, and his great compassion and understanding of children will always cause him to be loved by generations of young people. (pp. 92-3)

Keith Clark, "A Child of Mature Years: Walter de la Mare 1873-1956," in The Junior Bookshelf, *Vol. 37, No. 2, April, 1973, pp. 89-93.*

Sam Leaton Sebesta and William J. Iverson

In one of his fanciful short stories for children ["**The Lord Fish**"] Walter de la Mare comments: "But there is a music in the voice that tells more to those who understand it than can any words in a dictionary." Such word music is the triumph of his work, especially in his long book, ***The Three Royal Monkeys.*** From its beginning, it is filled with strange lulling language that must be read rhythmically aloud. . . . (p. 189)

The three sons set out for the Valley of Tishnar to find their father. Nod is separated from his brothers and captured by the Oomgar Mulga, a man. This relationship (chapters 9 through 12 in the book) forms one of the strangest, most captivating passages in all imaginative literature. Not until L. M. Boston's *A Stranger at Green Knowe,* wherein a Chinese boy and an escaped gorilla befriend each other in the woods of an English estate, do we find anything that tells so movingly of an animal and a human attempting to understand each other. . . .

If you develop a love for the sounds and rhythms of language through a book such as ***The Three Royal Monkeys,*** you have gained a great gift of aesthetic and communicative value. This facet of language has sometimes been neglected in modern teaching, although its power ought to be apparent as you witness the often fumbling attempts of modern rock lyricists to tap it. At any rate, the language of Walter de la Mare, borne by his animal kingdom, ought to be sampled. The book may have retreated in popularity, but we predict that it will return. (p. 190)

Sam Leaton Sebesta and William J. Iverson, "Fanciful Fiction," in their Literature for Thursday's Child, *Science Research Associates, Inc., 1975, pp. 177-214.*

Richard Adams

[*The following excerpt is from an essay in which Adams recalls his childhood reading and its influence on his epic fantasy* Watership Down.]

Only the other day I was reading an article . . . which threw out, almost *en passant,* and apparently as a truism, the remark that of course children need books which assure them of an established moral order—and this from a trendy young man, a lecturer in English at a university. For years of my childhood I found solace and delight in the poems of Walter de la Mare. These are informed throughout, in the most disturbing manner, by a deep sense of mankind's ultimate ignorance and insecurity. (**'The Children of Stare'** is a really frightening poem in my opinion.) De la Mare scarcely mentions Christianity—if indeed he can be said to mention it at all. Cold, ghosts, grief, pain and loss stand all about the little cocoon of bright warmth, which is everywhere pierced by a wild, numinous beauty, catalyst of fear and weeping. Why ever should this be comforting? First, I think, simply because the words, sounds and rhythms are so beautiful. John Mouldy in his cellar is beautiful in the same way as Agamemnon's dreadful death-cry from within the palace. Secondly, the poems possess and confer dignity—they make you feel, though perhaps unconsciously, that the human race is nobler and grander than you knew. . . . Thirdly, they tell the truth. I used to weep at the grief of the Mad Prince, of poor Robin and his wife, of Dame Hickory and Mrs Gill. But I also felt that this poet treated me as a potential adult and showed respect for me by telling me the truth—and all in words of storm, rainbow and wave. His sorrow was better than Mabel Lucie Attwell's reassurance. From de la Mare I derived early the idea that one must at all costs tell the truth to children, not so much about mere physical pain and fear but about the really unanswerable things—what Thomas Hardy called 'the essential grimness of the human situation'. (pp. 164-65)

[I can hear someone saying about *Watership Down,* surely] you derived from the Pilgrim's Progress the concept of Journey, didn't you? Perhaps I did—but here it is another book which I think of. No one told me about it. I had never heard of it. I found it by myself, in my prep. school library, at the age of eleven. It was a first edition (by Duckworth) and had at that time been extant only seventeen years—Walter de la Mare's ***The Three Mulla-Mulgars*** (now known for the worse as ***The Three Royal Monkeys***). For me, this great work was a milestone of profound importance. It opened my eyes. A tear springs to my eye as I think of what I owe to it. At the time, it seemed that this alone was a story and that all others were mere attempts at stories. I need not speak of the Mulgars' journey. From it I understood, darkly, that we are all wandering in the snow, to an unknown destination beyond darkness and hypnotic water. Never pretend otherwise. I understood, too, for the first time, that the greatest achievement of a great novel is to create, by feeling, selection and emphasis, a particular world, having its own colours, its own sun and moon, climate, atmosphere and values (how inadequate are words), more real than those of the actual world, to which the devoted reader can return again and again for delight and comfort. Years later, I was able to meet Walter de la Mare and thank him—thank God. Once only have I ever experienced the same thing with comparable force and passion. Seven years afterwards, at Oxford, the music of Chopin hit me like a thunderbolt and became for many months a coloured lens through which all the world was seen.

To try to copy *The Three Mulla-Mulgars* would be like trying to copy *King Lear.* But involuntarily, certain specific incidents and features of *Watership Down* undoubtedly reflect, *mutatis mutandis,* that unparalleled work—rather as the William books may be said to reflect *Huckleberry Finn.* Most obviously, of course, there is the weakling hero with the second sight who guides and saves his friends, sometimes despite their disbelief or contempt. Fiver is Ummanodda, no danger. And Fiver's meeting, in a trance, with the man putting up the board in memory of Hazel, recalls Nod's dream of the Oomgar's spelling-book, which led him to save the Moona-Mulgar who had fallen over the ledge during the fight with the eagles. The Black Rabbit of Inlé owes something to the Immanâla; though she is wicked and hateful, while the Black Rabbit is not. He is, rather, a counterpart of the Hindu Kali—the terrible but necessary death-aspect of God's face.

One thing of a different nature I owe to *The Three Mulla-Mulgars.* My family, all of them, scoffed and jeered—a shade harshly, I fancy—at my passion for it. No doubt I was a bore, but the pain taught me, once and for all, never to mock any child's feeling for any book—you never know what it may mean to him. And it drove the Mulgars underground, to germinate in silence and darkness—the best conditions for such a process, I dare say. (pp. 168-69)

> Richard Adams, *"Some Ingredients of 'Watership Down',"* in The Thorny Paradise: Writers on Writing for Children, *edited by Edward Blishen, Kestrel Books, 1975, pp. 163-73.*

Susan Cooper

[*Come Hither* is] one of the most remarkable books in the English language. . . . I've had my copy of this wonder for thirty years and must have turned to it at least as many times each year—sometimes for solace, sometimes for sunlight, always with an emotion that I have never quite been able to define. *Come Hither* is my talisman, my haunting: a distillation of the mysterious quality that sings out of all the books to which I've responded most deeply all my life—and that I dearly hope, as a writer, I might someday, somehow, be able to catch. But the quality is an evanescent as a rainbow; it will never stay to be examined. It's a kind of magic, but not from books which are necessarily *about* magic—not at all. What is it?

I don't know, but it's high time I tried to find out.

To begin at the beginning: *Come Hither* is magical not simply because it's a wonderfully far-ranging collection of verse put together by a very remarkable poet, but because it has an introduction and a set of notes half as long again as the verse. That doesn't sound very promising, I grant you. But the notes are no ordinary notes. They are the musings of a full and most agile mind, which wanders over hill and dale instead of keeping to the narrow path of scholarship. You read, for instance, an early poem which

is a kind of general wassail, entitled "Bring Us In Good Ale"—and you find as a note to it the engaging information that in 1512 the two young sons of the Earl of Northumberland were allowed for their daily breakfast " 'Half a Loif of houshold Brede, a Manchet, a Dysch of butter, a Pece of Saltfish, a Dysch of Sproits or iii White herrynge' "—and eight mugs of ale.

Or there's the note to Chaucer's lines about the month of May, when, as you will remember, "the foules singe / And . . . the floures ginnen for to springe." This transports de la Mare into five pages of beautifully random reflections about flowers, including the observation that Shakespeare never mentions foxgloves once in all his plays—though he names the rose fifty-seven times and the violet eighteen. The reason turns out to be that foxgloves dislike limestone and are rarely found in South Warwickshire. So that, says our editor, "it is possible . . . that Shakespeare when a child never saw a foxglove . . . and it is what we see early in life that comes back easiest later." (It is, indeed. And it is, I suspect, the root of what I'm talking about.)

Now, I don't know about you, but when I was reading scholarly editions of this and that at university, I was never blessed with footnotes like those. (pp. 498-99)

[In the introduction to *Come Hither,* which is called "The Story of This Book," the] boy, Simon, set out to find East Dene and instead came upon a house in a valley, at which he stared, down and down. And then he went down, to the house. Its name was inscribed in faded letters on the gateway: THRAE. It was an old, old house with embrasured windows, a round stone tower with a twirling weathervane, and a great overgrown garden. And an old lady lived there, called Miss Taroone.

Our boy came back to visit it again and again, growing bolder and going closer each time, and at length he met Miss Taroone and came to know her house with its multitude of rooms. He heard that she had once lived on another more ancient family estate called Sure Vine. He learned of some villages nearby called the Ten Laps, and was told that there was indeed a way to East Dene from this house—he would come to a Wall and would have to climb over.

But instead of going hunting for East Dene, he stayed to explore Miss Taroone's house. (p. 499)

[Miss Taroone tells] the boy about Nahum Tarune: Mr. Nahum. He was never quite sure of Mr. Nahum's relationship to her, but only that she had raised and taught him and that he had grown up in this house. One day she took Simon to the round room at the very top of the old stone tower, Nahum's room, and left him free to look at everything in it. It was the kind of marvelous room that you find described in books quite often, so often that I suspect every writer secretly hankers after it—or perhaps it's an image of the inside of any artist's mind. It was not unlike Merlin's room in *The Sword in the Stone.* . . . (pp. 499-500)

Every inch of space on the walls, in this cluttered room, was covered in pictures painted by the absent Mr. Nahum. Some were of Thrae, some painted in foreign parts; many were from his mind. " 'He has,' " said Miss Taroone, " 'his two worlds.' " Over and over, Simon would stare at the pictures, never quite understanding why each had a name and Roman numerals on the back—as, for instance, "BLAKE: CXLVII." Then one day, in one of the many bookcases in the room, he found a certain book.

It was "an enormous, thick, home-made-looking volume covered in a greenish shagreen or shark-skin. Scrawled in ungainly capitals on the strip of vellum pasted to the back of this book was its title: THEOTHERWORLDE." Simon—or Walter de la Mare—tells us that the book was full of rhymes and poems, some with Mr. Nahum's thoughts on them jotted in the margin, or a piece of prose bearing on a particular poem. Some had illuminated capitals, some were queerly spelled, some had names and numbers which linked with the pictures on the walls. Day after day the boy read them, as they took his fancy, and he learned to hear the music of the words and to see those pictures in them which were not on the walls.

And he began to realize that even when Mr. Nahum's pictures were about real things and places and people, they were still only of the places and people that the words made for him in his mind. He had, that is, to *imagine* all they told. So what he read remained as a single clear remembrance, as if his imagination had carried him away, like a magic carpet, into another world. He realized that Mr. Nahum had chosen only those poems which carried away his own imagination like that. And since they called to Simon's imagination, too, as the fowler's whistle calls to the wild duck, he sat down to copy them out and to make his own book.

So this inconsequential but unforgettable story leads to the collection of verse and prose which is **Come Hither,** the book which has haunted me, as reader and writer, since I was fourteen years old. And de la Mare's struggle to describe the *kind* of poems that he found in Nahum Tarune's book is my struggle to find out precisely what the quality is, in this book and others, which carries me so deeply into delight.

We never meet Nahum Tarune in the story of **Come Hither,** but he is all of us. Walter de la Mare has been playing with words. Nahum: human. Tarune: nature. Nahum Tarune is human nature. I don't really have the right kind of mind for anagrams, crossword puzzles, or word games, and I find allegory a very tiresome form; the more ingenious and convoluted, the more tiresome it becomes. But here, being biased I suppose, I find the parallels so deliberately clear that they have both charm and power. Thrae is the Earth, spelled, in effect, backward; Miss Taroone is Nature (Mother Nature, if you like); Sure Vine is the Universe; the villages called the Ten Laps are the Planets; and the ancestral home East Dene is Destiny.

It doesn't matter, all this; it doesn't affect the nature of what de la Mare is doing. But it does perhaps add a dimension to the way in which Miss Taroone speaks to the small boy she persists in calling Simon (or, perhaps, as a thoughtful friend of mine suggests, "my son"). " 'Remember,' " she says, " 'that, like Nahum, you are as old as the hills, which neither spend nor waste time, but dwell in it for ages, as if it were light or sunshine. Some day perhaps Nahum will shake himself free of Thrae altogether. I don't *know,* myself, Simon. This house is enough for me, and what I remember of Sure Vine, compared with which Thrae is but the smallest of bubbles in a large glass.' "

In the images of this story—in the old house set in its broad valley, with misted mountains all around and beyond them a glimpse of the sea, and in Nahum Tarune's great book that has in it all the best reading of a lifetime—I find something like a beckoning phrase of music, which sounds all too rarely but is wonderful to hear. Once upon a time I put such a phrase into a book of my own, as a recurrent herald of enchantment. Perhaps it was part of the *Come Hither* haunting.

What is it, the hearing of this music, the sense of being bewitched? It's not a matter simply of recognizing greatness or great talent. It isn't, as the jargon has it, a value judgment. It's subjective, idiosyncratic; perhaps it has something to do with form. I have that kind of gut response to a late Mozart symphony rather than to a Bach concerto grosso; to a Turner or a Renoir rather than to the formalities of the Flemish school. My appreciation of each, that is, is different—just as one finds different kinds of pleasure in reading different kinds of books. The appeal of a biography is different from that of a lyric poem; the appeal of a so-called realistic novel different from that of a so-called fantasy.

I say "so-called" because I've never been happy with either classification; classifying means drawing lines, and I find it hard to draw a line between any one novel and another. That magical shiver of response—I can't justify it by genre. (pp. 500-02)

That shiver, that *frisson* when I was growing up, came from legend, myth, and fairy tale and from a great deal of verse. My mother and my schools between them, thank God, sent poetry ringing through my head to leave most powerful echoes. (p. 502)

[For] me, when young and growing, that lovely shock came primarily from three things which are not "books" at all: from poetry, as I've said; from radio, which was at its peak as an imaginative medium in England when I was between ten and fifteen years old; and, above all, from the theater. My mother tells me that I was first taken to the theater when I was about three—to that Christmas institution in England known as the pantomime. I sat there enchanted, she says, not a whit puzzled by our transvestite tradition in which the hero of pantomime is played by a strapping girl and the hero's mother by a large hairy man. And when it was all over and the curtain came down, I sat unmoving in my seat, and I howled and howled. All the others left on their legs, but they had to carry me out. I couldn't believe that this wonderful, magical new world, in which I had been totally absorbed, had vanished away. I wanted to bring it back again. I suppose I've been trying to bring it back again, in one way or another, ever since.

It's horribly elusive, this same kind of sensation one has from certain books, poems, and works of art. Only the symptoms are easy to describe. The hair prickles on the back of the neck, and there is a hollowness in the throat and at the pit of the stomach—a great excitement that is a mixture of astonishment and delight. It's a little like catching sight unexpectedly of someone with whom you are very much in love. And the delight when it swamps you is full of echoes, carrying you away, as de la Mare said, "as if into another world." (pp. 503-04)

[Tough] and precise is what, to go back to our beginning,

the best books read by children have to be. That audience will settle for nothing less. . . .

Lucy Boston once wrote, "I believe children, even the youngest, love good language, and that they see, feel, understand and communicate more, not less, than grownups. Therefore I never write down to them, but try to evoke that new, brilliant awareness that is their world."

"That new, brilliant awareness"—only the poetic imagination can bring it back. The freshness of a child's vision of the world is what every artist strives to retain. That's what we're all after, painters and poets and composers and the authors of certain kinds of books. If we can capture it, if we can make our audience catch its breath, create that great stillness that comes over a visible audience at moments of pure theater—if we can do that just a few times in our lives, then we've done what we were put here to do. And the whole life of an artist, it seems to me, is captured at the end of Walter de la Mare's story of **Come Hither.** Perhaps that, in the end, is the reason why this story, like others of the same magical kind, can carry away the longing, striving adult just as it does the unwitting, rejoicing child. Listen now to the music, and the metaphor. (p. 506)

Susan Cooper, "Nahum Tarune's Book," in The Horn Book Magazine, *Vol. LVI, No. 5, October, 1980, pp. 497-507.*

Sheila A. Egoff

[**The Three Mulla-Mulgars**] is, in its own way, as unique as *Alice's Adventures in Wonderland,* both being works that cannot be imitated, much less duplicated. Nod, the little monkey in the sheepskin coat with nine ivory buttons, is not an ordinary monkey like the Banderlog in Kipling's *Jungle Books;* he has magic about him. De la Mare does not impute human speech to his monkeys. The Portuguese sailor tries to teach Nod human speech, which results in a kind of Mulgar-English, a linguistic tour-de-force that foreshadows Tolkien's use of linguistics in his fantasy. Nonetheless, Nod is a primitive in a primitive animal society. (pp. 107-08)

Nod really belongs to epic fantasy. He is the counterpart (as is Susan Cooper's Will Stanton) of a Sir Galahad or a Sir Gawaine. We enter with him into a world of fantasy where the spell is never broken, a world of astounding adventures, escapes, struggles, terror, evil, and even death—a world, in fact, which is universal. His is a spiritual odyssey and Nod reflects Walter de la Mare's basic philosophy that life is good and beautiful. It is through the beauty and refinement of de la Mare's thought and language that we see the universal in Nod's primitive nature. (p. 108)

Sheila A. Egoff, "Beast Tales and Animal Fantasy," in her Thursday's Child: Trends and Patterns in Contemporary Children's Literature, *American Library Association, 1981, pp. 105-118.*

Jon C. Stott

Although in his lifetime [Walter de la Mare] produced over eighty books for adults—novels, plays, poetry, and essays—he is chiefly remembered for his books for children. . . . De la Mare's best works for children can be divided into three categories: retellings of traditional stories, original stories, and poems.

Told Again and **Stories from the Bible** reflect de la Mare's great love of the traditional stories he heard as a child. In the former, he adapts nineteen folktales, including such favorites as "Cinderella," "The Sleeping Beauty," "Little Red Riding Hood," and "Jack and the Beanstalk." His versions are considerably longer than the originals, containing more dialogue, character development, and description. In this way, he is better able to give young readers a sense of the settings and the life-styles of times gone by. . . . While expanding on the Old Testament stories he included in [his] collection, de la Mare captured the rhythm of the originals as well as the spirit of the great events described.

De la Mare's own stories for children reflect his love of the old folktales; in fact, many of them are "literary folktales" incorporating into them character types and situations reminiscent of traditional tales. In **"Dick and the Beanstalk,"** a young boy who loved the stories he read discovers Jack's beanstalk, now dry and withered. However, when he climbs it, he discovers a descendant of Jack's giant and doesn't quite know what to do when the giant visits earth, causing many problems. Several stories make use of such traditional themes as the patient daughter (**"A Penny a Day"**) and the cruel master (**"The Three Sleeping Boys of Warwicksire"**). In the shorter pieces, the good, kind, and virtuous defeat the evil and selfish. (pp. 90-1)

The best known of de la Mare's longer works is **The Three Mulla-Mulgars.** . . . The story focuses on Nod, the smallest, youngest, but cleverest of the three brothers. It is, in fact, the story of his growth to maturity, and the adventures he experiences and the settings he passes through symbolize the stages of his growth. Although the story starts somewhat slowly, the pace soon picks up and readers find themselves both thrilled and deeply involved with the adventures and the small hero.

Because it is often specifically English in its descriptions and because it often deals with ideas and customs now considered somewhat old-fashioned, much of de la Mare's poetry for children appears difficult on first reading. However, even the outdated poems contain such beautiful word and sound patterns that the music itself is pleasing to the ear. The best of de la Mare's poems are those dealing with universal qualities of nature and haunting supernatural occurrences. In the former group, **"Seeds," "Snowflake," "Snow,"** and **"Silver"** are perhaps the best-known and loved. Such works as **"The Listeners"** and **"Nobody,"** with their delicate hints of the strange, unknown, and unseen elements of life, speak to imaginative, sensitive minds as forcefully today as they did when they were first written. Often the ability to feel the moods of the poems is as important as the ability to understand the meanings clearly. As de la Mare wrote, "We can, . . . particularly when we are young, delight in the sound of the words of a poem . . . without realizing its *full* meaning."

For young children, the reading of nearly all of de la Mare's poems will be a rich introduction to the beauties of the sounds and rhythms of language. The poems dealing with English landscape can serve as a complement to a reading of Frances Hodgson Burnett's *The Secret Garden.* Upper elementary aged school children who have enjoyed reading adventure stories about soldiers, sailors, and pirates will enjoy reading the poems on the same subject. **"Dick and the Beanstalk"** is an interesting follow-up to a reading of "Jack and the Beanstalk." Good readers who have responded to J. R. R. Tolkien's *The Hobbit* may find it interesting to compare Bilbo's journey to that of the young hero of ***The Three Mulla-Mulgars.*** (pp. 91-2)

> *Jon C. Stott, "Walter de la Mare," in his* Children's Literature from A to Z: A Guide for Parents and Teachers, *McGraw-Hill Book Company, 1984, pp. 90-2.*

Zena Sutherland and May Hill Arbuthnot

Adults and children of the English-speaking world lost a great lyric poet when Walter de la Mare died in 1956. (p. 301)

Many of his poems are difficult; nevertheless his work contains some poetry that should not be missed. Choose your favorite poems; try them with children; then try certain others that are beautiful but that are not so sure to be enjoyed at first hearing. Who knows what words will catch the imagination of children? When you are using the poetry of a great lyric poet, be adventurous and try a wide selection for the sake of that occasional child who may suddenly be carried away by the magic of poetry.

One characteristic of Walter de la Mare's poems is the use of the unanswered question which leaves the reader wondering. Many of his poems have this enigmatic quality. Of course, too much ambiguity may be discouraging to those children who are literal creatures and like things straight and plain. A little, however, stimulates children's imagination and provokes not only a healthy speculation but the ability to transcend the factual and go over into the world of dreams.

De la Mare could be direct and clear when he wished to, and his children are real flesh-and-blood children. The account of **"Poor Henry"** swallowing physic is as homely a bit of family life as you can find anywhere. Small children enjoy the matter-of-fact subject matter and the straightforward treatment of such poems as **"Chicken," "The Barber's,"** and the Elizabeth Ann parts of **"A Child's Day."** Even these poems for the youngest children, however, are illumined with little touches that invariably lift them above the world of the commonplace.

There are many nature poems in ***Rhymes and Verses.*** Throughout the poems you find intimate glimpses of flowers, birds, beasts, the sea, and the countryside—all caught and colored with the poet's own peculiar insight. No poetry is more intensely visual than de la Mare's. A "sunwashed drift of seabirds," "rain-sweet lilac on the spray," and, for another sensory experience, those "chuffling" pigs

making their "grizzling, gruzzling and greedy" sounds. . . .

The fairy poems, with a great range of mood and style, begin at nonsense level with such delightful absurdities as **"Tillie,"** the old woman who swallowed some magic fern seeds and has been floating around on the wind ever since.

That de la Mare's work for children has the same beauty found in his books for adults is not surprising when he himself said in his introduction to ***Bells and Grass,*** "I know well that only the rarest kind of best in anything can be good enough for the young." If anyone has given children "the rarest kind of best" in poetry, it is Walter de la Mare. (p. 302)

> *Zena Sutherland and May Hill Arbuthnot, "The Range of Poets for Children," in their* Children and Books, *seventh edition, Scott, Foresman and Company, 1986, pp. 297-320.*

John Rowe Townsend

One major twentieth-century poet did his best work for children, and dominated the field of children's poetry in the first half of the century. This was Walter de la Mare . . .

De la Mare's special quality as a poet is one that is widely desired and rarely possessed; an ability to recapture the childlike vision, to show things in words as they feel to a child. His craftsmanship was excellent to a degree that may have harmed his reputation in the long run. He could be and sometimes was more melodious than any other English poet except perhaps Tennyson, and it is easy to retain on the ear an impression of silvery delicacy rather than of force or substance. The corrective to this is to read ***Peacock Pie*** (the best book of all) and to note how often he is humorous, how often robust—look at ***The Ship of Rio***—and how he is perfectly capable of bouncy rhyme and down-to-earth diction if that is what the subject demands. He can manage the quick short line. . . . and the long one that holds itself up by subtle internal supports. . . . (p. 173)

De la Mare always rings true emotionally; he is never self-conscious, saccharine, coy or condescending—all of which are ways of being out of true. His effect on lesser verse-writers probably has not always been good, but a poet is not to be blamed for his emulators and imitators. I do not believe he is over-rated. (pp. 173-74)

> *John Rowe Townsend, "Craftsmen in Two Media," in his* Written for Children: An Outline of English-Language Children's Literature, *third revised edition, J. B. Lippincott, 1987, pp. 173-86.*

Roger Duvoisin

1904-1980

Swiss-born American author and illustrator of picture books, nonfiction, and retellings, and illustrator.

Major works include *Donkey-Donkey: The Troubles of a Silly Little Donkey* (1933), *White Snow, Bright Snow* (written by Alvin R. Tresselt, 1947), *Petunia* (1950), *The Happy Lion* (written by Louise Fatio, 1954), *Veronica* (1961), *Jasmine* (1973), *Crocus* (1977).

A prolific and internationally popular creator of books for children in preschool through the middle grades, Duvoisin is one of the most highly respected authors and artists in contemporary juvenile literature. Considered a versatile illustrator and masterful book designer who was also gifted as a literary stylist, he is often praised for the warmth, humor, and wisdom of his books as well as for his understanding of what appeals to children. Duvoisin is perhaps best known for contributing to the genre of the animal fable with several series of picture books featuring endearing barnyard and jungle animals who represent human feelings and foibles. These works, which spotlight such characters as Petunia, the archetypal silly goose; the Happy Lion, a good-natured animal mistakenly taken for ferocious created by Duvoisin and his wife, Louise Fatio; Veronica, a hippo who wants to be less noticeable; Jasmine, a nonconformist cow; and Crocus, a kind crocodile, address such themes as discovering self worth, celebrating uniqueness, and learning to overcome pride and greed. Several of these stories are considered classics, especially the eight books about the Happy Lion and the seven books with Petunia as their heroine. In addition to these works, Duvoisin wrote and illustrated informational books on national and international history, stories with holiday motifs and instruction on color, picture books on nature, and retellings of European folktales; he is also the creator of a well-received alphabet book which has as its basis the Old Testament story of Noah's Ark.

As well as receiving acclaim as an author and artist, Duvoisin was noted as the illustrator of approximately one hundred and fifty books by such authors as Daniel Defoe, Robert Louis Stevenson, Elizabeth Coatsworth, and Charlotte Zolotow. He is especially well known as the illustrator of eighteen picture books with nature themes by Alvin R. Tresselt; the first of these works, *White Snow, Bright Snow,* won the Caldecott Medal in 1948. In this book, Duvoisin uses an expressionistic style and a four-color scheme to depict the reactions of children and adults to an unexpected snowfall. As an illustrator, Duvoisin is often lauded for the variety of his mediums, styles, and printing techniques. He began his career as a watercolorist, but gradually began to use such mediums as gouache, acetate separations, and collage for his illustrations. Influenced by Matisse and other Impressionist painters, he is often recognized for his superior sense of color, economy of line, and the humor he achieves through subtle detail. Duvoisin encountered controversy for the pictures in William Rose Benet's *Mother Goose: A Comprehensive Collection of the Rhymes* (1936), which favor a nontraditional

approach relying on bright colors and reflecting a distinct Gallic influence; the book was later reissued with a new set of his drawings. However, most observers agree with critic Dorothy Waugh that Duvoisin was "a peerless illustrator for children," one whose sophisticated yet humorous pictures and clear and rhythmic texts consistently reflect his respect and affection for his audience. In 1956, Duvoisin and Fatio shared the first German Youth Literature Prize, the Deutscher Jugendliteraturpreis, for *The Happy Lion.* In 1966, Duvoisin received the Rutgers Award for Distinguished Contribution to Children's Literature. In 1968, he was named a highly commended illustrator by the Hans Christian Andersen Awards committee. He also received the University of Southern Mississippi Medallion in 1971 and the Kerlan Award in 1976, both for his body of work. In addition to receiving the Caldecott Medal for *White Snow, Bright Snow,* Duvoisin was presented with a second award from the Caldecott committee for *Hide and Seek Fog,* another collaboration with Tresselt which was named a Caldecott honor book in 1966.

(See also *Something about the Author,* Vols. 2, 23, 30; *Contemporary Authors New Revision Series,* Vol. 11; *Contemporary Authors,* Vols. 13-14, rev. ed., and Vol. 101 [obituary]; and *Dictionary of Literary Biography,* Vol. 61.)

AUTHOR'S COMMENTARY

[The following excerpt is from a speech which was originally delivered in July 1965.]

In the actual work of making a child's book, the artist had better keep his sense of humor and pleasure about him: if he forgets to do so, he may well end up with a book which will bore children. Therefore, I will mix fun and seriousness in trying to tell about my personal pleasures and problems in this delightful occupation of illustrating children's books. (p. 22)

Everyone who has improvised stories and pictures in the presence of a few children knows the fun one can have in that game. When this act has life and humor, the children's eager eyes and laughter are pleasant rewards. Even the bored looks which come to the children's faces when the story and the pictures lack inventiveness are part of the amusement. Bored looks spur one to higher feats of imagination in order to bring back the laughs.

The making of children's picture books is indeed like playing with children. The game is on even when the author-illustrator sits alone at his drawing table. For he is really not as lonely as he seems to be. He has his abstract public with him, as have artists in every field. In his case, it is a public made up of two kinds of children. First, there is the child *he* was, a child who is still very much present and who inspires him and helps him understand the other children. Second, there are the abstract children who are watching over his shoulder.

From White Snow, Bright Snow, *written by Alvin Tresselt. Illustrated by Roger Duvoisin.*

From his own childhood, he remembers the things, impressions, attitudes which impressed him most. He remembers his childhood conceptions of people, of animals, of scenes, and of books which were part of his world.

From the abstract children watching over his shoulder, he will have the fresh, unexpected, imaginative conceptions which they have expressed during games or conversations. In this give and take with his abstract public of children, the illustrator will learn to let his imagination flow more freely.

There is in the maker of children's books what is in most adults in their relations to children: that little sneaking desire to teach and to moralize, to pass on to children what we think of our world. A picture book is such a fine medium for this exercise that it is difficult to resist the temptation. Even if these sentiments are carefully hidden in the book they are generally there, and so much the better. The children's book maker has the added pleasure of believing that he has done more than merely entertain. Personally, I like to think that, while children read my books, they do not waste their time on the hundreds of toy trucks, cars, tractors, and bulldozers which fill most children's rooms nowadays, or on some of those books of useless facts. (pp. 22-3)

But there is also a serious aspect to the making of children's books, an aspect which, at times, demands very hard work. This other aspect of children's books concerns the illustrations from an artistic point of view. That is to say that while the artist desires to communicate his own pleasure to children, he wants to do so with illustrations that are original in their conceptions, that are well composed in their designs and colors. In this he is driven by his own need to experiment and to try to improve his art, and he is encouraged by the importance the art in children's books has acquired as an art form. (p. 24)

The modern picture book, then, must be considered as more than a vehicle to carry stories and pictures to children in order to amuse them and give food to their imagination—and to amuse their authors at the same time. It is also a most interesting medium for artists to experiment in with colors and design—to invent to their heart's content. This is why many talented artists have been attracted to the picture book, not only for the fun of it but also for the opportunities it offers for their art. The result is that the best children's books have become art creations without losing the particular qualities which give pleasure to children.

Imagine a layman listening to one artist as he explains to another artist what he is trying to do in working on a new book. What he may hear will make him wonder whether the poor child has not been completely overlooked in the problems the artist is trying to solve. These problems may pertain only to the proportions of margins to the interest of the white spaces and colored shapes, to the inventiveness of the design, to the relationship of the various colors, and other such problems.

Where is the child in all these things? Has he been sent to bed to leave the grownups to discuss serious things without being disturbed? The answer is that the child is very much present indeed. One of the reasons for making a page which is well designed is to tell the story with more simplicity, more verve, clarity, and impact; to give importance to what is important; to eliminate what destroys the freshness, the originality of the page; in other words, to make a page which will be more easily read by the child. A well-designed page will also educate the child's taste and his visual sense. A beautiful book is a beautiful object which the child may learn to love.

The modern children's book illustrator is not isolated from the turmoil of the art world around him. . . .

Roughly, the extraordinary things which happened to painting during the nineteenth and twentieth century—its evolution away from representation and toward pure abstraction—have made the art of illustration what it is today. (p. 25)

While the painters were slowly effecting the divorce of illustration from painting, dismembering the subject, planning its final murder, the professional book illustrators had a good time.

Illustrated books were popular during the nineteenth century. There were many professional illustrators of talent who were often accomplished craftsmen in wood or copper engraving and in the new reproduction process of stone lithography. These illustrations were printed in black, but were sometimes colored by hand. During the second half of the century, the printing of color overlays was perfected. But illustrators generally followed the tradition of realism and of closely following the text with exact literalness. (pp. 28-9)

Illustrations which impose the artist's conception of a novel with definitiveness and precise literalness come like a screen between the author and his readers. The illustrations interfere in a very unpleasant way with the readers' own dreams.

But illustrations, as done by the superior artists, are related to the text in a free, loose, subtle way; they leave the reader free to interpret the writing with complete freedom. And he has the added pleasure of doing the same with the illustrations. (p. 30)

Illustration profited much from abstract painting in spite of the opposition between the two. The treatments of surfaces, the use of space, the color relations, the free, dramatic forms and lines, etc., of abstract paintings teach much to the illustrator.

However, the children's book artist must think about all this within the very special art of picture books. Because making a picture book is like playing with children, the particular way children react to the world around them cannot be forgotten. This need not be a limitation; on the contrary, limitations are a challenge and a source of inventions.

With their uninhibited vision, children do not see the world as we do. While we see only what interests us, they see everything. They have made no choice yet. We do not see what sort of buttons a man we pass in the street has on his coat or how many there are, unless we are a button maker. But a child cares and will count the buttons if he can. He will care just as much about the tiny ladybug which falls accidentally on the dining room table as about the grownups who sit around it. More, in fact. The child's interests are infinite and he sees the tiniest details of his world as well as the biggest forms. And he does not say,

"I do not understand." He looks and sees. He lives among wonders and the children's book artist only has to take him by the hand, so to speak, to lead him toward the most imaginative adventures.

The child also has the tendency to enjoy this detailed world of his in terms of happenings, of things being done, in other words, in terms of stories.

In their own art, the children are not aware of abstract considerations. They are not concerned with color harmony or color contrast, with composition and design. Their art is only a sort of writing, however beautiful it might be sometimes. With it they tell a story. If a child is asked to explain a painting he has made, he will most likely tell what is happening in it. "This is a woman going to the market to buy fruit. This is a truck driver climbing on his truck. This is the sea, full of fish which the fisherman will catch." (pp. 31-2)

Another quality children possess is their love and understanding of the humorous side of things. This also can be a rich source of ideas for the maker of children's books. Not only can he laugh with the child as he makes his books, but he can tell the most serious and important things while he laughs.

I have said enough, I think, to show that the artist and author cannot complain that the making of children's books has limitations. Those limitations rather resemble a jail whose windows and doors open wide into a delightful paradise. The degree of talent of the children's book maker may be the only limitation.

In the art itself, I think we will see artists taking more and more liberties. Even abstract art can have a place in a child's book under certain circumstances. If the artist is inclined to search for his page designs and for his colors by using the elements of the story in rough, free, almost abstract forms, he will be tempted to leave his page almost in the rough abstract condition. The forms, the bright color surfaces which are not cut or soiled by details, the white spaces which remain pure have a freshness, a force, and an interest which they may lose when details and precisions are brought in. The artist may then be searching for a simpler and more ingenuous way of telling the necessary story.

When the artist writes his own story, he can conceive both his text and illustrations simultaneously, thus making the text and pictures help each other as they develop the story. He even can make his illustrations first, with great freedom, and get ideas for the text from them. In this case, the text may be like the threads the dressmaker uses to hold the pieces of material which will form the dress. (p. 32)

Roger Duvoisin, "Children's Book Illustration: The Pleasures and Problems," in Top of the News, *Vol. XXII, No. 1, November, 1965, pp. 22-33.*

GENERAL COMMENTARY

Dorothy Waugh

One of the most important attributes of an artist is the ability to enter into a mood; to absorb, mature, and completely comprehend it; then to give it expression: perhaps musical expression; or graphic, physical, dramatic, or literary expression. (p. 11)

The capable illustrator must, of course, have artistic mood-sensitiveness, and must be able to mature and express what he feels. If he is to do versatile types of work he must be able to plumb a variety of emotions. Besides, he must be able to take his initial impulse from an author, accepting the tone which the author has set, subjecting himself to it, expressing and interpreting it with a new fullness which brings added meaning to the author's statement—but always in the author's key. (pp. 11-12)

With the inept, inadequate illustrator it is as if the author walked down a road and the illustrator followed; the author said, "This is a large tree, green and full of shade"; and the illustrator echoed, "Tree; shade"; the author said, "It is dusk. A bent woman passes"; the illustrator echoed, "A woman. Here I have drawn her. I've put on her the kind of dress the encyclopedia calls for; I looked it up."

The illustrator who can rightly claim the title of artist follows the author in a much more sensitive mood; or accompanies him. The author says, "This is a large tree, green and full of shade"; the artist responds, "Largeness and shade, the calmness and coolness of shade; a largeness in breadth and height and depth, and in spiritual qualities; a largeness which makes details seem small and the wholeness great."

The author says, "It is dusk. A bent woman passes." The artist amplifies, in his own terms of expression. "A woman. She moves with a heavy heart. She is bending under the weight of some spiritual burden. She is a woman lost in the preponderance of nature, yet the center of all; the nucleus in incipient turmoil. I must express all that in my drawing."

I am trying to give a sense of difference—because so many indications show that few people in the children's book world are conscious of the difference—between the hack, who concerns himself with drawing physical objects, and the artist, who presents a pervading mood. There is a temptation to paraphrase the remark to Samuel, saying, "The hack looketh on the outward appearance, but the artist looketh on the heart."

To study Roger Duvoisin's illustrations with an eye for what he has added in atmosphere to the books he has illustrated—spiritual or emotional atmosphere, or mood—is a good exercise in the appreciation of art in contrast to hack work. His unusual versatility in mood-evaluation and mood-expression renders the contribution which he makes to an author's text particularly evident. (pp. 12-14)

In addition to the ability to sense, to develop, and to express a mood only one other ability, in any creative art, is absolutely essential. That is the ability to compose. Composition is the keeping of all parts in proportion and in position to achieve the desired whole—to make the parts unite, no single one left unneeded, all of them essential and contributing to an integral—often a centripetal—force. In reality, composing is an essential part of expressing a mood; yet it may be considered separately.

When so many people have learned to hear form in music; to know the difference between a mimic imitating sounds and a composer conceiving and delineating a symphony,

it seems strange that so many people fail to see the difference between a commonplace illustrator drawing objects and an artist presenting a spiritual whole of which each form, each direction and movement is a balanced part, in proportion to the entire expression, growing out of a given emotional impetus.

Especially is it strange that composition in drawings often goes unappreciated even by people who can see the difference between the effect of furniture scattered aimlessly about a room and the same furniture arranged for a cohesive visual balance, for heights, weights, color intensities, and textures which give the eye a movement that returns upon itself to create repose, or unity and completeness, in a plan having centers of interest, opposing forces, and axes—the same framework features which in a drawing make a whole out of all the parts.

Without intelligent, sensitive organization—in addition to mood presence—no expression is art. In other words, composition is so important that no talent whatever can give an expressionist in any creative field the right to the name of artist without the ability to compose. This is one of the abilities which Roger Duvoisin has to a high degree. (p. 15)

[A] Duvoisin illustration in which both composition and mood are plain is the drawing of hunter, dog and gun at the bottom of page 14 in [Douglas Rigby's] *Moustachio.* In composition the movement grows from the lower left in strong divergent lines upward to the right. Their strength is made powerful by the simplicity of the shapes; by the sharp contrast between darks and lights; by the definiteness of every form in this central active featured part of the composition. The movement of the attention is stopped, turned back, and held within the picture by two vertical tree trunks at the ends of the drawing. These have stationary power by means of their vertical stability and their bulk; and yet they are so softly presented, and so netted about by a loose lacework of merely suggested foliage, that they do not vie for attention with the main statement.

How effectively the shape and position of belt and powder horn give the upward-and-to-the-right turn to the hunter's figure. The upward-and-to-the-right movements of the drawing's stressed forms are like those in the growth of a plant—reminiscent of the way long blades of grass, starting from one root, reach, curve, and separate as they grow away from their common nucleus.

The mood of the drawing is one of humor, with a slightly quaint and fantastic tinge. It is not a forced, exaggerated, or superficial humor. It is gained by the merest touches: the delineation of the dog's eye; of the eye and eyebrow of the man, the tilt of his hat, the cut of his beard, and his positive melodramatic stance.

Humor is one of the emotions Roger Duvoisin has expressed successfully in many varying shades. Humor in dogs, cows, and other animals has really grown into a new area through his work. . . . (p. 17)

There is humor, when it is appropriate, in Duvoisin's people as well as in his animals. . . .

It is not the affected humor of the superimposed wart, the root-shaped hand, the noticeable clothes, the cuteness of trite paraphernalia; the humor is in the way the person in the drawing feels, the way he lives, and the way these conditions of life translate themselves into form, through the tilt of a head, the widening of an eye, the drop of a jaw or perhaps by means of a gesture or a posture which through the delicate throw of a muscle gives a figure violence, confidence, hesitancy, or languid grace.

If we speak of color, there again Duvoisin has an ability which is exceptional. Perhaps his years of designing fine silks are partly responsible for the rich breadth and the maturity of his color sense; though, on the other hand, it is improbable, of course, that the finest silk firm of two continents would have brought him here from Paris at the age of twenty-three had he not had outstanding talent along that line from the start. The books of Duvoisin's which have had appropriate manufacture show his color work with a beauty not often seen between book covers. (p. 18)

The abilities we have referred to so far are those of the artist as artist, or of the illustrator as illustrator. There are a number of specific applications of art to illustration for children, which work within limitations, or in accordance with releases, peculiarly their own.

Duvoisin says there are two ways of understanding and appreciating the child's viewpoint. One is through memory, the other through observation. If you can put yourself back into your childhood moods, or if you can watch children and tell them stories or read to them, you have a basis for selecting what will appeal to a child. He himself uses both of these methods. . . .

The books he read in French during his childhood included Jules Verne, Kipling, Cooper, Mark Twain, Stevenson, *Mother Goose, Peter Rabbit, Uncle Tom's Cabin, Alice in Wonderland, Thousand and One Nights, Moby Dick, Little Women;* and many more English and American classics; as well as La Fontaine, Grimms' and Andersen's fairy tales, and all the other European masterpieces. He also read all the lurid current trash which he could obtain for small coins. He enjoyed this with the same extravagant appreciation he gave to the other books. (p. 19)

When Duvoisin thinks now of those books he read as a child, he recalls the vastness, the wonder, the richness, and color which his child mind created; and in illustrating those or other stories he tries once again to live in the large lush land of imagination's childhood.

In watching children react to stories told or read aloud an author or an artist increases his sense of what feelings a child responds to most strongly and most quickly, Duvoisin says, telling of his own experiences with his children and their cousins. Things sad, happy, or funny, appeal to children most, he believes. The younger a child is the more he loves exaggeration and brash departures from fact. The older he grows, especially if he lives his hours among routine-ruled humdrum schools, the more he expects and even wants realism.

The vividness of Duvoisin's childhood memories are, without question, one of the greatest, if not the greatest, factor in making him a highly successful children's illustrator. His humor, his warmth, his imagination, his intellectual depth, and scholarly poise fit him for both this and his other lines of expression: his successes in adult illustrating—for the Heritage Club, for the first illustrated edi-

tion of W. H. Hudson, for *Fortune* and other magazines, for the *New Yorker* covers; for advertising for highclass magazines, for designing pottery and silks. But the ability to enter again into childhood's spiritual expanse is above anything else the thing which makes him peerless as an illustrator for children. (p. 20)

Dorothy Waugh, "Roger Duvoisin as Illustrator for Children," in The Horn Book Magazine, *Vol. XXIV, No. 1, January-February, 1948, pp. 11-22.*

Ruth E. Kane

Although Duvoisin's 16 other books are completely captivating, the writer feels that his warm cheerfulness, his imagination, and love of animals are, perhaps, best expressed in his four Petunia books. (p. 412)

Duvoisin does his illustrations first and then has the story follow. He tries to change from one book to another to bring infinite variety to his works. He simply delights in drawing animals. As a boy in Geneva, he felt handicapped because there were only deer in the city zoo. Consequently, he had to wait for the circus to come to town before he could draw his magnificent lions, elephants, and tigers.

Today, he can observe cats, ducks, guinea hens, horses, dogs, cows, and geese as well as the predators and woodland animals from his Somerset County home. However, he observes and sketches his lions, tigers, penguins, polar bears, and animals of this type at both the Bronx and Central Park Zoos in New York City. Since he likes to work with tempera and line drawings, he consequently thinks of animals which can be treated in line drawings.

Smiling gently, he said that it was simply amazing to an artist what a critic can see in, or read into, a book. In his future works he plans to try to get bolder and bolder in line composition and color. He plans further to work for more freshness. Duvoisin says that he thinks continuously of stories which will bring these things to fruition. Sometimes it is an old theme done over freshly which effects the desired objective. However, he ruefully admitted, ideas won't come when you want them to but appear when you least expect them.

Duvoisin has attained his present status as an artist for many reasons: One of these is his tremendous variety which can be demonstrated by **And There Was America** in contrast with **Petunia.** His work is bold and free—not at all stereotyped. There is nothing prissy, sissy-like, or cute about anything he draws. He makes use of direct bright, bold colors. His art has a sense of humor and an enviable visual freshness. His too, is a certain delightful spontaneity of craftsmanship, design, and color.

Duvoisin's has the same directness and simplicity as the Japanese manner of art. His is the direct line—sure, definite, and economical. There is no superfluity to be found in his illustrations.

His art may be likened to the playing of the piano: first, one learns the exercises; next, one goes through the effort to gain skill; and finally, the expert, playing, just lets the music flow out. So with his art, it starts, swells, flows, and then comes back. His angles are seen from an inventive way, and the body is seen likewise. Perhaps the essence of his books lies in every page's being a deliberate surprise.

Duvoisin is a perfectionist; rarely is he satisfied with his illustrations. . . . Sometimes in search of this perfection, he draws from models, but then his drawing loses that certain delightful creativity so typically Duvoisin. He is at his best when drawing from imagination.

His quest for the perfect is seen further in his making a dummy of every page of a book which he is creating. The dummy includes not only the pasted in type and sketches of his illustrations but specific directions concerning the binding, spacing, margins, exact position of the drawings, etc.

Because Duvoisin is an author as well as an artist [Louis Ansbacher has noted], "he understands the part illustration should play, and out of this perception and his intelligence he gives freely, unjealously, and as if in each case he were author as well as artist. . . ." (pp. 415-16)

> *Ruth E. Kane, "Roger Duvoisin—Distinguished Contributor to the World of Children's Literature," in* Elementary English, *Vol. XXXIII, No. 7, November, 1956, pp. 411-20.*

May Hill Arbuthnot

The Happy Lion stories have fascinating illustrations with details that make the French town where the stories take place just as familiar as the child's own home town. The lion, like the child, is cribbed and confined, but he has his own ideas. These he carries out gently but firmly, whether his project is going for a walk in the village or winning himself a beautiful lioness. With these *Happy Lion* stories, the husband-and-wife team of illustrator and author has made a real and lasting contribution to books for young children.

> *May Hill Arbuthnot, in a review of "The Happy Lion," in her* Children's Reading in the Home, *Scott, Foresman and Company, 1969, p. 64.*

Barbara Bader

At four, Roger Duvoisin's elder son drew himself into a story of a little boy whose drawings come to life. When he had trouble resolving it, Duvoisin père took it over and, drawing in the manner of a child, made what was to be his first book, *A Little Boy Was Drawing.* (p. 128)

The following year artists wandering in Woolworth's lighted on a little book selling for ten cents—Duvoisin's *Donkey-Donkey* in the original Whitman edition published by Sam Lowe, the first of its several embodiments. With sad-eyed good humor, *Donkey-Donkey* exemplifies the futility of trying to be what one is not. Discontented with the look of his ears, Donkey-donkey tries to hold them down like Hector the dog's; straight out like Fuzzy-fuzzy the lamb's, Phoebe the goat's, Fanny the cow's ("So many people *cannot* be wrong, Donkey-donkey"); and in front like Rosa the pig's. Expectably, ridicule and worse await him, but always with an extra fillip like the ornate Louis XV mirror that frames his foolishness.

If Donkey-donkey is foolish he is, to start with, "a nice little donkey"—an individual with feelings, as fallible as the next person. . . . [Expressing] feelings is Duvoisin's forte, and *Donkey-Donkey* is the book that said so.

Also evident already is that Duvoisin writes as slyly as he draws—"I suspect in fact that she just went to sleep," he remarks with Beatrix Potter punctiliousness when Rosa the pig, supposedly ruminating, fails to twitch an ear or flick an eyelid for two pages; and that, regardless, he composes not in words *or* in pictures but in images. During Rosa's doze, an inchworm traverses the top of the fence and Donkey-donkey, at first alert and expectant, rests his nose on it in baleful resignation, the one marking actual, the other psychological time. (p. 129)

Craftiness in line and tone and then splash! an explosion of color: the Heritage *Mother Goose.* Printers and production people cheered—"the book might have stepped out of an Italian or Soviet book shop"; buyers for big chains spoke darkly of 'sophistication'; reviewers divided, some regarding the break from tradition as a sacrilege; librarians were cautious—were Duvoisin's "hectic tempo" and brilliant color "suitable fare for the nursery"? (pp. 129-30)

Actually, only forty of the 160 pages are in color, and a more valid criticism would be that some of the designs are crowded and chaotic. At worst, the Old Woman Tossed Up in a Basket bears down on Peter, Peter, Pumpkin-Eater, the Three Wise Men of Gotham risk being crushed by the Barber Who Shaved the Mason, and the type gives ground to all four. But all is not anarchy and the excitement is infectious: not only has every rhyme a picture, but every picture has a point, be it only the cat's wary watchfulness in "I Love Little Pussy."

Duvoisin's signature is everywhere—in the inky upright script, the field-flower palette, the piquant pen notations—and everywhere is gaiety and vivacity. A Gallic Mother Goose.

During these same years and into the Forties, Duvoisin did advertising and editorial illustration, magazine covers, display design and murals, bringing to this so-called commercial work the very qualities that distinguish his books, and no less individuality. (p. 130)

Gradually Duvoisin gave up other work to concentrate on picturebooks—on picturebooks per se, not illustration, the only exceptions being works of the interest of Natalie Savage Carlson's *The Talking Cat* (Harper, 1952) and Robert Louis Stevenson's *Travels with a Donkey* (Limited Editions Club, 1957). (Only those who don't know *The Talking Cat* will question the pairing.) His doing so is obviously indicative of Duvoisin's bent; his being able to do so is symptomatic . . . the enormous expansion in the picture-book field that followed the war.

Of his work of the later Forties, the nature books Duvoisin did in collaboration with Alvin Tresselt for Lothrop are the most important, and in his oeuvre generally they hold a special place. (p. 133)

Children like them. They are not equally good, and a few, by either artistic or literary standards, are not very good at all, but children like them. They have a realness about them, compounded of integrity and immediacy, that overrides any momentary failure of execution. And it pays not always to strive for easy attractiveness: the colors in *Sun Up* (1949), an evocation of a hot summer day, are indeed muggy, and one perfectly understands the chickens taking shelter in the shadow of the barn, the cows in the shade of a tree; one senses why "everything hid from the burning sun." And yet they are the same three, red, yellow and dark blue, that Duvoisin uses in *White Snow, Bright Snow* to very different purpose. The same and not the same, for the colors—especially the red and the yellow—that are clear and at full strength in *White Snow, Bright Snow* are mixed by overprinting or muted by Ben Day tints in *Sun Up,* and in place of chill excitement comes torpor. (En masse, Duvoisin's books comprise an anthology of the possibilities of pre-separation, tints and other extra-studio techniques.)

Besides the four on the seasons, there were, through the Fifties and beyond, several others, among them *Wake-Up, Farm!* (1955) and *Wake-Up, City!* (1957), ideal springboards for small children, and a book that does almost the same thing for the beach, *I Saw the Sea Come In* (1954). But the one that has always been my favorite—it was a family favorite too—is *Follow the Road.*

Follow the Road opens on a spread rendered in black line and green wash, the green so deep that it blends with the black and gives the appearance of monochrome. What we see is a shadowed green world full of sharp details, a microcosm at once vast and intimate. Pulling it together is the meandering road, like no road and every road—or, like the scene itself, an abstraction.

Does such a lackadaisical dirt track have direction, extension? Is it really going somewhere? The little boy thinks so before he stops to play marbles; but turn the page and close to is the clay surface rimmed with wildflowers, a frog catching flies in the middle. Then a final curve and the road straightens out, heads through the trees toward the horizon, emerges black-topped and strung with telephone poles: "the road didn't stay, couldn't stay, not today."

The surface smoothens, widens, sports a center stripe, carries school bus and trailer truck, surges into the center of a big city . . . (pp. 133-34)

As the day draws to a close it slows down again, ambles past bandstand and fresh egg stand, carries the farmer on his tractor chugging home, whistling, the little boy pulling his wagon up the hill, puffing—his silhouette black against the red-streaked sky, the windows of his house beacons in the coming darkness. . . .

The text speaks for itself; lyrical and urgent, swinging from a shout to a whisper, always a voice, a presence, it is as fine as any of the many Tresselt has done. And Duvoisin fills it out, now in soft waves of country clover, now in the blank stares of tall buildings—grayed to highlight the bright street bustle and the cars in a child's red, yellow and blue.

In forty-one years, 1932-1972, Duvoisin illustrated by his own accounting 146 books, thirty-one of which he also wrote. (p. 134)

Unquestionably the best of the picturebooks are his, not necessarily because they are the best illustrated but because they are the best books. Consider *Petunia,* the story of a silly goose who equates the possession of a book with the acquisition of wisdom. She is the philosopher who can't see beyond his own stone, the expert who interprets his figures as facts, anyone who takes symbol for substance. (pp. 134-35)

Duvoisin's masterly line drawing of Petunia, eyes lowered, head high, book tucked under her arm, is justly famous.

Such clear bold line was . . . comparatively rare in the artist's earlier work; here it wiggles furiously for King the rooster's comb, thickens and thins as the animals stoop and stretch, and shoots off the top of the page as Petunia becomes still prouder and her neck grows still longer.

But single images don't tell the tale, their disposition in sequence does. In cartoon sequence, albeit around the double-page, across top or bottom, incorporating telling objects—in any of a variety of ways. The design is fluid and dramatic, the action is continuous: it is a picture-*story* par excellence.

As befits the strong line, the color is flat, sometimes clear and flat, sometimes extended by a full-strength mixture, a tint or a combination of the two—the deep green, the pink and the yellow-green respectively. And whether Petunia, all white except for her beak, is silhouetted against the colored background or the white itself forms the ground, white is the matrix—the wellspring and the cement—on the four-color as well as the one-color spreads, showing the drawings to advantage and unifying the design.

Drawing and design and dramatic action: follow Petunia's head as it makes a shallow sweep around the double-page and watch her expression change; see the tattered book, the bandaged neck, the doleful look—and the Rodin-thinker recovery.

It is all there in the pictures, the text could be a string of captions; but at its least it is something more. Petunia has just acquired the marvelous book:

> She slept with it   she swam with it.
>
> And knowing that she was so wise,
>
> Petunia also became proud.
>
> and prouder   and prouder   so proud
>
> that her neck stretched out several notches.

The words are parallel pictures in print and, keyed to the five pictures of Petunia, the rhythm, the stress, the pacing are dictated by the arrangement and spacing. (pp. 135-36)

Need it be said that [Duvoisin] always has an idea? In the case of *A for the Ark,* a web of ideas. The alphabet lends itself to the animals of the Ark; their entrance into the Ark suggests Noah's difficulties in keeping them in order, alphabetically and otherwise; the approaching storm brings darkening skies, haste, a final recapitulation before the Flood; and then the story takes over as it should, in three pages predominantly of text. But when the waters recede the animals must leave the Ark, and because Noah is acting in God's stead, the last shall be first. It becomes a game: "Can you tell now the names of the animals pictured with each letter . . . ?" ("If not, you will find them on the last page.") Majestically, the Roman capitals descend, each with an animal profiled in sinuous line.

The scheme of printing, in full-color process and two colors at alternate openings, plus the way Duvoisin uses it—modeling in full color, outlining and filling in with a flat wash otherwise—results in two distinct modes of illustration, as different as painting and drawing, which is in fact what they are. It is not the best design, perhaps, but it is a good, changing show. There is pith in the drawn pages, and even without the rich red of Noah's robe or the blue-black of the lowering clouds, there is drama in the painted ones.

Humor and affection shoulder each other throughout. The letter S brings the sheep into safe company; the wolves eye the weasels, "Both night thieves, but you cannot steal anyone from my Ark." If there is a recurrent motif, it is that the Lion and the Lamb shall lie down together alliteratively. But for sheer artistry, the back pages are the book's triumph. Here, svelter, are Veronica the hippopotamus and a dromedary with no less aplomb than The Camel Who Took a Walk (other Duvoisin troupers); and, blocked in clear, vivid hues, the capitals offsetting them, with a strip of color balancing, bordering, at the middle.

Of all the characters Duvoisin has drawn into being, probably the favorite of children is the Happy Lion, the joint creation of the artist and his wife, Louise Fatio. Petunia has dash, sang-froid, even a certain sex appeal; the happy lion has friendliness and a friend, François. There is nothing new in the idea of an importunate bear, a reluctant dragon or a sociable lion being mistaken for fierce; what matter? its very persistence as a theme attests to its durability. Besides, children, we know, are always new. (pp. 137-39)

A gentle parable told and drawn with spirit, *The Happy Lion* is a minor classic. Others in the series have more plot and less to say—though, so persuasive is the star of the little zoo, no less appeal to children.

Over the years art changed, printing practices changed, and Duvoisin's work changed—as one can see in the successive appearances of Petunia and the Happy Lion. What one cannot do is date a book by any single factor: different material continued to elicit different treatment. In 1965 there appeared, among others, *Hide and Seek Fog* (text by Alvin Tresselt, Lothrop), pure mood in watercolors printed by full-color process, and *The Rain Puddle* (text by Adelaide Holl, Lothrop), of which Duvoisin said: "What attracts me to this story is that it has the charming ingenuousness of a little folk tale, and I have tried to keep my illustrations just as simple." Composed of a few flat cut-out forms accented with line, they appear throughout on the right-hand page opposite the text, one of the simplest possible arrangements too. Speaking of Duvoisin, editors invariably praise his craftsmanship; the sensibility is there for anyone to see. (p. 139)

> *Barbara Bader, "Roger Duvoisin," in her* American Picturebooks from Noah's Ark to the Beast Within, *Macmillan Publishing Co., Inc., 1976, pp. 128-39.*

Marcus Crouch

It is perhaps not quite as perverse as it may seem to remember Duvoisin first as a writer. Like Ardizzone he wrote many of his own texts, and like Ardizzone too he had a rare facility with words. He wrote very directly, utterly without affectation, and with a fine feeling for the simple, melodious, right-sounding word and phrase. Aspiring writers could do a lot worse than study in detail the balanced cadences of his uncrowded and unpretentious pages.

But it is of course as an illustrator that he will be remembered with greatest affection. (pp. 5-6)

His lasting reputation is based on a dozen or so of his own

From A for the Ark, *written and illustrated by Roger Duvoisin.*

picture books and those written by Louise Fatio, and a few picture books by other writers with whom he found himself specially in harmony: notably those by Adelaide Holl, Mary Calhoun, Charlotte Zolotow and Alvin Tresselt. . . . Of all these, English children will recall with warmest affection the animal characters: The Happy Lion, Petunia, Veronica and Crocus. . . . All these animals have in common candour, friendliness, goodwill. Petunia, the goose, may not be the cleverest creature in the farmyard—not to put too fine a point she is plain stupid—but her intentions are good and she is even capable of learning by her dreadful mistakes. There is a moral in *Petunia* as there is in all Duvoisin's books and in his wife's, but it is a simple, uncontroversial one which is not imposed on the reader. There is more complexity in Louise Fatio's **'Happy Lion'** stories. The Lion reflects the gentle pacific philosophy of the Duvoisins, but he is a subtle character, an animal with things on his mind, and one who is not prepared to be put off with easy solutions.

In Duvoisin's work the word and the thought, the environment and the philosophy, are inseparable from the graphic image. Well as he wrote he thought through his drawing hand, in line and colour. Of all the book-artists working in America in his time he most readily accepted the discipline of the printed page and turned it to positive advantage. He was less fond than some of double-spreads, but he took immense pains over the balance of pages, floating his narrative across the two elements of each opening and maintaining the tension up to and beyond the turning of the page. When he does use a double-spread, as in the title-page of **Petunia** where that supergoose thrusts her eager neck diagonally from corner to corner, it is the more effective for its rarity. Except perhaps in some of the early American books, produced in the halcyon days, his use of colour, although powerful, was economical. He was supremely the professional worker and he made no unreasonable demands on printer or block-maker. (pp. 6-7)

Duvoisin himself—and it was one of his many endearing traits—clung obstinately to his origins. He moved to America at 23 and became a naturalised American citizen in 1938, but to the end of his life he and his wife spoke French in private and on every other possible occasion. He remained French in his thought processes and in his individual preferences. Perhaps, paradoxically, it was this which enabled him to speak so directly and easily to children of all races. What makes him so supremely successful in communicating with the young is, above all, his respect for his audience. He was profoundly influenced by the ideas of his compatriot Piaget and believed, like him, that the child was not an adult-manqué but an individual with an individual's rights, his own personality and thought-structure. Duvoisin did not try to evolve some graphic equivalent of Piaget's educational theories. His understanding of those theories enabled him to deal with children without any of the usual generation-gap impediments. (p. 7)

Marcus Crouch, "From Petunia, Veronica and Crocus—With Love," in The Junior Bookshelf, Vol. 45, No. 1, February, 1981, pp. 5-7.

TITLE COMMENTARY

A Little Boy Was Drawing (1932)

Quite one of the jolliest [picture books] this year in color and text, and with that touch of nonsense without which no picture book is complete, is **A Little Boy Was Drawing. . . .** The title is the story; a little boy draws, and the things he draws come to life, with very funny results. Turning the pages one can almost see the child, with his tongue stuck out, exultantly tracing the mice and tigers and policemen which later bring him such trouble. The tale is amusing and the pictures delightful, spilling over with colors that really do recall the joys of one's first cheap paint box.

Margery Bianco, "New Picture Books Full of Gayety and Color," in New York Herald Tribune Books, November 13, 1932, p. 8.

The story of Tom's visit to the Land of Wonders where his painted mice and cats and people are alive is one of those imaginative books which come only every so often. The pictures are vivid and exactly like the "primitive" art a child turns out on a rainy afternoon with his paint-box. (pp. 844-45)

Nancy Evans, in a review of "A Little Boy Was Drawing," in The Bookman, New York, Vol. LXXV, No. 8, December, 1932, pp. 844-45.

Donkey-Donkey, The Troubles of a Silly Little Donkey (1933)

The publisher's jacket copy says that this was first published in 1933, that it was among the first of the Caldecott Medalist's picture books. Books usually go out of print because they don't sell well and if such was the case with **Donkey-Donkey,** it probably didn't attract enough wear and tear to justify replacements. Its story goes on past the preschoolers' predictable point of restlessness as the vain little donkey seeks repeated advice from both people and the other farm animals about the most attractive angle at which to wear his ungainly ears. The illustrations have all the signals that are still a part of Duvoisin's work: swift, slightly exaggerated lines; color laid on in controlled splashes; small, amusing secondary details forming a visual subplot in the pictures. Students of children's literature will be able to trace the evolution of the artist's storytelling, especially in comparing this to the most recent of his comic animal fantasies. But it still seems too long to hold the initially intended audience.

Lillian N. Gerhardt, in a review of "Donkey-Donkey," in Library Journal, Vol. 93, No. 13, July, 1968, p. 2728.

A baby's bookshelf is better small: half-a-dozen favourites, tried and true, are much more rewarding than a new book every day. But when the time comes to add to the store, there is a bewildering choice—hundreds of almost identical stories, all gaily got up and lovingly drawn. The largest pile is given over to farmyard dramas, and many of Roger Duvoisin's stories are among them. It seems the more surprising that one of his nicest efforts, **Donkey-donkey,** first published in America in 1933, is only now available in England. Mr. Duvoisin's more recent work is sometimes woolly; *Donkey-donkey* is witty, and sharp. . . . [A] slight enough tale, but beautifully drawn; the Duvoisin trick of showing the passage of time by the progress of a caterpillar along a wall, or a fly across a pig's back, has never been brought off better.

"Modern Baby's Bookshelf," in The Times Literary Supplement, *No. 3536, December 4, 1969, p. 1397.*

The Three Sneezes and Other Swiss Tales   (1941)

Walter Duranty once said that he believed folklore to be one of the keys to the character of a nation. Most of us do not feel competent to analyze the national and racial elements in a folk tale, but all of us, children and adults alike, take pleasure in noting characteristic details which distinguish the fairy and folk tales of one part of the world from those of another.

Many of the tales from the Swiss provinces are similar to those of the surrounding countries, because, as Mr. Duvoisin reminds us, so many people—Celts, Gauls, Romans and Germans—have helped to make the small country of Switzerland. These Swiss versions of well-known stories have been eliminated except in a few instances. Other stories have their origin in local beliefs and superstitions; the Alps are peopled by the Bergmänlein, the little men of the mountains; on the farms and in the mountain châlets are the family dwarfs, the "servants," as French Switzerland calls them, who are rewarded by a jar of milk for their household labors. The caves shelter fairies, not princely ones, but a simple fairy folk whose maidens were not above marrying herdsmen to assume the duties of a mountaineer's wife. Glaciers and avalanches, of course, were readily explained as the vengeance of supernatural beings. All these types are represented as well as the tales which grew out of friendly rivalry between villages and made good-natured fun of a neighboring town, such as **"The Bad Joke That Ended Well"** and **"The Foolish Folk."** The stories are divided into "Swiss French Tales" and "Tales from German Switzerland," all have a hearty peasant flavor. Simple, dramatic and full of humor, they will be welcomed by children and by the story teller.

Mr. Duvoisin, who was brought up in Switzerland and heard these tales as a child, has caught their lively humor in his drawings.

Anne T. Eaton, in a review of "The Three Sneezes and Other Swiss Tales," in The New York Times Book Review, *September 28, 1941, p. 12.*

Mr. Duvoisin, himself of Swiss origin, has gathered together a group of folk tales and legends as interesting, as well-written and delightfully illustrated as any we have had for years. Most of the stories have a sly "dig in the ribs" kind of humour. Others are a little more sinister, as many south-eastern European stories are, but all have an atmosphere born of the ever-present mountains.

As illustrator Mr. Duvoisin is not well known in this country, and perhaps the success of this volume will persuade the publishers to issue some other volumes containing pictures in the bold colours in which this artist excels.

A review of "The Three Sneezes and Other Swiss Tales," in The Junior Bookshelf, *Vol. 8, No. 2, July, 1944, p. 76.*

They Put Out to Sea: The Story of the Map   (1943)

Just as soon as a boy or girl begins to study geography or to draw maps in school, this book comes with impetus and direction. How did the map begin and how did it grow? What was the world like when Hecataeus of Miletus drew the map—here sketched—that shows all the lands men knew in his day? What made the Phoenicians sail so far? By showing, in rapid sentences and strong little pictures, how Hanno set out from Carthage, what cities he started as his ships paused to put off workmen, what terrors they encountered with wild men—who were quite possibly chimpanzees—a ten-year-old sees the map growing under his eyes. So he does with each succeeding experience—traveling with Pytheas and finding the way to the Tin Islands and the amber country, not only to help the Greek traders, but with a general curiosity such as now sends scientists on exploring expeditions. So they go with others: Alexander setting out to conquer the world, Ptolemy drawing the world's most beautiful map so far—and then the great darkness coming with barbarians from the north, so that all the Greeks and Romans had learned about the world was lost. The Crusades come in: they will be remembered when later reading reaches them. The Polos appear, Prince Henry, the great admiral. The story pauses with Magellan's name more famous than that of Columbus; the largest continents have been drawn in their proper places on the globe.

Pictures have kept pace, and the map appears as it was drawn at each period. Every now and then a brilliantly colored scene stretches across two pages. There are several excellent books for somewhat older readers on this general subject, but this one a ten-year-old, or even a younger child, takes happily, now that the map is part of a family breakfast table.

May Lamberton Becker, in a review of "They Put Out to Sea," in New York Herald Tribune Weekly Book Review, *February 20, 1944, p. 5.*

From the earliest traders to Magellan the account is woven together as the map grows and it reads as well as the most exciting adventure yarn. Simple and graphic in style with emphasis upon anecdote and conversation, lively illustrations in black and white and color by the author. Good index. Highly recommended for older boys and girls. Simpler than Lucas' *Vast Horizons* which it resembles somewhat in subject matter, this should fill a real need in the collection for the eight- to eleven-year-olds.

Margaret C. Scoggin, in a review of "They Put Out to Sea," in Library Journal, *Vol. 69, March 15, 1944, p. 264.*

It is a great pity that the excellent production and illustration of this book is not matched by equally inspired storytelling. From the earliest times to the end of Magellan's last voyage the efforts of man to discover more about the world in which he lived are traced. The Phoenicians, Alexander the Great, Marco Polo, Henry the Navigator, Columbus, Magellan and many others appear in these pages, but the epic quality of their adventures is often obscured by writing down, by padding, by trivial and unreal conversation, by a dull and pedestrian style which robs them not only of their quality but even of their dignity. The author has been diligent in his collection of information, but he might have been better advised to seek a collaborator to weave his gleanings into a more lively and exciting pattern. In short, as illustrator Mr. Duvoisin is superb, but as writer he is not a success in this book. (pp. 174-75)

A review of "They Put Out to Sea," in The Junior Bookshelf, *Vol. 11, No. 4, December, 1947, pp. 174-75.*

The Christmas Whale (1945)

There have been so many silly pointless stories and pictures about Santa Claus and his reindeer that we approached this one with misgivings. By the third or fourth page we found ourself laughing out loud. This is a really amusing picture book. It gets funnier and funnier as it goes on.

It seems that one year, just before Christmas, the reindeer were smitten with influenza. The picture shows all eight of them lying neatly in eight very elegant beds with red and white counterpanes drawn up to their chins. Obviously they would not be able to draw the sleigh for Santa Claus. Then who would? Much worried, Santa Claus asked all the Arctic dwellers to carry him on his annual journey round the world, but no one of them could. They simply were not equipped for it. Then a cod thought of the Kindly Whale. "Her back is as broad as an iceberg," he said, "she is as strong as the waves in a storm, and she is as fast as the wind. Go ask her." Santa Claus asked the Kindly Whale and the Whale agreed. Everyone helped with the loading of hundreds and thousands of packages, all neatly done up in red paper. Look at the picture where the bears, seals, porpoises, cods, and various other animals are carrying the packages to the beach. Then turn the pages quickly and look at the one where the tugs are pushing and pulling the Kindly Whale into the pier at New York. Anyone who has ever sailed out of or come into New York in a liner knows every detail of that scene. Then follow the gay red maps and see for yourself that Santa Claus and the Kindly Whale remembered every harbor in the whole round world. The Whale was very tired when they got back to the North Pole: "The icy cold waters of the North had never felt so deliciously refreshing." "After all," said Mrs. Santa Claus, "whales are very decorative." . . .

Good design and an unfailing humor will make this book just as refreshing to fathers and mothers as it will be pleasing to the children themselves.

Mary Gould Davis, "Santa's Helper," in The Saturday Review of Literature, *Vol. XXVIII, No. 49, December 8, 1945, p. 40.*

Chanticleer, The Real Story of the Famous Rooster (1947)

This is a disappointment from Roger Duvoisin—a rather

muddling story of the rooster who thought he was responsible for the sun's rising, and of what happened when the alarm clock and the owl and the sun himself decided to prove him wrong. Fantasy, elaborating on a familiar folk tale—and not quite coming off. But the gay and entertaining pictures carry the story along.

A review of "Chanticleer," in Virginia Kirkus' Bookshop Service, *Vol. XV, No. 20, October 15, 1947, p. 576.*

White Snow, Bright Snow (1947)

[*White Snow, Bright Snow was written by Alvin R. Tresselt.*]

AUTHOR'S COMMENTARY

[*The following excerpt is from Duvoisin's Caldecott acceptance speech, originally delivered on 15 June 1948.*]

It is surprising that the pictures for **White Snow Bright Snow** have been so honored, for after such a winter everyone should be tired of snow, even in a children's book. . . . Now that the award has been made, I can safely say what I have known all along, that the book brought the winter upon us. This conclusion has been arrived at by simply putting two and two together. It was the first time that I had the opportunity to illustrate a book about snow and it was also the first time that I ever saw so much snow in one winter. (p. 293)

The only good thing that the book brought this winter is the assurance that never again will our elders dare mention the Blizzard of Eighty-Eight! Ours was better.

But, if all that trouble did not prevent **White Snow Bright Snow** illustrations from winning a great honor, it is not only because they found enough good friends in the South and West who could easily dismiss the black side of white snow, nor even for their quality as illustrations, but also, I think, because the childhood love for snow, like all childhood memories, is strong enough in all of us to make us open our hearts to everything connected with snow.

When the snow begins to fall, a few timid flakes at first, and then the heavy whirling mass of white which buries everything, our pleasure in looking out the window is very complex. It is partly the pleasure of seeing fields and woods being transformed into a beautiful landscape of fairy tale, but in it, too, is the secret childhood urge to go out and feel the snow, to plunge our hands into it, to make snowballs and snowmen. (pp. 293-94)

How children love snow! Nothing in the world can be as completely satisfying to them as snow. Nothing can lend itself so well to the fancies of their imagination—not even sand on the beach, not even a muddy puddle after the rain. They can jump into snow from the porch railing, they can war upon each other with snowballs or break windows, close the driveway with that four-foot snowball, build forts, tunnels, snowmen—why, even sleigh and ski over it! (p. 295)

No wonder then that a book about snow can win some affection, and no wonder that the illustrator's old love for snow will come out of him when he is asked to paint snow on the pages of a book. Besides, what looks more like snow

Petunia and Charles were married on Christmas day. The barnyard had never seen so much dancing, singing, and feasting.

114

It was a very, very merry Christmas.

From Petunia's Christmas, *written and illustrated by Roger Duvoisin. Reproduced from* Petunia the Silly Goose Stories *by Roger Duvoisin.*

than the white pages of a book? All the artist has to do is to let the white speak for itself. A red spot on the page and you have the feeling of a red brick house whose roof is confused with the snowy hills behind. In the snow landscape everything is guessed rather than clearly seen, and the white page will be the perfect snow landscape if hardly anything is added to it, if the spaces composed on it are suggested rather than actually drawn. It's like the solid black page which I remember having seen in a joke book somewhere, with the caption: "Chimney-sweep in a tunnel at midnight."

The illustrator, and also the writer of children's books, is thus lucky in his work because much of it consists of recalling the wonderful and charming impressions of his childhood so that he may pass them on to children of new generations; to re-create for them the world which made his own childhood happy. That is why many children's writers or artists start their career by doing a book for their own children. Publishers like to say this in their advertising, but it is generally true, at least when the children's book artist *has* children.

Children's writers and illustrators are like all other grown-ups. They are very sentimental about their childhood memories. They distort them unconsciously to fit their changing conception of life. These memories grow and evolve and go very, very far sometimes from the original thing, and when translated into a book, they sometimes meet the discouraging bored look of the child because they

do not present to him a real child's world but a child's world seen through grownups' eyes.

Parents commit the same mistake when they insist on giving children the toys and picture books which they loved when young, for children's tastes change as the things around them change. If we give a child a toy car in the shape of the old-fashioned automobiles which made us happy, he will be scornful. What he wants is a toy car in the shape of the modern streamlined automobile. (pp. 295-96)

The ***White Snow Bright Snow*** book will have a luckier history, I hope, for industrial designers will never be able to streamline snowflakes, at least not in the foreseeable future.

Perhaps it is only illustrations for stories that are purely imaginative, like Tenniel's illustrations for *Alice in Wonderland,* which can live on for a long, long time, and never seem dull and outdated.

So the illustrator and the writer of children's books must find that compromise, that good balance, between what he wants to give out of his own memories and what he knows the children of today want and are interested in.

The illustrator of children's books has another disappointment sometimes. He can go on making every effort to do tasteful illustrations (in which endeavor he may or may not succeed, of course) and he will always be astounded to see what sort of things children may love. For taste, as educated grownups know it, is not a children's affair. They do not have good taste or bad taste; they simply are not conscious that there is such a thing. They will be fond of the most frightful illustrations just as they will love good ones. What they like is an illustration that suggests something which their imagination can grasp and build upon.

After working very hard all day to make a satisfying set of illustrations, I am often made thoughtful by the gleam of joy I see in my son's eyes when he comes home with a one-foot pile of comics which he has traded with a friend (the one source of comics parents cannot control). I have seldom seen a child open a good book with the same enthusiasm with which he plunges into a gorgeous pile of comics. Why is that? The reason is, it seems to me, that too often the writer and the illustrator, in their effort to give tasteful things to children, are too restrained, and do not go all the way with this abundance of imaginative situations which the children love.

I remember a talk I heard at the last annual children's book exhibition at the New York Library by Mr. Donald Adams, and with which I completely agree. He said that the books we remember and love best are the purely imaginative stories. And even history can be presented in an imaginative way like fiction, while keeping an eye on the accuracy of the statements.

Stories, short, up-to-date, and extraordinarily abundant—unfortunately also too often coarse, silly and tough—are what they find in comics. But it is possible to combine good taste with this abundance, and it is my dream to find the time and the talent to do some good books which can compete in a child's estimation with the comics.

I can find a good example in my own boyhood reading of how and why illustrated literature may be preferred to the best, and its effect. The classic struggle which takes place in many homes between children who try to smuggle in this literature and the parents who try to weed it out was going on in our own home between my father, my brother and me.

There was at that time a cheap little publication which caused the despair of parents with its popularity among children. It cost two cents and for that small sum we could plunge into the weekly illustrated paradise of shooting and extravagant rides, hair-raising murder and adventures, the hero of which was Texas Jack, the pitiless enemy of criminal cowboys and outlaws (pronounced in French *coveboas* and *ootlavs*). It was the Heigh-Ho Silver of those days. It must have been written and illustrated by a Frenchman who had never come to America and his stories were all the more fanciful and unhampered by true facts. None of the lessons of history about America which we had in school could affect our extraordinary and over-romantic conception of the land of perpetual and gorgeous adventures. (pp. 298-99)

Well, we never missed an issue of Texas Jack. And as I said, all our history lessons never stamped out completely our Texas-Jack conception of America, because history was presented to us as a dead thing. Texas Jack, cheaply written as the story was, was alive. When I came to America a few years later, it was not in the land of Washington, Jefferson, and Lincoln that I landed—it was in the land of Texas Jack. And to this day, since I have never been to the Southwest, my idea of that country is colored by Texas

Jack, right or wrong. As a matter of fact, I think that that conception would even survive a visit to the West, so deeply have these wild fictions taken root in my memory.

I remember that when I first visited the Adirondacks, I expected to find something similar to the image I had formed in my mind when reading Fenimore Cooper who was, after Texas Jack, one of my favorite authors about America. Even though the descriptions of Cooper were fine and accurate, the illustrations of the book were not, as I remember them; the illustrator had never seen America, I am sure. His forests were more like the mysterious forests of Tom Thumb or other fairy tale illustrations, than those of the Adirondacks, and I was vaguely disappointed when I went there to find something quite different, even though I was impressed by the beauty of the country.

And I am sure that American children have also just as wrong a conception of the rest of the world if they read too much about it in cheap, inaccurate fiction which does not combine imagination with accuracy.

And so the juvenile book artist should have the tact to guide the child while giving him what he likes and wants, should fully satisfy his hungry imagination without distorting his conception of the world about him. It is only by giving children all that their imagination will take that he can get to see in their eye this gleam of joy which shows their complete response to a picture or a book.

Another influence picture books must have, it seems to me, is counterbalancing the too great love that children have for mechanical things in opposition to things of nature. I think that we shall never put in the hands of children enough picture books about nature, and we must take the trouble to control the number of books they read about gadgets just as we must take the trouble to see that they do not read too much cheap literature. Of course, this is a quite personal opinion which is based on my own observation. In spite of all we hear about them, machines are dead things. They are but toys, even the ones that grownups love. Things of nature are live things, like people, animals, flowers, mountains. To study nature, to learn how to know it well, makes a child mature more rapidly. An animal is not a mechanical toy to play with. It is a creature which has its own personality and its reactions, habits, likes and dislikes must be taken into consideration. To study it requires an intellectual effort from the child which he does not make in reading about mechanical things or playing with them. To read about nature is to learn about life. A man who knows about life is more mature than a man who knows only about machines. Only books, illustrated books about life, can counteract the ever-present mania of most children for mechanical things—a childish mania which too many of them carry into their later life. Unfortunately, just as children will too often discard a good book for a silly one, they will too often drop the good book to concentrate on a catalog for a new model motor car. This must be fought not by forbidding the mechanical toys or automobile catalog, but by surrounding children with pictures and books which give them a sense of nature, a sense of their own relation to it. (pp. 300-02)

I do not want to end without saying that Mr. Alvin Tresselt must have his share of the honor conferred upon **White Snow Bright Snow**. It is his story after all, and a charming and well-done story it is. When an illustrator is given a *good* story to illustrate, his job is made pleasant and easier. The story is to a picture book what the silk is to a textile pattern. You can cover up poor material with a flashy pattern only to a certain extent. It will fool no one very long. (p. 303)

> *Roger Duvoisin "Caldecott Acceptance Paper—1947," in* The Horn Book Magazine, *Vol. XXIV, No. 4, July-August, 1948, pp. 293-303.*

Never shall I forget the afternoon I came alone in a motor, from far in Westchester to my home on Morningside. For the year's first snowfall went just ahead of us, traveling at the same pace. From estates and suburban gardens, slum tenements and school gates, children came, holding up their hands to catch the flakes in gestures almost ritualistic, performing the spontaneous dance with which generations have greeted the first snow. Had I not seen them I would still have known the first snow was falling: all the way along the air had a joyful humming note that, once heard, is forever recognized.

All this and more one finds in this simple narrative with its introductory poem "Softly, gently in the secret night, down from the North came the quiet white." These colored pictures are merry in themselves yet full of memories for any one who has in his own childhood or that of his children run out to greet the annual marvel of the snow. This farmer reaches for a snow shovel, this postman for his high boots; this policeman gets his feet wet and his wife makes him a poultice of mustard; these rabbits take to their holes. But the children dance and try to "catch the lacy snowflakes on their tongues." All night the flakes descend. Next morning, what brightness! What forts and statues! Then the sun shines, the marvel melts, the rabbits return, the grownups get to work—and the children begin to watch for the first robin.

> *A review of "White Snow, Bright Snow," in* New York Herald Tribune Weekly Book Review, *November 16, 1947, p. 8.*

Alvin Tresselt sets the mood in his charming verses for *White Snow,* but it is Mr. Duvoisin who makes the snow fall on the soft blue pages of this lovely book—a revelation to children who have never known the wonder and excitement of a first snowfall—a miracle to those who watch for it every year that its mystery, magic and fun have at last been captured in a picture book. Brilliant splashes of red and yellow bring out all the gaiety and humor which pervade the book.

> *Anne Carroll Moore, in a review of "White Snow, Bright Snow," in* The Horn Book Magazine, *Vol. XXIV, No. 1, January-February, 1948, p. 25.*

The artistic attitude of Duvoisin in *White Snow* is expressive rather than realistic. He chooses only primary red and yellow as dominant hues to depict people, houses, and natural surroundings that would in reality include more color choices. The artist in fact once said, "The fewer the colors, the greater the challenge." The expressive approach is also seen in the policeman's house, for which the illustrator used cutaway views that endow the audience with super-

human powers to see through walls into bathroom and kitchen. The case against realism in *White Snow* is clinched by the illustrator's use of different proportion systems for shapes and even for different figures in the same compositions to imply depth.

This case against realism does not imply that Duvoisin created a fantasy world. Recognizable organic and geometric shapes appear in abundance in this book, and all humans, animals, and buildings have idealized proportion. While idealized shape seems realistic in [Elmer and Berta Hader's] *The Big Snow,* figures in *White Snow* are simplified, with flat, shallow depth to give artistic impressions much like those in [Virginia Lee Burton's] *The Little House.* Note for instance that Duvoisin simplifies houses and people as did Burton. . . . Use of ground colorations for effect on the audience is also similar to Burton's: dirty gray sets the mood for dark fall and winter scenes, and the cleanest of whites is used for clear winter skies and for the coming of spring.

Many illustrations by Duvoisin employ natural proportion in sizes and amounts of shapes, overlapping, and audience perspectives. Figures lost in the binding's gutter would undoubtedly have added balance between shapes within some double-page spreads. In some cases, though, rabbits appear too large in relation to children nearby or a house seems very small for its owner standing outside. These digressions are good examples for children of hierarchic proportion used by this illustrator. . . . This disparity helps us understand that on both pages all figures are vignettes viewed from different distances and not shown in the same setting with the same depth, as they may seem at first glance.

In one illustration Duvoisin uses *distorted proportion,* in which characteristics of a shape are grossly overstated in relation to its other parts or to other figures. . . . Distorted proportion can . . . render a shape as humorous, which is the reaction of most children to Duvoisin's automobile on page 23. Its geometrical shape is absurdly distorted to look like the organic shape of a "big fat raisin" because the snow has fallen on it. The car also takes on an open shape that allows the ground space to penetrate most appropriately to imply the depth of the snow all around. This bit of distorted proportion appears in a scene with otherwise natural proportion implying much depth in the townscape. The contrast enhances children's enjoyment of *White Snow*'s most popular illustration.

Duvoisin often expressed his artistic ideas successfully within a single system of proportion but on occasion rather unsuccessfully with confusing combinations of systems. As an artist moving away from realistic toward simplified shape, he presents for children an important step in art appreciation, bridging the work of the Haders and Ezra Jack Keats. (pp. 161-62)

> *Lyn Allen Lacy, "Shape, 'The Big Snow,' 'White Snow Bright Snow,' and 'The Snowy Day'," in her* Art and Design in Children's Picture Books, *American Library Association, 1986, pp. 144-177.*

The Four Corners of the World (1948)

In this colorful little book for 8-to-12-year-olds, Mr. Duvoisin gives us a glimpse of Pizarro's boyhood and of the restless ambition that led him to the New World. The setbacks and hardships of his first unsuccessful attempts to reach the fabled Incan empire are vividly portrayed. Then comes the landing on the Peruvian coast and the march to Atahualpa's camp. A simple but clear sketch of Incan customs is given by the Spaniards' guides. Mr. Duvoisin ends his story with Atahualpa's murder, two years before the founding of Lima. The book is enriched by delightful drawings in color, and in black and white.

> Nina Brown Baker, in a review of "The Four Corners of the World," in The New York Times Book Review, November 14, 1948, p. 5.

With brilliant dramatic pictures and in vivid language, Roger Duvoisin tells again the story of the young Spanish swineherd who became a great conqueror. Pizarro stands out as a real person whose dreams and wishes at last came true but whose search for the Land of Gold involved cruel hardships and fierce conflicts. The story moves swiftly, following the facts of history but with much direct speech. It will grip the attention of children of the middle age group. In spite of Pizarro's compelling personality, it will create sympathy for the hapless Indians in his path and for the last great Inca Emperor.

> Alice M. Jordan, in a review of "The Four Corners of the World," in The Horn Book Magazine, Vol. XXV, No. 1, January-February, 1949, p. 46.

Petunia (1950)

Doubtless this rare nonsense-picture book began on the Duvoisin farm, where perhaps a silly goose did once find a book belonging to their son. With sparkling wit and wisdom, the little scene has been built into a gay story, full of the repeated acts of error children love. The bold, modern pictures give us this artist at his best. Brilliant colors may add to the sales appeal, but it is the clear bold line, so seldom seen before in Mr. Duvoisin's work, that is so able and admirable.

Petunia, a book-owner so proud that her neck grows right off the page, tries to be wise for all the barnyard creatures. In every case, her advice is wrong, but she has a Book. So she keeps on trying. Has she not heard Mr. Pumpkin say, "He who owns books and loves them is wise?"

But by the last page, Petunia says, "It was not enough to carry wisdom under my wing. I must put it in my mind and in my heart. And to do that, I must learn to read."

You know, Mr. Duvoisin, we reviewers never can feel so sure as you and Petunia about this matter of reading. Nevertheless, your merry pages carry a very special Book Week message, and your story has that point, wit, and body which makes it outstanding among picture books.

> "A Wise Goose," in New York Herald Tribune Book Review, November 12, 1950, p. 9.

A not-very subtle plug for learning to read in a story that lacks either humor or charm. Not recommended.

> A review of "Petunia," in Bulletin of the Children's Book Center, Vol. IV, No. 6, May, 1951, p. 42.

This charming story has the blend of humour and good sense associated with Munro Leaf. Mr. Duvoisin's art, however, is all his own. He has a nice choice of words. His drawing has a confident simplicity and gaiety. It is wonderful what expression he can achieve in simple line. He uses the frame of the page as an integral part of his design. This is in fact a "designed" picture-book, sophisticated in its technique, but completely suitable to children. It deserves to be enormously successful.

> A review of "Petunia," in The Junior Bookshelf, Vol. 22, No. 5, November, 1958, p. 265.

This story and pictures of Petunia, the silly goose who tried to be wise, appeals immensely to children's sense of humour. . . . [Petunia's] conceit grows at such a pace that her head in the air disappears off the top of the page. Petunia's eventual downfall, with the reappearance of her head into the picture, is thoroughly enjoyed by the five-and six-year-olds. Her conversion to reading "so that she can be truly wise" naturally cuts no ice with the children. At the same time it does not detract at all from a hilarious story told in good easy prose and the gayest of pictures.

> M. Chambers, in a review of "Petunia," in The School Librarian and School Library Review, Vol. 9, No. 4, March, 1959, p. 326.

Petunia and the Song (1951)

"Those who sing must be very happy," sighed Petunia, for she could only honk. We laugh at her amazing attitudes of longing, as she envies one singer after another—cricket, rooster, canary, woodthrush. Then she hears the farmer's wife singing a song about one Petunia. It makes her try every possible way to get into the farmhouse. She even tries late at night—which leads her to catch the apple thief and get a remarkable reward. The words and music of the song are given.

We like Petunia's silly doings, which will interest not the youngest picture-book lookers, but those of about six to nine. We like the way the artist spreads her huge form in bold, masterful lines, all over the pages, with pattern and style very clear for young eyes. The little moral at the end—"some people are meant to sing, others to be sung to"—slightly disappoints us, for we have clung to the belief that almost any one CAN be taught to sing. If, out at the Duvoisin farm, they really did try Petunia with a Victrola record, we believe their results.

> A review of "Petunia and the Song," in New York Herald Tribune Book Review, November 11, 1951, p. 12.

Petunia's Christmas (1952)

That resourceful big goose, whose life was changed by finding a book . . . and who found out what to do when one can't sing . . . , now finds herself a husband. We are ever so glad to see her again, drawn in Mr. Duvoisin's most dashing style, in hundreds of funny poses.

Duvoisin at his desk.

The way the story is connected with Christmas will delight children of various ages, probably those from five to ten the most. For Petunia earned her Charles by making and selling Christmas wreaths and tree decorations. The way she displayed them is hilarious; she looks in one picture like the very inventive toy-sellers of Mexico and Spain. There is a fine variety of mood—the delicacy of the cold winter woods, the gaudy horror of Petunia painted like a fairytale monster, the crowded fun of the barnyard wedding on Christmas Day. There is a masterly economy of line in the back view of the two after the rescue, and in such "shots" of Petunia alone as on the cloth binding.

This gay nonsense book, all Christmas red and green, will gather a still wider audience for a most original heroine.

> *"Unusual Gifts for All Ages," in* New York Herald Tribune Book Review, *November 16, 1952, p. 26.*

The third Petunia book is the best to date, supremely well drawn, with that self-effacing mastery of draughtsmanship which is Roger Duvoisin's characteristic, and supremely funny. Petunia the intelligent goose finds that Charles the gander is being fattened up for Christmas. Her efforts to rescue him, successful of course, lead to some delightfully ludicrous situations. Petunia is so much a goose that her ungooselike behaviour is the more funny. The picture of Charles and Petunia going out "together over the hill" is surely this fine artist's best drawing. Beautifully designed this is essentially a book for children. No knowing nudges for the adult reader here.

> *A review of "Petunia's Christmas," in* The Junior Bookshelf, *Vol. 24, No. 5, November, 1960, p. 288.*

A for the Ark   (1952)

For many years I have been an ardent admirer of the work of Roger Duvoisin. Realizing that I could write happily about any one of a great number of books adorned by his distinguished hand, I chose one in particular. The battered and coverless picture book that lies in my lap at the moment is *A for the Ark.* Its dilapidated condition is eloquent proof that it has been the loved choice of countless small readers and embryo artists long before I seized upon it. And this gives me added pleasure in choosing to write of it now.

Perhaps a long-founded admiration for good lettering has somewhat influenced my choice. I must admit that the beautiful basic shapeliness and balance of these Roman capitals gives me deep satisfaction. When coupled with Roger Duvoisin's lively, sensitive and masterly draughtsmanship, there is a treat for the eye on every page!

Every other double-spread of this picture alphabet is in full color, the lower half of each page being devoted to a continuous sort of picture-frieze while the upper part carries the bold, simple text and elegant capitals in alternate shades of blue and coral red. The entire treatment is deceptively simple, with Roger Duvoisin's inimitable vitality and freedom of line. Each double-spread has a satisfying sense of balance and design that never interferes with the legibility of the text but carries the eye on comfortably, along with the gradually accumulating alphabet, and readily invites the turning of the page.

With the utmost economy of means, either in color, tone or line, Duvoisin portrays a mood and gives marvelous characterization of each animal called into the Ark. With an apparent flick of his pen he shows us the supercilious stateliness of the llamas, the eager inquisitiveness of the foxes and the slinkiness of the leopards. We can literally hear the thundering of the horses' hooves, the clatter of goat feet, and feel the beautiful rhythmic jump of the kangaroos. And then there are the sly touches of humor: the flowers in Mrs. Kangaroo's pocket, the swaying angle of the polite black bears, the little leaping frogs, that sideways glance of the wolf at the ferret, and the whole company depicted again on the endpapers!

The drama of the Noah's Ark story moves consistently and progressively with the gathering clouds growing bigger and blacker on every page. In the color pages, the deepening ominous tones are intensified by the glorious red touch, now large, now small, that is Noah's robe.

There seems to be just the right amount of detail in the pictures, plus a certain amount of informative natural history, for a young child. But there is never a sense of overcrowding. The wide blank spaces are carefully planned and play their part. The vitality and humor of the line drawings beside the colorful lettered squares at the end are a feast for the eye, whatever the age of the viewer.

As with many of Mr. Duvoisin's books for children, I love the refreshing spirit of fun, of pure enjoyment, that pervades every page. What delight he must have had doing them, I think, in spite of the inevitable problems that every illustrator encounters. His joy in the smallest detail, in each of his characters—four-footed or two, in *A for the Ark,* is infectious and unmistakable. Who would not want to join up with that memorable alphabetical boatload! (pp. 110-11)

Nora S. Unwin, in a review of "A for the Ark," in The Horn Book Magazine, *Vol. XXXV, No. 2, April, 1959, pp. 110-11.*

Roger Duvoisin's Ark ABC is a frolic, drawn with his enormous virtuosity and his endless humour. Beautifully coloured, excellently reproduced, it is a great delight, and the selection of material is resourceful. There are weaknesses. It was surely an error of judgment, in a book for the smallest children, to introduce a different set of animals in the final "recap." This will lead to bewilderment. And in an excellently brief text, why include gratuitous inaccurate information? One example only, what made Mr. Duvoisin think pelicans can't fly? (pp. 206-07)

A review of "A for the Ark," in The Junior Bookshelf, *Vol. 25, No. 4, October, 1961, pp. 206-07.*

ABC books and retellings of the story of Noah have proliferated in past decades, but *A for the Ark* remains unique for its originality in integrating the timeless narrative into an alphabet book; for the beauty, drama, and humor of its illustrations; and for the imaginative experience it offers to children.

Ethel L. Heins, in a review of "A for the Ark," in The Horn Book Magazine, *Vol. LXIII, No. 2, March-April, 1987, p. 237.*

Petunia Takes a Trip (1953)

When a big white goose landed at the busy intersection of a large city, a taxi-driver cried, "Petunia! It's Petunia!" This will be the greeting of Petunia's many fans who have already enjoyed her surprising adventures in preceding stories. This time Petunia flies off to discover where the airplane goes which flies over the farm each day. In the city the taxi driver and a friendly policeman show her the sights, large boats, large buildings, large houses, until Petunia begins to feel smaller and smaller. Finally, her friends put her on the train for home. . . .

Mr. Duvoisin's story and drawings are so convincing that everything Petunia feels and does seems completely logical. She eats a triple-decker sandwich at the cafeteria, rides in the taxicab and in all ways shows what a capable, poised adventurer she is. This book about her will delight her old friends among children and win her new ones.

Lois Palmer, "Goose's Tale," in The New York Times Book Review, *November 15, 1953, p. 42.*

From the beginning, we have rooted for the goose Petunia. She is such a goose! And so wonderfully well drawn. And always up to some adult adventure which no other goose ever has had in a picture book.

For its nonsense and clever pictures this belongs on the picturebook shelf, and for the goose-eye glimpses of New York. But our favorite Petunia books are the first one, in which she learned to read, and the very delightful last one, *Petunia's Christmas.*

Louise S. Bechtel, in a review of "Petunia Takes a Trip," in New York Herald Tribune Book Review, *November 22, 1953, p. 18.*

The first book about Petunia, the cultured goose, was masterly. It had not only a delightful heroine and superb drawing but also a real story. The heroine remains the same, the drawing is as good as anyone could ask, the story is very thin. . . . The incidentals are excellent however. Petunia doing calisthenics—and lovers of vocabulary-control need not worry; no child would fail to understand the meaning—Petunia eating a triple-decker sandwich, Petunia in the train—few artists could be more funny, or more accurate, for in the most ungooselike situations Petunia remains all goose.

A review of "Petunia Takes a Trip," in The Junior Bookshelf, *Vol. 24, No. 1, January, 1960, p. 26.*

Easter Treat (1954)

We love the Duvoisin **"Petunia"** books not only for their very clever art, but for their stories. They are jolly picture books with original points and plots. This new two-color book is labeled for ages four to six, and possibly that age would be amused to know what Santa did one Easter: how he came to the big city in clothes quite different from his Christmas clothes; how he proved he really was Santa, and went home with lots of Easter presents for Mrs. Santa. It all seemed to us too slight, not able to create an addition to the Santa myth which would greatly impress children of an age to believe in him.

> *Louise S. Bechtel, in a review of "Easter Treat," in* New York Herald Tribune Book Review, *April 4, 1954, p. 10.*

Blithely turning tradition upside down, Roger Duvoisin dresses Santa Claus in tweeds and sends him out into the world for an Easter escapade. Yearning for a whiff of spring, Santa comes incognito to the big city. . . . Admittedly the story is slight, but it has a daffy kind of logic that should please children who remember Santa Claus all through the year. They will be further convinced when they see the pictures of him admiring the tulips, listening to the robins and arguing with bewildered cops.

> *Ellen Lewis Buell, "Spring Visit," in* The New York Times Book Review, *April 11, 1954, p. 26.*

The Happy Lion (1954)

[*The Happy Lion was written by Louise Fatio.*]

A lion on the lam is a fine inspiration to youthful dreams of glory, especially if it is as amiable a creature as the happy lion of this picture book. Inmate of a zoo in a little French town, he is on the most cordial terms with all the townspeople—or so he thought until the day he found his cage door open and sauntered out to return the visits his many friends had made. His reception by the grown-ups is all very bewildering to the lion. It is Francois, the keeper's small son, who calmly resolves the mutual misunderstanding.

The initial situation is not entirely unfamiliar in children's books, but Louise Fatio has brought to it a nice sense of timing and has pointed up the comedy with a touch of satire. Roger Duvoisin has portrayed an ingratiating lion and a typical French village in a *crise* with all his customary Gallic wit.

> *Ellen Lewis Buell, "Bewildered Caller," in* The New York Times Book Review, *August 22, 1954, p. 22.*

In a gay, simple story, appealing to ages four to seven for a look-and-listen book, children will meet a most characterful lion, and will laugh at the changes in his expression, and the humorous doings in the town. They also will get a delightful glimpse of provincial France, in a lovely birds'

eye view of town and zoo, and in street scenes where their parents balconies, the baskets, bags, long loaves of bread, that taken together mean France, and small children can learn one bit of French: "Bonjour."

> *Louise S. Bechtel, in a review of "The Happy Lion," in* New York Herald Tribune Book Review, *September 5, 1954, p. 7.*

Story and illustrations combine to make this an engaging picture book. In rhythmic prose, which makes skilled use of repetition, word sounds, and humor, the wife of Roger Duvoisin tells the tale of an amiable lion who lives in a zoo in a little French town. . . .

The illustrations, broad in scope and large in perspective, have delightful detail and a quality of humor as ingratiating as that of the story.

> *Elizabeth Nesbitt, in a review of "The Happy Lion," in* The Saturday Review, New York, *Vol. XXXVII, No. 46, November 13, 1954, p. 66.*

Two Lonely Ducks, A Counting Book (1955)

Two Lonely Ducks . . . is an instructive as well as a beautiful picture book that will teach children how to count up to ten. This is accomplished in Mr. Duvoisin's own inimitable way by means of line-and-wash drawings coupled with rhythmic counting phrases in the text.

The author of **Petunia** has another lovely book to his credit—a counting book that is artistic and informative.

> *Rae Emerson Donlon, in a review of "Two Lonely Ducks," in* The Christian Science Monitor, *May 12, 1955, p. 11.*

I cannot think of a happier way of learning to count than by turning the pages of this delightful and beautiful little picture book. A new picture book by Roger Duvoisin is always an event, and this one is a major one for spring 1955. The flowing expressive line, the sensitive texture and tone, the simplicity and bold grace of the design shine out on every page. Roger Duvoisin does more with white space than most illustrators with a profusion of detail. A few lines, a few discreet touches of color and there is conveyed a marvelous feeling of the countryside where the two lonely white ducks set up housekeeping and end up with a fine family.

> *Mario Cimino, in a review of "Two Lonely Ducks," in* The Saturday Review, New York, *Vol. XXXVIII, No. 20, May 14, 1955, p. 47.*

Roger Duvoisin is so resourceful and inventive that it seems unnecessary for him to join in the present craze for counting books, at best not much more than an excuse for a book. In the event he manages to put a surprising amount of variety into two ducks, ten eggs and ten ducklings, drawing with customary strength and warmth, but most of us would have preferred something a bit more difficult and more funny. (p. 166)

> *A review of "Two Lonely Ducks," in* The Junior Bookshelf, *Vol. 30, No. 3, June, 1966, pp. 165-66.*

One Thousand Christmas Beards   (1955)

A natural for the Christmas season shows another of Roger Duvoisin's pleasant quirks of the imagination as Santa becomes actively distressed about all the other Santas who are trying to pose as him. Going on the warpath, the real Santa unmasks them all and is triumphant until his wife makes him realize that the others, too, help bring cheer to all who can't see Santa himself. The beards are returned. The author's pictures on each page are in seasonal colors.

> *A review of "One Thousand Christmas Beards," in* Virginia Kirkus' Service, *Vol. XXIII, No. 16, August 15, 1955, p. 592.*

That eternal question asked by the curious younger child who sees so many Santa Clauses around at Christmas, is answered by Mr. Duvoisin in an original funny story. . . . The solution, and [Santa's] wife's argument, will make every one happy. The funny pictures, full of action, with their bright red and green colors, are just right to go under a Christmas tree.

> *Louise S. Bechtel, in a review of "One Thousand Christmas Beards," in* New York Herald Tribune Book Review, *December 11, 1955, p. 8.*

All that [this] book succeeds in doing is divesting Santa and his helpers of any vestige of Christmas spirit. Walters' *The Real Santa Claus* (Lothrop, 1950) is a better book for helping young children to understand why there are so many Santas around at Christmas time.

> *A review of "One Thousand Christmas Beards," in* Bulletin of the Children's Book Center, *Vol. IX, No. 5, January, 1956, p. 59.*

The House of Four Seasons   (1956)

What a delightful way to present color combinations to the picture-book age! What a delightful book for any one who enjoys color and has ever puzzled over the ideal shade for his house or his room or even for just a piece of furniture! No one can ever decide on the loveliest, just like the father, mother and children in this family when they want the perfect color for their house in every season. They decide to experiment with all the colors but they find they can buy only yellow, blue and red. Daubing bold splashes of these singly and together on sketches of their house they discover how many color combinations are possible on the quaint old house. Each color looks beautiful, for a particular season and they argue as families do. Then father finds the perfect solution as he twirls all the colors together to show the one that contains all the others. The house "was very beautiful" and so is Mr. Duvoisin's feast of color which fairly shouts with joy in clear, bright pigment even on the end papers. We are not surprised that "when it was all finished the birds flew and sang in all the bushes and the old owl came back to live in an old tree near by."

> *"An Honor to Bright Color," in* New York

His home was not the hot and dangerous plains of Africa
where hunters lie in wait with their guns,
it was a lovely French town with brown tile roofs and gray shutters.
The happy lion had a house in the town zoo, all for himself,
with a large rock garden surrounded by a moat,
in the middle of a park with flower beds and a bandstand.

From The Happy Lion, *written by Louise Fatio. Illustrated by Roger Duvoisin.*

Herald Tribune Book Review, *May 13, 1956, p. 16.*

What a riot of color excites the eye and kindles the imagination in this beautiful and ingenious picture book, intended to acquaint young children with colors and their combinations. . . . It takes Father, crossing colors to show how they change and spinning them to show the one color which contains all the rest, to find the perfect one for their house, in this gayest and loveliest of Duvoisin creations.

Polly Goodwin, in a review of "The House of Four Seasons," in Chicago Tribune, *June 17, 1956, p. 11.*

Roger Duvoisin has spun a little story out of the three-colour process and illustrated it with some of his mastery. . . .

The idea is rather better than the execution, but still this is a sensible unpretentious book, written with economy and illustrated, if not with exuberance at least with great competence and a little spirit.

A review of "The House of Four Seasons," in The Junior Bookshelf, *Vol. 24, No. 4, October, 1960, p. 214.*

Petunia, Beware! (1958)

Another delightful interlude with that silly goose, Petunia. A firm believer that the grass *is* greener on the other side of home, Petunia intrepidly wanders off to the hill top where, not only is the grass parched and dry, but where at every step a hungry animal eyes Petunia thinking that she would make a more than ample dinner. Petunia's predicament turns out to be a treat for the reader as it includes him in an adventure through Roger Duvoisin's green, green fields, brilliantly alive with colored growing things, and with a whole repertoire of utterly beguiling animals. Suspense, wisdom, and warm humor—a must.

A review of "Petunia, Beware!" in Virginia Kirkus' Service, *Vol. XXVI, No. 13, July 1, 1958, p. 451.*

[Petunia's] journeying follows a repetitive folk-tale pattern as one after another of her friendly animal neighbors warns her of unfriendly ones at large, and as she finds ever again that the grass isn't a bit greener. A concluding wild scramble and the earlier serene wanderings have animated pictorial interpretation, in lively black and white and in a bright burst of colors. Amusing for preschool storytelling.

Virginia Haviland, in a review of "Petunia, Beware!" in The Horn Book Magazine, *Vol. XXXIV, No. 5, October, 1958, p. 377.*

Petunia is certainly one of the immortals of goosedom, holding a place in children's affections close to that of the Golden Goose and Jemima Puddleduck. There is great fun both in the story and pictures of her latest adventure, not unlike Jemima's, which came about because she was very silly and only wanted what she didn't have. . . . Poor Petunia! She met not only fox but weasel, raccoon and bobcat, and would never have returned to decide that

"her home grass was the best grass she had ever tasted" but for the lucky fact that all four enemies wanted her so ardently that a wild fracas ensued. Very satisfactory as an ending for the picture-book age.

"Riches in Verse and Story to Stimulate Eager Eyes and Minds," in New York Herald Tribune Book Review, *November 2, 1958, p. 3.*

Day and Night (1960)

Since Day, a poodle in the Pennyfull household, never went out at night, and Night, an owl living in a near-by wood, slept all day, their friendship, which began one twilight when Day rescued Night from a marauding fox, seemed doomed from the beginning. After dark Night hung around outside Day's window WHOO-ING away, and Day howled back at him, to the irritation of the senior Pennyfulls, who wanted to sleep and understood not a word of such animal conversation. Night and Day would have been parted forever had young Bob Pennyfull not grasped the situation and invented a perfect solution. The result was a happy one for both Day and Night (and also for the Senior Pennyfulls), and each animal was able to share all his secrets with the other until "between them they knew all about night and day." For children of the picture-book age this offers a brief diversion and in color effective sketches of the dark woods in shifting pattern of night and day.

"Wishes, Supposings, Puns," in New York Herald Tribune Book Review, *May 8, 1960, p. 30.*

A poodle named Day and an owl named Night are allowed to continue their early dawn conversations in Mr. Duvoisin's fantasy, thanks to the intervention of a sympathetic small boy. The notion is a bit tricky, as if it were based on reversed Cole Porter word-play. It is as an artist that Mr. Duvoisin makes the brightest comments about his chief characters, who emerge, respectively, all quivering curly-cues and solemn eyes. Incidentally, the final resolution does not seem quite credible by the conversational standards of dogs, owls, or humans. But 4-8's may well find it no less logical than adults find Thurber's dealings with the same subjects.

Melvin Maddocks, "Furry Tales," in The Christian Science Monitor, *May 12, 1960, p. 4B.*

Veronica (1961)

Like *Hubert the Travelling Hippopotamus* Veronica leaves her own environment to achieve some degree of individuality in the realm of people. But, unlike Hubert, Veronica is a purely fictional hippo with definite ulterior motives. Indistinguishable from her brethren in the swamps, she heads for the city where, to mingled astonishment, chagrin and delight, she stops traffic, consumes a vegetable cart, bathes in the city fountain, parks at a fire hydrant and requires an army of people to push her through the jail entrance. Relieved to be back with her fellow hippos, Veronica's exciting stories gain her a special place among her own kind. These hilarious events visualized in sublimely mirthful colored illustrations make this a real winner.

> *A review of "Veronica," in* Virginia Kirkus' Service, *Vol. XXIX, No. 12, June 15, 1961, p. 497.*

Add now to that special zoo of animal characters which Roger Duvoisin has created with brush and pen Veronica, a young, ambitious hippopotamus. Although, as Mr. Duvoisin tells us blandly, "Hippopotamuses can sometimes be very conspicuous," Veronica suffers from a feeling of anonymity among her innumerable relatives and that is easy to understand from Mr. Duvoisin's pictures. Longing for fame, she invades a city and eventually emerges, after some rather remarkable adventures, with the realization that one can, after all, be *too* conspicuous. Young readers and listeners, many of whom also like to be seen and heard, may interpret this idea any way they like. In any case, they will undoubtedly find Veronica—snoozing casually in a city street, hiding behind a park bench, being literally bulldozed into jail, very funny.

> *Ellen Lewis Buell, "Traveling Two," in* The New York Times Book Review, *August 27, 1961, p. 22.*

Clever, beautifully colored drawings of bizarre predicaments due to Veronica's monstrous hulk keep this from being just one more tale of an animal suffering from an excess of human emotion.

> *Virginia Haviland, in a review of "Veronica," in* The Horn Book Magazine, *Vol. XXXVII, No. 5, October, 1961, p. 433.*

The Happy Hunter (1961)

Now with the hunting season upon us the tender-hearted can take comfort from Roger Duvoisin's pictorial comedy about a reluctant Nimrod. From his little house on the edge of the forest Mr. Bobbin watches the hunters go by and thinks "it must be nice to look so big and bold and to walk through the forests, across field, up the hills and down the valleys." So he starts out with a fine new gun but he has reckoned without his own soft heart. How he manages *not* to bag even one animal that season and in many to follow, and how the animals repay his kindness makes a gentle, funny story for all but the bloodthirsty. Noteworthy, too, are Mr. Duvoisin's serenely beautiful November landscapes.

> *Ellen Lewis Buell, "Reluctant Nimrod," in* The New York Times Book Review, *October 29, 1961, p. 42.*

A repetitive tale about Mr. Bobbin who makes sure that each hunting day ends in the escape of rabbit or squirrel or 'possum; when he retires from active life, the animals miss him so much that they come in a body to visit him at home. An idyllic American countryside, with towering trees and rustic interiors, is illustrated in a pointilliste style, in muted greens and yellows, which is unusual and charming.

> *Margery Fisher, in a review of "The Happy Hunter," in* Growing Point, *Vol. 1, No. 6, December, 1962, p. 93.*

Our Veronica Goes to Petunia's Farm (1962)

Mr. Duvoisin is in top form as author and illustrator of **Our Veronica Goes to Petunia's Farm.** In her second book the happy hippo is not so happy. Oh, the farm is beautiful, the mud is just right for wallowing, the meadow grass green and tasty—but the barnyard animals are unfriendly. Never having seen a hippopotamus, they think Veronica is a fat, ugly outsider—a "foreigner." Our Veronica wastes away until each animal's timid gesture of friendship puts her back on her feet. A slightly grave story but grand in meaning and illustration.

> *George A. Woods, in a review of "Our Veronica Goes to Petunia's Farm," in* The New York Times Book Review, *November 11, 1962, p. 56.*

Spring Snow (1963)

Round-faced Mr. Pippin sat reading his paper while smiley-faced Mrs. Pippin sat knitting some socks. In almost-spring, giant snow flakes—which constitute too many of the illustrations—fill the sky. The Pippins begin shovelling their drive, and are buried up to their knees, their waists, their heads,—gone. Angry Mr. Sun melts the snow, and the good old Pippins come smilingly to life along with their barnyard menagerie. While the illustrations are skillfully designed, this slight, snow-bound book is not comparable to other works of this esteemed author-illustrator.

> *A review of "Spring Snow," in* Virginia Kirkus' Service, *Vol. XXXI, No. 4, February 15, 1963, p. 182.*

Roger Duvoisin has a nice, slight idea, about the Spring snow which fell briefly but alarmingly, and in theory the gradual emergence of Mr. and Mrs. Peppin and their farmstead under the rays of the sun is funny. In practice it is not quite well enough done. To mention just one detail—if so much of each page is to be blank white to represent snow, then that page must be opaque; the whole idea becomes pointless if, as here, one can see the next page's print ghost-like through the white.

> *A review of "Spring Snow," in* The Junior Bookshelf, *Vol. 30, No. 2, April, 1966, p. 113.*

Roger Duvoisin illustrates the process of the glaring sun melting the snow with great humour, little tufts sticking out of the snow are gradually revealed, page by page, as the farm animals, while the snow sinks lower and disappears and the Peppins go back to their fire. This is a very entertaining book in which the blue and grey illustrations and the text fit together to make a very satisfying whole, each being equally important to the book. The lively text has lots of repetition, so that even a non reader can join in and enjoy helping to tell the story. A very simple but attractive book.

> *S. P., in a review of "Spring Snow," in* Children's Book Review, *Vol. IV, No. 1, Spring, 1974, p. 15.*

Lonely Veronica (1963)

Veronica, the intrepid hippo of **Our Veronica Goes to Petunia's Farm** is on the loose again. This time she is in New York doing exactly what most boys, some girls, and almost no hippopotamus would enjoy. "She could watch the bulldozers, the cranes, and the steam shovels pull, dig, build and demolish," giving her author-artist a wonderful opportunity to show his love of bold design, colors, and changing textures amid the geometry of high New York. How Veronica gets stranded in a half-built tower above the clouds, finds a friend, food and another occupation should bring giggles and sighs of relief to the 4-7's.

> Guernsey LePelley, "Seeworthy Fun and Otter Nonsense," in The Christian Science Monitor, November 14, 1963, p. 2B.

An artist of lesser inventiveness and humor might have difficulty in keeping such a character as Veronica the hippopotamus in pursuit of acceptable anthropomorphic adventures—but not Mr. Duvoisin. Here he reveals how Veronica came to leave Africa and find the farm home described in the preceding book. When men bulldozed through the hippopotamuses' contented river country, the hippos held a conference in which the elders decided that the good old days were gone. But Veronica was young and said, " 'I want to see the good *new* days.' " This spirit carried her, as the pet of the machine crew, all the way to the jungle of New York and fantastic involvement in high-rise construction. The four-color pictures and alternating ones in black and white with their great good humor and brilliance of tones will prove immensely entertaining.

> Virginia Haviland, in a review of "Lonely Veronica," in The Horn Book Magazine, Vol. XXXIX, No. 6, December, 1963, p. 591.

It is painful to be less than enthusiastic about Roger Duvoisin, but his latest Veronica book is not among his best. The colours are often horribly garish, and the fun which Mr. Duvoisin squeezes out of the incongruity of a hippopotamus in an urban setting is stretched to the limit. There are good things, notably the last idyllic picture of Veronica at peace on the farm, but on this occasion they have to be looked for.

> A review of "Lonely Veronica," in The Junior Bookshelf, Vol. 28, No. 4, October, 1964, p. 225.

Veronica's Smile (1964)

Everyone else on the farm is useful except Veronica, who is bored and depressed with nothing to do. A hippo can be handy, she finds, as her cavernous mouth serves as a hideaway for a scared rabbit; a nest for orphaned pheasant chicks; jail for a marauding weasel; a weapon against Old-Ogre Bear and, in his most glorious achievement, an ark for the farmer's son. The story's point is that we all do the best we can with what we have—and Veronica does it very well. Mr. Duvoisin does even better in colorfully portraying the farmyard and woodland life.

> George A. Woods, in a review of "Veronica's Smile," in The New York Times Book Review, October 4, 1964, p. 26.

Roger Duvoisin is always the professional, but he is not always equally happy in inspiration. After several recent books on a low level of humour and spontaneity he finds his best form again in **Veronica's Smile**. . . . The drawing is beautiful in its extreme simplicity and so is the writing.

> A review of "Veronica's Smile," in The Junior Bookshelf, Vol. 29, No. 4, August, 1965, p. 209.

Hide and Seek Fog (1965)

[Hide and Seek Fog *was written by Alvin Tresselt.*]

The inviting title and book jacket picture of children at play on a hazy shore will beckon each child who spies this book. He won't be disappointed when he listens to this poetic mood piece describing a New England village as it waits for a long and heavy fog to pass. He will feel the chill and dampness as he studies Roger Duvoisin's exquisite water colors, a total departure from the overly familiar style of the artist some of whose recent books have looked as if he tossed them together before he gulped down his morning coffee and rushed out the door to do something more important. The ethereal beauty of fog on the landscape is sustained even on the endpapers and on the title-page which depicts the fishing boats in the harbor. The opening pages sparkle in brilliant blue; then the fog descends on sea and shore. The fishermen come home, the holiday visitors grumble and the children play indoors. The text falters occasionally but not enough to mar the feeling of suspended motion throughout the village. " . . . the fog twisted about the cottages like slow-motion smoke. It dulled the rusty scraping of the beach grass. It muffled the chattery talk of the low tide waves." There are several fine picture books about the atmosphere along the New England coast. This takes its place among them and has a quality all its own. (pp. 956-57)

> Patricia H. Allen, in a review of "Hide and Seek Fog," in Library Journal, Vol. 90, No. 4, February 15, 1965, pp. 956-67.

A companion volume to this author and artist's **White Snow Bright Snow,** this is even more successful in bringing to children the misty feeling of a fog that settled down on a Cape Cod village and transformed it for three days. Young people in coastal towns and villages, or the cities so often blanketed by fog or smog, will find special meaning in the book.

Its pictures differ in style from the artist's usual ones. There are misty figures of children and adults moving with the grace of a ballet through the fog. There are also brightly colored scenes indoors by the fire and outdoors when the sun returns.

> Alice Dalgliesh, in a review of "Hide and Seek Fog," in Saturday Review, Vol. XLVIII, No. 13, March 27, 1965, p. 33.

Mr. Tresselt's poetic prose, characteristic of his other stories describing seasonal experiences, is simple, direct, friendly. Mr. Duvoisin's illustrations, however, are a departure from his previous work for children. As shadowy shapes and muted shades move, haunting and ephemeral, through floating, "cotton-wool" mist, who can say what surprises lie in wait beyond the gray haze? Another distinguished achievement by the author-illustrator team.

> *Priscilla L. Moulton, in a review of "Hide and Seek Fog," in* The Horn Book Magazine, *Vol. XLI, No. 2, April, 1965, p. 164.*

Petunia, I Love You   (1965)

Raccoon, looking at Petunia, the goose, sees a wonderful feast, so he invites her for a walk, planning by guile to forestall any danger from her powerful wings. When Petunia continually saves Raccoon from the results of the backfiring of his wily schemes, he is forced to give up his wicked plans, to thank Petunia, and to swear to be her truest friend forever. A fable that is endlessly funny to little children is told with a touch of sophistication in text and in pictures—some in strong, flat colors.

> *Ruth Hill Viguers, in a review of "Petunia, I Love You," in* The Horn Book Magazine, *Vol. XLII, No. 2, April, 1966, p. 189.*

We all love Petunia, too, and with no ulterior motives. Raccoon thought she was pretty enough to eat, and wanted to do just that. There is, however, a special providence to protect foolish geese, and Raccoon falls—quite literally—into his own traps. Petunia, whose head may not be too bright but who has her heart in the right place, rescues him to provide a most satisfying happy ending. All this is done with unobtrusive good style, both in words and in pictures. No one packs so much character into a few words and lines as Mr. Duvoisin. He is beyond question the master in his own line of country, and a generous contributor to the joy of nations.

> *A review of "Petunia, I Love You," in* The Junior Bookshelf, *Vol. 31, No. 1, February, 1967, p. 32.*

The Missing Milkman   (1967)

The milkman isn't really missing. He has just gone fishing with Sylvia, his dachshund, and Amelia, his truck. One day, irked by the same tedious routine—turning left and right on the same streets, stopping and starting at the same houses and chatting about the same thing with the same housewives—he loads up and cuts out for the open country. A week off swimming and fishing where the world is green and blue; where the kingfishers fly and bears steal ice cream is the right kind of a holiday to revive a milkman's morale. Roger Duvoisin has told a pleasant, perceptive story and dedicated it to all the milkmen who rarely miss a day on their routes. His blithe and brightly colored illustrations have a vitality that helps keep a long and leisurely text from lagging too much. (pp. 27-8)

> *Margaret F. O'Connell, in a review of "The Missing Milkman," in* The New York Times Book Review, *March 12, 1967, pp. 27-8.*

There is an attractive immorality about the milkman's spontaneous escape, accompanied by his dog Sylvia and his truck Amelia, to an isolated bear kingdom, where he can fish and enjoy a Thoreau-like life-style far from the maddening housewives' incessant prattle. When he re-

turns it isn't because he's run out of dairy products to eat (after sharing them, in a brotherly way, with the bears), but because after a taste of privacy and idyllic isolation, he misses the jabbering ladies. Togetherness triumphs.

Thus [Duvoisin, pursuing the theme of] . . . the urge to privacy and escape from group pressures [reaches the] conclusion: "You MUST go home again." It is, I suppose, one way of conditioning children to accept the awful truth about modern living and the "loss of self" with resignation. But what if the milkman had stayed with the bears. . . .

> *Barbara Novak O'Doherty, "Earthbound," in* Book Week—The Washington Post, *June 18, 1967, p. 14.*

What Is Right for Tulip   (1969)

An utterly relaxed bear asleep in the snow, a dreamy smile on his face—every Roger Duvoisin animal carries his unmistakable hallmark. ***What is Right for Tulip . . .*** has more than its share of Duvoisin animal personalities and visual wit. A crocodile, dragon, rhinoceros, a bunch of hens, and Tulip the bear himself appear as pro and con examples of what is the right thing to do. It is a lesson (in full color, of course) that is far too fascinating to irk even the oldest of the 4-7 age group.

> *Pamela Marsh, "A Glance at the Winners," in* The Christian Science Monitor, *November 6, 1969, p. B1.*

Roger Duvoisin's latest picture-book boasts attractive illustrations which are, however, far less dazzling than those he did, for example, for Dayton's ***Earth and Sky*** (Harper, 1969); similarly, the book fails to sustain a mood with the success of such previous Duvoisin titles as ***Petunia*** and ***Veronica.*** The slight storyline seeks to contrast what appeals to a polar bear with what children and other animals enjoy. For example, Tulip the polar bear is shown to enjoy washing in icy water, while the cat washes herself without water and Bill washes himself in his shower with a washcloth, brush, and soap. The text is marred by digressions: e.g., after showing how different animals wash, eat, and greet others, Duvoisin embarks on a consideration of which animals—dragons among them, Tulip not mentioned—share and which don't. Such inconsistencies probably wouldn't bother young listeners, and they would like the delightfully colored pictures. But the book as a whole is very skimpy fare.

> *Pat Byars, in a review of "What Is Right for Tulip," in* School Library Journal, *Vol. 16, No. 6, February, 1970, p. 69.*

Veronica and the Birthday Present   (1971)

Duvoisin's dashing pictures have far more zing than this uninspired, tedious tale about Veronica, the hippopotamus of amiable character whose exploits generally teach a lesson. In this appearance she befriends a "white as sugar icing" kitten named Candy. Veronica won't stay with Mr. and Mrs. Pumpkin unless Candy is there too, but Candy belongs to Mr. and Mrs. Applegreen. After prolonged treks back and forth between the two families, the two are reunited on the Pumpkin farm, and Mr. Applegreen brings his wife a new kitten—Candy's twin, Periwinkle. Veronica is more likable in, among others, **Veronica's Smile** and **Our Veronica Goes to Petunia's Farm.** (pp. 63-4)

> *Cary M. Ormond, in a review of "Veronica and the Birthday Present," in* School Library Journal, *Vol. 18, No. 9, May, 1972, pp. 63-4.*

What a pleasure it is to welcome another Veronica book from this talented writer and artist, especially as this is as good as any in the series. . . . The repetition of the action, the delicious words heard in the names of the animals and the expletives of the farmer, the perfect marriage of picture and text, combine to make great appeal to the three and four-year-old. Altogether this is a very happy little story, funny and touching at the same time. . . .

> *C. Martin, in a review of "Veronica and the Birthday Present," in* The Junior Bookshelf, *Vol. 36, No. 3, June, 1972, p. 153.*

The Crocodile in the Tree   (1972)

In Roger Duvoisin's stories accord among the animals is generally the rule, but sometimes the human characters take a while to get hold of the right end of the stick. When Bertha the duck brings a crocodile to live in Farmer Sweetpeas's barnyard there is a brief moment of panic among the other animals, but they are quick to recognize the friendly intentions of the newcomer. Mrs. Sweetpeas, however, is terrified when he appears out of a pile of hay and gives her his sweetest smile, and it is only after a long siege that he finally wins her heart. **The Crocodile in the Tree** is as kindly and humorous as all Mr Duvoisin's books, and his pictures are a riot of colour and activity.

> *"In the Garden of Eden," in* The Times Literary Supplement, *No. 3687, November 3, 1972, p. 1327.*

A deliciously absurd story about a duck who befriends a crocodile living upside down in a tree. She takes him to the farmyard where, despite his crocodile reputation, his pleasant ways win over first the other animals and then, through their shared interest in beautiful flowers, the farmer's wife and her husband. It is all told in Roger Duvoisin's inimitable way, as though the most outrageous impossibilities were an everyday matter. Crocodiles and their tears being what they are, there is an element of suspense till we finally discover that this crocodile, at least, is genuinely altruistic.

> *M. Hobbs, in a review of "The Crocodile in the Tree," in* The Junior Bookshelf, *Vol. 37, No. 1, February, 1973, p. 18.*

Duvoisin's illustrations carry along the light-hearted story which is as good as his Petunia and Veronica tales. Since most children enjoy alligator stories, this one, which places the animal in an unlikely situation, should be a popular selection for story hours. (p. 108)

> *Dorothy E. Lovelock, in a review of "The Crocodile in the Tree," in* School Library Journal, *Vol. 20, No. 2, October, 1973, pp. 107-08.*

Jasmine   (1973)

When Jasmine the raspberry-colored cow starts parading around the barnyard in a fancy bonnet, the other animals call her good-for-nothing, pretentious and sick, but it doesn't take long after they discover that the Pumpkin attic is full of old hats before they are all similarly attired. Nonconformist Jasmine then removes her hat, provoking the same reaction of outrage followed by emulation, and then—maddeningly—puts it back on. A plot to pull off the offending badge of individuality is foiled when Anne Pumpkin appears to take a picture of "the queen of the barnyard . . . who did not mind NOT being like everyone else." It's an accurate enough reflection of fashion dynamics, though it seems to us that Jasmine, who can't abide BEING like everyone else, is just as silly as the rest of them. She does, of course, provide Duvoisin with occasion for dressing up his rainbow of livestock in a fetchingly ludicrous assortment of feathers, ribbons and lace.

> *A review of "Jasmine," in* Kirkus Reviews, *Vol. XLI, No. 18, September 15, 1973, p. 1030.*

Duvoisin's gay pictures are always charming, and his heroine here is a particularly captivating plump pink cow, Jasmine, who finds and wears an old hat. . . . The message is that one should dare to be different, but the story line is thin, especially in the concluding episode, in which the sight of a camera convinces all the barnyard to shift to amity. (pp. 108-09)

> *Zena Sutherland, in a review of "Jasmine," in* Bulletin of the Center for Children's Books, *Vol. 27, No. 7, March, 1974, pp. 108-09.*

See What I Am   (1974)

A conversation among the colors, in which each hue sings its own praises until finally they all agree that "none of us can do without the others." Their speeches are poetic verging on precious ("See how bright I am. I am the chrysanthemums that cheer the autumn gardens. I am the yellow cat who sleeps in the sun . . . "). But at the foot of each page Max the Cat adds some deflating criticism, rejecting each color one after another until they get together—with individual color separations that are eventually merged into a "full" color page—to make him his proper three-toned self. This all adds up to a reasonably clever demonstration of elementary color theory and even color printing, but it would have been better if "red" did not appear as a pastel pink and better still if Duvoisin's impish collages were not so out of sync with his gentle "lovely" prose. Somewhat hokier than the usual Duvoisin. (pp. 938-39)

> *A review of "See What I Am," in* Kirkus Reviews, *Vol. XLII, No. 17, September 1, 1974, pp. 938-39.*

Max is a good-looking kitten, if he does say so himself. That is not clear, however, when you see him all yellow, blue, red or even black. In white he disappears save for his eyes and claws, and in the binary green of blue plus yellow, or the purple of red plus blue, he is in danger of becoming a laughingstock among mice. Once in the full harmony of four-color superposition on the clean white page, Max is himself: "white with yellowish-reddish, black spots and blue eyes." You *are* good-looking, Max, and you present lightly and well, with a bit of sly sermon, how a few colors form the richer images we see. For families with new readers or small listeners, here is a pleasant and meaningful book.

> *Philip Morrison and Phylis Morrison, in a review of "See What I Am," in* Scientific American, *Vol. 231, No. 6, December, 1974, p. 148.*

Petunia's Treasure (1975)

Petunia the goose finds a trunk at the bottom of the river and decides that it is a treasure chest. What happens when she returns to the barnyard with her news and the animals expect their rich friend to give them each a gift makes a happy tale in the best Duvoisin tradition. Petunia is as bright and sassy as when she first appeared in 1950. Duvoisin's humorous full-color illustrations will captivate children who enjoyed the earlier Petunia books. (pp. 41-2)

> *Margaret Maxwell, in a review of "Petunia's Treasure," in* School Library Journal, *Vol. 22, No. 4, December, 1975, pp. 41-2.*

A slight tale must depend on the author's lively, colorful pictures for its appeal; dependably, Duvoisin provides frisky, familiar barnyard beasts in great variety, drawn with masterful humor and vigor. (p. 95)

> *Zena Sutherland, in a review of "Petunia's Treasure," in* Bulletin of the Center for Children's Books, *Vol. 29, No. 6, February, 1976, pp. 94-5.*

This pleasant book follows the style of its four predecessors. Emphasis is laid firmly on the funny side of acquisitive folly, rather than on drawing a moral. It is careless plotting, though, that we see no sign of the rainstorm which apparently overturned the trunk, revealing its emptiness, between Petunia's two visits to the riverbed.

> *R. Baines, in a review of "Petunia's Treasure," in* The Junior Bookshelf, *Vol. 41, No. 3, June, 1977, p. 153.*

Periwinkle (1976)

Duvoisin's muted, dappled backgrounds are a pleasant and fit reflection of giraffe Periwinkle's loneliness, but page after page spotlighting the awkward, long-necked creature stretching this way or that is simply boring. And the story, about an English-speaking giraffe longing for someone to talk to, is essentially a long-winded statement of a minor moral. When Periwinkle finds Lotus, a frog who also speaks English, their mutual delight soon gives way to anger as both insist on doing all the talking; another fight ensues when both, overpolite, insist on listening; somehow it takes Periwinkle rescuing Lotus from a hungry jackal for the two to begin talking *with* each other. A talented reader-aloud might make a good show of the conversations, but scintillating they're not.

> *A review of "Periwinkle," in* Kirkus Reviews, *Vol. XLIV, No. 17, September 1, 1976, p. 970.*

The softly colored pictures, paint and collage, are attractive if repetitive, but the text is a bit forced. There is no explanation of how Periwinkle has achieved her freedom; there's a slight message about give and take in communication, and some humor in the communications failure, but the plot is not very substantial.

> *Zena Sutherland, in a review of "Periwinkle," in* Bulletin of the Center for Children's Books, *Vol. 30, No. 7, March, 1977, p. 105.*

Crocus (1977)

Roger Duvoisin's new book shows how far he has moved from *The Happy Lion* and *Petunia* into the world of modern illustrators—a softening of colour and background, reminiscent of the Japanese children's artists, here emanates in splendid pink and yellow cows, blue and brown horses, and a violet dog with pink spots against delicate pastel washes. The Crocodile in the Tree, now named as Crocus, has obtained the farm's respect by his teeth. When they have to be removed, he feels and indeed is insignificant. The Sweetpeas family realise the trouble and get him crocodile dentures, with a happy restoration of the status quo.

> *M. Hobbs, in a review of "Crocus," in* The Junior Bookshelf, *Vol. 42, No. 1, February, 1978, p. 13.*

Crocus, Duvoisin's *Crocodile in the Tree,* is back, now firmly ensconced on the farm of Mr. and Mrs. Sweetpeas with his canine, feline, and equine friends. The illustrations are better than ever, particularly the two-page spread of Crocus stretched full length in all his green greenness. However, the lesson this time—that everyone needs some attribute in order to feel important—may be a bit on the double-edged side as Crocus' prized possession is his set of intimidating teeth.

> *Merrie Lou Cohen, in a review of "Crocus," in* School Library Journal, *Vol. 24, No. 8, April, 1978, p. 68.*

Snowy and Woody (1979)

In this simple, unprepossessing picture book, a bird friend's tales of fields and flowers entice polar bear Snowy to go South. And the same bird wisely intervenes when Snowy meets brown bear Woody and the two begin to fight. "Be friends instead and help each other," shrieks Kitty from the skies, and thereafter Woody covers Snowy's conspicuous white hide whenever a helicopter or airplane goes by. Snowy gets a chance to return the favor come winter, but by then each bear is feeling an inward pull to his accustomed winter headquarters—Woody to his cave and Snowy to his Arctic ice pack. Unmodulated and altogether unexceptional, but the story holds up because it is neither arbitrarily concocted nor underlined with meaning.

> *A review of "Snowy and Woody," in* Kirkus Reviews, *Vol. XLVII, No. 19, October 1, 1979, p. 1140.*

Duvoisin uses the story of two bears to inculcate gently the

From Hide and Seek Fog, *written by Alvin Tresselt. Illustrated by Roger Duvoisin.*

concept of protective coloration in nature. . . . While the trek south may give erroneous ideas to the lap audience, the story is appealing because of its simple, direct style, its theme of mutual help, and its illustrations, delicate in hues, strong in line and texture.

> *Zena Sutherland, in a review of "Snowy and Woody," in* Bulletin of the Center for Children's Books, *Vol. 33, No. 8, April, 1980, p. 149.*

The Importance of Crocus (1980)

Crocus, for those unfortunate enough to have missed Roger Duvoisin's two earlier books, is a crocodile; not the terror of the swamps but an amiable and much-liked member of the farmyard community. In this third book Crocus tries to match himself against the other farm animals and finds that, in, for example, giving milk or climbing trees, he falls sadly short. Only when he does the things a crocodile excels in does he discover that there is a role for him in a world of specialists. Mr. Duvoisin draws and writes as well as ever.

> *M. Crouch, in a review of "The Importance of Crocus," in* The Junior Bookshelf, *Vol. 45, No. 1, February, 1981, p. 11.*

Crocus is a benign, bright green crocodile that lives on the Sweetpeas' farm. . . . [He] feels useless and clumsy until

the Sweetpeas build a pond on the property, and then he is in his element, swimming and protecting the ducks and geese from foxes and other predators. Duvoisin was born in 1900, and this is the last book completed before his death in 1980; it has simplicity and mellowness, qualities that seem to be produced by great age. The illustrations are vintage Duvoisin; lively colors, soft focus, varied scale, all spread generously across double-page spreads.

> *Mary B. Nickerson, in a review of "The Importance of Crocus," in* School Library Journal, *Vol. 28, No. 2, October, 1981, p. 127.*

Petunia the Silly Goose Stories (1987)

When Roger Duvoisin died in 1980 . . . , few noted the loss of a modern master of the picture book. Yet this author-artist almost single-handedly brought American children's book illustration up to date. Beginning with *A Little Boy Was Drawing,* Duvoisin was the first in the United States to adopt the innovations of the School of Paris to books for young readers. Born in Geneva, he studied in Switzerland and France (one of his classmates was Alberto Giacometti) before moving to New York to work for a textile firm. His master was always Henri Matisse whose admiration for children's artistic sensibilities guided much of Duvoisin's work for boys and girls.

Duvoisin was that rarity in the juvenile book market—an intellectual. He read extensively in child psychology and quietly incorporated Jean Piaget's discoveries into his picture books. He was fascinated by how the young view their world through spontaneous, quick impressions. He also found boys and girls more sophisticated than their elders, less sentimental, less conventional, far more imaginative, and certainly more humorous.

Although one of the most honored of all children's book illustrators, Duvoisin never produced one masterpiece, no *Millions of Cats,* no *Madeline,* no *Where the Wild Things Are.* The book for which he received the Caldecott Medal, **White Snow, Bright Snow** by Alvin Tresselt, is a relatively minor effort. One must consider his entire body of work to fully appreciate his extraordinary contribution to the form. Perhaps his most enduring character is Petunia the goose, heroine of several delightful picture books which Duvoisin both wrote and illustrated and which have just been collected in a single volume. ***Petunia: The Silly Goose Stories*** is Duvoisin at his best.

Duvoisin was one of only a few illustrators as adroit with words as with drawing. A shrewd fabulist, he wrote in a clear, rhythmic, stately style. Petunia and her barnyard companions suffer human passions—pride, greed, vanity, selfishness. In the first of these five tales, Petunia fools herself into believing that by possessing a book she has acquired wisdom. In **"Petunia, Beware!"** (reminiscent of Beatrix Potter's *The Tale of Jemima Puddleduck* and perhaps the best in the collection), the silly goose narrowly escapes with her life to learn that the grass is not greener on the other side. The treasure of **"Petunia's Treasure"** proves to be only fool's gold. The weakest of the stories, but no less charming than the others, is **"Petunia Takes a Trip,"** a simple introduction to the wonders of the big city. **"Petunia's Christmas,"** which describes the goose's devotion to Charles the gander, is one of the tenderest love stories in all of juvenile literature.

The same gentle wit and wisdom is evident everywhere in the lively pictures. Like all great masters of the picture book, Duvoisin says as much with his illustrations as with his words. Experienced as a textile, ceramic and poster designer, Duvoisin brought to his children's work a sophisticated understanding of what could and could not be done with the limitations of color separation. He beautifully juggled various screens and overprintings to produce an impressive range of texture and hue. He was a master in the use of the white of the page.

Fortunately he was never clever for its own sake. His visual virtuosity never distracts the young reader from the enjoyment of the story. He once admitted that it was not easy to be simple. Yet his picture books seem so effortless. He could define character or landscape with only a few deft strokes of the pen and some swatches of overlapping primary colors. In the present edition, some of the black-and-white pictures have been newly color separated by another artist, but happily none of these changes clashes with Duvoisin's original intentions. Perhaps there can be no better way to introduce young readers to Roger Duvoisin's legacy than through these stories of Petunia the silly goose.

> *Michael Patrick Hearn, "Honk, If You Like Petunia," in* Book World—The Washington Post, *July 12, 1987, p. 9.*

Mem Fox
1946-

(Born Merrion Frances Partridge) Australian author of picture books.

Major titles include *Possum Magic* (1983), *Wilfrid Gordon McDonald Partridge* (1984), *Koala Lou* (1987), *Night Noises* (1988).

Often considered Australia's most popular contemporary writer for children, Fox is celebrated for creating picture books which feature Australian settings and characters and are noted for using rhythm, rhyme, and repetition to present young readers with such themes as the importance of memories and the power of love. A nationally and internationally known storyteller as well as an actress and drama teacher, she brings a strong dramatic sense to her books through their scriptlike texts. Her works, which Fox designs to reassure children and to introduce them to reading in a pleasurable way, are either pure fantasy, strict realism, or a combination of both. Featuring both human and animal characters in stories which receive either humorous or serious treatments and often spotlight the elderly, the books characteristically center on female protagonists who help others or receive positive reinforcement for their actions. An unusual feature of Fox's works is her inclusion of positive adult figures who aid the young protagonists through love, attention, and problem-solving abilities. Fox is perhaps best known as the author of her first picture book, *Possum Magic* (1983), which is considered a classic of recent Australian children's literature as well as one of its most successful bestsellers. Describing how the grandmother of Hush the possum makes her invisible by bush magic and how the pair set off on a rollicking culinary tour of Australia in order to find the antidote, the story describes a variety of locales and dishes; the popularity of *Possum Magic* in Australia has spawned an industry of clothing, calendars, bedding, and other items.

In addition to *Possum Magic,* Fox is the creator of several other notable works for young readers. Her second book, *Wilfrid Gordon McDonald Partridge,* is the only one of her titles to feature a male protagonist; taking his name from Fox's father, young Wilfrid gathers a basket full of items that he hopes will trigger the memories lost by his friend, elderly Miss Nancy. In *Night Noises,* another popular title featuring an elderly protagonist, Fox presents another tender sharing between young and old: Lillie Laseby, nearly ninety, snoozes at home and dreams of the important events in her life as the noises of the evening continue to build; the noises are revealed to be Lillie's friends and relatives who have come to celebrate her birthday. Fox received a mixed reception for *With Love, at Christmas* (1988), a miracle story in which the elderly protagonist is found dead by her family. However, Fox is credited with creating one of her most charming works with *Koala Lou:* set in the Australian bush, the story describes how a young koala bear tries to get the attention of her weary yet sympathetic mother by becoming a contestant in the Bush Olympics. Fox is also the author of such works as the adventures of a miniature girl, a cumulative tale about an ob-

servant hen and a hungry fox, a picture book in verse that uses the rhyming pattern of "The House That Jack Built" to describe how a well-meaning family gets carried away in their attempt to provide one of their members with a new wardrobe, and a picture book designed to present children fearful of nuclear war with a hopeful message; she has also written an informational book for adults on teaching drama to children. *Possum Magic* received the New South Wales Premier's Literary Award for best children's book and the Australian Children's Book Award, picture book of the year highly commended, both in 1984, while *Wilfrid Gordon McDonald Partridge* was short-listed for Picture Book of the Year, Australia, in 1985.

(See also *Something about the Author,* Vol. 51 and *Contemporary Authors,* Vol. 127.)

AUTHOR'S COMMENTARY

Like St. Paul, I too have seen the light! It happened at a National Language Arts Conference in Western Australia in 1979. I went to the conference as a lecturer in drama to talk about storytelling but what I learned about reading literally changed my life. . . .

Let's begin at the beginning. We know that the child is father to the man, or in my case, mother to the woman. I was a fortunate child who grew up in a typical Language-Arts-Ideal-Home. I'm the living product of the book-filled house, with parents who read and valued literature, parents whom I often observed at their own desks, writing, and parents who made time to share and listen to the things that we children were reading and writing. (p. 18)

I am now a mother myself and I've tried to create a literary past for my Chloë that's as rich as my own was. . . . Through books she bonded with my husband and me, and through my husband and me she bonded with books. That's been very important to me as a writer. . . . (p. 19)

So, in 1979, before my Age of Enlightenment, I knew about being a child and being a mother, but I didn't know about being a teacher of reading. . . . I have discovered that I'm a sort of two-headed teacher of reading: I teach reading, as most of us do, using other people's texts; but I also teach reading by virtue of being a writer for young children. . . .

What *do* I know about reading and what difference does it make? By now I guess we all know about the three cueing systems that we use in order to make sense of print:

    1. a. knowledge of the world (semantic),
       b. knowledge of language (syntactic), and
       c. knowledge of print (graphophonic).

                                      (p. 20)

Let's look at the three cueing systems: the first is "knowledge of the world." I was aware of that when I wrote *Possum Magic.* I built on the familiar, such as Vegemite sandwiches, but I also felt a duty to extend the horizons of my readers by including all the state capitals of Australia and by making it clear that Tasmania was an island state:

> "You look wonderful, you precious possum!" said
> Grandma Poss. "Next stop. Tasmania!" And over
> the sea they went.

It was done on purpose. I was teaching reading by providing information that would become prior knowledge in their subsequent reading of other texts.

The second cueing system is "knowledge of language." The children I write for are so young that they're still immersed in the rhyme and rhythm of nursery rhymes and playground rhymes. I wanted to build on that background, to connect that world to the world of books, so I included rhyme in *Possum Magic,* right there, in the middle of the prose:

> She looked into this book and she looked into that.
> There was magic for thin and magic for fat,
> magic for tall and magic for small,
> but the magic she was looking for wasn't there at
> all.

In my local newspaper, the *Adelaide Advertiser* on August 20th, 1983 the children's literature critic wrote,

> If I dislike the way the story every now and then
> falls suddenly into rhyme and just as suddenly out
> again, that is a small and perhaps purely personal
> fault to find with what is almost perfection.

But it's the rhyming that children love, and remember! (pp. 21-2)

And now to the third of our cueing systems, "knowledge of print." I have never yet written a "Dan-can-fan-the-man" book and, of course, I never will. I am aware however, that some attention, somewhere along the line, has to be paid to graphophonics. In my second book, **Wilfrid Gordon McDonald Partridge,** I had a huge battle with the publishers—a battle I lost—over the names of the old people. I wanted "Mrs. Morgan who played the organ"; "Mr. Lawry who told scary stories"; "Mrs. Hicks who walked with wooden sticks"; and "Mr. Bryant who had a voice like a giant." I could see the teaching possibilities. I could see the learning possibilities. I was imbued with the fire of the knowledge of the reading process! To my sorrow we now have Mrs. Jordan playing the organ, Mr. Tippet being crazy about cricket, and so on. The publishers thought rhyming names were beyond the realms of reality. Boo, hiss! I do think, seriously, that publishers of children's fiction in this country and elsewhere would do well to attend a language arts conference or two. They have much to learn.

I don't simplify vocabulary because I don't feel hidebound by the graphophonic cueing system. I know that meaning isn't difficult to grasp because we read in chunks, so I never worried about the apparently long words in **Possum Magic** such as "invisible," "pavlova," "lamington," or "Vegemite sandwiches." (A "lamington" is a delicious, typically Australian, chocolate-and-coconut sponge cake.) When I read **Possum Magic** to five year olds, I have to prepare the muscles in my face not to smile when I come to the sentence: "In Hobart, late one night, they saw a lamington on a plate" because there's nearly always a heartfelt chorus of "Arrrh, yu-u-u-m!" It's the "Arrrh, yu-u-u-m!" that teaches the kids how to read, not the length of the world "lamington."

Reading one book teaches us how to read another. It's one of the "prior knowledge" factors in reading. So, along with knowledge of the world, and language, and print, children need to develop a knowledge of how books work. That's why **Possum Magic** starts with "Once upon a time" because children have heard it before and will hear it again. That's why **Possum Magic** is an archetypal quest story: it prepares its readers for Victor Kelleher's *Master of the Grove* (Great Britain: Kestrel, 1982), Tolkien's *Lord of the Rings* (London: Allen and Unwin, 1954), the Arthurian legends, and the Odyssey of Homer.

What else do I know about the reading process? I know that rhythm and repetition are important as an aid to prediction so I used them to extremes in **Hattie and the Fox,** a book I adore even though I wrote it. Hattie, by the way, connects to children's pasts through the story of the Little Red Hen, and Pat Hutchins' *Rosie's Walk* (London: Puffin, 1970) and is a foundation for the future of Chaucer's Chaunticleer and Dame Partlett in "The Nun's Priest's Tale." I try to remember my place in the continuum of literature, acting as a carefully built bridge between past and future. (pp. 22-3)

Another thing I know about reading . . . is that we read in chunks and our prime aim is to make meaning. I try therefore to write *meaning*fully. [I am creating] an antinuclear-war allegory written again for the picture-book form. It's called *Swans and Peacocks* [later published as **Feathers and Fools**]. (p. 24)

I couldn't have written that story had I not read Hans Christian Andersen, the Bible, Rudyard Kipling, and John Keats' "La Belle Dame Sans Merci"! I deliberately included an overtly literary vocabulary. . . .

E. B. White (1969), the author of *Charlotte's Web* (London: Penguin, 1970) believes that

> Anybody who writes down to children is simply wasting . . . time. You have to write up, not down. Children are demanding. They are the most attentive, curious, eager, observant, sensitive, quick, and generally congenial readers on earth. They accept . . . anything as long as it is presented honestly, fearlessly, and clearly. In *Charlotte's Web* I gave them a literate spider and they took that. Some writers for children deliberately avoid using words they think a child doesn't know. This emasculates the prose and I suspect bores the reader. Children love words that give them a hard time, provided they are in a context that absorbs their attention.

I have now covered what I *know* about reading—except to add that some books help children to learn to read, and some help them to want to read. I'm aware of writing both sorts of books. Sometimes, as in **Koala Lou** (my favorite!) which has a strong emotional pull as well as a repeating catchphrase, I kill two birds with one stone so that my readers, I hope, will both learn to read, and want to read because of it. (pp. 25-6)

Firstly, I'm a parent. I remember all that bonding between Chloë and Malcolm and books and me. So I write *about* relationships. I'm sure a love of reading is closely connected to a love of the feeling of being read to by someone you love.

I write for the child-within-the-parent who is reading to the child. I'd like adults to remember the best bits of their childhood as they read my books. I always write with adult readers in mind because my readers are often too young to read on their own. That's why there's the adult joke about "pumpkin scones in Brisbane" in **Possum Magic.** (The wife of the Premier of Queensland, whose capital is Brisbane, is famous for her pumpkin scones!) That's why the mother is so warm, and understanding and middle-class-controlled for most of the book called: **Just Like That,** until at the end she's yelling her damn head off while the kid stands there, just like that. I can hear, in that story, the adult-reader and the child-listener building up to a crescendo of a relationship as they read it. If I can help along the bonding between parents and children through my books, I have a hunch I'll be helping along the bonding between children and literature. (p. 26)

I have some other hunches about reading. I know from watching Chloë that it's the emotional content in the material that she reads which makes her go on reading and reading and reading. (p. 27)

So I try not to write pap. I think of Chloë and her books . . . and I try to write *guts* instead.

That's why I wrote in **Possum Magic:** "Grandma Poss looked miserable. 'Don't worry,' said Hush. 'I don't mind.' But in her heart of hearts she did." The problem is there, admitted, but later resolved. The question which arises is where is the emotional content in most basal readers? The conflict? The fear? The heartache? The humor?

While conflict, fear, heartache, and humor may be desirable, they are not, by themselves, sufficient to hold the attention of readers or listeners. I've discovered that, through storytelling. The plot may be filled with blood and guts, but it's fine writing that keeps the audience rapt: it's exquisitely constructed sentences; it's carefully honed cadences; it's the marvellous satisfaction of the sensual rhythm of perfect prose. . . . (p. 28)

Now, my penultimate point: it's about role models in children's fiction. I've had lots of letters from kids who think that the possum, Hush, is male: "I like it when *he* gets invisible." Hush is a "she," but because most heroes are male, the assumption is already there in a five-year-old *girl* that Hush is male. I'm distressed by that. Pride in oneself is important. If you're a girl and girls seem unimportant, and you're only five, it's a hard road ahead. I have determined therefore to have only female protagonists for the rest of my writing life. "Wilfrid Gordon McDonald Partridge" was an aberration because it's my father's real name and I love him and I loved the rhythm of that name.

It's been said that the liberation of women can only come about through the concurrent liberation of men, so I keep in mind all the time that I'm writing for boys as well as girls. When Wilfrid Gordon says to Mr. Tippett who is crazy about cricket: "What's a memory?", Mr. Tippett replies unashamedly: "Something that makes you cry, my boy, something that makes you cry." The message to my male reader is "You can howl if you want to, sweetheart. It's OK." Daisy O'Grady in **Guess What,** is a wonderfully *revolting* witch. Koala Lou, in her training for the Bush Olympics, is seen to lift weights and to hang from a branch with one arm at a time, in a very macho manner. **Arabella,** the smallest girl in the world, is wildly active, in a physical sense, in every picture, on every page. Sophie, in my life-and-death story, is seen to make furniture in her grandfather's workshop. My sister is a superb carpenter and upholsterer besides being a language arts consultant in London. What a fantastic role model for all children. I just had to put her in a book!

I feel a tremendous responsibility to remove the inadequacy felt by female readers all their lives. (pp. 29-30)

At last—my final point! The illustrations. As a writer of picture books, where would I be without the pictures? But it isn't only I who would be lost, it's all the young readers for whom my books are springboards to literacy. The appeal of books, I've noticed, from Chloë, myself and my husband, and the many other children (!) I've observed, is not just in the rhyme, rhythm, and repetition, nor in the plot, nor in the emotional content, nor even in the fine, nonsexist writing—it's in the pictures. We mustn't insult the aesthetic intelligence of our young readers. Books that delight the eye first, may later delight the ear, the heart, and the mind but it is the *eye* first. So, while we're all busily writing in order to teach reading, I believe we're wasting our time utterly if the integrity of our texts is not matched by a similar integrity in the artwork. (pp. 30-1)

I like kids. I like them very much. I have enormous respect for their intelligence and ability, and high hopes for their future. I haven't mentioned that before, but it is pivotal to my writing. Secondly, I'm happy that within the me who writes for children there is also a child, a parent, a teacher, a storyteller, and a woman because each of these provides me with different information and a unique perspective. The total picture I have as a writer leads me to believe that loving relationships, fine writing, and stunning illustrations make learning to read an easy pleasure.

Here endeth the lesson. (p. 31)

Mem Fox, "The Teacher Disguised as Writer, in Hot Pursuit of Literacy," in Language Arts, *Vol. 64, No. 1, January, 1987, pp. 18-32.*

GENERAL COMMENTARY

Jill Brislan

Young children are entranced by Mem Fox's stories, and delighted by her characters. . . .

How is it that a writer whose first book ***Possum magic*** was published as recently as 1983 is so widely read and praised? And how is it that teachers, parents and librarians find her books so easy and rewarding to read aloud?

The answer lies, I believe, in her strong background as a storyteller and, formerly, as a drama teacher and actor. (p. 95)

The influence of drama can be seen in Mem Fox's writing in the way she presents her characters, shows the conflicts or contrasts between them in dialogue and situation, and in her strong evocative images. Her text works in a way similar to that of a script for a play, in that it suggests or implies emotion, facial expression, gesture and movement, and even setting, costume and effects. Her work shows awareness of the social nature of dramatic performance and the immediacy of its appeal to children.

Fox's characters are presented actively rather than passively: we are not so much *told* about them but rather *shown* them—thinking, feeling and doing.

Fox introduces the main character(s) by name and appearance in the opening sentence and, straight after that, those characters who provide contrast or conflict. Perhaps the best example of this is ***Wilfrid Gordon McDonald Partridge:***

> There was once a small boy called Wilfrid Gordon McDonald Partridge and what's more he wasn't very old either.

The six old people, or the contrasting characters, are each shown in terms of Wilfrid Gordon's relationships with and intense interest in them—in particular with Miss Nancy:

> But his favourite person of all was Miss Nancy Alison Delacourt Cooper because she had four names just as he did. He called her Miss Nancy and told her all his secrets.

When Wilfrid Gordon hears that Miss Nancy has lost her memory his concern and decision to help are manifested in his actions. His conflict is not *whether* to help Miss Nancy but *how* to. (pp. 95-6)

The dramatic technique of selective use of dialogue is used by Mem Fox in five stories: to emphasize a significant part of the plot and to reveal character and relationships.

The first time dialogue is used in ***Possum magic*** is to emphasize quite magically that Hush is tired of being invisible, and also to convey her trust in Grandma Poss:

> But one day, quite unexpectedly, Hush said 'Grandma, I want to know what I look like. Please could you make me visible again'.
>
> 'Of course I can,' said Grandma Poss, and she began to look through her magic books.
>
> (p. 96)

The use of dialogue to provide a dramatic focus can be seen in ***Hattie and the fox*** and ***Just like that.*** Hattie's first speech is:

> 'Goodness gracious me!
> I can see a nose in the bushes!'

and each subsequent speech expands with each new piece of observed information about the fox—while the other animals simply repeat themselves. The one-way communication directed at Harriet by her mother has the effect of focussing the reader's or listener's attention on Harriet.

Perhaps the most important thing common to both storytelling and drama performances is their social nature. Both need a gathering of people: one or more to tell the story, or to act in the play, and one or more to listen or to be the audience. So the audience is as much a part of the performance as the performer.

Similarly, a picture book is by its nature social. It is meant to be read aloud by an adult or older child to a child who cannot yet read, or read by a school child who is learning to read.

In Mem Fox's stories there are no outsiders. Fox presents a world where the character who represents a child's point of view belongs to a social group, which offers security and safety. Within this world, there is opportunity for risk-taking, helping others and even adventure. Since the child-character's emotions and experiences are expressed directly and immediately as has been shown above, the child-reader becomes involved in the story, laughing at a joke in ***Sail away,*** or utterly still in Hush's night of sadness in ***Possum magic.***

The child-character, whether in human or animal guise, has a conflict or a problem that is usually within his/her capacity to solve, such as finding a lost memory (***Wilfrid***); being friends again (***Just like that***); being different (***Arabella***); or just has fun. There is always a viable adult available to help (***Wilfrid***), or to actually solve the problem (***Possum magic***). Little Nell is both the little one and the adult—showing her big brother and everyone else in ***Sail away*** what to do.

The cultural aspect of Fox's world is also significant. The child's own environment is celebrated in her books: in Australian settings (beach, bush and backyard); animals (dingos and possums); food (vegemite sandwich); and even a bush ballad (***Sail away***). This further allows a reader or listener to feel at home.

The stories lend themselves to dramatization. Children of five or six enjoy pretending they're a giant like Mr Drysdale, or a mother saying 'Harriet, you'll drive me wild,' or the cow scaring away the fox. Children of eight or nine could act out the story of ***Wilfrid.*** In fact ***Wilfrid*** was successfully adapted for the stage, and performed to 18,000 enthusiastic young Adelaide children in 1987. (p. 97)

Mem Fox gives her readers the storyteller's gift of undivided attention. She achieves this through her tone, language and a simple, flowing storyline.

The author's tone or attitude to her stories and her audience is one of love, reassurance, good humour and confidence in her power to communicate. (p. 99)

Fox's attitude is reflected in the love and attention her adult-characters give to child-characters, like Grandma Poss with Hush, and the old people with Wilfrid. That the child reciprocates in kind, and that no-one is perfect, is shown in *Just like that* until:

> . . . later that night they were the best of friends.
> And that is where the story ends.

Most of all Mem Fox appeals direct to a child's imagination through her choice of words. The text is uncluttered: no word is superfluous and each word is given meaning. This has the effect of creating a space in children's minds which their imagination is free to fill. Examples of this are the magic that made Hush invisible and what it would be like to be invisible; the scary stories that Mr Hosking tells and what sorts of stories are scary; and names like Hush and Wilfrid Gordon McDonald Partridge.

She also encourages learning new words and what they mean, as Wilfrid Gordon learns what memory means and how Miss Nancy's loss of memory affects him. (pp. 99-100)

A close hearing of each story reveals that the text has been honed so as to suggest speech rhythms and appropriate pauses and silences—not to mention implied dynamics such as a big, loud voice for Mr Drysdale and a low, soft voice for Hush. It is no surprise to learn that Fox makes a practice of reading her drafts aloud to adults and 'kids in schools'.

Fox successfully incorporates storytelling aspects such as quiet opening, clear plot, food, magic, repetition, rhyme, surprise and quiet closing.

The stories begin quietly and simply, as in *Hattie and the fox:*

> Hattie was a big black hen.

This book provides a good example of a clear plot: a hen warns the other animals about a strange creature hidden in the bushes but they take no notice until the creature jumps out at them. . . .

Repetition and its cumulative effect not only hold a child's attention but can form the structure of the stories. For instance *Arabella* comprises four four-line verses, the first verse having an extra line:

> Arabella was the smallest girl in the world.
> **She had** a pillow **just like yours,**
> **And** a plant **just like mine.**
> **She had** a bath **that's just like ours,**
> **And** a mirror **oh, so fine!**

The bold face shows the words that are repeated in the next verses, leading to the joyful surprise of 'a story just like ours'.

The structure of *Wilfrid Gordon McDonald Partridge* is more subtle, being prose and consists of repetition and variation of key words and phrases, and even whole sentences. The story begins and ends with the same phrases: 'a small boy' who 'wasn't very old either!' 'What's a memory?' asks the small boy six times, and receives six different replies. (p. 100)

'Memory' and 'remember' appear nine and six times respectively, thus emphasising the theme. The effect is not so obvious as might be thought, as the focus in each sentence is on what Wilfrid Gordon is feeling, thinking, seeing, hearing and touching. Thus repetition both reinforces the storyline and delights the ear. The sense of hearing is highlighted by Fox's use of rhythm and rhyme. . . . (pp. 100-01)

Surprises and smiles are also important in the structure of Fox's stories. Surprises enhance the climax, such as the cow's sudden "MOO!" which frightens the fox away in *Hattie and the fox* after which all the animals, who've been talking a great deal, are 'so surprised' they fall quite silent. After setting out to *'see'* the boat race in Perth, the crew of the 'Dinki Di' not only take part in the race but incidentally win it *(Sail away)*. Smiles or their equivalent convey the mood of the climax, as when Wilfrid Gordon and Miss Nancy 'smiled and smiled'.

And the stories have satisfying endings to bring them to a calm close, for instance *Just like that:*

> And that is where the story ends.

I have sought to show that Mem Fox's books reveal a story from a child's perspective. By the use of dramatic and storytelling aspects, she has the ability to reach a child's imagination and encourage an empathetic response. I believe that in these respects her work represents a distinctive contribution to Australian writing for children. (p. 101)

> *Jill Brislan, "Mem Fox: Magic Writer," in*
> Orana, *Vol. 24, No. 2, May, 1988, pp. 95-101.*

TITLE COMMENTARY

Possum Magic (1983)

"Picture books," says Australian children's author Mem Fox, "are so . . . hard. You use so few words you must choose the very best." Sparse text, a clean plot line, an obvious climax and Julie Vivas' delightful, star-sprinkled illustrations are the ingredients Fox uses to brew *Possum Magic,* a spirited if somewhat nationalistic romp of a tale that, since its publication in 1983, has become far and away the best-selling contemporary Australian children's book.

To keep Hush the Possum safe from snakes, Grandma Poss—famous for her bush magic—makes her invisible. "What adventures Hush had!" But when Hush wants to become visible again, Grandma's magic inexplicably fails. The trick, it turns out, is to eat the right kind of food, "people food—not possum food," and so the pair set off on a rollicking tour of Australian state capitals and cuisine, sampling all the classic dishes from Vegemite sandwiches in Darwin to desserts like pavlova in Perth and lamingtons in Hobart (map and glossary provided). The magic works, of course, and the starry-eyed possums and their bush friends hold an annual feast from then on "just to make sure that Hush stayed visible forever."

> *Elizabeth Ward, "Picture Books for a Summer's Day," in* Book World—The Washington Post, *August 9, 1987, p. 6.*

Although the characters, locales, and vocabulary are thoroughly Australian, **Possum Magic** has universal appeal. Fox chooses her words carefully, making readers believe that certain foods just might be magical. Vivas uses a variety of techniques, including splatter painting and washes to create full- and double-page watercolor illustrations which complement the text and will entrance readers. A perfect choice for storytimes, but also useful for curriculum enrichment, thanks to a simplified map and glossary.

> *Jeanette Larson, in a review of "Possum Magic," in* School Library Journal, *Vol. 34, No. 4, December, 1987, p. 73.*

This agreeable tale from down under is peppered with "Australia-isms," but there is a zest to the story that transcends the language barrier. . . . The art captures the experience of being invisible as an "unseen," outlined Hush slides down a kangaroo's back and is almost squashed by a koala. Vivas' eminently likable pictures, featuring soft watercolors that spill across the pages, are striking standouts against the expanses of the white backgrounds. Fun for individual readers or as a supplement to units on Australia.

> *Ilene Cooper, in a review of "Possum Magic," in* Booklist, *Vol. 84, No. 7, December 1, 1987, p. 631.*

While Vegemite, Pavlova, and other taste sensations may not appear on the average American diet, readers' enjoyment of the story should not be hampered; the mere sounds of the foods are evocative, and a brief glossary is provided. The tiny stars of magic, scratchy lines depicting invisible Hush, and the rounded shapes of the Australian menagerie shown in full-color illustrations have a wonderfully comfortable, almost lackadaisical feeling to them, standing out effectively against a stark white background. Young readers will automatically befriend little Hush and Grandma Poss with her spectacles, star-spangled apron, and magic. But the real magicians are Mem Fox and Julie Vivas. As in their earlier **Wilfrid Gordon McDonald Partridge** they fuse text and illustrations together so masterfully one might almost think they've used sleight of hand. Presto chango: one enchanting book. (p. 53)

> *Karen Jameyson, in a review of "Possum Magic," in* The Horn Book Magazine, *Vol. LXIV, No. 1, January-February, 1988, pp. 52-3.*

Wilfrid Gordon McDonald Partridge (1984)

After young Wilfrid overhears his parents discussing Miss Nancy's memory loss, he asks all his friends in the old people's home next door, "What's a memory?" Each has a different answer. For one it is something warm; for another something that makes you sad; and for still another, something that makes you laugh. Hoping to help Miss Nancy,

Wilfrid gathers a basketful of objects which seem to embody these definitions—an egg for warmth, a hairy puppet for laughter, and his grandfather's medal for sorrow. As Miss Nancy's old fingers gently handle the collection, each item does, indeed, bring back happy memories of her girlhood. The brief text blends the physical feel of Wilfrid's treasures and the wistful nostalgia of the associations they bring to Miss Nancy. More striking, perhaps, are [Julie Vivas's] illustrations with the arresting volume of the figures and the sympathetic humor in the depiction of the baggy pants and drooping socks of the elderly but still mobile senior citizens. The pictures are washed in soft tans, mauves, and blues in a muted tonality that underscores the less vigorous life of Wilfrid's older companions. Arranged usually in a double-page spread format, the pictures flow easily across the pages in a pleasant variety of size and composition and are suffused with the artist's pleasure in the shapes of the human body, be it the lithe but knobby knees of the young or the bulging bellies and rounded shoulders of the old. (pp. 47-8)

> *Ethel R. Twichell, in a review of "Wilfrid Gordon McDonald Partridge," in* The Horn Book Magazine, *Vol. LXII, No. 1, January-February, 1986, pp. 47-8.*

Arabella (1986)

I found this book something of an oddity: Arabella's miniature stature allows the artist and reader to observe familiar objects as larger than life whilst the short text listing the articles has a pleasing pattern and rhythm and rhyme but [Vicky Kitanov's] pictures tell a far more imaginative story. So, a soap dish becomes a boat with cotton wool stick oars, and ice cream becomes something from which to build a snowman. But the final picture showing Arabella standing in the palm of dad's hand between his and mum's large smiling faces, and captioned with 'She had a story just like ours, with an ending—oh so fine.' I found rather puzzling.

> *Jill Bennett, in a review of "Arabella the Smallest Girl in the World," in* Books for Keeps, *No. 43, March, 1987, p. 10.*

Hattie and the Fox (1986)

Hattie the Hen announces that she sees a nose in the bushes, to which her barnyard friends respond: "Good grief!" "Well, well!" "Who cares?" "So what?" and "What next?" What's next are the eyes, ears, legs, and body of a hungry fox. The fox lunges, Hattie flies, and the goose, pig, sheep, and horse panic. But the cow moos so loudly that the fox is frightened away. Bright, whimsical tissue collage and crayon illustrations [by Patricia Mullins] add zest to this simple cumulative tale, and reveal more action than is expressed by the text alone. The repetition of the urbane animals' responses creates a rhythm which is energized by the fox' arrival. **Hattie and the Fox** combines a refreshing visual presentation with a classic form to make a terrific choice for reading aloud to very young children, or for those just beginning to read on their own.

> *Carolyn Noah, in a review of "Hattie and the*

Fox," in School Library Journal, *Vol. 33, No. 8, May, 1987, p. 84.*

The delightful repetition of the remarks and the obvious stupidity of the animals will be enjoyable, no doubt, to the lap-sitters, but even more outstanding are the illustrations. They are done in tissue-paper collage, touched with line, and show, with remarkable solidity and strong color, a particularly splendid pig, blasé cow, droopy sheep, and sly fox. An excellent picture book for the very young.

Ann A. Flowers, in a review of "Hattie and the Fox," in The Horn Book Magazine, *Vol. LXIII, No. 3, May-June, 1987, p. 329.*

A tiny story is developed with a fine sense of timing, and hen, horse, pig and cow and the others are all drawn with much freedom and animation. The book comes from Australia, but we would never know it. In subject and presentation it speaks with an international voice. Very good indeed.

M. Crouch, in a review of "Hattie and the Fox," in The Junior Bookshelf, *Vol. 52, No. 2, April, 1988, p. 80.*

Koala Lou (1987)

AUTHOR'S COMMENTARY

One of the worst aspects of being a writer is that editors and other people keep asking me to write. I have little imagination, and I can't write to order. Some writers, when asked to write a story for four-year-old girls on the theme of friendships at kindergarten, can do it at the flick of a word processor. Not me. One of the reasons I hate writing picture books is because getting the idea is so difficult. Recently an editor asked me to write a series of books on warm family relationships. Not just one book—a whole series! I laughed and told him I'd probably written my last picture book as I hadn't had an idea for over a year.

If I have no imagination, where do the ideas come from? (p. 288)

My first book, *Possum Magic*, did not win the Picture Book of the Year Award—the Australian equivalent of the Caldecott Medal—although it was highly praised and very popular. This should not have been devastating. I was an adult after all, aged thirty-eight. Nevertheless, the day after the awards I cried like a child. Coming in second with "highly commended" wasn't enough. I understand looking back that writing *Koala Lou* was a way of coming to terms with this major disappointment.

This kind of process is typical of my writing. The ideas leap into my head from real life, and if they don't, I don't write. I'm not one of those disciplined writers who sit down at a blank piece of paper or a blank computer screen and say, "Right! I'm not moving until I've written five hundred words." I could sit there for a month without writing a word. My imagination is, on the whole, a blank.

Eventually the first sentence appears, but it may be a while before the second squeezes itself onto the page. I find writing picture books such torture that my shoulders ache with the tension of trying to choose the right words to put in the right places. I hate the narrow confines of a picture book. There's no room to move. A picture book text is like a sonnet: small, powerful, and tightly disciplined. It's like a short, smooth plank of wood when seen beside the luxuriant oak tree of a novel. So why don't I write a novel? I might if I had an idea.

Part of the reason I find picture books so difficult is that I've been exposed to two of the best examples of writing in the English language: the Bible, because my parents were missionaries in Africa; and Shakespeare, because I spent three years at a drama school in London. So I have a deep understanding of the sound and the feel of the English language. However, I am not actually William Shakespeare, a fact which frustrates me every time I sit down to write. Shakespeare gets the rhythm right every time. Why, oh, why can't I?

Most of the drafts of *Koala Lou* focused on the problem of rhythm. I spent whole days working on single sentences, reading them aloud, rewriting them, and reading them aloud again. It drove me mad. To use a musical analogy, I could hear the tunes in my head, but I couldn't reproduce them on paper. It made me despondent. Why did I care? Why do I always care? (pp. 289-90)

[One] reason for caring is that I know children need an abundance of stunning books to ease the development of their literacy. My aim is for children to become literate without realizing what's happening to them. This can come about only if the material they read is among the best available, with terrific plots, great characters, magnificent themes, outrageous humor, clear settings, superb illustrations, and lastly—my own favorite—fine writing, which includes the perfection of Shakespearean and biblical rhythms within ordinary Australian prose. I live in terror of the possibility that I might be responsible for the literacy standards of an entire nation.

Koala Lou is a mere 488 words, yet it took me two years to write: forty-nine drafts for a story that fits on to one side of an 8½-by-11-inch piece of paper. I'm not surprised that I hate writing picture books: it's easy to do badly and difficult to do well. With *Koala Lou* I lived by the maxim that the secret of good writing is rewriting and made changes to the text every time I read it. (pp. 290-91)

When I rewrite, how do I know what I need to change? For me, rewriting is often synonymous with retalking. I read my drafts to any audience I can pin down: schoolchildren, my family, my other friends, my editors, my students, my colleagues, and my agent. They're my sounding boards. For example, I had written: " 'On your marks,' said the kookaburra. 'Get set—go!' " Then a friend pointed out that since there was only one koala, the line should read: " 'On your mark.' " Also, I didn't have any times recorded for Koala Klaws's rapid climb to the top until a year-seven class in Brighton, South Australia, said, "How fast was Koala Klaws? And how high did she climb?" Until then I hadn't thought about it, nor had I realized that anyone would be interested. (p. 292)

I couldn't have written *Koala Lou* on my own. I had to talk it through. I always need people to talk to when I'm writing a book—about the content, not the style. I can rewrite stylistically by reading aloud in private, but I can't tell by myself which bits of the content are confusing, boring, or irrelevant. Someone has to help me.

As a writer for children, I can't help wearing my teaching hat. I know that rhyme, rhythm, and repetition make learning to read a pleasure. The recurring line, " 'Koala Lou, I DO love you' " is there for literary reasons: it sounds warm, and it develops the characters. But it's also there for learning-to-read reasons. I know that children who listen to the story will quickly join in on that line and be able to read it, if it is pointed out to them a couple of times. I am always excited by the idea of creating readers as I create text.

Finally, I am also interested in a book's emotional content. Emotion is to picture books as flour is to bread. I'm thrilled when adults suddenly howl at the end of **Koala Lou.** It makes me dare to think it might be a good book. Good books, I contend, have as much to do with the effect they have on the reader as with any other criterion. If we don't laugh, gasp, block our ears, sigh, vomit, giggle, curl our toes, sympathize, feel pain, weep, or shiver during the reading of a picture book, then surely the writer has wasted our time, our money, and our precious trees. If I read a picture book and remain in the same emotional state I was in before I read it, then for me the book has failed. It's a here-today-and-gone-tomorrow book.

I'm surprised time and again by the lack of emotion in some of the published picture books I've seen. Their blandness reminds me of still waters running shallow. It's as if their authors had nothing to say but said it anyway. I've done the same myself more than once. I haven't much to say, all things considered, and the struggle to say it is so painful I now think twice before I begin. (pp. 293-94)

Eventually the book is published. It takes time. I wrote **Koala Lou** over a span of two years, between August 1983 and September 1985. (p. 294)

As I was putting together this article, I thought I'd merely be providing a candid view of my love/hate relationship with picture books. But there's been something else nagging at the back of my mind all along, and I've only just realized what it is. My real reason for putting all this on paper is to explain why I feel so uncontrollably murderous when I experience the sweet condescension of those who say: "I think I'll write a picture book one day, when I have the time." (p. 296)

Mem Fox, "Writing Picture Books: A Love/ Hate Relationship," in The Horn Book Magazine, *Vol. LXVI, No. 3, May-June, 1990, pp. 288-96.*

Mem Fox plays amusingly with a universal theme in this gentle tale set in the Australian bush. Koala Lou feels bereft when her mother becomes preoccupied with a growing brood of younger koala children. In her desire to recapture her mother's attention and affection, the enterprising Koala Lou decides to become a contestant in the Bush Olympics. The training efforts of the determined young competitor are conveyed with a storyteller's sure touch for phrasing and pacing. "She jogged and puffed and lifted weights and panted. She hung from a branch with one claw at a time till she ached." Pamela Lofts creates a sympathetic, sometimes zany, cast of animal participants and observers, adding many humorous touches in the attire and actions of the animals. There's a jaunti-

ness in Koala Lou's untied red sneakers and in the assorted hats worn to the Olympics and tossed high in celebration. There's also a surreal quality to the soft purple and orange tones of the tall, gnarled gum tree that is the focus of Koala Lou's efforts. Lofts is particularly dynamic in her page designs, incorporating a frame of varying size in each right-hand page; the action spills out of the frame, but the viewer has a sense of looking into the story. Koala Lou doesn't win the race to the top of the gum tree "in spite of all her training and her hoping." As she snuffles off home, having "cried her heart out," the story ends most satisfyingly with her mother's warm embrace and the longed for words, " 'Koala Lou, I DO love you!' " A first-rate choice for bedtime, story hour, or reading aloud. (pp. 757-58)

Margaret A. Bush, in a review of "Koala Lou," in The Horn Book Magazine, *Vol. 65, No. 6, November-December, 1989, pp. 757-58.*

A loving, warm story. . . . Koala Lou is appealing and truly believable, the kind of child who often gets overlooked because of her unassuming nature. Her mother is caring, sensitive, and frazzled, and she is able to sense and respond to her children's needs. Fox brings out the best in her characters, and also conveys an important message about competition without being strident or didactic. Lofts' illustrations are realistic, whimsical, and almost textured; she gives an additional depth to the animal characters by making their faces (especially the eyes) so expressive. Her colors are bright, vivid, and almost exotic; however, the vibrant tones contrast sharply against the soft and gentle story, and jar readers from Fox' semi-cocoonlike setting. While it is unfortunate that the color tone doesn't match the mood of the story, the book as a whole is enjoyable.

Jane Dyer Cook, in a review of "Koala Lou," in School Library Journal, *Vol. 36, No. 1, January, 1990, p. 80.*

With Love, at Christmas   (1988)

The elderly Mrs. Cavallaro always shops early for the presents for her family, lovingly wrapping each one, writing "With love, at Christmas" on each tag and tucking them into a special trunk. But this year, Mrs. Cavallaro keeps hearing about families with no presents and children without food; she gives away the presents before she knows what she is doing. She weeps when she realizes that she has no gifts for her loved ones. But the night before Christmas, she goes to her trunk, and it is no longer empty—a holy baby on a bed of straw is lying there. The next morning, her family finds the presents in the trunk, with Mrs. Cavallaro slumped dead over them. By the author of the acclaimed **Possum Magic,** this story is a failed attempt to choreograph a modern-day miracle. The ending is shocking, and [Gary Lippincott's] paintings, while carefully executed, do not convey the pathos of the story.

A review of "With Love, at Christmas," in Publishers Weekly, *Vol. 234, No. 14, September 30, 1988, p. 64.*

This disturbing story with near photo-realist watercolors tells of a Christmas miracle. . . . While some readers may applaud the generous spirit of Mrs. Cavallaro, others may ask why she had to die, or whether the miraculous return of the presents with "with love, at Christmas" tags makes up for the loss of the story's main character. (pp. 33-4)

> *Susan Helper, in a review of "With Love, at Christmas," in* School Library Journal, *Vol. 35, No. 2, October, 1988, pp. 33-4.*

Night Noises (1988)

Another tender, good-humored encounter between young and old from the author of **Wilfrid Gordon McDonald Partridge.** As old Lily Laceby dozes peacefully in her armchair, her barrel-shaped dog, Butch Aggie, pricks an ear at the quiet click of car doors outside, cocks her head to the crunch of feet on the garden path, bristles at the mutter of voices, rumbles at the rattle of the doorknob, and finally breaks into barking when fists pound on the door. Lily wakes with a start, gets up and lets in—a horde of family and friends wishing her a "Happy Birthday!" "Are you really ninety?" whispers Emily, her great-great-granddaughter. "Inside I'm only four-and-a-half, like you," Lily answers, "but don't tell anyone." Fox builds up the suspense expertly, and [Terry] Denton follows her lead in the richly-colored, scribbly illustrations. Butch Aggie's increasing alertness plays off against Lilly's slightly rumpled serenity in a way that will rivet young readers as dreamy scenes from Lily's life parade past in a wordless series of side panels. Emily looks older than four and a half, but that's a minor bobble in this happy collaboration.

> *John Peters, in a review of "Night Noises," in* School Library Journal, *Vol. 35, No. 13, September, 1989, p. 225.*

Like most of the books by either Mem Fox or Terry Denton, **Night Noises** does not have an immediate impact on the reader. It is more subtle than that. This is a book which grows on you with each reading. . . .

Mem Fox's story telling skills, as usual, are excellent with the words rolling off the tongue—spiced as they are with alliteration, repetition and onomatopoeia. . . .

This is a delightful book which can work on a number of levels and hence grow with the child. While pre-schoolers will enjoy the tension and excitement of working out what is making the noises, and the fun of the party which follows, older children will be able to move onto the next level and appreciate the warmth of the message about youth and old age and the importance of the memories which bring the two together.

> *Stephanie Owen Reeder, in a review of "Night Noises," in* Magpies, *Vol. 5, No. 1, March, 1990, p. 27.*

Feathers and Fools (1988)

Long ago and far away there was a pride of magnificent peacocks and a flock of elegant swans . . . There is a beautiful directness about this anti-nuclear-war fable. A peacock urges his pride to fear the swans because they are different. So when the peacocks arm themselves with sharpened feathers, the swans in fear do the same. For both, the more arrows they stockpile the more terrified they become, until an innocent act by one of the swans panics the peacocks into attack. Almost everyone is destroyed, then . . .

Well, the book condemns: the suspicion of others who are different, a gullible belief in leaders who advocate conflict, and the madness of an arms race or of any escalating antagonism. In the end it celebrates the simplicity of friendship and asserts the necessity for trust. This is an argument which applies to nations, families and schoolyards.

This book's storyline is unerring; the focus and mood of Lorraine Ellis's images, in her first major children's book, make them apt and powerful; and subtle shifts of tone move us to feel the author's message. 'Today's kids are terrified of nuclear war," says Mem Fox and she offers **Feathers & Fools** in a spirit of hope.

> *Don Pemberton, in a review of "Feathers & Fools," in* Magpies, *Vol. 5, No. 1, March, 1990, p. 31.*

Shoes from Grandpa (1988)

With a keen appreciation of zany possibilities in the familiar, Mem Fox has used the rhythmic patterns suggested by "The House That Jack Built" to describe the outfitting of one young girl by a family with more heart than taste. The results are hilarious, as one by one the relatives search for garments to complement—or compete with—the pair of shoes provided by Grandpa. Here, for example, is mother's offering: "I'll buy you a skirt that won't show the dirt, / to go with the socks from the local shops, / to go with the shoes from Grandpa." Fortunately, Jessie, who is as down-to-earth as her name, manages to retain her equilibrium, thank all politely, and then request the one item that she wants more than anything else: a pair of jeans. The illustrations [by Patricia Mullins], torn-paper collages, are as lively as the text, giving concrete reality to the catalogue of garments. The choice of medium was inspired, for it allows the artist to extend the text, adding subtly to the characterization of each participant through his or her selections. Once again, Mem Fox and Patricia Mullins prove that they are a formidable duo whose combined talents are not only compatible but also mutually enriching. (pp. 187-88)

> *Mary M. Burns, in a review of "Shoes from Grandpa," in* The Horn Book Magazine, *Vol. LXVI, No. 2, March-April, 1990, pp. 187-88.*

In this humorous suburban variation on "The House that Jack Built," Grandpa gets things started off with a pair of new shoes, Dad offers "socks from the local shops," and Mom buys "a skirt that won't show the dirt." As each of Jessie's relatives gets into the act, the rhythmic cumulative tale builds momentum. . . . Either in story hour or reading on their own, youngsters will enjoy seeing Jessie's free spirit triumph over her family's overly enthusiastic good intentions.

> *Carey Ayres, in a review of "Shoes from Grandpa," in* School Library Journal, *Vol. 36, No. 4, April, 1990, p. 89.*

Roy Gerrard

1935-

English author and illustrator of picture books.

Major works include *The Favershams* (1982), *Sir Cedric* (1984), *Sir Francis Drake: His Daring Deeds* (1988).

The creator of humorous picture books in verse with historical settings, Gerrard is recognized for writing and illustrating satires of medieval life, the Victorian and Edwardian ages, and the American West with whimsy and affection. Stylish and sophisticated stories which characteristically include playful balladic texts and watercolors featuring foreshortened human characters who appear against lavishly detailed backgrounds, the works are noted for their droll, gentle renderings of English values and behavior and for the quality and technical skill of their illustrations. Gerrard is perhaps best known as the creator of *The Favershams* (1982), a story which takes Charles Augustus Faversham, a Victorian upper-class gentleman, from birth to old age, and for his two books about a polite but courageous medieval knight, *Sir Cedric* and *Sir Cedric Rides Again* (1986). With *Sir Francis Drake: His Daring Deeds,* Gerrard describes the life of the explorer in selected episodes from Drake's career which stress the less bloody aspects of his life. Gerrard also spoofs the Hollywood Western with *Rosie and the Rustlers* (1989), the tale of a rancher and her hired hands who track down their stolen herd with the help of their Cherokee friends, and has provided the illustrations for *Matilda Jane* (1981), a picture book written by his wife, author Jean Gerrard, in which a small girl comments wryly on her holiday in a Victorian seaside town. Although Gerrard is questioned for presenting young readers with instances of nudity in *The Favershams* and *Sir Cedric Rides Again* and has been accused of racial sterotyping in *Sir Frances Drake* and *Rosie and the Rustlers,* he is often acknowledged for his strongly pacifistic themes and for the success of his humor. Especially influenced as an author and illustrator by Edward Lear and Lewis Carroll, Gerrard is also a well known oil painter who often exhibits internationally and has taught art in English elementary and high schools. Gerrard received the Mother Goose Award runner-up for *Matilda Jane* in 1982 and the "Fiera di Bologna" children's graphic art prize from the Bologna Children's Book Fair in 1983 as well as several other awards for his illustrations.

(See also *Something about the Author,* Vol. 45 and *Contemporary Authors,* Vol. 110.)

AUTHOR'S COMMENTARY

[The following excerpt is from an interview by Jean Russell.]

Even children's book enthusiasts will not recognise the name of . . . Roy Gerrard, because **Matilda Jane** is his first picture book. So excited were we by the delicate, whimsical Victorian illustrations, that for the first time in the 16 year history of *Books for Your Children* we . . .

placed an unknown illustrator on our cover—which we normally reserve for established artists. Not that Roy Gerrard is not an established artist, he is well known as a painter. . . .

Each of the pictures in **Matilda Jane** accompanies a jaunty verse written by [Gerrard's] wife Jean, which begins "It astonishes me said Matilda with glee . . . " and as it goes on Matilda becomes more and more astonished as her weeks holiday at the Victorian seaside town progresses.

> the way grown-ups look
> when they enter the sea
> with their trousers rolled up
> and their skirts held high
> it's hard not to smile
> or to laugh, but I'll try.

When I visited Roy and Jean Gerrard in their tiny gritstone village on the edge of the moors above Manchester they explained how it had come about. "Someone saw my painting at my one man show" said Roy "and suggested that they could be expanded into a picture book. It had never occurred to me, but then once the idea was there it just took off." Jean, who is head of a remedial reading unit in a large comprehensive school, explains. "I knew that the children love to latch on to words, words they can get their tongue round. They love to recognise a long word and repeat it, hence the phrase 'it astonishes me' ". In *Matilda Jane* the words were done first and then Roy did the pictures to fit round them". . . .

Roy has been influenced by Edward Lear: "he has a Victorian sense of whimsy which I like. I am greatly influenced by the Victorian city of Manchester. As a boy I was brought up 12 miles outside Manchester and as a child always thought of it as a magical city, the streetlife, the trams, horses, and cobblestone." "Oh Roy" interrupted Jean. "There weren't cobblestones and horses when you were a boy, you make it sound as if you're about 90." "It felt like that" Roy continued. "I have this need to look backwards, all my watercolours are fantasy and reminiscences. I used to work in oils but gave it up about 10 years ago when I decided to give up painting and I destroyed all my existing work. Then in 1972 I was immobilised for several weeks after a climbing accident and started tinkering around with small watercolours. I became obsessive and in about 3 years had arrived at my true style of small, highly detailed watercolours, remorselessly whimsical and often Victorian/Edwardian subjects."

> *Jean Russell, "Cover Artist: Roy Gerrard," in* Books for Your Children, *Vol. 16, No. 2, Summer, 1981, p. 4.*

TITLE COMMENTARY

Matilda Jane (1981)

[Matilda Jane *was written by Jean Gerrard.*]

Two paramount points about this most unusual picture/story book—the meticulous details of the Edwardian scenes on the railway and at the seaside, with their picture-postcard colours, and the energy of the verses, governed as they are by the repeated phrase 'It astonishes me' which introduces a child's shrewd and at times caustic comments on the family outing. How amazing it is that they have travelled so far in a day, that the landlady's cat is so changeable in its behaviour, that the train stays on its rails and, above all, that in spite of seaside delights, it is pleasant to be home again. A delectable book.

> *Margery Fisher, in a review of "Matilda Jane," in* Growing Point, *Vol. 20, No. 3, September, 1981, p. 3950.*

Jean Gerrard has written a clever and fluent poem, which never sets a foot outside its Edwardian context, about a child's visit to the seaside. Its neat stanzas are nicely matched by her husband's careful and detailed watercolours. Everything here is calculated. Tram, bandstand, boarding house, pier—here is the essence of a bygone holiday in all its fascinating horror. Whether children will like it is questionable, but it will find many admirers of more mature years, the old to whom it will recall past joys and younger adults who have taken up the early years of the century from a curious imagined nostalgia.

> *M. Crouch, in a review of "Matilda Jane," in* The Junior Bookshelf, *Vol. 45, No. 6, December, 1981, p. 243.*

The rhymes on one page move quickly and urge readers to look on to the next page, where minutely detailed wa-

From The Favershams, *written and illustrated by Roy Gerrard.*

tercolors show in vivid colors the accoutrements of living and vacationing at a seashore resort in Edwardian England. The abundant detail of gingerbread trim on houses, wallpaper patterns and bathing costumes are whimsically pleasing. The only detail detracting from the book is that the rhyme pages frame the words in an elegant montage of objects—flowers, seashells, a house front—but the same frames are repeated, rather than using a new one for each page. It would seem that the wealth of detail runs unfortunately short.

> *Ruth K. MacDonald, in a review of "Matilda Jane," in* School Library Journal, *Vol. 28, No. 8, April, 1982, p. 58.*

The Favershams (1982)

Roy Gerrard has a passion for Victoriana, and *The Favershams* is a curious and delightful product of his consuming interest. We follow the story of Charles Augustus Faversham from birth to serene old age, in drawings which are scholarly, exact and charming and in verse which is a great deal better than most of the rhyming texts of picture-books. Charles' career follows the pattern of the Victorian upper classes: the Army, action followed by decoration by the Queen herself, love and marriage, an adventurous honeymoon, service in India, big-game hunting, family life, retirement to a career as an author, an occasional lapse from the traditions of his time and class (nude bathing!). This is good fun, gentle satire, a relevant comment on a period of history, all in one happy book. Mr. Gerrard has a formidable technique, but not everyone will like his characteristic style with its curious foreshortening; those who yield to its charms will find the book a rare and distinctive pleasure.

> *M. Crouch, in a review of "The Favershams,"*
> *in* The Junior Bookshelf, *Vol. 46, No. 6, December, 1982, p. 220.*

A quirky picture book, apparently a spoof on the life and times of Victorian England, features the adventures of Charles Augustus Faversham. . . . The story is told in relentless iambic tetrameter, doggerel in effect. Outstanding, however, are the illustrations. Human figures are grossly foreshortened and distorted, and Charles's troops look like toy soldiers; but the textures of fabrics, rugs, laces, wallpaper, and even the monstrous crocodile that Charles has shot are brilliantly rendered, while the dark, muted reds and browns are certainly Victorian in feeling. A picture book for children old enough to appreciate the humor.

> *Ann A. Flowers, in a review of "The Favershams," in* The Horn Book Magazine, *Vol. LIX, No. 5, October, 1983, p. 562.*

A loving satire on the life of the ruling class in Victorian England. . . . Roy Gerrard is besotted with the moral rectitude of the Victorians. You may laugh, his characters seem to be saying—and we do, as we delve into the marvellously detailed pictures of the Favershams playing tennis with fly-swat bats, cycling on steeds too lofty for their short legs, or sipping tea dwarfed by the soaring architecture of the tea rooms. A treasure-trove of Victoriana, this, just as *Sir Cedric,* his most recent book, is the most debunking, yet secretly admiring, look at the absurdities of chivalry since Sheila Sancha's *Knight after Knight.*

> *Elaine Moss, in a review of "The Favershams" in her* Picture Books for Young People 9-13, *revised edition, The Thimble Press, 1985, p. 43.*

Sir Cedric (1984)

[*Sir Cedric*] is crammed not only with jingling quatrains recounting stirring deeds, but also with pictures of breathtaking intricacy and verve—rather as if Richard Dadd had illustrated *The Book of Hours.* The story of knights, maidens and castles rattles along tremendously; there are a few digs for the adult reader (including a knowledgable reference to *droit de seigneur*), but developing a plot and pointing a moral remain the priority. The role-models may seem robustly traditional, but even without the illustrations, appearances are vividly created:

> Matilda, though fat, was a princess, you see,
> and could have any man that she chose,
> But Black Ned was badtempered, dirty and mean,
> and had hairs growing out of his nose. . . .

[The] story resolves itself into a historical romance: Matilda thrills to Sir Cedric's muscular arms ("he was little, but wiry and strong"). There is gore offstage, but at the climax

a wonderful Bayeux-tapestry battle is terminated by cucumber sandwiches and tea, while Black Ned is forgiven and repents. For the moral at the end, Cedric and Matilda are translated, immobile in monochrome, into a splendid memorial tomb.

The illustrations . . . may make *Sir Cedric* a classic, but the text deserves attention too: it is tough-minded, funny and convincing. An authorial eyebrow is raised at the "silliness" of formal combat; the duties and abuse of knightly authority are firmly sketched. Like the best children's books, it will age with its reader.

> *Roy Foster, "Costume Drama," in* The Times Literary Supplement, *No. 4253, October 5, 1984, p. 1139.*

Parody in the tenderly romantic mock-biography of a dauntless knight who rescues Princess Matilda from her gaoler, Black Ned, and marries her. The joke lies in Cedric's small size, exaggerated by his posture on a huge elongated charger, and the satirical suggestions in such details as the cucumber sandwiches eaten on the journey and the bourgeois atmosphere of the chivalric union. In mock-medieval scenes in bland colour, highly decorated and comically Victorian in detail, the two chubby lovers stand out in all their incongruous social smugness. An adult joke, certainly, which older children should appreciate for its stylish expression both in words and in pictures.

> *Margery Fisher, in a review of "Sir Cedric," in* Growing Point, *Vol. 23, No. 4, November, 1984, p. 4347.*

Mr. Gerrard's lavish illustrations incorporate his verses in their design, and neither is complete without the other. And the combination of words and pictures says something very different from what each tells alone.

Sir Cedric is bald, round-faced and sports a mustache. Fat Matilda isn't fat at all, she's just not a Tennysonian wraith. All the characters are small and shaped like thumbs, the horses have very long legs, and only Black Ned has a full head of hair and full beard. The landscapes and peasants echo Pieter Brueghel, the forest echoes Albrecht Dürer, also William Blake and William Morris. The confrontation between the armies of Sir Cedric and Black Ned cites the Battle of Hastings and looks like the Bayeux tapestry. (The quatrain for this dire but bloodless scene tells how, when the battle ended, the army sat down for tea.)

Sir Cedric, then, is very English, humorous and civilized. Its composed and engrossing surface overlays much complication and disarray, just like those level English lawns where the seed is scattered of a season and then rolled for 500 years.

> *Laurance Wieder, in a review of "Sir Cedric," in* The New York Times Book Review, *November 4, 1984, p. 23.*

Sir Cedric Rides Again (1986)

The little knight whose flamboyant rescue of the fair Matilda was so opulently depicted and charmingly described in *Sir Cedric* is back with a feisty daughter, who also needs rescuing when she's captured by Arab bandits. This time the rescuer is an apparent wimp, Hubert the Hopeless.

Gerrard's wonderfully detailed watercolors of a legendary medieval landscape embellished with lovely decorative borders are somewhat less elegantly decorative here, and his plot is in the same mold as the earlier one. But his adroitly rhyming ever. A book to pore over, read aloud, and share with delight.

A review of "Sir Cedric Rides Again," in Kirkus Reviews, *Vol. LIV, No. 20, October 15, 1986, p. 1576.*

In his second book about Sir Cedric, Roy Gerrard's verse bounces along cheerfully. . . . The illustrations are lively, rather in the Noggin the Nog mould, but the moment when the captive ladies "feared a fate worse than death" is troubling. Abdul tells Edwina that she will be "wife twenty-three" while one plump bare-breasted girl whispers laughingly behind her hand to another. The sexual and racial undertones unsettle because they distract from the story and invite speculation and inquiry more mature than the likely readership, a misjudgment which leaves a faintly unpleasant taste. . . .

Lachlan Mackinnon, "Exotic Excursions," in The Times Literary Supplement, *No. 4369, December 26, 1986, p. 1458.*

Let Sir Cedric's fans prepare to chortle through a new adventure in Gerrard's medieval never-never land. . . . Though feminists may cringe at the lady-in-distress theme, it's hard to take offense at such a mocking version of convention. A period pastiche with something of the Victorian era in the telling as well as the design, this romp pleases the ear, the eye, and the funny bone.

Carolyn Phelan, in a review of "Sir Cedric Rides Again," in Booklist, *Vol. 83, No. 9, January 1, 1987, p. 708.*

Sir Francis Drake: His Daring Deeds (1988)

The challenges of creating books for younger children about historical events and the figures who have shaped them have attracted a number of writer/illustrators, among them Joe Lasker and Aliki, who have both done fine books on social customs in the Middle Ages, and Diane Stanley in her handsome biography *Peter the Great.* These books have not compromised the complexity of the historical material or underestimated the capacity of younger readers to be fascinated by the events, people, places and things of the past.

The life of Sir Francis Drake, the first Englishman to circumnavigate the globe, one of the destroyers of the Spanish Armada, privateer for Queen Elizabeth I, does not seem a suitable subject for a picture book. How does one begin to tell the life of that remarkable adventurer without including some of the bloody chapters that brought him fame and fortune in the first place—and, if one chooses to recount some of those episodes, how should they be represented pictorially?

There is, too, the matter of scope: how much of Drake's story should the writer tell? Does one begin, for instance, with his impoverished youth and his early hatred of Roman Catholicism? How much of the cultural backdrop against which his exploits are being recreated needs to be sketched in for the reader to make some historical sense of Drake's actions? The whole enterprise seems fraught with problems in as brief and visual a form as the picture book.

Yet Roy Gerrard's verse jumps blithely into the action, beginning when Drake was 10 (though some sources say he was 13), went to sea for the first time,

And flabbergasted all the crew
by quickly learning what to do.

He fathomed ways of wind and tide,
in storms he just brushed fear aside.
He taught himself to read a map—
lion-hearted little chap!

Within another page, Drake has made 27 voyages and become the captain of his own vessel, and, within another, he has been given his first taste of Spanish treachery in Mexico, which is meant, it seems, to justify his battles with the Spanish from then on; he wanted to show them "that *Drake* was boss." We see his ship sinking a Spanish galleon, but we're told he "treated prisoners well" because "though revenge was on his mind, / he found it hard to be unkind." (Tell that to Thomas Doughty whom Drake had executed when he thought Doughty was plotting against him on the trip around the world!) Perhaps that explains why, when he "caught some Spanish chaps" deep in the jungle of Panama "whose mules / bore bulging sacks of gold and jewels," Drake, who is in the foreground of the picture with drawn sword, holds back while one of his men merely clubs a conquistador into submission.

There are other equally baffling scenes in *Sir Francis Drake,* such as the one in which Drake, somewhere in South America, "went ashore to have a nap / but local tribes had set a trap." Why would he need to land for a nap? And, oh, those treacherous Indians, ganging up like that on Drake and his chums! And why, on Drake's voyage around the world, would he burn two of his ships, Mr. Gerrard explains, "to cook their meat / (and dry their clothes and toast their feet)"?

Alas, once one starts trying to make literal sense of the fragments Mr. Gerrard has chosen from Drake's life, the text quickly loses its credibility. Finally, as an American reader, one wonders if this is trying to pass for a fragment of unreconstructed national history in Thatcher England. Mr. Gerrard is a well-known British author and illustrator, and this book first appeared in Britain. Or is he perhaps putting us on?

I think not, because there doesn't seem to be any ironic edge to the text, and the illustrations are sincerely affectionate toward their main subject, though Mr. Gerrard continues to depict adults as quaintly distorted, as in his earlier books. . . . They're all head and torso on legs without thighs, and their strangeness becomes even more pronounced when juxtaposed with the "normal" proportions of his exquisitely wrought backgrounds. While this mannerism is certainly interesting and, in other circumstances, valid, here it limits rather than enriches the story, trivializing the very events Mr. Gerrard wishes to celebrate. It is all the more disappointing because he is clearly a gifted illustrator. Even the best graphics could not stir

From Sir Cedric, *written and illustrated by Roy Gerrard.*

this becalmed book: it needs a thoughtful text to fill its sails.

John Cech, in a review of "Sir Francis Drake," in The New York Times Book Review, April 10, 1988, p. 38.

Roy Gerrard's little people are always endearing, however much they confound the facts of anatomy, and certainly his chubby Francis Drake is irresistible. We mustn't take his account of the 'daring deeds' too literally: there is more artistic truth than sound fact in them. But he has drawn the ships with great gusto, and he captures the spirit of high adventure. There is a splendid storm scene, and the double-spread of Drake rounding the Horn is enough to make anyone shiver. How nice for him to get home to a welcome from a doll-like Elizabeth surrounded by her courtiers (everyone of them a portrait). I commend too the miniature (after Hilliard) which adorns the title-page. The verse narrative is not too awful.

M. Crouch, in a review of "Sir Francis Drake," in The Junior Bookshelf, Vol. 52, No. 3, June, 1988, p. 130.

Sir Francis Drake has never been so appealing as he is in this exuberant tale. . . . The playful, tongue-in-cheek humor of the text perfectly matches Gerrard's majestic and detailed illustrations which fill these pages with visual adventures. The expansiveness of line provides depth, and the intricacies of design and juxtapositions of textures create pages to pore over again and again. The infinite variety of the sea is captured differently in each illustration, and even the placement of the text on the page or its enclosure in decorative borders adds to the integrity of the composition. Hues of blue and brown dominate the pictures, but lush greens capture the mood of the tropics and enter into the earth and sea tones in other settings. Rusty reds highlight everything from Drake's hair and beard, to details of sailors' uniforms and ship decorations, to flames destroying Spanish ships and towns. Children will also delight in the language, from "flabbergasted" on the first page to the final battle against the Spanish Armada when "The discombobulated foe / decided it was time to go." A book that children will love to discover and explore.

Kay E. Vandergrift, in a review of "Sir Francis Drake: His Daring Deeds," in School Library Journal, Vol. 34, No. 11, August, 1988, p. 81.

Rosie and the Rustlers   (1989)

"Where the mountains meet the prairie, where the men are wild and hairy / There's a little ranch where Rosie Jones is boss. / It's a place that's neat and cozy, and the boys employed by Rosie / Work extremely hard, to stop her getting cross." With this balladic kick-off, Gerrard launches another historic spoof illustrated with his signature wit. When Rosie's hearty crew leaves the ranch unprotected to visit their Cherokee friends, Greasy Ben's outlaw band steals the herd. The subsequent chase scene leads Rosie, her boys, and the viewer through some spectacular Western scenery, a perfect showcase for the artist's favorite play with contrasting perspectives—diminutive, tall-hatted humans against cacti or dazzling bluffs. Both the patterned landscapes and detailed portraits make this one of Gerrard's best, while the verses, syllabically crowded and sometimes hokey as they are, will round up young listeners by the dozen.

Betsy Hearne, in a review of "Rosie and the Rustlers," in Bulletin of the Center for Children's Books, *Vol. 43, No. 3, November, 1989, p. 55.*

Gerrard has employed his mastery of the story-told-in-whimsical-verse to subjects as diverse as his fictional ballads about Sir Cedric and the exploits of Sir Francis Drake. Now he presents a parody of a Hollywood western—a story, unremarkable in itself, about how Rosie's six "boys," who have names like Fancy Dan, Salad Sam, and Mad McGhee, get the best of the miscreants who are after their herd. What *is* remarkable, however, is Gerrard's ever-clever versifying, of the sort to leave readers startled with admiration at the end of each neatly scanned, concise stanza; and his exquisitely designed and executed watercolors, with wonderfully evocative landscapes peopled by his funny little tall-hatted characters and full of nifty details—a teddy bear in Utah Jim's upper bunk, or the nine outlaws escaping on horses with what must be *almost* 36 tangled legs. Ironically, Gerrard's effort to simultaneously caricature and counteract stereotypical thinking is less than perfectly successful: although she's the boss, Rosie never actually does much, while the boys "Work extremely hard, to stop her getting cross"; and it's the friendly Cherokee who can track the rustlers across impossible terrain. Still, like Rosie's celebration at the end, enormous fun. (pp. 1669-70)

A review of "Rosie and the Rustlers," in Kirkus Reviews, *Vol. LVII, No. 22, November 15, 1989, pp. 1669-70.*

The author-artist's now familiar solid, chunky figures and humorous verse work especially well in this rollicking spoof of old Wild West ways and mores. . . . Vast panoramic scenes of foothills and buttes, saguaro cacti and roiling clouds—not to mention voluminous ten-gallon hats that sweep the skies—are a perfect foil for the droll, doll-like faces of the characters. A book that will be enjoyed at story hours as much for its visual fun as for its word play. (pp. 188-89)

Nancy Vasilakis, in a review of "Rosie and the Rustlers," in The Horn Book Magazine, *Vol. LXVI, No. 2, March-April, 1990, pp. 188-89.*

Kevin Henkes

1960-

American author and illustrator of picture books and fiction.

Major works include *Grandpa and Bo* (1986), *Two Under Par* (1987), *Sheila Rae, the Brave* (1987), *Chester's Way* (1988).

The creator of picture books featuring human or animal characters as well as contemporary realistic fiction for middle graders, Henkes is often praised for his understanding of children and their world and for his sensitivity toward their thoughts and feelings. He is perhaps best known for his picture books, characteristically gentle, humorous works which feature both real children and mice children as their protagonists. Henkes addresses such subjects as sibling rivalry, friendship, relationships with relatives, boredom, bathtime, a child's first waking moments, the joys of being alone, and the exploration of the senses in these books, which are often noted for their warmth, tenderness, and wit. He often focuses on situations where bossy youngsters, often older siblings, get their comeuppance and learn their limitations, and is well known for creating spunky heroines and likeable younger children with whom young readers can readily identify. For example, in one of Henkes's most popular works, *Sheila Rae, the Brave,* boastful mouse Sheila gets lost on the way home because she has decided to walk backwards with her eyes closed; she is rescued by her timid little sister Louise who has been following her and who, in the process, discovers her own bravery.

In addition to his picture books, Henkes is also the author and illustrator of several stories which are acknowledged for their presentation of caring families and empathetic treatment of emotional issues. Henkes is credited with not providing overly easy answers for his young protagonists, usually ten-year-old boys and girls whose experiences in their families, such as learning how to accept change and to become more compassionate, aid in their maturation. As an illustrator, Henkes frequently uses soft watercolors and delicate pen and pencil lines in pictures which are occasionally framed or bordered. He is consistently celebrated for the expressive quality of his characters, especially his cartoonlike animals, which have been compared to the early work of Maurice Sendak. Henkes's recent picture book *Shhhh* (1989) premiered his first use of acrylics in paintings which depict the atmosphere of the early morning.

(See also *Something about the Author,* Vol. 43 and *Contemporary Authors,* Vol. 114.)

TITLE COMMENTARY

All Alone (1981)

How does a child learn that he can spend profitable time alone, without friends or television—even without books? *All Alone* addresses this problem. The young boy who ap-

pears in each of the soft landscapes, drawn in gray pastels, finds that when he is alone, he notices more about what his senses of sight, hearing and smell can tell him. He asks himself questions. He thinks, imagines and talks in figurative languages: "I can be tall enough to taste the sky." It is difficult to portray introspection that is not too wistful or pensive. The author-artist tries to avoid the negative side of these emotions by drawing almost exclusively the back of the boy's head or his profile. The cover, however, does have a three-quarter face portrait. One of the last things the boy wonders about is what his friends are doing. No hermit he. It is good to be alone "for just a while." *All Alone* is a book that can help a child who has experienced similar feelings to understand and express himself, but will not be an all-occasion favorite.

Elizabeth Holtze, in a review of "All Alone," in School Library Journal, *Vol. 28, No. 1, September, 1981, p. 108.*

A little boy muses on the pleasures of being outdoors alone—in a remake of of umpteen vapid picture-book evocations. The text ranges from the plain and apt ("I feel the sun's heat all over me") to the plainly conventional ("I think of favorite things I've done); from the nicely suggestive ("When it's just me, I ask myself questions I can't answer") to the insistently meaningful ("When I'm alone, I look at myself inside and out. No one looks just like me or thinks just like I do"). Henkes paints with a delicate palette—the coloring is the most distinctive thing about the book—and the illustrations have a degree of feeling. But the text is simply a wash-out.

A review of "All Alone," in Kirkus Reviews, *Vol. XLIX, No. 24, December 15, 1981, p. 1517.*

At age 21, Henkes has already won prizes for the kind of paintings that enchant one in his first book. Muted colors, delicate lines reflect the sensitivity in the text. It's not a story per se, but the musing of a small boy, walking in the woods all by himself. When he's alone, he hears the trees breathe in the wind; he can change, grow tall enough to taste the sky or small enough to hide from a dragonfly behind a stone. He can think and pretend and wonder. Soon, he begins to wonder what his friends are doing and readers know that only sometimes he likes to be alone. The quietly lovely book can encourage children to avail themselves of what everyone needs: private moments, "all alone."

A review of "All Alone," in Publishers Weekly, *Vol. 220, No. 25, December 18, 1981, p. 70.*

Clean Enough (1982)

There is nothing wrong with a quiet book *per se,* but to appeal to children a book must have enough charm to raise it above the ho-hum level. I'm afraid this book doesn't succeed in capturing that elusive element. My question on finishing the book was "So what?" and neither of our book-loving preschoolers at home have asked me to read it again. The illustrations are nice enough, as is the story of a little boy's bathtime, but that's not enough to warrant adding it to your collection, unless you have a sizeable budget.

Maureen O'Connor, in a review of "Clean Enough," in Children's Book Review Service, *Vol. 10, No. 9, April, 1982, p. 82.*

Boy takes bath. That's what transpires in this highly successful picture book meant for young listeners (rather than readers), and it's likely to reach and to please them. The nuances of humor that lie beyond the matter-of-fact account enhance the book for adult viewers without violating the integrity of communication with the primary audience. The affectionate drawings in soft pencil are complemented nicely with blue and (skin toned) beige; the equally affectionate narrative is first person, and low-key. Only those who find frontal nudity inappropriate in a book about a small child bathing will not want to buy this book.

Joan W. Blos, in a review of "Clean Enough," in School Library Journal, *Vol. 29, No. 2, October, 1982, p. 141.*

The bathroom looks old fashioned and the taps are peculiar, but otherwise all is straightforward and decorous: both the loo and the boy's genitals are placed with discretion. He entertains the family cat, and us, by his thoughts on the difficult task of getting the water temperature just right. He discovers that sensations change as he gets older, and recalls the time when he was really naughty, using his father's shaving cream to decorate himself and his surroundings as he squeezed it from its tube.

This is an agreeable book which any damp and towel-wrapped toddler should enjoy as it snuggles on an adult's knee.

R. Barnes, in a review of "Clean Enough," in The Junior Bookshelf, *Vol. 47, No. 6, December, 1983, p. 236.*

Margaret and Taylor (1983)

Margaret and Taylor are brother and sister, seven-or-so and four. In format—pages of text, some black-and-white drawings, seven short chapters—the book looks to be for late-second/early-third graders. In all but a couple of the episodes, Margaret is out to put something over on Taylor, sometimes by a mean trick. She encourages, even urges him to open an envelope addressed to "The Tippet Family"—then keeps trying to get Mother to punish him. They go to the store to buy a present for Grandpa's birthday, and when he follows her lead and looks at other things, she reproaches him with forgetting Grandpa's birthday. True, he has a comeback—he's still carrying, for Grandpa, some leaves he collected. But what's the point? Margaret's nastiness, interpretable also as just plain sick, doesn't make for pleasant reading—and it's small consolation that Taylor isn't as totally bested as she intends. In two of the post-Grandpa's-party chapters, Margaret refuses to tie Taylor's balloon to his wrist (so he loses it—and then she loses hers too); agreeing to give him part of her leftover cake, she gives him hardly more than a crumb (then, forgetfully, leaves her piece behind). The one cheering passage is the family joke that Grandpa plays on Margaret and Taylor both. Otherwise, more dispiriting than anything else.

A review of "Margaret & Taylor," in Kirkus Reviews, *Vol. LI, No. 17, September 1, 1983, p. 162.*

Henkes's story and ebullient drawings bring Margaret and her little brother Taylor immediately into the reader's company. Margaret is *so mean!* setting the smaller child up for a fall but landing in the trap herself. . . . [Margaret's] ploys keep interest at a height, with their unexpected, merry and satisfying failures. She is an object lesson to superior siblings, and Taylor is a likable younger brother whom readers will root for, especially those put-upon like him—boys or girls. Hooray for Taylor.

A review of "Margaret & Taylor," in Publishers Weekly, *Vol. 224, No. 20, November 11, 1983, p. 47.*

The large type, open format and abundance of illustrations give the appearance of an easy reader; however, because of the unsettled conflict that exists between [the] siblings, adult explanation and discussion may be required. In any event, the stories will provoke thoughts about feelings and sibling rivalry. Sensitive pencil drawings, rather than the text, provide insight into the personalities of arrogant Margaret and vulnerable Taylor. The textless story of a surprise birthday party for their grandfather comes alive through these drawings. Adults will understand Margaret—but children will cheer for Taylor.

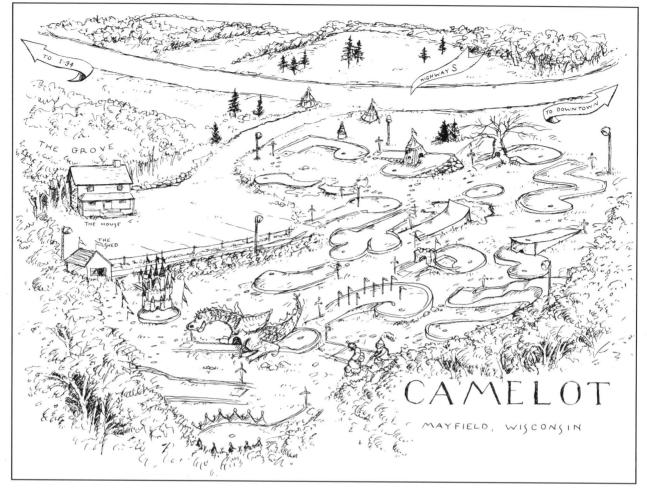

From Two Under Par, *written and illustrated by Kevin Henkes.*

Paula J. Zsiray, in a review of "Margaret & Taylor," in School Library Journal, *Vol. 30, No. 6, February, 1984, p. 72.*

Return to Sender   (1984)

Confident that he will get a reply, Whitaker Murphy writes a letter to TV superhero Frogman. The reply comes, but from an unexpected source. Whitaker's scantily addressed letter is picked up at the post office by Barney the mail carrier, who knows Whitaker will be disappointed if he doesn't get an answer and so writes back himself. This starts a correspondence between Whitaker and Frogman's ghostwriter—one that continues to puzzle Mr. and Mrs. Murphy, who try to persuade Whitaker there is something suspicious about the letters. Whitaker confides in Barney that he is fervently looking for a sign to indicate the reality of Frogman. Barney, realizing his culpability, sets out to provide one. Ironically, the words "Frogman Lives" painted on a water tower prove just the opposite to Whitaker—he has seen Barney fooling around with graffiti on a bridge. In a very sudden (and confusing) turnabout, Whitaker goes from feeling tricked to appreciating Barney's efforts in helping him grow up. The Frogman hook is a clever one, spicing up the usual family fare, al-

though Whitaker seems a little old to believe in Frogman with such intensity, while Barney is much too old to be defacing public property. However, the story line has child appeal, and the large print will attract readers in an age group for which fiction is scarce.

Ilene Cooper, in a review of "Return to Sender," in Booklist, *Vol. 80, No. 19, June 1, 1984, p. 1398.*

"It all started when Whitaker Murphy sent a letter to Frogman," the story begins; although his parents assure him that a television superhero isn't likely to answer, Whitaker does get an answer. Readers (who will probably enjoy being in the know) are aware that it's Barney, a sympathetic mailman, who's answered. And that's the start of an amusing story that is marred slightly by the silliness of postcard messages from vacationing kin, but readers should enjoy Whitaker's credulity, Barney's kindness, and even the oversize graffito . . . that mars the view but makes Whitaker understand he has a friend.

Zena Sutherland, in a review of "Return to Sender," in Bulletin of the Center for Children's Books, *Vol. 38, No. 1, September, 1984, p. 7.*

The plot, although slight, is innocuous, and some readers may identify with Whitaker's hero worship. There are real problems, however, with the characterizations, particularly of adults. Whitaker's mother doesn't encourage his imagination and while Barney does, he is portrayed as childish, often spilling food and drink on the mail and, in an act of gross vandalism, spray painting the city water tower in order to prove Frogman's existence. There is some humor, mainly slapstick or at someone's expense. Unmemorable.

> *Jeanette Larson, in a review of "Return to Sender," in* School Library Journal, *Vol. 31, No. 1, September, 1984, p. 118.*

Bailey Goes Camping (1985)

Bailey's siblings are going with the Bunny Scouts on a camping trip that sounds like a lot of fun: "All we do is eat hot dogs and live in a tent and go swimming and fishing and hunt for bears and tell ghost stories and fall asleep under the stars." Bailey wants to go too, but he's too young. Papa's assurance that "it's not *that* great" is small comfort to Bailey. Of much more interest is Mama's observation that he can do all of those things right here at home. So, it's hot dogs for lunch, a homemade tent to play in, swimming and fishing in the bathtub, and a bear hunt and ghost stories with Daddy before bedtime. Jaunty pen-and-wash drawings go along with the simple story. Bailey and his family (all rabbits) have a disarmingly innocent look; that and the pictures' pastel hues and country prints add up to a cozy, comfortable book that will leave youngsters smiling at Bailey's good luck in having such a wise, comforting mother.

> *Denise M. Wilms, in a review of "Bailey Goes Camping," in* Booklist, *Vol. 82, No. 2, September 15, 1985, p. 134.*

It isn't often that a book comes along that *truly* captures the world of the small child. [*Bailey Goes Camping*] does this successfully with wit and warmth. A book that is a cinch to delight both children and adults.

> *Anne Devereaux Jordan Crouse, in a review of "Bailey Goes Camping," in* Children's Book Review Service, *Vol. 14, No. 3, November, 1985, p. 25.*

The pale blues, grays, purples and soft yellows of the watercolor and pencil drawings are a soothing complement to the quiet text. Illustrations are bordered and centered; text appears opposite or below the artwork. The rabbits, who show human expressions, are drawn in a simple cartoon style, with human clothing and household accoutrements. An enjoyable read-aloud book for small preschool groups or before bedtime.

> *Dawna Lisa Buchanan-Berrigan, in a review of "Bailey Goes Camping," in* School Library Journal, *Vol. 32, No. 4, December, 1985, p. 74.*

Grandpa and Bo (1986)

Henkes' latest picture book is a welcome addition to his growing list of accomplishments. As in his earlier books,

Henkes' soft pencil drawings accurately convey the story's mood of quiet simplicity.

It was summer. This meant Bo would be staying with his Grandpa as he did every summer. It was the only time they saw each other, except for every other Christmas. They were together all day long—playing ball, gardening, cooking, whittling, taking long walks, and fishing under a shaded tree. Bo's favorite time was when Grandpa told stories about his childhood and taught Bo the names he gave the things around them. The nicest part of the whole summer was the special summer Christmas they shared, since this year they wouldn't be together for Christmas.

The summer passed quickly. The corn grew as tall as Grandpa, and the nights became cooler. The night before Bo was to leave, he and Grandpa each made a wish on a shooting star—and without a word they knew they had wished for the very same thing.

As is Henkes' style, he takes an ordinary childhood memory and gently textures it with a number of touching details to demonstrate how special the memory is, e.g., the relationship between this boy and his grandfather. However, the understated nature of the illustrations and the story makes this a picture book that may have more appeal to reminiscing adults than to young children.

> *A review of "Grandpa and Bo," in* Kirkus Reviews, *Vol. LIV, No. 4, February 15, 1986, p. 303.*

A warm, affectionate portrayal of a loving relationship between a boy and his grandfather. . . . Quiet pencil drawings with soft edges and a nostalgic ambience accompany the story. This is low-key but rich; feelings are close to the surface, ready to touch anyone who comes along.

> *Denise M. Wilms, in a review of "Grandpa & Bo," in* Booklist, *Vol. 82, No. 13, March 1, 1986, p. 1018.*

Soft drawings, grays on cream paper, with some black lines, are neatly framed and face pages on which the type is set off by ample space. The story of a small boy's summer spent with a beloved grandfather on a farm (where Grandpa seems to live alone but have all his time free) is low-keyed and gentle. This won't have the appeal of action or humor, but it's a pleasant book about a relationship and a situation, and the read-aloud audience should enjoy the way Grandpa names flora and fauna, and the way he and Bo celebrate Christmas on a summer night to make up for being apart on the holiday.

> *A review of "Grandpa and Bo," in* Bulletin of the Center for Children's Books, *Vol. 39, No. 9, May, 1986, p. 167.*

A Weekend with Wendell (1986)

The pitfalls of having company over the weekend are divertingly recounted by Henkes with good humor and charm. Sophie greets her mother's announcement that Wendell is spending the weekend with silence. They play house together, and Wendell is the mother, the father *and* the five children—he makes Sophie be the dog. They play hospital, and Wendell gets to be doctor, nurse and patient—Sophie is the desk clerk. When they play bakery,

Sophie gets to be a sweet roll. Wendell is a houseguest with presence, and Sophie puts up with him until he gives her a new hairdo with shaving cream. Then Sophie invites Wendell to play firefighter, and *he's* the burning building. Sophie turns the hose on him, and her assertiveness pays off. A friendship is born under the rainbow umbrella formed by sunlight on the water. Henkes keeps text to a minimum and lets the postures of his mice children speak volumes. Sophie's quivering eyebrows alone could carry most of this tale.

> *A review of "A Weekend with Wendell," in* Publishers Weekly, *Vol. 230, No. 4, July 25, 1986, p. 187.*

The joke goes on a little too long, but there is plenty of humor here, both textual and visual. The pen-and-ink drawings colored in spiffy pastels are full of fun, with sly expressions worth noting. Any parent will sympathize with Sophie's mother and father, who are glad to see Wendell gone, no matter how much Sophie misses him in the end.

> *Ilene Cooper, in a review of "A Weekend with Wendell," in* Booklist, *Vol. 83, No. 1, September 1, 1986, p. 62.*

This story of mischievous mouse-boy Wendell, parked over the weekend with mouse-girl Sophie's parents while his own are out of town, sounds as if the author has been eavesdropping on children at play. . . . The soft, neatly framed watercolors complement the funny text with the characters' expressive faces and postures, extending the story without overwhelming it. This is a hilarious read-aloud and could prove a turning point in the life of a bossy child—or a mousy one. (pp. 27-8)

> *Betsy Hearne, in a review of "A Weekend with Wendell," in* Bulletin of the Center for Children's Books, *Vol. 40, No. 2, October, 1986, pp. 27-8.*

Once Around the Block (1987)

A lighthearted treatment of what is, for many children, a serious problem—boredom! Annie has nothing to do. Finally, her mother suggests she take a walk around the block till Papa comes home. To each neighbor, she repeats her litany: "My best friend Bea is on vacation. Mama is busy with baby Phil. Cornelius has fleas. There's nothing good on television. And I've been waiting for Papa to come home from work for hours." Each diverts her with a small gift of cookies, flowers, or sympathetic suggestions ("Why don't you take your shoes off and run your toes through my grass?"). When she gets home, Papa is waiting for her with the same complaint she's been making—a masterstroke of child appeal on the part of the author. Not only is this a child-like and funny story, but [illustrator Victoria] Chess takes full graphic advantage of the scenario, as is her wont. The dog never appears without its leg up for a scratch; the characters are a warm, homely lot, and the setting a varied, old-fashioned neighborhood to envy. Every child should have such a block to circle when they're lonely.

> *Betsy Hearne, in a review of "Once Around the Block," in* Bulletin of the Center for Chil-

dren's Books, *Vol. 40, No. 7, March, 1987, p. 126.*

As in his other books, Henkes creates a comfortable story with understated, believable characters and events. Chess has toned down her usual dramatic style to fit the mood—to be sure, some colors are still garish, and everyone still looks like a pop-eyed lunatic, but she has made facial expressions gentler than is her wont, and set the tale in a neat, quiet, well-tended neighborhood.

Boredom is generally countered in picture books by wild flights of fancy (see Stevenson's *There's nothing to do!,* 1986, for a recent example); here's a satisfactory alternative treatment.

> *A review of "Once Around the Block," in* Kirkus Reviews, *Vol. LV, No. 8, April 15, 1987, p. 638.*

Two Under Par (1987)

Wedge is a slightly overweight boy, age 10, who stows away presents in a box that he hopes to someday give to his father. His mother Sally says she doesn't even know who his father is and she expects Wedge to adapt to his new stepfather, King, and King's son Andrew. Wedge's window overlooks King's miniature golf course, where castle marks the 18th hole. The boy doesn't like anything about his new life and being part of a family; he finds King to be a homely buffoon, and Sally, who is pregnant, no longer available to him. The complicated process of learning acceptance and being accepted is one Henkes explores with confidence and care; his novelist's hand is as sure as his illustrative talents. In this touching and funny book, there are no easy or sudden solutions—just a sense of isolation slipping away, as Wedge reaches out and receives much more than he expects. (pp. 84-5)

> *A review of "Two Under Par," in* Publishers Weekly, *Vol. 231, No. 8, March 13, 1987, pp. 84-5.*

[Despite] Wedge's raw feelings, his new family continues to bond with each other; the simple passage of time takes its toll on Wedge's determination not to accept change. Finally Wedge realizes that King is the father figure he has always longed for. Although Henkes' story is brief and simple, it reflects a great deal of sensitivity to emotional issues and doesn't take any shortcuts in characterizing Wedge's transformation. There is no overnight solution here; rather it is the inevitability of circumstances that forges the change in Wedge, much as it does in real life.

> *Denise M. Wilms, in a review of "Two Under Par," in* Booklist, *Vol. 83, No. 19, June 1, 1987, p. 1522.*

Wedge is ten, fat, and unhappy. He feeds his unhappiness, downing cans of instant whipped cream at a sitting. He is miserable because his mother has a new husband, a tall, skinny man ten years her senior, with a five-year-old son who is skinny too. . . . Henke's handling of Wedge's problems is masterful and shows a keen understanding of childhood. In only a few pages, readers will see Wedge grow and mature and come to appreciate his almost all-new family. Wedge's parents are refreshingly decent people who try hard, make errors, but ultimately succeed in helping to bring Wedge around. Readers are left with the impression that Wedge is a good kid who learns to adapt to life as it is. Still, there's that weight problem, and perhaps Henkes will take that up in another volume.

> *Robert Unsworth, in a review of "Two Under Par," in* School Library Journal, *Vol. 33, No. 10, June-July, 1987, p. 96.*

Sheila Rae, the Brave (1987)

A mouse both boastful and fearless, Sheila Rae decides to go home from school by taking a new route. She walks backwards with her eyes closed, growls at dogs and cats, climbs trees, turns new corners and crosses different streets—and ends up in the middle of unfamiliar territory. Lost and sad, she thinks of home, her parents and her timid sister Louise. As soon as she cries for help, who should appear but Louise, who swings down from a tree branch and saves Sheila Rae from harm. She had followed her older sister, and *she* knows the way back. Everything that happens here is completely credible, hence appealing to kids' intuitions—most get carried away sometimes and learn their limitations the hard way. Henkes's illustrations show brightly hued forests, mellow graffiti-scrawled fences and one very confident character. Sheila Rae. But little Louise steals the show.

> *A review of "Sheila Rae, the Brave," in* Publishers Weekly, *Vol. 231, No. 25, June 26, 1987, p. 71.*

Fearless mouse Sheila Rae is not afraid of anything, and she flaunts her confidence by confronting real and imagined terrors daily (her imagined ones are particularly creative and funny). Finally Sheila Rae decides on a new challenge: she will go home from school a new way. When she gets hopelessly lost, her courage falters, but scaredy-cat little sister Louise has been surreptitiously following Sheila Rae, and proves her own bravery by leading her sister safely home. Louise mimics her sister's undaunted style all the way home ("She growled at stray dogs, and bared her teeth at stray cats"), thus providing a strong language pattern for new readers. Bouncy watercolors in spring-like colors with some pen-and-ink detailing highlight Sheila Rae's bravado in an engaging and amusing way, and Henkes provides Sheila Rae, Louise, and their school friends with highly expressive faces. Children will respond to both the humor of the story and the illustrations and to the challenge of facing fears head-on. Librarians can share this one with small groups or recommend it for patrons without fear, for children will love it.

> *David Gale, in a review of "Sheila Rae, the Brave," in* School Library Journal, *Vol. 34, No. 1, September, 1987, p. 164.*

A seamless offering, this will both touch and tickle little ones. Henkes packs plenty of appeal into his watercolors outlined in pen and ink and coaxes maximum expressions from the thin lines and dots that serve as the mice's features. Let's see more of these spunky heroines.

> *Ilene Cooper, in a review of "Sheila Rae, the Brave," in* Booklist, *Vol. 84, No. 1, September 1, 1987, p. 64.*

The Zebra Wall (1988)

The author of several picture books and novels . . . tells how Adine Verlob, ten and the oldest of five sisters, adapts to two new arrivals to the household: a baby brother and her mother's older sister.

Everyone is delighted with the baby, even though his room must be repainted: the family has been expecting another girl. Adine is less happy about Aunt Irene: 50-ish, newly divorced, and with a propensity for uncomfortable observations and smelly brown cigarettes (Henkes suffuses the book with cigarette smoke, for reasons that are never made clear), as well as a mania for cats. When it seems that she's going to share Adine's room indefinitely, Adine vows to do anything to get rid of her, until an overheard telephone conversation gives her a new understanding of Irene's vulnerability.

Although the plot is fresh and has some resonant, truthful moments, this is unevenly written. The Midwestern working-class setting is authentic, but not very sympathetic. There are well-realized characters, especially Adine's parents and Aunt Irene, but others (including Adine's sisters) hardly emerge from the background. A mixed effort. (pp. 362-63)

> *A review of "The Zebra Wall," in* Kirkus Reviews, *Vol. LVI, No. 5, March 1, 1988, pp. 362-63.*

Henkes' story presents a loving, creative family with

Chester and Wilson and Lilly,
Lilly and Wilson and Chester.
That's the way it was....

From Chester's Way, *written and illustrated by Kevin Henkes.*

Adine Vorlob, a sensitive, intelligent youngster as the main character. The arrival of a sixth child provides the catalyst which helps ten-year-old Adine understand her eccentric and bossy Aunt Irene. As the oldest, Adine has participated in the traditional creation of a special nursery wall to celebrate the first initial of each of her five sisters, all named alphabetically from B to E. All of the family is convinced that a sixth female will join the line. The title announces a surprising change. Aunt Irene comes to care for the girls while their mother is in the hospital and stays to help out afterwards, much to the children's dismay. With her sisters, Adine plots to get Aunt Irene to leave, but in the end learns compassion and understanding. Henkes' characters are well drawn and appealingly unusual. As in *Two Under Par,* he writes with humor about a caring family. Fans of Beverly Cleary and Betsy Byars will enjoy this newest Henkes selection. (pp. 100-01)

> *Renée Steinberg, in a review of "The Zebra Wall," in* School Library Journal, *Vol. 34, No. 8, April, 1988, pp. 100-01.*

Kevin Henkes has brought a fresh new family to young readers. The Vorlobs—Mother, Dad, Aunt Irene, and the five girls (Bernice, Carla, Dot, Effie, and our heroine, the first-born Adine)—come to life as rather eccentric, funny, and creative individuals. . . . Adine and Aunt Irene, who subtly battle for leadership but become friends through adversity, and Deedee, Aunt Irene's cat, assume key roles in the novel in which adjustment and compromise are central to a satisfying and believable conclusion. The story is told through gentle humor and embodies genuine understanding of a ten-year-old's fears. A beguiling story peopled with true characters.

> *Elizabeth S. Watson, in a review of "The Zebra Wall," in* The Horn Book Magazine, *Vol. LXIV, No. 3, May-June, 1988, p. 352.*

Chester's Way (1988)

Chester, a mouse, is almost *too* good: he does everything just so—from double-knotting his shoes to carrying a first-aid kit. His friend Wilson is just like him; they are always together. When Lilly, an imaginative hellion, moves in next door, they find her too uproarious to play with—till the day she scares away some bullies who are pestering them; but when they finally get to know Lilly, they find her creativity makes life more interesting—and, of course, she has something to learn from them as well.

The reversal of the stereotype here is hardly novel, but Henkes' pungent dialogue is amusing, and his illustrations engaging. Using two or three vignettes per page, he represents his characters mouse-size, which emphasizes what comically tidy, particular little people Chester and Wilson are. This should double well as an easy reader.

> *A review of "Chester's Way," in* Kirkus Reviews, *Vol. LVI, No. 12, June 15, 1988, p. 898.*

Henkes's vision of friendship captures the essence of the childlike; his mice live in a sunny, imaginative world mixed with secure routines and the safety of known factors. The story unwinds at a deliberate pace; every sentence is either downright funny or dense with playful, deadpan humor. The artist/author, as always, gently

grants room for differences between people (the turn-around in *A Weekend with Wendell,* for example, and the reconciliation between Wedge and his stepfather in *Two Under Par*). Behind each book is a wide-open heart, one readers can't help but respond to, that makes all of Henkes's books—and especially this one—of special value to children.

> *A review of "Chester's Way," in* Publishers Weekly, *Vol. 234, No. 2, July 8, 1988, p. 53.*

Kevin Henkes, well known for his strong empathy with the feelings of children, has shown his characters as delightful little mice, expressive physically as well as verbally. The virtues of variety and experimentation, on the one hand, and friendship, on the other, are deftly handled in the amusing, believable story.

> *Ann A. Flowers, in a review of "Chester's Way," in* The Horn Book Magazine, *Vol. LXIV, No. 5, September-October, 1988, p. 616.*

Jessica (1989)

Jessica is the imaginary friend of a girl named Ruthie, whose parents constantly remind her, "There is no Jessica." But Ruthie knows better, and Jessica is included in every aspect of the girl's play. Then Ruthie goes to kindergarten and, despite her parents wishes to the contrary, takes Jessica with her. It's a confusing day, and just as Ruthie's woes are about to be desperately compounded (the children have to choose *real* partners), a classmate introduces herself as "Jessica." She becomes as close a friend to Ruthie as her imaginary namesake. The story is characteristically on target in its reflections of the inventive ways in which children play; Henkes never falters as he outlines the logic and reasoning behind Ruthie's affection for her invisible playmate. But the denouement seems hasty, especially given all the care that has led up to it. Nevertheless, Henkes's scenes of Ruthie and her two Jessicas are visions of fun (although his people do have a bit of Karen Gundersheimer and Maurice Sendak to their marching stances), and despite the ending, readers will find plenty of pleasure within these pages.

> *A review of "Jessica," in* Publishers Weekly, *Vol. 235, No. 2, January 13, 1989, p. 90.*

Jessica may be invisible, but there's nothing unreal about the strong friendship Ruthie shares with her, vignettes of which are pictured in tiny, tidy, line-and-watercolor illustrations scattered cleanly and cleverly among the text. This is an exceptionally well designed picture book, with a witty use of white space and an imaginative variety of type and line placement. For example, the line "And if Ruthie was glad, Jessica felt exactly the same" tootles out of Ruthie's horn as she blithely marches through a meadow of wildflowers. Henke's felicitous prose makes this a prime pick for reading aloud to kids and their significant others, invisible or not.

> *Roger Sutton, in a review of "Jessica," in* Bulletin of the Center for Children's Books, *Vol. 42, No. 6, February, 1989, p. 148.*

The concluding page, like a charming pas de deux, depicts

the two small girls repeating many of the games which Ruthie once played with her invisible friend, bringing the story full circle to a satisfying conclusion. The illustrations are thoroughly engaging: small figures defined by delicate, expressive, agile pen lines and enriched by the authoritative use of watercolor are set against carefully limned but not overpowering backgrounds. Not one extraneous element in text or pictures mars the lyrical, joyous tone, reminiscent but not imitative of Sendak's illustrations for *A Hole Is to Dig.* Ruthie's empowering is one that every small child can understand and celebrate. She is her own person and one worth knowing.

> *Mary M. Burns, in a review of "Jessica," in* The Horn Book Magazine, *Vol. LXV, No. 3, May-June, 1989, p. 357.*

Shhhh (1989)

In an affecting, stylistic departure from his often joyous watercolors, Henkes uses acrylic paints to create the hushed world of a child's first waking moments. A girl notes that the rest of the household is still asleep, from her stuffed animals and family pets to a baby sister in a crib and her parents. Reaching for her toy horn, she blasts them all awake—and is she punished? No, the final scene shows the loving family gathered together. The text is all mood—unlike Henkes's other works, which tell more of a story—and the paintings convey that tenderness in dusky morning tones and broad sweeps of the brush. How rewarding to watch an artist stretch, and achieve another perfect fit.

> *A review of "SHHHH," in* Publishers Weekly, *Vol. 235, No. 23, June 9, 1989, p. 65.*

Henkes' story will tickle preschoolers, who are often early birds, though parents may have darker opinions of such outbursts. It's all in fun, however, and the thick acrylic paintings, a change from the artist's usual watercolors, convey both the peaceful stillness and the burst of energy that morning brings.

> *Denise Wilms, in a review of "Shhhh," in* Booklist, *Vol. 85, No. 22, August, 1989, p. 1977.*

Henkes' muted acrylics perfectly capture the hushed mood of the quiet, sleeping house. Not to be missed are his "sacked out" stuffed animals and an unusual overhead view of the child peeking at a sleeping baby. The final double-page spread, in which pets, parents, and children greet each other and the morning, is bathed in soft lavenders and blues. Cozy, warm, and reminiscent of lazy weekend mornings in many a child's world, the book will be equally at home as a lap book or in a preschool story time. The text is spare, but offers opportunities for participation both in the initial "shhhh" of the tiptoeing child and the following noise and clatter of wake-up time.

> *Gail C. Ross, in a review of "Shhhh," in* School Library Journal, *Vol. 31, No. 1, January, 1990, p. 83.*

S(usan) E(loise) Hinton

1948-

American author of fiction and screenwriter.

Major works include *The Outsiders* (1967), *Rumble Fish* (1976), *Tex* (1980), *Taming the Star Runner* (1988).

Often considered the most successful novelist for the junior high and high school audience, Hinton is credited with creating the genre of young adult literature with the publication of her first book, *The Outsiders,* at the age of seventeen. Although not a prolific author, she is acclaimed for writing powerful and insightful contemporary realistic fiction about adolescent males in hostile social environments which is often acknowledged for its authenticity, candor, and appeal to young adults, especially teenage boys. Hinton is often lauded for her success in eliciting the desire to read in young people for whom literature has little or no interest, and her works are often used in classroom settings due to their popularity with both readers and nonreaders. Although her books include topical elements such as gang violence and drug abuse, Hinton focuses more on character and theme, an attribute praised for contributing to the universality of her works. Hinton, who writes her books from a male first-person viewpoint and often explores fraternal and semi-fraternal relationships, is often falsely identified as a man due to her understanding of the male psyche.

When Hinton began her literary career with *The Outsiders,* she was prompted to fill a need for books that deal realistically with the lives of teenagers. Based around events that occured in her high school in Tulsa, Oklahoma, the novel describes the rivalry between two gangs, the lower-middle-class greasers and the upper-class Socs (for Socials), a conflict which leads to the deaths of members of both gangs. Narrated by fourteen-year-old Ponyboy, a sensitive, orphaned greaser who tells the story in retrospect, *The Outsiders* explores the camaraderie, loyalty, and affection that lies behind the gang mystique while pointing out both the likenesses in the feelings of the opposing groups and the futility of gang violence; through his encounters with death, Ponyboy learns that he does not have to remain an outsider. Initially regarded as controversial for its unflinching portrayal of disaffected youth, the novel is now recognized as a classic of juvenile literature as well as a unique accomplishment for so young a writer. In her subsequent books, Hinton continues to depict the survival and maturation of her adolescent male protagonists, tough yet tender lower-class boys who live in and around Tulsa and who grow by making difficult decisions. Hinton addresses such themes as appearance versus reality, the need to be loved and to belong, the meaning of honor, and the limits of friendship in a prose style noted initially for its urgency but more recently for its more controlled, mature quality. Underlying Hinton's works is her depiction of society as a claustrophobic and often fatal environment which contributes to the fear and hostility felt by her characters. Although she has been accused of sexism for inadequately developing several of the young women in her books, Hinton is often praised for the over-

all superiority of her characterizations and for her sensitivity toward the feelings and needs of the young. She has also written the screenplays for feature films based on the first four of her books. In 1988, Hinton received the first Young Adult Services Division/*School Library Journal* Author Award from the American Library Association.

(See also *CLR,* Vol. 3; *Contemporary Literary Criticism,* Vol. 30; *Something about the Author,* Vols. 19, 58; and *Contemporary Authors,* Vols. 81-84.)

AUTHOR'S COMMENTARY

[The following excerpt is from an interview by William Walsh.]

W. W. How does a sixteen-year-old come to write a novel that is such a best seller and such a popular novel?

S. E. H. I've been practicing writing for eight years. I started in grade school, and I had written a couple of other novels before *The Outsiders.* It was just the first I ever tried to publish.

W. W. Tell us the story of why you sent this one out, when you hadn't sent any others.

S. E. H. The mother of a girlfriend of mine writes children's books, and she read *The Outsiders* and liked it. She said she would give me the name of her agency and told me to send it to them to see what they could do with it. Finally, I thought it would be worth a try, and I did send it.

W. W. Did this inspire you to burn the midnight oil?

S. E. H. Oh, no. It inspired me so greatly that I was unable to write for four years. I had a super case of "first novel block." I could not write for four years. I could not use the typewriter, even to write a letter, even though I taught myself to type when I was in the sixth grade. I love to write, but for four years, I could not. I was a teenage writer, which is very similar to being a teenage werewolf. People are always watching you for signs of "things." I was put in the spotlight. I can understand complications people have who are suddenly famous overnight. Even though the amount of fame I got was very small, compared to that of a lot of people at the same age, it was enough to really bother me.

W. W. Where did you get the material to write the story, *The Outsiders?*

S. E. H. Well, it dealt with a situation I had in high school: The Socialist-Greasers thing, which is a very small part, because I went to a large high school and everybody was divided up into different camps. The Socialists and the Greasers were actually just the extremes. There were all kinds of middle groups like the "artsy-craftsy" people; the "student council" people; "greasy socialists," and "socialist-greasers." It was a complicated social situation. I thought it was a very dumb situation, on top of that.

W. W. Did you belong to one of these groups yourself?

S. E. H. No. Even the nonconformists would not have me, because I wouldn't conform. But I had friends from all different groups. I thought it was dumb; but nobody questioned it.

W. W. You were accepted, though, by people in all the different groups?

S. E. H. Yes, Well, everyone looked at me sort of strangely, but I was accepted. I was a pretty good fighter; I did not scream when the police chased us; and I had a pretty good-sized switchblade knife that everybody liked. I was treated as one of the guys. I got my tooth chipped when I was hit in the face with a bottle. I had an interesting adolescence.

W. W. There's a crucial scene in the book where Johnnycake is dying in the hospital. He sees Ponyboy and he says, "Stay gold, Ponyboy; stay gold." Now, we remember, earlier on, that they were taught Robert Frost's poem, "Nothing Gold Can Stay." Did you have anything else in mind beyond that?

S. E. H. Not really. While I was writing the book, I had no idea of plot structure—I still don't, I can't plot my way out of the Safe-Way Store—but I know my characters. And, during the book, I would go so far as to say to my friends, "I'm writing a book; this is what's happened so far. What should happen next?" And they would tell me something, and I'd stick it in. The fire scene was something somebody told me ("Hey! Make the church catch on

fire!" "Okay, I'll do that."). But, as far as the poem goes, I was working on my book in a creative writing class (which I made a "D" in because I was writing my book and not doing my class work), and I read the Robert Frost poem. I enjoyed it, and thought it was appropriate for my book and I stuck it in. I liked the feeling of it, the enthusiasm and the innocence and everything you lose as you get older. You lose your emotional commitments and I think that's what Frost had in mind. That's what I had in mind, even though I probably could not have articulated it at that time.

W. W. Was there a Ponyboy Curtis? I mean, I know you say there was a general situation, but. . . .

S. E. H. Not really. I couldn't point out any kid that I knew as a child and say that that was Ponyboy; but he was very much like I was at that age. Maybe a lot of things happened to him that happened to different friends of mine. Not all of his experiences were one person's experiences. I just incorporated them. I've learned as a writer that any character you write is going to turn out to be some aspect of yourself, so there's an awful lot of me in Dallas Winston as well as Ponyboy Curtis. I don't think as a writer you can really, truthfully, say this person is so-and-so; it has to be filtered through your mind, so it is some part of you.

W. W. You said before that you couldn't plot your way out of Safe-Way and that, very often, others suggested elements of plot that you would put into the novel. Were the characters the same way? Do you have a clear idea of the character?

S. E. H. I have an absolutely clear conception of my characters. If they walked through the door, I wouldn't be surprised. I know their birthdays, what they like to eat for breakfast; I know what kind of dreams they have; I know their hair color, their eye color. . . . I'm a very strong character writer, but that is only myself. There are other writers, like Ray Bradbury, who are idea writers; there are people who are atmosphere writers; people who can do intricate plots. Everybody has his own strong point. Mine is character.

W. W. When you wrote *That Was Then,* did it also come out of some personal experience?

S. E. H. It's hard to say because you mix up things that have happened to other people with your own experiences, and you take what your own experiences might have been and dramatize them into something completely different. You get your characters from different places. Like Mark, one of the main characters in *That Was Then.* His personality was taken directly from a cat I had (people think this is a cute, funny, little writer-thing you say). I actually got his personality from a cat, as much as I can get a personality from a human being. Later, I was talking to my sister (who is also a cat-person) and told her I had gotten Mark from Rabbit—my cat—and she said, "Oh, yes. I see that." Rabbit had beautiful beer-colored eyes that I had to incorporate into the character. And he's a completely amoral little animal. What was good for him was good; what was bad for him was bad. He had no judgments, so far as how his actions might affect other people.

W. W. This mixing up your life with other people's and

then sorting it out in a book, does that help you understand yourself or your experiences better?

S. E. H. Sometimes. But it takes several years to look back on it and see what you were actually saying; I feel like the theme in *That Was Then* was "growth is betrayal" and, even though I knew that was what I wanted to say, when I got through with it, I was satisfied that I had it said. I still could not put it into words until four or five years later.

W. W. You said it better than you knew. I think many writers have that experience. A lot of what you're doing is unconscious or subconscious.

S. E. H. It is completely subconscious; and later you can look back and say, "I did this," or "I did that." Like in *Rumblefish,* I had somebody remark upon the color symbolism I used (black and white motif) and I didn't realize that I had done it until I looked back and saw; not only with the color blindness of the motorcycle boy, but the different things of black and white and black and white that go out through the story.

W. W. Speaking about *Rumblefish,* at one point Rusty James becomes color blind. Is there a set parallel we're supposed to see?

S. E. H. There's supposed to be, even more so, at the end of the book when he's talking to Steve and he starts listening to the ocean; he doesn't hear Steve. And the motorcycle boy was notoriously bad on his hearing. I thought it would be interesting to show two completely different people, one very complex, one very simple, who went through the same battering set of circumstances and came out relatively the same at the end, even though the cause and the effect worked on completely different things. This kind of numbness—Rusty James didn't care if he saw Steven, didn't care about anything; he liked sitting there looking at the ocean all day—was somewhat the same regarding the motorcycle boy's detachment that he would just see things and not get involved with anything. He didn't belong anywhere. I enjoyed doing that book because I felt it was a challenge to me as a writer. It would have been very easy for me to write a sequel to *The Outsiders* or a sequel to *That Was Then* and go into *The Curtis Boys Visit the Farm* and that sort of thing, but I wanted to do something different and Rusty James is different. He's not articulate, observant, or intelligent. It is difficult to write a book from his point of view. As a writer, I was very happy with the book.

W. W. That's an interesting thing you said. The feeling you get from reading *Rumblefish* is quite different from the feeling you get from *The Outsiders* and also from *That Was Then.* They are all first-person narrations, and it seems that it is the narrator who is changing in each case, and the world appears different, as each person sees it.

S. E. H. I try to do that. I could take Ponyboy Curtis and change his name to "Jim Smith" or something and write another book from the same person's point of view; but that's not stretching yourself as a writer, and I want to do that. At the same time, I still want to reach my own audience. I write for kids who don't usually read a book, so I feel that *Rumblefish* is written on two different levels, when it's one. Just a simple, straight story, a little action thing, how Rusty James couldn't let go of the good old

days of the gangs, and how that destroyed him. But I still feel, at least from the letters I've gotten from kids, they realize there's something else there, even if they don't know what it is. They think, "I've got to think about that. Maybe I don't know what it means, but it's something to think about and maybe I'll come back to it later." I think I accomplished what I set out to do with *Rumblefish.*

W. W. Do any of the youngsters who write to you ask you about their own writing?

S. E. H. Yes, they do. A lot of them want to write and don't know where to begin. I always say that, first of all, they've got to read. Just read everything. I never studied writing consciously. But if you read a lot, like I did, subconsciously, structure is going to drop into your head, whether it's sentence structure, paragraph structure, chapter structure, or novel structure. Pretty soon, you're going to know where things go—where the climax is supposed to be, where the ending's supposed to be, how to get there, how to describe people. You can absorb it subconsciously. I, personally, never tried to copy any one person's style because I feel you should write the way you think. But reading lots of different styles will expose you to different ways of thinking. My big recommendation is to read and then practice. Write yourself. I wrote for eight years before I wrote *The Outsiders.* I advise writing for oneself. If you don't want to read it, nobody else is going to read it. Once you do that and get somebody else's opinion, just start sending it away.

W. W. Who's your favorite character—of your own? Or your favorite book?

S. E. H. That's hard to say because *The Outsiders* sort of made my fame, but I see so many things wrong with it as a writer that I can't say that's the best writing I've ever done. Another thing, it's been very hard for me to accept the fact that it's very likely that the first book I've ever written will be the book I'll be known for ("Oh, you're the person who wrote *The Outsiders*"). As far as characters go, although Mark is not a particularly admirable character, I feel he's a very vivid character in *That Was Then;* and that silly motorcycle boy who just drove me nuts—would not leave me be—I saw his picture in *Life Magazine* just as I described it in the book when Rusty James is going into the drugstore and he's reading a magazine. I had to write that book and describe the motorcycle boy; I probably still do not do him justice. It's hard, like when you ask someone, "Which is your favorite child?" (pp. 32-7)

W. W. All of your character-narrators are first person, male.

S. E. H. I can't write from a female point of view. I've tried it, but I can't do it. It's just that when I was growing up, all my close friends were guys. I identified with the male culture; I was a tomboy; and, while I realize now I used to think I had a male mind, I think I just had a female mind that didn't conform to the female culture at that time. It's just a thing I feel very comfortable with, and I realize I reach all my audience that way. While girls will read boys' books, boys very often will not read girls' books; so one can appeal to both of them that way. It's very likely I will continue to write from the male point of view.

W. W. You don't think there's a great deal of difference, then, between the point of view of a fifteen year-old boy and a fifteen year-old girl?

S. E. H. Not as much as you would think, really. It's amazing the similarities among the letters I get from guys and girls. If they could just realize that this artificial barrier between them is almost just socially set up, that their wishes, their dreams and everything are very similar, they could communicate a lot better. (pp. 37-8)

> *S. E. Hinton and William Walsh, in an interview in* From Writers to Students: The Pleasures and Pains of Writing, *edited by M. Jerry Weiss, International Reading Association, 1979, pp. 32-8.*

GENERAL COMMENTARY

Gene Lyons

Quick, name the only American novelist whose books have inspired both the Walt Disney studios and Francis Coppola to adapt them to film? . . . Give up? If there's a teen-ager on the premises, ask the kid. Odds are good that S. E. Hinton is a household name around your place, whether you knew it or not. (p. 105)

The appeal of Hinton's novels is obvious. . . . The narrator-hero of each is a tough-tender 14- to 16-year-old loner making his perilous way through a violent, caste-ridden world almost depopulated of grownups. "It's a kid's fantasy not to have adults around," says Hinton. While recklessness generally gets punished, her books are never moralistic—all manner of parental rules are broken with impunity. Hers are tales of honor, emotional kinship, loyalty and betrayal. "For a tough kid," says Rusty-James, younger brother of a heroic and doomed character in *Rumble Fish* known only as the Motorcycle Boy. "I had a bad habit of getting attached to people." Hinton has never read Hemingway and says she never will, because English teachers compare her style to his. But it's Raymond Chandler and Ross Macdonald she needs to avoid. Her young toughs are private eyes in training. (pp. 105-06)

> *Gene Lyons, "On Tulsa's Mean Streets in* Newsweek, *Vol. C, No. 15, October 11, 1982, pp. 105-06.*

Cynthia Rose

As an author of youth fiction, Hinton is somewhat unique in that she penned her first book, *The Outsiders,* when she herself was only seventeen. Its publication enabled her to major in education at the University of Tulsa, where she met her husband and made the decision to take up teaching. During the summer following her graduation from college, Hinton wrote a second book (*That Was Then, This Is Now*), following it four years later with *Rumble Fish* and four years after that with *Tex.*

These books have been widely hailed (not least by their teenage readership) for their 'realism', but in fact all of them are extremely stylised and consistently repetitive in their concerns. Each is told in the first person by a young male narrator, and their quickly paced action is set in a neo-mythical world inhabited only by teenage protagonists and antagonists. Hinton claims that she began *The Outsiders* to see if she could construct such a world: "a world outside the narrow confines of school, with no parents or authority figures . . . a place where kids live by their own rules". The result of her efforts is hardly 'naturalistic'. But the consistency with which adults are rendered absent or impotent . . . is unimportant. It conforms to adolescent wish-fulfilment and provides a clear arena in which characters can wrestle with the central dilemma of youth: learning to distinguish appearance from reality.

In all Hinton's novels, 'appearance' takes the venerated form of an illusory group identity—the gang—while 'reality' is the lonelier pursuit of self-realisation. It's a realisation which always leads the heroes to oppose the kind of mindlessness and impulse towards self-destruction which perpetuate the gangs. The protagonists are 'heroic' by inherited teenage standards. Like the casts of youth films from *Blackboard Jungle* (1955) to Jonathan Kaplan's *Over the Edge* (1979), even the losers talk hip and act tough. But the books' plot twists are always engineered so that abstract concepts such as freedom or individual dignity can niggle away at the edge of the narrator's inarticulate ruminations. Much of their questioning is sparked by economic ramifications—all of Hinton's characters are 'white trash'. (p. 238)

Bryon's story (*That Was Then, This Is Now,* the best of Hinton's quartet) was written in 1971 and, though set in the late 60s, it incorporates contemporary circumstances which have altered something of its subject's situation. ("Besides, now it was hard to tell a Soc from a greaser. Now the greasers wore their hair down on their foreheads instead of combed back . . . And the Socs were trying to look poor. They wore old jeans and shirts with the shirt-tails out just like the greasers always had because they couldn't afford anything else".) Hinton herself is from a middle-class rather than a sub-blue collar background. But her characterisation of the emotional claustrophobia and relentlessly limited prospects of the poor white world—where sacrifice so often defines love—is her most impressive literary achievement. The plot of *Tex,* for instance, hinges on its title character's slow grasp of how much his older brother Mason has given up to buy him a future which will 'matter'. It's a theme developed since *The Outsiders,* where Ponyboy Curtis comes to understand that his eldest brother Darrel is strict and straight out of necessity rather than from choice.

Like Mary Renault, Susan Hinton is a woman imagining how young men feel, speak and interact—and her heroes sometimes err on the side of over-sensitivity and poetic perception. (Ponyboy's spontaneous recitation of an entire Robert Frost poem to Johnny in *The Outsiders* and the Motorcycle Boy's stilted self-explications in *Rumble Fish* are two outstanding examples.) A more unsettling characteristic is the machismo lavished on all the male characters at the expense both of natural adolescent awkwardness and of their female counterparts. It seems likely that Hinton's writing has been influenced in this respect by Jim Carroll's *The Basketball Diaries.* First published in 1963, the *Diaries* were an even bigger-selling youth success than Hinton's books; they are also genuine in the sense that their author *is* a reformed junkie and street hustler writing from personal experience. More to the point, perhaps, is his sex—from a man, street macho and street slang issue with a different authority and resonance. But, like Hinton's format, the *Diaries* feature a first-person narration and a keen 'evaluation' of events. The major difference is that the *Diaries* are not structured to provide moral conclusions; Hinton's books self-evidently are.

Yet their female characters very much take a back seat until the appearance of the articulate Jamie in *Tex.* The novels are all set in period, albeit written with the psychology of hindsight, and the female roles fulfil the good girl/bad girl stereotype in a manner which recalls nothing so much as *West Side Story.* (pp. 238-39)

The confusing jolts of teen love—suddenly overwhelming and just as suddenly blank—are, however, acutely rendered. Bryon loses his feeling for Cathy as soon as he is forced to betray the best friend who was jealous of her "I wondered impersonally why I didn't love her any more. But it didn't seem to matter"). The hero of *Rumble Fish,* Rusty-James, has to break up with long-time girlfriend Patty when she finds out that he has been seeing someone else—it's a matter of pride, and this time the pride is hers. The fatalism with which Rusty-James is left typifies the way each novel ends: reality can't be avoided; it has to be faced whether it is an economic limitation or a romantic disappointment.

Most of the differences between the sexes which Hinton emphasises are valid, even if she takes them too far into stereotype. But the ultra-romantic imposition of the gang myth on the fictitious small towns she pictures is unquestionably reactionary. Life's real outsiders—whether disenfranchised by class or through ignorance—can only lose if they interpret their inheritance as 'turf' when those with real power will always envision it as a market. Hinton's homilies may be constructed to demonstrate that real courage consists in facing up to real problems, whatever their size or solubility. But she attracts and holds the interest of her young public through the same glamorisation of the 'outlaw' stance and the 'cool' delinquent utilised by a long line of predecessors with considerably less lofty aims. (p. 239)

Cynthia Rose, "Rebels Redux: The Fiction of S. E. Hinton," in Monthly Film Bulletin, *Vol. 50, No. 596, September, 1983, pp. 238-39.*

Cin Forshay-Lunsford

[*The following excerpt is from an interview by Patty Campbell with Forshay-Lunsford, a young adult novelist who began her first book,* Walk through Cold Fire *(1985), as a high school senior. Campbell notes of Forshay-Lunsford and Hinton, "There are some striking similarities between* The Outsiders *and* Walk through Cold Fire *both in theme, plot, and character, and in the circumstance of both authors having been suddenly thrust as teenagers into the literary spotlight."*]

P: How old were you when you first read *The Outsiders?*

C: Twelve, in eighth grade. And I reread it a year or two later at fourteen. I liked it the first time I read it, but the second time I was just totally infatuated with it. I guess it was more relevant for my life the second time. I admire Susie Hinton a lot. I love her stories—especially *Rumblefish.* I fell in love with the Motorcycle Boy. To me that type is like the perfect guy, all tough and rugged and

wacko on the outside and underneath very tender and intellectual.

P: These kinds of characters, like your gang, The Outlaws, have become almost American mythic prototypes.

C: Like James Dean. Like the Matt Dillon image, which S. E. Hinton really helped make. In our society that tough rock and roll, heavy metal leather jacket image is the epitome of rebellion. Of turning your back on regular morals. And I think that's what a lot of the characters in *The Outsiders* do. Or maybe the world turns its back on them. Anyway, I've always loved S. E. Hinton's work, and I admired her so much. . . . I think her writing is absolutely beautiful.

P: You know people are calling her the Grand Old Lady of YA Fiction?

C: I would *hate* that, if I was her! I mean, she's a young person, no way is she *old.* . . .

P: The Queen of the Young Adult Novel, maybe.

C: Yeah, that's a lot better.

Cin Forshay–Lunsford and Patty Campbell in an interview in Wilson Library Bulletin, *Vol. 60, No. 1, September, 1985, p. 63.*

Michael Malone

America at its saddest and dangerously silliest has the adolescent soul of a grade-B cowboy movie—violent and sentimental, morally and mentally simplistic. . . . [No] doubt that's why the four Young Adult novels of S. E. Hinton have sold millions of copies and have made their rough-tender way into successful Hollywood movies. . . . The novels—*The Outsiders; That Was Then, This is Now; Rumble Fish;* and *Tex*—are touted on their covers as heroic tales of "the young and the restless," as "strikingly realistic portraits of modern kids trying to make it in a rough world." (p. 276)

Hinton was 17 when she wrote *The Outsiders,* and the characters, she says, were "loosely based" on people she knew. "When I was growing up, most of my close friends were boys," she remarked in an interview in *The New York Times.* "In those days girls were mainly concerned about getting their hair done and lining their eyes. It was such a passive society. Girls got their status from their boyfriends. They weren't interested in doing anything on their own." They certainly don't do anything on their own in Hinton's books—indeed they scarcely put in an appearance, although the male narrators frequently comment on how nice their hair looks. Nor are adults much in evidence. In this world the stories, like the streets, belong almost exclusively to tribes of adolescent males, to accounts of their tender camaraderie, reckless rebellion, macho warfare and often tragic fates.

It is difficult, if not horrifying, to think that the millions of 12-year-olds reading these "strikingly realistic portraits of modern kids" find any more in them than the most remote connections to their own lives, for Hinton's boys are usually impoverished, are often thugs and thieves, are variously abandoned by parents, brutalized by policemen, jailed, stabbed to death, shot to death, burned to death and so routinely beaten nearly to death that they think it's a drag to have to rush to the hospital for something as trivial as a fractured skull. When his chest is cut so deeply in a gang fight that he can see "white bone gleaming through," Rusty-James of **Rumble Fish** grits his teeth ("Ain't all that bad") while his brother douses whiskey on the wound ("He's been hurt worse than this"). These are "lean hard" "tough as nails"—or rather "tuff" as nails—"cool" 14-year-olds. Misery, lawlessness and violence are served up matter-of-factly to palates presumably so jaded by screen violence that it seems there are no squeamish stomachs left among the prepubescent. "The Dingo is a pretty rough hangout; there's always a fight going on there and once a girl got shot" (**The Outsiders**). "The last guy who was killed in the gangfights was a Packer. He had been fifteen" (**Rumble Fish**). Bryon, narrator of **That Was Then, This is Now,** comments blandly: "We fought with chains and we fought Socs and we fought other grease gangs. It was a normal childhood. . . . So that was how we lived, stealing stuff and selling stuff." Other boyish pastimes mentioned are drunken poker games, car theft, drag racing, pool hustling and "jumping hippies and blacks." The horrendous life of Bryon's former girlfriend is summed up in a paragraph and dismissed as nothing unusual: "Her husband didn't have a job, her brothers were both in jail, her old man was drunk all the time, and her father-in-law was always slapping her bottom. . . . They weren't so different from most of the families in our neighborhood."

Tragedy is parenthetical, introduced in a dependent clause: "Since Mom and Dad were killed in an auto wreck . . . " (**The Outsiders**). Even in **Tex,** the most recent, the least riddled with gang romance and the best of the books, Tex (a pleasant fellow, given to believable classroom pranks and adolescent worries) is forced at gunpoint to drive an escaped killer to the state line. He rolls the truck into a ditch, enabling the pursuing police to blow the young convict away in a barrage of crossfire. Only a week or so later, Tex himself is critically shot in the stomach while accompanying a friend on a drug deal. Tex has only gone along for the ride because he's upset. He's upset because his brother has just blurted out that their Pop is not really Tex's father; his real father was a no-good rodeo cowboy with whom Mom had a one-night stand to spite Pop when he was in prison for bootlegging.

In **That Was Then, This is Now** "golden dangerous Mark," the narrator's best buddy, also discovers that he is mistaken about his parentage—his real father turns out to be another rodeo cowboy. Bryon tells us about it like this: "Mark had lived at my house ever since I was ten and he was nine and his parents shot each other in a drunken argument Later we learn the argument was over Mark's parentage; the shots were fatal, and the child, hiding under the porch, heard it all. As Mark recalls: "And then they start yelling and I hear this sound like a couple of firecrackers. And I think, well, I can go live with Bryon and his old lady. . . . I didn't like livin' at home." The desire to leave home is a sentiment with which most teen-agers can empathize, but few are given so graphic an opportunity to do so. Nor do the majority, I hope, respond to family indifference like Dallas Winston of **The Outsiders,** who "lied, cheated, stole, rolled drunks, jumped small kids," even if they occasionally feel the same way about their parents: "What do they matter? Shoot, my old man don't give a hang whether I'm in jail or dead in a car wreck or drunk in the gutter. That don't bother me none."

What is clear from the recurrent themes of Hinton's novels, like the discovery of mysterious parentage, is that despite their modern, colloquial tone, they are fairy tale adventures (Luke Skywalker's father is really Darth Vader), and their rumbles as exotic as jousts in *Ivanhoe* or pirate wars in *Treasure Island.* What is curious is that grown-ups insist on the books' veracity. Hinton announces, "The real boy like Dallas Winston was shot and killed by the police for having stolen a car." Tim Hunter, director of the film *Tex,* says he was drawn to Hinton's work because of the way she weaves social problems "into the fabric of a realistic story."

In fact, the fabric is mythic. There are no verisimilar settings. Presumably the books take place near Tulsa, Oklahoma (the films do), but place names are never mentioned, and were it not for occasional references to rodeos, one would have little notion of the Western ambiance so evident in the movie versions. Characters live in "the neighborhood"; sometimes they go to "the city" or to "the country." The city is bacchanalian: "There were lots of people and noise and lights and you could feel energy coming off things, even buildings" (**Rumble Fish**). The country is pastoral: "The clouds were pink and meadowlarks were singing" (**The Outsiders**). Temporal location is equally vague. **The Outsiders,** published in 1967, might as easily have been written ten years earlier, in the fifties of its real progenitor, James Dean movies. True, some parenthetical hippies are up to some druggy no-good in **That Was Then, This Is Now** (1971), but the Motorcycle Boy in **Rumble Fish** (1975) might have ridden right off the screen of *The Wild One.* Far from strikingly realistic in literary form, these novels are romances, mythologizing the tragic beauty of violent youth, as the flashy surrealism of Francis Ford Coppola's *Rumble Fish,* with its film noir symbolism and spooky soundtrack, all too reverently attests.

Moreover, while praised for its "lean Hemingway style" and natural dialogue, Hinton's prose can be as fervid, mawkish and ornate as any nineteenth-century romance, although this is less true in the later books, especially **Tex.** The heightened language of her young narrators intensifies the glamour and sentiment of their stories, but it will not strike readers as everyday school-locker lingo. Ponyboy, 14, and Bryon, 16, fling adjectives and archaic phrases ("Hence his name," "Heaven forbid") around like Barbara Cartland. Bryon notes that his friend Mark's "strangely sinister innocence was gone." Ponyboy describes his brother, Sodapop, as having "a finely drawn, sensitive face that somehow manages to be reckless and thoughtful at the same time," as well as "lively, dancing, recklessly laughing eyes." Ponyboy is also given to quoting from memory long snatches of Robert Frost's "Nothing Gold Can Stay," and to using words like "merrily," "gallant" and "elfish." Of course, Bryon and Ponyboy point out to us that although they seem to spend all their time hanging out with the gang, they are both honor students: "I make good grades and have a high IQ." But even Rusty-James of **Rumble Fish,** stuck in "dumb classes" and, by his own admission, no student ("Math ain't never been my strong point"), waxes poetical: "I wouldn't have her to hold anymore, soft but strong in my arms." Sententious moralizing coats the pages: "That was what he wanted. For somebody to tell him 'No.' . . . If his old man had just belted him—just once, he might still be alive." "You start wondering why, and you get old." "We see the same sunset."

The lyricism, the lack of novelistic detail, the static iconography of Hinton's books keep the clutter of creation from interfering with the sources of their obviously persistent appeal—their rapid action (mostly violent) unfettered by the demands of a plot, their intense emotions (mostly heavy) and their clear-cut moral maps. Hinton's fictional universe is as black-and-white as an old cowboy film. *The Outsiders* is the ur-text. In it there are Socs (Socials) and there are greasers; unlike that of the warring Hatfields and McCoys, Montagues and Capulets, Jets and Sharks, this eternal enmity is neither familial nor racial, but financial. Socs are rich, greasers are poor; Socs are "the in crowd," greasers are "the outsiders." Socs always wear madras and English Leather and drive Mustangs or Corvairs. They always "jump greasers and wreck houses and throw beerblasts for kicks." That's pretty much all we get to know about Socs; they're just the enemy. A Soc girl, Cherry Valance, makes a brief appearance to point out to Ponyboy, "We have troubles you never even heard of," but those troubles are not explored; instead she schematizes neatly: "You greasers have a different set of values. You're more emotional. We're sophisticated—cool to the point of not feeling anything." Given this fundamental difference (and despite the fact that they see the same sunset), Cherry is obliged to warn Ponyboy: "If I see you in the hall . . . and don't say hi, well, it's not personal. . . . We couldn't let our parents see us with you all."

Our heroes, greasers, are also initially defined by their appearance and their style of antisocial behavior: "We steal things and drive old souped-up cars and hold up gas stations once in a while . . . just like we leave our shirttails out and wear leather jackets." But popular culture has taught us to interpret this style with sympathy, if not rabid infatuation. The narrators pay continual, indeed obsessive, attention to their own and their friends' appearance. We hear constantly about "strange golden eyes," "light-brown, almost-red hair," faces like "some Greek god come to earth." They are always asking and reassuring each other about their good looks, particularly the beauty of their hair.

Funky costume and flamboyant hairstyle have long been the outward signs of inward romantic rebellion—from Shelley's flowing locks and open collars through Ginsberg's sandals to Elvis's sideburns—and Ponyboy's identifying himself through his hair oil ("I am a greaser") announces his place in a tradition that goes back to Brontë's crush on Heathcliff, and associates him with such suffering gods as James Dean. It's significant that many of the young men who played in Coppola's 1982 film of *The Outsiders* were to become adolescent idols within the next few years: [Matt] Dillon, Rob Lowe, Tom Cruise, Emilio Estevez, Patrick Swayze. A leather jacket, bloody knuckles and a sensitive soul is an irresistible combination. Pain and sadness help too.

There is no sweeter sorrow than the self-pity of our teens, no pain more rhapsodized than our adolescent anguish; adults simply lose the will to sustain such *Sturm und Drang.* Like the protagonists of all *Bildungsromans,* Hinton's leather-jacketed young Werthers are lyrical on the subject of their psychic aches and pains. Tough as nails on the street, yeah, hey—but alone in the dark, they're as naked and afraid in a world they never made as any Herman Hesse hero. Confused, lonely, slighted, they share with, they feel for, their readers that most profound pubescent emotion: "I don't belong." In the classic apprenticeship novel, the youngster—Tonio Kröger, Stephen Dedalus, Paul Morel, Eugene Gant—experiences and reflects on this sense of alienation and so grows to understand the particular difference that is his self. When, in *The Outsiders,* Ponyboy tells us, "I cried passionately, 'It ain't fair that we have all the rough breaks,' " his *cri de coeur,* like the novel's title, suggests the tribal rather than personal thrust of Hinton's use of the theme, as well as its simplistic economic nature. ("You can't win because they've got all the breaks.") In Hinton's books, selfhood is subsumed in the tribal gang. "It was great, we were a bunch of people making up one big person" (*That Was Then, This Is Now*). "Why did the Socs hate us so much? We left them alone." "It wasn't fair for the Socs to have everything. We were as good as they were" (*The Outsiders*). So magically does the gang incorporate its members that in the opening of *The Outsiders* it miraculously appears out of the night to save Ponyboy from the motiveless malignity of a carful of Socs: "All the noise I had heard was the gang coming to rescue me." "Somehow the gang sensed what had happened."

The gang is the family: "We're almost as close as brothers." And in contrast to "a snarling, distrustful, bickering pack like the Socs," greaser gangs are unfailingly loyal and free of rivalry. Maybe they have "too much energy, too much feeling, with no way to blow it off " except through marauding violence, but with one another they are as gentle as maidens on a Victorian valentine, innocently sleeping with their arms around each other, choking with tenderness for one another's pain. Johnny in *The Outsiders* is the most vulnerable, most pathetically hurt gang member (the Sal Mineo part in *Rebel Without a Cause;* for his film of *The Outsiders,* Coppola even found in Ralph Macchio an actor who looks just like Mineo). Ponyboy's solicitude for him is shared by even the toughest of the greasers. He is "a little dark puppy that has been kicked too many times and is lost in a crowd of strangers. . . . His father was always beating him up, and his mother ignored him. . . . If it hadn't been for the gang, Johnny would never have known what love and affection are." Like Mineo's Plato, Johnnycake is clearly pegged for tearful sacrifice. And sure enough—having accidentally stabbed a Soc to death and then redeemed himself by saving some children from a burning church—he dies from burns and a broken back after a series of heart-rending hospital-bed scenes. As might be expected in fiction for adolescents, the blood brother bond supersedes all other emotional commitments. *That Was Then, This Is Now* opens, "Mark and me went down to the bar"; and Bryon's love for Mark, like the love of Beowulf or Roland for their companions, runs like a lyric refrain through the novel.

These characters do sometimes have girlfriends, but their erotic relationships come nowhere near the power of male camaraderie. Hinton reports she almost didn't agree to sell *Tex* to Walt Disney Productions because she "thought they'd really sugar it up, take out all the sex, drugs and violence," but there is actually far less sex in her books than in the films made from them. Her instinct, conscious or not, that young readers could take endless physical violence and heartbreak but would be embarrassed by physical passion is quite sound. On the page of **Rumble Fish,** Rusty-James tells us of his visit to Patty, "I just sat there holding her and sometimes kissed the top of her head"; on the screen this becomes a torrid tumble on a couch. Rusty-James's description, "There were some girls [at the lake] and we built a fire and went swimming," becomes on screen an orgiastic montage of naked bodies. Similarly, unlike the films, the books are as free of profanity as *Heidi.* We are told people "talk awful dirty," but the only curses we hear are almost comically mild: "Glory!" "Shoot!" "Oh blast it!" Indeed, gang members warn the younger ones to avoid "bad habits" like cursing. They may smoke cigarettes, integral to the image, but they don't much care for booze and are leery of drugs. As well they might be. M & M, *That Was Then, This is Now's* counterpart to the doomed Johnnycake, takes LSD, goes psychotic, is hospitalized (the doctor announces solemnly, "He may have lost his mind forever") and is told that his chromosomes are so messed up that he must forget his dream of a large family.

In *Rebel Without a Cause,* James Dean is trying to cope with a new society, with a new girl, with his parents, with adult authority. He copes in part by means of wry humor, a detachment that is missing in Hinton's books and in the films made from them. Rather than ask her characters to cope with adults, wryly or otherwise, Hinton either removes them or removes their authority. The Oedipal struggle is displaced to older siblings. Ponyboy's parents are dead; he lives with and is supported by his big brother, Darry, a football star who gave up college to keep the family together. Ponyboy fears and idolizes him. Tex's mother

Publicity shot of Hinton.

is dead (after a fight with his father, she walked off in the snow to go dancing, caught pneumonia and quickly succumbed), and his father forgets for months at a time to return home or to send money. Tex lives with and is supported by his older brother, Mace, a basketball star, whom he fears and admires. Rusty-James's mother ran away; his father, once a lawyer, is a hopeless drunk on welfare who wanders in and out of the house mumbling, "What strange lives you two lead," to Rusty-James and his idolized older brother, the Motorcycle Boy (about whom Hinton seems to feel much as Lady Caroline Lamb felt about Byron: "Mad, bad and dangerous to know"). Like Dallas Winston, the Motorcycle Boy is shot to death by the police, leaving the hero to inherit his romantic mantle—even to the extent of going color-blind. Bryon has no father but does have a mother, depicted as a model of saintly virtue. She behaves, however, with a remarkable lack of maternal responsibility or even curiosity. Not only do Bryon and Mark sometimes not "come home for weeks" without being reprimanded but their being beaten black and blue elicits little concern. Mom notices ten stitches in Mark's head: "How did that happen?" "And Mark answered, 'Fight,' and the subject was dropped. That was a good thing about Mom—she'd cry over a dog with a piece of glass in his paw but remained unhysterical when we came home clobbered. . . . Parents never know what all their kids do. . . . It's a law." The laws of Hinton's books are the laws of the cowboy movies, the laws of romance.

According to a children's librarian in Connecticut, Hinton and Judy Blume have long been the most popular authors of "reluctant readers" in the junior-high age group, youngsters who generally "wouldn't be caught dead in a library." Hinton's books "go out by themselves," without having to be recommended by adults or assigned by teachers or cleverly packaged (*"Swiss Family Robinson* is about survival—just like *Rambo"*). (pp. 276-78, 280)

The successful marketing of Young Adult fiction to teenage consumers is defended by some, who point out that the choice is not between an adolescent's reading *Tex* and reading *Sons and Lovers* but between reading *Tex* and reading nothing. Librarians are deeply concerned about the drop in reading once children reach high school or even junior high. "They come to the library only when it's time to research a school assignment," one told me. The causes are doubtless varied, but the hope is that those who did acquire the habit of reading for fun in grade school will rediscover it in their later teens. Meanwhile, the spinning stands of Harlequin Romances and movie tie-ins may keep the idea of reading alive and the books of S. E. Hinton in circulation. Asked if she would ever consider branching out into adult fiction as Judy Blume has, Hinton said she didn't find adults as interesting, because adolescence is "the time of the most rapid change, when ideals are clashing against the walls of compromise." That she is able to evoke for her audience how teen-agers feel about those clashes is indisputable. She once remarked, "Ponyboy is how I felt at 14." There are millions of Ponyboys out there, soulfully dreaming, sentimental, cool. (p. 280)

Michael Malone, "Tough Puppies," in The Nation, *New York, Vol. 242, No. 9, March 8, 1986, pp. 276-78, 280.*

Margery Fisher

When young people play central parts in adventure stories, their motives and actions are as a rule suitably moderated nor are they expected to concern themselves with elaborate points of honour. Yet this is an area where the emotional strength of junior adventures, so often timid and inadequate, could be deepened if the concept of honour in its universal sense were to be recognised. A remarkable film of 1955, *Rebel without a Cause,* claimed as 'new realism' when it was first screened, showed delinquent boys and girls in the mid-teens proving their worth in 'chicken' contests whose violence, distorted as it is by social pressures, does express a genuine personal pride: the dares and challenges of the groups of Hell's Angels today, leading to criminal actions, have a distant debased origin in the concept of honour. The remarkable novels of S. E. Hinton—for instance, *The Outsiders* and *That Was Then, This Is Now*—describe the operation of honour as it exists within American city gangs with a passionate conviction one looks for in vain in many similar contemporary adventure fictions. (p. 79)

> Margery Fisher, "Honour and the Unattainable Ideal," in her The Bright Face of Danger, The Horn Book, Inc., 1986, pp. 63-80.

Randall K. Mills

Examining stories from literature is one powerful way of helping students work at the task of personal growth. Egan (1978) has stated that adolescents have a great need to identify with heroes and that they do this best through stories. Specifically, he points out that stories can help adolescents develop awareness of their strengths and weaknesses in a manner which will help them prepare for adulthood. He calls adolescence the romantic stage and states that, "stories have a crucial characteristic that makes them ideal for this stage—they are ego-supporting". S. E. Hinton's *The Outsiders* and *That Was Then, This Is Now* lend themselves well to this process.

The Outsiders is a story of a boy growing up in contemporary America and revolves around three major conflicts. The first concerns the narrator's (Ponyboy Curtis) attempt to deal with his inner feelings. Like many adolescents, he finds the struggle a difficult and lonely experience. . . .

A second important conflict in the story deals with the struggle among members of his family. Ponyboy's mother and father are dead, and he lives with his older brothers, Darrel and Sodapop. Much of the story focuses on Ponyboy's difficult relationship with his older brother, Darrel. (p. 642)

A third conflict examines the tension between the rich and poor kids in his community. Ponyboy and his family and friends live on the poor side of town and are called greasers by the rich kids who are called Socs by Ponyboy's group. (p. 643)

A pivotal part of the story concerns Johnny's death and Ponyboy's acceptance of the fact. For several weeks, Ponyboy could not face the reality of Johnny's death until he found a note left for him by Johnny. The note referred to a poem Ponyboy had told Johnny about while they were hiding, Robert Frost's "Nothing Gold Can Stay." . . . It

is this powerful note that finally gives Ponyboy the courage to face life with all its sorrows and defeats. Significantly, Ponyboy begins his journey by beginning to write this story for an English composition class.

The Outsiders can be used to examine the difficulties adolescents face in dealing with authority, as well as with their own inner feelings. Specifically, students might be asked to explore the tension between Ponyboy and his older brother, Darrel. The following questions help probe the problem:

1. What were some of Ponyboy's feelings toward his older brother's authority? Quote passages to support your opinions.
2. Discuss which of Ponyboy's feelings toward authority were appropriate or inappropriate. Explain.
3. What were Darrel's feelings toward Ponyboy? Cite passages to support your opinions.
4. In what ways were Darrel's feelings and actions toward Ponyboy appropriate and inappropriate? Explain.

Concerning the exploration of social conflict, students can be asked to answer the following questions:

1. What were some possible reasons for the conflict between the two groups in the story? Find passages to support your arguments.
2. Discuss Ponyboy's feelings toward the Socs. Quote passages which indicate how he felt.
3. Were there ways for Ponyboy and his family to improve their social position? How realistic were their chances of improvement?
4. Discuss Ponyboy's attitude toward people from the outside who tried to help the "greasers."
5. What role does the story suggest education has to play in helping people live better lives? Explain.

A later novel, *That Was Then, This Is Now,* is also hard-hitting and realistic. It leaves one with a deep sense of life's uncertainties. The main character and narrator, Bryon Douglas, is a typical adolescent, at least in his view of the world. . . . However, Bryon's neighborhood is very similar to Ponyboy's in *The Outsiders.* In this story, Bryon's best friend, Mark, becomes involved in selling drugs. Although Bryon thinks of Mark as a brother, he chooses to turn Mark in because of the influence of a new friend, Cathy, and the devastating effect drugs are having on young kids. Like all of Hinton's stories, this one is about growing up, which means making difficult decisions about important matters. However, unlike many such stories, this one does not indicate whether choosing to go through the pain of growing up is worth it. . . . Adolescents reading this story will appreciate and be strengthened by Hinton's honesty and authenticity.

That Was Then, This Is Now is an invitation for adolescents to critically investigate life. Although there is an emphasis on the drug problem in this novel, the personal growth aspect of the story may be more significant for adolescents to examine. In general, perhaps if more emphasis is placed on personal growth in schools, there would be less of a drug problem.

Specifically, students can be asked to examine Bryon's personal conflict leading to his decision to turn his best friend in to the police. Some questions students might be asked to think about are:

1. What were Bryon's alternatives to turning Mark in?
2. Why didn't he choose other possibilities?
3. Do you think Bryon's decision was right? Explain.
4. How does Bryon's struggle to grow up coincide with real life? Explain.

Schools have the obligation to create better individuals, and the use of stories such as those by S. E. Hinton can help students enhance their personal development. (pp. 643-45)

> *Randall K. Mills, "The Novels of S. E. Hinton: Springboard to Personal Growth for Adolescents," in* Adolescence, *Vol. XXII, No. 87, Fall, 1987, pp. 641-46.*

Jay Daly

In April 1967 the Viking Press brought out a book called *The Outsiders,* by S. E. Hinton, and the world of young adult writing and publishing would never be the same. This is not an exaggeration. In more ways than one, *The Outsiders* has become the most successful, and the most emulated, young adult book of all time.

The situation was ripe, in the mid-sixties, for the arrival of something like *The Outsiders,* although no one knew it at the time. There had been a "young adult" genre for many years, dominated by books like Maureen Daly's *Seventeenth Summer,* dreamy-eyed stories of carefree youth where the major problem was whether so-and-so would ask our heroine to the prom in sufficient time for her to locate a prom gown. Or there were cautionary tales to warn us that, if we were not good, and we all know what "good" meant, we would never get to the prom at all.

Into this sterile chiffon-and-orchids environment then came *The Outsiders.* Nobody worries about the prom in *The Outsiders;* they're more concerned with just staying alive till June. They're also concerned with peer pressures, social status, abusive parents, and the ever-present threat of violence. What in the world was this? It certainly wasn't the same picture of the teenage wonder years that the "young adult" genre projected (and no one ever lived). Welcome to real life.

There is a perception now that *The Outsiders* was published to immediate teenage accolades, but such was not the case. In fact, because the book was so different from what the publishers considered "young adult" material, it was at first sent out with the general trade, or adult, releases, where it disappeared into the murk. It was only gradually, as the word from the hinterlands drifted in, that the publishers realized the book was finding its word-of-mouth fame among the very teenagers whose lives it depicted. The rest, as they say, is history.

The grass-roots success of *The Outsiders* paved the way for writers like Paul Zindel, Richard Peck, M. E. Kerr, Paula Danziger, and Robert Cormier. It set off a wail of controversy from those who thought that there was enough real life in real life without also putting it into books. It caused many lesser writers to make the mistake

of wandering off in search of the "formula" for her success, and it sent publishers scurrying off in search of other teenaged writer-oracles; everyone wanted a piece of "the next S. E. Hinton." In truth, of course, there is no formula, and it is not likely that there will be "another" S. E. Hinton.

There are now perhaps ten million copies of Hinton books in print. *The Outsiders,* itself now twenty years old, no longer a teenager, continues to be the best selling of all Hinton's books. Clearly there is more to this than the novelty of its publication in those pre-Hinton, Mary-Jane-Goes-to-the-Prom years. In fact there is something in *The Outsiders,* as there is in the other Hinton books, that transcends the restrictions of time and place, that speaks to the reader directly. It has nothing to do with the age of the author, and little to do with the so-called "realism" of the setting. It does, however, have very much to do with the characters she creates, their humanity, and it has everything to do with her honesty. Her characters are orphans and outlaws and, as the song says, "to live outside the law you must be honest." If there is a formula to S. E. Hinton books it is only this: to tell the truth.

There is also something that is quintessentially American about S. E. Hinton. Her books are all set in the real American heartland, the urban frontier, and her characters are American pilgrim-orphans, believers in the dream of perfection, of an American paradise on earth. Francis Ford Coppola, who filmed and cowrote, with Hinton, the screen versions of *The Outsiders* and *Rumble Fish,* called her "a real American novelist," straight out of the tradition that runs from Herman Melville right up through J. D. Salinger, and beyond. The myth of the American hero, of the outlaw-individualist, of the "gallant," lives on in the eyes of Ponyboy Curtis and Johnny Cade.

None of this would matter, though, if it were not based on real characters. None of this would count if we did not believe that her books tell the truth, not so much about beer parties and gang fights, but about what it feels like to be a teenager, caught between childhood and adulthood, always on the outside looking in at a world that is very far from being a paradise on earth. pp. (i-iii)

[Most of the controversy about *The Outsiders* came about because it] grew to be identified with something called "The New Realism" in young adult writing. The term—New Realism—was added later, but the fear—that books for teenagers were getting a little too realistic for their own good—was beginning to be heard more and more frequently during the time after the publication of *The Outsiders.* Indeed there are many who fix the point at which young adult writing changed, and changed utterly—from the cautionary Mary-Jane-Goes-to-the-Prom book to the attempt at serious and authentic portrayal of life as it is—with the publication of *The Outsiders.* Such a radical change could not be expected to go unchallenged. . . .

The irony is that, while the debate team focused on the gangs and the violence, the smoking and the beer drinking—all dreaded evidence of the New Realism—the major thrust of *The Outsiders* had nothing to do with realism at all. The real message of the book is its uncompromising idealism. The real reason the book struck such a responsive chord in its young readers (and continues to strike that chord) was that it captured so well the idealism of that time of life. Of all the young adult novels of that period, *The Outsiders* is by far the most idealistic, the least concerned with the strictly realistic. In its search for innocence, for heroes, for that Garden of Eden that seems to slip further away as youth fades into adulthood, *The Outsiders* is a book for dreamers, not realists. And youth is the time of dreamers.

On its surface at least, *The Outsiders* is indeed a novel about the friction between social classes, in this case between the greasers and the Socs. It is also about the hunger for status, for a place in the pecking order, both inside and outside these groups. And it is about the violence that is so much a part of that particular place and time of life. These concerns are not, however, what make the book come alive. The book comes to life through its characters and situations, their almost painful yearnings and loyalties, their honesty. . . . With all the talk of clichés and melodrama, why does this book continue to speak to new generations of young readers? Idealism alone, after all, is not enough. Nor is sincerity. Think of all the sincere, idealistic books in dustbins and yard sales around the country. The continuing popularity, the continuing interest derives, I think, from the fortunate combination of achievements by the young Susie Hinton in three essential categories: the hand of the storyteller . . . ; the continuing credibility of the characters; and the honesty, the sincerity . . . embodied in the themes of the book, each of which reduces, finally, to the yearning to "stay gold." (pp. 17-8)

The orphans of *The Outsiders* are outlaws and dreamers. They're like "that tragic boy," Peter Pan, in J. M. Barrie's turn-of-the-century play. The Boy Who Would Not Grow Up. Peter Pan, and his group of orphans, the lost boys, rejected by their parents, make their own world of heroics and adventure. They have their own Never Land, where they belong. Wendy, like Cherry with her busy-ness, cannot prevent herself from changing, until she suddenly turns around to discover that she is "old, Peter. I am ever so much more than twenty." Peter Pan, on the other hand, stays pure; he never grows up. He stays gold.

Likewise do the lost boys in *The Outsiders* form their own, more perfect world in the world of the gang. They dream of the perfection they know must exist, their Never Land, that perhaps they even once had and lost, where things are gold, where Johnny Cade can find his "ordinary people," where Ponyboy's parents remain golden and young. The striking thing about these orphans is that they use it to their advantage; they are dreamers and they use their abandonment to feed their dreams. Life intervenes, of course, and their dreams will never come true, but that's only because they have such high standards. They want perfection. Like Peter Pan, they want to stay gold forever. (p. 34)

Ponyboy recites [the Robert Frost poem "Nothing Gold Can Stay"] for Johnny on page 85. They are at the church, and have just been witness to a lyrical dawn . . . The poem captures a feeling that is important to Ponyboy, though he's not sure of all of it. "He meant more to it than I'm gettin," he says, "I always remembered it because I never quite got what he meant by it." Ponyboy, who has the capacity to be a little slow when it serves to advance the story, needs Johnny to validate the poem for him, in his letter at the end of the book. "[H]e meant you're gold when you're a kid, like green. When you're a kid every-

thing's new, dawn. It's just when you get used to everything that it's day." The only way to stay gold, then, is to stay a kid, or at least to retain that childlike wonder, that innocence, which continues to make the world new. The key to staying gold then, in Johnny's view, is to stay, like Peter Pan, a child.

If this is indeed the case, then it creates problems. To stay at a Peter Pan level of innocence is to be retarded (in all senses of the word). All of us are in fact more like Wendy than like Peter; we lose gradually that limber quality of youth, the idealism and innocence, the ability, so to speak, to fly. To the extent that we retain some of this capacity we are blessed, but to retain it fully is impossible. Not just because "nothing gold can stay," but also because it would be unnatural to do so. Innocence cannot escape coming to terms with life, which does not necessarily mean being corrupted. The opposite of innocence is—not corruption, of course—but knowledge.

Worse yet, innocence/youth/idealism carried to such extremes is not innocence/youth/idealism at all. It is usually a more selfish, and sometimes dangerous, thing. Look at Ponyboy's selfish attitude toward Darry early in the book. This is an attitude that is innocent of the most elementary awareness of another human being. When he sees Darry cry, and feels his hurting inside, it is suddenly a loss of innocence, a falling into knowledge of the real world, but it's a far better condition he falls into than that he left behind.

It is no accident that those literary heroes who stay gold, who retain their innocence unnaturally, lead lives whose effect upon others is often far from innocent. There is something inhuman about them. Think of Melville's Billy Budd, or Lennie in Steinbeck's *Of Mice and Men.* Their very innocence tends to lead them always toward, in Lennie's words, "another bad thing." It's as if they can't help but hurt people in the end. J. M. Barrie, once again, at the end of *Peter and Wendy,* describes his creation Peter, who would not grow up, as forever "young and innocent," but then he also adds, "And heartless."

The Frost poem is in fact not so much about the fleeting nature of youth, or even life, as it is about the Fall. Notice those repeating verbs, "subside . . . sank . . . goes down." The loss of Eden, of that state of perfection of which the "gold" of the poem is but a cruel reminder, this is the real knowledge in the poem, as it is in *The Outsiders.* When Ponyboy remembers his parents, it is always in a kind of misty Garden of Eden setting . . . It's been only eight months since they died, but already they seem to have entered into a golden mythology. The book's idealism invents that place "in the country" of sunsets and ordinary people, but in fact—after the Fall—such a place cannot exist, not in this life.

Which brings us to the one way of staying gold that works. It is the only way of achieving the perfection that was promised. It involves memory, and the shifting of emphasis in Frost's last line from "gold" to "stay." Nothing gold can *stay.* Rather than agree that Ponyboy's image of perfection cannot exist in this world, the book agrees only that it cannot stay here. By dying Johnny stays gold in a way he could never have achieved in life. Even Dally becomes a gallant in death, frozen in time forever under the streetlights of the park like a carved figure from Keats's "Ode on a Grecian Urn."

Most of all, Ponyboy's parents stay perfect parents in a world sadly lacking in parental perfection. They will be young and golden and love him always. His mother in particular remains "beautiful and golden," perfect in a way she could not have remained in life. It is an irony that only by abandoning him could she become for him that symbol of perfection that Ponyboy, and all the others, so desperately need. In the words of the Keats poem: "She cannot fade, though thou hast not thy bliss, / For ever wilt thou love, and she be fair!"

In the pages of *The Outsiders,* and in Ponyboy's memory, she remains, as the song goes, forever young. She stays gold. It's a cruel sort of perfection, but for the idealistic heroes of all the Hinton books (up until *Tex*), who prize perfection so highly, it's the only kind of Paradise they know. (pp. 35-7)

That Was Then, This Is Now is, in nearly everyone's view, a much more disciplined novel than *The Outsiders.* . . . [We] have something that is much more advanced, more mature, and better balanced than *The Outsiders,* that is more cool and studied and less emotional, but it lacks something. It lacks the spark, the élan vital that made *The Outsiders'* triumph over clichés so complete. *That Was Then, This Is Now* is simply a novel so "disciplined" that it almost seems wrestled with, brought by the ears to publication like a recalcitrant child. It's technically better, maybe, but it's not *better.*

At the same time we mustn't lose track of the fact that we are dealing with the work of a twenty-year-old author. In any other case we'd be cheering her future to come. Perhaps it's not fair, but the fact of the matter is that *The Outsiders* will always be treated like a precocious teenager while *That Was Then, This Is Now,* scarcely older, will be held to more sophisticated standards. On the other hand, it's a tribute to the book that we happily apply these standards without giving much thought to the age of the author. (pp. 42-3)

Time and change play a formidable role in the book. They join to form [critic] Michael Cart's statement of the book's theme: growth can be a dangerous process. Dangerous but necessary. It seems almost an attempt to repudiate the "stay gold" message of *The Outsiders.* It is as if Hinton—so sensitive to the faults of *The Outsiders,* the emotionalism and the apotheosis of youth—made a conscious effort to go the other way. You want discipline? Here's discipline. You want realism? Here's realism.

That Was Then, This Is Now turns the Peter Pan vision of the world inside out, and chooses instead to inspect the more unhealthy side of eternal youth. Times change, the book says; grow with them or be left behind. It's a brutal and unsentimental message and, as the events of the story prove, the rejection of idealism, the hardheaded choice to move on, may not be the real answer, either. The events imply that changing may not be very much better (other than the gift of staying out of jail) than staying behind.

Hinton has found, in her letters and talks over the years, that no other book has provoked the kind of discussion of motives and personal disagreements about character that *That Was Then, This Is Now* provokes. It is not a book that comes to a very comfortable conclusion. She made hard choices, herself, in composing the book (that discipline, again) and the reader must make some hard choices, as well.

The preoccupation with time and youth and change is a restatement of the Peter Pan dream; it was such a part of *The Outsiders,* such an idealistic and winning attitude of that book's most inspired characters, that it is not unexpected, surely, to have it make a new appearance in the next book. What is a bit surprising is the new attitude of the author toward it. All the boys in *The Outsiders* who will not grow up are given a lesson in acceptable behavior by *That Was Then, This Is Now.* We saw earlier that eternal youth, staying gold, was an impossibility, perhaps even a condition that was best left unrealized. *That Was Then, This Is Now* attempts to show why.

Mark is the Peter Pan holdover from *The Outsiders.* He's the one with the youthful, nothing-can-touch-me attitude toward life. "Mark always came through everything untouched, unworried, unaffected." He's the "innocent lion," with the Peter Pan view that the world is made for flying, not for worrying. Bryon is defensive; Mark is puzzled that anyone would need such an attitude.

> Bryon: "Pow! Care about somebody, give a damn for another person, and you get blasted. How come it's like that?"
>
> Mark: "You got me, Bryon. I never thought about it. I guess 'cause nothin' bad has ever happened to me."

This, don't forget, from someone whose parents have murdered each other in a scene that adds a point or two to the old charge of melodrama, still alive and kicking from *The Outsiders.* "Nothing bad has ever happened to me." Peter Pan, all the way.

Dallas Winston got to be Peter Pan, as did Johnny Cade, and so even—at least in desire—did Ponyboy, but Mark is not permitted that grace. In *That Was Then, This Is Now,* Mark is the avatar of youth, an exalted station in *The Outsiders* but an honor that has since lost much of its glow. Mark delivers the message, one of the unmistakable messages of *The Outsiders*: "You gotta just take things as they come, and quit trying to reason them out. Bryon, you never used to worry about things. Man, I been gettin' worried about you. You start wonderin' why and you get old." Sounds like Peter Pan talking to Wendy. And he failed to make his point with her, too.

Bryon keeps talking about how he is growing, changing, even maturing, but he is never completely convincing. He talks a good game, but he just doesn't yet know how to live it. "Do you ever get the feeling that the whole thing is changing?" Mark asks, and Bryon agrees, but the change, and—more important—their response to it, is out of their hands. They're powerless, finally. Both of them give up. (pp. 49-51)

There is much to admire in *That Was Then, This Is Now;* the discipline of the writing shows the serious side of a growing talent. The expansion of themes and techniques, later used to better effect, give promise that such achievements will be forthcoming. There is the good dialogue and the occasionally striking stylistic touches we had come to expect from the author of *The Outsiders:* the description of Angela, for example, whose "eye makeup [ran] down her face in dark streaks . . . like she was behind bars";

and of Angela, again, who had "the kind of face that would probably be strikingly beautiful even if she shaved her head," which, of course, they later do.

The book is indeed "disturbing," but it also gives the impression of something a little less acceptable, something forced, manipulated. We have no right to expect a repeat of the golden idealism of *The Outsiders,* but we do have a right to expect that the new characters be faithfully drawn, that they achieve their bitterness rather than have it gifted upon them.

There are many thematic similarities between *That Was Then, This Is Now* and *Rumble Fish,* not the least of which is the subservience of mortals to the demands of time and fate. This is a classical theme, drawn from Greek tragedy. "You don't know what's comin'," Mark says. "Nobody does." Why is it that Bryon Douglas seems so empty, then, even manipulated, while Rusty-James, equally doomed by events he cannot control, seems heroic and human by comparison? One answer is that Bryon lacks that essential element of Greek tragedy, the tragic flaw, that human quirk of personality (whether it be pride or loyalty or whatever) that would allow him to participate in the tragedy. The character of Bryon Douglas has been washed clean of such human quirks, other than perhaps selfishness, so that what is left seems strangely hollow, and the tragedy lacks a human face.

The problem with *That Was Then, This Is Now* is that it is too much like its main character, Bryon Douglas. It has the discipline and strength of character to resist the easy choices, the convenient idealism. But it needs to be more like Mark the guardian lion. It needs to keep the faith. It needs to care more, and reason less. That's what *Rumble Fish* does. (pp. 59-60)

Rumble Fish, Hinton's slightest book, is in fact her most ambitious. The message of the book, the world of the book, is presented by suggestion, in brief scenes of brief phrases. The inarticulate longing of her narrator makes her earlier heroes seem almost self-satisfied by comparison. The success or failure of this book rests with its ability to bring the reader into contact, not so much with the motivations of the characters or the answers to their particular problems, but with the mythic element of life itself, with the element of mystery for which there are no answers other than belief. For *Rumble Fish* to succeed, one must respond finally with a tingling at the top of the spine, the body's signal that it has been in touch with a successful work of art. (p. 70)

There is not much cause and effect in this story. In *The Outsiders* there is a random element to the act of violence that triggers the story, the stabbing in the park, but once that has occurred, the rest of the story proceeds with absolute fidelity to the motivations of its characters. Once Johnny stabs Bob, everyone behaves exactly as they would be expected to behave, and the story gathers momentum toward its proper conclusion. In *Rumble Fish* there is no such turning point, no crucial act or omission (unless it is the simple returning to town of the Motorcycle Boy) after which the action of the story becomes inevitable. Instead it is all random, and it is all inevitable. Like a Greek tragedy dressed in modern black leather and denim, *Rumble Fish* is the story of human subservience to fate, to a destiny over which, finally, there can be no control. (pp. 70-71)

[Rusty-James's friend] Steve says of the Motorcycle Boy, "[H]e is the only person I have ever met who is like somebody out of a book. To look like that, and be good at everything, and all that." Thus does one of the book's characters state the main problem about the Motorcycle Boy. People in books should not themselves appear to come out of books; that's too much of a jump for any character to make, and the Motorcycle Boy, who doesn't make the river at the book's end, doesn't make the jump into fully realized existence either. He's just too distant, too idealized, too detached, and finally too inhuman to be taken seriously as a character. (p. 84)

The problem of the Motorcycle Boy is the problem of trying to create a larger-than-life character—the saint, the seer, the mystic—and at the same time have that character animated by the common spark of humanity we all recognize. Not many writers are able to pull this off. . . .

Ordinarily this should prove fatal to a novel, a major character who fails to break through two dimensions into at least the suggestion of a rounded existence, but not so in *Rumble Fish. Rumble Fish* succeeds in spite of the Motorcycle Boy because *Rumble Fish* is not the Motorcycle Boy's story at all . . . It's Rusty-James's story, actually, and from the point of view of the reader's allegiance, it is the Motorcycle Boy who plays squire to Rusty-James's knight, and not the other way around. . . . The spark of humanity that is missing in the Motorcycle Boy is a roaring fire in Rusty-James, and it is our concern with this conflagration that gives the book its impact. We imagine that the main thrust of the story is about the Motorcycle Boy, but in this we are fooled (intellectually, not emotionally) by a sleight of hand. . . . [Upon] closer inspection, all the themes of the book, even those having to do with perfection and perfect knighthood, are concerns of the character of Rusty-James as well as the Motorcycle Boy. If we sometimes cringe at the behavior of the Motorcycle Boy, we never look away, because in fact it is never the Motorcycle Boy we are truly looking at. What we are looking at is a distorted mirror, "a distorted glass" reflection of Rusty-James.

In the end we respond to *Rumble Fish* in a much deeper way than we do to *That Was Then, This Is Now.* It's an emotional, almost a physical response, as opposed to the more rational, intellectual reaction that the other book prompted. Whatever its defects, whatever its ambitions only partly achieved, *Rumble Fish* works as a novel. In its appeal to the mythic element in life, in its living, breathing creation of the pilgrim character of Rusty-James, the book works. And there is a name usually given to this kind of success. It is called art. (pp. 86-87)

[There] is little doubt that, as an example of mature, polished storytelling, *Tex* is Hinton's most successful effort. All the discipline and control she had to force into *That Was Then, This Is Now* is here brought effortlessly to bear. *Tex* doesn't take the chances that *Rumble Fish* took, but it knows what chances it is willing to take and how to handle them.

In fact *Tex* is clearly the most seamless of her books. The voice is consistent and appropriate throughout. It is Tex's voice, Tex's consciousness. The controlling, manipulating hand of the author is far in the background. For us, the readers, it has disappeared.

This is a style of writing that puts the welfare of the book, and the integrity of the book's voice, above its own need to show off. The most successful fiction—that which will last beyond one day in the sun—always seems to work its magic upon the reader in concealment, lying in wait like an enemy agent, familiar and friendly and certainly unsuspected, until at some point it explodes into an awareness that is truly subversive, that shakes the foundations of the reader's version of comfortable reality. *Tex's* subversion is a modest one, as befits a book of such "unexpected contentment," but in its own way, in the conclusions it draws, the world view that gradually comes into focus behind its exceptional main character, it is as meaningful, and as important, as the shattering monochrome vision of *Rumble Fish.* (p. 94)

We are inside Tex's head and with his thoughts from the first line. Once inside his head we never leave; we're coaxed into believing in that voice from the start, and the voice never falters, so our belief remains strong. It's clear that just one "clanger," just one miscalculation of what the character might do or say in a given situation, can destroy the illusion of reality and the reader's complicity in making that illusion seem real. Many's the novel that one such foolish move has reduced from the miraculous to the merely good. *Tex,* whether it be miraculous or not, at least makes no foolish moves.

S. E. Hinton knows Tex, intimately. She knows how he thinks and, like a good actor drawing on the experience of her own emotion to animate a character, how he feels. Consequently, the voice does not seem contrived; it is a true voice. (p. 98)

The theme of innocence, of staying gold, arises in *Tex* nearly unchanged from its statement in *The Outsiders* (and its counter-statement in *That Was Then, This Is Now*). As long as Tex stays "simple-minded," as long as he stays a kid, he stays gold. "I ain't going to outgrow [the fair]," he says to Mace. "I'll think the Fair is fun no matter how old I get." It's Peter Pan again, but Peter's solution, as we saw in *The Outsiders,* is incompatible with life in the real world. One cannot stay gold and stay around. Tex, who is from the beginning one who will stay around and knows it, must make another, more realistic solution. This is where *Tex* takes over and expands upon *The Outsiders.* This is where *Tex* is, in many ways, the summation statement of the unresolved concerns of all three earlier books.

Tex is a character study, and it is an action novel, but at its core it is also a novel of ideas. Not surprisingly, the ideas the novel feels impelled to grapple with are those we have seen before, the troubling, unresolved problems of *The Outsiders, That Was Then, This Is Now,* and to some extent *Rumble Fish.* And *Tex* the novel is like Tex the character; it wants to find solutions to these problems; it wants to make a working arrangement that will let them all live in the real world. To do so it must deal directly with problems of the real world that have left earlier characters bitter, or puzzled, or just numb. (pp. 102-03)

What Tex has that the other characters lack is that rare generosity of his, that ability to break out of the prison of himself and to feel a sympathy for others. Rusty-James had some of this talent, too, but he invested it all in the Motorcycle Boy and when he lost the Motorcycle Boy he lost everything. Tex doesn't have any preferred invest-

ments; he seems to invest in everybody. As a result, his stock never falls, he's always got someone to hope for, and something to look forward to. It's never anything major, but that's the point, that's where his "contentment" comes from. He knows, as Huck Finn put it, how "to keep still," to concentrate on doing the work that needs to be done, on cultivating the garden.

The lesson of *Candide,* and of *Tex,* is that, after all the talking and philosophizing, life requires work. It is not—nor should it ever be mistaken for—a gift that comes fully valued and ready to be cashed in. There's nothing hereditary about success in life; it's no one's birthright, and it's just as available to Tulsa orphans as to anyone else, if they are willing to work at it. "Let's work without speculating," says one of the characters at the end of *Candide.* Let's quit talking and get to work. It is significant that, as the novel ends, Tex's first real job, at the Kencaide Quarter Horse farm, begins. (pp. 110-11)

> *Jay Daly, in his* Presenting S. E. Hinton,
> *Twayne Publishers, 1987, 128 p.*

Michele Landsberg

[S. E. Hinton's] books are read and reread avidly by young teenage boys—perhaps the only books which can claim such a ready audience among this least-reading-motivated group.

The characters in S. E. Hinton's books have an undeniably forceful presence, preposterous though they may be; the ardent, almost sexually adoring descriptions of her teenage delinquent heroes lend a feverish animation to the fan-magazine prose. The fourteen-year-old first-person narrator of *The Outsiders,* Ponyboy, introduces himself proudly as a "greaser," a wrong-side-of-the-tracks tough kid and orphan who glories in his class warfare with the privileged middle-class kids in town. Two pages into the first chapter, Ponyboy has already boasted about his lovely hair and greenish-gray eyes, his good build, his "high I.Q. and everything," and his unique ability to "dig movies and books." Then Ponyboy describes his sixteen-year-old brother Sodapop in these words: "He's movie-star kind of handsome, with a finely drawn, sensitive face that somehow manages to be reckless and thoughtful at the same time. He's got dark gold hair that he combs back—long and silky and straight—and in the summer the sun bleaches it to a shining wheat gold. His eyes are dark brown, lively, dancing, recklessly laughing eyes that can be gentle and sympathetic one moment and blazing with anger the next . . . ."

As the monologue of a tough street kid, and a male one at that, this is simply absurd. So is the weary repetition of stock phrases meant to show the humane decency of the older members of the gang towards the younger ones: On every other page, one of these paragons, affectionate and amused, will "cock an eyebrow and ruffle the hair" of a younger one.

It's easy to see why this burble is swallowed whole, and eagerly, and repeatedly, by young boys. For one thing, the unbridled impulsivity of the delinquent is inherently fascinating to teenagers. I remember the wave of popularity enjoyed by an adult mass market paperback in the 1950s, *The Amboy Dukes.* I read it myself at age eleven for its shock value and for the heady sense it gave of teenagers living in complete defiance of adults. Hinton's work, furthermore, flatters the egos of young male readers with its barely-subliminal sexual praise, and lets them escape into the fantasized glory of attention and approval from an older teenage tough. Adult criticism is neatly fended off by the fact that the delinquent heroes (Tex, Ponyboy) are clever at school, talented readers, disapproving of drugs, good athletes, and invariably develop worthy crushes on middle-class girls with clean hair. (pp. 214-15)

Michele Landsberg, "Growing Up," in her Reading for the Love of It: Best Books for Young Readers, *Prentice Hall Press, 1987, pp. 201-28.*

Linda Waddle

Any librarian who serves young adults (and that would mean most librarians in school, public, and university libraries) should be aware that Hinton has probably turned more kids onto reading than any other author. She began writing when she was fifteen, drawing her characters from observations of the teenagers around her, in Tulsa, Oklahoma. In her first book, *The Outsiders,* there were members of gangs—losers without parental guidance—whose loyalty and love for each other sustain them in a hostile world.

More than twenty years and three books later, her characters and their worlds still speak to young adults. There are still "outsiders" who identify with Ponyboy and Rusty James and who find support and validation in those characters. There are still "insiders" who find insight into and understanding of situations and people not known from personal experience. (p. 64)

Linda Waddle, "School Media Matters," in Wilson Library Bulletin, *Vol. 62, No. 9, May, 1988, pp. 64-5.*

Sue Tait and Christy Tyson

This summer the American Library Association gave a new award: The YASD/*School library journal* Author Achievement Award is given to an author "whose book or books, over a period of time, have been accepted by young adults as an authentic voice that continues to illuminate their experiences and emotions, giving insight into their lives (and enabling them to) understand themselves, the world in which they live, and their relationship with others and with society." The first winner was S. E. Hinton. Her books speak directly to our issue of independence and belonging. In *The Outsiders* the narrator finds his family, his sense of belonging, in the gang but he also finds that he must think for himself, must make decisions for himself, must become independent with all its terrors and promises. Hinton's other books as well speak of the struggle to become separate and the need to belong, to love and to be loved in its most inclusive sense. These novels have been staples of young adult work since they were published, and it is very fitting that she and her work be recognized by this first award. Young Adult work is noted for its ephemeral nature, but Hinton's books go beyond the topical, speaking to the deep needs of the young teenager. (pp. 55-6)

Sue Tait and Christy Tyson, in a review of "The Outsiders," and Others in Emergency

Librarian, Vol. 16, No. 2, November-December, 1988, pp. 55-6.

TITLE COMMENTARY

The Outsiders (1967)

What barrier separates the teen-age outcast—call him "greaser" or what you will—from the rest of American society, when race is not a factor? Seventeen-year-old novelist S. E. Hinton explores that question in an emotionally charged story for young people, *The Outsiders.*

Ponyboy, Hinton's fourteen-year-old protagonist, travels with the greasers—long-haired, tough kids bound together by passionate loyalty and affection. Sometimes Ponyboy ponders the differences between his own crowd and the Socs (or Socials). . . .

Ponyboy comes to learn that the Socs have problems, too, even if they are another magnitude. There is Bob, good-looking and intelligent, whose well-to-do parents could never say "no" to him, never set limits, who instead would blame themselves whenever he did something wrong. He is killed in a gang fight, and still they ask whether it was because somehow they had failed to "give him enough."

Yet the respectable world that will accommodate to Bob and the Socs shows only contempt for the greasers, striking out symbolically when unable to do greater damage. (p. 201)

Like Salinger's Holden Caulfield, Ponyboy is a romantic. He watches sunsets and looks at the stars and aches for something better. He muses that the moon he sees from his back steps is the same one that a Soc girl he admires can see from her patio on the other side of town. But as much as the sensitive, thoughtful Ponyboy resembles Holden, his milieu is irrevocably different. All around him are hostility and fear, along with distrust for the "system." As the story ends he sees a buddy shot down by the police under a street light. It was too late for him, but was it too late to tell other boys who are mean and tough and hate the world that there is still good in it—and would they believe you? "Someone should tell their side of the story," declares Ponyboy. "Maybe people would understand then, and wouldn't be so quick to judge a boy by the amount of hair oil he wore."

Admittedly, this is not on all counts a remarkable book. The dialogue sometimes rings false, and the message may be a shade too profound to be mouthed by teen-aged "hoods." Still there is little of the pretentiousness here, the whining tone, that characterizes the first statements of youthful authors.

Beyond this, such a book has relevance for today's attempts to reach the adolescent "outsiders" and provide them with a second chance. (pp. 201-02)

William Jay Jacobs, "Reaching the Unreached," in Teachers College Record, *Vol. 69, No. 2, November, 1967, pp. 201-02.*

Here is a powerful story, described as "about teen-agers, for teen-agers, by a teen-ager." It deals with gang rivalry and rumbles, but also leaves the reader with incisive portraits of individual boys growing up in a hostile environment with their own standards of courage and loyalty. (pp. 174-75)

The story shows boys of many varieties, still undecided which way they are going—on toward violence and crime or perhaps back to school, but then what? The characters are unforgettable, the action dramatic and moving. (p. 175)

> *May Hill Arbuthnot, in a review of "The Outsiders," in her* Children's Reading in the Home, *Scott, Foresman and Company,, 1969, pp. 174-75.*

Eventually, the protagonists in [Mildred Lee's] *The Skating Rink* and **The Outsiders** look within to find meaning in life, but the growth depends on a significant other person. . . .

The significant other in Ponyboy Curtis' life is not an adult, although he is an "outsider." Johnny, "a little dark puppy that has been kicked too many times," lives outside the world of the high school prom. Both Ponyboy and Johnny, the outsiders, are from a neighborhood where youth live by their own rules, in a world where there are no adult authority figures. In this setting marred by street violence, the young Ponyboy is torn between making something of himself or becoming like the other Greasers. Not till his best friend Johnny dies, after rescuing children from a fire, does Ponyboy grow in compassion and understanding. Johnny's last words, written in a note, suggest awareness: "Don't be so bugged over being a greaser. You still have a lot of time to make yourself be what you want. There's still lots of good in the world." Through his encounter with death, Ponyboy Curtis realizes there is a place for him in the world; he does not have to remain an outsider. (p. 59)

> *Linda O. Morgan, "Insight through Suffering: Cruelty in Adolescent Fiction about Boys," in* English Journal, *Vol. 69, No. 9, December, 1980, pp. 56-9.*

With a few exceptions, fiction evidently shows adults playing a negative or indifferent role in teenage identity formation. How does the peer group compare?

Some writers—Susan Hinton for example—have turned the group itself, its interactions and meanings, into the subject matter of a novel. Hinton's teenage groups grow up too fast, leading grim lives on the wrong side of the law; they carry knives and guns and are no strangers to violence or murder. The main character in **The Outsiders,** Ponyboy, is a member of a 'greaser' gang. The events of the novel develop out of the rivalry between the working-class greasers and the 'socs' or 'socials' who live on the better side of town. . . . Toughness is exaggerated and the beauties of friendship and kinship are sentimentalized by frequent repetition. There are also rather heavily delivered messages about young people, particularly the poor ones, being helplessly drawn into the inner-city whirlpool of violence and crime and missing the opportunity to discover the worthwhile things in life.

Theorists have acknowledged the role of social class in determining young people's behaviour and identity: adolescence is not merely a psychological or biological event, nor do all adolescents, as we once assumed, belong to a single

subculture characterized chiefly by its opposition to adults and the status quo. There are differences among young people themselves, often as a direct result of their class origins. Hinton's novel does recognize such distinctions, but without examining them in any depth, using the stereotypes of working and middle class simply as justification for the hostility between the two gangs. In fact she proceeds to overthrow the significance of the class barrier by pointing to the futility of gang warfare and exposing the myths behind the stereotypes. The greasers, for example, imagine that the working class has a monopoly of life's problems, but Ponyboy is made to see that, while the socs have the edge financially, they experience their troubles too. The gang ideal itself begins to ring hollow: teenagers who break allegiance to their own gang in order to speak on equal terms with a member of the opposing force are shown to be the most admirable and mature. Ponyboy finds himself more flattered to be known by his own name than 'grease'—the call name of the gang. Although appearance, dress and habits of speech, as well as emotional support and physical protection derive from the gang, family and closest friends are probably more important. (pp. 114-15)

> *Susan Thompson, "Images of Adolescence: Part II," in* Signal, *No. 35, May, 1981, pp. 108-25.*

[**The Outsiders** is] a groundbreaking book in the New Realism for adolescent readers. . . . The formulaic plot is occasionally melodramatic, and some incidents seem very unlikely. They are so implausible as to be almost ludicrous upon reflection, but, interestingly, they hold up well during reading, probably because the author makes Pony's concerns and the warm relationship between the brothers seem very real. The author's occasional editorializing about the faults of society injects a startling didactic element into an otherwise quite emotionally engaging story. The author succeeds in making potentially unsympathetic characters believable and likeable. Vocabulary is fairly easy, some use of street language contributes authenticity to the setting and simple interest, and the street code comes through clearly. (pp. 495-96)

> *Alethea K. Helbig and Agnes Regan Perkins, "The Outsiders," in their* Dictionary of American Children's Fiction, 1960-1984: Recent Books of Recognized Merit, *Greenwood Press, 1986, pp. 495-96.*

That Was Then, This Is Now (1971)

Mark's parents had shot each other when Mark was nine. He has lived with Bryon since then, and Bryon, who tells the story with the same directness and honesty that made **The Outsiders** so appealing to teen-agers, feels that Mark is his brother. But when he sees the effect of drugs on a gentle, friendly younger boy and discovers Mark is a pusher, he calls the police. He hates himself for the betrayal of his friend, but he's been a tough kid on the fringe of delinquency and he's aware of what happens beyond that fringe. The situation is harsh, yet the story has no minatory stridency. The writing has perception; the characters are wholly believable.

> *Zena Sutherland, in a review of "That Was*

Then, This Is Now," in Saturday Review, *Vol. LIV, No. 25, June 19, 1971, p. 27.*

That Was Then, This Is Now is a searing and terrible account of what life can be like for east-side youths in an American town—on the look out for easy money, for chicks, for drink, for the fast car to hot-wire and, sometimes, for hard drugs. This is a book which is both violent and tender, a book in which the hero, Bryon, grows from being a kid, when he "had all the answers", into a young manhood beset by questions. . . . A starkly realistic book, a punch from the shoulder which leaves the reader considerably shaken.

> *"Punching from the Shoulder," in* The Times Literary Supplement, *No. 3634, October 22, 1971, p. 1318.*

Susan Hinton's burning conviction carries her through a story of car-thefts, murder and acid-trips in which once again a first-person narrative gives the reader little respite from emotion. Yet although Charlie's Bar and his pool alley, the senseless car parade and the hippie commune are real enough as settings, the story is not basically about violence. This is the means, not the end; the theme is more complex and universal. Bryon and Mark, both sixteen, have been brought up together; they live as brothers, until the time when Bryon begins to grow up and his social attitudes to change, while Mark, the golden-eyed amoral lion, remains the uncaring petty thief he has always been. It is obvious that they will soon grow apart but the change is brutally sudden. . . . The book could have been merely a sensational street-drama: it is in fact a thoughtful and thought-provoking novel.

> *Margery Fisher, in a review of "That Was Then, This Is Now," in* Growing Point, *Vol. 10, No. 7, January, 1972, p. 1866.*

Rumble Fish (1975)

The greaser gangs are no longer where it's at, but S. E. Hinton still can't get over them. At least she has the insight to build this around another kid who can't either—Rusty James, a born down-and-outer whose self-description ("I ain't never been a particularly smart person") is an understatement. Here Rusty-James, now just "bumming around," is describing events of five or six years back. Even then the gangs had been broken up by dope, but he couldn't help trying to live up to the rep of his older brother, Motorcycle Boy, a kid who engineers his own destruction with such detachment that his sanity can only be debated in metaphysical terms. Rusty-James himself is a lot easier to figure. Sliced up the side in a knife fight, smashed over the head by two muggers, barely ambulatory throughout and always headed for the next confrontation, he is far realer than he has any right to be. Hinton knows how to plunge us right into his dead-end mentality—his inability to verbalize much of anything, to come to grips with his anger about his alcoholic father and the mother who deserted him, even his distance from his own feelings. Even the luridly symbolic climax—when Motorcycle Boy is shot by a vengeful cop after burglarizing a pet store to liberate the Siamese fighting fish (rumblefish, to him)—works better than you would suppose. Hinton, on her own turf, is still unbeatable, although she

seems to have no more of a future, or even a present, than Rusty-James has. Not to be confused with a nostalgia piece . . . this is a remarkably preserved specimen of rebel-without-a-cause nihilism.

> *A review of "Rumble Fish," in* Kirkus Reviews, *Vol. XLIII, No. 20, October 15, 1975, p. 1193.*

While this is as convincing a picture of brother love as is **The Outsiders,** it is a less balanced book. Believable, written convincingly in first person, the story line is less a plot than a picture of personality disintegration. Memorable, but with no relief from depression, no note of hope, no variation on the theme.

> *Zena Sutherland, in a review of "Rumble Fish," in* Bulletin of the Center for Children's Books, *Vol. 29, No. 4, December, 1975, p. 63.*

The author's portrayal of men and women is decidedly sexist. The machismo creed is heavily reinforced by Rusty James' refusal to cry, his need to keep up a tough-hood front, his faith that his strong hands are more valuable than a good mind. Girlfriend Patty is jealous and manipulative, turning her tears on and off at will. Girls are classified as "good," cheapies to mess around with, pretty possessions, housewives or runaway mothers.

Behind a colorful and action-packed facade, Ms. Hinton promotes negative images and values. (pp. 215-16)

> *A review of "Rumble Fish," in* Human—and Anti-Human—Values in Children's Books, *edited by The CIBC Racism and Sexism Resource Center for Educators, The Racism and Sexism Resource Center for Educators, 1976, pp. 215-16.*

Tex (1979)

Hinton's style has matured since she exploded onto the YA scene in 1967 with **The Outsiders.** In **Tex,** the raw energy for which Hinton has justifiably reaped praise has not been tamed—its been cultivated, and the result is a fine, solidly constructed, and well-paced story. Fourteen-year-old Tex lives with his 17-year-old brother Mason in a rural area. Their father hasn't been home in five months, and the relationship between the two boys is tense. Each has his own problems, fears, and growing pains which keep him alienated from his brother, until a dramatic and terrifying experience forces them to seek comfort and support from each other. With Tex, Mason, their father, friends, and neighbors, Hinton has created a cast of distinct personalities. Personal discoveries emerge from the action in a natural, unpretentious, and non-didactic way as Hinton explores questions about responsibility, friendship, desire, and communication.

> *Marilyn Kaye, in a review of "Tex," in* School Library Journal, *Vol. 26, No. 3, November, 1979, p. 88.*

Tex is a tale of coping with and surviving the trials and uncertainties of adolescence. Tex himself faces odds, to be sure: His father is a rodeo cowboy who's rarely around, and Tex and his older brother Mason must make do for themselves; he's got troubles at school and scuffles with his friends. Worse, though, he and Mason have problems that won't go away: In Tex's view, Mason is bossy and mean; moreover, he's sold their horses, in order to keep them going and the animals from starving.

Problems abound, in other words, and those aren't the only ones the author places on Tex's shoulders. He and Mason are held up and kidnapped by a hitchhiker (though clever Tex extricates them from the predicament); girl friend Jamie alternately asks for and rejects sex; there's a question about Tex's true parentage; at the end, Tex has a shoot-out with a drug pusher.

There's too much going on here. Even by the standards of today's fiction, S. E. Hinton's vision of contemporary teen-age life is riper than warrants belief.

Nevertheless, there are good things. The scene, the American Southwest, is rendered keenly. Mason, the older brother, is more than he seems to Tex, and Miss Hinton permits us to see it. The bewilderments of adolescence are often painfully caught. Yet *Tex* smacks, somehow, of Snoopy's "It Was a Dark and Stormy Night," busier and more melodramatic than the real life it purports to show. Perhaps it's like this these days, but *Tex* makes the case unconvincingly.

> *Paxton Davis, in a review of "Tex," in* The New York Times Book Review, *December 16, 1979, p. 23.*

Susan Hinton's attention has always been directed towards the crucial, changing relationships of adolescence but in the thirteen years since the first publication of *The Outsiders,* when the young author was writing to some extent from her own experience, she has taken a larger canvas on which to group more varied characters. *Tex* has a wider spread than her earlier books, first and most obviously in the geographical sense, because her setting here is Oklahoma farmland rather than city streets. This is something more than just an extended background. The tensions between Tex McCormick, who is fifteen, and his protective older brother Mason, are no less urgent and claustrophobic than those operating in the urban gangs of the earlier books, but they have an added force because of the isolation of the brothers in the dusty roads and paddocks where Tex rides his horse and his motor-bike, where the two of them wait for their restless father to return. Each summer the head of the household, a widower, has disappeared in search of an elusive fame and fortune at fairs and rodeos, leaving Mason to stretch inadequate funds and worry over the effect on Tex of their precarious life. Mason, a local basket-ball champion, is determined to escape by way of an athletic scholarship to college; frustration and anxiety drive him to illness, and in practical terms to the desperate measure of selling the horses, an action which brings to a head Tex's growing need to assert himself, to deny Mason's anxious control and claim his own identity.

Tex is a true survivor. Accepting insecurity and domestic hardship, this rough, explosive boy has an unexpected contentment which the author has brilliantly conveyed through his reactions to the important and the minor crises of his fifteenth summer and autumn. At school, he finally seals his long loyalty to his friend Johnny Collins (a friendship opposed by Johnny's conventional father) with a dangerous exploit on his bike. At home, he watches

Mace with new insight and helps him—with a murderous hitch-hiker and with Mace's weakly criminal friend Lem—almost by virtue of his cheerful approach to life as it is and not as he would like it to be.

Susan Hinton has shown in this book that first-person narrative can work. Tex's manner—blunt, colloquial, exploratory and openly egotistical—suits the setting and builds up the boy's character so that his view of his peers and of the adults who affect his life seems natural and inevitable. After he and his brother have narrowly escaped from the hitch-hiker, Mason asks him 'You don't think that you could ever turn out like that?' and Tex answers 'Well, I don't think so, but then nothing really bad has ever happened to me.' In the end he has to face a past history as distressing as that described by their attacker, but in facing it he wins the right to be himself. In soliloquy, in reported dialogue, in the plain account of day after day, Tex has opened his character to the reader together with a view of a landscape, a house, a city and a group of friends, neighbours, associates. Phrases and sentences seemingly casual and unstudied have been carefully devised to carry clues to personality and event in a totally natural way. . . . In this new book Susan Hinton has achieved that illusion of reality which any fiction writer aspires to and which few ever completely achieve. (pp. 3686-87)

> *Margery Fisher, in a review of "Tex," in* Growing Point, *Vol. 19, No. 1, May, 1980, pp. 3686-87.*

S. E. Hinton, . . . it seems to me, gets right to the heart of how and why people behave towards one another, in this case two teenage brothers in rural Oklahoma (a state to avoid like the plague, if this book is anything to go by). *Tex* is the first of her books that I've read, but it certainly won't be the last. [It's] a brilliant study of a fraternal relationship: moving, powerful, funny, and entirely convincing. It's odd, really, that the novel works so well when so many of the elements in the story are highly theatrical. The young narrator-hero, among other things, is kidnapped by a deranged gunman, is shot by a desperate junkie, and discovers that he isn't really his father's son. Each of these events would have sufficed for a novel on its own and it takes some courage to pack them all into one book. But a writer as good as Hinton can carry it off effortlessly; one believes implicitly in the characters and cares what happens to them. (p. 121)

> *Lance Salway, in a letter to Nancy Chambers, in* Signal, *No. 32, May, 1980, pp. 120-22.*

Taming the Star Runner (1988)

Ever since the publication of *The Outsiders,* it has been generally agreed that no one can speak to the adolescent psyche the way S. E. Hinton can. Her first novel since *Tex* shows readers evidence that she hasn't lost her touch. The hero, Travis, like the protagonists in all her novels, is an outcast. After an altercation with his stepfather that lands him in juvenile hall, Travis is sent to live with an uncle who owns a horse ranch in Oklahoma. There he develops an interest in a girl who runs a riding school. He is fascinated by the huge half-wild horse, The Star Runner, whom she is attempting to train, instinctively understanding that the animal and he share the same fierce need not to be controlled. His own wild bursts of temper cause trouble for him again until he realizes the steep price he has to pay for them. Although the story isn't as clearly focused as some of the author's previous ones and lacks the inherent energy of its predecessors, the characterizations are stellar, and the writing demonstrates a greater level of maturity, perhaps mirroring the author's own coming of age. It is difficult, in fact, not to think of this novel as somewhat autobiographical because her sixteen-year-old hero has written a novel that is accepted for publication. The account of Travis's first meeting with his editor is funny and revealing. Particularly telling are the editor's comments on his manuscript: "The narrative flowed, there was a strong sense of place, and his characters—well, his characters were wonderfully realized human beings, everyone would come away from his book convinced that these people really existed." (pp. 78-9)

> *Nancy Vasilakis, in a review of "Taming the Star Runner," in* The Horn Book Magazine, *Vol. LXV, No. 1, January-February, 1989, pp. 78-9.*

His boot felt empty without his knife in it," begins S. E. Hinton's fifth novel, *Taming the Star Runner.* A young hood, desperately tough and desperately vulnerable, is on his way to exile on his uncle's horse ranch—and in one paragraph the reader is back in familiar Hinton country after a hiatus of 10 years. What bearing does this new book have on the literary and popular reputation of Susan Eloise Hinton, who at 16 wrote *The Outsiders,* a novel that, in 1967, gave birth to the new realism in adolescent literature, and who has since achieved almost mythical status as the grand dame of young adult novelists?

Ms. Hinton has produced another story of a tough young Galahad in black T-shirt and leather jacket. The pattern is familiar, but her genius lies in that she has been able to give each of the five protagonists she has drawn from this mythic model a unique voice and a unique story.

In *Taming the Star Runner,* 15-year-old Travis conceals his budding talent as a writer under a carefully cool exterior. When he nearly kills his stepfather in a fight, he is sent to his Uncle Ken's horse ranch, and there he finds himself very much out of his milieu. It's "invisible-man time again" with the "hick jocks and hick nerds" at school. Out of loneliness, he begins to hang around the horse barn where 18-year-old Casey Kencaide has a riding school. Watching her dominate her dangerous stallion, Star Runner, he falls in love with her but keeps it to himself. Unexpectedly, Travis gets a letter from a publisher accepting a novel that he has written. He is ecstatic, but has trouble finding someone to share his pleasure. When Casey wins a difficult jumping competition with Star Runner at a horse show, he kisses her and she grudgingly admits what he had felt was the "strange tie, bond, fate, between them."

The sky darkens as Travis's old friend Joe comes fleeing the city, terrified by his part in a double murder. Travis realizes that he may have escaped from his old life just in time. Then, when a tornado strikes, Star Runner leaps the fence and gallops off across the fields with Casey and Travis in wild, exultant pursuit in a Jeep. Lightening crashes, and Travis and Casey are knocked unconscious. They awake to an empty pasture and a smell of burning

flesh. The reader is left to surmise that the mystical Star Runner has been killed. Later, Travis finds that something wild has gone out of his passion for Casey, but that they have become close friends. As the book ends, the young man has reached some contentment with his life and is about to begin a second novel.

Taming the Star Runner is remarkable for its drive and the wry sweetness and authenticity of its voice. Gone is the golden idealism of the earlier works, perhaps because here Ms. Hinton observes, rather than participates, in the innocence of her characters. The autobiographical passages that give glimpses of a past painful time in her own adolescence are most interesting: the young writer bumbling through an awkward first lunch with the publisher or becoming inarticulate at a television interview.

The symbolism of the horse is less successful. At first, Star Runner is seen as demonic, even erotic, but later Travis muses on him as an alien being from space. In the chase he seems to become a nameless wild force out of control, perhaps creativity itself. The symbol never quite comes into focus and consequently fails to carry its weight in the plot, leaving the ending unclear—a fault that young adult readers find particularly annoying.

Because *Taming the Star Runner* is also a more mature and difficult work, it may not be as wildly popular as the other Hinton books have continued to be with succeeding generations. Are those novels stuck in time? A check with youth librarians across the country shows that Hinton readers are younger than they used to be, and if *The Outsiders* is no longer the cult novel it once was, perhaps that is because so many teachers are using it in the classroom. But S. E. Hinton continues to grow in strength as a young adult novelist.

> *Patty Campbell, in a review of "Taming the Star Runner," in* The New York Times Book Review, *April 2, 1989, p. 26.*

S. E. Hinton's first novel, *The outsiders,* was published in 1967 when she was seventeen. Travis Harris, the hero of her new novel, is a child of tough urban America as she was, and he too is a writer, only sixteen when his first novel is accepted. Suspicions of disguised and indirect autobiography are bound to arise. But in the words of another Hinton title, 'That was then, this is now,' and there is no trace of nostalgia to cloud the book's realistic and convincing presentation of the very different 1980s teenage culture. What is clearly first-hand, authentic and fascinating is the author's knowledge of precocious writing prowess. She marvellously conveys the fractious and explosive energies of giftedness, equally in Travis himself and in the horses and young horsewomen with whom he unexpectedly finds himself working. . . . In her mature writing, S. E. Hinton has a wider range and a mellower, less urgent voice, but has lost none of her insight into raw life growing. *Taming the star runner* is a tough, eventful, gripping story and an exhilarating portrait of endangered but victorious talent.

> *Peter Hollindale, in a review of "Taming the Star Runner," in* The School Librarian, *Vol. 37, No. 4, November, 1989, p. 160.*

Margaret O(ldroyd) Hyde

1917-

American author of nonfiction, editor, and scriptwriter.

Major works include *Animal Clocks and Compasses: From Animal Migration to Space Travel* (1960), *Mind Drugs* (1968), *Know Your Feelings* (1975), *Speak Out on Rape!* (1976), *AIDS: What Does It Mean to You?* (1986).

Applauded for providing young readers with comprehensive and enjoyable introductions to timely subjects in the social, biological, physical, and mechanical sciences, Hyde is a prolific author acknowledged for examining complex, often controversial topics in an objective and accessible manner. Focusing on current world problems and recent scientific developments, especially as they relate to her audience of upper elementary school through high school readers, she addresses such subjects as animals; psychology, human behavior, and the mind; the earth, the environment, and overpopulation; the human body and sexuality; computers and robots; alcohol and drugs; crime; juvenile and adult rights; death; genetics; terrorism; transportation; and energy. Hyde structures her books as overviews of their subjects; many of these works include a history of the topic, a current assessment, examples of case studies and experiments, a sampling of suggestions for improvement, and theories about the future of the issue. Praised for her lucid prose style, she is often noted for providing her readers with valuable appended matter such as further reading lists, glossaries, and reprints of related documents.

Originally intending to become a doctor, Hyde reluctantly abandoned her premed studies when her parents objected to the unsuitability of the medical profession for women; she studied zoology and psychology and taught science education for several years before becoming a full-time writer. Hyde is often celebrated both for the depth of her research and for the significance of her information. Her research has taken her to space labs, crisis centers, observatories, operating rooms, and other locations, and she consults frequently with professionals and specialists, several of whom are credited as collaborators; she has written a number of titles with child psychologist Elizabeth Held Forsyth and has also collaborated with her husband and her two sons. Hyde updates her books on a regular basis, and several of her works have gone into revised editions. In addition to her nonfiction, Hyde is the author of a work of fiction, *Playtime for Nancy* (1941), and is the adapter of an ecological history of the deserts of the world by Italian photographer Folco Quilici. She is also the editor of *Mind Drugs,* a work about juvenile drug abuse considered among the most outstanding in its field, and has written scripts for the television series *Animal Secrets.* Hyde won the Thomas Alva Edison Mass Media Award for the best children's science book of the year in 1961 for *Animal Clocks and Compasses* and was named an honorary doctor of letters by Beaver College in 1971.

(See also *Contemporary Literary Criticism,* Vol. 21; *Something about the Author,* Vols. 1, 42; *Something about the Author Autobiography Series,* Vol. 8; *Contemporary Au-*

thors New Revision Series, Vol. 1; and *Contemporary Authors,* Vols. 1-4, rev. ed.)

AUTHOR'S COMMENTARY

[The following excerpt is from an interview by Patty Campbell.]

Question: what young adult author has written for teens since 1953, has sixty-one books to her credit, and gets better all the time? No, it's not Jeanette Eyerly, or Lois Duncan, or even Janet Quinn-Harkin. Margaret O. Hyde is that prolific, long-running writer, with thirty-eight of those sixty-one books still in print. For over thirty years Hyde has used her scientific training, her skill at organization, and her meticulous research to produce a stream of excellent books for junior high readers on the social and biological sciences. Her subjects are as current as the evening news, and she goes straight to the cutting edge by garnering much of her material from the experts and organizations who are making that news. ***Mind Drugs,*** now into its fifth edition, has long been the standard work for teens on substance abuse, and her recent ***AIDS: What Does It Mean to You?*** is the best yet on that topic for young readers. She has the gift of making complex matters easy to understand. This column once referred to her as "that elegant and dependable workhorse."

Yet, because nonfiction is the unglamorous stepchild of adolescent literature she is seldom seen at publishers' parties or on the library conference lecture circuit, and while Richard Peck, Robert Cormier, and Paula Danziger are familiar faces, few of us have ever met Margaret Hyde. So to remedy the invisibility of this important writer, this month the "Young Adult Perplex" interviewed her by telephone from her home in Vermont.

As we talked, I could visualize her sitting in her office, looking out into the woods (because I *have* met her, although I had to go to Canada to do it). Peg Hyde is an imposing woman with a strong and kindly face; she looks exactly the way you always hoped the principal would look when you were in second grade. Her conversation is as organized as her writing, but warm and genial. My first question made her chuckle. "Did you write as a teenager?"

"No, I never even thought of it." Her only C in college was in English composition, although she always had A's and B's in chemistry and biology. So she was convinced that she couldn't write. When a colleague at Columbia University, where she was teaching one summer, invited her to do a sixth-grade science book for his textbook series she flatly refused. But he encouraged her, and with help she struggled through. Later, when she was at home with two young sons, she attempted a Wonder Book (a series similar to the Golden Books). "I must have written 200 before I got one published," she remembers ruefully. Its title was *Playtime for Nancy,* and it was to be her only foray into fiction. She sold it for $200, no royalties. Many years later she spotted it in a supermarket rack and discovered that it had even gone into French translation.

But the book from which she dates her career is *Flight Today and Tomorrow.* Deciding that writing for an older audience would give her a chance to use her science background, she leaped in with an approach that in retrospect seems audacious. "I look back and gulp!" She had the reader piloting the plane, although she herself had never flown. But then, using a technique that was to serve her well, she ran the manuscript past an authority, a commercial pilot, to make sure she had gotten it right. She sent it to three publishers, and the third, McGraw-Hill, accepted it on condition that she would write others for them. Her relationship with McGraw-Hill and their Junior Books Division editor, Helene Frye, was a long and productive one, and ended only when the publisher closed the division. Hyde then went to Franklin Watts, and later branched out to several others. Nowadays at any one time she usually has three or four manuscripts in various stages with as many different publishers.

This highly successful writer had originally wanted to be a doctor. She did her pre-med studies in three years at Beaver College, but her family was not impressed. They felt that medicine was unsuitable for a girl, so, bowing to their wishes reluctantly, she went on to Columbia University to work toward a master's degree in zoology and psychology. But sexism again intervened. When it began to seem that as a woman it would be very hard for her to get a job in genetics, her major field of interest, she switched at the last minute to teaching. Ironically, she eventually did teach at both Columbia and Temple Universities (as well as the Shipley School in Bryn Mawr), where she showed student teachers how to present science to different grade levels. After her marriage she continued teaching science education for awhile, but when her boys began to grow up she switched to writing exclusively, using their nap times and evenings for her work.

How does she choose those late breaking subjects for her books? "Editors call with ideas, or when I speak to school groups, teachers or librarians or students will make suggestions. If a subject really appeals to me and I feel it needs doing, then I will go ahead with it. One time when I talked to a group of young people there were four who stayed afterward and begged me to do books on certain subjects." As a result she later wrote on child abuse, suicide, and the problems of children whose parents are divorced. Only very occasionally has she been unable to interest a publisher in a topic she considers important—fire safety and arson, for example. . . . Working with current social problems imposes its own pressures. "I usually rush and hurry and get it out before the thing changes," she says.

Hyde's working methods are interesting for other information professionals. At any one time she is collecting material for four or five new book ideas and several revisions of existing books. Each is assigned its own big plastic milk carton or bushel basket, into which Hyde tosses newspaper and magazine clippings, letters, articles, pamphlets, notes of names and organizations, etc.

She usually collects for a year or two before actually beginning the book. Then the next step is to divide the material into project chapters, usually ten: "A history, what's happening in the field today, what people can do about it, where they can go for help, and what may happen tomorrow." By this point Hyde will have a contract with a publisher, and she switches her information-gathering into high gear. She gets addresses from the library and writes a great many letters requesting information from organizations, hospitals, and experts in the field, whose names she has previously culled from newspapers and television. She gets new books and government documents from the library of the university of Vermont, and buys what she cannot find there. She contacts her senators and asks for updates on the government material. But phone calls and visits with scientists and doctors are her primary resource. Her most famous informant has been Linus Pauling, but many other leading doctors and scientists have helped her. She finds them very generous with material: "One Nobel Prize winner sent me something and said, 'This is the only copy I have, so please be sure to return it.'" Often she is invited to learn about her subject firsthand. A famous heart surgeon had her in to watch an operation, and stood her so close to the operating table that blood spurted onto her sterile gown. She had to remind herself that she was told to fall backwards if she were going to faint.

The sheer volume of material is overwhelming at times, admits Hyde. Piles of papers accumulate around each of her three computers—two in the work rooms and one in her bedroom—as she moves from one to another to organize her information and double-check facts. (And at the same time she may be revising another book and proofreading or indexing a third.) When the manuscript reaches first draft, she sends it back to her informants to be checked for accuracy. Like most writers, she works best in the morning, and "by the afternoon I get into errands." In the evenings she often files material, a job she can do while watching TV. As the deadline approaches on a book, she steps up the pace, working all day, every day. The writing of a book takes between four and six months, and publishers' production time can be as long as a year, so a book must often be updated once again just before it reaches final form.

Hyde has worked with several joint authors. Most recently she has combined forces with a neighbor, Elizabeth Forsyth, who left her private practice as a psychiatrist to write full time. Forsyth brings her background and knowledge to the partnership in such books as *Know Your Feelings* and *Suicide: The Hidden Epidemic,* although Hyde does most of the actual writing. Other coauthors have been sons Bruce and Lawrence (three books each) and even husband Edwin once, in 1955. (pp. 74-5)

> *Patty Campbell, in an interview with Margaret Hyde, in* Wilson Library Bulletin, *Vol. 102, No. 8, April, 1988, pp. 74-5.*

TITLE COMMENTARY

Flight Today and Tomorrow (1953)

A fairly simple introduction to some of the basic principles of flight and some advances that have been made in the development of various types of planes. The author writes as if the reader were standing with her on the field of a large airport—a point of view which becomes confusing when she keeps directing the reader to "look" and there are no accompanying pictures at which to look. An excellent bibliography at the end will suggest to the reader other, more detailed, books on the same subject.

> *A review of "Flight Today and Tomorrow," in* Bulletin of the Children's Book Center, *Vol. 7, No. 6, February, 1953, p. 46.*

A satisfactory once-over-lightly on flight. . . . A personalized narrative puts the reader in the pilot's position and the flights he goes on rise from a monoplane to a moon-bound rocket. All possible essentials, for so short a book, are well presented, and its unique contribution is its overall view instead of a particular aspect, of all flight. But for more grounding in special branches look at the books suggested in the bibliography.

> *A review of "Flight Today and Tomorrow," in* Virginia Kirkus' Bookshop Service, *Vol. XXI, No. 16, August 15, 1953, p. 539.*

This book on flight is quite comprehensive—covering an introduction to the basic science of flight, private planes, commercial planes, military planes, engine types, jets, rockets, navigation, blind flying, the social and economic significance of aviation, and even space travel.

The style is simplified, to make the complex subject matter comprehensible. . . .

No child can go wrong reading this book unless he tries to fly a real plane without a wee bit more instruction.

In the chapter on actual piloting, the pilot, among other things, violates CAA regulations by busting into a cloud on a VFR flight, and "corrects" for a spin with control manipulation that would have put the light ship into a disastrous outside loop.

> *John Lewellen, "Science of Flight," in* Chicago Tribune, *December 27, 1953, p. 9.*

[*The following excerpt is a review of the revised edition published in 1970.*]

A broad and cursory whirlwind tour through aviation from astronauts to seagulls and Bernouilli to Sikorski. Crammed with facts and little anecdotes, apparently to keep the story moving, the book skims the tops of numerous waves but never seems to get its feet wet. . . . [It] appears to be primarily a rewrite and a "brought-up-to-date version of the original '53 edition." Although primarily accurate and broad in scope, it lacks verve, imagination, and "punch."

> *Richard H. Weller, in a review of "Flight Today and Tomorrow," in* Appraisal: Children's Science Books, *Vol. 5, No. 1, Winter, 1972, p. 20.*

Atoms Today and Tomorrow (1955)

Young people—and adults too—will find *Atoms Today and Tomorrow* informative, accurate and unexpectedly pleasant reading. Unlike so many books on atomic energy, this one does not foster fear and frustration. There are no pictures of menacing mushroom clouds, blasted buildings and pathetically maimed humans. But there are illustrations [by Clifford N. Geary], dozens of them, accurately and artistically drawn, and, with the text, they tell an up-to-the-minute story of the many peace-time uses of atomic energy.

Mrs. Hyde discusses frankly the serious hazards of working with radioactive materials, but she stresses the elaborate safeguards provided to all workers. As new applications of radioactive materials are found, more workers will be needed. An important contribution of this book may be the encouragement of young people to enter careers in atomic industries and professions. Recommended to librarians, guidance counselors and science teachers for discussion with teen-agers.

> *Alfred D. Beck, "Here to Stay," in* The New York Times Book Review, *August 28, 1955, p. 16.*

[*The following excerpt is a review of the revised edition published in 1959.*]

Margaret Hyde . . . writes an explicit and pertinent account of the atom, its dangers and potentials. Based on the hypothesis that man is now confronted with the choice of how and to what extent atomic energy should be used, this text presents a clear and informative exposition of what, so far, is being done and to what one may look in the future. An exceedingly difficult topic is handled here with admirable clarity and impartiality in this text which is as morally challenging as it is scientifically precise.

> *A review of "Atoms Today and Tomorrow," in* Virginia Kirkus' Service, *Vol. XXVI, No. 23, December 1, 1958, p. 873.*

[*The following excerpt is a review of the revised edition published in 1966.*]

This is an interesting, accurate, and readable account of the atomic age and its future. Although she includes no new material, the author has joined in a smooth-flowing fashion the great variety of applications in which nuclear knowledge has and will be utilized. Examples are taken from cancer research, tracer studies in plants and animals, mutation of plants and animals, industrial applications, nuclear reactors, electrical power production, and many more. The author makes no attempt to be quantitative. Considerable emphasis is placed on the careful handling required in the use of radioactive materials. The important role of health physics in the atomic age is stressed. The book concludes with advice for the reader on how he may be part of the atomic age either as a participant or part of an informed public. (pp. 4352, 4354)

[*Editor's note, Library Journal*]: There has been a good deal of revision of the second edition of 1959 to bring it up to date. Some chapters are almost completely rewritten, others have new paragraphs added, and only a few have minor editing. (p. 4354)

> *Phillip W. Alley, in a review of "Atoms Today & Tomorrow," in* Library Journal, *Vol. 91, No. 16, September 15, 1966, pp. 4352, 4354.*

[*The following excerpt is a review of the revised edition published in 1970 and coauthored with Bruce G. Hyde.*]

The intent of this book is to give "young readers" (age unspecified) some familiarity with peacetime uses of atomic energy. The treatment is broad but superficial. Written in a familiar, colloquial style, the book is descriptive rather than explanatory. We are told, for example, that health physicists use instruments called "Cutie Pie" and "Pee Wee"—but not what they are used for nor how they work. On the credit side, the authors do cover a wide variety of applications and mention both sides of the controversies about the safety of nuclear power stations, and the effects of low dosage of radiation. There is virtually no mention of military applications—a fact that this reviewer counts as favorable. (pp. 255-56)

> *A review of "Atoms Today and Tomorrow," in* Science Books: A Quarterly Review, *Vol. 6, No. 3, December, 1970, pp. 255-56.*

Medicine in Action: Today and Tomorrow   (1956)

This is an illuminating book for the teen-ager who might be thinking of medicine as a career, or who is curious about this amazing science. Also, the adult layman who knows little about modern medical practices and miracles, but would like to have a discussion of them in understandable language and entertaining style will find this a rewarding book. It discusses the work of those in medical careers, the thrilling adventure of searching for new wonder drugs in far places, and the advances made in treating mental illness. It closes with a challenge and with a hope that with the aid of modern medicine mankind will continue to grow healthier and happier.

> *M. M., in a review of "Medicine in Action," in*

The Saturday Review, *New York, Vol. XL, No. 7, February 16, 1957, p. 53.*

Modern medicine is a highly developed and complicated science, which means that behind and beside the doctor stand many highly trained people who are not M.D.'s. Nurse, laboratory technician, medical artist, x-ray technician, medical social worker, occupational therapist, medical secretary, hospital administrator, librarian are but a few of those who play an important part in the medical world. The major portion of this excellent book on the world of medicine is devoted to discussing these careers and how a young person may prepare for them. The author has devoted a chapter, in many cases, to each category and at the end of the book has summarized in a set of tables the many careers that do not require the long and arduous preparation necessary to become a surgeon or a medical specialist.

This is an extremely valuable and informative book for vocational guidance, as well as an instructive one for the general reader who wants to know more about the team of which the doctor is the captain.

> *Frank G. Slaughter, "Doctors' Helpers," in* The New York Times Book Review, *February 24, 1957, p. 31.*

[*The following excerpt is a review of the revised edition published in 1964.*]

A revision of a very useful and popular career-guidance narrative . . . , carefully updated. The very readable text gives a clear overview of the medical profession including the work of doctors, nurses, technicians, pharmacologists, therapists, aids, psychiatrists, social workers, etc. A tabular appendix lists for each position or activity the length and nature of instruction or training, the place of employment, and the source of additional information obtainable by correspondence. Indispensable in school and public libraries.

> *A review of "Medicine in Action," in* Science Books: A Quarterly Review, *Vol. 1, No. 1, April, 1965, p. 37.*

Off into Space! Science for Young Space Travelers (1959)

An excellent book on "space science" for the eight-to-twelve age group. The youngster is introduced to authentic conditions as they will be (at least as nearly as can now be predicted) on a space-ship and is taken, in imagination, to the Moon and back. Vignettes of scenes on other planets are given, all according to the best current theories on the matter. The author may be a little too optimistic in describing the Martian landscape as including plants, without feeling the need for a cautious qualification such as a "perhaps."

> *Isaac Asimov, in a review of "Off into Space!" in* The Horn Book Magazine, *Vol. XXXV, No. 3, June, 1959, p. 227.*

In a personal, direct style, readers are told about space suits, life and food on a space station, conditions and facts about the moon and other planets. Basic information about gravity and atmospheric conditions is given; simple experiments on air pressure and eating habits in space. Of special appeal is the difficulty of playing an imaginary baseball game on the moon. (pp. 2223-24)

> *Lois Anderson, in a review of "Off into Space!" in* Library Journal, *Vol. 84, No. 13, July, 1959, pp. 2223-24.*

Information about space travel, the solar system, gravity and atmosphere, and the principles that make rocket ships operate is given in a very informal and simplified writing style. The author uses the device of discussing these aspects of space as though they were being encountered by a traveler, and the auxiliary device of an imaginary film (which does not clearly distinguish known fact from speculation) shown at a space station. Some suggestions are given for elementary home demonstrations of basic principles: a glass of water covered with heavy paper and turned upside down, for example, as a demonstration of air pressure. The explanations are not as comprehensive as those of such authors as Nephew and Bendick, but the simple terminology and the format make the book more useful for the third and fourth grade readers. (pp. 148-49)

> *A review of "Off into Space!" in* Bulletin of the Center for Children's Books, *Vol. XIII, No. 19, May, 1960, pp. 148-49.*

[*The following excerpt is a review of the revised edition published in 1969.*]

Off into Space will interest many young readers. Various aspects of space science are discussed and some experiments are suggested. The narrative is written in such a way that the reader becomes involved in imaginary space research projects and voyages. The illustrations [by Bernice Myers] are attractive, but since most of them probably were made for the first edition, many of those that deal with spacecraft are out of date. Illustrations should have been revised, where necessary to look like actual spacecraft and more recent speculative designs that the young reader has seen on television and in current magazines. Although the edition probably was in press prior to the Apollo II expedition, the text could have been updated to incorporate other findings of the Gemini and Apollo programs.

> *A review of "Off into Space! Science for Young Space Travelers," in* Science Books: A Quarterly Review, *Vol. 5, No. 3, December, 1969, p. 275.*

Animal Clocks and Compasses: From Animal Migration to Space Travel   (1960)

The fascinating phenomenon of animal time telling and direction finding is described in this text which should interest even the most indifferent students of animal, fish, bird and insect behavior. How herons determine the changing of tides, how pigeons find their homes, how crabs tell time, these and many other examples of the keen intuitive mechanisms that govern non-human life are illustrated. Margaret Hyde provides the reader with the possibility of observing animal clocks and compasses himself, by providing him with suggestions of where to watch and how. . . . [This] is an invitation to an intriguing and educational hobby.

> *A review of "Animal Clocks and Compasses," in* Virginia Kirkus' Service, *Vol. XXVIII, No. 13, July 1, 1960, p. 503.*

Miss Hyde compiles . . . fascinating nature information . . . in a book which combines much of what is given in Will Barker's *Wintersleeping Wild Life* and Sigmund Lavine's *Strange Travelers,* both excellent studies. Hers is equally authoritative and lively and goes beyond obvious facts of hibernation and migration to the *why* and *how* of living clocks—timing by tide, light, animal radar or echo-location—suggesting possible use of the principle of hibernation for man in spaceships, and outlining science projects based on observation of earthworms, frogs, flies, and birds. Included are bibliography, index, and small explicit sketches [by P. A. Hutchison] of species discussed (less striking than Carl Burger's drawings for the Barker book). (pp. 65-6)

> *Virginia Haviland, in a review of "Animal Clocks and Compasses: From Animal Migration to Space Travel," in* The Horn Book Magazine, *Vol. XXXVII, No. 1, February, 1961, pp. 65-6.*

With her sure instinct for the dramatic and fascinating questions in science, Margaret Hyde . . . discusses the built-in clocks and compasses in animals. What makes the fiddler crab know when it is high tide or low tide? How does the grunion know precisely the right wave, the one which reaches further up the beach, before depositing its eggs? What guides the salmon, the eel, the plover and the albatross, and many mammals in their migrations? What happens when oysters from New Haven waters, used to opening their widest at the time of New Haven's high tide, are transported to Chicago and keep the New Haven time for a while but gradually adjust? Is all this built in, or do outside influences affect them? What guides the warbler which flies in the night from Germany to its African wintering place? All these and many other remarkable phenomena arouse interest in what we do not know and what experiments are being carried on to solve some of these problems.

> *Margaret Sherwood Libby, in a review of "Animal Clocks and Compasses," in* Lively Arts and Book Review, *May 7, 1961, p. 36.*

This Crowded Planet   (1961)

A prolific "future directed" author well known for such lucid scientific books as *Exploring Earth and Space, From Submarines to Satellites, Atoms Today and Tomorrow,* etc., focuses now on our own planet and its incredible population explosion, and how scientists are preparing to tap new channels in order to overcome the startling imbalance between people and resources. We first "look to the earth", then the sea, and finally to the sky, and watch ingenious ideas take shape as all three areas are probed for the food, minerals and energy necessary for life. Water can be farmed as well as mined. Great mineral treasures lie beneath the earth's surface and forests can be planned and preserved. Outer space may hold some of the answers for man's survival, certainly such ancient elements as the sun and the rain will some day be controlled for maximum output. Realistic, yet optimistic, this is a timely and worthwhile summary of man's struggle with his environment.

A review of "This Crowded Planet," in Virginia Kirkus' Service, Vol. XXIX, No. 14, July 15, 1961, p. 622.

It is encouraging to see an author present a lively book for young teen-agers on a serious world problem—run away population growth and its threat to exceed the world's resources to support it. The author ably presents both the dimensions of the problem and the prospects for meeting it through expansion of resources and food supply. The challenge this offers research scientists is well described. But, probably because it is a delicate subject, the author sidesteps what may be the biggest challenge of all—that of holding population growth in check. Thus she tends to make the possible solution of the population versus resources problem appear easier than is likely to be the case.

Robert C. Cowen, "Acoustics, Etc.," in The Christian Science Monitor, November 17, 1961, p. 8B.

Psychology in Action   (with Edward S. Marks, 1967)

Amateur psychology is a universal hobby if not an avocation in this day and age. Disagreeable acquaintances are now called "sick" or "paranoid" by those who would discredit an adversary and at the same time appear both charitable (condescending) and informed. *Psychology in Action* fills the obvious gap which exists between the frivolous use of this terminology and its actual meaning. More important, it describes the dimensions and functions of psychology and psychologists in layman's terms. It not only defines the popular but poorly understood terminology, but shows clearly the triumphs and limitations of this inexact science.

Psychology does more than cure the mentally sick or disturbed. It functions as a positive guide for students in career selection, for industry in recruiting and assigning personnel and in the more intimate family and marital relationships. Possibly too much space is allocated to testing and test interpretation—and an understandably chauvinistic tone prevails throughout. Nevertheless this book will give a teen-ager insight into a subject which, rightly or wrongly, will have a great effect on his future.

Robert W. O'Connell, in a review of "Psychology in Action," in The New York Times Book Review, May 7, 1967, p. 34.

Collaboration between an experienced author of science books for young readers and a clinical psychologist has produced a short, highly readable introductory overview designed to convey to the uninitiated a sense of both the diversity of subject matter and the range of application of psychology as a vocational choice. The emphasis throughout is on the practical aspects of work in the clinical field, counseling, learning, dealing with problems appearing on the social scene, such as racial prejudice, and the ways in which psychologists are called upon to meet the challenge of manned space flight. Illustrations [by Carolyn Cather] add to the interest as well as the clarity of presentation. With a few notable exceptions (for example, the role of psychologists in the burgeoning field of sleep and dream

investigations) most of the major trends and research areas are identified. It is the intent of the authors to stimulate interest in the subject and to suggest sources for further information in the additional reading list provided. The style lacks the sense of drama and excitement that a vista-opening work should contain, but it will serve its purpose in providing a balanced and intelligent survey of a very complex field.

A review of "Psychology in Action," in Science Books: A Quarterly Review, Vol. 3, No. 2, September, 1967, p. 85.

[*The following excerpts are reviews of the revised edition published in 1976.*]

The second edition of this basic psychology text has been updated to include expanded articles on career choices. The authors emphasize that psychology is a many-faceted science which is not confined solely to laboratories or just concerned with statistics. There are chapters on the psychologists' tools, educational guidance, and considerable attention is given to the new fields of mental health and family counseling. An appended bibliography and index make this a good introductory title.

Janet Bell, in a review of "Psychology in Action," in School Library Journal, Vol. 23, No. 3, November, 1976, p. 70.

This book is for students who want to know what psychologists do, or who wish to major in psychology. It is exceptionally well written and interesting. The authors' lively presentation of different branches of psychology (research, clinical, counseling) and their accurate coverage of these areas will go a long way in dispelling the stereotypes surrounding psychology. Hyde and Marks use the jargon of researchers (e.g., independent/dependent variables, operational definitions) and explain a variety of therapeutic techniques (e.g., psychoanalytic, client-centered, behavioral) in an entertaining and exceptionally clear manner. They describe numerous ethical and methodological issues which confront researchers in many areas of research, such as perception, learning, testing and motivation. Separate chapters cover learning (conditioning, language, creativity), testing (intelligence, achievement, personality), counseling (career, school), social psychology (prejudice, group dynamics) and careers in psychology (requirements at undergraduate/graduate levels of study, areas of specialization). Every high school counselor (and even university instructors) involved with students considering psychology as a major should have and recommend this book.

Gregory T. Fouts, in a review of "Psychology in Action," in Science Books & Films, Vol. XIII, No. 1, May, 1977, p. 4.

Mind Drugs   (1968)

There are few speakers more in demand on the college-high-school-churchgroup circuit than those who profess to an expertise on drugs. Everyone is concerned about drug abuse—teen-agers, college kids, parents, teachers, ministers, lawyers, doctors, police officers. Everyone is searching for information, advice, and any "answers" that may be available.

Mind Drugs . . . is an attempt to provide some facts for those interested in drug abuse. It is reasonably short, but not superficial. The style is "popular" (in the nonpejorative sense), but should not offend the sensibilities of the intelligent reader, young or old. Its facts are, so far as I can tell, generally correct.

The contributors are a mixed lot: four psychiatrists, two psychologists, and a young doctor who has been medical director of the hippie clinic in the Haight-Ashbury section of San Francisco. Mrs. Hyde (who doubles as editor and author of three of the chapters) is not only a professional writer but a teacher and a director of the Northeast Mental Health Clinic of Philadelphia.

The description of the various "mind drugs" is good—and, in some respects, exemplary. The section by William McGlothlin on marijuana ("grass"), for example, is a model of clarity, discussing all of the important points with fairness, an economy of words, and dispassion without becoming either pompous or dull.

The book is primarily about young people—why they use drugs, what drugs do for and to them (good and bad), and some of the ways a person might be helped to kick his drug habit. It points out the semantic traps in defining "addiction," how complex the medico-legal ramifications are, how psychedelic "trips" can be pleasant or (unpredictably) catastrophic. It reminds us that it is not necessary for someone to suffer a psychotic break after the use of hallucinogens. It shows us how hard it is for LSD users to love even *one* other person, let alone "the world" or "humanity."

My major complaint about this useful volume is that it never gives in-depth reasons why youngsters take drugs; nor does it stress the alternative, non-drug challenges and satisfactions that might be provided by society. Juvenile drug abuse, in many ways, is like the inner city problem. In both instances, definite political, social, economic and psychological forces breed antisocial defiance and self-destruction, with incalculable loss to the individual and society. The proposed solutions to these problems have been heartbreakingly simplistic and unimaginative. Legal penalties are supposed to provide a deterrent or retribution—but have failed miserably, even in these respects, and cannot hope to eradicate the basic troubles. Preoccupation with secondary manifestations has blinded us to causes, with the dismal failure that might have been predicted. As the respected authority on addiction, Dr. Lawrence Kolb, has put it: "Our approach so far has produced tragedy, disease and crime."

It is perhaps unfair to ask for definitive solutions from a book of this type, although some suggestions are offered. We must still ask ourselves why our children resort to drugs—and how we can change the world so they will no longer feel this need. Perhaps, if reality could be made less ugly, young people would not seek escape in perceptual distortions, hallucinations and stupor.

> *Louis Lasagna, "The Grass Isn't Greener," in* The New York Times Book Review, *November 3, 1968, p. 3.*

[*The following excerpt is a review of the revised edition published in 1972.*]

This revised edition has been carefully updated to include recent social trends and much has been added on methadone treatment. A detailed list of " 'Drug' Related Terms" replaces the first edition's more elementary glossary, and "Where to Get Help" now covers the whole country but provides less specific information on each area. Additions include "Sources of Further Information" (a list of agencies) and a complete 13-page section on "Psychoactive Drugs" in outline and chart form, compiled from the Haight-Ashbury Free Medical Clinic and the *Journal of Psychedelic Drugs,* which covers everything from LSD to baby wood rose seeds and animal tranquilizers. However, the first edition's "Turning on Without Drugs" has unfortunately been omitted, so keeping both editions is recommended.

> *Nancy Clements Benham, in a review of "Mind Drugs," in* School Library Journal, *Vol. 19, No. 8, April, 1973, p. 75.*

[*The following excerpts are reviews of the revised edition published in 1974.*]

With the exception of the chapter on drug abuse and social values, all chapters in this new edition have been rewritten, at least in part, to incorporate more up-to-date information, and a new—somewhat idealistic—chapter on natural alternatives to drug use has been added. The appended lists of places to get help, suggestions for further reading, and "drug"-related terms have also been revised. The 1972 second edition is not enough out of date to warrant replacement, but the third edition is recommended for collections needing additional or new copies.

> *A review "Mind Drugs," in* The Booklist, *Vol. 71, No. 8, December 15, 1974, p. 419.*

This is a fine book, although this third edition is only occasionally different from the second edition. Unfortunately, few research studies have added to our knowledge since that time. Various contributors note that bootleg hallucinogens (and other drugs) are frequently "not as advertised." Treatments, therefore, formerly prescribed for acute drug reactions may today be harmful rather than helpful. Methadone treatment of heroin is described, but methadone abuse is discussed minimally. The recent evidence of markedly increased methadone deaths is ignored, and readers should be aware that methadone in high doses can cause a "high," it can be used with heroin, and the resultant condition is very difficult to treat.

> *A review of "Mind Drugs," in* Science Books: A Quarterly Review, *Vol. X, No. 4, March, 1975, p. 316.*

[*The following excerpt is a review of the revised edition published in 1981.*]

This latest edition of *Mind Drugs* is an excellent book for anyone with an interest in up-to-date information concerning the use and abuse of drugs. It extensively covers the problems of youth that lead to drug use and gives available alternatives. Many effects of mind drugs are described, and the difference between addiction and habituation is explained. The authors are experienced in working with addicts, and they describe the type of person most apt to become involved with drugs and develop underlying reasons for such involvement. The authors bring out that attitudes about addiction are changing with the increased recognition that the addict is a sick person. When the addict is so viewed rather than as a criminal, treatment becomes important. The establishment of methadone and rehabilitation centers and their contribution is well covered. More importantly, the book indicates the extent of the drug culture, and the fact that society will have to cope with it for the foreseeable future. It is hoped that the problem will lessen as improvements are made in our educational methods, attitudes, and treatment.

> *Rob S. McCutcheon, in a review of "Mind Drugs," in* Science Books & Films, *Vol. 17, No. 3, January/February, 1982, p. 155.*

[*The following excerpts are reviews of the revised edition published in 1986.*]

The fifth edition of Margaret O. Hyde's **Mind Drugs** is welcome both for what is carried over from the previous edition and for what is new. Most of the chapters, written by various experts, remain substantially the same. David Smith's "Contemporary Patterns of Youth and Drug Abuse" has naturally been updated, Ms. Hyde has revised William McGlothlin's chapter on marijuana, and she has added a chapter (right up at the beginning) on cocaine—including, of course, crack—which had only received a couple of pages in the fourth edition. Her chapter on drugs and driving has also been revised, now including material on M.A.D.D. and S.A.D.D., but dropping the chart on blood alcohol levels and effects on feelings and behavior. In the additional material at the end of the book, the section on "Where to get help" has been dropped, the chart on psychoactive drugs revised and more uniformly set up, "Drug-related Terms" have of course changed and the section is now called "Street Language," S.A.D.D.'s Contract for Life is included, and the sections on "Suggestions for Further Reading" and "Sources of Further Information" remain, in updated form.

This remains one of the most readable and broadly based books on the subject for young people, and has the added appeal of not ignoring the "adult" legal drugs of nicotine and alcohol. Its greatest asset remains its straightforward, concerned, non-judgmental approach.

> *Daphne Ann Hamilton, in a review of "Mind Drugs," in* Appraisal: Science Books for Young People, *Vol. 20, No. 3, Summer, 1987, p. 47.*

This book, now in its fifth edition, is outstanding in many respects. It presents a comprehensive and objective overview of all aspects of the drug scene, and although the writing in places will be difficult for some younger readers, should be must reading for all school-aged youngsters twelve and older. Reading the book section by section and discussing its contents with a parent, teacher, or some other respected adult would be an ideal way to benefit most from it. Virtually all mind-altering drugs now in use, including crack, and in addition the legal drugs alcohol and tobacco, are discussed in detail. A unique feature is a section devoted to positive alternatives to drug use. Far too often the anti-drug message includes only negatives, whereas something positive to fill the void left by discontinuing drug use is also sorely needed. A list of street language related to drugs; tables of psychoactive drugs, their psychological and physiological effects, methods of use,

etc.; a bibliography; sources of additional information; a copy of SADD's contract for life; and an index are included. The book is highly recommended for classroom use, the junior and senior high and local public libraries, and for home study as well.

> *A. H. D., Jr., in a review of "Mind Drugs," in* Appraisal: Science Books for Young People, *Vol. 20, No. 3, Summer, 1987, p. 47.*

The Earth in Action (1969)

The central theme of the book as stated by the title is approached several times by the author. However she rebounds into a variety of unrelated topics and secondary beginnings that leave a reader in a state of confusion. Approaching the earth as visitors from another planet, to begin the description of earth, could represent a reasonable technique to introduce concepts of size, position, and origin. But by interjecting additional approaches, the thought continuity is interrupted. Disproportionate emphases, mixing comparisons and scales for comparison, and littering the pages with imprecise adjectives, presents evidence both of padding and of rambling. Using the word "tremendous" three times in two consecutive sentences, contributes little toward understanding or knowledge. Several of the photographs are excellent; many illustrations should have been omitted; a few are reproduced two or more times (the book cover photograph is printed in reverse on p. 83; the same end papers at the front and back of the book are reprinted on p. 16). The remainder of the illustrations compound confusion (concepts of the sea floor) and are not properly related to the text (pp. 48, 60). There is some evidence of editorializing: "Radiation ocean dumps pollute sea water." A figure caption which is located on p. 22 belongs near the text reference on p. 124. The statement, "This theory comes closer to satisfying both the laws of astronomy and the words of the Bible than any of the others," referring to the planetismal hypothesis, is inappropriate and unsubstantiated. This is another unfortunate attempt to cover too much material in a small book which is loaded with miscellaneous and often irrelevant illustrations.

> *A review of "The Earth in Action," in* Science Books: A Quarterly Review, *Vol. 5, No. 4, March, 1970, p. 319.*

A valuable, very up-to-date book that portrays the earth as a dynamic, constantly changing phenomenon and that consistently illustrates the true nature of science by giving observable facts and then the theories or explanations for the phenomena observed. The book is filled with photographs, detailed explanatory drawings and light sketches to illustrate many of the concepts presented. There are two chapters on oceanographic research that will capture the imagination of any reader. Unfortunately, no attention is paid to the subject of caves or the action of underground waters. Ending on a positive note, the book indicates that it is time for man to use his knowledge about the earth to insure that it remains a livable place. Essentially a condensation and incorporation of much of the material found in separate volumes, such as those in the Time-Life series—Milne's *Mountains* (1962), Bergamini's *The Universe* (1966), Ley's *The Poles* (1962), etc.—this book would be a fine supplement to earth science programs, but would also be good for leisure reading.

Donald J. Schmidt, in a review of "The Earth in Action," in School Library Journal, *Vol. 16, No. 9, May, 1970, p. 84.*

For Pollution Fighters Only   (1971)

This is a fine primer for citizen action aimed at amelioration of environmental pollution. Mrs. Hyde has easily and coherently introduced the base concepts of spaceship earth—the interrelatedness of everything in a finite, essentially closed system. Her seven-page treatment of the life-support system of the biosphere is as good as this reviewer has seen for this audience. Subsequent chapters deal with individual pollution problems such as those affecting lake and wetland systems as well as the more typical ones such as water, air, noise, and solid wastes. Final chapters treat examples of community efforts to fight pollution, suggestions for positive action by any individual or community group, and private and public sources of information and political response to articulated needs. Most impressive is a responsible, common sense chapter decrying emotionalism without facts, quick and easy solutions to complex problems, doomsdayers, overreaction by environmentalists, and the like. With but a few not too serious exceptions, the material is technically accurate, up-to-date and well-written. Recent examples of pollution problems from mercury in Lake St. Clair to the crown of thorns starfish infestation add to the book's interest. It is ideal for class use in discussion and preparation for action programs of individual and community involvement.

A review of "For Pollution Fighters Only," in Science Books: A Quarterly Review, *Vol. 7, No. 3, December, 1971, p. 191.*

The book is well written, well organized, and offers an excellent summary of today's outstanding problems in the area of environmental pollution; yet it leaves much to be desired in its approach to the solution of these problems. The text emphasizes the complexity of ecological relationships, and offers examples of well-intentioned "improvements" that have been far outweighed by their long-term negative effects; yet the book offers several rather simplistic suggestions for "pollution fighters" without attempting to evaluate their potential negative side effects. In most localities, for example, more pollution might be generated by transporting trash to appropriate recycling facilities then by simply discarding it. Perhaps most unfortunate, in terms of the book's overall purpose and approach, is the fact that self-education is nowhere listed among the many actions that "pollution fighters" ought to take in order to improve their environment. For without some fundamental knowledge of chemistry, biology, economics, sociology, and other relevant disciplines it is difficult to imagine how young people can ever be integrated into the leadership of an effective "environmental revolution." This book seems to imply that the good intentions and dedicated activism of wide-eyed Aquarians are adequate to meet the challenge at hand. I doubt it. (pp. 20-1)

Ronald J. Kley, in a review of "For Pollution Fighters Only," in Appraisal: Children's Sci-

ence Books, *Vol. 5, No. 1, Winter, 1972, pp. 20-1.*

Know about Drugs   (with Bruce G. Hyde, 1971)

The authors simplistically and condescendingly describe various reactions to such drugs as nicotine, marijuana, LSD, and barbiturates and the ways these chemicals affect different people depending on amounts, kind, and when and why they are taken. The examples given to warn young people against the dangers of drugs are so exaggerated that they will induce laughter more readily than caution: e.g., "Picture a rock singer relaxing . . . with some alcoholic drinks, then [he] pops a few barbiturates into his mouth. . . . The barbiturates produce nausea, causing vomiting, in which the singer may choke to death." Only mature readers will appreciate the writers' psychological framework, and no one will appreciate [Bill Morrison's] mundane illustrations. A more informative and clearly written book for the age group is Geoffrey Austrian's *The Truth About Drugs* (Doubleday, 1970). (pp. 77-8)

Eleanor Frome, in a review of "Know about Drugs," in School Library Journal, *Vol. 18, No. 9, May, 1972, pp. 77-8.*

[*The following excerpt is a review of the revised edition published in 1979.*]

The second edition of Hyde's **Know About Drugs** revises and updates the original title, containing much more material than was first presented. In clear detail, the authors examine drug use and abuse, paying attention to cocaine, heroin, and the current favorite, PCP. Without moralizing, they frequently use a storytelling technique to emphasize the psychological factors. The scope is broad but inclusive and two-color illustrations [by Bill Morrison] complement the succinct style necessary for the age group concerned.

Janet B. Wojnaroski, in a review of "Know about Drugs," in School Library Journal, *Vol. 26, No. 7, March, 1980, p. 132.*

VD: The Silent Epidemic   (1973; revised edition as VD-STD: The Silent Epidemic)

A concise, general account of venereal diseases and their history, causes, symptoms, and treatments. Though all types are mentioned, emphasis is placed on gonorrhea and syphilis, which are the most serious. The author repeatedly stresses the importance of consulting a physician if there is *any* evidence of VD, since treating the disease in its early stages avoids the complications which arise in advanced cases. Also covered are blindness, brain damage, etc., which can result if certain diseases do not receive professional attention, and the possibility of an infected mother-to-be passing the sickness on to her child. The book does not preach standards of sexual behavior; in fact, it denounces the attitude that "nice" people can't get "the clap." Young people, who are afraid or embarrassed to confide in their parents or family doctors, will find the section on clinics and hotlines helpful for information and to keep their problems confidential. Libraries disseminating VD pamphlets from health agencies will probably find nothing new here; however, those unequipped to inform students about this illness, which is afflicting an ever-growing number of young people, will want this title.

Linda Johnson, in a review of "VD: The Silent Epidemic," in School Library Journal, *Vol. 19, No. 9, May, 1973, p. 80.*

In a no-nonsense, no-threat, no-coyness book, Margaret Hyde gives straightforward treatment to a subject of increasing concern to the young, since statistics show that in the United States as well as in other countries it is the young who are the primary victims of venereal diseases. . . . There is no note of censure in the author's acceptance of the fact that today's young people are frank about sexual matters (nor of approbation) since her concern is with eradication of the epidemic rather than deprecation.

Zena Sutherland, in a review of "VD: The Silent Epidemic," in Bulletin of the Center for Children's Books, *Vol. 27, No. 1, September, 1973, p. 10.*

Hyde's factual approach to venereal disease avoids scare tactics and preaching and provides a very readable account for young people or even those who are older. The major venereal diseases, their symptoms and modes of spread are accurately described in a manner useful to one who fears he or she has contracted VD. Readers are encouraged to seek medical advice quickly. The information provided should also help readers avoid contracting VD. Brief summaries of control methods and research programs are presented. Intelligent parents should encourage their children to become familiar with the information in this book, and it is a good supplementary source for physical education and hygiene courses.

A review of "V.D.: The Silent Epidemic," in Science Books: A Quarterly Review, *Vol. IX, No. 4, March, 1974, p. 312.*

[*The following excerpts are reviews of the revised edition published in 1983.*]

This revised edition of **VD: The Silent Epidemic** has been thoroughly rewritten, updated, and reorganized in light of current knowledge about sexually transmitted diseases. Coverage of genital herpes and the consequences of STDs on newborns has been greatly expanded, adding to the value of a concise introduction for younger readers or for those not able to manage fuller accounts. A list of HELP (a program service of the American Social Health Association) chapters for herpes victims and index appended.

Sally Estes, in a review of "VD-STD: The Silent Epidemic," in Booklist, *Vol. 79, No. 14, March 15, 1983, p. 955.*

There are several important and effective changes in Hyde's revision of **VD: the Silent Epidemic.** First and most obvious, the term *sexually transmitted disease* (STD) is used instead of *venereal disease.* This is in line with the move toward ridding diseases such as genital herpes, trichomoniasis and scabies of the stigma that syphilis and gonorrhea have carried. Secondly, Hyde gives space to 11 of the most common and important STDs and makes mention of approximately 8 more. Third, this new edition responds to the growing problem of genital herpes (Herpes

Simplex II) by providing clear, descriptive information plus a listing of "some HELP chapters for herpes victims." The result is a subtle but positive change in overall presentation. While the 1973 edition came across with a "here are the facts—now let's go get 'em" attitude, the new edition reaches out for attitudinal changes and general awareness. (According to Hyde, ¼ of the estimated 20 million who will be victims of STD this year will fall into the YA age group.) This is an excellent purchase to update collections and for older reluctant readers. However, Eric Johnson's *VD* (Lippincott, 1978) is still a first choice because of the inclusion of physiological diagrams, case study photographs, question and answer chapters and overall coverage.

Laurie Bowden, in a review of "VD-STD: The Silent Epidemic," in School Library Journal, *Vol. 30, No. 6, February, 1984, p. 82.*

Alcohol: Drink or Drug? (1974)

Emphasizing the detrimental effects of this potentially addictive drug, Hyde offers a sweeping survey of alcohol and alcoholism. Covered are: a brief history of the substance; its physiological effects; the production of and differences among beer, wine, and distilled spirits; drinking and driving; predisposition toward alcoholism; and organizations to help alcoholics and their families. Hyde's prose is frequently cumbersome and occasionally flawed by obvious remarks. However, there are no comparable books for the age group, and those for older readers—Ayers and Milgrams' superficial *The Teenager and Alcohol* (Richards Rosen, 1970) and Cain's preachy *Young People and Drinking: the Use and Abuse of Beverage Alcohols* (John Day, 1963)—are not reliable sources. Despite its deficiencies, Hyde's objective treatment is needed, especially since ". . . some estimates indicate that one of every 15 young people will become an alcoholic."

Leah Deland Stenson, in a review of "Alcohol: Drink or Drug?" in School Library Journal, *Vol. 21, No. 1, September, 1974, p. 85.*

Although alcohol and alcoholism are usually discussed in books about drugs, few give as much information as is contained in this detailed and objective survey. There is no moralizing; in the several chapters on alcoholism, the author describes the damaging effects of abuse, the problems of the alcoholic, and the dangers of behavior—while drunk—that are aggravated by false confidence that is drug-induced. There are, however, suggestions for storage of beer and discriminating amongst wines in the separate chapters on those forms of alcoholic drink, since the text takes no stand upon drinking and points out that many people drink lightly with no ill effect. A sensible and moderate book, marred only by the close-set type; a fairly lengthy list of suggestions for additional reading and an index are appended.

Zena Sutherland, in a review of "Alcohol: Drink or Drug?" in Bulletin of the Center for Children's Books, *Vol. 28, No. 3, November, 1974, p. 44.*

Hotline! (1974)

An introduction to telephone hotlines, which serve as sources of information, solace, help with crises or long-term problems, or referral for more help. Hyde discusses the proliferation during the late '60's and early '70's of volunteer-run hotlines, often arising out of drug abuse or suicide prevention programs. She describes types of hotlines; how calls are handled; how hotline staffs are trained; and how to organize and fund a hotline. There is an extensive "National Directory of Hotline Services" arranged by state and city; however, hotlines are born and die so frequently that any list is always out of date. A good starting point for YA's working on hotlines as well as those who need to make calls.

> *Dolores King, in a review of "Hotline," in* School Library Journal, *Vol. 21, No. 8, April, 1975, p. 76.*

[*The following excerpt is a review of the revised edition published in 1976.*]

The revision in this edition is substantial in some sections of the book, and several chapters have been added, including one on hotlines for runaways (followed by a list of runaway centers, divided by states). As before, a general discussion of hotlines—how they began, how they operate—precedes separate chapters on hotlines for different needs, such as drug help, rape crisis, suicide, etc. Some sources of help are cited within the text, but full information is given in the appendices: a bibliography, an index, a national directory of hotline services, a directory of child protection hotlines, and a list of newsletters and publications. Case histories and examples of telephone conversations are included in a book that is objective, informative, and well organized.

> *Zena Sutherland, in a review of "Hotline!" in* Bulletin of the Center for Children's Books, *Vol. 30, No. 4, December, 1976, p. 58.*

Know Your Feelings (with Elizabeth Held Forsyth, 1975)

This is less the advice book that the second person title would indicate than a slack sort of introduction to the psychology of emotions—namely anger, aggression, love, fear, happiness and depression. In a typical objective YA overview, the chapter on different types and definitions of aggression says an inconsequential little about the work of a lot of people—Robert Jay Lifton, Erich Fromm, Louis Leakey, Freud, Adler, Dr. Harlow of the Madison monkeys, Lorenz, Jane Goodall and Jose Delgado—leading nowhere except to some lame and impractical concluding suggestions for reducing violence. ("Instead of living in large, impersonal cities, it might help if people could live in smaller communities.") The chapter on love (surely not a basic reaction like anger or fear) is even flabbier, full of non-sequiturs and generalizations on the order of "Some describe sex as a raw quantity of energy, while love accepts the faults of the loved one without being blind to them." Elsewhere we're informed that happiness comes from within, not from amusement or material goods, and when advice is offered it's not much help. (Though phobias are described as irrational and beyond the control of reason even when recognized, a person with a mother-condi-

tioned fear of thunder is told to "consult your local weatherman or your librarian about the small percentage of people who are killed by lightning.") Ending up with a catalog of methods for "changing awareness"—concentrate on deep breathing or on a mantra such as Om; look into biofeedback—this may impress some for its coverage, but surely the days when a mushy rehash is considered good enough for YA's are over. (pp. 129-30)

> *A review of "Know Your Feelings," in* Kirkus Reviews *Vol. XLIII, No. 3, February 1, 1975, pp. 129-30.*

The word "feelings" is overworked today. Feelings are hard to understand and very often confusing, yet all life's decisions are based on them. Every individual is unique and complex.

Know Your Feelings . . . is a book which tries to help individuals explore their feelings and to determine the sources of anxiety, love, depression, anger, and fear. This is one of the few books at the young adult level which could help them explore and understand their own feelings and learn how to live life more fully. The information is authentic: the author has written many science-related books; the co-author is a child psychiatrist.

Know Your Feelings can be used as supplementary material in science, social studies, social problems, and health. An index and a list of books for further reading are included. A very readable and "down to earth" presentation of a complex subject.

> *Sister Mary Columba, in a review of "Know Your Feelings," in* Best Sellers, *Vol. 35, No. 4, July, 1975, p. 97.*

In attempting to discuss man's basic emotions and explain them for young people, ***Know Your Feelings*** fails to be more than an unexceptional survey, a rather boring coverage of a potentially exciting subject. Among the feelings included are: anger, aggression, love, fear, happiness, sadness, and depression. Each is defined insofar as it can be; scientific research into it is mentioned; and situations where it arises are discussed, unfortunately in an overly obvious, uninteresting way. Psychological terms are frequently used without sufficient explanation; clichés do nothing to add to the undistinguished writing style. One chapter devoted to changing awareness attempts to interest readers in meditation and biofeedback, but it, too, fails to explore the potential of its topic.

> *Sonia Brotman, in a review of "Know Your Feelings," in* Appraisal: Children's Science Books, *Vol. 8, No. 3, Fall, 1975, p. 17.*

Speak Out on Rape! (1976)

As usual Hyde has done a good deal of research and very little in the way of organization or analysis. Conclusions are even scarcer, though that might be only prudent here where she repeatedly refers to the inconclusiveness of research to date. Feminist assertions that rape is an outgrowth of our sexist society and that much preventive advice restricts women's rightful freedom are mentioned without endorsement or rejection; and unlike Brownmiller's more polemical *Against Our Will* (1975), which asserts that rapists are motivated by power needs and that victims should fight back, Hyde leaves both questions open and compiles no profile of the typical attacker, though she devotes chapters to indiscriminately reviewing different theories and viewpoints on both. (The one characteristic, she reports, which seems to ward off attack is an air of confidence.) Hyde does emphasize the severe emotional damage suffered by victims and the common ignorance or callousness toward such feelings on the part of medical and legal professionals. Here the NOW task force and other women's groups can be supportive, and Hyde lists a number which provided her with help and material. Her stated purpose is to alert young women to the prevalence of the problem and the sources of help; to that end, despite its shortcomings, **Speak Out On Rape!** must be counted a first step worth taking.

> *A review of "Speak Out on Rape!" in* Kirkus Reviews, *Vol. XLIV, No. 4, February 15, 1976, p. 207.*

Comprehensive research into what is known about the topic, good organization, and an excellent bibliography outweigh the frequently awkward writing and occasionally sloppy scholarship (Hyde refers to one article as "recent" without supplying a date when, in fact, it was published in 1960). Everything young people might want to find out about this subject is covered, and further references and resources supplied. Competent coverage on an important topic neglected until now.

> *Joan Scherer Brewer, in a review of "Speak Out on Rape!" in* School Library Journal, *Vol. 22, No. 8, April, 1976, p. 90.*

Hyde examines what is and is not known about rape, hoping to "encourage understanding, both of the need for research and for action." Unlike some current feminist writers, Hyde does not treat rape as a political action or as class warfare between the sexes; rather she treats it as a violent crime of assault assuming epidemic proportions and involving all of society. The author examines some of the myths concerning rapists and their victims (i.e., that women generally provoke rape), reasons why many rapes are never reported, medical and psychological needs of the victim and the antiquated but changing legal procedures wherein the victim often becomes the criminal defending her honor and rapist more often than not is set free. Many questions are raised but few are answered, primarily because so little is known—a point the author continually stresses. Some recent and current research efforts are described, but the book is seriously flawed by the lack of adequate references. (Either studies are referred to anonymously or, where attributed by name, the reference is absent.) Hyde urges a change in the attitude of police and medical personnel toward victims and the need for supportive therapy, hot lines and rape crisis centers. Michigan's recently revised model rape law is printed in an appendix and discussed in the text. Finally, suggested methods of protection against and prevention of rape are reviewed along with examples and consideration of opposing viewpoints on resistance.

> *Rhoda E. Taylor, in a review of "Speak Out on Rape!" in* Science Books & Films, *Vol. XII, No. 3, December, 1976, p. 133.*

Juvenile Justice and Injustice (1977)

A prolific author of books for young people reviews the quality of American juvenile justice and its response to increasing youth crime. Punctuating her discussion with sample case studies, Hyde surveys the early history of the current system; describes punishment inconsistencies, some stemming from confusion about the meaning of the term delinquency itself; looks at the system's reaction to female delinquents and youth gangs; and paints a grim picture of problems juveniles face in courts overburdened by less serious, status offenders (runaways, truants, etc.) and plagued by insufficient staff and rising costs. A look at some current state and federal efforts to improve matters completes a thought-provoking, realistic, ultimately hopeful assessment. Appendices include the text and purpose statement of the 1974 Juvenile Justice and Delinquency Prevention Act and a noteworthy selection of further readings.

> *A review of "Juvenile Justice and Injustice," in* Booklist, *Vol. 74, No. 4, October 15, 1977, p. 368.*

In a detailed discussion of the laws and practices that apply to minors in the United States, Hyde is objective about inadequacies, critical in evaluating programs, and realistic in describing possible solutions. However, the material is not as well organized as it has been in her earlier books, and the solid pages of type, inadequately leaded, are oppressive. The book discusses delinquency, gangs, alternatives to the courts, and abuses and inequities of treatment of juveniles in our legal system and its attendant social programs. A bibliography, an index, and a rather extensive list of resource agencies are provided. (pp. 96-7)

> *Zena Sutherland, in a review of "Juvenile Justice and Injustice," in* Bulletin of the Center for Children's Books, *Vol. 31, No. 6, February, 1978, pp. 96-7.*

[*The following excerpt is a review of the revised edition published in 1983.*]

While this is a well-organized, readable report on aspects of juvenile involvement in the justice system, libraries owning the 1977 edition will not need it as only one chapter, "The Violent Offender," is new. The emotional and complicated influences—societal, economic, judicial, attitudinal—which affect the treatment of juvenile offenders are explored with objectivity. Examples are given of programs which have demonstrated effectiveness in reducing numbers of offenders and of recidivists, including some in which the thrust is diversion from detention and incarceration. Appendixes include lists of other resources, organizations, state agencies; and the text of the national Juvenile Justice Delinquency Prevention Act of 1974.

> *Wanna M. Ernst, in a review of "Juvenile Justice and Injustice," in* School Library Journal, *Vol. 29, No. 10, August, 1983, p. 76.*

Brainwashing and Other Forms of Mind Control (1977)

Like Elizabeth Hall's *From Pigeons to People*, this is a serious discussion of various approaches to behavior shaping; although the two books cover much of the same material,

Hall's focus is psychological and Hyde's is sociological. Both books are excellent, and each author considers sociological and psychological facets; the difference is in emphasis. Hyde discusses religious cults, behavior modification in prisons, and legal precedents as well as theories of behavior shaping, hypnosis, therapy, meditation, and political brainwashing. The text is thoughtful and objective, the writing style straightforward, the topic one that should appeal to a large audience. A bibliography, a glossary, and an index are included.

> *Zena Sutherland, in a review of "Brainwashing and Other Forms of Mind Control," in* Bulletin of the Center for Children's Books, *Vol. 31, No. 3, November, 1977, p. 49.*

An objective, well-researched account of the sociological effects of behavior modification which complements Elizabeth Hall's discussion of the psychological aspects of "be mod" in *From Pigeons to People: a Look at Behavior Shaping* (Houghton, 1975). Hyde discusses the benefits as well as the possible abuses of behavior control, psychosurgery, biofeedback, hypnosis, and commercial mind control courses. The motivation for membership in religious cults and the theory behind brainwashing techniques are explained. The chapter on neuroanatomy suffers from a lack of illustrations but, over all, this provides clear and timely information on an area of psychology that is of particular interest to teens.

> *Paula Hogan, in a review of "Brainwashing and Other Forms of Mind Control," in* School Library Journal, *Vol. 24, No. 7, March, 1978, p. 137.*

Fears and Phobias (1977; revised edition as *Horror, Fright and Panic: Emotions that Affect Our Lives*)

This explores at book length a topic—human fears and phobias and the distinction between the two—which receives general treatment in Hyde and Forsyth's *Know Your Feelings.* Hyde uses good examples drawn from classical research and recent psychoanalytic and behavioral experimentation to discuss common fears (including the fear of death) and to explain fear in terms of its relationship to other emotions and to abnormal behavior. Some knowledge of psychological jargon is helpful but not mandatory to understanding these basic concepts, which are clearly, concisely, and objectively presented here.

> *Cheryl Hillmer, in a review of "Fears and Phobias," in* School Library Journal, *Vol. 24, No. 6, February, 1978, p. 65.*

Hyde has written an informative, quasi-technical dissertation on human fear. While specific clues as to the purpose of the book are notably lacking, I presume the book is offered as a calm overview of the range of common human fear reactions, from mild anxiety to the state of extreme panic, with the implied intention of saying to the reader, "Fear is normal, and help is available for you if you do need it to combat your own particular fear problem." The title does not suggest a self-help book, and the author's presentation seems to be slightly in the academic vein, with a modest amount of footnotes, suggestions for further reading and an index. The print is somewhat oversized,

and the chapters are presented in small, readable segments. . . . The information presented is pertinent to the topic at hand, and is summarized expertly but with numerous intext citations and experimental descriptions and a great deal of "who believes this or that" professional name-dropping. Although the chapter about death and dying was disappointingly bland to me, Chapter 8, "Are Your Fears Different?" is the most valuable in the book.

> *Leonard D. Godwin, in a review of "Fears and Phobias," in* Science Books & Films, *Vol. XIV, No. 3, December, 1978, p. 178.*

[*The following excerpts are reviews of the revised edition published in 1987 and coauthored with Elizabeth H. Forsyth.*]

Directed at young adults, this brief book about common fearful emotions has a potential audience in older readers as well. For example, adult discussion groups might use it as general background, and even therapists and counselors might offer clients a copy as part of an orientation to fear and panic. Well written, informative, and exceptionally well balanced between example and theory, this book whets one's appetite for more information. Unfortunately, only general references for further reading are given, and the primary literature on which the book is based is not cited. Nonetheless, the authors have combined scholarly talents with an ability to communicate. They have synthesized, even homogenized, many diverse sources. The result is a self-help book that does not pander but, rather, skillfully integrates necessary definitions into an absorbing account of fears and how to deal with them.

> *J. F. Campbell, in a review of "Horror, Fright & Panic!: Emotions that Affect Our Lives," in* Science Books & Films, *Vol. 24, No. 1, September/October, 1988, p. 20.*

Fear is an emotional response which occurs in all mammals, and the authors examine how it serves a biological purpose when it does not become exaggerated. However, fear has an adverse reaction on an estimated fifty million Americans who suffer from irrational worries, and according to a recent survey, anxiety accounts for over ten percent of all visits to medical doctors. In the past ten years, anti-anxiety drugs like Valium have been one of the most frequently prescribed drugs in the United States.

This work is a revised edition of *Fears and Phobias,* published in 1977. This revision includes updated information on issues which face a high-tech society, such as nuclear war, AIDS, terrorism, etc. The authors stress that, while the nature of a fear may differ with time, the emotional response in an individual remains about the same.

In addition to fears and anxieties, the authors examine phobias, stress, and ways to overcome these. There is a chapter on death and dying.

Similar to that of the author's others books, the text is clear and augmented by case studies or examples to which young people can relate. Perhaps the original title should not have been changed, for most of the book's contents is centered around fears and anxieties.

Supplementing this book are a glossary, index and bibliography. The majority of the books listed in the bibliography have publication dates within the past ten years.

The authors are well known and respected for their writings for young people in the social sciences. This work upholds the author's reputation for writing good and concise informative books. (pp. 33-4)

> *Jeanette Lambert, in a review of "Horror, Fright and Panic: Emotions That Affect Our Lives," in* Appraisal: Science Books for Young People, *Vol. 21, No. 4, Fall, 1988, pp. 33-4.*

At one time or another every child has felt the emotions associated with fear, and children are often keenly interested in knowing about fright and fears. For the teacher or parent who wants to read an introductory book on the general topic of fear, this book is a good place to start. It deals with a large number of fear-related topics, and does so in an informative, yet low-key manner.

Emphasis is upon a rational, intelligent understanding of the topic rather than sensationalism or theatrics. . . .

A skillful teacher or parent could probably use this book to open up the topic of fear through guided discussions with young people. Topics such as death, stress, and anxiety are presented in a context which encourages rational thought about subjects so often avoided or treated irrationally.

This is a first rate acquisition for any home or school library, and should be made available to the interested, juvenile reader. Merely reading a book of this quality could be of use to juvenile readers who are looking for a reliable, authoritative discussion of fears and emotions.

> *Clarence C. Truesdell, in a review of "Horror, Fright and Panic: Emotions That Affect Our Lives," in* Appraisal: Science Books for Young People, *Vol. 21, No. 4, Fall, 1988, p. 34.*

Addictions: Gambling, Smoking, Cocaine Use, and Others (1978)

Taking a broad definition of addiction, Hyde presents a well-researched, across-the-board treatment that includes cigarettes, gambling, food (over- and under-indulging), caffeine, cocaine and amphetamines, alcohol, barbiturates, and heroin. For each she provides up-to-date information on the characteristics of an addict, scientific research, and other aspects pertinent to the individual problem. She also explores the marijuana controversy, noting that addiction is apparently one of the less important issues and reporting on research into physical and psychological effects. She concludes with a look at positive addiction—jogging, cycling, and meditation used as mental strengthening. Concise, well-organized, and non-preachy. Sources of further information and suggestions for further reading appended.

> *A review of "Addictions: Gambling, Smoking, Cocaine Use, and Others," in* Booklist, *Vol. 75, No. 1, September 1, 1978, p. 39.*

Is addiction a matter of chemistry, social learning, or a basic human deficiency? This has been a question of concern and a matter of controversy for some time. While *Addictions* will not put the problem to rest, it is an excellent introduction to the concept of addictive behavior. Hyde's basic premise is that cigarette smoking, compulsive gambling, coffee drinking, food intake, and even jogging are similar, and that we should encourage positive addictions while discouraging undesirable ones. The weakness of the book is the inconsistent content, with some chapters more complete than others which are quite superficial. For example, alcohol, barbiturates, and tranquilizers are treated in one chapter. There is also a lack of documentation. Many resources, including interviews and research studies, are cited, but it would be impossible to locate them without any bibliographic material. The text is relatively short but the writing generally easy to follow. It is certainly suitable for high school audiences and valuable toward initiating discussion. (pp. 11-12)

> *Paul Leung, in a review of "Addictions: Gambling, Smoking, Cocaine Use, and Others," in* Science Books & Films, *Vol. XV, No. 1, May, 1979, pp. 11-12.*

Suicide: The Hidden Epidemic (with Elizabeth Held Forsyth, 1978)

A helpful selection of additional readings and a state-by-state listing of suicide-prevention/crisis-intervention centers back up a solid examination of one of the major causes of death in America—suicide. Emphasizing the complex, controversial nature of their subject, the collaborators . . . discuss the misconceptions surrounding it, describe suicidal patterns, simplify principal causation theories, and explain some of the psychological factors that may motivate the act. Broader in scope than Klagsbrun's *Too Young to Die: Youth and Suicide,* Hyde and Forsyth's treatment still singles out teenage suicide for special attention in a separate chapter, while sections on suicide notes, interpretation of statistics, and clues for identifying a person who needs aid extend the coverage further. Although much information is given, occasional convoluted explanations and some oblique examples make this a demanding introduction.

> *A review of "Suicide: The Hidden Epidemic," in* Booklist, *Vol. 75, No. 4, October 15, 1978, p. 368.*

This is a very clear, matter-of-fact yet sensitive approach to a timely subject. Suicide is one of the ten major causes of death in the United States, and one of the three leading causes of death for people in their late teens and early twenties. Margaret Hyde, an experienced and responsible science writer, is joined by Elizabeth Held Forsyth, a psychiatrist. Their account is low key but very serious in tone, concise but not superficial. Finding an excellent balance, their treatment is both thorough and practical, covering psychological theories and patterns of suicides and giving specific advice for detecting potential suicides and responding in a helpful and appropriate way. Myths about suicide are explained; the possible causes are explored. A list of suicide prevention centers arranged by state is included, as well as a list for further reading. The clarity and excellent organization of the text are highlighted and reinforced by the layout and the use of bold faced type to accent topics and chapter headings. This is aimed at the same audience as that of *Too Young to Die* by Klagsbrun (Houghton, 1976), but this covers a wider scope, and contains so much accessible information that it is highly recommended for school and public libraries.

Christine McDonnell, in a review of "Suicide: The Hidden Epidemic," in Appraisal: Children's Science Books, *Vol. 12, No. 2, Spring, 1979, p. 28.*

A thorough, well-written, well-organized, well-documented account of the theories about suicide, and the patterns of thought that characterize the suicidal person. It is made clear, at the outset, that reading or talking about suicide does not cause one to commit suicide. In fact, it is the premise of this detailed book, that understanding the suicidal mind may help to prevent attempted suicides. Ten chapters containing case history illustrations and diagnostic clues guide the reader to understand the psychological profiles of suicidal persons, the attitudes that promote suicidal behavior, statistics and research findings. An excellent selection of suggested readings is included, along with a comprehensive listing of State Suicide Prevention/Crisis Intervention Centers throughout the U.S. The book is as important for teachers to read as it may be to the adolescents needing such help. (pp. 28-9)

Robert J. Stein, in a review of "Suicide: The Hidden Epidemic," in Appraisal: Children's Science Books, *Vol. 12, No. 2, Spring, 1979, pp. 28-9.*

[The following excerpt is a review of the revised edition published in 1986.]

Suicide: The Hidden Epidemic emphasizes straightforward information. An update of a 1978 publication, it is a collaborative effort from a practiced writing team—Margaret O. Hyde, author of more than 50 juvenile/young adult titles on social and medical issues, and child psychiatrist Elizabeth Forsyth.

Theories advanced to account for suicidal behavior, attitudes toward taking one's life that have evolved over time, and common motivational factors—loss, genetic predisposition, environmental stress, depressive illness—are considered in lucid, concisely written chapters with well-identified subsections that should be a boon to students who want ready access to facts.

Fallacious statements and outright myths ("people who talk about suicide don't take their lives" or "December has the highest rate of suicides") are debunked, and particular problems adolescents may have that can underlie self-destructive behavior are brought to the fore. A discussion of suicide notes is also included.

As is usual in treatments authored or coauthored by Hyde, brief information of a practical nature is incorporated; in this case, it is a chapter discussing suicide danger signals and advice on how to approach someone in the throes of a suicidal crisis. No documentation has been furnished, but a state-by-state listing of suicide prevention/crisis centers and a suggested list of titles and audiovisuals are appended.

Stephanie Zvirin, "The YA Connection: Suicide and Youth," in Booklist, *Vol. 83, No. 7, December 1, 1986, p. 566.*

Know about Alcohol (1978)

More and more heavy drinkers are people under twenty; more and more accidents that are fatal and are caused by drinking have people under twenty as victims; the number of children who are drinking is increasing. Hyde does not preach; she explains why people drink, why they are affected in different ways and at different rates. She describes the effects of alcohol on the body and suggests some ways in which alcoholics can be identified, and she gives information about organizations that help alcoholics. One chapter poses problems and gives multiple choice answers for questions of personal decision such as what to do if one is a baby sitter and a drunken parent offers a ride home, or if there is an alcoholic in the family and one wants to help. Straightforward in style, the book gives no unusual information, but it covers many aspects of the problem and it is written with clarity and objectivity. A list of places to obtain further information, a reading list, and an index are appended. (pp. 119-20)

Zena Sutherland, in a review of "Know about Alcohol," in Bulletin of the Center for Children's Books, *Vol. 32, No. 7, March, 1979, pp. 119-20.*

Alcohol's use, abuse and effects on the body are discussed in this introduction for intermediate grade students. The author emphasizes her feeling that knowing the facts about alcohol (if they are presented in an unbiased manner) will help young people to make intelligent decisions; a section of hypothetical situations involving young people and alcohol is included, along with discussions of possible ways to handle them. There are many good titles currently available on the subject. The Silversteins' *Alcoholism* (Lippincott, 1975) is a much fuller treatment and Judith Seixas' *Alcohol—What It Is, What It Does* (Greenwillow, 1977) presents the same material—for a slightly younger audience—more succinctly, but Hyde's book is still a good choice.

Kathryn Weisman, in a review of "Know about Alcohol," in School Library Journal, *Vol. 25, No. 7, March, 1979, p. 140.*

Everyone's Trash Problem: Nuclear Wastes (with Bruce G. Hyde, 1979)

As the title suggests, nuclear waste disposal is everyone's problem. While the future of nuclear power is being hotly debated, it is important that every citizen be as informed as possible about the issue. Unfortunately, information about the disposal of radioactive wastes has been highly technical and difficult to evaluate. The authors have done an outstanding job of stripping away the mystery and technical jargon to explain the essence of the problem, why it exists and what can be done about it. Without trying to bias the reader either for or against nuclear power, the authors simply provide the basic education needed to intelligently discuss the issue so that readers can investigate further and make up their own minds. The book contains an excellent glossary that will help readers better understand the terminology used in the literature today. In addition, there is a comprehensive index, sources of further information and suggestions for additional reading. This book would make excellent collateral reading for any high school or adult education program dealing with current sociotechnological issues.

> *Floyd D. Jury, in a review of "Everyone's Trash Problem: Nuclear Wastes," in* Science Books & Films, *Vol. XV, No. 4, March, 1980, p. 217.*

My Friend Wants to Run Away (1979)

This carefully written book for junior and senior high school students could be helpful to college students and general audiences as well. It would serve as an excellent basis for discussion for health, home economics and psychology classes. Hyde uses case histories of runaways, which add to the book's appeal and enhances reader interest. Her approach to problems is practical and realistic, and she has a good grasp of contemporary issues in the adolescent underground and the socially disorganized family. Her tone is hopeful and she suggests that there is more than one way to deal with a seemingly impossible problem. My only criticism is of one history in which a runaway girl's class is informed that she has been sexually molested. I assume that she would have a very difficult time attending this class and school if she returned to her family. On the whole, however, the book is highly recommended.

> *Michael Beck, in a review of "My Friend Wants to Run Away," in* Science Books & Films, *Vol. XV, No. 5, May, 1980, p. 274.*

The vocabulary in [this] book is aimed at the middle elementary grades but the examples of sexual abuse are more appropriate to an older age group. The chapter subheadings—"Cathy Ran in Fear," "Jennie: Alone and Pregnant," "Marci Had a Funny Uncle," and "Bob Ran Away to Have More Fun"—are suggestive of slick magazines. In most instances the solutions are too pat. Readers are introduced to Cathy, Marci and company in the first chapter and then must hunt for their stories in later chapters. . . . Unless Hyde is needed for high/low readers, [Arnold Madison's *Runaway Teens*] is better.

> *Joan L. Dobson, in a review of "My Friend Wants to Run Away," in* School Library Journal, *Vol. 27, No. 2, October, 1980, p. 156.*

Cry Softly! The Story of Child Abuse (1980)

Cry Softly! discusses child abuse, with definitions of physical, emotional and sexual abuse, chapters on victims and perpetrators and summaries of the relevant history of attitudes toward and treatment of children. There are separate chapters on children of long ago, yesterday's England and America. Emphasis on the teaching of parenting and the encouragement of parent-infant bonding are offered as possible directions for prevention. Saying that child abuse hurts everyone, as statistics show that today's abused child may well become tomorrow's criminal, Hyde encourages any young person to take action when child abuse is suspected. There is information on hot lines, social agencies and Parents Anonymous, with addresses to write to for more information. With child abuse reaching epidemic proportions, this problem of course cannot be overstated,

and *Cry Softly!* is an acceptable introduction. However, Dolan's *Child Abuse* (Watts, 1980) is a more extensive treatment of the same material.

> *Linda Rombough, in a review of "Cry Softly!: The Story of Child Abuse," in* School Library Journal, *Vol. 27, No. 6, February, 1981, p. 75.*

This oversimplified description of child abuse and child abusers, historical and current, can be useful to a teacher who suspects that a child is being hurt at home but who cannot get the child to discuss her or his situation.

The book will make clear to a child that child abuse is common among all socio-economic groups, that parents can be taught to stop abusing children (there are groups involved in such counseling), and that children can also approach such organizations and reach help. . . .

Since abused children are rarely trusting enough to step forward and confide in a teacher, this book may help open the conversational door.

> *Lyla Hoffman, in a review of "Cry Softly! The Story of Child Abuse," in* Interracial Books for Children Bulletin, *Vol. 12, Nos. 4 & 5, 1981, p. 38.*

[*The following excerpt is a review of the revised edition published in 1986.*]

In her revision of the 1980 title, Hyde discusses the various forms of abuse—physical (including neglect), sexual, and emotional—and provides non-sensational examples of each. She includes stress and parental kidnapping as newer forms of child abuse. Three chapters are devoted to an extensive history of child abuse. The final two chapters discuss what young adults and adults can do to prevent child abuse. Hyde's "Suggestions for Further Reading," which includes both fiction and nonfiction, is one of the best lists available. This edition is more specific than the original title, with newer statistics, more examples, and a longer list of helping agencies. Elaine Landau's *Child Abuse* (Messner, 1985) is written for the same age group and contains much of the same information in a similar format. The major difference is that while Landau discusses adolescent abuse, the runaway, and suicidal reactions, she does not cover the history of child abuse. Both are excellent report books and smooth reading for browsers. *Cry Softly!* is especially appropriate for teens who are interested in community involvement, since Hyde recommends several ways in which individuals can help prevent child abuse.

> *Karen Radtke, in a review of "Cry Softly!: The Story of Child Abuse," in* School Library Journal, *Vol. 33, No. 1, September, 1986, p. 136.*

Energy: The New Look (1981)

Some people will be tempted to dismiss Margaret Hyde's book as just another one on energy. This is unwise; she has done an unusually balanced job of describing advantages and problems for a fairly large number of possible energy sources, without revealing herself as either strongly against or frenziedly for any of them (unless her omission of all but a few passing words about nuclear fission should be interpreted that way). She mentions the resulting pollution and the difficulties in supply of wood as well as its renewability; the problems with mining, transportation, and the "greenhouse" effect of coal, along with its plenty; the huge investments required by solar and wind power, along with their "free" supply. I was a little uneasy about her phrasing at one point: In the hydrogen chapter she says that "at the present" it takes more energy to separate the element from its compounds than it yields when burned as fuel. Since the chief source compound is water, which is also the product of burning, there is no hope whatever that this fact will be changed in the future unless the first law of thermodynamics proves to be wrong; in that case all bets would be off, and we might as well start trying perpetual motion machines. We would have to start physics all over from the proverbial square one. With list of energy information hotlines, bibliography, and index. (pp. 458-59)

> *Harry C. Stubbs, in a review of "Energy: The New Look," in* The Horn Book Magazine, *Vol. LVII, No. 4, August, 1981, pp. 458-49.*

Hyde provides a good background primer to introduce the lay reader to the energy issue. She explores topics such as new fuels from plants, harnessing the wind, energy from hydrogen and synthetic fuel from coal. The material is presented in a clear, literary style and in very simple terms. The end of the text contains titles for further reading and the appendix includes telephone numbers of energy "hotline" services. The chapter on energy conservation is of special interest because it contains practical information on how to conserve energy, raising such questions as, Are unused areas heated, cooled or lighted needlessly? Does more insulation save heat? Although the book is relatively short, it is a good beginning for those interested in and concerned about future energy sources.

> *Robert Messina, in a review of "Energy: The New Look," in* Science Books & Films, *Vol. 17, No. 1, September/October, 1981, p. 25.*

My Friend Has Four Parents (1981)

With her customary brisk efficiency and sympathetic perception, Hyde discusses and advises on some of the problems that arise for children who must adjust to stepfamilies; single-parent homes; divorce, with the several custody arrangements that may obtain; and the growing phenomenon of parental kidnapping. She describes the ways in which children react to these problems, using many fictional examples, and suggests ways of helping oneself or getting help if adjustment seems difficult or impossible. A useful, sensible book closes with an index, a divided bibliography, and a list that includes both organizations readers may wish to join and sources from which they may get helpful information or actual counseling.

> *Zena Sutherland, in a review of "My Friend Has Four Parents," in* Bulletin of the Center for Children's Books, *Vol. 35, No. 6, February, 1982, p. 109.*

This boring book about divorce, which meanders through the issues of separation, loss and family reconstruction, will not appeal to its intended audience.

The author tries to present every aspect of divorce, including parental irresponsibility, manipulation of children and rivalry with the new parent, but this is done superficially. At no time are kids allowed to speak directly for themselves. Children of divorce are presented as cases, and the reader gets no sense of the emotions involved.

In several instances, the book raises issues that are potentially scarey to children from divorced families—sexual abuse, kidnapping, custody fights—and leaves these issues unresolved. For example, the author advises children who are sexually abused by stepfathers to "discuss it with your own parent." This is not an easy thing for a child to do!

On occasion, the language suggests a subtly negative judgment of divorced families, implying that there are "normal" roles in nuclear families, that there are "natural" parents, and that divorce is "bad luck." The economic and emotional struggles of single parents are not validated, and there is no mention of the growing number of parents who, after marriage, discover that they are lesbian or gay.

The book reads like an article on "How Divorce Affects Children" in a psychology journal. When I gave it to a twelve-year-old friend whose parents had separated, she left it unfinished, stating, "It's dull . . . just facts. It says things like a robot. I want to know how kids *feel*." I agree. A far better book on divorce, written by seventh and eighth graders, is *The Kids' Book of Divorce* available from Stephen Greene Press. . . .

> *Jan M. Goodman, in a review of "My Friend Has Four Parents," in* Interracial Books for Children Bulletin, *Vol. 14, No. 6, 1983, p. 20.*

Computers That Think? The Search for Artificial Intelligence (1982; revised edition as Artificial Intelligence: A Revision of Computers That Think?)

Beginning with the question, "Do computers think?" Hyde goes on to explore the intelligence capacities of both computers and robots and looks at them vis à vis the human brain. Also included in her discussion are the ways these intelligent machines do their work, the numerous jobs they now perform, their potential for the public, and the futuristic query that troubles many people—How bright should computers be allowed to become? Because this book looks at artificial intelligence from a less mechanical, more theoretical view than most computer literature, it is a valuable addition to the genre. The numerous black-and-white photographs are exceptionally well reproduced for a book of this kind. Suggested reading list of adult books appended.

> *Ilene Cooper, in a review of "Computers that Think? The Search for Artificial Intelligence," in* Booklist, *Vol. 78, No. 19, June 1, 1982, p. 1313.*

This overview of man's attempts to understand and simulate human intelligence provides interesting speculation into the future of research in this area, its implications and the controversy that surrounds whether computers can "think." . . . The author generally provides clear, concise information, unfortunately assuming at times that readers are familiar with computer terminology. No glossary is included. Of particular value is the history of the development of microcomputers. The illustrations are excellent choices. This timely book will feed the curiosity and imagination of computer "whiz kids."

Marsha Swantko, in a review of "Computers That Think?: The Search for Artificial Intelligence," in School Library Journal, *Vol. 29, No. 2, October, 1982, p. 162.*

[*The following excerpts are reviews of the revised edition published in 1986.*]

A revision of **Computers that Think?,** this book presents an upbeat, optimistic overview for beginners. However, little more than ten per cent of this revision represents new material. A general introduction to AL research with examples of what has been accomplished and varying definitions of *intelligence* as the term applies to automation are included, as are passages on binary processing, the history of computers, robots, equipping computers with sight, speech and hearing, reading comprehension of computers, expert systems, and the debate over human control of computer systems. Most of the revision is accomplished through an essentially new first chapter and new closings for each of the other chapters; most illustrations have been carried over from the original, with fewer than ten new pictures replacing the handful that have been dropped. Although her text is readable, Hyde is too glib in her presentation of AI research and does not explain the problems involved or the potential for failure as well as Dorothy Hinshaw Patent's *The Quest for Artificial Intelligence* (HBJ, 1986). While **Artificial Intelligence** is suitable as a basic introduction to the field, libraries that already own **Computers that Think?** will find the original adequate and will be better off purchasing Patent's book. (pp. 89-90)

Jeffrey A. French, in a review of "Artificial Intelligence," in School Library Journal, *Vol. 33, No. 3, November, 1986, pp. 89-90.*

Margaret Hyde has written a fine overview of the state-of-the-art in artificial intelligence. She begins by defining artificial intelligence and reviewing the history of computing. Questions of importance which Hyde raises include how smart can machines really become, will we ever understand human intelligence, and current scientific thinking is that animals are smarter than humans have previously considered, so can we really judge intelligence other than human? Great detail is provided on the subject of robotics. Hyde describes the speed and efficiency of robots in industrial uses as well as proposed uses in space for exploration or mining the surface of planets. She mentions the replacement of people by robots in a positive nonthreatening way, explaining that the jobs are hazardous to begin with. She also devotes a considerable portion of the book to describing computer technology which aids in medical diagnosis, or reading machines like the Kurzweil Reading Machine which help the blind and physically handicapped. She ends the text with speculation about fifth-generation computers and expert systems. Included are many fine black-and-white photographs illustrating changes in computers throughout the 20th century. My only regret is that I did not have a chance to see the earlier edition, **Computers that Think?,** to compare it with the revision. Hyde is very upbeat, and minimizes any negative questions one might have about the uses of artificial intelligence.

D. R. H., in a review of "Artificial Intelligence," in Appraisal: Science Books for Young People, *Vol. 20, No. 1, Winter, 1987, p. 35.*

Foster Care and Adoption   (1982)

In seven concise chapters, Hyde explores the problem of unwanted children who fall through the holes in our social fabric. Her coverage is occasionally too generalized, especially in the historical background, but the emotional trauma of entering a foster home or, worse, several in a row, is clearly laid out, as are controversies over the advisability of moving children on to strangers' care rather than putting money into preventive support for the biological families. The discussion of adoption mentions the recent practice of surrogate mothers and the issues raised, as well as the need most adopted children have shown to trace their biological roots. While social agencies come in for some documented criticism, the point of view seems fairly balanced. Appended are lists of special-interest groups, agencies that specialize in children with special needs, some agencies that specialize in international adoptions, groups interested in searching for biological parents and for biological children, and books for further reading. A good start for researchers on projects or on their own. (pp. 1525-26)

Betsy Hearne, in a review of "Foster Care and Adoption," in Booklist, *Vol. 78, No. 22, August, 1982, pp. 1525-26.*

The subject of adoption and foster care has seldom had as dull and confusing a treatment as this one, written from an adult point of view and in a style that would have little appeal even at a high-school level. The author asks us to consider the rights and wrongs of several extreme case histories in which agonizing decisions must be made about separating children from their biological parents—issues with much right *and* wrong on both sides. While the jacket describes the book as "drawing heavily on actual case histories," many of them do not ring true—they seem contrived to prove a particular point. There is a good list of sources for further information, bibliography and index, but there are no illustrations, and the solid black cover with chilling white lettering and only a touch of red in a small spiral design is not inviting either. DuPrau's *Adoption: the Facts, Feelings, and Issues of a Double Heritage* (Messner, 1981), which includes information on foster care as well, deals on a more personal level with what it's like to be an adoptee and is much more readable and informative.

Karen Ritter, in a review of "Foster Care and Adoption," in School Library Journal, *Vol. 29, No. 2, October, 1982, p. 162.*

The Rights of the Victim   (1983)

In her usual briskly informative style, Hyde discusses the plight, role, and rights of victims of violent crime, noting that attitudes towards victims are changing. Though she includes a brief historical review, her focus is on the present day as she examines such aspects of the problem as the reasons blame is often placed on victims and the feelings of victims themselves, before addressing ways in which individuals as well as social and government programs can help victims of crime. Her concluding chapter gives advice on how to reduce the risk of becoming a victim. An introductory account that is especially valuable for its appended matter, which includes suggestions for further reading, sources of additional information, a directory of offices of state crime victim compensation, a glossary, and an index.

> *Sally Estes, in a review of "The Rights of the Victim," in* Booklist, *Vol. 79, No. 14, March 15, 1983, p. 955.*

Because the American system of justice is oriented toward the rights of the accused, government has traditionally taken little recognition of the welfare of the victim, and little responsibility for victims. Statistics from the Bureau of Justice show that murder occurs in our country at the rate of one every 24 minutes; rape, one every 7 minutes; home burglary every 10 seconds, etc. There are, therefore, thousands of victims; the processes of litigation and imprisonment cost taxpayers millions. Who helps the victim? Can those victimized help themselves? Is there anything one can do to avert victimization? Hyde discusses the historical relationship of the criminal to victims, gives some answers to the questions posed here, and describes some of the growing number of programs that have been instituted on behalf of victims of crimes. The crisp and informative text should be useful because of the facts it gives about what help is available and what precautions one can take in specific circumstances.

> *Zena Sutherland, in a review of "The Rights of the Victim," in* Bulletin of the Center for Children's Books, *Vol. 36, No. 8, April, 1983, p. 151.*

Know about Smoking (1983)

Because it's so much harder to stop smoking than to resist starting, Hyde encourages 9 to 12 year olds to stay in the nonsmoking majority. Reiterating that smoking is on the decline overall, her tone is positive, providing nonsmokers with real answers to peer pressure from friends who are hooked. Like earlier books on the evils of tobacco (*To Smoke or Not to Smoke* [Lothrop, 1969] by Terry and Horn; *Smoking and You* [Messner, 1977] by Madison; *Tobacco: What It Is, What It Does* [Greenwillow, 1981] by Seixas), Hyde includes the history of consumption, research on risks, misleading advertising. Unlike the others, she adds role-playing situations in which children can learn how to refuse a cigarette or to ask someone nearby to quit in their presence. (pp. 73-4)

> *Symme J. Benoff, in a review of "Know about Smoking," in* School Library Journal, *Vol. 30, No. 6, February, 1984, pp. 73-4.*

Hyde's goal is to inform young people about the hazards of smoking. She uses role-playing dialogue throughout the text to effectively teach kids how to resist peer pressure. Some of the health hazards that Hyde mentions include the build-up of carbon monoxide in the blood stream, effects on the unborn child, and emphysema. She also mentions that smoking doubles the risk of heart attack and is connected to more than 80 percent of lung cancer deaths. The social problems related to smoking are also covered, including bad breath, smelly clothing, reduced athletic

stamina, stained teeth, and environmental pollution. (The American Lung Association has found that a burning cigarette releases more harmful particles than the smoke that is inhaled.) A 1982 survey showed that the percentage of high-school seniors who smoke had dropped from 29 to 20 in the previous four years. Only about 25 percent of the population smokes, and two-thirds would like to stop, despite the fact that half of the billboards in this country advertise cigarettes. This is a well-written . . . book that is designed to convince kids not to smoke. It ends by suggesting various avenues of help for the person who has already started.

> *Bernice D. Lyon, in a review of "Know about Smoking," in* Science Books & Films, *Vol. 20, No. 3, February, 1985, p. 156.*

Is This Kid "Crazy"? Understanding Unusual Behavior (1983)

Most psychology books for this age group fall in two categories: self-help books for the stresses of teenage years or textbook descriptions of the varieties of mental functioning. In an innovative departure from the mold, Hyde presents brief sketches that illustrate behavior termed *crazy* and deals with people's reactions to it. Dictionary descriptions of hyperactivity, autism, schizophrenia, depression, anorexia nervosa/bulimia and general emotional disturbances come to life in dramatic vignettes of typical behavior under these conditions. Hyde describes the experiences of the mentally ill, the feelings of their friends and family and current scientific knowledge and treatment. Most notable are the steady reminders that the mentally ill are not to be feared, hated or shunned, but understood. This book's greatest strength is its plea for humanitarian values. (pp. 124-25)

> *Nancy J. Horner, in a review of "Is This Kid 'Crazy'?: Understanding Unusual Behavior," in* School Library Journal, *Vol. 30, No. 8, April, 1984, pp. 124-25.*

Good-natured, logical discussion of the possible causes, symptoms and remedies of several mental health problems that affect young people. . . . In adolescence especially, being considered "normal" is extremely important. Hyde gives many plausible reasons for behavior that children and teens might consider weird or strange. A list of mental health terms, a bibliography and a list of adolescent clinics in the United States and Canada are also included at the book's conclusion. My one complaint is that CIP data states the volume is indexed; it is not. Although the table of contents is reasonably clear, an index should definitely have been included. Otherwise, this is a low-key, conversational introduction to various mental health disorders.

> *Debbie Earl, in a review of "Is This Kid 'Crazy'? Understanding Unusual Behavior," in* Voice of Youth Advocates, *Vol. 7, No. 2, June, 1984, p. 110.*

Sexual Abuse: Let's Talk About It (1984)

There's not much here to qualify this as a "science book," but it a superior piece of work all the same! The more squeamish among us might like to brush it aside as one more trendy but repellent topic, and some might even object to it as "unsuitable" for a children's collection, but a wise children's or YA librarian will buy multiple copies and display them casually but openly. Such a book can do a world of good even if it never gets checked out: it is likely in fact to be one of those "let's giggle over this in the back of the stacks" items, picked up by children with morbid curiosities, or by those hoping to be titillated.

It is not either morbid or titillating, however—the message of abuse cited are carefully worded and circumspect, but the message is repeated over and over again that children "have rights to the privacy of the parts of their bodies that are covered by bathing suits," and that they can and should say "Don't do that!" to parents, trusted adults, older siblings, strangers, or anyone else who might violate that privacy. Children of all ages need to hear this message.

Listings of child sexual abuse treatment centers, community support organizations, resource centers make this a valuable tool for teens, parents, and library reference staffers. Highly recommended.

> *Susanne S. Sullivan, in a review of "Sexual Abuse: Let's Talk About It," in* Appraisal: Science Books for Young People, *Vol. 17, No. 3, Fall, 1984, p. 26.*

Here's a straight-forward, honest, and sensitive approach to a problem that directly affects at least one out of every ten children in the United States today. Will talking about sexual abuse frighten children? Not if it is done in a gentle and understanding way, asserts Ms. Hyde, the book's author. Since sexual abuse sometimes occurs in infancy, education should begin early. Parents can teach their children about sexual abuse in much the same way as they teach about fire safety, traffic safety, and other safety precautions. Child psychiatrists agree with Ms. Hyde that sexual abuse needs to be discussed. The author's treatment of the subject is timely and right on target. (p. 26)

Through anecdotes and actual case studies, the author explains the different forms of sexual abuse, including incest, and gives healthy ways to deal with the problem. Young adults will relate well to her approach; parents and teachers can borrow the anecdotes in discussing the topic (playing "what if") with young children. The author repeats several important messages throughout the text which will help victims of sexual abuse to overcome their feelings of guilt and shame. "You are not alone in your problem . . . It is not your fault . . . Do not keep it a secret—get help, etc."

The book has no illustrations, but does include a short bibliography, a list of child sexual abuse treatment centers (by state), sources of more information, and a list of regional child abuse centers. The bibliography gives materials for both elementary and secondary students. A book list for parents is needed and should include *No More Secrets* and *The Silent Children*. Despite this omission, the book is still a tremendous resource for young adults, parents, and teachers. Every school library should have at least one copy. (p. 27)

> *Martha T. Kane, in a review of "Sexual Abuse: Let's Talk About It," in* Appraisal: Science Books for Young People, *Vol. 17, No. 3, Fall, 1984, pp. 26-7.*

At times, Hyde seems to be talking to parents more than children, but any child reading the book will not find this an obstacle. This book is an essential addition to collections serving young people, as it contains important material in an informative but non-threatening way that has been previously unavailable to children. Hyde has the delicate touch necessary to unmask a monstrous problem and help the child victims deal with it. Let's hope it gets into the hands of those who need it.

> *Mary Lynn Copan, in a review of "Sexual Abuse: Let's Talk About It," in* School Library Journal, *Vol. 31, No. 3, November, 1984, p. 132.*

[*The following excerpt is a review of the revised edition published in 1987.*]

Although the text and internal statistics remain largely unchanged from the 1984 edition, Hyde has added some new information to what was one of the earliest (and still most accessible) teenage treatments of sexual abuse. The predominant alteration is the addition of a section recognizing boys as victims of abuse, presented as a kind of parallel to the chapter entitled "Binny's Story," which focuses on a young girl. Using the experiences of a teenager named Bob (whose story Hyde admits may not be typical), the author explains how sex role stereotypes add an extra burden to young male victims. Also new in this edition are Hyde's consideration of the controversial use of closed-circuit television and videotaped testimony in trials and her description of Marvel Comics' new *Amazing Spider-man and Power Pack* that has been used so successfully to teach young people about sexual abuse. The bibliography shows some change as well. No documentation; index.

> *Stephanie Zvirin, in a review of "Sexual Abuse: Let's Talk About It," in* Booklist, *Vol. 84, No. 12, February 15, 1988, p. 990.*

Cloning and the New Genetics (with Lawrence E. Hyde, 1984)

The book was decidedly worth writing; the word *clone* has recently suffered a lot of mistreatment, and its real meanings and possibilities badly need clarification. The book *In His Image: The Cloning of a Man* by David M. Rorvik, which probably caused more misunderstanding on this subject among uncritical readers than anything else in recent years, was published as fact; of course, it is not. It is now widely regarded as science fiction, which I don't consider a very valid description, either; but I will accept responsibility for helping to straighten matters out by highly recommending *Cloning and the New Genetics.*

Early in the book, the authors not only explain carefully just what a clone is but make very clear just how natural the cloning process is with many organisms and how human beings have been using it in agriculture for centuries. They make clear that this use is not an unnatural intrusion on the prerogatives of the Almighty; it would be more fair to describe it as acceptance of the responsibility incurred by acquiring knowledge. (One wonders whether the objection some people express to research is based on their fear of the likelihood of increased human responsibility.) The greater part of the book explains in fair detail how such processes as gene splicing and recombinant DNA manipulation are carried out and the uses to which such techniques can be put. The authors do specify some of the possible dangers, which seem to me a small price to pay for the potential benefits. I have never yet called a book required reading, except for the classes I teach, but I feel very much like saying that everyone should read this one before accepting adult responsibilities in a democracy. You don't, of course, have to share my views—but read the book before you reject them. With glossary, bibliography, and index. (pp. 787-88)

> Harry C. Stubbs, in a review of "Cloning and the New Genetics," in The Horn Book Magazine, Vol. LX, No. 6, November-December, 1984, pp. 787-88.

Cloning and the New Genetics is a good book about cloning and genetic engineering. There are far better books on the subject, but this one provides an overview which is essentially nontechnical and, consequently, makes the subject accessible to a wide audience. The writing flows well, and the book is largely in the style of newspaper or magazine reporting written for the average reader, but not especially for the young reader.

One of the outstanding features which makes this book particularly instructive for the young reader, however, is the author's fairly consistent use of the names of scientists who are associated with various types of research. Readers are given names of scientists, as well as where they are actually doing their research. This pattern of reporting lends a sense of immediacy to the writing, and tends to engage the thoughtful reader. Young readers should soon learn that scientific knowledge is the result of a great deal of research conducted by real people, who are also scientists. I believe this to be an important feature of this book. Young readers should find this a useful book because of the factual material presented. They will find the book interesting because of the writing and coordinated illustrations. Diagrams and photographs add considerably, and help explicate complex concepts. More careful editing could have caught the blooper on page 43. A photograph of a computer and CRT is used to illustrate the text which describes a gene synthesizer. This is one of the few instances where text and illustrations fail to reinforce each other.

Chapter eight comes to grips with the inevitable issue of human clones. One can easily visualize heated classroom discussions over this chapter, which fairly thoroughly considers the issues raised by its title: "Cloning A Man?" Ethical questions are brought up, as are many of the commonly-believed fallacies relating to human clones. A very good book about a complex, timely subject of great importance. Well worth having in the school library.

> Clarence C. Truesdell, in a review of "Cloning and the New Genetics," in Appraisal: Science Books for Young People, Vol. 18, No. 2, Spring, 1985, p. 23.

[This] book cannot be recommended because it contains serious errors of fact: in chapter one, after correctly defining a clone and pointing out that all organisms in a clone contain the same genetic material (p. 13), the authors in-

correctly equate parthenogenesis with cloning; they consider the progeny of a clutch of unfertilized fish or reptile eggs to be a clone (pp. 17-20)! Since cloning is the main subject of this book, such an error is inexcusable. There are other misconceptions and ambiguities, such as "the armadillo, a mammal, reproduces asexually routinely" (p. 18). There is a misleading description of the manufacture of human growth hormone (p. 62) and faulty definitions of nuclear transplantation and of tissue culture (in the glossary). After a description of embryo transplants in cattle and humans, the authors mention that "people often confuse this technique with cloning" (p. 22). True, and this book is likely to add to their confusion.

> I. J. Lorch, in a review of "Cloning and the New Genetics," in Science Books & Films, Vol. 21, No. 1, September / October, 1985, p. 23.

Missing Children   (with Lawrence E. Hyde, 1985)

With the aid of a coauthor, a frequent contributor of books on important social concerns turns her attention to missing children—a problem she indicates has reached epidemic proportions in the U.S. today. Dividing these children into three categories—runaways; youngsters abducted for purposes of sexual exploitation, black market adoption, etc.; and individuals kidnapped by one of their own parents, usually as a consequence of a marital break-up—the authors sketch the nature of each kind of "missing" and explore the effects on both the young person and the parents involved. Careful not to sensationalize, they incorporate numerous real-life cases (Adam Walsh, Etan Patz) and look at measures currently being taken to locate the lost and aid the runaway, describing several activist groups and listing some 50 additional organizations, agencies, and hot lines in an appended section. A concisely written text that presents information as it raises awareness. Illustrated with black-and-white photographs. Suggested readings and an index are appended.

> Stephanie Zvirin, in a review of "Missing Children," in Booklist, Vol. 82, No. 4, October 15, 1985, p. 325.

Cancer in the Young: A Sense of Hope   (with Lawrence E. Hyde, 1985)

This book is factual and clearly written, but it is unclear for whom it is intended, and no introduction is offered to clarify this point. The book describes much of the progress made in the medical treatment of childhood cancer and carries a properly hopeful tone. However, major relevant texts are not cited, and the general area of behavioral medicine and psychosocial aspects of pediatric oncology are slighted—a serious offense in 1985. For example, mention is made of bone marrow aspirations and lumbar punctures as painful procedures that children with cancer must undergo, but the impressive work on hypnosis, relaxation training, and other behavioral techniques of pain reduction is not cited; neither is the concept of multidisciplinary psychosocial care dealt with. The book is inappropriate for most pediatric cancer patients, who tend to be young children, and adolescents cannot be expected to wade through 96 pages to get to the few bits of information that concern them. The book might be suited for parent education except that it covers information already dealt with in other books and pamphlets and, once again, the parent of a child with leukemia would do better to read a pamphlet on leukemia than peruse a book that contains much irrelevant information. In sum, this is a book without a substantial audience that rehashes information already well covered elsewhere. The authors themselves may be aware of the lack of audience, as the back cover first talks about cancer in general, stating that someone in the reader's family may suffer from it. This is misleading, of course, for although adult cancer is common, pediatric cancer is extremely rare—a fact cited in the next paragraph.

Jonathan S. Kellerman, in a review of "Cancer in the Young: A Sense of Hope," in Science Books & Films, *Vol. 21, No. 4, March / April, 1986, p. 219.*

The Hydes have written a book that handles an emotional subject—cancer in children—in a simple and direct way. Although childhood cancer is really very rare (only 3-4 of 100,000 die each year), its coverage in the media has exposed many more children and their families to the reality of the disease's effects, as well as to the myths and phobias surrounding the word "cancer." The book presents honest answers to frequent questions children ask: Is cancer contagious? Will everyone who has cancer die? Can it be cured? Will I get it? The book includes facts about the disease, its forms and possible treatments. Short stories about real cancer patients help develop awareness of the upsets and emotional traumas, as well as the raw courage, of children with cancer. It is an excellent resource for families who may know someone with cancer, or may be facing the disease themselves. It is a reassuring overview of a serious health problem; but treated in a positive way, and filled with hope. Cancer patients, whether young or old, need support from friends and families. The stories in this book, the facts presented clearly—all help to dispel the fear generated by misconceptions. They show children that they needn't be afraid, just be a friend. There are extended chapters on newsletters and resources allowing children to share their feelings with other patients. There are also chapters on camps and other fun for young cancer patients. The end sections of the book include a glossary of cancer / medical terms, a list of suggested readings by grade level, further information sources on organizations and centers that help families of cancer patients, an annotated listing of nationwide camps, and an index. (pp. 29-30)

Beverley Mattei, in a review of "Cancer in the Young—A Sense of Hope," in Appraisal: Science Books for Young People, *Vol. 19, No. 2, Spring, 1986, pp. 29-30.*

The Hydes have written a wonderful book about nearly every aspect of cancer in children. The book provides information about almost every question on this topic that one might ask. The scientific presentation is up-to-date, accurate, and complete. . . .

My only concern is that the book may not be suitable for younger children, those for whom it might have had the most direct appeal and interest. No photographs, illustra-

tions, or visual materials of any kind interrupt the text. Also, the reading level seems high to me. The authors explain every scientific concept carefully, but do so without pulling any punches with their terminology. In their apparent efforts to be completely clear and honest with their readers, they sometimes have a tendency to tell more than the younger reader may be able to comprehend.

I find it difficult to fault such a courageous, sincere, serious effort dealing with this important subject. I have little doubt that the book will be a great success with parents, educators, and more sophisticated younger readers. Still, I wish that the editors had found a way to make the work more accessible and more appealing to the very large number of other young readers who do not fall into these categories.

David E. Newton, in a review of "Cancer in the Young—A Sense of Hope," in Appraisal: Science Books for Young People, *Vol. 19, No. 2, Spring, 1986, p. 30.*

AIDS: What Does It Mean to You? (with Elizabeth H. Forsyth, 1986)

This nifty little book has nine short chapters, each of which is interesting and some of which contain more scientific information than others. It could be used by students from junior high school up. It contains very little technical information, making the book unsuitable as a high school biology text. Even though the book has a 1986 copyright, by the last half of 1986, many new developments in AIDS research and treatment had occurred that are not in the book. For instance, it is now known that people with ARC (AIDS-related complex) stand a 10 percent chance every year of developing full-blown AIDS. Second, a new drug, AZT (azidothymidine), has been shown to improve the symptoms and possibly the immune dysfunction of AIDS patients; it was released in October 1986 for use on a specific subgroup of patients. Amid these hopeful developments, spread of the disease is continuing, and heterosexual transmission has been identified, which is altering sexual behavior probably forever. Violence is being directed against homosexual men in certain parts of the country because of an increase in AIDS anxiety or what the book calls the "epidemic of fear." Yet the basic messages here are valid, and the book is a good introduction to the subject. A chapter on plagues of the past is concise and informative and gives a good historical perspective. The final chapter, "Battling the Spread of AIDS," demonstrates the number of agencies involved worldwide in the fight against this unusual virus. . . . [The] book will be a lifetime reminder of how we viewed a landmark disease at its inception.

Joseph F. John, in a review of "AIDS: What Does It Mean to You?" in Science Books & Films, *Vol. 22, No. 4, March / April, 1987, p. 234.*

This is a problematic book, one which might have been labelled satisfactory if it were all that were available on this pressing topic, but which pales so dramatically beside the Silversteins' *AIDS: Deadly Threat* that I don't want to recommend it. Hyde chooses to emphasize the "mystery", misinformation, and the public distrust of medical authorities regarding this frightening epidemic, but simply does not have the medical expertise that could (and should!) lay those fears to rest.

It seems odd, for example, to talk about "How is AIDS spread" before offering any background on immune systems or the nature of viruses. It seems more odd to discuss the spread of AIDS with only one brief mention of anal intercourse. (Note that the term does not appear in either the index or the glossary. Is this timidity or irresponsibility?) It seems sensational and superfluous to include a chapter on the horrors of past plagues.

Hyde offers repeated qualifications about what "seems" or "may" be known about AIDS. She labels "hysteria" the fears about sharing swimming pools, public restrooms, and school classes with AIDS victims, but then quotes "experts" who recommend extra chlorination in swimming pools used by homosexuals, and chlorine bleach solutions to be used in cleaning public facilities. She then follows the whole discussion with the warning that " 'No case has been documented' which is not as comforting as 'This could never happen'."

There is but one six-page chapter with any real medical information and that is sketchy and superficial. The glossary is taken from the Congressional Office of Technology Assessment and will be difficult reading for most students. There is no bibliography.

Overall this book is more likely to spread suspicion and misunderstanding than to clarify the issue, and librarians would do better to buy multiple copies of the new Silverstein book and leave this one behind. (pp. 32-3)

> *Susanne S. Sullivan, in a review of "AIDS: What Does It Mean to You?"* Appraisal: Science Books for Young People, *Vol. 20, No. 2, Spring, 1987, pp. 32-3.*

What a great joy to find *two* highly commendable books on AIDS in a single review session. Like the Silversteins' book on this topic, the Hyde and Forsyth text is a masterly treatment of a difficult and profoundly important issue in health sciences.

In comparison with the Silversteins' book, the Hyde and Forsyth text is somewhat more oriented toward the personal issues of the disease. This is not to say that a careful, accurate discussion of the medical aspects of the disease is omitted. The reader will be able to learn all the technical information that he or she might want or need from this book.

But the authors do a really outstanding job of showing how, above all, AIDS is a personal tragedy for those who contract it and those whose lives are touched by it. The chapters entitled "Living with AIDS" and "Michael Callen: A Personal Report" carry statements that are as moving as anything I've seen in the general press. The two chapters are, by themselves, worth the price of the book . . . which is a must for your shelves in any case.

> *David E. Newton, in a review of "AIDS: What Does It Mean to You?" in* Appraisal: Science Books for Young People, *Vol. 20, No. 2, Spring, 1987, p. 33.*

[The following excerpts are reviews of the revised edition published in 1987.]

A revision of the 1986 title is a testament both to the rapidity with which new information about AIDS has been garnered and to the responsible competence of the authors. The revision has been careful and thorough, with a more logical arrangement of chapters, revision and updating of material within chapters, and infusion of information based on new research findings and records. Most of the changes are in the introductory chapter and in the chapter on "Medical Progress." As in the first book, the authors maintain a calm tone and a scientific attitude. Appended are a glossary, an index, a list of groups offering AIDS information and support, and—a new feature—a copy of the Surgeon General's report on AIDS.

> *Zena Sutherland, in a review of "AIDS: What Does It Mean to You?" in* Bulletin of the Center for Children's Books, *Vol. 40, No. 10, June, 1987, p. 190.*

About 20% of Hyde and Forsyth's 1986 title has been revised, and the updated book includes reports and statistics from late 1986, including the Surgeon General's Report on AIDS and the report of the National Academy of Sciences. Michael Callen's heartbreaking 1983 account of the plight of an AIDS victim is repeated, with an encouraging 1986 report that he is alive and helping others through the National Association of People With AIDS. Late research on HTLV-IV is reported. While this updating is effective, the prose still suffers from many qualifiers and too much use of the passive voice, making the reading lackluster and harder to follow than necessary. Charts and maps are not always placed with the corresponding text. Glossary, index, list of AIDS hotlines, and support groups are appended. Sexual knowledge is assumed, and terms such as "anal intercourse" are not in the glossary or index. The Silversteins' *AIDS: Deadly Threat* (Enslow, 1986) is better written, but is outdated by this revision. (pp. 95-6)

> *Anne Osborn, in a review of "AIDS: What Does It Mean to You?" in* School Library Journal, *Vol. 33, No. 11, August, 1987, pp. 95-6.*

Terrorism: A Special Kind of Violence (with **Elizabeth H. Forsyth, 1987**)

"The bottom line is that terrorism works and there's no end in sight."

Though more Americans die each year in their bathtubs, or trying to cross the street, terrorist attacks have had a disproportionate effect on international tourism and many other economic activities. The authors paint a gloomy picture; often backed by national governments, terrorists have built bureaucracies, established training schools, even organized formal conferences. Terrorism has become an integral part of some cultures, passed on from parent to child. Forsyth, a forensic psychiatrist, presents a psychological portrait of the typical terrorist, and also discusses the variety of ways hostages respond to terrorist kidnapping. Anti-terrorist activities are only sketched; new techniques and equipment receive very brief mention, and "counterterrorism" as an occupation is not discussed.

Recent examples, and a bibliography full of new titles, make this potentially useful as an update for more thoroughgoing studies such as Harris' *The New Terrorism* (Messner, 1983).

> *A review of "Terrorism: A Special Kind of Violence," in* Kirkus Reviews, *Vol. LV, No. 3, February 1, 1987, p. 230.*

A whirlwind view of world terrorism from a U.S. perspective. Informative and sure to spark reactions, this book tries to establish a historic perspective for the use of random force. Trying to unravel a very complex topic, the authors describe well-known terrorists such as Carlos and the mercenary nature of their activities. Much emphasis in this account is placed on the Arab-Israeli conflict as a source for terrorist activity. The explanation is clear, and the misunderstanding and disagreement that further blur the Islamic world to Westerners is demystified and explained skillfully and concisely. Perhaps the most interesting part of the book is the section that deals with the victims of terrorist kidnapping and the psychological difficulties that they face. While the book does pose the question of whether terrorism can ever be justified, there is no doubt that the authors condemn it under all circumstances and see it as a threat to the Western world in particular and civilization in general. This is a timely and concise overview. . . .

> *Steve Matthews, in a review of "Terrorism: A Special Kind of Violence," in* School Library Journal, *Vol. 33, No. 8, May, 1987, p. 112.*

Terrorism is a frightening, violent and escalating problem that seems to fascinate as well as repel us. Teenagers, who live in this world of increasing violence, are attracted by the drama of terrorist acts and by the fact that many terrorists are under 20. In this short book, Hyde, . . . and psychiatrist Forsyth explore several different aspects of terrorism. The authors use many very current examples, such as the *Achille-Lauro* incident and even the alleged arms-for-hostages deal with Iran to illustrate their points.

The book begins with chapters defining and classifying terrorism and tracing its history back to Robespierre, 19th century revolutionary Russian, and the Boxers in China. The discussion of young terrorists reveals distressing facts about Irish and Middle Eastern teens, indoctrinated by bitter adults, who are innocently anxious to die for "the Cause." . . .

Two interesting chapters concern the psychology of the terrorist and the psychological interplay between terrorists and their hostages. Both are illustrated with current examples. The controversy over terrorism's coverage by the media is also a concern. How much should the news media reveal and when? Are they interfering with rescues, giving terrorists wanted publicity? Do they incite further terrorism? The last chapter goes over several ideas for preventing and combating terrorism, thus rounding out a thought-provoking probe into this strange and violent world. There is a good list of further reading and an extensive index. Though some YAs may be confused by the many foreign names and numerous incidents cited, the basic information is clear and to-the-point. This is a worthwhile addition.

> *Paula J. Lacey, in a review of "Terrorism: A*

> *Special Kind of Violence," in* Voice of Youth Advocates, *Vol. 10, No. 5, December, 1987, p. 250.*

Know about AIDS (with Elizabeth H. Forsyth, 1987)

Technically defined, this book is propaganda. It tries repeatedly and in different contexts to promote life-saving "safe sex" and to encourage compassionate but self-protective behavior toward AIDS patients. No effort is made to place avoidance of AIDS within any larger context of sexual values; the implicit assumption is that most readers already engage or soon will in promiscuous sexual intercourse. Current knowledge about AIDS is correctly presented. The technical problems of making and using an AIDS vaccine are well summarized. The problem of AIDS in Africa is also discussed. Although I recommend this book, I have a few problems with it. The authors refer to "safe sex," but the term is missing from the index, although "condom" appears with one entry where it is defined as a "protective sheath." Also, the vocabulary ("immune deficiency," "mobilizing defense systems") is too difficult for the average child of eight or for the poor reader of 12, the ages for which the book claims to be targeted. In addition, there are fewer than 50 pages of text, and the illustrations [by Debora Weber] contribute little except to show persons of different ages, sexes, and ethnicity—evidently for reader identification. Finally, the cover picture shows two figures sharing confidences and possibly handling a needle, although the drawing is so poorly done it's hard to tell. Fighting the epidemic, not the sufferers, is the authors' plea. "No one is invulnerable" is their message. How to persuade young people who feel omnipotent is another matter.

> *Joanna D. Denko, in a review of "Know About AIDS," in* Science Books & Films, *Vol. 23, No. 5, May / June, 1987, p. 302.*

Hyde and Forsyth, authors of *AIDS: What Does It Mean to You?* for teens, here attempt—with marginal success—to reassure younger children that their risks of exposure to the virus are slight, and to have compassion for people with AIDS. They include no sexual information at all, so that when references are made to the use of condoms for "safe sex," young readers will have no internal reference point. The writing is choppy and repetitious. The authors do explain why it is taking so long to develop a vaccine and argue effectively against mandatory testing, exclusion of AIDS victims from schools, and quarantine. One chapter, a fictionalized case study of a family who takes a child with AIDS into their home, confuses with contradictory messages. While the parents stress that there is no risk of contracting AIDS by casual contact, their actions say just the opposite. "Just to be safe," they do not allow clothing or food to be shared, and the child is not permitted to swim in the family pool, promoting serious misconceptions. The bibliography is an odd assortment of nonfiction relating to blood, immunities, and drugs and fiction dealing with death, homosexuality, and hemophilia. (pp. 108-09)

> *Anne Osborn, in a review of "Know about AIDS," in* School Library Journal, *Vol. 34, No. 3, November, 1987, pp. 108-09.*

AIDS education for middle-grade children which is so general and vague that young readers may not glean enough information to safeguard themselves. In addition, the author's tone may well offend homosexuals, blacks, Hispanics and the poor. The young reader in search of accurate, timely, nonjudgmental information will be better served by Silversteins' *AIDS: Deadly Threat.*

Hyde cautions, "Some groups of people behave in ways that expose others to AIDS," and writes, "AIDS seems to be spread by behavior that is unacceptable to many people . . . Many people have strong negative feelings about [homosexuals] and may call them names such as 'faggot,' 'queer,' or 'fairy'." True perhaps, but not very useful. In another section, Hyde relates: "In 1987 more than 70 percent of the cases of women with AIDS occurred among blacks and Hispanics. There are more poor people and intravenous drug users . . . in these groups than in the general population . . . Stopping the spread of AIDS among people who care more about getting food and / or drugs each day than about their future health is very difficult." . . . Suggestions for further reading are dated and list only one title (also by Hyde!) on the topic of AIDS.

> *A review of "Know About AIDS," in* Kirkus Reviews, *Vol. VI, No. 22, November 15, 1987, p. 1629.*

Teen Sex   (1988)

Hyde's point of view becomes clear from the outset of this book: sex is not bad (the opposite, in fact), but lack of information or responsibility about sex "can mean bad things." Because there are literally millions of teenage parents, the issue is worth exploring. In this slim but informational volume are discussions about the historical influences on our attitudes, analysis of mixed messages, reasons teens have sex and discussion of birth control, pregnancy options and sexually transmitted diseases. Perhaps most telling is Hyde's matter-of-fact listing of ways in which uninformed people try to prevent pregnancy, including standing during intercourse or jumping up and down afterward.

> *A review of "Teen Sex," in* Publishers Weekly, *Vol. 233, No. 20, May 20, 1988, p. 94.*

A discussion emphasizing the problems of teenage pregnancy and the danger of contracting AIDS, this book also includes a useful academic approach to the sexuality of young people today. The history of sexual mores, examples of sexual dilemmas, and practical advice on being responsible make up an appreciable part of *Teen Sex.* Plain, if sometimes awkward writing gets its message across. It will be useful as a source of information for term papers, and for its up-to-date discussion of AIDS. However, many of the books in the bibliography are outdated because they do not discuss AIDS. *Changing Bodies, Changing Lives* (Random, 1988) covers some of the same material for a slightly older age range. (pp. 206, 208)

> *Ann Scarpellino, in a review of "Teen Sex," in* School Library Journal, *Vol. 35, No. 1, September, 1988, pp. 206, 208.*

Alcohol: Uses and Abuses   (1988)

Hyde describes the medical and social problems that alcohol causes alcoholics and the community in which they live, based on reputable statistics and studies. Using hypothetical cases and simulated situations, she equips readers with information on how to get help for the alcoholic, how to get help for themselves as children of alcoholics, and how to act in social situations, emphasizing that sometimes there are no right answers and that not all stories have a happy ending. Appendixes include a list of telephone numbers of organizations that help alcoholics; telephone numbers of Al-Anon / Alateen in the United States, Canada, the United Kingdom and Ireland; a bibliography of both fiction and nonfiction titles; a glossary; and an index. A few black-and-white photographs, diagrams, and cartoon drawings decorate the text. A *Sixpack and a Fake I.D.* (M. Evans, 1986) by Susan and Daniel Cohen talks more personably and directly about the problems of teenage drinking. *Living with a Parent Who Drinks Too Much* (Greenwillow, 1979) by Judith Seixas does not discuss the community problems or provide the historical background that Hyde does. Hyde, while not completely detached, speaks less emotionally and deals equally with being a child of an alcoholic and with teenage drinking.

> *Martha Gordon, in a review of "Alcohol: Uses and Abuses," in* School Library Journal, *Vol. 35, No. 1, September, 1988, p. 206.*

The Homeless: Profiling the Problem   (1989)

The subject of the homeless in this land of plenty has loomed large as a national disgrace. Hyde offers here a basic introduction which defines the problem and suggests solutions. First, dispelling the myth that most homeless people choose to be homeless, Hyde outlines the horrid conditions of living without shelter. Lack of good medical care, poor diet, and exposure to the elements prove to be overwhelming obstacles to a person without the most basic need, a home. The homeless are often mentally ill or teenage runaways. Yet an increasing number of families, and thus children, have no place to call home. Suggested solutions include the construction of more low-cost housing, better screening of mental patients before release, and increased involvement of community volunteers. This is a simple and accessible book which provides a number of brief but heartrending examples to demonstrate the personal dimensions of the problem. This volume would be good to use with Elaine Landau's more emotional *The Homeless* (Messner, 1987). The black-and-white photos are evocative but not essential. The "How to Give or Get Help" section is quite useful.

> *Steve Matthews, in a review of "The Homeless: Profiling the Problem," in* School Library Journal, *Vol. 35, No. 9, May, 1989, p. 130.*

This brief book profiles the problem of the homeless in urban America, mainly in New York City. Numerous cases illustrate the many dimensions of homelessness. The author describes the homeless as victims of domestic violence, single men and women of all ages unable to afford housing, families with children unable to afford housing, deinstitutionalized mentally ill, alcohol and drug users, runaways, and throwaways. These cases encourage young readers to empathize with the homeless. The author's solution to the problem is volunteers who are committed to helping these unfortunate people. Several significant attempts to service the homeless are presented in a final chapter as are the addresses of agencies and services young people can contact. While no one can fault the motives of citizens trying to help their brothers and sisters after they become homeless, the question of preventing homelessness is not addressed. The massive social and political changes required to provide all children with appropriate and meaningful education and skills to help prevent joblessness and homelessness are ignored in this book. The dramatic redistribution of wealth through taxation and development of social programs common to other countries, such as Sweden, are not mentioned. In the present political climate in the United States, gentle kindness comes from volunteers, when what is needed as well is serious political change to prevent homelessness.

> *David L. Ellison, in a review of "The Homeless: Profiling the Problem," in* Science Books & Films, *Vol. 24, No. 5, May / June, 1989, p. 297.*

Meeting Death   (with Lawrence E. Hyde, 1989)

This slim volume is yet another title on the death education bandwagon. The Hydes have written a disappointingly simplistic text replete with generalizations, faulty logic, and loaded phrases (e.g., "playing G-d" in reference to artificial life support systems). The chapters do not flow smoothly and placement of certain information is not logical, such as inclusion of a definition of death in a chapter unrelated to the topic.

The authors contend that death education enables people to deal with death rationally. Yet in this volume they mix the rational (stages of dying, transplants) with irrelevant folklore (ghosts and superstitions). The requisite information on death is included, but not in an organized or interesting manner, except for the resources lists at the end of the text. We have come to expect better writing from these authors and need not settle for less.

> *Frances Ruth Weinstein, in a review of "Meeting Death," in* Voice of Youth Advocates, *Vol. 12, No. 4, October, 1989, p. 235.*

Drug Wars   (1990)

Has the drug scene in America changed? Hyde says yes, and she describes the new violence and despair that widespread use of crank and crack have brought to the U.S. She gives a sane and well-focused overview of the major problem drugs, a history of the war against each, and some tough decisions that must be made to control their use. In the first chapter on cocaine and its derivatives, the focus is on the ready availability of crack and the havoc it has caused. In subsequent chapters on heroin, marijuana, alcohol, and cigarettes, Hyde reviews the possible effects of the drug, and explains what has been done to discourage or stop its use. Perhaps the most important discussion comes in the final two chapters, which portray the difficulty of winning a war against mind-altering substances. Hyde explores many solutions: sealing U.S. borders, destroying all domestic production, prosecuting users, and legalization. It is clear, by the book's end, that drug abuse is not a new phenomenon and that solving the current violent turn will not be easy. No discussion of hallucinogens is included other than in the "Controlled Substances-Uses and Effects" chart at the end.

> *Steve Matthews, in a review of "Drug Wars," in* School Library Journal, *Vol. 36, No. 6, June, 1990, p. 141.*

Diana Wynne Jones

1934-

English author of fiction, short stories, and plays, and editor.

Major works include *Eight Days of Luke* (1975), *Charmed Life* (1977), *Dogsbody* (1977), and *The Homeward Bounders* (1981).

Praised as an especially original writer of distinctive, sophisticated fantasies for readers in the middle grades through high school, Jones is a prolific author acclaimed for creating inventive, insightful, and powerful books which blend realism with the supernatural and serious themes with high comedy. Compared favorably with E. Nesbit and Joan Aiken, she is the writer of such popular works as *Dogsbody* (1975), the story of how Sirius the Dog Star redeems himself when he is sent to earth as a real dog after being falsely accused of murder, *The Homeward Bounders* (1981), a novel set in nineteenth-century England which describes how thirteen-year-old Jamie becomes caught in a sinister wargame involving mysterious superhumans and alternate worlds, and two series, the Dalemark and Chrestomanci cycles. The first of these series, a trilogy which outlines the history and prehistory of a fictitious medieval country beset by civil war, includes *Cart and Cwidder* (1975), *Drowned Ammet* (1977), and *The Spellcoats* (1979), while the second, a quartet comprised of *Charmed Life* (1977), *The Magicians of Caprona* (1980), *Witch Week* (1982), and *The Lives of Christopher Chant* (1988), is set both in mythical Europe and in present-day England and describes a world where magic is legalized under the guardianship of the enigmatic necromancer Chrestomanci.

Characteristically incorporating mythological and fairy-tale themes, motifs, and characters in her works as well as elements taken from science fiction and the political and romance novel, Jones uses the reactions of her protagonists to magical events to reveal their giftedness and inner strength. Her main characters, often displaced, unhappy boys and girls whose parents or guardians are either absent or hostile, learn to cope with their problems through their encounters with the extraordinary and discover their own identities in the process. Besides her exploration of the relationship between children and adults, Jones addresses such issues as the use and misuse of power, the nature of time, the struggle between good and evil, and the importance of loyalty, courage, and compassion. Although her works contain situations involving horror, tragedy, and death, Jones balances her inclusion of these instances with humor, wit, literary jokes, and slapstick action, elements noted for underscoring the characteristic exuberance and charm of her books. In addition to her novels, Jones has written fantasies for primary graders and several plays for children; she has also written and edited collections of short stories for older readers and is the author of an adult novel. Critic Marcus Crouch has written, "Among the post-war generation of children's writers none is more individual and more unpredictable than Diana Wynne Jones." Jones was commended for the Car-

negie Medal in 1975 for *Dogsbody* and in 1977 for *Charmed Life,* a work for which she won the Guardian Award in 1978; she was also commended for the latter in 1977 for *Power of Three. Archer's Song* was named a *Boston Globe-Horn Book* Award honor book in 1984, a designation received by *Howl's Moving Castle* in 1986.

(See also *Contemporary Literary Criticism,* Vol. 26; *Something about the Author,* Vol. 9; *Something about the Author Autobiography Series,* Vol. 7; *Contemporary Authors New Revision Series,* Vol. 26; and *Contemporary Authors,* Vols. 49-52.)

AUTHOR'S COMMENTARY

From my window I can see a steep stretch of woodland, which is really the garden of a big terrace of flats. I have watched it for five years now. It is full of children who appear to be mad. A group of girls totter down the slope. Each is wearing a skirt of her mother's and holding a home-made crown on to her head. Every so often, they all stop and shake hands. Further along, another group of girls wander among the bushes. Some bushes seem to terrify them. They clutch one another and scream. But they seem quite unaware of the bush beside them where three boys are crouching, armed with guns, and do not even look when one boy throws up both arms and dies. The girls in crowns seem equally unaware of four other boys struggling on their bellies up the gentle slope towards them. These boys seem to be in the last stages of exhaustion. One of the four dies as the girls pass and the others roll back down the slope. The rest of the wood is full of similar groups. They are there day after day, tirelessly and all apparently insane.

Of course we all know at once that each group is playing a different game of *'Let's Pretend'*. But anyone who watches this wood, or anywhere else where children habitually play, will quite soon notice a number of things, all of which ought to have great importance for anyone who is interested in writing for children.

The first thing is how *often* children play these kind of games. It seems to be something they need to do. You can see they need to because they are all so happy. That second group of girls is only pretending to be frightened. None of the groups are quarrelling or crying—only screaming, dying and ignoring one another. The next most important fact is that the children are all in groups. . . . Acting out a *'Let's Pretend'* [seems] to be a social act. I am sure that it is when I see how sexist the various games are. None of these children seem to have heard of Women's Lib. The girls say *'Let's pretend we're all queens,'* and the boys, *'Pretend we're soldiers'*—and though I haven't a notion why the other girls are screaming at bushes, they are not playing with the boys. It really does seem as if *'Let's Pretend'* games are children's way of practising being a girl or a boy—as they see it—as well as learning how to behave in a group.

You can see this is true when a quarrel breaks out. All the quarrels in the wood happen—with someone in tears and someone else bleating *'I'm not playing!'*—when the children are trying to play a game like hide and seek or building a tree house, which does not involve make-believe. The rules allow both sexes to combine in these games. And it is hopeless. All children under about thirteen are so *bad* at co-operating. I watch them in exasperation, each one running about as if they were the only child there, without the slightest notion of how to get together with the rest. They really do seem to need some sort of *'Let's Pretend'* to make them combine. And the thing which seems to allow them to get together is the thing which makes the games seem so mad to an onlooker: they at once seem to enter a sort of enchanted circle, where they are in control and nothing outside matters.

Now a book is another form of this enchanted circle. Any book, whether realistic or fantasy, is a self-contained world with the reader in control (if you do not like the game the writer is playing, you can always stop reading). My feeling is that children get most from books which work along the same lines as they do—in other words, by *'Let's Pretend'*. I am not saying that a fantasy needs to ape children's games, but I do think it should be like them in a number of important respects. Above all, it should be as exciting and engrossing as the games in the wood. I aim to be as gripped by the book I am writing as I hope any reader will be. I want to know what happens next. If it bores me, I stop. But a book has an additional asset: it seems to be real. If you say a thing is real in a book, then in that book it *is* real. This is splendid, but it can also be

a snare. I find I have to control any fantasy I write by constantly remembering the sort of things children do in their games.

Notice, for instance, that the children in the wood are very wisely not pretending too many things at once. They say *'Pretend we're all queens,'* or *'Pretend we're explorers'*, and part of the point of what follows is to find out what this entails. In the same way, I find it works best to suppose just one thing: *'Pretend you are a ghost'*, or *'Pretend your chemistry set works magic'*, or *'Pretend this dog is the Dog Star'*. Then I go on to explore the implications of this supposition. Quite often, I am totally surprised by the result.

I also bear constantly in mind the fact that pretending is a thing most usefully done in groups. It is done to show you how to get on with one another. When I write a book, it seems useful to extend the group to include both sexes, so that both girls and boys can enjoy it, but I do not find I can completely ignore the one-sex nature of the games in the wood. Oddly enough, this means that if I want a neutral character, not particularly girlish or boyish, I have to use a boy. A neutral girl would strike most girl readers as a tomboy. Otherwise, it is obvious that all other characters in a fantasy ought to be very real and clear and individual, and to interact profoundly—real colourful people, behaving as people do. The three girls, for instance, in *The Time of the Ghost,* strange as they are, are all drawn from life. One of them was me.

The third thing I bear in mind is the peculiar happiness of the children wandering in the wood. They are killing one another, terrifying one another and (as queens) despising one another and everybody else too. And they are loving it. This mixture of nastiness and happiness is typical of most children and makes wonderful opportunities for a writer. Your story can be violent, serious and funny, all at once—indeed I think it *should* be—and the stronger in all three the better. Fantasy can deal with death, malice and violence in the same way that the children in the wood are doing. You make clear that it is make-believe. And by showing it applies to nobody, you show that it applies to everyone. It is the way all fairy tales work.

But when all is said and done, there is an aspect to fantasy which defies description. Those children in the wood are going to grow up and remember that they played there. They will not remember what they were playing or who pretended what. But they will remember the wood, with the big city all round it, in a special, vivid way. It does seem that a fantasy, working out in its own terms, stretching you beyond the normal concerns of your own life, gains you a peculiar charge of energy which inexplicably enriches you. At least, this is my ideal of a fantasy, and I am always trying to write it. (pp. 4-5)

Diana Wynne Jones, "Far Out Fantasy," in Books for Your Children, *Vol. 16, No. 3, Autumn/Winter, 1981, pp. 4-5.*

GENERAL COMMENTARY

Gillian Spraggs

Diana Wynne Jones's children's novel *Cart and Cwidder* is set in an imaginary land somewhat similar to late-mediaeval Europe in its culture and social structure.

Moril, the hero, is the son of a travelling musician. His father, Clennen, who is secretly a freedom fighter, is murdered at the orders of a brutal baron, and Moril inherits his greatest treasure: a big 'cwidder', or lute-like instrument, that has been handed down from a near-legendary ancestor. The original owner of the cwidder has left a reputation as a powerful wizard; gradually Moril discovers how to use the instrument so that he too can perform marvels.

The process of learning to use the cwidder is closely tied to Moril's progress in self-understanding and maturity. (p. 17)

Strong emotion is not enough, nor is a righteous cause; he must learn to use the cwidder with strict integrity and awareness. The end of the book sees Moril continuing his quest for maturity and mastery of the cwidder.

Cart and Cwidder offers the reader a gripping story of magical adventure, with some intriguing and persuasive glimpses of a pastiche-archaic society. It also contains elements of fable: using the central image of the cwidder, Diana Wynne Jones explores ideas about the imagination, especially the imagination of the artist. The artist, after all, is the only true magician: able to translate imaginings, no matter how fantastic, into form by the power of his artistry. But art that is self-indulgent and rejecting of reality is ineffective: it is the flavour of things as they are that convinces, and potent art, no matter how fantastic the subject-matter, is always informed by the artist's grasp on, and emotional responsiveness to, life. Like the magician, but in a less tangible way, the artist has power—power to entrance people's imaginations, move their emotions, alter their perceptions. And like all power, this is liable to misuse: the artist is required to avoid falsity, to be honest in his art, and therefore, primarily, with himself. Closest to the magician of all artists is the fantasist, since there are no limits on his scope—except the limitations of his powers of evocation, his ability to give his creations, in J. R. R. Tolkien's phrase, 'the inner consistency of reality'; and the more fantastic his creations, the greater a challenge this becomes.

Not all of Diana Wynne Jones's extensive output of fantasy novels communicate the texture of reality in the same degree; though all, even the most light-hearted trifles, share in this quality to some extent. *Cart and Cwidder* itself falls a little short in one respect. Towards the end of the book Moril has seen his father murdered, his brother arrested on a capital offence, his mother separated from him by distance and changed loyalties; but though his sense of bereavement is touched on, the reader is never really confronted with a grief proportionate to what has happened to him. In this connexion it is instructive to compare the book with another modern fantasy novel for children, William Mayne's *Earthfasts* (1966), in which experiences of alienation, first of a boy who is torn by magic from his own time, later of another who sees, as he thinks, his best friend's death at his side, are expressed very perceptively and feelingly. However, if Diana Wynne Jones fails in *Cart and Cwidder* to cope fully with the emotional demands of her hero's experiences, she still shows a fine gift for evoking both the humdrum details of family life in a crowded tilt-cart and the wilder manifestations of magical power; and as she is well aware, the detailed realism with which everyday life is delineated greatly fortifies

the conviction carried by the fantastic elements in the story.

It is not to deny its solid virtues to describe *Cart and Cwidder* as a children's fantasy of a fairly conventional kind. However, one of Diana Wynne Jones's most striking qualities as a fantasy writer, which has become more in evidence as her output has grown, is her remarkable inventiveness and her willingness to take risks. She is always ready to gamble on her ability to lend conviction to the wildest idea. This is well illustrated by *The Spellcoats,* in which she returns to the world of *Cart and Cwidder,* this time to a period long before Moril's. To begin with, the story is outwardly a fairly conventional one, a family adventure with serious overtones in an archaic land torn by war: but gradually we discover that the narrator is not writing the story but weaving it into coats, using a convention taught her by her lost mother; we share her discovery that the story-telling coats have magical potency (hence the title), and that she and her brothers and sister are, on their mother's side, more than merely human. This far-fetched tale, in which a young man is turned into a clay image, evil wizards catch the souls of the dead in nets, and the heroine finds out that she has a river for a grandfather, is superbly written, and commands total acceptance by the reader.

Interestingly enough, in view of her unsatisfactory handling of this theme in *Cart and Cwidder,* experiences of displacement and alienation crop up repeatedly in Diana Wynne Jones's writing. In *Dogsbody* the stars and planets are envisaged as governed by spiritual rulers, like the mediaeval Intelligences. The ruler of Sirius, the Dogstar, is overthrown by treachery and finds himself on Earth in the body of a dog desperately attempting to find a lost object of power and clear his name. I must confess to some irritation with the conceptual framework of this book—what glimpses we catch of the behaviour of stars show this as disappointingly similar to the more banal activities of humans—but Sirius's experiences as a dog are vividly imagined and his doomed relationship with the girl who befriends him is movingly portrayed.

In *The Homeward Bounders* Diana Wynne Jones takes the theme of alienation a stage further. In this almost outrageously ingenious story, young Jamie, a lower-middle-class lad from the reign of Queen Victoria, trespasses in the mysterious Old Fort and discovers an appalling secret: the world we know is nothing more than a playing board for a colossal war game, controlled by *Them,* sinister superhuman beings with no check save their own arbitrary rules. As a result of his discovery, he is treated as a discarded playing piece: he is condemned by *Them* to life as a Homeward Bounder, doomed to pass continually through a seemingly endless series of parallel worlds, on each of which a different game is being played. He has been told that if he can get home to his own world then he can 'enter play again in the normal manner'. But when he does return home it is too late—a hundred years too late. His family are dead and he himself to all appearances is slightly younger than his own great-nephew. He will always be a displaced person now. In the end, Jamie finds a way of turning *Their* rules back on *Them* and breaking *Their* hold on the universe: but though he can free others, there is no remedy for his personal tragedy. In this book Diana Wynne Jones allows the heartbreak to emerge and stir the reader; but *The Homeward Bounders* does have a weakness, and this lies in its postulates. *They* are supposed to have established *Their* power over the worlds by draining these of reality and taking it all to *Themselves*. This was done by chaining Prometheus (not actually named in the book) to his rock: since he knows all the worlds but cannot go to them, only remember them, they gradually lose their reality. Jamie alone is able to release Prometheus because after discovering that his own world has effectively vanished, no worlds are real to him any more. This all sounds very impressive, but it is hard not to notice that it relies for its effect on making extremely vague use of difficult abstractions like 'reality'.

It is hard to imagine a state of dislocation more extreme than Jamie's, but Diana Wynne Jones has done so. *The Time of the Ghost* opens with a brilliantly persuasive depiction of the experience of being a disembodied ghost. Moreover, not only is the heroine out of her body, but she could be one of four sisters and she doesn't know which. The ghost and the reader are kept guessing for most of the book, just as they are kept in suspense over the ghost's ultimate fate. The book is something of a *tour de force;* though Diana Wynne Jones is guilty of a measure of sleight of hand in sustaining the uncertainty as to the ghost's identity.

Two of Diana Wynne Jones's most enjoyable books are *Charmed Life* and *Witch Week,* both of which feature the stylish trouble-shooting enchanter Chrestomanci. *Charmed Life* is set in a world parallel to our own; magic is commonplace, and institutes for magical research are funded by the State. Young Cat is a duffer at spells, whereas his elder sister Gwendolen seems exceptionally gifted. But as the story progresses, Cat is forced to recognise that in reality he himself is a powerful natural magician, and that his unprincipled elder sister is making evil use of magic that she draws from him. In this book magic may be seen as a correlative for power. Cat must learn to face up to his sister's lack of care for him and take over responsibility for using his magical potential.

Similar ideas are explored in *Witch Week,* which is again set in a parallel world, this time a rather different one. Again, magic is a generally accepted phenomenon; but in this world the practice of it is proscribed, and to be a witch is to be mercilessly hunted down and burned alive. Class 2Y at Larwood House School, a government boarding school for witch orphans and other problem children, are well aware of the dangers; nevertheless, at least one pupil is plainly indulging in magic. Eventually, after a wickedly funny sequence of mishaps, Class 2Y rescue themselves on the brink of collective immolation and set their world to rights. Once again the right use of power is a crucial issue—discussed more explicitly in this book than in *Charmed Life.* A secondary theme is the sense of personal inadequacy and inability to fit in which breeds that familiar sensation of persecution and exclusion which for most people is especially intense during adolescence. The revelation, towards the end of *Witch Week,* that nearly everyone in this witch-hunting world is secretly a witch, is persuasive and deeply reassuring, as well as comical.

Both these books possess in full measure a quality with which all Diana Wynne Jones's books are generously endowed: humour. This is something which it is hard to communicate adequately in the context of a critical arti-cle: above all else, her books are *fun.* Read them; especially the ones I have mentioned, but also the others. If you have any sympathy for fantasy, and any trace of a sense of humour, you are certain to enjoy them. (pp. 18-22)

> *Gillian Spraggs, "True Dreams: The Fantasy Fiction of Diana Wynne Jones," in* The Use of English, *Vol. 34, No. 3, Summer, 1983, pp. 17-22.*

Fiona Lafferty

Diana Wynne Jones's books overflow with magic, mystery and suspense. They tell of fantastic adventures in this world and in parallel fantasy worlds and portray events in the past, present and future—often simultaneously. Her stories feature witches, wizards and warlocks, ghosts, space-age time travellers, mythological characters and, just very occasionally, ordinary people.

It is perhaps strange then that her passion for such exuberant and rich fantasy sprang from a childhood starved of books. She grew up during the post-war years of austerity when books were scarce, a situation exacerbated by her father, whom she describes as miserly, and who thought he was fulfilling his obligation to provide his three daughters with books by buying a complete set of Arthur Ransome novels and giving them one to share each Christmas. So Diana Wynne Jones eventually started writing, aged twelve, out of desperation to have something to read aloud to her sisters.

Although she didn't have anything published for another thirty or more years . . . , these early attempts obviously provided valuable experience. Her books read aloud well—many even demand to be read out loud—and she still believes this to be a vital factor in successful writing for children. She checks every word, line and paragraph for the cadence because she is aware that young children get bogged down in long sentences and pages of description. However, she never underestimates her readers, convinced as she is that children can follow the most complex plots if the story is flowing well. She has more difficulty, she says, making her plots simple enough for adults to follow!

Diana Wynne Jones chose to write fantasy, firstly because she had been starved of it as a child and, secondly, because she feels books should provide something other than reality. This is not to suggest that her books aren't firmly rooted in reality, albeit a rather distorted reality. She creates fantastic worlds and situations, but her characters are very real and the ways they behave are entirely plausible.

In fact she admits that she thinks the idea of worlds co-existing outside our own could actually be a possibility. One book in which she uses this idea is *Homeward Bounders,* an incredibly complex novel inspired by the Dungeons and Dragons type of wargames. Diana adds a new dimension to the idea by creating a situation in which real people from the supposedly real world get caught up as random factors in a game played by 'players' in a superior world, and are then sent into different worlds at the throw of a dice, while all the time hoping to arrive back in their own home world.

The real reason, however, that Diana Wynne Jones chooses to use the device of fantasy worlds is, she says, because it is 'such a splendid way of making our own world strange'. She feels that the age-group for which she mostly writes is slightly blasé, and she thinks 'it's very good for people to turn round and look at their own environment and ways of thinking'.

She doesn't write books simply to be enjoyed, which of course they are, but says 'I always want to try and help people to do something as well—show them that this is a mighty strange place we inhabit'. One example of a book that manages to do just that is *Archer's Goon,* in which seven wizards control various aspects of life in the town where Howard Sykes and his family live. Each wizard can tune into the Sykes's household and watch their every move, and can make their lives unbearable by, for instance, turning off the power, or creating continuous sound from radios, TVs and musical instruments. That this book was written in 1984 was no accident. Diana Wynne Jones intended this fantastic idea to act as a metaphor for what happens in real life, where governments can control people.

On the other hand, she dislikes the overtly didactic approach of books that she remembers from her own childhood, but feels strongly enough about certain things to want to keep her readers aware of them. Nuclear war is one such subject, the implications of which are touched on in *Homeward Bounders* and crop up again in her latest book *A Tale of Time City,* another very complex novel in which the three main characters travel backwards and forwards in history from a city that controls time.

Diana Wynne Jones feels that fantasy has an advantage over super-realism in that it can enable a child to look at a problem or unpleasant situation from a distance and often with a sense of humour. After all, humour is often used with very serious subjects, as in jokes—which children tell all the time. For example, the victimization of individual children in school is the essential theme of *Witch Week.* The reason some children in Class 2Y of Larwood House are being victimized is because they are witches rather than because of any difference of race, colour or religion. 'Children do get victimized and everybody accepts it in the dreadful way children do.' What the writer must do is 'not concentrate on that as the essential thing but remove it as a metaphor. People being persecuted for witchcraft is the same, only on a fantasy level.'

She believes that children often resist attempts by adults to help them come to terms with problems by giving them books that mirror their situations, for the very reason that they are too close to reality. She says 'you can actually hurt people by thrusting their noses into a situation that has been very painful. This is where fantasy scores, because you can remove the situation into a realm where you can walk all round it and it releases you so you can think about it.'

One of the drawbacks of writing for children is the number of adults—publishers, teachers, librarians, parents—that have to be satisfied before a book actually reaches the children for whom it is intended. 'Adults,' she feels, 'often have these arbitrary rules, like "all adults must be good" '. When she started writing she says 'you were only allowed one sinful adult and this had to be the villain . . . otherwise they all had to be saints, and this seemed to me to be unrealistic.' She felt that one thing that children's books

could do was to help children to deal with the adults that they have to spend about half their existence coping with. The adults in her books are often extremely unpleasant and frequently get away with their unpleasantness. For example the aunt, uncle and cousins who are David's guardians in *The Eight Days of Luke* do not hide their dislike of him or their irritation at having to look after him during the school holidays. Yet they demand that he should be grateful for this appalling treatment. Although Diana Wynne Jones sees this as one of the sins adults as parents have, she feels that 'it's easier to point out how terrible these people are if they are aunts and uncles and stepfathers rather than mothers and fathers'.

Diana Wynne Jones's books convey in a subtle way a certain morality—good triumphs over evil—which springs from her preference for happy endings. She is, she says, more concerned with 'people coming to terms with the nastiness in themselves'. The magic in her stories is a strong metaphor for power, ranging from supernatural power in the form of witchcraft, as in the books featuring the wizard Chrestomanci (*Charmed Life, Magicians of Caprona* and *Witch Week*), to the more human or earthly power in, for example, *The Ogre Downstairs,* in which the magic is contained in a seemingly ordinary chemistry set. The ways in which characters use and misuse magic are similar to the ways in which real people use and abuse power. The characters who misuse magic power in her stories get their comeuppance, but, she says, 'this very often happens in natural ways, as a natural consequence of misusing power in the first place. You've only got to follow the logic through . . . and this can be very extreme.' For example in *The Ogre Downstairs,* which is about children who hate their stepfather, the logic of the situation leads to the point where there are actually two murder attempts. 'On the other hand,' she points out, 'usually the logic comes slapping back at you . . . and if you get yourself into an extreme situation then extremely nasty things happen to you, so that the situation itself is a moral one.'

Many of Diana Wynne Jones's books centre round myth or use mythology as a base, whether it's the straightforward 'Puss in Boots' ending to *Wilkin's Tooth,* the more detailed Norse mythology pervading *The Eight Days of Luke,* or the creation of the mythical country Dalemark in *Cart and Cwidder, Drowned Ammet* and *The Spellcoats.* What she relishes about myths is 'that they keep appearing and that they have a tremendous amount of meaning for almost everyone in different ways'. From the writer's point of view they are a gift because, she says, 'they come to pieces like Lego and you can use little bits. You can take those out and make use of them and, of course, they're common property. You need only refer to them sometimes and people will get the point.'

Diana Wynne Jones reads a lot of science fiction, believing it almost impossible to separate it into a different genre to fantasy. She loves the play of ideas, often deep philosophical ideas, that science fiction provides, and delights in coming across new twists, even if she is occasionally annoyed at not having thought of them first. Not that she could ever be accused of being short of ideas. If anything her problem is having too many ideas, and she sometimes has difficulty separating them out to form a book. She is a prolific writer and has published a novel almost every year since 1973, and very often more than one. She finds that as she is writing one another is growing up under-neath, so that books are often written in pairs; for example *Homeward Bounders* and *The Time of the Ghost* (a romantic ghost story for older readers) were written in quick succession, as were *Archer's Goon* and *Fire and Hemlock.* That these two pairs form opposite sides of a coin in terms of style and subject matter points to another feature of Diana Wynne Jones's writing. She likes to explore new ideas and experiment with new concepts in each book. For this reason she finds it difficult to go back to situations she has already written about and write sequels, except in the case of Chrestomanci, whom she feels to be full of possibilities. When I spoke to her she was correcting proofs of a new Chrestomanci novel—a 'prequel' to *Charmed Life*—which goes back to tell the story of his childhood.

It would be impossible to talk about Diana Wynne Jones and her books without mentioning her sense of humour. She has a loud, infectious laugh and loves making other people laugh. She learnt early on that children love to laugh and recalls her own children spending much time rolling about on the floor laughing at awful jokes. Much of her humour comes in the language she uses—playing with words is second nature to her and she points out that most children's jokes are based on terrible puns. She confesses to laughing uproariously while writing, much to the consternation of her family, and recounts how she fell off the sofa laughing at a bit in *Howl's Moving Castle.* What better assurance that her readers will do the same?

No one would recommend that a child be deprived of books in general and imaginative fiction in particular. But perhaps Diana Wynne Jones's fans should be grateful that she did not come across C. S. Lewis's 'Narnia' stories as a child. For, had she discovered these, who knows, she may not then have felt the same urgency to create fantasy of her own. Then thousands of children (not to mention adults) would have been deprived of some of the most inventive fantasy imaginable. (pp. 2-5)

Fiona Lafferty, "Realms of Fantasy: An Interview with Diana Wynne Jones," in British Book News Children's Books, *Winter, 1987, pp. 2-5.*

Michele Landsberg

Diana Wynne Jones is a British fantasist of astonishing originality and power. She is equally adept at those mind-opening reversals of perceptions (*The Power of Three*) that make *The Borrowers* outstanding, and at wittily elaborate magical farces (*Witch Week* and *The Magicians of Caprona*). Like Joan Aiken, she happily borrows from myth, legend, and folk tale for her basic plot ingredients. But so accomplished is she at sleight-of-hand and bewildering complications that they exist just out of sight, submerged like the concrete underpinnings of a fantastically ornate bridge.

The Homeward Bounders, in fact, is based on the craze for fantasy and war gaming, and is a bracing antidote to the excesses of both. Not till halfway through *The Homeward Bounders* does it become clear that the first-person hero, thirteen-year-old Jamie Hamilton, has been permanently exiled from his nineteenth-century English working-class home by a shadowy group of futuristic gamers who play "The Real and Ancient Game" with real people and overlapping worlds.

Struggling through endless worlds, some more tormented than others, Jamie begins to discover other Homeward Bounders, who, like him, are doomed to walk the boundaries of the worlds forever. Among them are legendary or mythological figures like Prometheus, the Flying Dutchman, the Wandering Jew—all of them plausibly entangled in the complex plot, and all of them springing into a curious new life in Wynne Jones's hands.

Just as **The Homeward Bounders** is tailor-made for the youth who can't be coaxed to read anything but Dungeons and Dragons handbooks or sci-fi, **Dogsbody** may entice a girl who's stuck on animal stories to reach a little further. The story begins when Sirius, the dog star, a hothead among the stellar beings, is exiled by a heavenly court of judgment for an alleged murder and for the accidental loss of a "zoi," an object of supreme magical power. Sirius is cast down to earth in the form of a newborn puppy, an unwanted byblow who turns up (red ears and all) in a pedigree setter's litter.

Sirius grows to dog's estate, and his growing strength and understanding are brilliantly delineated from the dog's eye point of view—albeit a supernatural dog who just happens to be cared for by a lonely orphan girl, Kathleen, living with her unlovable aunt, uncle, and cousins.

Sirius's dawning realization that he is a fallen star on a mysterious earthly mission is perfectly integrated with his clumsy, enthusiastic growth from puppyhood. Somehow, Wynne Jones conveys a doggy nature of wagging optimism that perfectly accords with the boundless energy of an astral lord. Sirius's growth, not coincidentally, parallels a child's development into maturity and skill, and also the progress of the meek, almost Cinderellalike Kathleen toward self-assertion and independence. As in all Wynne Jones's books, the narrative suspense is muscular enough to carry the reader right through mazes of bewildering plot twists. **Dogsbody** is, however, one of her more coherent and accessible fantasies, a sometimes rueful, sometimes lyrical journey toward self-knowledge. (pp. 175-76)

Michele Landsberg, "Fantasy," in her Reading for the Love of It: Best Books for Young Readers, *Prentice Hall Press, 1987, pp. 157-82.*

TITLE COMMENTARY

Wilkin's Tooth (1973; U.S. edition as **Witch's Business**)

A fresh, entertaining fantasy by a new writer worth watching, about two children who set up "Own Back Limited" hoping to earn money by wreaking revenge for others. The results are unexpected, involving a properly sinister and rather interesting witch, and with a climax pinched unashamedly from Puss in Boots.

"Novellas for Under-Nines," in The Times Literary Supplement, *No. 3709, April 6, 1973, p. 387.*

Frank and Jess find themselves without pocket money because they have broken a chair, so they set up an "Own Back" Agency Ltd. in their back shed. Their first customer is the local bully and gang leader Buster who asks them to get him one of Vernon Wilkin's teeth in revenge. They oblige, but use a milk tooth belonging to Vernon's young brother. Imagine their consternation when the child's face begins to swell at an alarming rate and they discover that Buster is involved with Biddy the local witch. The plot concerns their breaking of her power and settling various scores as they go. This is fantasy, but I did feel it was a case of someone jumping on the bandwaggon. Had Joan Aiken written it, the story would have sparkled, but as it is the result is rather pedestrian. However, perhaps children of nine to twelve who enjoy "adventure" books will read this, but it will do little to stimulate their imaginations, and it does rather hark on the material things of life. One scene which should have been really funny, the chase over the croquet lawn, is almost dismal. (pp. 270-71)

J. Murphy, in a review of "Wilkin's Tooth," in The Junior Bookshelf, *Vol. 37, No. 4, August, 1973, pp. 270-71.*

[**Witch's Business**] is typical of a kind of TV story style—two-dimensional, linear, endlessly this-happened-then-that-happened. Talk, events, background, acquire no reality. . . . There is a claim here for the actuality of evil, and I am not persuaded. However, the way in which a child's total world is conveyed is impressive: its obliviousness to adult ways and solutions. No authority but the child's own is ever recognized and adults are never appealed to, no matter how serious the trouble or great the need, as if such an appeal must be useless. When an adult does speak, it is as though a large empty building had uttered sensible sounds. The old "Our Gang" movies suggested the same sealed mini- or parallel world. Here it is frightening rather than comic, and that's good. (p. 26)

Christopher Davis, "There's the Devil to Pay," in The New York Times Book Review, *May 5, 1974, pp. 22, 24, 26.*

The Ogre Downstairs (1974)

Domestic comedy is rarer than one would like, partly perhaps because it demands a maturity of approach that is not always deemed necessary for young readers. *The ogre downstairs* will be wasted if it is not accorded the widest possible readership—not that young readers won't appreciate it but their elders should not miss it either. Like E. Nesbit, Diana Wynne Jones uses magical events as a way of revealing character; by the way people react to extraordinary happenings you see what they are like and how they change. Here are two families faced with the need to unite and fiercely resenting it. When Mrs. Brent married Jack Macintyre, her children—Caspar, Gwinny and Johnny—found his sons Douglas and Malcolm unutterably stiff and stuck up, while the Macintyre boys thought the Brents noisy and uncivilised. Something had to be done, but the dour martinet whom his step-children thought entirely worthy of the title of Ogre was as bewildered as their mother, who had been used to treating her children in a relaxed way. Magic saved the day—a layer of ingredients at the bottom of the two apparently harmless chemistry sets which the Ogre, as a gesture of good will, gave to Malcolm and Johnny. Labels like *Misc. pulv.*, *Petr. Philos.* and *Dens drac.* meant nothing to the children until experiments revealed their peculiar properties; and with each surprising chemical reaction the hostile offspring drew a little nearer to understanding one another. To carry off

this idea without being either silly or didactic would have been beyond many writers but Diana Wynne Jones, with the brilliantly successful **Wilkin's Tooth** behind her, is quite equal to making us believe her new fantasy. Here is the result of spilling part of the phial labelled *Animal Spirits* in Johnny's Magicator set:

> But the toffee-bar took no notice. It stretched several times more, rather harder. Then, quite suddenly, the white and yellow paper split in two along the top of it. The toffee inside wriggled a little, and then it crawled out from the paper, a smooth yellow-brown strip.
>
> "I'll have to catch you", Gwinny said firmly. She reached out, not quite so firmly, and tried to take hold of the toffee-bar. It must have seen her hand coming. Its limber brown body jack-knifed and leapt away from her fingers. In a flash, it had jumped off the table, wriggled over the floor, and gone to earth in a shelf of library books.

To say any more would be to spoil this gorgeously funny, shrewd family story for intending readers, but I must offer one word of advice. A knowledge of the Greek alphabet (no more) will add to the enjoyment of pages 182-3.

Margery Fisher, in a review of "The Ogre Downstairs," in Growing Point, *Vol. 13, No. 1, May, 1974, p. 2399.*

In **The Ogre Downstairs** Diana Wynne Jones goes to town on something . . . practical: a magic chemistry set. . . . This may not sound like anything very much, but the adventures are beautifully propelled and sustained by Mrs Wynne Jones's imagination, working much on the level of Wells's Magic Shop. Who could resist animated toffee bars that seek the warmth of a radiator and melt, eat sweaters and can't easily be drowned? The children fly, shrink and change colour, but none of this seems overdone: the physical consequences of each experiment are described in ingenious detail, and the last episode involving Dragon's Teeth warriors in the shape of crash-helmeted toughs who mushroom up from the ground talking joke-Greek ('Λετμι αττεμ') is a fine stroke. Having found the fantasy in her first book a little breathless and uncontrolled, I am happy to report that **The Ogre Downstairs** is an unqualified success. (p. 738)

John Fuller, "Schemers," in New Statesman, *Vol. 87, No. 2253, May 24, 1974, pp. 738-39.*

I liked Diana Wynne Jones's idea of chemistry sets containing curious chemicals such as Parv.pulv. and Irid. col. being instrumental in domestic fantasy, but I felt that some of the end-products of the experiments were unfortunate—a question of being ill-fitted to context rather than intrinsically bad. I could believe in Elevation, Invisibility, Swopped Bodies and—from Petr. Philos. (Peter Fillus to the children)—the magical attributes of the Philosopher's Stone. I was bored by and incredulous of animated toffy bars and dust-balls. . . .

Several excellent and original ideas have been used, but somehow they don't seem to jell into a really convincing whole. There is plenty of enjoyment to be had though, both from the experiments and the changing relationships between the children and their parents.

Margot Petts, in a review of "The Ogre Down-

stairs," in Children's Book Review, *Vol. IV, No. 2, Summer, 1974, p. 65.*

Eight Days of Luke (1975)

Diana Wynne Jones, who showed her talent for exploiting the tensions that exist between adults and children to create hilarious situations in **The Ogre Downstairs,** has now gone one step further and woven a mythological dimension into the plot of her latest book. David is obliged to spend all school holidays with his horrid relatives who make it quite clear that he is not wanted, but still insist that he should be grateful to them. At meal-times, when they are not getting at him, they are vying with each other to see who can make themselves out to be the most ill. This activity David secretly calls "the illness contest", and he keep a mental scoresheet to see who wins each round. On one occasion he is banished to the bottom of the garden and, while indulging his hatred of the five adults in the household, he inadvertently summons up Luke, who becomes his friend and ally, albeit a dangerous one. Gradually David gets involved in helping Luke to evade some menacing pursuers.

The book is shot through with the most delightful humour, the effect of which is both immediate and rewardingly cumulative. All the loose ends are tied up in the final chapter when it becomes clear that, in helping Luke, David has also been extricated from the toils of his relatives. Diana Wynne Jones clarifies the identity of Luke's pursuers and their link with Norse mythology on which the plot has been built, and in doing so defends herself against the charge of willful obscurity which has been levelled at some writers of fantasy. While admiring the ingenuity of her puzzle, I admit to being more interested by the gloriously comic superstructure that has been erected upon it: an immensely enjoyable and dramatic story which should not be missed.

> *Lesley Croome, "Dangerous Wishes," in* The Times Literary Supplement, *No. 3813, April 4, 1975, p. 365.*

After sending up witchcraft and 'scientific' magic in her first two books, Diana Wynne Jones has chosen a mythological theme for her best book yet. . . .

The plot develops and harmonises with Norse mythology: children who know their legends will enjoy solving the mystery, and those who don't will probably become interested, as the plot is related to the names of the days of the week and shows how they are derived. This is more unified and less cluttered than the author's previous books, and well within the Nesbit tradition, combining magic events with an unhappy family situation. The story ends with both magic and personal problems resolved. An outstanding, original fantasy which ought to be one of the year's best books.

> *Jessica Kemball-Cook, in a review of "Eight Days of Luke," in* Children's Book Review, *Vol. V, No. 2, Summer, 1975, p. 61.*

As always, Jones's characters are attractive and interesting. The reader truly cares what happens to them. The friendship of Astrid and David is a warm and caring one made even more intriguing by its unexpectedness. The

Norse allegory is clearly and concisely explained in the afterward. This is an early example of Jones's work, just released in the United States. While it doesn't show the polish of her later novels, it's still a fascinating look at an alternate reality, seen with her unique vision.

> *Penny Blubaugh, in a review of "Eight Days of Luke," in* Voice of Youth Advocates, *Vol. 11, No. 6, February, 1989, p. 295.*

Cart and Cwidder (1975)

The making of large imaginary worlds, whole kingdoms with their landscape, their peoples and their politics (usually medieval, these, with barons, and kings good and bad) is a recurrent form of story. **Cart and Cwidder** is just such a story. North and south are at logger-heads; vile tyranny crushes the south. Clennan, the travelling singer with his cart, journeys between the two. He and his children are just entertainers, busking in one town after another for their bread—or so the children think, but Clennan is not only what he seems.

A fantasy adventure, especially one that culminates in the gathering of armies, epic fashion, invites comparison with *The Hobbit;* but this is not another derivative book, for Diana Wynne Jones has a subject of her own to involve us in. Not the eternal war of good and evil, as in Tolkien, but the mysterious power of song is at the heart of her story. For one of the instruments in Clennan's cart is a huge old cwidder, that once belonged to one of the heroes of his songs, and if played with passion enough this instrument does strange things. The book tells us not only how Clennan's children escaped their enemies, and brought home the true heir to his kingdom, but also how Moril learnt about the power of the cwidder, and the use and abuse to which it could be put by such as he. This deeper strand, though handled with a light touch, gives subtlety and thoughtfulness to a story that is otherwise full of such sunny charm that only the villainous Tholian is hard to believe in.

> *Jill Paton Walsh, "Epic Ventures," in* The Times Literary Supplement, *No. 3826, July 11, 1975, p. 764.*

Classic adventure is seldom hampered by social morality. In a treasure hunt the seeker is, by prescriptive right, the hero: the holder—dragon or man—is in the wrong. Since *Treasure Island* this has been one of the strongest conventions of the adventure story. The ethics of aggression have been in the past accorded a similar ambiguity; a certain concept of honour, differing in its nature from country to country or from period to period, has been considered reason enough for one antagonist to be accounted hero and another, villain. Today, political and social sensitiveness is making its mark on children's stories, not only in the kind of adventure (like J. M. Marks's stories, for example) with a topical, contemporary setting, but also in fantasy and space adventure. The change is particularly interesting in regard to **Cart and Cwidder,** for here the old chivalric idea of honour and a modern liberal attitude are interwoven. The villains—as so often in adventure stories nowadays—are those who curtail freedom (everybody's bogy, in fact). They are the corrupt, totalitarian earls of the South, in an unnamed country, engaged in a protracted

Cold War with the North, where people can be themselves. Between the two sharply divided cultures and countries moves a travelling entertainer, Clennen the Singer, with his family earning money with music of all kinds and carrying personal messages, some of them not quite what they seem. Clennen's children, and especially thoughtful Moril, have always wondered about the passengers Clennen takes from time to time, and Kialan, a strangely unsociable youth, intrigues them particularly. Kialan in fact shows himself to be a true friend when Clennen is killed by enemies from his past, Dagner the eldest son is arrested for spying and upon Moril falls the responsibility for taking cart and cwidder further North—the cart in which their few possessions are housed, the cwidder which Moril is afraid to play. For this ancient instrument has, as he is slowly discovering, a mysterious power to oppose deceit and self-seeking; and when he finds the courage to play it, the extreme peril to Kialan and to Northern freedom is averted. This slow-moving, allusive, enigmatic tale has a chivalric atmosphere, conveyed in details of costume, in slightly archaic idiom, in the rustic settings and medieval-type settlements and in the moral attitudes of Clennen and of Moril; the modern concern for liberty has been given almost an Arthurian gloss. (pp. 2708-09)

> *Margery Fisher, in a review of "Cart and Cwidder," in* Growing Point, *Vol. 14, No. 4, October, 1975, pp. 2708-09.*

The vocabulary of fantasy has become familiar to the contemporary reader who will find in this book nothing new. North and South of an imaginary kingdom are at war; the names are vaguely Nordic, the setting vaguely medieval. (p. 69)

Ms. Jones's work is highly derivative. This is particularly unfortunate with regard to her style. One of the surest marks of second-rate fantasy is the presence of formal speech-patterns ineptly handled and apparently only half-understood by the author. Ms. Jones interrupts her "high" speech with frequent modern slang, apparently without any suspicion of incongruity.

This lack of linguistic sensitivity is paralleled by what I can only call a lack of emotional authenticity. Even the hangings and murders, of which the story has quite a few, have a passionless air about them: that is, their violence is taken distrubingly for granted and arouses no convincing depth either of sympathy or of revulsion in the characters. The moral problem of violence is thus in essence avoided: violence becomes merely a counter in the plot. The fantasy kingdom is too ill-realized to make us care about its affairs, although this need not be the case even in a small-scale fantasy: witness the marvellously realized landscapes and people in Peter Beagle's *The Last Unicorn.* Ms. Jones's characters have a mechanical, derivative quality. One cannot escape a suspicion that even the "magic" element of the ancient cwidder is included because magic is a stock ingredient in the fantasy formula. I have never read an author whose style and story were so empty of real magic.

A reviewer appears graceless when he finds nothing in a book to praise, but I must accept this unsavory responsibility. *Real* fantasy can nourish a child's imagination on so high a level, can awaken him to beauty, to grief, to

moral passion. One searches in vain for these excellences here. *Cart and Cwidder* is a sort of fantasy paint-by-numbers set. (p. 70)

> *Ruth Nichols, in a review of "Cart and Cwidder," in* The World of Children's Books, *Vol. III, No. 1, 1978, pp. 69-70.*

Dogsbody (1975)

Dogsbody has as its point of departure dissension among the Heavenly Bodies, during which the Dog Star, falsely accused of murder and the loss of a Zoi, is condemned to be born on earth as a pup so that he may search for the sacred object, which has fallen as a meteorite. The red-eared mongrels born to Mrs. Partridge's pedigree labrador are dumped in the river, but several survive. Sirius himself is rescued by Kathleen, a waif from Ireland taken in unwillingly by stony-hearted Mrs. Duffield, who sees in this relative of her husband's a useful domestic slave. Child and dog endure blows and insults, and Sirius suffers a persecution from the heavens which he only understands after he has remembered, piece-meal, his own origin. Like all Diana Wynne Jones's fantasies, this is a confident, intricate interweaving of contemporary family tensions and alliances with flashes of extra-human activity, as stars and planets join in the search for the Zoi and make their several contributions to the final unravelling of plot and counter-plot. The parallel between Duffie's cruelty to Kathleen and the ruthless actions of Sirius's Companion is significant. The conflict is not a moral so much as a psychological one, and the fantasy, with its constant emphasis on light and darkness, is there to make a point about human behaviour. (pp. 2771-72)

> *Margery Fisher, in a review of "Dogsbody," in* Growing Point, *Vol. 14, No. 6, December, 1975, pp. 2771-72.*

[The plot of *Dogsbody*] sounds fabricated, airy-fairy stuff, but in fact the authoress is singularly successful in combining the fabulous with everyday reality, in making both convincing, in presenting good human values, all in a fast moving story with a well shaped plot. This will certainly prove to be one of the best stories for ten- to twelve-year-olds published in 1975.

> *Norman Culpan, in a review of "Dogsbody," in* The School Librarian, *Vol. 24, No. 1, March, 1976, p. 36.*

Dogsbody is about Sirius, the hot-tempered star, framed and found guilty of the murder of a young luminary by striking him with a Zoi which is lost in the process. He is banished to the body of a creature in the sphere where the missing Zoi is thought to have fallen. Sirius will be reinstated if he retrieves the Zoi during the life span of the creature; if not, he will simply die when it dies. . . .

The idea is quite ingenious and gives Diana Wynne Jones scope for her invention, but some important things elude her, such as convincing human dialogue and moments of pathos. Confusing shifts of tone from serious to comic put the dramatic tension at risk, and the attempt to combine so many strands—stellar, canine, human, and the troubles in Ireland—overtaxes the author, even though in the end she neatly resolves the dichotomy of Sirius and Kathleen moving in their respective but interacting spheres.

> *Graham Hammond, "Death Duties," in* The Times Literary Supplement, *No. 3864, April 2, 1976, p. 383.*

Successfully combined, the disparate elements of the fantasy are given down-to-earth verisimilitude and humorous expression in Sirius' canine experiences; and the story, fast-moving, and full of suspense, is rich in character contrast—human, animal, and extra-terrestrial. (p. 320)

> *Paul Heins, in a review of "Dogsbody," in* The Horn Book Magazine, *Vol. LIII, No. 3, June, 1977, pp. 319-20.*

A reissue of this 1975 publication is welcome, for it is one of Jones' most polished, whole, humorous, and deeply touching works. Her intricate plotting requires attention (some brushing up on ancient Celtic gods and celestial bodies might clarify matters), but is is always compelling. A large cast of characters is superbly developed, both by economical and acute verbal description and through actions. The value of deep and unconditional love is a clear and resonant, but never oppressive, theme. Best of all, the interplay between Sirius' nature as a powerful effulgence and his nature as a canine is funny enough to provoke belly laughter. By the bittersweet ending, the reader is ready to buy into Jones' cosmology unreservedly. This is a book worth reading and re-reading, and which will need no promoting to Jones' fans. (p. 295)

> *Ann Welton, in a review of "Dogsbody," in* Voice of Youth Advocates, *Vol. 11, No. 6, February, 1989, pp. 294-95.*

Power of Three (1976)

Diana Wynne Jones has a remarkable ability to grasp the basic elements of myth or fairytale, twist them sharply, then fit them without undue strain into patterns of her own making. In *Power of Three,* her most ambitious book yet, she has marched onto that dangerous, old, but not very straight Celtic track along which so many others have strayed recently. Still, if she has not quite avoided all the pitfalls her version is highly distinctive, funny, exciting and with one marvellous twist. It is about the peoples who mythologically and historically have displaced each other within the British Isles. Her heroes—and so for this book, the norm—are three children of the Mound People (the little folk to us) who help to bring their own people together with their traditional enemies, the moon-worshipping Dorig on the one hand, the awkward and noisy Giants on the other, in face of a common threat to their homeland, the Moor. The surprise comes when we realize that what appears to have been an imaginary country is in fact our own; and that the Giants with their mysterious magics and even more mysterious habits are actually our human selves.

This book tackles large themes, from ecology to international and racial understanding, taking in the individual's struggle to understand and use his particular gifts on the way. Some of it is brilliant; but ultimately it is perhaps too neatly resolved to be wholly satisfactory or even believable. Still, if in her refusal to leave her audience enough

Jones at work, 1988.

uncertainties Mrs Wynne Jones is the victim of her own intelligence let us be grateful for it. In this kind of book such observation and such wit are rare.

> *Penelope Farmer, "Self-Examination," in* The Times Literary Supplement, *No. 3864, April 2, 1976, p. 383.*

[The theme] of war and peace lies behind the intricate plot of *Power of Three.* In moorland country, somewhere in South-East England, three races co-exist, on uneasy or antagonistic terms, each assuming its supremacy. . . . Fantasy and reality interact in a story in which water-shortage and water-spells each affect the working out of the curse in the second generation until the three races learn to respect one another's needs and identity. This is not altogether an easy book to read, because of the profusion of characters and the enigmatic way the author directs her narrative; but attentive readers will find in it, as they will have found in all her books, that at the bottom of it all lies that microcosm of the Family, with its tensions and its claustrophobic relationships, which can serve as a mirror reflecting the condition of Man as a whole.

> *Margery Fisher, in a review of "Power of Three," in* Growing Point, *Vol. 15, No. 3, September, 1976, p. 2936.*

In an intricate fantasy, with many strands of conflict, magical forces impinge on a place in modern England which needs to develop a new water supply. . . . The three children who figure in the adventure are the gifted sons and daughter of Gest, leader of Garholt in the land of Mounds, and of the Wise Woman of Adara. Although largely in the background, the mother is a strongly felt presence of wisdom and loving protectiveness. Two of the children have psychic powers, and one of them—who believes himself to be "unspeakably ordinary"—is discovered in a crisis to have the rarest gift of all. A heroic journey to discuss the flooding with the Dorig king involves the three children and the two young Giants in crucial matters of life and death, a rich mélange of actions and counter-actions which move the story to high peaks of drama. Modern speech and the quarrels of children inject humor into the storytelling but are somewhat at odds with the otherworldliness; there is humor also in the characterizations and the action. (pp. 47-8)

> *Virginia Haviland, in a review of "Power of Three," in* The Horn Book Magazine, *Vol. LIV, No. 1, February, 1978, pp. 47-8.*

Another story from this successful creator of fantasy and magic, which is inventive, exciting and immensely pictorial. These words, used to praise, could however be the basis of a criticism of the book. It appears, on reading the book, that the author sees every scene as in a film, and she transfers the image on to the written page most vividly and successfully. The trouble arises when the action becomes peopled with too many characters, and in order to paint them in she has to litter the book with proper names, Gair, Ayna, Ceri, Garholt, Dorig, Otmounders, Adara, Gest etc, etc, sometimes as many as forty or fifty to a page, and so the narrative becomes stilted and disjointed as the words intrude on the wonderful story she weaves. Oh, for the film of the book, when the creatures of the marsh would rise in the mist, when the Giants would make their surprising entrance, and when the dwellers on the Moor could be seen with their beautifully worked golden collars and all the other fascinating inventions of Diana Wynne Jones.

> *E. A. A., in a review of "Power of Three," in* Book Window, *Vol. 5, No. 2, Spring, 1978, p. 31.*

Charmed Life (1977)

To the reviewer's jaded palate, stories set in invented other worlds, involving magical apprenticeships and witchcraft contests, are scarcely more welcome than yesterday's cold fillet of a fenny snake, so it is a pleasant surprise to come across a really enjoyable example, one that avoids portentous moralizing or mythologizing in favour of a rapid and remarkably sustained comic action. Diana Wynne Jones's **Charmed Life,** in spite of touches of Joan Aiken and, in the final chapters, C. S. Lewis, is an outstandingly inventive and entertaining novel, which never for a moment loses its characteristic pace and verve. Its setting is a world whose culture has evolved through magic rather than technology, where taxpayers subsidize research into spells and warlocks appeal to their MPs when deprived of their powers. There are some splendid set pieces of witchery, such as the havoc caused during a dull sermon when the sober figures in the stained glass windows run riot, and a stone crusader thumbs his nose at the vicar. The comic in-

vention is at once prolific yet well-disciplined, and the presentation of a parallel scheme of things is much strengthened by the introduction of a heroine from our own world, who finds the Edwardian garters, petticoats and boot-buttons all too much for her. The plot combines real surprise with psychological and fictional consistency—you must wait till the very end for the opening mysteries to be explained. Altogether a delightful book. . . .

> *Julia Briggs, "Spells of Power," in* The Times Literary Supplement, *No. 3915, March 25, 1977, p. 348.*

To sustain on a convincing level a tale of complex family relationships and extraordinary happenings in an impossible cosmos demands considerable expertise if the story is not to crumble into whimsy or unacceptable absurdity. Diana Wynne Jones never falters as Cat Chant works his way through a fair number of his nine lives, hampered by a jealous sister and perplexed by the amazing wizardry of the great Chrestomanci. Here is a world in which dragon's blood is at a premium, a girl is turned into a frog, the figures in a stained glass window come to life, and woods march Birnam fashion to the very walls of Chrestomanci Castle.

Wizards and necromancers the characters of this lively story may be but they shed few of their normal human characteristics: such manifestations as envy and anger, affection and loyalty are still the mainsprings of action. Action? There is plenty of it and, as an explosive climax to so much toil and trouble, there is a glorious battle when Chrestomanci's enemies discover his Achilles Heel. But the real triumph is Cat's: he is finally honoured as that rarity, a nine-lifed enchanter. (pp. 303-04)

> *G. Bott, in a review of "Charmed Life," in* The Junior Bookshelf, *Vol. 41, No. 5, October, 1977, pp. 303-04.*

A kind of maddening brilliance about the work of this author captivates me. The stories are metaphors of possibility in a universe where magic is normal and the unexpected commonplace. If you have ever wished you could turn someone into a toad, you can if you are Gwendolen Chant, and the logic of magical propositions is as inexorable as any other kind. The comedy is cheerful, the writing witty, and someone will examine it all further and at great length soon. In case you have missed the earlier titles, begin here, now. (pp. 363-64)

> *Margaret Meek, in a review of "Charmed Life," in* The School Librarian, *Vol. 25, No. 4, December, 1977, pp. 363-64.*

[Jones] writes with exceptional finesse—whether establishing the atmosphere of the castle, orchestrating large confrontations, or filling in the domestic scene with vital incidentals. But the framing ideas are weak. The notion of alternate worlds with duplicate populations is commonplace, if functional, and not worth all her meticulous, anticlimactic unraveling. And the revelation that the enigmatic Chrestomanci is a "government employee," charged with keeping other witches in check so they don't muck up the world (this in a world where only the rich have cars), is both disappointingly tame and disturbingly paternalistic.

A review of "Charmed Life," in Kirkus Reviews, *Vol. XLVI, No. 4, February 15, 1978, p. 177.*

A fantasy set in a mythical England where witches (certified or accredited) are commonplace, as are soothsayers and clairvoyants. The plot follows the fortunes and misfortunes of Cat Chant, who appears to be a shy, ordinary boy bossed around by older sister Gwendolen, a witch. After the two are orphaned and adopted by the mysterious Chrestomanci, it becomes clear that Gwen has been using her magic for more than just mischief. Summoning Janet, a 20th-Century time-traveler to take her place at Chrestomanci's Castle and leaving Cat behind, Gwen goes off in search of greater power. Through the confidence Cat gains from his new friendship with Janet, he is revealed, in a resounding finale, as a rare nine-lived enchanter. Despite this satisfying conclusion and the often light-hearted way the author combines several classic themes—the struggle between good and evil, the use and abuse of power, discovering one's true identity and potential—far too much is left unexplained and the pacing is jerky, preventing the fantasy from being totally successful.

Cyrisse Jaffee, in a review of "Charmed Life," in School Library Journal, *Vol. 24, No. 8, April, 1978, p. 94.*

Drowned Ammet (1977)

In this companion to Jones' *Cart and Cwidder, Drowned Ammet* is a benevolent, Neptune-like sea god who, with his female counterpart, rides to the rescue of three young people fleeing by boat from dangerous and repressive political conditions in their homeland. The setting, a different section of the same imagined group of late medieval earldoms as the earlier book, is interesting, and the main characters—the strong, active girl, Hildy, and the Oliver-like, streetwise Mitt, who appealingly represents the deserving but downtrodden poor—are generally well portrayed. However, the story falls victim to its author's excesses. For example, Mitt's concern for social justice is admirable, but when, as a six- or seven-year-old, Jones gives him lines like "Can't the poor people get together and tell the rich ones where to get off?" it all starts to sound unlikely. And, in the last third of the book, when the old gods get almost hyperactive and demonstrate a truly impressive array of tricks (e.g., instant island raising) the plot goes beyond credulity. Although *Drowned Ammet* has it's appealing moments, Jones has not been able to shape them into a satisfying whole; both Ursula Le Guin's *Earthsea* trilogy and Lloyd Alexander's Prydain series are better crafted examples of historical fantasy.

Chuck Schacht, in a review of "Drowned Ammet," in School Library Journal, *Vol. 24, No. 8, April, 1978, p. 85.*

She is a clever and witty writer, Diana Wynne Jones—too clever in some of her books; you admire the means, ultimately not so much the ends. Not so, however, with her latest book *Drowned Ammet,* set like the earlier *Cart and Cwidder* in the mythical country of Dalemark. . . .

The origins of [the story] are anthropological rather than mythological perhaps, some familiar enough but all properly rooted in a living and integrated plot. The evoking of magical powers is strong, idiosyncratic and interesting. With water the prevailing image, I am reminded of Dannie Abse's dictum on poetry, that like a stream it should be clear right down to the depths, yet leave you in the end not quite able to touch bottom. For this is clear water all right; you can see what the author is doing, follow the progression and recognize the sources of her ideas. None the less you do find yourself floating sometimes; there is enough that is whispered and hinted at, that you can almost hear and see and yet not quite. Perhaps the mythical setting helps give to it its integrity—even if there is less scope for fireworks, it does mean that the author does not have to strain to connect sceptical age and impossible event. Nor is any humour sacrificed in the process. There is no whimsy in her invented land; this book is as sharp about people as her others, sharper in some respects.

Diana Wynne Jones has always been an exceptionally inventive writer, but the invention here seems particularly unforced. I especially like villainous, yet not quite villainous Al and his somewhat ambiguous demise; and also Mitt's longed-for country which he recognizes by smell as much as sight or sound—though the description of this is nearer poetry than invention.

Penelope Farmer, "Dalemark Festivities," in The Times Literary Supplement, *No. 3966, April 7, 1978, p. 377.*

Watching a novelist really getting it all together is one of the great pleasures of life. This is why I so hugely enjoyed Diana Wynne Jones's latest story set in the land of Holand—itself surely ranking as one of the best examples of 'sub-creation' of recent years. . . . Magic—springing from the customs associated with Poor Old Ammet and Libby Beer, themselves symbolic of greater moral forces—is not used arbitrarily but to further the developing insights of the main characters. Humour and near-farce intermingle with vivid danger and action; relationships and responsibilities are portrayed squarely and unsentimentally. There are echoes towards the end of Masefield and Le Guin—nevertheless, the whole brew is unique. It is a story which illustrates perfectly Jill Paton Walsh's image of 'the rainbow surface'—for here indeed is a brilliant outside with real pressure behind it.

Dennis Hamley, in a review of "Drowned Ammet," in The School Librarian, *Vol. 26, No. 2, June, 1978, p. 161.*

Who Got Rid of Angus Flint? (1978)

Who Got Rid of Angus Flint? is straight situation comedy. Angus Flint is the unbearable visitor who comes to stay (because he has left his wife) and proceeds to disrupt the whole household. Eventually, even the furniture turns against him. There is some nicely observed domestic detail here, but occasionally one senses that what appeared hilarious when it happened to one's own kith and kin can sometimes seem a trifle forced when set down as amusement for the reader.

Geoff Tomlinson, "Laughing Matters," in The Times Educational Supplement, *No. 3309, December 1, 1978, p. 24.*

This is a very different story from those normally associated with this gifted author. It is really a short story . . . about an impossible guest who picks people up by their hair, and will not allow the members of his host's family to do anything which they want to do. It is told in the first person by one of the children of the house, and although the family do all in their power to get rid of him, it is left to the household furniture to turn nasty—the tables knocking him, the chairs herding him into other chairs, and the piano kicking out with its pedals. The text is interpolated with handwritten messages or criticisms of the way his sister is telling the tale by her younger brother. This unusual lay-out and the absurdity of the story should appeal to readers. . . .

> B. Clark, in a review of "Who Got Rid of Angus Flint?" in The Junior Bookshelf, Vol. 43, No. 1, February, 1979, p. 33.

The Spellcoats (1979)

Diana Wynne Jones has already written twice about the country of Dalemark. In this new, and remarkable, book she explores some of its prehistory, the archaeological evidence for which consists of two woven coats into which a narrative had been worked. The Spellcoats is the story of that weaving and of the weaver.

Stories of imagined worlds are acceptable only so far as they present inhabitants with whom we can feel some bond of sympathy. Miss Wynne Jones captures our interest and concern from the first page. Here is a united and reasonably happy family, father and three boys, two girls, living in a small and mainly hostile community, the village of Shelling. This stands on the bank of the river, and the river dominates their lives and puts a bound to their experience. War comes to the country, and father and the eldest son go off to fight for the King. In their absence life becomes harder and the villagers more hostile. The trouble is that the children are fair and blue-eyed, the rest of the village dark, and the Heathen invaders are also fair. When news comes of father's death, and Gull the brother comes home an empty shell, a crisis comes. The children launch themselves on to a river in flood, and exchange the maliginity of their neighbours for the perils of water and the unknown. From their old life they rescue only the household gods, the Undying.

In the adventures which follow, supernatural forces and dark magic are skilfully balanced against the everyday quarrels, affections and fun of family life. These are seen through the eyes of Tanaqui, the weaver, a girl of character whose role is to be the intermediary between the living and the dead. She, for all her impatience and quick temper, has the gift of seeing both sides of the story, and through her the fortunes of natives and Heathen are united against a common enemy.

There are some spine-chilling moments and a fine climax, and a conclusion which is not too tidy, leaving the imagination many loose ends to work upon. In fact this is one of those books which goes on in the mind long after the last page has been scanned. If such are to your taste, you have to thank Miss Wynne Jones' philosophy as much as her knowledge of character and her skill in narrative. It is a big book, long and continuously demanding of attention and a degree of surrender. (pp. 221-22)

> M. Crouch, in a review of "The Spellcoats," in The Junior Bookshelf, Vol. 43, No. 4, August, 1979, pp. 221-22.

As the fantasy genre fastens its grip on children's writing its landscapes seem to be growing more shadowy and indistinct. The detailed, concrete worlds of Tolkien and le Guin, in which topography, social, economic, religious and political structure, language, flora and fauna are slowly and painstakingly given the solidity of the pavement outside the reader's front door, have given way to a sort of generalized other country with pseudo-medieval village or tribal communities, stark ranges of mountains, enclosed valleys, decadent cities, sinister priesthoods and wars and rumours of wars.

Diana Wynne Jones' Dalemark, for instance, seems insubstantial, at the service of her stories rather than served by them. I found The Spellcoats . . . somewhat flimsy. The central symbol of the river is a strong one, and is skilfully kept at the forefront of the book, but the characters are bland and uninteresting, their human qualities dwarfed by their magical ones.

Diana Wynne Jones's best work, Charmed Life, Dogsbody and Eight Days of Luke, has had a quirky humour which the short, flat sentences of The Spellcoats cannot convey, and a subtlety which here turns to cleverness. The magic confuses rather than clarifies.

> Neil Philip, "Stark Mountains, Haunted Valleys," in The Times Educational Supplement, No. 3312, November 30, 1979, p. 25.

The characterizations of the two kings are convincing; so are those of Tanaqui, Robin, and their brothers, who slowly discover their magical powers and are fascinating for their strong relationships with one another. The complex and difficult plot is sometimes confused and blurred, but the spellcoats (Tanaqui's rugcoats) and the Undying, which are integral parts of the story, are ingenious and original.

> Ann A. Flowers, in a review of "The Spellcoats," in The Horn Book Magazine, Vol. LV, No. 6, December, 1979, p. 669.

The Magicians of Caprona (1980)

Like Joan Aiken, the author has a remarkable talent for creating a time which never was yet which seems believably familiar. The fantasy is set in the imaginary duchy of Caprona, located in the vicinity of Siena, Pisa, and Florence. It has its own history and geography, fluctuating in consonance with the squabbling neighboring city-states. As the story opens, Caprona has fallen upon evil times: The powers of the Montanas and the Petrocchis, the two chief "spell-houses," are declining; a wicked enchanter is at work undermining the charms which once defended the city from its foes, and the longstanding rivalry between the principal families prevents a united stand against the forces of evil. Then young Tonino Montana, who—unlike the rest of his family—was dismally slow in learning spells, discovers a possible solution: Find the correct words to the angelic tune brought straight from heaven centuries before as a guarantee of perpetual peace and strength. The enchanter Chrestomanci, the enigmatic and fascinating personality developed in *Charmed Life,* plays a less dominant role in the Capronian capers, yet his presence serves as a necessary element in the resolution of the problems. A gorgeous concoction of humor, suspense, and romance, the narrative has the gusto and pace of a commedia dell'arte production. (pp. 407-08)

> *Mary M. Burns, in a review of "The Magicians of Caprona," in* The Horn Book Magazine, *Vol. LVI, No. 4, August, 1980, pp. 407-08.*

What a brilliant and talented writer this is! She breaks all the usual rules of fantasy with impunity, secure in her own virtuosity. (p. 192)

Miss Wynne Jones tells a magnificent story for all it is worth, but she is far more than a master narrator. She has created a whole world, consistent in all its details, and peopled it with living and fascinating beings, clever and perverse, comic and eccentric. There are some wonderful moments, the best perhaps being a terrifying Punch and Judy show, although the State visit of the Montana and the Petrocchi to the Ducal palace runs it close, but these are not isolated inventions; they spring from the natural reactions of people and events and places.

Funny and frightening and profoundly exciting as this story is, it demands of the reader total surrender. It is not an easy book. Casual and lazy readers will give up early. For those who persist, children and adults, alike, the rewards are very great. Miss Wynne Jones has set a standard for 1980 which will take some beating. (pp. 192-93)

> *M. Crouch, in a review of "The Magicians of Caprona," in* The Junior Bookshelf, *Vol. 44, No. 4, August, 1980, pp. 192-93.*

Jones sets this in the ununified Italy of a world "parallel to ours, where magic is as normal as mathematics, and things are generally more old-fashioned" and she directs it like a manic opera, as the varied but uniformly voluble members of the closely-knit extended Montana family cope in frenetic counterpoint with one crisis after another. (The enemy is invading, the children are kidnapped, the cat ate the fish.) The most theatrical scene occurs fairly early on, when the Montanas in full force confront the hated Petrocci clan, their rivals in spell-casting, in a knock-'em-down, zap-'em-to-pieces contest of shape-changing magic. The battle occurs because each family believes the other guilty of kidnapping, but in fact an outside enchanter has imprisoned the youngest Montana and the youngest Petrocci to tie up both families' defensive spells while three other states invade their native Caprona. As little Tonino Montana and Angelica Petrocci discover to their terror and discomfort, the enchantress behind the plot against Caprona is the Duchess herself. . . . [Her] evil genius proves so powerful that it takes the Duke, the now-united magician families, the Montana cat Benvenuto, and a guest appearance by the great Chrestomanci of *Charmed Life* to reduce her to her true rat's form and dispatch her accordingly. Jones carries off the performance with real finesse and a great show of brio. However, the absence of moral, intellectual, or (especially) emotional grounding might be an impediment to reader engagement.

> *A review of "The Magicians of Caprona," in* Kirkus Reviews, *Vol. XLVIII, No. 17, September 1, 1980, p. 1163.*

The Four Grannies (1980)

Diana Wynne Jones, in *The Four Grannies,* starts with a promising situation. Because of their parents' previous marriages, Emily and Erg have four grandmothers: one stern, one anxious, one selfish and one feebly saintly. When the parents go away, all four grannies come to look after the children. The prospect is uncomfortable and the things get worse when Erg's invention, made from stray bits of household equipment, develops magic powers, apparently turning Emily into a large teddy bear. Erg's efforts to keep this a secret from the grannies are entertaining and result in the production of one magically amalgamated Supergranny who combines the annoying characteristics of all four.

Much of the action is lively, reinforced by some spirited drawings from Thelma Lambert. But the final effect is somewhat wooden. Diana Wynne Jones is one of the most inventive and original of modern writers for children, but her abilities seem cramped here. The grannies fall between two stools, being neither believable characters nor satisfyingly monstrous monsters, and the plot is solved unsatisfactorily and abruptly, by an accident. It is a fairly entertaining book, but it falls short of that comic glee at which it so clearly aims.

> *Gillian Cross, "Beginning Books," in* The Times Literary Supplement, *No. 4042, September 19, 1980, p. 1026.*

The Homeward Bounders (1981)

The Homeward Bounders is a fantasy novel with elements of science fiction, in which Diana Wynne Jones develops the idea of war gaming by playing with live characters in an infinite number of different worlds. As in her previous novels, her apparently inexhaustible imagination takes in many moods and themes. The book contains terror, humour, adventure, everyday problems of survival and references to mythical characters.

The story begins in our own world in 1879 when thirteen-year-old Jamie stumbles unknowingly into forbidden territory and witnesses "Them" (faceless grey-cloaked figures) playing a mysterious game involving minute worlds, huge dice and complicated machines. This is the "Real Place" from which They control what goes on in different worlds, having previously absorbed the reality of those worlds. The details of this are only revealed later, but Jamie has already seen too much and must be "discarded" to the "Bounds" between the worlds. There are, of course, certain rules: he may not "enter play" in any world and every time a move ends in his field of play, he will be transferred remorselessly on to another field of play. He is allowed to return home—if he can find home—and only then can he re-enter play. He has become a "Homeward Bounder". The full horror of the implications of this is only gradually revealed to the reader, as Jamie relates his experiences in a pleasantly chatty, intimate style which subtly emphasizes his terror, loneliness and his longing for home.

Jamie passes through a hundred worlds, some welcoming, others hostile, before returning home but it is one hundred years later and he is still a thirteen-year-old. He has met numerous vividly drawn characters: Helen with the magical Hand of Uquar, Joris, the demon-hunter, the mythical Titan chained endlessly to his rock, Ahasuerus, the Wandering Jew and The Flying Dutchman.

It is a complex story with many different threads running through it. The early allusions to characters and situations in the latter part of the story may well be missed on a first reading. The recurrence of the anchor symbol, references to mythology and the emphasis on Hope, are important elements in the understanding of the story. "Hope is an anchor" Ahasuerus states prophetically: "If you cast hope aside . . . all evil is cast out with it".

It is only when Jamie is totally bereft of hope that he unwittingly frees the Titan and begins to understand Ahasuerus' prophecy and the states of the worlds. The final battle against Them can now be won; the worlds can become real again. But Jamie is condemned to walk the bounds for ever, as the anchor which will secure the continuing survival of the worlds.

It is not an easy book to read and many of the ideas may be difficult for all but the most dedicated reader to grasp. But for that reader, the story is strangely compelling—rather like a monster jigsaw puzzle in which the reader can become totally and intensely absorbed.

> *Judith Elkin, "Walking the Bounds," in* The Times Literary Supplement, *No. 4069, March 27, 1981, p. 339.*

Good and evil are in opposition on a cosmic and a local scale at the same time in **The Homeward Bounders.** The extraordinary power of this narrative is the result of strong feeling combined with brilliant technique. The author does not lay down her theme or her plot bluntly but allows the shape and point of the story to come to the reader clue by clue, as events are suffered, and assessed, by the victims of 'Them' and most of all by young Jamie, central among the Homeward Bounders. The idea that 'They' are playing an enormous, multi-part war-game with whole worlds is chillingly real because of Jamie's words and actions, as he slowly realises the penalties of being a random piece on the board, gathering information from the people he meets—dark, enigmatic Helen and the acquiescent slave Joris among them—and using intellect and emotion in judging the enemy's weakness and deciding on his special duty for the future. At times Jamie seems, simply, the questing, questioning spirit of Man, and this is confirmed by his bitterly real dealings with the Promethean sufferer who encourages his independence of mind: at other times he is a boy driven by gigantic, inexplicable forces. This is not a book that could have an 'ending' as such, but it has a conclusion, and one that sums up the elusive hints and emotional tides of a book precise and perceptive in details and immensely powerful as a whole.

> *Margery Fisher, in a review of "The Homeward Bounders," in* Growing Point, *Vol. 20, No. 1, May, 1981, p. 3882.*

This many-leveled book can be enjoyed as pure adventure but also as an allegory with its folkloric and mythical allusions, its plays on words like "bound" and the evil, amoral *They* and the war games *They* play, with human beings as game pieces. Even though the story bogs down at times, it then conveys the frustration and boredom Jamie endures. A satisfying tale and one that "Dungeons and Dragons" fans ought to especially enjoy.

> *Mary I. Purucker, in a review of "The Homeward Bounders," in* School Library Journal, *Vol. 28, No. 1, September, 1981, p. 137.*

Combining elements of science fiction, folklore, and mythology, the author has created a fantasy with overtones of allegory. . . . In spite of its tragic overtones, the story is never lugubrious; the originality of its concepts is intriguing, and the realism of its presentation gives it verisimilitude. But because of the haphazard quality of Jamie's experiences, the narrative pace is somewhat disjointed and makes many demands of the reader.

> *Paul Heins, in a review of "The Homeward Bounders," in* The Horn Book Magazine, *Vol. LVII, No. 5, October, 1981, p. 542.*

The Time of the Ghost   (1981)

Diana Wynne Jones is a prolific novelist of enormous range who can raise hairs on the back of the neck one minute, belly laughs the next. A certain untidyness and self-indulgent prolixty have characterized many of her novels to date, especially the group set in an imaginary medieval period. But she also writes about modern children, witty, abrasive, articulate, often neglected, always resilient: they need to be resilient if they are to cope with the emantions of the paranormal that threaten their lives.

Diana Wynne Jones's new novel, **The Time of the Ghost,** is one of her modern stories. The title is instantly forgettable one may think as one picks up this book but as, three hours later and in a state of bewildered admiration one lays it down again, realization dawns: the title pinpoints the theme exactly. Mrs Wynne Jones is skillfully exploring time—and the ghost.

In the conventional literary ghost story it is the ghost of past happenings that rises, walks, haunts the present demanding retribution. Diana Wynne Jones defies this convention; for here it is from the present that a ghost returns to a period seven years past, desperate to avert a catastrophe in its own "now".

To explain, or to try to explain: the ghost that hovers unhappily among the three Melford sisters in their joyless rooms in a boys' boarding school is a lost memory, yellowish, amorphous with a voice trying always to break through. It is urgently seeking to recover its identity; is it Sally the fourth (absent) sister, and if so, why isn't it embodied? For the ghost knows Sally is not *yet* dead. But is a Sally-in-the-future in danger? The body of a young woman lying unconscious in a hospital bed after an accident could be that Sally of the future. The accident might have been connected with the Melfords' black magic practices (in which the boys from the school had joined). Monigan, the greedy spirit they raised, may finally be claiming the life of one of the Melfords, seven years hence.

The ghost/lost memory of the young woman in the hospital bed must somehow intervene in the past to divert Monigan's curse.

Not since K. M. Briggs, that great folklorist and author of *Kate Crackernuts,* has the supernatural been so firmly and convincingly handled. But here the horror of dealing with evil spirits, the blood rites, the elemental disturbances lie cheek-by-jowl with a richly humorous story in which three schoolgirls, determined to catch the attention of their over-busy parents for once, send off the fourth sister to see whether "Himself " and Phyllis will notice Sally is missing. *The Time of the Ghost* is a great feat of imaginative writing. It will be a thousand pities if, like the ghost of Sally, it fails to float over the artificial barriers of the adolescents' world to attract the attention of adults.

Elaine Moss, "Ghostly Forms," in The Times Literary Supplement, *No. 4103, November 20, 1981, p. 1354.*

Atmosphere is all, in true ghost stories. Motive and situation may be infinitely plausible, characters carefully shown to be vulnerable, but the thrill, the conviction of ghostliness, depends on less detectable, less tangible elements, on appropriate combinations of words and rhythms and on such *selected* details of place and circumstance as will strike at the senses. Too little atmosphere and the story will fall flat: too much, and it will turn into farce. In *The Time of the Ghost* Diana Wynne Jones shows impeccable control of her material. In particular, she uses description scrupulously so that we get to know just as much of the school buildings and the surrounding country as we need, and no more. Emotion and atmosphere grow out of these settings. . . . The turmoil of humans close in birth and rearing, passionately different in temperament, at once dictates and is dictated by the ghost-element in the story, whose complexities tease the mind and harry the heart while weird, flickering humour eases the tension. This unorthodox 'ghost story' has more real supernatural terror in it than hundreds of more usual hauntings.

Margery Fisher, in a review of "The Time of the Ghost," in Growing Point, *Vol. 20, No. 5, January, 1982, p. 3992.*

[Apart] from the personalities of the girls the book's charm lies in its weirdly hilarious vignettes of the school and its boys, the family life of the girls, and often and just as entertainingly in the combination of both. A sinister thread does come to the surface occasionally but one never knows how seriously to regard it and perhaps the readers may feel cheated at the end, but not many will mind. Miss Wynne Jones has broken the rules of fantasy before and got away with it. If single adjectives are required, there is a choice of whacky, grotty or kooky, but certainly not grotesque, mind-boggling or quaint. (p. 34)

A. R. Williams, in a review of "The Time of the Ghost," in The Junior Bookshelf, *Vol. 46, No. 1, February, 1982, pp. 33-4.*

Witch Week (1982)

Diana Wynne Jones has returned to the fast-moving pace and immensely entertaining tone of *Charmed Life* in this latest book. The time is, more-or-less, our familiar present-day world, but heavily steeped in witchcraft, and in a period of suppression: witchcraft is illegal, witches are burned on bonfires and the Inquisitors are an everyday threat.

Set within the enclosed community of a boarding school, the action centres on class 2Y who, at the age of about twelve, are just discovering their own witchcraft, some reluctantly, some delightedly, others unwittingly and with hilarious results. The story begins with a note to the teacher of 2Y, saying "Someone in this class is a witch." An innocuous-enough comment but not when witchcraft is punishable by burning. The teacher broods on the implications of the note and the children write their private daily diaries, revealing, although somewhat obscurely, their individual feelings, viewpoints and relationships. In the first few pages, the reader is offered a huge amount of instant background detail and is likely to be totally committed to this outrageous story.

It transpires that there is more than one witch in the class, and this idea allows free rein to Diana Wynne Jones's vividly inventive imagination, as she explores the children's varied, yet largely uncontrolled magic, set against their constant fear of discovery. As usual she manages to follow several parallel threads without any loss of impetus or blurring of characters. There is Nan who has a peculiar gift of tongues which leads to her apparently uncontrollable and stomach-turning description of school dinners, while seated at the top table with the Headmistress and important guests. Yet this is the gift which proves vital at the final climax of the story. There is Charles, the loner, who turns out to be a very powerful, but very self-interested witch, who first discovers the extent of his power when he calls all the shoes in the school (hundreds of them) into the school hall, in an attempt to find his trainers, but quite unsuccessfully, as Nirupan has already turned them into a chocolate cake which the class bully has eaten, spikes and all.

Fear of the Inquisitors finally drives the children to call the powerful Enchanter, Chrestomanci, to their aid. He needs all his powers and that of the witches in 2Y to sort out what has gone wrong with their world. This is a theme familiar in the author's earlier books: parallel worlds split from each other at a significant point in history and thence develop separately. But in this case, two worlds have not split cleanly, leaving one world with an unequal share of outlawed witchcraft still partly attached to an almost identical world with too little witchcraft. Chrestomanci has to find the point in history where things went wrong and try to unify the two worlds.

This is a much less demanding book than *The Homeward Bounders,* but it contains a great deal of very entertaining reading, which will appeal to many children. The story romps along, the dialogue is excellent and the characters carefully observed. These are real characters whom you might find in any second year in a comprehensive school, but drawn large in this vivid world of magic. The reader is left wondering how normal teachers actually manage without magical powers.

Judith Elkin, "School Charms," in The Times Literary Supplement, *No. 4138, July 23, 1982, p. 794.*

Comic witches are fashionable just now—likewise comic ghosts and familiars of various kinds. Fortunately, for every facetious tale centred on a broomstick-version of the banana-skin joke, there is one which uses humour as a way to set the anarchic impulses of youth in a new light. Like the necromantic academies described in recent years by Barbara Willard and Jill Murphy, Larwood House School is plagued by magic going awry but in **Witch Week** the magic is not a curriculum subject but a secret and forbidden undercurrent. This is one of those fantasies which describe in familiar and concrete terms an alternative world, one which diverged from our own back in the past when legislation against witches had to take into account the persistence of a genetic freak. . . . Diana Wynne Jones takes everyday incidents (lost running-shoes, illicit night-expeditions, water-fights) and gives them an edge of weird improbability, while the familiar rivalries and alliances of schooldays are made strangely urgent by the impending investigations from staff and outsiders. There seems no limit to this author's inventive energy; ingenious in plot, with a mock-casual twist at the end, her new book offers one more rollicking and provocative study of human behaviour.

> *Margery Fisher, in a review of "Witch Week,"*
> in Growing Point, *Vol. 21, No. 4, November,*
> *1982, p. 3984.*

Among the post-war generation of children's writers none is more individual and more unpredictable than Diana Wynne Jones. Of her next book all one can be sure of is that it will be exciting, amusing and unlike the last. For one who treads the tricky paths of fantasy that is saying quite a lot.

In some ways the society shown in **Witch Week** is not unlike that of present-day England. Larwood House School is, in a nasty way, similar to other boarding schools. The pupils are not much more horrid than others; the teachers are odd, but then some of them are in real life. But something is wrong, as if we were looking at reality through a distorting glass. There is this preoccupation with witchcraft. And in an apparently civilized society witches, of all ages and both sexes, are burnt. With the Inquisitor ready to move in at a moment's notice, no wonder that witches and their probable fate occupy more than a fair share of the children's thoughts. (p. 231)

Adults, who often find it more difficult than children to accept incongruities, may be bothered that so revolting a subject as death by burning can be treated in a funny way. I must admit that one or two things in this story stuck in my throat; on the other hand I also found myself laughing aloud, and that doesn't often happen. The invention, of character and incident (and the two are interlinked), is brilliant, the writing, and especially the dialogue, beautifully controlled. An offbeat masterpiece. (p. 232)

> *M. Crouch, in a review of "Witch Week," in*
> The Junior Bookshelf, *Vol. 46, No. 6, December, 1982, pp. 231-32.*

Archer's Goon (1984)

When Quentin Sykes refuses to write his quarterly quota of words for the mysterious Mountjoy, he and his family

learn it can be inconvenient—and even dangerous—to defy the commands of imperious magicians. Unwittingly and unwillingly involved in a wizardly power struggle, the family Sykes discovers that nothing is as it seems and that no one can be trusted. One of the strengths of this story lies in Jones' ability to create memorable, idiosyncratic characters with swift, sure strokes of detail. Although there are many players, each is an individual rendered with insight and wit. It is a mad world Jones has created, unpredictable and spiced with unexpected humor. The complicated and surprising plot, involved and quickly paced, is fugal in design. Brim full of the kind of seemingly effortless creativity which marks a confident writer who revels in her ability to spin improbable yarns, **Archer's Goon** leaves readers wanting more.

> *Holly Sanhuber, in a review of "Archer's*
> *Goon," in* School Library Journal, *Vol. 30,*
> *No. 7, March, 1984, p. 160.*

Though the writing in **Archer's Goon** is fine and the scenes and characters fresh and well-drawn, the convolutions of the plot and sheer numbers of characters make the whole difficult to juggle. It is fast-paced and comic, which keeps you turning the pages, but is finally only a self-indulgent romp from an author who has been seduced by, and has lost control to, her own extravagant inventions. Still, it's a cheery tale and children will probably like it a lot.

> *Natalie Babbitt, "Writings of Passage: The*
> *Young and the Restless," in* Book World—
> The Washington Post, *May 13, 1984, p. 18.*

Though previous science fiction titles by Jones have proven innovative and interesting, **Archer's Goon**'s erratic structure, confusing plot, and uninteresting action make it a title most YAs would not choose for leisure reading. . . . **Archer's Goon** presents a naughty little girl, named Awful; a series of zany characters, and a hint of mystery to entice readers; yet its plot is so unbelievable and its protagonists so unlikeable that a YA reader would be hard put to finish the title. In addition to its reading defects, there is the problem of readership: while older teens would reject the title because of the youth of its protagonists and the corny character of a little girl named Awful, the younger ones would be too confused by the tangled plot to be satisfied with the book.

> *Diane C. Donovan, in a review of "Archer's*
> *Goon," in* Voice of Youth Advocates, *Vol. 7,*
> *No. 2, June, 1984, p. 101.*

Jones is an accomplished writer; what difficulties there are in the text seem rather minor. The mysterious seven at times verge on the grotesque. The grossly fat, leather-wearing Shine, who farms crime, may be a bit too threatening for a juvenile, for example. And the novel does encourage a mildly paranoic worldview, since there is indeed a cabalistic conspiracy out there somewhere. And finally, there are a fair number of Briticisms which might present some problems for the seventh graders and up the book is designed for.

On the other hand, **Archer's Goon** does create moments of believable suspense with which its intended audience will probably feel deep empathy. The characters do develop a sense of life, even though several touch on being stereotypes—Howard's kid sister, for instance. And the plot itself works through a number of convolutions with some skill. My only complaints are that the nature of the mysterious seven is never quite fully explained, and that the novel's resolution seems more temporary than permanent—several of the nastier wizard-types are successfully eliminated, but the central problem (and the remaining wizards) remain. Still, the book is pleasant, tightly plotted, with occasional forays into wit and discussions of the power of words.

Michael R. Collings, "Amusing Paranoia," in Fantasy Review, *Vol. 8, No. 1, January, 1985, p. 45.*

Fire and Hemlock   (1984)

Polly Whittacker has two conflicting sets of childhood memories; one is boringly normal, and the other is infused with the friendship of cellist Thomas Lynn. Although Mr. Lynn introduces her to books and music, his company also brings danger, and ultimately a kind of amnesia, which seems to be linked to the sinister folks of Hunston House and an enigmatic painting. If *Fire and Hemlock* is not so fast-paced and exuberantly humorous as some of Jones' earlier work, it shows an impressive awareness of character interaction and development. Jones draws telling portraits: Polly's mother, who blames others for her own inadequacies; her father, weak and bemused by self deception; astrigent granny and Polly herself, whose growth to womanhood is gracefully portrayed. The friendship between Polly and Tom parallels that growth and is detailed with warmth, humor and realism. The elegiac tone, the leisurely pace and the difficult narrative structure (an extended flashback) will not appeal to some readers, yet the careful orchestration of suspense, the creation of a mood of forboding and mystery will capture others who are able to immerse themselves in the book's complexities. This is a haunting, thought-provoking story, which, like the painting of the title, seems to change focus each time it is viewed. The characters perform a stately dance macabre to the strains of the British ballads "Tam Lin" and "Thomas the Rhymer," in which the implacably cold creatures of another world overreach themselves because they do not understand the steadfastness of human love. In the denouement, as elsewhere, nothing is certain. It seems that to lose is to win, to let go is to hold, and to become bereft is to be granted healing, hope and happiness. (pp. 167-68)

Holly Sanhuber, in a review of "Fire and Hemlock," in School Library Journal, *Vol. 31, No. 2, October, 1984, pp. 167-68.*

Jones is a British author of several highly recommended books. This novel deserves equal acclaim. It is the story of a college-age girl puzzling over recent clues about her past that don't seem to correspond with the facts. The remainder of the novel is a series of flashbacks as she attempts to recreate the crucial events in her past that have led to this confusing situation. The plot becomes an intricate romantic fantasy filled with mystery, magic, sorcery and intrigue as the girl is drawn into an unusual relationship with an older man.

There is much here to interest the younger reader, especially girls, since they would more easily identify with the main character and her memories of growing up. Whoever reads it hopefully will respond to the message throughout the book advocating the joys of reading as found in Tolkein, Dumas, fairy tales, folk ballads, *The Golden Bough,* and many other works.

Though marketed for younger readers, it is a well-written book for anyone. Adults can appreciate the finely-crafted plot, their own shared memories of the painful process of growing up, and the deepening mysteries that unfold. Reality shades hazily into magic and the lack of sharp distinctions between the two add much enjoyment to *Fire and Hemlock.*

Gary Zacharias, in a review of "Fire and Hemlock," in Fantasy Review, *Vol. 8, No. 5, May, 1985, p. 19.*

Wynne Jones has written her way comfortably into **Fire and Hemlock** (. . . her first [novel] for older teenagers) by starting with a ten-year-old and watching her grow up. The expedient is the only simple thing about the book. Nominally, the whole history is in flashback, effortlessly recalled by Polly as she lounges on her bed at Granny's house, putting off packing for her fourth term at Oxford, and wondering who it was that gave her the strange photo of hemlock and burning hay that hangs over her head. This first chapter is perfunctory, and the book is two-thirds done before we return to the present-day Polly, almost as if the author herself did not know the answer, and had to write the story to find out.

The mystery provokes such doubts. Characters, major and minor, constantly and inexplicably change roles. The Fairies only pretend to observe human social conventions; but are the humans any less perfidious? Which are the humans anyway? A pervasive instability disturbs the reading. Polly's Granny, for example, begins as a dry, dependable old lady, "upright as the Queen Mother" and redolent of shortbread. She passes through a fidgety, superstitious phase, and emerges at last as a fearless and wise white witch. If old Mrs Whittacker knew from the first what she is constrained to reveal at the eleventh hour, why did she not rouse herself at once? It is laid on her not to remember, and history itself has been tampered with; but is it the imminence of the ninth Hallowe'en that starts to loosen the spell, or is it that the author finished her book with a subtle understanding of its immense complexity, but failed to go back and write this into the beginning?

The character of Polly, on the other hand, develops with commendable steadiness. Her relationship with Tom Lynn is daringly conceived, delicately shaped and unfailingly fascinating. What it means, however, is perpetually in doubt. The text is explicitly organized by a straightforward fairy-tale pattern derived from the ballads of "Tam Lin" and "Thomas the Rhymer". Yet sinister, inverted interpretations forcibly suggest themselves: the book is Polly's nightmare of adulthood; or Polly has inherited her mother's paranoia and never knows it; or else the Fairies are indeed real, and Tom and Granny are part of their malevolent conspiracy, with Polly the dupe of a vampiric race that preys upon the human heart. Or Polly is a Fairy too, possibly even Tom and Lorelei's daughter. Pressed, the puzzle yields such plausible solutions, none complete, none satisfying. In a mystical duel informed by imagery from T. S. Eliot's *Burnt Norton,* Polly gains a courageous victory, but in such a questionable world the consolation is slight.

Colin Greenland, "Nine Hallowe'ens," in The Times Literary Supplement, *No. 4313, November 29, 1985, p. 1358.*

Warlock at the Wheel and Other Stories (1984)

In this collection of eight stories, Jones exhibits her ability to work successfully within the framework of a short format. The humorous title story features a warlock in search of lost magical powers. This story and **"The Sage of Theare"** give readers further glimpses of that unconventional wizard, Chrestomanci, introduced in Jones' *Charmed Life* **"Auntie Bea's Day Out"** resembles a compact *Mary Poppins* with a contemporary flair. **"No One"** shows a robot's confrontation with automation, while **"The Fluffy Pink Toadstool"** explores whims and excesses in a family. Jones often mixes humor with the dark side of human nature, as seen in **"Carruthers"** and **"A Plague of Peacocks."** **"Dragon Reserve, Home Eight"** has finely drawn characters and rich thematic material, suggesting it as a candidate for expansion into a full-length novel. It is the most complex story in the book. Four of these stories have previously appeared in earlier British publications. Readers will find this collection widely varied in story line, with the ingenuity of young people—good and bad—frequently emphasized. Dialogue is lively and uncontrived. Jones' strength as a writer of fantasy is shown in her ability to make characters who are part of the most unlikely situations seem reachable and credible. An exciting collection which sustains reader interest throughout. (pp. 97-8)

Karen P. Smith, in a review of "Warlock at the Wheel and Other Stories," in School Library Journal, *Vol. 31, No. 8, April, 1985, pp. 97-8.*

A selection of eight short fantasy stories by Jones that maintains the standard of charm and unexpectedness of her novels. In **"The Plague of Peacocks"** only Daniel Emanuel is able to drive the nosey and overbearing Platts out of town. Once he realizes that the Platts remind him of peacocks hundreds of peacocks appear to nest on the Platts lawn until they leave. Fluffy pink toadstools grow all over the house when Mother gets into a health food craze. Father finally says he cannot live in a house with pink toadstools and will leave unless she gets rid of them in **"The Fluffy Pink Toadstool."** Overbearing Auntie Bea in **"Auntie Bea's Day Out"** is certain that she can picnic on the island despite the No Trespassing signs. The children notice the strange happenings and go home but Auntie Bea is determined to stay and vanishes as does the island. It is a while before the family finds out what happened to her. Then there is **"Carruthers"** a magical walking stick that only speaks to Elizabeth. Knowing Carruthers gets Elizabeth in a lot of trouble until she discovers what Carruthers really is. In **"No One"** a computerized house and a robot fight between themselves to see who will run the house with disastrous results until they must unite to save Edward, their human occupant from a kidnapping.

This is a charming collection full of unique "people." Jones has a gift for creating unusual circumstances and surprising endings that fantasy fans will really enjoy.

Jean Kaufman, in a review of "Warlock at the Wheel and Other Stories," in Voice of Youth Advocates, *Vol. 8, No. 2, June, 1985, p. 139.*

These eight stories by a master of fantasy show an exuberance of imagination that is almost overwhelming and is reminiscent of the work of Joan Aiken. Many themes are favorites with this author; several of the stories deal with alternate worlds—as in *The Homeward Bounders.* Chrestomanci, the urbane master magician from *Charmed Life,* appears in two tales, including the title story, **"Warlock at the Wheel,"** the hilarious account of a renegade warlock who gets his comeuppance at the hands of a magic car, a bratty child, and her very large and protective dog. In **"A Plague of Peacocks"** a little boy with supernatural powers wreaks a perfect revenge on a busybody couple. The confines of the short story, however, do not always allow the author enough room for expansion. In **"Dragon Reserve, Home Eight"** there are telepathic dragons, a confederation of planets, a polyandrous society, an elite corps of military, a strong-willed fourteen-year-old heroine with magic powers, and an attack by evil slavers—all in twenty-nine pages. A splendid story, it would have made an even more splendid novel. But the reader will undoubtedly revel in the rich collection of magical tales. (pp. 453-54)

Ann A. Flowers, in a review of "Warlock at the Wheel and Other Stories," in The Horn Book Magazine, *Vol. LXI, No. 4, July/August, 1985, pp. 453-54.*

Howl's Moving Castle (1986)

Wizard Howl's black-chimneyed castle which lurches about the countryside is only one of the oddities in a story that all but denies synopsis. In the heroine, Sophie, transformed by the Witch of the Waste into an elderly woman during most of the book, and in the hero, Howl, who indulges in long scented baths and has a reputation for eating the hearts of young females, emerge a pair of colorful and unstereotypical personalities. The author, well-known for *Archer's Goon* and *Dogsbody,* extracts every possible ounce of humor and entertainment from the unlikely combination. The plot does not so much unfold as erupt, as meddlesome Sophie sets to right the frightful disorder of Howl's castle where she has taken refuge during her enchantment and where she attempts to break the strange contract between Howl and the fire demon, Calcifer. She fends off a menacing scarecrow and plunges around in seven league boots while scolding yet endearing herself to Howl's chaotic household. Wit and humor glint from the pages as does the author's dexterity in making a prodigious assortment of spells seem a part of everyday life. Thunderous displays of magic reverberate as Howl and the Witch of the Waste reach their final confrontation, but it is the growing romance of Sophie and Howl—who bicker, argue, and sulk—which gives warmth to the almost brittle facility of the fantastic plot and provides the story's engaging appeal and happy ending. (pp. 331-32)

Ethel R. Twichell, in a review of "Howl's Moving Castle," in The Horn Book Magazine, *Vol. LXII, No. 3, May/June, 1986, pp. 331-32.*

[This is an] intricate, humorous and puzzling tale of fantasy and adventure which should both challenge and involve readers. Jones has created an engaging set of characters and found a new use for many of the appurtenances of fairy tales—seven league boots and invisible cloaks, among others. At times, the action becomes so complex that readers may have to go back to see what actually happened, and at the end so many loose ends have to be tied up at once that it's dizzying. Yet Jones' inventiveness never fails, and her conclusion is infinitely satisfying.

Sara Miller, in a review of "Howl's Moving Castle," in School Library Journal, *Vol. 32, No. 10, August, 1986, p. 101.*

Diana Wynne Jones's eighteenth book is a very accomplished and assured fantasy. Set in the fairy world of Ingary, **Howl's Moving Castle** creates a land filled with magic spells, charmed suits of clothes, seven-league boots, demons, witches and wizards. At the same time, the book ingeniously updates a number of fairytale themes and motifs. . . . The two worlds, Ingary and Wales, set each other off to good effect and the interchange between them is carefully controlled without seeming over contrived. The range of strange characters and adventures is striking and there are some impressive descriptions of magical effects such as that of a storm of magic with jumping packets, seething powders and a guitar playing itself tunelessly. Sophie's transformation into an old woman is particularly well handled as part of a consistently inventive and often very amusing novel which can be warmly recommended to readers of eleven upwards.

Emma Letley, "A Storm of Magic," in The Times Literary Supplement, *No. 4367, December 12, 1986, p. 1410.*

The dislocation of personality is aptly illustrated here by the several doors of the castle, which open on to different places and times; the fact that the castle not only pivots but also actually travels increases the possibilities of dramatic action and developing relationships between Sophie Hatter, whose curiosity leads her into the castle, and the necromancer Howl, whose reputation for battening on the souls of young girls proves to be unjustified. In romantic terms this is the story of an unlikely love flourishing against pretty stiff odds, largely because of a young woman's good sense and tenacity. In terms of fantasy it is an absorbing sequence of conflict and incantation, with a finely drawn Witch of the Waste, an utterly original and comical fire-demon and an assortment of landscapes and interiors which have that uniquely persuasive oddity special to Diana Wynne Jones. I was totally captivated by this story, by its inventive vivacity, by the shot-silk variations on traditional magic themes and, above all, by the special, tender, spontaneous humour which asserts positively the enduring virtues of the human spirit. (pp. 4772-73)

Margery Fisher, in a review of "Howl's Moving Castle," in Growing Point, *Vol. 25, No. 6, March, 1987, pp. 4772-73.*

A Tale of Time City **(1987)**

High-spirited time travel fantasy that is sure to delight its readers. When 11-year-old Vivian Smith is evacuated from London in 1939, she expects to end up in the peaceful British countryside. Instead she is kidnapped by two

youthful time travellers who mistake her for the "Time Lady" and whisk her off to Time City, a richly imagined alternative world which exists in time but not in history. Time City observers, Viv learns, have reason to believe that the Time Lady, the wife of the founder of Time City—a mysterious Merlin figure—is at large in history and is busily altering it, thereby endangering not only the historical world but Time City itself. If Vivian is to return to her own world and time, it will be necessary for her to help her kidnappers foil the Time Lady first. That almost nothing—whether person or incident—is precisely what it appears to be at first encounter both complicates Vivian's task and delights readers. This ability to surprise has become a Diana Wynne Jones signature, as have her unflagging inventiveness and almost uncanny ability to create imaginary worlds of resounding reality, a capacity based in part on her attention to detail and in part on her capacity to create believable and sympathetic characters. All of these gifts are in abundant evidence in **A Tale of Time City** which is, accordingly, absolutely first-rate entertainment. And to her fans, this will be one of the few things about her new book which will come as no surprise!

Michael Cart, in a review of "A Tale of Time City," in School Library Journal, *Vol. 34, No. 1, September, 1987, p. 196.*

A Tale of Time City is Diana Wynne Jones's nineteenth novel and one of her most exuberant. The title is well chosen. In the style of her first rather helter-skelter books, and in contrast to more sombre recent publications like **Fire and Hemlock,** the 285 pages of **A Tale** are all story. . . .

At times the book rather resembles an enormously extended episode of *Dr. Who,* with grotesque dangers almost flippantly survived, and time-travel paradoxes knocking everyone for loops. Now and then the piled-up complexities of Wynne Jones's story interact negatively with the streamlined thinness of texture her swift and reckless pacing necessarily entails, so that occasional moments of confusion are inevitable. Younger readers, being perhaps less likely than adults to question the patchwork quilt of science fiction and fantasy that underlies the tale, may find its dazzling speed exhilarating, its grotesqueries unshocking. At the story's close, they will also find a lesson or two.

Present from the first as a burly bad-tempered tutor, Faber John recovers his memory in the nick—more accurately the end—of time, and confounds the ambitions of the power-seeking family responsible for all the tumult. Selfishness is laid bare and punished, but with compassion; and Vivian brings the attention of the assembled adults of Time City sharply to bear on the subject of their collective guardianship. After the hilarity and the confusion—time-travel stories, especially those built on paradoxes, are inherently difficult to narrate with any clarity—a mellow and familial glow suffuses the final pages. It is a mark of Wynne Jones's highly deliberate craft that this humane closing seems perfectly in order, and thoroughly welcome.

John Clute, "Approaching Unstable Eras," in The Times Literary Supplement, *No. 4416, November 20-26, 1987, p. 1283.*

This is a book recommended only to those school librarians who serve a readership already committed to the work of Diana Wynne Jones. It is a demanding read, with literary and historical references which will be lost on the inexperienced reader. There is a tremendous amount of detail, particularly in the descriptions of Time City, which leaves vivid images in the mind, and the reader must be prepared to meet the author half-way and work with the young protagonists through the problems and situations which face them.

> *Sheila Ray, in a review of "A Tale of Time City," in* The School Librarian, *Vol. 36, No. 2, May, 1988, p. 64.*

The Lives of Christopher Chant (1988)

Christopher's dreams project him into strange worlds—he calls them "the Anywheres"—which are only a bit odder than his home, where Mother and Father communicate for the most part through notes. Like Christopher, the reader is projected into a tailspin journey, never knowing what twists and turns lie ahead. A kindly uncle is in reality a scoundrel, and a questionable governess eventually becomes a friend; Christopher discovers that he has extraordinary powers of enchantment and the gift of nine lives. A prequel to **Charmed Life,** the story is concerned with Chrestomanci's youthful adventures with Millie—his wife in the earlier book and now a goddess who escapes from captivity in the Anywheres—and with a final and glorious battle. Marvelously funny moments sparkle throughout as whole castles are levitated and lowered with massive creakings and clouds of plaster and as the most ornery of cats slashes and claws his way into the reader's affection. The author moves a large and captivating cast of characters around with a choreographer's skill and gives to an enchanter's apprenticeship the same homely qualities one might need to master driving a car. Although the plot is almost labyrinthine and occasionally confusing, the individual episodes are wonderfully entertaining. To read the book, you must resign yourself to the impossible and let a born storyteller weave her own brand of magic. (pp. 208-09)

> *Ethel R. Twichell, in a review of "The Lives of Christopher Chant," in* The Horn Book Magazine, *Vol. LXIV, No. 2, March/April, 1988, pp. 208-09.*

[This] story runs swiftly along with the most good-humoured acceptance of magic. Those of serious temper can read it as a study in the development of a boy from childhood to maturity; those who are romantically inclined can ponder over the friendship which grows between Christopher, who takes magic pretty casually, and his boon companion, the Little Goddess, whose divinity may be dangerous to her when she grows up. The exuberant inventiveness in the book is felt in the characterisation—of the boy and girl, of Gabriel the wraith-like controller of enchantment, most of all perhaps of the forthright cat Throckmorten who is vital in the defence of Christopher's stronghold when it is besieged by the dreaded Dright and his evil band. It is felt in the details which make each scene memorable, from the Egyptian-style buildings of Asheth to the dripping wet, recognisable World B and the splendidly uninhibited magic which Christopher as a beginner greatly enjoys. In fact he is revealed as the next Chrestomanci-elect and readers of *A Charmed Life* will be fascinated to see the working of an unusual apprenticeship in an alternative world of wizard-ry and its expressions of levitation, misdirection or kinetic power.

> *Margery Fisher, in a review of "The Lives of Christopher Chant," in* Growing Point, *Vol. 27, No. 5, January, 1989, p. 5092.*

In this exuberant fantasy the magician Christopher Chant is living through his awkward boyhood, painfully sorting good from bad among those who wish to harness or exploit his nascent powers, and slowly accepting his vocation as the next Chrestomanci (a Nine-lifed Enchanter)—the author marvellously conveys his gradual change from reluctant sulkiness to relish. Christopher is also learning the hardest of real-life childhood lessons: to see himself through other people's eyes.

The book's exceptional narrative energy successfully mingles high comedy and deep seriousness, enchantment and naturalism, wild invention and deadpan normality. Its flavour is well illustrated by the literary jokes. In mischievous parody of the cricket match in *England, Their England,* Chrestomanci Castle plays the village team, whose most destructive weapon is 'a demonically cunning spin bowler', the village blacksmith: Christopher, who is mad on cricket, soon sees *him* off. A little more pathos surrounds the Living Goddess Asheth, who longs to attend a proper boarding school like Larwood House, the scene of dorm adventures for her fictional heroine Millie. But some of the verbal jokes are much more acidic, like the name of Eleven's godlike overlord. It may need a medievalist to catch the full echoes of 'Dright', but his disconcerting nature as a slippery overweening tyrant will be comprehensible to every reader. The whole book works this way: very few authors can blend such wit, subtlety and sophistication with such accessibility and vivid entertainment.

> *Peter Hollindale, in a review of "The Lives of Christopher Chant," in* The Signal Selection of Children's Books, 1988, *The Thimble Press, 1989, p. 41.*

Chair Person (1989)

[**Chair Person** is] full of hilarity and wit. An ancient armchair turns into a bumbling but self-opinionated individual, retaining the coffee, ink and ketchup stains of his previous existence, also the extruding stuffing (as a beard). His information and vocabulary have been learnt from TV, in front of which he has spent all his life. No outlandish machines here, just pure magic in a story much enhanced by the illustrator [Glenys Ambrus].

> *Joyce Banks, in a review of "Chair Person," in* The School Librarian, *Vol. 37, No. 3, August, 1989, p. 104.*

Diana Wynne Jones has written a lively fantasy about an old chair which comes to life and causes chaos. The action is fast-moving, and the characterisation of the Chair Person is good: he is clumsy, larger than life and we remain uncertain as to whether he is friend or enemy. Other characters are somewhat stereotyped, but adequately portrayed. The characterisation of Auntie Christa, an organising charitable busybody, is amusing.

Children are likely to respond to the humour in the descriptions of the chaos created by the Chair Person, of the vast quantities of food which he eats messily, and of the party games which go disastrously wrong when he joins in. As an average, undemanding book, this is perhaps worth buying: to encourage the 7-9 age-group to read by themselves.

> *S. M. Ashburner, in a review of "Chair Person," in* The Junior Bookshelf, *Vol. 3, No. 5, October, 1989, p. 227.*

Robert Lipsyte

1938-

American author of fiction and nonfiction.

Major works include *The Contender* (1967), *Assignment: Sports* (1970), *One Fat Summer* (1977), *Free to Be Muhammad Ali* (1978).

A writer for the junior high and high school audience whose works often utilize sports as subject or background, Lipsyte is recognized as an insightful author who combines enthusiastic coverage of sports with a perceptive awareness of human nature and social issues. Acknowledged as the creator of contemporary realistic fiction noted for its strong characterizations and absorbing narratives, he characteristically focuses on the struggle of individuals to develop their self-confidence and sense of self-worth in the face of often hostile forces within society. His black and white male adolescent protagonists learn to care about themselves and others through their experiences both on and off the playing field. Although not considered a controversial author, Lipsyte includes such elements as brutality, drugs, and abortion in his works but in a manner usually considered restrained and relevant to his plots. His nonfiction, unsentimental profiles of sports figures, is also praised for its perceptiveness and literary quality.

Lipsyte is perhaps best known as the author of *The Contender* (1967), his first novel for young adults. Considered a classic of the genre, the story describes how Alfred Brooks, a Harlem teenager who aspires toward a better life by training to be a boxer, realizes that he has the inner strength needed to better himself beyond the confines of the ring. As a white author writing about the black experience during a time when the subject was only beginning to be explored in young adult literature, Lipsyte is credited with vividly and authentically describing the worlds of boxing and ghetto life; during the course of the novel, he also addresses such issues as black militancy and the concerns of white merchants in black communities. Lipsyte is also well known for his autobiographical trilogy about Bobby Marks, an overweight youngster with a wise mouth, a vivid imagination, and a confidence problem. Set during the 1950s, the novels take Bobby from the ages of fourteen to eighteen and demonstrate how Bobby becomes a thin, independent young man who is unafraid to stand up for the what he believes. An author of adult fiction and nonfiction as well as a journalist and screenwriter, Lipsyte brings his background as a sports reporter and internationally syndicated sports columnist to his works for young people. In the informational book *Assignment: Sports,* a collection of twenty-four vignettes based loosely on some of his columns, Lipsyte is noted for his distinctive choice of subjects and his authoritative writing style. One of the figures profiled in this work is Muhammad Ali, who later became the subject of the biography *Free to Be Muhammad Ali,* a book considered outstanding for its depth of coverage regarding both the man and his times. In addition to several awards for his journalism, Lipsyte won the Child Study Children's Book Award in 1967 for *The Contender.*

(See also *Contemporary Literary Criticism,* Vol. 21; *Something about the Author,* Vol. 5; *Contemporary Authors New Revision Series,* Vol. 8; and *Contemporary Authors,* Vols. 19-20, rev. ed.)

AUTHOR'S COMMENTARY

[The following excerpt is from an interview by Betty Miles.]

Sports is, or should be, just one of the things people do—an integral part of life, but only one aspect of it. Sports is a good experience. It's fun. It ought to be inexpensive and accessible to everybody. Kids should go out and play, test and extend their bodies, feel good about what they can achieve on their own or with a team. And children's books about sports should encourage that approach.

Instead, adults try to make sports into a metaphor—a preparation for life. We endow sports with mystical qualities that don't exist and raise unreal expectations about what it can do. At the same time, by making sports into a metaphor, we devalue it for itself. It's no wonder that the kids who read sports books are confused by them. The things that happen to people in the books bear very little relation to their own experiences and anxieties in real life. So the kids read them and wonder, "What's wrong with me?"

What the books don't say is that in our society, sports is a negative experience for most boys and almost all girls. Soon after they start school, at an age when they have no other standards on which to judge themselves, we force children to judge each other on their bodies, which is the thing that everyone's most scared about. They're required to define themselves on the basis of competitive physical ability.

Sports is the basic way kids learn sex roles. Traditionally, the boys are sent out into the arena to prove themselves and the girls are given the baton to cheer them on. The boys now begin a series of qualifications for the rest of their lives, which are called cuts. Somewhere along the line, most boys will get cut. They'll be deemed unworthy boys, and they'll see themselves as inferior because they weren't chosen; they didn't make the team. At a time when they needed it, they didn't get the approval that mattered. (pp. 43-4)

The people who are writing and producing and selling [sports] books are people who have been bent by the system themselves. Most of them hate or are awed by sports because *they* were rejected, and they produce books which reinforce the idea that if you don't make it in sports you're a failure as a person, instead of reaching out to kids through books that say "It's OK—you're in better shape than you think you are. We've all come through this, and most people survive."

I'd like to see sports books for children that would take away some of the pressures they feel and defuse the sense of competition and rejection. To do this, I think the books must acknowledge children's real fears about sports.

The first, perhaps ultimate, fear is of being ridiculed—the fear that everyone's going to laugh at you because you're not good. Children know that when they're ridiculed for not catching a ball, they're being ridiculed for their bodies. I think this is much worse than being laughed at for reading badly or whatever. You're being totally rejected as a person. . . . Books that talk about people's fear of being hit with a ball, getting knocked down or punched or trampled would help children see that their own fears are not unusual.

A third fear that kids have about sports is of disappointing their parents. . . . Books could help to free kids from the idea that they should do sports to please their parents. (pp. 44-5)

Finally, there's the basic, overall fear of not measuring up in sports—of not being man enough, or woman enough. This may be the most meaningless definition of being a worthy person in our society.

I don't think we have to make any rules for sports books for children beyond asking that they present some sense of truth about the role of sports in our lives. But most books perpetuate the old myths. Even in the new, trendy sports stories, where problems like pregnancy, dope, and so on are admitted, the basic point that comes across to the reader is that if you're willing to take orders, if you're

determined to succeed, everything else will work itself out. Blacks and whites will get together, the coach will be understanding, poor kids will get rich, and the team will win the championship. Kids who read these books wonder why such things don't seem to happen in real life, to them or to people they know. Most of them, no matter how hard they push themselves, will never make the team, and of those who do, many will discover that the coach is a tyrant who exploits his players and that the brotherhood of sports they've read so much about doesn't exist. (pp. 45-6)

The myth that sports is a way out of the slums has been exploded. But as long as there's a Rocky image, as long as the books lionize one or two real kids like Sugar Ray Leonard who've made it, we're saying to all the others, "It's your fault for staying poor. It's not society's fault. You didn't try hard enough. You didn't listen to coach. You didn't play hurt."

One of the most sainted names in sports literature is John R. Tunis. He was ahead of his time. He wrote about cooperation; he said that winning isn't the only thing, that doing your best is what matters. But he, too, pushed the myth that a real man plays hurt

Sports biographies for children, which perpetuate all these myths, are really the junk food of publishing. They're all too easy to produce. You get scissors and a paste pot, raid the newspapers for false biographies of the hero of the moment—and sports writers never were trustworthy in terms of biographical material—and make a book. The trouble is that teachers and librarians feel justified in pushing these biographies at kids because "it gets them reading." But the kids who get hooked on them aren't going to be able to move on to books in which every other adjective isn't "immortal" or "fabulous" and every sentence doesn't end with an exclamation mark. Or in which every hero's success isn't simply a matter of hard work and determination. (p. 46)

The basic questions of what sports figures are like have hardly even entered adult sports books. And when they do, as in Jim Bouton's *Ball Four,* you have many people saying that the book should not have been published. Not because anything in it is untrue, but because they feel that kids should not be exposed to such truths about their heroes. They feel it's more important to have false heroes than it is to know the truth. And then, of course, teachers don't suggest adult books like this to kids, because they worry about running into problems with parents about the language. But I think that if they'd read some of these books along with the kids, kids would profit from them and enjoy them. *Ball Four* is a charming book; it's one big Valentine to baseball. *Life on the Run,* by Bill Bradley, is a good book. *Paper Lion,* by George Plimpton. A very nice book called *Heaven Is a Playground,* about black basketball players, by Rick Telander. These books tend to be honest. There's no reason that books like them could not be written specifically for kids. I'd like to see that.

Trying to reform sports books for children is discouraging, but you've got to start somewhere. That's what we do as writers. If we can reach one kid, affect some program somewhere, wake up one teacher, it's probably worthwhile. We should be trying to write books that acknowledge kids' fears about sports and say that other people, even heroes, share them. Books in which nice guys do finish last and it doesn't matter. In which making the team doesn't end all the problems and the team doesn't win all the games. Books that integrate sports into the rest of life. If we write more truthfully about sports, perhaps we can encourage kids to relax and have fun with each other—to challenge themselves for the pleasure of it, without self-doubt and without fear. (p. 47)

> Robert Lipsyte, "Robert Lipsyte on Kids/Sports/Books," in Children's literature in education, *Vol. 11, No. 1, Spring, 1980, pp. 43-7.*

GENERAL COMMENTARY

Sari Feldman

Lipsyte, currently known for his popular young adult novels, is no newcomer to the daily grind of writing. From 1957 to 1971 he was a sports reporter and columnist at the *New York Times.* Lipsyte did not suffer from false hero worship or misconceptions about the role sports plays in the lives of Americans and, if anything, he was particularly attuned to the sociological significance of sports in our society. His career spanned a time that saw the professional athlete change from a symbol of virtuous values to entertainment celebrity. He regrets that the genuine importance of athletics cannot filter through the commercial media hype that emphasizes the sports figure as superstar. "But I feel the whole sports thing has gotten away from what the real value of sports is which is: (1) to get people healthy and in good shape and (2) (this is where women have particularly suffered) to teach you how to work with people you don't necessarily like."

Another strong concern of Lipsyte's is that many youth, minority youth in particular, buy into this superstar image and hype that so few can attain, and turn away from education and other careers. (p. 198)

While Lipsyte was writing for the *New York Times* he had his first young adult novel published. *The Contender* is the story of Alfred Brooks, a young black growing up in Harlem who aspires to a better life than the ghetto can offer by training to be a boxer. The self-discipline and personal courage Alfred displays become the real rewards of the experience

The Contender may seem quite sentimental, but in 1967 the realities of urban life were just beginning to be revealed, particularly to teenagers. The optimism of *The Contender* reflects the social vision of the "Great Society," a vision that remains unrealized. Today the well-meaning white adults of the novel are seen in a more sophisticated light and could be viewed as paternalistic or inadvertently exploiting impoverished neighborhoods and impressionable youth. It is the themes of *The Contender* and the vivid sports action that keep the book pertinent to a 1980 audience. "I think today *The Contender* is a girl gymnast in a well-to-do suburban high school," Lipsyte acknowledges.

The Contender owes its inspiration to a chance meeting with an aging boxing manager in Las Vegas. "He was old, he was going blind, kind of shuffling through the scene and he began to reminisce and he talked about this gym that he had once owned that was up three flights of stairs on

the Lower East Side," Lipsyte recalled. "He used to sit at the top of those stairs listening to boys come up the steps and he could judge whether or not they would ever be contenders. He could tell because he was waiting for the boy who came up alone, one set of footsteps, a boy who came at night and a boy who came up scared, the footsteps kind of scurrying, or at least not confident. That boy was going to conquer his fear because he was so desperate to become somebody."

This image stayed in Lipsyte's mind and started him thinking about the word *contender* in a very symbolic way. What are the moments in life that are equivalent to "going up the stairs"? His ruminations led to the development of the Brooks character.

Today a white author might not risk creating a central black character. "In retrospect," Lipsyte revealed, "I'm appalled at my arrogance that I could have, I'm not so sure I should have." At that time Lipsyte had just come out of an intensive nine months with Dick Gregory, getting an exposure to black culture and gaining confidence to realistically relate to and write about the black experience. They coauthored *Nigger,* Gregory's autobiography of his early years and personal struggles. "Just from working on *Nigger,* talking to him (Gregory), meeting his friends, listening to reminiscences, talking about the sense of being black, I felt that maybe I could present a story in a reportorial way."

In a more recent novel, *Jack and Jill,* Lipsyte once again concerned himself with ghetto life. In this case Hector, a Hispanic gang leader from the South Bronx, dreams of revitalizing his community through the autonomous control of a housing project. Rather than tell this story through Hector, Lipsyte created from his sports knowledge Jack Ryder, a high school baseball star. Jack and Hector are brought together through Jillian, a teenage photographer concerned with conditions in the South Bronx. "I didn't really feel that I could take a Hispanic character and do a book from the Hispanic point of view. I just hadn't logged the time as I had with *The Contender.*"

His second young adult novel, *One Fat Summer,* is about the summer Bobby Marks loses weight and gains self-esteem. The novel's humor and compassion make it easy for teenagers to identify with Bobby's personal problems. For Lipsyte the novel had deeper meaning because the story and character of Bobby Marks are autobiographical. "I always thought that I would write about the summer I had lost a lot of weight and had never been able to. Suddenly I was able to write some 24 years later," he disclosed.

The novel is set in 1952 but neither the historical time frame nor Bobby's naive character interfere with the sensitive portrayal of adolescent insecurities. "I really wanted to write about kids and their bodies. While the pressures and feelings might have been different in the 1950s, the internal thoughts on how one viewed his or her own body and how one viewed oneself in relation to friends and parents probably never changed." (pp. 199-200)

Body image and its effects on self-image play a significant part in Lipsyte's young adult novels. Although he claims not to be familiar with adolescent theory, he is completely in touch with the dynamics of body image. "During adolescence you don't have the mind and the soul you're going to have later so your body is really your manifestation of you, at least how people are going to judge you."

A second stage of adolescent development is the focus of his two most recent young adult novels, *Jack and Jill* and *The Summerboy.* In each book an older adolescent moves beyond personal needs, converting his narcissistic concerns for self into a concern for the outside world. In the hands of a less skilled writer these stories could have been doctrinaire, but Lipsyte's absorbing plots, strong characterizations, and insights into individuals' motivations create fine works of social realism.

In *The Summerboy* Bobby is forced to work with women laundry workers as his punishment for damaging a truck. Firsthand experience enlightens him to the women's unjust and inequitable working conditions, and Bobby makes a grand, heroic gesture on behalf of his coworkers. "Bobby Marks was sort of pre-ordained to do that because Bobby Marks is a person who lives as a hero in his own daydream. He's a continuing character in his own mind and he's a hero waiting for an event." (pp. 200-01)

Fiction as social commentary has some of its roots in the works of John Steinbeck, a writer that drew Lipsyte as a boy. "For some reason his (Steinbeck's) accessibility, his compassion for people, his outrage, somehow made it seem that there was a way to be a writer and still not be just a fantasist, just a storyteller, that there be kind of a social purpose." (p. 201)

Speaking on familiar ground, Lipsyte attacks sports biography as an example of the type of book arbitrarily pushed on different groups, in this case boys. "It (sports biography) has no relation to the guy's life, it is probably poorly written, probably written by some underpaid sports writer who pasted together some clippings from some second rate newspaper and it is presented to the kid and the kid reads it. So they give kids these bad sports biographies, junk food biographies and they are prepared for more junk food biographies. I don't think they're necessarily going to progress."

Free to Be Muhammad Ali is Lipsyte's own sports biography, an in-depth portrait of not only Ali's rise to fame but also the controversy and racism that surrounded Ali's career. This kind of biography was made possible by the intimate and mutually respectful relationship they enjoyed during Lipsyte's years with the *New York Times. Free to Be. . .* is not a secondhand account but personal observation that calls upon the reader to interpret the social and political climate surrounding the Ali mystique.

Young adult literature has certainly had positive impact on encouraging young people to read. Lipsyte reflects, "Maybe you should think of this kind of literature as a bridge between people who have just learned to read, reading children's books and reading textbooks, and to prepare them for the next step which is for a lifetime of reading, and give them books that pertain particularly to their own lives."

Young adult authors operate under certain constraints. They have less freedom in subject matter and presentation, and need to be less obscure stylistically and still not sacrifice quality. Above all, Lipsyte feels that young adult authors must be truthful not only in their facts but also in characterizations and life situations. "If you assume that your audience has substantially less experience than you do, then you're under a kind of pressure to be truthful in ways that you may or may not have to be truthful in books for an older audience."

For many years Robert Lipsyte was surrounded by great sports figures and other media personalities. He rejects the notion that teens need idols like these to emulate. "I don't think that we need heroes, I think that we need people who inspire us to be better ourselves." Today teenagers may be finding peer-heroes within young adult novels. Robert Lipsyte has created such characters with courage, determination, humor, and the ability to survive adolescence. Therein could be the major impact of his work. (pp. 201-02)

> *Sari Feldman, "Up the Stairs Alone: Robert Lipsyte on Writing for Young Adults," in* Top of the News, *Vol. 39, No. 2, Winter, 1983, pp. 198-202.*

TITLE COMMENTARY

The Contender (1967)

Boxing can be an ugly, brutal business, but to Alfred, a Harlem high school dropout, it represents a last-ditch effort to avoid a dead-end life as a grocery boy, addict or criminal. In virtual desperation, he throws himself into training and becomes a skilled fighter but ultimately finds that he lacks the "killer instinct" for boxing. He decides, however, to transfer the competitive spirit to life outside the ring, determining to return to school and work in a recreation center to improve the life of youngsters in the ghetto. Admirably, the author tries to portray Alfred's world through the boy's own eyes, and like *Durango Street,* in his own language, but too often Mr. Lipsyte oversimplifies. For instance, white characters are paragons of interest and devotion; black nationalist ideas invariably come from the mouths of addicts and thugs, thus constituting a kind of guilt by association. Most important, only one way of responding to complicated problems is made to appear valid. Alfred's decision to compete by conventional methods is considered by the author to be the only proper action and is pitted against the attitude of Alfred's unsuccessful friends that, in any case, "Whitey" won't let you make it in his world. The implication whether intended or not, is that Alfred's friends are the chief cause of their own trouble. Such assignment of blame, however, makes the very real pressures that provoke these feelings in the ghetto teen-agers seem trivial. As a sports story, this is a superior, engrossing, insider's book; but as social commentary on problems in a Negro ghetto, it is a superficial, outsider's book which doesn't increase real understanding. But the book is worth trying out to see how the Alfreds react.

> *Susan O'Neal, in a review of "The Contender," in* School Library Journal, *Vol. 14, No. 3, November, 1967, p. 78.*

Far too many writers of fiction for the young seem to believe their primary function is to teach rather than to create textures of experience which are their own reasons for being. In this first novel for young readers, Robert Lipsyte, a sports writer for The New York Times, alternates between these two roles.

Lacking the requisite killer instinct, [Alfred, a] newly inner-directed black youngster, abandons the idea of boxing as a profession, but is now able to return to school, rescue a junkie friend and aim at taking part in a black-run recreation center for other ghetto children who may also learn in the ring that "anyone can be taught how to fight. A contender, that you have to do yourself."

On this homiletic level, the material is so neatly and obviously manipulated that virtue will have to be its own reward because *The Contender*—as a whole—fails as believable fiction. In several of its parts, however, didacticism recedes, and lo, there is life! In particular, whenever Lipsyte writes about boxing itself he indicates how intensely evocative he can be and he moves the reader beyond maxims into participation.

Lipsyte is most convincing in his unfolding of the inner transformation of a boy gone slack into a boxer gradually responding to different and compelling rhythms as he is driven by self-stretching imperatives, as emotional as they are physical. Within his factitious outer framework Lipsyte occasionally lets his main character become palpable.

It is when he leaves the gym and the ring that Lipsyte is too often content to map the road to salvation, rather than explore much more deeply the present ghetto terrain of his dropout. Can the lessons in more-than-survival that are learned in the ring be as easily applied as *The Contender* promises in neighborhoods where the rules of the game and the odds are set by distant outside societal forces? If the Horatio Alger approach is to be at all relevant in a work of fiction set in the ghetto, it needs to be considerably updated and treated with much less naiveté than here.

> *Nat Hentoff, in a review of "The Contender,"* in The New York Times Book Review, *November 12, 1967, p. 42.*

In his descriptive study on the emergence and nature of the junior novel [a doctoral dissertation entitled "A Definition of the Role of the Junior Novel Based on Analyses of Thirty Selected Novels"], Stephen Dunning has cited some consistent characteristics of the genre which are clearly to be found in *The Contender.* There is a good bit of didacticism, but it is not out of proportion and Lipsyte on occasion places two adult pontificators, Spoon and Uncle Wilson, in slightly ironic postures. Spoon occasionally recognizes that he is preaching, and Uncle Wilson is the object of some ribbing by the boys to whom he is giving the good word. Dunning's contention that the junior novel is "consistently wholesome" can also be related to the work, but Lipsyte has again handled the matter of taboos with restraint and imagination. Concern with drugs, sex, poverty, and violence are found throughout the novel, as well as some speculation on the value of religious belief, but none of these is dwelled on at length, and profanity and other objectionable language are avoided. Thus some no-no's are there but fit nicely into the total texture of the work.

As Dunning claimed, the junior novel is constantly updated. The content of the work, alienated young people searching for a place in a modern urban setting, is relevant as is Lipsyte's accurate reproduction of the idiom and syntax of the Harlem resident, both teenage and adult. The novel is presented with stylistic simplicity and brevity, which are also in Dunning's list of characteristics, and the author's skillful mixing of extended descriptions with suspense and action, especially in the early phases of the novel, meets yet another criterion.

Dorothy Pettit's admirable study of the well-written novel for adolescents [a doctoral dissertation entitled "A Study of the Qualities of Literary Excellence Which Characterize Selected Fiction for Younger Adolescents"] has established the theme of the search for self-identity as the most consistent characteristic of such works. This theme is clearly at the center of *The Contender.* In the final chapter, Alfred, the protagonist, feels that he has found himself enough to be able to attempt to persuade his friend James to give himself up to the police and to begin an attempt to overcome his drug addiction. . . . More tribute to the author lies in the fact that in his search for himself, Alfred has scaled no Matterhorn peaks at the novel's conclusion (as has, for instance, Rudi Matt in Ullman's *Banner in the Sky*). Instead we find the *process of becoming* the focus of the work, as Pettit has said it should. Alfred hasn't really accomplished anything startling at the conclusion of the novel, and the lack of outer evidence that he has now "become somebody" is to Lipsyte's further credit. His (Alfred's) gains are modest and his successes frequently tainted with fear, reproach, and self-depreciation. His achievements are tentative, as is appropriate to the time, setting, and action of the work.

Another crucial theme, that of male adolescent friendship, is also well symbolized. Alfred has two such relationships during the novel, but it is the complex aspects of such friendship, doubt, suspicion, cynicism, despair, which are emphasized instead of the superficial and melodramatic comradeship found in many "books for boys." There is further no triumphal resolution to be found as the result of such friendship. Again the tentative nature of Alfred's relationships with his friends closely corresponds with what *is* among teenage boys. (pp. 116-18)

In both thematic and stylistic matters, Lipsyte's novel illustrates some of the more recent directions taken by junior novels written most recently.

The environment developed in the novel is not one customarily found in earlier ones. It is an urban one and focuses most specifically on filth and squalor of a black ghetto. Moreover, the plot produces no "emergence" from the setting; the main characters in the work will apparently remain in their present living situation. Attendant to this environment is found treatment of problems endured by those who must live there, especially the teenagers of a lower class minority group. Several contemporary concerns are evident: the plight and self-concept of the school dropout, the militancy of some blacks, the fearful espousal of an "Uncle Tom" status quo of others, the concerns of white merchants in a black community, all are found in *The Contender* and are clearly related to Alfred's continuing search for self. Most interesting of these is the continuing presence of white policemen in the black community, and what their presence means to the inhabitants of the ghetto. Once again, Lipsyte has neither extoled nor damned the police. He has merely included them as factors in the life of a boy such as Alfred Brooks.

Several junior novels written in the 1960's have sometimes dealt with taboos in the service of literary realism, and *The Contender* is no exception. It goes without saying that some contemporary concerns must be carefully handled in a junior novel in order to meet the criterion of "wholesomeness" of which Dunning has reminded us. In my opinion, Lipsyte has done a masterful job of reconciling "controversial" issues with the realities of censorship. Throughout the novel a good deal of brutality, cruelty, and violence is described. The characterization of Alfred's peer, Major, illustrates a young black who has pretty largely turned to violence as *his* answer. The use of drugs and alcohol is also an important factor. Alfred and his friends smoke marijuana and drink cheap wine at an all-night party and James, Alfred's closest friend, has become addicted to heroin. Sexual involvement is also suggested in the description of the party. But all of these inclusions are made both with great restraint and with direct relevance to Alfred's growth and change as a human being. They are there because they *belong* there and not for faddish or sensationalistic reasons.

In his inclusion of the generation gap as one of the thematic concerns of the novel, Lipsyte is simultaneously dealing with a concern of profound significance to young and old people of today, and venturing into an area of adolescent fiction which Dunning claimed to be one of its most glaring weaknesses: adult-adolescent relations. The portrayal of Uncle Wilson in his frustrations and confusion during a confrontation with two youths, one a college student, the other a dropout, symbolizes a highly vexing contemporary problem. Throughout the novel Alfred confronts a variety of adults: his manager, his Jewish boss, Uncle Wilson, his aunt-guardian, and a black ex-fighter school teacher. They all influence his attitudes and decisions. Some of my undergraduate students have stated the conviction that this is a novel as much about adults as teenagers. In my opinion, Lipsyte has avoided many of the stereotypes found in earlier junior novels in his adult characterizations. They are not unmitigated bumblers, but they are not totally "with it" either. They are complex.

As significant as new thematic directions in this novel are the departures from the rigid stylistic conventions to be found in *The Contender*. There is little of the quasi-Victorian sentimentality of past adolescent works. The carefully drawn pictures of ghetto life accentuate its grimness and resultant dearth of hope. In his awareness of taboos, the author doesn't go all the way, but some of his Harlem descriptions are reminiscent of James Baldwin in *Go Tell It On The Mountain*. Beyond this, the knowledge Lipsyte has acquired through years of sports reporting has aided him in creating valid images of stifling gymnasia, seedy, threadbare boxing arenas, and the physical pain and mental anguish of first training for, then competing in boxing matches. The narrative is also made more complex and enjoyable by the mixing of relevant memories of the past and idealistic speculations of the future in Alfred's mind. Flashback is used frequently and effectively to give those reveries dramatic intensity. And, as has been mentioned previously, the author has done an impressive job of reproducing several New York City dialects, especially that of the Harlem Negro.

As an inducement to the inveterate symbol hunters in the teaching gentry, *The Contender* provides a couple of fairly obvious ones. Comprehending the significance of the continued use of the cave and the stairs in the novel will not constitute an overly frustrating task for large numbers of early adolescent readers. Their placing in the novel and the care taken with their description make them relatively easy to place in clear symbolic perspective.

In case some readers (of this essay, that is) think that I am drumming this novel as a Nobel Prize contender, let me hasten to the claim that there are some weaknesses in the work. There is a good bit of moralizing about the virtues of an establishment-oriented good life here, especially in pronouncements by Spoon (the ex-fighter, now teacher), Donatelli (the hard-nosed, fatherly manager), and the already much-maligned Uncle Wilson. Lipsyte may also be called to question for presenting so many whites with good-guy images. Some balance is needed for the indulgent boss, the manager, the manager's dentist friend, and the "friendly cops" who applaud Alfred's morning run through the park. But many of the apparent weaknesses in the novel can be at least partially related to the limitations which continue to be inherent to the genre itself. I have tried to make it evident that I do not feel them to be overwhelming. (pp. 118-19)

> *John S. Simmons, "Lipsyte's 'Contender': Another Look at the Junior Novel," in* Elementary English, *Vol. XLIX, No. 1, January, 1972, pp. 116-19.*

In *The Fire Next Time*, Black writer James Baldwin (1970) describing the search for his place in a threatening world, articulated the fearful problem of giving direction to his young life. He was Black; he lived in Harlem; his talents were few.

> When I tried to assess my capabilities, I realized that I had almost none. In order to achieve like I wanted, I had been dealt, it seemed to me, the worst possible hand. I could not become a prize fighter—many of us tried but few succeeded. I could not sing. I could not dance. . . . The only other possibility seemed to involve my becoming one of the sordid people on the avenue, who were not really as sordid as I imagined but who frightened me terribly.

These fears and pressures to choose among questionable alternatives seem to be the adolescent heritage of too many of Harlem's young people. Alfred Brooks, central character of Lipsyte's award winning novel *The Contender,* finds himself in similar circumstances. He is a school dropout; the pressures of the avenue are mounting; he too can't sing or dance. He decides to search for a place in the sun in the boxing ring. In his quest to become a contender, Alfred learns much about himself and those around him. He also learns to make peace with himself as a man and as a Black.

If Alfred Brooks were not Black, he would be concerned only with the universal questions that trouble all adolescents: Am I worth something? What am I capable of that will earn the respect of my peers? Alfred Brooks, however, shows how one young man comes to peace with his Blackness. While being Black limits his choice of direction, it also conditions his relationship to his peers. Will he be part of the young protest movement? Should he work for a White store owner? Should he give his life to the church as a means of bearing the White man's burden? (p. 693)

Alfred's seeking to be a contender is what carries him to manhood. In the course of his search, the reader gets a good idea of what a Black adolescent must contend with in her/his quest for identity.

For the classroom teacher, Lipsyte's book is invaluable. More than one Alfred Brooks sits in our classrooms. Alfred's problems are everybody's in the ghetto. Just seeing that is the first step in a young person's coming to terms with herself or himself. It is nice to know that one is not alone. Alfred's solutions may not be for everyone, but they are solutions that young people can hold up for their own individual viewing. Readers with limited skills may not be able to make it through Baldwin's writings, but they can handle *The Contender*. (pp. 693-94)

> *Saul Bachner, "Three Junior Novels on the Black Experience," in* Journal of Reading, *Vol. 24, No. 8, May, 1981, pp. 692-95.*

Assignment: Sports (1970)

Not tips but performance—by the *New York Times* sportswriter whose *Contender* bespoke four years covering the likes of Muhammed Ali. Not that there's anybody like Ali: in fast-clip impressions from pre-Liston to post-title he's "the onliest boxer in history people asked questions like a senator." The line-up is seasonal, with a little personal journal-ese by Lipsyte introducing each, from the Mets' first spring training (also Lipsyte's first big assignment, a bigger than usual first) to, well, "Winter Thoughts of a Bush-League Ballplayer" who's ahead of the long-lost game except when "the air is faintly touched with the smell of the outfield grass." Spring brings crew racing too, and the Kentucky Derby, and in summer "Arnold Palmer Tees Off," in winter "Jake the Snake Is Hot On Ice"—but some of Lipsyte's best pieces are illimitable, like the tale of Bozo Miller, the world's champion eater, and the 'no-sob-story' "Athletes in Wheelchairs Compete for the Paralympic Team." "I found in sports a very rich field for writing," observes once-great Russian weight-lifter Vlasov, and so has Lipsyte; countering the 'fun and games' aspersion, he notes that "politics, race, religion, money, the law—all play roles in sports." He's tackled all of them, and here he takes on "The 1968 Olympics: The Reds and the Blacks and the Gold" in a sequence of vivid vignettes. Stanley Woodward's *Sportswriter* tells more about the metier, and so, indirectly, does John Tunis' autobiography; but this is the best of the field—for example.

> *A review of "Assignment: Sports," in* Kirkus Reviews, *Vol. XXXVIII, No. 9, May 1, 1970, p. 520.*

With the skill of a fine fiction writer for nuance, [Lipsyte] brings to life "rabbit-quick rookies" making "impossible leaping catches—always when the coaches weren't looking." In a few sparse lines he illuminates Arnold Palmer who frowns "down at the grass, flattening it with a glance" while putting "on his white glove, flexing his fingers eleven times until the leather surrendered to the shape of his left hand."

In his detached style and writing rhythms, Lipsyte makes *Assignment: Sports* the unsentimental report about sports figures and sports. "The sweetness drained out of the after-

noon," he writes in a long piece about Muhammad Ali. Not only does this image pungently rise off the printed page, it is the quintessence of what the book is about—the winners, the losers, the in-betweeners. In 24 stories separated into four sections—Spring, Summer, Fall, Winter—a division that seems arbitrary rather than actual—the book makes it because finally you realize that only the background is sports.

Which means you don't have to be a fan or even knowledgeable about sports to understand Lipsyte's own admission that "the crowd roared with a bloodlust that never fails to frighten me at prizefights." . . .

This is no-nonsense writing in a field too often drowned in bathos and outright dishonesty. Even Lipsyte's choice of subjects—a 15-year-old caddying in his first pro tournament, a world's champion eater, girl athletes in wheelchairs competing for the Paralympic Team—shows a writer concerned about characters, what they think and feel and how they act in human circumstances.

The "new journalism," this non-fiction style is called in our time. It is, in fact, an old technique, used by the best fiction writers since the genre was invented. Robert Lipsyte's public will need no reminder of his skills in this department. Readers meeting him for the first time, regardless of age-group, have a rare treat in store.

> *Sam Elkin, in a review of "Assignment: Sports," in* The New York Times Book Review, *May 31, 1970, p. 14.*

Any adolescent who has enjoyed *The Contender* will need no introduction to Robert Lipsyte's new book or encouragement to read it. The same careful control of language, the same ability to develop a well-rounded character through conflict with a sport are evident in *Assignment: Sports*. . . .

Robert Lipsyte never castigates, never ridicules, and rarely praises his characters. *Assignment: Sports* is the author's impressions of a variety of human beings participating in sports or talking about participation. As a reader completes each article, he senses Robert Lipsyte's insight on human frailty. The effect is devastating. Pretense is stripped away and the athlete is revealed as Lipsyte sees him. Lipsyte's ability to capsulize life effectively permeates *Assignment: Sports*. It is a rare skill and adds immeasureably to a reader's enjoyment. . . .

I hope Robert Lipsyte's publishers will soon give us more from this great talent.

> *John N. Conner, in a review of "Assignment: Sports," in* English Journal, *Vol. 60, No. 4, April, 1971, p. 529.*

One Fat Summer (1977)

Fourteen-year-old Bobby Marks is fat—exactly how fat he's not sure since he always jumps off the scale as the 200 mark rolls by. Then one summer, at the New Jersey lake resort where his parents vacation, Bobby lands a job mowing lawns and loses the requisite number of pounds to gain a new self-image. Of course, it's not quite that easy: he has to contend with a flinty, cheapskate employer as well as a gang of local greasers headed by a psycho ex-Marine who has it in for him (Bobby is left naked in the middle of the lake, roughed up, and threatened at gunpoint). His self-deprecating delivery where every joke is at his own expense is awfully funny at times and the dialogue (a lot of pseudo-cool "ranking out") catches the early 1950's better than all the references to ponytails, polio, and pop songs of the era. However, Bobby's eye is so fixed on the pointer of his scale that he's hardly aware of or concerned about anything else (e.g., his older sister's affair with a muscle-bound Adonis or the widening rift in his parents' relationship). His self-absorption grows tiresome, and while often entertaining, this adds up to a lot of empty calories.

> *Jane Abramson, in a review of "One Fat Summer," in* School Library Journal, *Vol. 23, No. 7, March, 1977, p. 152.*

[Lipsyte's] first-person narrative gives us an inner perspective of Bobby's thoughts and feelings. Refreshingly, he is neither precocious nor off-beat, in the manner of so many teen-age protagonists, but simply a normal boy in abnormal circumstances.

Bobby, however, is Lipsyte's only fully realized character; the supporting cast shifts in and out of the reader's focus, not only because of the plot, but also because our perception of them varies. For example, Bobby's father is alternately stiff, compassionate, machine-like and impulsive. His mother is sharp, sensitive, but sometimes blindly overprotective. In one way, these contrasting qualities reflect the changing ways in which Bobby sees them. In another way, they're confusing.

Nonetheless, the dramatic movement of Bobby's metamorphosis is effectively rendered. As the summer progresses, he sheds pounds and illusions in equal measure, and in the process, both his mind and body begin to shape up. His long struggle culminates in the realization that he has the independence to meet life on his terms—and that's a weighty enough idea for anyone.

> *Stephen Krensky, in a review of "One Fat Summer," in* The New York Times Book Review, *July 10, 1977, p. 20.*

Romances were among the very first stories to be told. People like to hear them because they have happy endings, and the tellers of romances are willing to exaggerate just enough to make the stories more interesting than real life. A basic part of the romance is a quest of some sort. In the course of the quest, the protagonist will experience doubts and will undergo severe trials, but he or she will be successful in the end. This success will be all the more appreciated because of the difficulties that the protagonist has suffered. The extremes of suffering and succeeding are characteristic of the romance. In good moments, it is like a happy daydream, but in bad moments it resembles a nightmare. (p. 205)

[Today], when a literary piece is referred to as a romance, it usually contains either or both adventure and love.

The romance is appealing to teenagers because it is matched in several ways to their roles in life. The symbols that are used often relate to youthfulness and hope, and, in keeping with this, many of the protagonists, even in the traditional and classic tales, are in their teens. Modern young adults are at an age when they leave home or antici-

pate leaving to embark on a new way of life. It is more likely to be called "moving out" than "going on a romantic quest," but the results are much the same. And seeking and securing a "true love" usually—but not always—takes up a greater proportion of the time and energy of the young than of middle-aged adults. And the exaggeration that is part of the romantic mode is quite honestly felt by young people. Never at any other stage of life do people feel their emotions quite so intensely. (pp. 205-06)

Another teenage characteristic particularly appropriate to the romantic mode is the optimism of youth. Whether or not young people, either as a group or as individuals, are really more optimistic than their elders, they are presumed to be so, and a writer doing the same story for adults might be more tempted to present it as irony than as romance. (p. 206)

It is a distinguishing feature of the adventure-romance that the happy ending is achieved only after the hero has proven his or her worth by undergoing a crisis or an ordeal. Usually as part of the ordeal the hero must make a sacrifice, must be wounded, or must leave some part of his or her body, even if it is only sweat or tears. The real loss is that of innocence, but it is usually symbolized by a physical loss . . . What is purchased with the suffering of the hero is nearly always some kind of wisdom, even though wisdom is not what the hero set out to find.

The adventure-romance has elements applicable to the task of entering the adult world, which all young people anticipate. The story pattern includes the three stages of formal initiation as practiced in many cultures. First, the young and innocent person is separated both physically and spiritually from the nurturing love of friends and family. Then, during this separation, the hero, who embodies noble qualities, undergoes a test of courage and stamina that may be either mental, psychological, or physical. In the final stage the young person is reunited with former friends and family in a new role of increased status.

How this archetypal initiation rite can be translated into a modern, somewhat realistic story for young adults is shown through Robert Lipsyte's **One Fat Summer.** It is the story of a quest for self-respect. When the protagonist begins it, he is quite unaware of the magnitude of his undertaking. As part of the quest, he is isolated from his family. The suffering that he undergoes is something that no one else could do for him, but it makes the victory that much sweeter. (pp. 206-07)

[Bobby's] loss of weight is his tangible reward, but, more important than this is his coming to know himself and to understand, at least partially, the motives of the half-dozen people who play significant roles in his life that summer. This understanding brings him relief from the fears that had haunted him during all the summers his family had spent at Rumson Lake.

Bobby does not lose weight or come to these understandings without the central struggle or ordeal that is at the heart of all romances. His physical ordeal is the task of keeping Dr. Kahn's huge hillside lawn immaculate. (p. 207)

As befits the mode of romance, the place that Bobby works is both idyllic and far removed from the small houses and cottages that make up the middle-class beach community that he is accustomed to. Dr. Kahn's house is on the other side of the lake, and at first Bobby's family and friends do not know that he is working. When Bobby first looks at Dr. Kahn's lawn it is "like a velvet sea, a green velvet sea that flowed up from the gray shore of the county road to surround a great white house with white columns. The house looked like a proud clipper ship riding the crest of the ocean."

A more important challenge than that of the lawn is the one that Bobby meets in the ex-Marine Willie Rumson who is the kind of villain that appears in nearly all romances. It is in keeping with the romance pattern that the characters, other than the protagonist, are one-sided. They are either villains or angels. Since a romance is essentially the story of one person's achievement and development, everything else is a condensation. For the sake of efficiency, the personalities of the supporting characters are shown through symbols, metaphors, and significant details, all of which highlight the qualities that are important to the story. (Dr. Kahn, Bobby's employer, is presented as such a negative stereotype, though, that some readers have been offended.)

It is not usually the villain whom the hero has to defeat ultimately, but the villain stands in the way of the real accomplishment and gives the hero an enemy upon whom to focus. Without some scary, nightmarish, and usually life-threatening incident, the happy ending could not be appreciated. At first, Willie and his friends just tease Bobby calling him "The Crisco Kid" because he's "fat in the can," and asking him if he has a license to drag that trailer behind him. But then Willie can't get a job, and he decides that he wants to be Dr. Kahn's yard worker. He demands that Bobby quit the job, and, when it becomes apparent that he won't, Willie and his buddies get mean.

In keeping with the form of the romance it is significant in the ordeal that follows that Bobby experiences something similar to what in the traditional romance would have been a vision. He has been stripped of his clothes and left on an island in the lake. Symbolically the peaceful setting of the lake has changed into something fearsome. The night "exploded with thunder and lightning and the wind drove nails of rain" into his naked body. Bobby is lying in the mud and puddles where they dumped him and he thinks he's going to drown, but then he hears a voice. . . .

> "ON YOUR FEET. YOU'RE NOT GONNA
> LET THOSE BASTARDS KILL YOU. YOU
> BEAT THE LAWN, YOU CAN BEAT THEM.
> YOU'RE TOUGH. YOU RAN, YOU FOUGHT,
> YOU'LL DO IT AGAIN. YOU'LL DO IT TILL
> YOU WIN."
> I recognized the voice.
> Captain Marks, Commander Marks, Big Bob
>   Marks.
> It was me.
> I stood up.

Another element of the romance is that the protagonists put forth efforts on their own behalf. By standing up, Bobby proves that he is willing to do this and is, therefore, worthy of outside help. As it often does in the romance, the outside help comes from an unexpected source. A cousin of Willie's arrives in a canoe and takes Bobby back to Rumson Beach. All that Bobby loses in the ordeal is a sock. What he finds is a new kind of confidence. This pre-

pares him for the final confrontation with Willie Rumson. . . . Bobby wins the fight, but this physical act is only a symbolic way of showing the emotional victory that Bobby achieves over his own misunderstandings and fears.

The whole experience gives him enough confidence to face Dr. Kahn at last and ask him for the pay that was originally advertised for the job:

> He stared at me. Just like he did the very first time, a lifetime ago. But those shotgun eyes didn't scare me anymore.
> "You should pay me for this summer," said Dr. Kahn. "I've watched you change from a miserable fat boy into a fairly presentable young man. On my lawn. On my time."
> "You didn't do it, Dr. Kahn. I did it."

This last statement sums up a prime requisite for a modern young adult romance. The hero has to accomplish the task and it has to be one that readers can respect and at the same time imagine themselves accomplishing. (pp. 208-09)

> *Kenneth L. Donelson and Alleen Pace Nilsen, "The Old Romanticism of Wishing and Winning, in their* Literature for Today's Young Adults, *Scott, Foresman and Company, 1980, pp. 205-227.*

Free to Be Muhammad Ali   (1978)

As a sports writer for the *New York Times* Robert Lipsyte has covered Muhammad Ali's boxing career from its beginning; through the anecdotes he shares and the remarks of the never silent Ali, Lipsyte presents a warm and personal look at the Champ. Facing head-on the controversies that have attended Ali's tumultuous career, the author offers insightful background material on the climate of boxing in the 1960s and on the civil unrest and growing disturbance over the Vietnam war—issues on which Ali took definite and, at the time, unpopular stands. Lipsyte's involving delivery avoids the cynicism found in other biographies of the Champ and presents a sensitive look at this boxing legend in an excellent addition to sports collections.

> *A review of "Free to Be Muhammad Ali," in* Booklist, *Vol. 75, No. 3, October 1, 1978, p. 303.*

Lipsyte's been in Ali's corner, as reporter and friend, since 1964, and this forthright, fair-minded biography nicely chronicles the champ's highly publicized career, circling in on the man's genuine talents and pointing out much of the "fakelore" as well-three versions of the Olympic medal story, for example. The approach requires a mature reader (Ali's "vanity has always bordered on narcissism"), able to comprehend the political climate of the Sixties, when the champ asserted his rights as an individual—to convert, to change his name, to refuse induction—and suffered undeserved recriminations from sportswriters, boxing associations, and the U.S. Army. Lipsyte doesn't dance away from the contradictions in his personality, and although he clearly acknowledges Ali's world-wide appeal and popularity, he doesn't muddle his account with the rhetoric of the literary heavyweights. No mention of the second Spinks fight, however, which limits this even before publication. A contender nonetheless.

A review of "Free to Be Muhammad Ali," in Kirkus Reviews, *Vol. XLVI, No. 22, November 15, 1978, p. 1256.*

Of those sports journalists who have covered Muhammad Ali throughout his turbulent career, Robert Lipsyte consistently has provided the most lucid and perceptive accounts. Neither siding with critics who castigated Ali during his exile from boxing, nor accepting without reservation the bombast of Ali's mythologizers, Mr. Lipsyte's portraits of the heavy-weight champion have been both revealing and temperate. Its brevity notwithstanding, *Free to Be Muhammad Ali* adheres to those standards. . . .

What one finally derives from this slim biography is a sense not only of Ali's mercurial personality, but also of the affection and respect the author feels for him as an athlete and as a man. Without suppressing Ali's largesse and athletic ability or his hucksterism, Mr. Lipsyte presents a thoughtful, complex portrait of one of America's greatest athletes. He does so with taste and an honest resolve to delve beyond the usual level of puffery and jock hype, which in his own field makes him almost as unique as Ali.

Mel Watkins, in a review of "Free to Be Muhammad Ali," in The New York Times Book Review, *March 4, 1979, p. 32.*

Summer Rules (1981)

The slogan of the Happy Valley Bungalow Colony was "More in 'Fifty-four!" but sixteen-year-old Bobby wanted less of the Happy Valley Day Camp. The protagonist of *One Fat Summer* tells the story; he had other plans for the summer, but his father had insisted on this job as a camp counselor because he didn't want Bobby spending the summer with the rough, tough Rumsons of the first book. Bobby's toughest job was trying to cope with the spoiled, hostile Harley, age nine, motherless child of one of the family that runs the camp. Much of the book is concerned with Bobby's romance with Harley's cousin Sheila, a romance that quickly loses its appeal, and throughout the story Lipsyte paints an acidly candid picture of camp life, but the climax of the story is serious and dramatic: Bobby knows that a fire at the camp was started by Harley, rather than Willie Rumson, released from an institution, confused by shock treatments, and a natural suspect because of his previous record. Shall Bobby let Willie go to jail—which might benefit society—or tell what he knows and have Harley take the merited blame—which might do further damage to his already-disturbed personality? Although not difficult reading, this is a sophisticated story, provocative and perceptive.

Zena Sutherland, in a review of "Summer Rules," in Bulletin of the Center for Children's Books, *Vol. 34, No. 8, April, 1981, p. 156.*

My enthusiasm for this book is boundless. Robert Lipsyte is the adolescent male's answer to Judy Blume, universally loved by young girls. (p. 79)

He is a heavyweight in the field of children's literature. Nevertheless, he writes for kids, not for prestigious awards. His dialogue is earthy and humorous in a kid-smart vein, his characters are recognizable, and his plots compelling.

Summer Rules is about sixteen year old Bobby Marks' summer as a counselor at Happy Valley Day Camp in the 1950's. Crucial characters include his parents, imperfect separately, but together able to give the family a balance of warmth and authority that one would like to see more of today. And there is Bobby's nineteen year old sister Michele, sophisticated beyond his endurance. From this background events unfold through Bobby's point of view. Very interesting is a *boy's* encounter with first love. The concept of responsibility becomes a major battle in Bobby's life. Loyalty to old friends brings trouble, and in the end, the cold bare fact of truth is the glue that Bobby hangs onto when values become overwhelmingly confused.

Summer Rules leaves you feeling good about families, and about kids growing up. My sincerest compliments to author Robert Lipsyte for what could become a classic series. (pp. 79-80)

Gail Tansill Lambert, in a review of "Summer Rules," in Best Sellers, *Vol. 41, No. 2, May, 1981, pp. 79-80.*

Summer Rules is disappointing, especially in light of *The Contender* and *One Fat Summer.* Bobby Marks is a much more credible protagonist in *One Fat Summer* than in its sequel, *Summer Rules.* (p. 30)

The situation at the day camp is unrealistic. The man who runs it is a principal during the academic year; here he manipulates his counselors and is in turn manipulated by his six-year-old nephew, a holy terror who frightens the other youngsters as well as the adults. In addition, Bobby falls in love with a girl who's interested but hard to reach. Suddenly, the two are so close that Bobby realizes he's not ready for total commitment. The girl has quickly become the pursuer, and the reader is not prepared for the abruptness of the change. When the man who terrorizes Bobby in *One Fat Summer* returns to the scene, he has become a zombie, a victim of shock therapy to make him more socially acceptable. All of this fits as part of the plot, but it seems extremely contrived.

Some scenes, however, are quite effective. Bobby gets drunk at a counselors' party, and his thoughts, speech, and actions are typical. Too, the scenes between Bobby and his dad are well done. Bobby feels an ambivalence that he is not sure how to handle. Some readers may be drawn to the novel because it is Lipsyte's or because they recognize Bobby Marks, but it will not be a best seller. (pp. 30-1)

William G. McBride, in a review of "Summer Rules," in Voice of Youth Advocates, *Vol. 4, No. 2, June, 1981, pp. 30-1.*

Jock and Jill (1982)

Jock is looking forward to his last big high school baseball game, especially because his team is playing in Yankee

Stadium in the finals of the Metro Area competition. There are several serious problems on his mind, however: he's fallen suddenly in love with Jillian and has become just as suddenly alienated by learning she's a drug user; he's worried about whether or not he ought to be letting the team doctor give him pain-killer shots so freely; most of all he's concerned about a tragic situation (decrepit buildings, with small children left alone in them—tied to a radiator because their mother had to go out to get piece-work to bring back) that Jill led him to and that Hector, a young Puerto Rican, is determined to change. Somehow, all of this plus a macho team coach and a retarded younger brother and breaking up with another girl and convincing the Mayor of New York to work with Hector and the Big Game all fit into a well-written story about a nice guy who becomes a concerned adult; there's so much going on, it shouldn't work, but Lipsyte handles the various elements with control and balance and it works very well indeed.

Zena Sutherland, in a review of "Jock and Jill," in Bulletin of the Center for Children's Books, *Vol. 35, No. 8, April, 1982, p. 152.*

Robert Lipsyte, who used to be a sports columnist for The New York Times, has a number of pitches to make in this engaging and didactic novel. Sports "medicine," he wants us to know, can be almost as hazardous to your health as the "medicine" you buy in glassine bags on Times Square or 125th Street. The "doctors" we meet in this book medicate an inning at a time. Sports "values"—"Achievement. Attaining an objective. Going the distance. Reaching the goal."—are not unworthy; they depend on what you want to achieve and how far you are willing to go and whether you should. Beyond such values are enduring human chords, as played on a harmonium not to be heard in a Bronx professional ballpark.

On the big game, Mr. Lipsyte is superb. He is equally superb on the wretchedness of the South Bronx, about which Hector refuses to despair. On class antagonism and personal trust, he is deft. On the subject of drugs, he is severe and minatory and persuasive. On sex, he is forgiving. On other joys, he zings. He tries too hard to teach, as if our heads were drums, but what he insists that we know is crucial; it implies that most venerable of Buddhist virtues, reciprocity. Which means fairness.

John Leonard, "Resisting the Pitch," in The New York Times Book Review, *April 25, 1982, p. 34.*

This is not a sports novel. Baseball plays only a minor role in the novel, and the juvenile-sounding title is definitely misleading. Jack is a finely-drawn character whose future is certainly in baseball, but that doesn't make him a dumb jock or exempt him from the human race. One of Lipsyte's points is that an athlete is human and has concerns not related to athletics. Jack is typical in that he has girl trouble and parent trouble, and he enjoys the occasional off-color locker room banter. He is unusual in his openly-expressed love for his parents and his mentally retarded brother. But what really shows Jack's maturity is his interest in the plight of some extremely poor people he doesn't even know. The book is frank in some places, but the central message of establishing priorities is very important to younger readers as well as older ones. Highly recommended.

Earl Lomax, in a review of "Jock and Jill," in The ALAN Review, *Vol. 11, No. 1, Fall, 1983, p. 27.*

The Summerboy (1982)

Bob Marks, the narrator and protagonist of **One Fat Summer** and **Summer Rules,** is eighteen now, and again he sets his story against the background of a small community where his family has come for so many vacations. This time his parents are away because of his father's illness, and Bob gets a job at the local laundry whose owner, Roger Sinclair, asks him to keep an eye on the workers. The one girl Bob fancies scornfully accuses Bob of being a spy for Sinclair and she rejects every friendly overture. Conditions *are* bad; no safety rules are observed in repairing malfunctioning equipment. After an elderly woman is hurt, Bob (who angrily confronts Sinclair with the fact that his affair with Joanie—Bob's best friend—has resulted in an abortion arranged by Bob) rallies to support some angry workers and is instrumental, by threatening a strike, in getting Sinclair to make improvements. The story ends realistically: Bob's fired, and although he's been a catalyst for change, he leaves the laundry staff rejoicing as he walks away, still an outsider, still a summerboy. Although this has the appeal of a sequel, it stands on its own as a narrative; like the earlier books, this deals in a sophisticated way with serious issues, but is lightened by the humor of the breezy dialogue. The characterization and style have depth and polish.

Zena Sutherland, in a review of "The Summerboy," in Bulletin of the Center for Children's Books, *Vol. 36, No. 1, September, 1982, p. 15.*

[Bobby's experiences during the summer] up to his heroic-finale confrontation with Sinclair and rousing call-to-arms to the workers. This loses Bobby his job (what the hell, the summer was ending anyway) but it wins the workers a significant victory in their incipient struggle for safer working conditions. It's corny in outline and just as corny in the preemptive ironies of the telling (Bobby fantasizes about fiction and film, where the heroes maintain a more glamorous mien)—yet, beyond the calculable series appeal, Lipsyte can be counted on to put a sharp edge on his observations of '50s mores, and to wring some real feeling from Bobby's adolescent rue.

A review of "The Summerboy," in Kirkus Reviews, *Vol. L, No. 17, September 1, 1982, p. 1001.*

Until recently, the vast majority of children's book writers were non-Jewish and their books had rural, homespun, wholesome themes. Only in the last decade have writers like Lipsyte, Judy Blume and Deborah Hautzig created anything akin to the Jewish novels that have been a mainstay of adult fiction for so long. Bobby Marks is a character out of early Roth—wry, introspective. Even slimmed-down, he is more of an observer than a doer, and he delights the reader with the engaging urban freshness of his point of view. We sense from the beginning that not much will come of his crush on blond, feisty Diana, a factory girl who regards him as a stool pigeon for the boss. More moving is Bobby's nonromantic friendship with Joanie, who is involved in an ultimately disastrous affair with a married man. (Bobby helps her when she needs an abortion, more an act of courage and personal loyalty back in the 1950s, when the book takes place, than it might be today.) If there is a problem with *The Summerboy,* it is that the factory owner, Roger Sinclair, is perhaps too much of a villain and gets too decisive and satisfying a comeuppance. But one readily forgives that because of the well-paced plot and the truthful ironies of Bobby's perceptions of the world. One of the few male writers in the young-adult field, Lipsyte writes books that teen-agers who loved *Catcher in the Rye* and don't know where to turn next will appreciate.

Norma Klein, "Not for Teens Only," in The Nation, *New York, Vol. 236, No. 10, March 12, 1983, pp. 312-14.*

Markoosie

1942-

(Full name Markoosie Patsaug) Canadian author of fiction.

The following entry presents criticism of *Harpoon of the Hunter*.

Recognized as the first Canadian Eskimo author of fiction, Markoosie is lauded for the creation of his sole book *Harpoon of the Hunter* (1970), a young adult novel which describes the initiation of a sixteen-year-old Inuit boy into manhood. Acclaimed as the first work to bridge the gap between Eskimo oral tradition and literature in English, the story has been compared to Greek tragedy for depicting in a gripping, moving fashion the themes of the unyielding quality of fate and the eventuality of death as part of life. Set in the Arctic in a time when it was populated exclusively by Eskimos, *Harpoon of the Hunter* is the story of how teenage Kamik accompanies a small band of hunters in a quest to destroy the rabid polar bear that has attacked their settlement. Left the only survivor after the bear attacks again, Kamik, who suffers terrible hardships as he attempts to return home armed only with his harpoon, is saved by Eskimos from another camp from an attack by a second bear. Kamik, his mother, and his fiancée join the people of his own camp as they travel across the ice to join a larger settlement; however, as they are crossing the ice, Kamik loses his mother and future wife and decides to commit suicide with his harpoon in order to find the peace of which his late father had spoken.

Told episodically in a terse style characterized by its concentration on action rather than on description or characterization, *Harpoon of the Hunter* is praised both for its immediacy and for its successful portrayal of the courage of the Eskimos as they struggle to survive against nature. Although the novel is considered controversial for presenting young people with a brutal and somber picture of life, it is also defended for providing its readers with an authentic picture of Inuit lifestyle and philosophy. Markoosie, who uses a single name in the tradition of his people, was inspired by the novels of the Canadian writer Farley Mowat to create a book which would keep alive the stories of the Inuits and bring them to a larger audience. Basing his novel on an Eskimo tale which has been handed down for generations, Markoosie first published *Harpoon of the Hunter* in syllabics in the newletter *Inuttituut,* a federally-funded magazine translated as *Eskimo Way* which was founded to assist the Eskimo people in developing a written literature from their oral tradition. In addition to *Harpoon of the Hunter*, Markoosie is the author of a short adult novel about the contemporary North which was published in *Inuttituut* in 1973 as well as an article on piloting; the first Canadian Eskimo to hold a commercial pilot's license, he is a bush pilot in northern Canada and has served as a translator and officer for several Inuit associations as well as an administrator for the government of Quebec.

(See also *Contemporary Authors,* Vol. 101.)

Alan Cooke

The story is simple enough. Most of the men in a little village set out to kill a rabid polar bear. Kamik, the hero of the story, is the only survivor of this expedition, and, against all odds, makes his way home again. Meantime, those remaining in the village had sought help from neighbours who live across a dangerous strait and, in the end, everyone decides to move to the other settlement. Among those who perish in the crossing are Kamik's mother and the girl he has decided to marry. There is an impressive dignity in Kamik's decision to take his own life in this final despair, after enduring through stubbornness and skill all of his earlier hardships.

This account of hardship and survival—survival of the community, not of individuals—is presented as "a story of life in the old days, not as it has appeared to southern eyes, but as it has survived in the memory of the Eskimos themselves." If that be so, life in the old days was a bleak and harrowing succession of disasters, for this story is as grim as anything by Zola. There is no hint at all of the good nature and the cheerfulness with which Eskimos faced adversity, and no suggestion that life was ever anything but a violent struggle.

It is this reviewer's impression that the book has been over-edited, for the distinctive quality that an Eskimo gives to his use of English has virtually disappeared. But there remain many passages of moving simplicity.

> *Alan Cooke, in a review of "Harpoon of the Hunter," in* The Canadian Forum, *Vol. LI, No. 605, June, 1971, p. 33.*

Anne Craggs

Harpoon of the Hunter is a starkly simple story. . . . Though plot and character development may appear minimal to some the book portrays more than just the story of one boy testing his manhood. From its terse, direct language emerges the picture of the basic struggle for survival which each man and beast must daily face in a land uncompromising in its vast harshness. Death is accepted as an integral part of the battle to live. The bleakness of the Barrens, naked in their intensity, remains with the reader long after he has finished the story. . . . (p. 35)

> *Anne Craggs, in a review of "Harpoon of the Hunter," in* In Review: Canadian Books for Children, *Vol. 5, No. 3, Summer, 1971, pp. 34-5.*

F. Bruemmer

[*Harpoon of the Hunter*] is a stark, violent tale, well told. With its theme of inexorable fate it shares the spirit of classic Greek tragedy. Only here, in the Arctic, fate and nature are one, pitiless and powerful. It is a gripping story, quickly paced, fascinating to read.

Unfortunately, the book is occasionally flawed by improbabilities and even inaccuracies. The late Joe Panipakuttuk of Pond Inlet wrote several stories for "Inuttituut", accounts that are vividly authentic, written by a man who has known and experienced the events he writes about. Markoosie is a younger man, raised in a settlement environment, yet his tale is set in the time before whites came to the Arctic.

When he describes in the book how a camp elder rather authoritatively calls "a meeting of the entire people", he is projecting, I think, present settlement (white-influenced) customs into the past. As two Eskimos approach the igloos of another camp, "hundreds of people" come to greet them. Only in the Bering Strait region could such large camps have been found.

These are small, though jarring points. But when the author says: "Wolves and musk oxen roam the land, living on anything they can kill", he lets drama override the facts. Musk oxen are fairly mild herbivores. Another disturbing note is the use of the harpoon to kill polar bears. Eskimos, whenever possible, used spears to hunt bears. And when the author says that Kamik ". . . took his harpoon, and struck the bear again and again," he is stating an impossibility. It is the characteristic of a harpoon that, driven into an animal, it cannot be pulled out again.

On the whole, though, this is an enjoyable book, hopefully the first of many to be written by Eskimo authors. (pp. iv-v)

> *F. Bruemmer, in a review of "Harpoon of the Hunter," in* Canadian Geographical Journal, *Vol. LXXXIII, No. 2, August, 1971, pp. IV-V.*

James McNeill

Out of generations of unrelenting struggle for survival as a race in a bleak land has come a story that is destined to be read for many years to come. *Harpoon of the Hunter* was a first and Markoosie, the author, is a first, the first Canadian Eskimo to write an original novel. (p. 9)

When I began work with the Eskimo people in 1967 for the Federal Government, part of my charge was "to assist them to develop a written literature from their own rich oral tradition." I went north to meet the people, look for talent and find material for *Inuttituut,* the Eskimo language magazine we founded. Response was slow at first, but gradually material began to come in—old stories, memories on tape, songs and some poetry. We typed our first book in syllabics from a tape, the 123 page *Autobiography of John Ayaruaq.* It was the first book ever printed in Eskimo for enjoyment reading only. A copy was given to every family in the North. It was well accepted and became a sort of catalyst—a challenge to people to write longer material.

I heard that Markoosie had read the book and had begun writing, and I quickly got in touch with him. Yes, the answer was, and would I be interested in it when it was finished? Of course it was some time before a traveller from the North looked me up and handed me a bulky envelope full of paper. With the help of several Eskimo friends, the manuscript enclosed was carefully read. It was the breakthrough we had all been waiting for. We published Markoosie's novel in Eskimo in *Inuttituut* in installments, all the while seeking a publisher for an English translation.

Many were interested but most were afraid of publishing an unknown Canadian author. One man was not. He was Robin Strachan of McGill University Press. He found it had a quality and a magic of its very own. This was not a white man describing an Eskimo situation. Here was one of "the people", an *Inuit* telling a story. True, it was fiction, but it described the human drama of the Arctic against a background of reality. It was the first novel to come from an ancient people and the first in Canada to be typeset by computer.

Harpoon of the Hunter is a simple, spare story of adventure and suspense which begins when the survival of a community is threatened by a rabid white bear. The bear kills some sled dogs, but the wise old men know that it is only the beginning. In time all the animals will become infected, including the game animals, and starvation will follow. The bear must die. But before it is killed a long chase, full of danger and death, follows. As the story unfolds, Kamik, a young unmarried man becomes a hero. The ending is one of complete surprise. It is perhaps a bit shocking to southern readers, but it is truly Eskimo.

Markoosie is a small, shy man. He speaks slowly and deliberately in a low voice. His spoken English is punctuated with time saving phrases used by pilots and radio operators. This is natural because Markoosie is a bush pilot, if bush pilot is the correct description of a man who flies over a world of treeless tundra, glacier scraped islands and the ice-chocked channels between them. His dream of becoming a pilot was realized in 1968 when he graduated from Sky Harbour Air Services training centre in Goderich, Ontario. . . .

Markoosie has flown hundreds of miles over his country, carrying oil searchers, administrators, wildlife specialists, students and patients.

Other courses in instrument flying and navigation followed. Between these and during long waits when weather conditions did not allow him to fly, Markoosie wrote. In addition to *Harpoon of the Hunter,* he has completed a short novel called *Wings of Mercy,* which is now being published as a serial in *Inuttituut.* This is a pilot's story of cooperation between the *Inuit* and *Kabluna* when tragedy strikes in the modern North.

There will be many more stories from the agile mind of Markoosie. He has a foot in two worlds—the old and the new, and he is not torn between them. He chooses what he wants from both. (pp. 9-10)

> *James McNeill, "Profile," in* In Review: Canadian Books for Children, *Vol. 7, No. 3, Summer, 1973, pp. 9-10.*

Sheila Egoff

Of the many possible variations on the theme of conflict against the wilderness, Eskimo life has proved especially fruitful. Perhaps it is because the struggle of human beings with nature is here revealed at its starkest. Or it may be because Eskimo life is so far removed from ordinary experience as almost to guarantee that only authors who really know their subject will dare to write about it. And who should know it better than an Eskimo? The first piece of Eskimo fiction to be published in English is *Harpoon of the Hunter* by Markoosie, who writes of the adventures of a sixteen-year-old boy in the not-so-distant past as if he had lived them himself.

The word 'survive' occurs frequently in the story:

> Maybe they would be lucky and get a polar bear. But Kamik knew that hunting bear is not easy. He knew that many times hunters come back empty handed after many sunrises of chase, sweat, and exhausting work. Bear hunting is the hardest thing in the north. The bear, if cornered, can kill many good dogs or men, if he gets the chance. But that is life. To survive in this wild land, man and beast kill for food. This is the land where the strong survive. The weak do not survive.

But even the strong are defeated here, thus making *Harpoon of the Hunter* one of the most sombre as well as moving experiences in Canadian children's books. The artless style, almost devoid of adjectives and adverbs, matches the landscape, which is empty of all but threats to life, except for the people who live and love and help one another. The form of this novelette is sophisticated and dramatic. It moves in brief episodes, from the hunters who go in search of a rabid bear, to events in the base camp, to the people who go for help, to the wounded bear itself. Together these episodes make a perfect whole. (p. 159)

> *Sheila Egoff, "Tales of Outdoor Life and Adventure," in her* The Republic of Childhood: A Critical Guide to Canadian Children's Literature in English, *second edition, Oxford University Press, Canadian Branch, 1975, pp. 154-74.*

Irma McDonough

[*Harpoon of the Hunter* is] a starkly simple story of Kamik's first polar bear hunt at the age of 16—which he does not survive. Many readers of the book recoil from the brutality they find in it and object to its being available to children. The justification for the plot is the life it reflects, interpreted by a man whose experience includes the very conditions faced by his ancestors. The imperatives of their lives developed out of their cunning responses to their circumstances. The Inuit are survivors: they have made a workable adaptation to their environment. That life includes tragic death is an accepted eventuality—and Inuit children are not spared this knowledge; indeed they prepare for it. Nothing is hidden from them. And if this naked truth is too stark for southern sensibilities at least it is the truth. The Native people do not compartmentalize people into ageistic boxes; the continuum of life allows for experiences splashing across boundaries that they do not recognize anyway, anymore than they recognize geographic boundaries. People at any age are still people and require consideration only in that light. That approach is foreign to so-called civilized Canadians who "clean up" the Native legends, so that children will not be exposed to the dynamic sexuality or the hard reality inherent in Native lives and legends, and reality can creep upon them in slow degrees until Santa Claus is finally dead and Harlequin romances can take over. (pp. 10-11)

> *Irma McDonough, in a review of "Harpoon of the Hunter," in* In Review: Canadian Books for Young People, *Vol. 16, No. 2, April, 1982, pp. 10-11.*

Norma Fox Mazer

1931-

(Born Diane Norma Fox) American author of fiction and short stories.

Major works include *A Figure of Speech* (1973), *Saturday, the Twelfth of October* (1975), *Dear Bill, Remember Me? And Other Stories* (1976), *Taking Terri Mueller* (1981), *After the Rain* (1987).

Respected as an especially versatile and literate author of contemporary realistic fiction and short stories for middle graders and young adults, Mazer is credited as one of the first writers to present her audience with strong and independent female protagonists, young women whose confrontations with ethical dilemmas and personal relationships bring out their inner strength. Her works are often noted for the relevance of Mazer's subjects, which include kidnapping, child abuse, teenage sexuality, and the affects of the Vietnam war, for her success with characterization, and for the moving and thought-provoking qualities of her books. Often about middle-class families, her books characteristically focus on the often antagonistic relationships between mothers and daughters; she also consistently depicts relationships between teenage lovers, several of whom are star-crossed; her inclusion of two adolescents living together in *Someone to Love* (1983) is credited as the first in young adult fiction. One of Mazer's most prominent themes is independence as a necessary and positive change; in their search for selfhood, her characters often break away from parents and guardians, or from the negative influence of males with whom they have had relationships. Mazer's protagonists, who are often considered outsiders, consistently face both personal and societal hypocrisy; in *Taking Terri Mueller,* for example, a young woman discovers that she has been deceived by the father who had kidnapped her nine years earlier when he was refused custody. In addition, Mazer often involves her characters with the poor and the elderly and has them encounter such harsh issues as sickness, death, and grief. However, Mazer informs young people throughout her works that they can cope with and survive the difficulties of life by relying on the strength within and by living truthfully and lovingly.

A prose stylist noted for writing economically and conversationally, Mazer is often acknowledged for her experimentation with form: using narratives in first, second, and third person and representing the points of view of several of her characters, including adults, each of her books is considered stylistically unique; she also embellishes her texts with such features as letters, newspaper articles, and journal entries. Among her works, Mazer has written two collections of short stories which reflect themes similar to those of her fiction, two novels on which she collaborated with her husband, young adult author Harry Mazer, and a novel which blends fantasy and science fiction. *A Figure of Speech* was a finalist for the National Book Award in 1974, while both *Saturday, the Twelfth of October* and *Dear Bill, Remember Me?* won Lewis Carroll Shelf Awards in 1976 and 1978 respectively; *Dear Bill* also won

the Christopher Award in 1977. *Taking Terri Mueller* won the Edgar Allan Poe Award in 1982 and *After the Rain* was named a Newbery honor book in 1988.

(See also *Contemporary Literary Criticism,* Vol. 26; *Something about the Author,* Vol. 24; *Something about the Author Autobiography Series,* Vol. 1; *Contemporary Authors New Revision Series,* Vol. 12; and *Contemporary Authors,* Vols. 69-72.)

AUTHOR'S COMMENTARY

[The following excerpt is from a speech which was originally delivered on 24 June 1984.]

Back in [the] early days when I was trying to write, I didn't think about the past. I had enough to handle with the present. I certainly didn't think that I was living a privileged life. We didn't have much money, we drove an old car, we lived in an old house, and for recreation we went sledding or camping with the kids. What I did have was a husband and three kids I dearly loved. But still . . . the one thing in life I really wanted, to become a writer, was as distant, as impossible, as my becoming a movie star. Yet I couldn't stop dreaming about it, couldn't stop scribbling.

In his wonderful autobiography, the English critic and short story writer V. S. Pritchett says of himself as a young man, "I found I simply wanted to write anything. . . . I had read that one writes because one has something to say. I could not see that I had anything to say except that I was alive." And he goes on, "I simply wanted to write two or three sentences even as banal as the advertisement on a sauce bottle, and see them in print with my name beneath them."

I read Pritchett's remark many years after I sat on [my] couch struggling to write a few words, and I saw that he had described my state of mind exactly. I had nothing but a love of words and, from some mysterious place, the will to keep trying. In fact, in those early years, one of the things that most frightened me was that I, too, thought I had nothing to say with my writing. What was it that I could say that anyone would want to listen to? What did I know? Who was I to say *anything?* I was unknown, unimportant, unpublished. A person of authority only to my kids. Respected only by my husband. (p. 161)

I think my first duty as a writer is to know how to tell a story, how to capture and entertain my readers. I want to write good books, I don't want to write products. I don't want to write books that fit neatly into slots, interchangeable books—we're seeing a lot of those these days. Product books which have less and less to do with the writer and more and more to do with marketing. I assume these books are, in the most basic sense, entertaining. That is, they do have story in its elemental form. I want to entertain, too; I don't consider that a dirty word. The story, the line of the story, the plot, if you will, is the basic ingredient of entertainment.

But a book written only to entertain, only to distract, a book without something worth saying underlying the story will have a robotlike quality. It will lack the heart beating at its center that is so necessary for a story to be more than a diversion, that will keep the story living in the reader's mind.

I love stories. I'm convinced that everyone does, and whether we recognize it or not, each of us tells stories. A day doesn't pass when we don't put our lives into story. Most often these stories are ephemeral, of the moment. They are the recognition, the highlighting of the minutiae of our daily lives.

But other stories embed themselves in our hearts. A story isn't an event, but the telling of the event . . . and not the bone-dry factual telling, but the event as seen through the eyes and heart of the teller.

Almost as soon as children can talk, they will begin to tell stories. My son started talking with the germ of a story. After pointing and grunting for two years to get everything he wanted, he woke up one morning, looked at the mobile hanging over his crib, and said quite clearly, "My Daddy do dat." All the basic elements of a story were present in that little sentence—a character, action, a conclusion.

The desire of the child to tell is not learned. It simply exists from the moment the child has language. And as the language becomes more complex, so, too, will the story and the levels on which the story is told and perceived. Since we all begin as storytellers and story listeners, reading ought to be a natural progression. Today, of course, television is one of the chief sources of stories. There is no denying the power of the acted story, yet for those who love reading, it's a rare TV show that can replace the book. At a school where I spoke, a young boy said to me that when he read he "walked beside the characters." I've never forgotten that. It has become a kind of touchstone for me—am I writing books for the young where they can walk beside the characters?

When I first began writing, I wrote blindly, wanting only to put down words on paper. The first real lesson I learned about writing was that I needed to—and did—have something to say. That something was there, inside me, waiting to be called out. That struggle, I think—not only for the writer, but just for living in this world with self-respect—is to find what's uniquely one's own: the real, the true things one thinks, which reflect one's own view of the world, one's own experiences, one's own perceptions and visions.

When I start asking myself that most basic question—What do I really believe?—the emphasis is on *really.* I need to get past the first thoughts, the surface slog, the pat phrases, the pet ideas, the banal and the slick, the easy answers.

My method, if it can be called that, when I'm thinking, when I'm planning a book, when I'm working out characterizations, or when I want to know what I think this book is really saying, is to talk to myself on paper. This means all barriers down, no "writerly" stuff, no looking for the right word, the phrase that will resound, the beautifully constructed sentence. It means pouring out what's in my mind, what's beneath the surface, all those unique, not nice, and but-what-if-no-one-else-agrees-with-me thoughts.

I learned to pour out this way a long time ago. I learned this out of painful necessity when Harry and I, terrified and crazily optimistic, launched ourselves into the world of free-lance writers. He quit his job, our sole source of income, and we set out to provide for ourselves and our, by now, four children through our writing.

At that point I *had* to write, not out of love of words, anymore, not out of pride and vanity, but because I had to bring in my share of the money needed for our family. And out of days of sitting frozen in front of the typewriter, tears coming because I knew I'd never make it and our dream would shatter, came this method of "get it out." It's still the way I draft—get it out, get it on paper. Never mind what it sounds like, just get it down so I have something to work with, so I can rewrite, so I can clear my mind for other things to enter.

Any writing that intends to make an impression has to be informed by what the writer believes, not what she thinks she ought to believe. Every word, every sentence she puts down ought to be laid on the solid foundation of her point of view. Point of view, what the writer thinks, should never be spelled out in a novel, yet it is intricately, I should say inextricably, tied to the development of plot and the working out of character. And those two, in turn, are so closely intertwined for me that I am at a loss when someone asks me which comes first, plot or character.

The fact is that they act one upon the other, and one of the challenges of writing for the young adult market today is to create honest characters who come alive while at the same time developing a plot which will keep a generation of kids brought up on TV turning the pages of a book. (pp. 163-65)

Approaching a new book is always a time for chills. I still wonder, can I do it? Am I capable of writing a real novel? Will I do this story justice? Will I write a book people enjoy reading? What does this story *mean?* And why am I even writing this book? Aren't there enough books in the world already?

No, I guess not. I think we all share an ancient and common need to make order out of the chaos of life. The story, the book, the novel does this for us by bringing order to events that, in life, might be random, purposeless, even meaningless.

In my own life, it seems that events are never finished until I've either told them or written about them, sometimes accurately, more often not.

For instance, in **Summer Girls, Love Boys,** there's a story called **"Florrie, Adelina, and Carmella."** It's a story about women working in a factory, their exploitation and their friendship. I worked in that factory, and I knew those women. It was a brief but important time of my life, and I always wanted to write about it. It took me a great many years to find the way to do it, but all that time it was always somewhere waiting in my mind.

In that story, I was very conscious of the connection of memory to story. But in **When We First Met,** which is a Romeo and Juliet story with Jenny Pennoyer from *A Figure of Speech,* the situation for me was entirely different. At that point in the early work, where the story was bare bones in my mind—boy and girl whose families hate each other fall in love—I had no idea how the story connected to me. But while I was planning and writing, all kinds of connections arose. And those connections were often in the form of remembered or half-remembered stories from my childhood. (pp. 165-66)

One . . . example: in **Someone to Love,** there's a scene toward the end of the book when Nina returns from a visit to her family and finds her lover, Mitch, has had his hair cut, nearly shaved off. She's shocked, he seems all at once to be someone she doesn't know. In fact, of course, he *is* someone she doesn't know, but she doesn't yet realize this.

I've realized that haircutting occurs frequently in my stories. In the title story of **Summer Girls, Love Boys,** the heroine at the end cuts her hair: a symbolic gesture. She's coming out from behind the masks, facing the world still with fear, but bravely. Maybe the way we all face the world. This haircutting goes back to when I was thirteen and my older sister cut my hair. I'll never forget going to school the next day and hearing several classmates say, "I didn't recognize you!" That was wonderful for me. It was what I wanted—to be transformed, not really to be someone else, but to be different than I was. Don't all adolescents long for transformation?

That adolescent me, that girl who was, as I remember her, insecure, unsure, dreaming, yearning, longing, that girl who was hard on herself, who was cowardly and brave,

who was confused and determined—that girl who was me—still exists. I call on her when I write. I am the me of today—the person who has become a woman, a mother, a writer. Yet I am the me of all those other days as well. I believe in the reality of that past.

I believe there is more than one reality. Our memories are real. Our dreams are real. Our fantasies are real. All the life of our mind is real. No wonder we are eternally fascinated, charmed, troubled, and moved by stories. This is because, at its best, the story springs from inside ourselves and speaks to the inner life of the listener or reader.

As we enter a story, as we begin reading a novel, it's as if we are standing outside a house in the darkness, our noses pressed to a window. Gradually the lights will go on in every room, and we will be privileged to see what's happening there. How people talk to each other, what they do, how they love and hate, and make up and cry, and try and fail, and try again.

Unexpected things happen, we're surprised into laughter or tears. And all the time, beneath the surface, we're wondering, "Well, what does it all mean?" The storyteller may tell the story at first for the sheer joy of being a storyteller, of being a writer, but finally she, like the listener, like the reader, wants more. And so, writer and reader both press on toward the ending to find out what happens and what it signifies.

We live in a difficult world. It can be sad, frustrating, and irrational, and no more so than for the young. They, with their energy and impatience and idealism, want answers and solutions. And usually there are no answers, or at any rate, none which will solve the world's problems either rapidly, completely, or very well. Mostly we all stumble along, we do the best we can, and we hope and believe—more and more I think against all evidence—that somehow goodness will prevail. And meanwhile, in a little way, we can often find sanity and hope in stories, in books and novels.

The poet, writer, and teacher Paul Zweig said: "All stories beckon us out of the visible. . . . The story is like wind filtering through cracks in the wall: it gives evidence of the vastness."

I am moved every time I read that—by the whole thought, by the way Zweig brought together the homely natural metaphor of the wall and wind to express something far more profound, and I am moved, perhaps most of all, by that single phrase, "the vastness." That, for me, sums up and expresses the world—the entire mysterious, beautiful, terrifying, awful, lovely world in which we are privileged to live.

And in that world I believe that stories and storytelling are as basic to human life as singing and dancing . . . that stories are as essential to our lives as food and water, as sleep, dreams, and love. (pp. 166-67)

Norma Fox Mazer, "Growing Up with Stories," in Top of the News, *Vol. 41, No. 2, Winter, 1985, pp. 157-67.*

GENERAL COMMENTARY

Suzanne Freeman

It's not hard to see why Norma Fox Mazer has found a place among the most popular writers for young adults these days. At her best, Mazer can cut right to the bone of teenage troubles and then show us how the wounds will heal. She can set down the everyday scenes of her characters' lives in images that are scalpel-sharp. In Mazer's books, we find lovers who cheat and fathers who cry. We find elephant jokes and pink champagne. We find college students who live in apartments which smell of cats and we find high school kids who walk through corridors which smell of "lysol, oregano (pizza for lunch again) and cigarette smoke." What's apparent throughout all of this is that Mazer has taken great care to get to know the world she writes about. She delves into the very heart of it with a sure and practiced hand. . . .

In its sharpest moments, Norma Fox Mazer's writing can etch a place in our hearts. In the passages that are perhaps not so well-honed, her people and their stories still manage to make us care. And that is no small achievement.

> *Suzanne Freeman, "The Truth about the Teens," in* Book World—The Washington Post, *April 10, 1983, p. 10.*

Sally Holmes Holtze

Trissy Beers, the heroine of Norma Fox Mazer's first novel, *I, Trissy,* and the daughter of separated parents, finds a note that she's not supposed to see. It is left with a homemade chocolate cake in her father's bachelor apartment. The note is from a woman, obviously one who is used to the apartment, and evidently one who has spent the night with Trissy's father.

What does Trissy do? She does the kind of thing heroines of books for children and young adults didn't generally do in the year *I, Trissy* was published; she plunges both hands into the cake, squeezes and mashes it, and then smears chocolate frosting handprints all over the walls of the apartment.

Few heroines before Trissy strayed as far as she does from more conventional heroines: less passionate protagonists who never came up against the kind of emotionally upsetting situation that Trissy did and who would not have reacted that way if they had. Some children's authors before Mazer had written on realistic topics and given their protagonists first-person narratives to describe their problematical lives. But when *I, Trissy* and Norma Fox Mazer's other early works appeared, it was still unusual to find strong, independent protagonists describing their very contemporary problems.

I, Trissy is a book for a younger audience than most of Mazer's novels, which fall into the young adult category, usually defined as books for readers twelve and older. However, the book shares with Mazer's later works the realism that was prevalent among young adult novels emerging at the time of its publication, as well as strong, independent heroines and the innovative style of her young adult novels. (pp. 1-2)

One of the most consistent aspects of her work is inconsistency; that is, she is a relentless experimenter with forms.

Many fiction writers publish an unpolished first novel that hints of the promise of a later, more mature style; their later books show a development of that same style. Mazer's first book, however, is a polished, first-person narrative. She abandons this form in her second book, which is third-person prose that is sometimes awkwardly written. Thus, she is likely to disregard the groundwork she has laid for her stylistic development in one book in order to try something completely different in the next. She will tailor a book's individual style to suit its subject. Yet, some elements of the idiosyncratic prose forms that contribute to her personal style pervade almost all her work.

The kind of prose Mazer excels in is realistic, contemporary fiction that explores relationships among middle-class people, especially those between a woman and a girl. Lou Willett Stanek commented in [*Media and Methods,* September 1976] on the dearth of books about such relationships, especially mother-daughter ones. Mazer has gone a long way toward filling this gap; this kind of writing is her forte. She frequently discusses the concerns of intelligent, independent-minded young women who confront their problems. She does not limit herself to such topics and characters, however, and the topic of her individual works seems to determine the forms and structure of her prose. (pp. 19-20)

In *I, Trissy,* Mazer's first novel, she uses a variety of literary devices to create a vivid character, Trissy Beers, who at age eleven constantly gets into trouble and feels that life is unfair to her. She's a fresh girl by anyone's standards, talking back to teachers and parents, but she is also perceptive, sensitive, and a talented writer. In the course of the novel she comes to terms with her parents' separation, finally acknowledging what she had not wanted to believe at first. She tells herself, "Open your eyes."

It is hard to draw many conclusions about Mazer's prose style from her first novel; it is easy to see that she is interested in experimenting with technique. The entire book is written on Trissy's typewriter. There are dramatic scenes, set up like scenes from a play; stories Trissy concocts; lists; compositions written for school; imaginary newspaper articles; and finally, a diary entry. The entire book reads like a diary or journal, as Trissy is recording her thoughts on a typewriter. Later in the 1970s, so many young adult protagonists told their stories through letters or diaries that the device became trite. Indeed, during those later years the technique became so common that a reviewer would pick up a new book, recognize the diary form, and just hope for something special, something with a little depth.

In *I, Trissy,* which may have set an example for later writers of the many journal-like or epistolary novels, readers do find depth; they find a fine story, a humorous, touching one; a protagonist to care about; and a fast-paced, lively reading experience. The many fresh and varied forms make for enjoyable reading, and the facsimile pages of double-spaced typing add to the book's tone. In most of her books Mazer employs some of the literary forms she uses in *I, Trissy,* but only in this first novel are the forms used exclusively, without the explication of third- or first-person narrative. (pp. 20-1)

Mazer's next book, *A Figure of Speech,* has only one break from conventional narrative in it: a list of "assets" and "liabilities" that the protagonist, thirteen-year-old

Jenny, assigns to herself. Interestingly, Mazer re-uses in the list a complaint that Trissy made in *I, Trissy:* Jenny points out that she is not liked as much by her parents as the other children in the family are. The rest of the book consists of third-person narrative, from Jenny's point of view, for the most part; the narrative is sometimes told from her grandfather's point of view. (p. 22)

There are some awkwardnesses, some flaws; the strength of the narrative is somewhat diluted by the switching from Jenny to Carl Pennoyer. . . . Mazer has a tendency, more than do other authors of young adult literature, to present the thoughts of adults—often of mothers, but in this case, of Grandfather Pennoyer—instead of just the thoughts of the teenage protagonists. The power of the narrative is weakened because the focus on Jenny's thoughts and concerns is neglected. Instead of learning of Carl's feelings through Jenny, we are distracted from Jenny's feelings by the change in narrator. (p. 24)

A Figure of Speech affords our first example of Mazer's third-person, descriptive style. The care she takes with these passages demonstrates her ability to write such prose at this stage in her development. An example of this rich prose is the death imagery that begins the chapter in which Grandfather dies: Mazer uses words and phrases like "clammy," "chill," "grass stiff with silver frost," "deep hush," and "cold ground." Her later books, however, largely eschew descriptive prose and concentrate on techniques that get her closer to her characters' thoughts.

Mazer's third book is utterly different from either of the books that came before it. It is ambitious and complicated; there are several ways to categorize it. *Saturday, the Twelfth of October* is a book of "biological realism," that is, it discusses the menarche; it is a fantasy that presents an entire fictitious matriarchal society; and it is a time-travel novel.

The book came out in 1975, when there was a profusion of stories about girls going through puberty; many authors seemed to be following the lead of Judy Blume, who discussed menstruation in her popular 1970 novel, *Are You There, God? It's Me, Margaret.* Many young adult books published at that time that featured a teenage girl included a scene of "biological realism," as one reviewer commented, in "stories that do not need it." The seemingly obligatory scenes were frequently whimsically added to an unrelated story, and they were beginning to be tiresome. In *Saturday, the Twelfth of October,* however, the subject is crucial to the book.

The menarche is important to the novel because Mazer has created in her fantasy novel an entire culture in which the menarche plays an important part. The details of the fictitious, prehistoric society are so believable that one might expect to pick up *The Golden Bough,* the seminal book on comparative religion and mythology, and find Mazer's society described there. Her matriarchal world includes its own religion, folklore, names, speech, customs, and rituals of birth, death, and coming of age. Zan Ford, the protagonist of *Saturday,* wishes, alone, for her own menarche in contemporary American society, when the event is considered unmentionable. Then she is thrown back in time to a culture where, she discovers with delight, a girl's coming of age is a joyous occasion. There is a great deal of depth to Mazer's matriarchal culture, with carefully thought-out explanations of not only the day-to-day workings of the society, but the customs of mourning and burial, the procedure of healing the sick, and the inclusion of evil spirits as well as a higher god. (pp. 25-6)

Last, but not least, the novel is a time-travel fantasy. Zan, a contemporary fourteen-year-old in an agitated state of mind, runs to a spot in a park and finds herself thrown back to prehistoric times. She stays with the tribal people for almost a year, but on her return to modern-day civilization, she finds that she has been gone for only a day. The portrayal of another time period is successful, but the portrayal of the back-and-forth journeys themselves is less so. Mazer describes traveling through time in terms of elemental changes such as sounds Zan hears and sensations she experiences: "Then a storm of darkness descended on her, wings of darkness spinning and tossing her in a blur of silver and black." The lack of precision in the description of what exactly is happening may enhance the mysterious effect of the process, but the vagueness is unsatisfying. In this case, Mazer has tried for something a little different and failed. (pp. 26-7)

Up in Seth's Room . . . is a book that Mazer wrote in order to address a specific topic: sexuality among teenagers. (p. 30)

Though Mazer set out to write the book about a certain external subject, the novel is none the weaker for it. Mazer couldn't be closer to her protagonist than she is in *Up in Seth's Room,* with the authentic voice of Finn. In this novel Mazer hits her stride. Finn is pressured by everyone, by her best friend (to go out with Jerry), by her parents (to drop Seth), by, finally, Seth (to sleep with him); but Finn is an independent-minded, strong character who faces her problems and the pressures put upon her and works them out, making a few concessions to her parents, but none to her integrity.

The book has a strong, mature style, with just a few awkward moments. As in *Saturday, the Twelfth of October,* Mazer's descriptions do not always succeed in making the thought processes of her characters understandable to the reader. (pp. 30-1)

[Mazer's *Mrs. Fish, Ape, and Me, the Dump Queen*] is for readers aged eight to twelve, younger than Mazer's usual young adult audience, and the heroine is elementary-school-age. Joyce is an outsider, and Mazer captures that quality extremely well. Joyce is accustomed to the way she is treated by other children, and yet she can be hurt; she still remains open to possible friendship. She is an admirable character who knows what is important, who is respectful of her skeptical Old Dad but who is strong enough to lead him to open up to a new person in both of their lives—Mrs. Fish, the eccentric, even outlandish custodian of Joyce's school.

The entire novel is told in a strong, first-person narrative, a point of view that Mazer has not used since *Dear Bill, Remember Me?* She does not waste words; the result is a direct, compelling reading experience. The narrative voice allows readers to feel close to Joyce, to detect her perception and sensitivity. (p. 34)

Mazer switches effortlessly back to her younger audience, the audience of *I, Trissy,* with this novel; she addresses the younger age group so well that it is easy to forget that she writes primarily for young adults. Mazer's young protagonists are quite different from her fifteen-year-old heroines; rather than being concerned with romantic relationships, the younger characters are concerned with such subjects as having and losing a best friend. Trissy temporarily loses her friend Steffi in *I, Trissy,* and Joyce finds, loses, and regains the friendship of Lacey in **Mrs. Fish.**

Mrs. Fish is a poignant, serious book that explores the pain of being an outsider and allows us to come to know a lovable character; and the happy ending, unconventional because Mrs. Fish and Old Dad are going to live together, though unmarried, is quite welcome. (p. 35)

Pete Greenwood of **Downtown** is only the second male protagonist to appear in one of Mazer's novels, after Derek of **The Solid Gold Kid.** . . . The book does not exhibit much change in Mazer's style; although she excels at writing about girls, Pete is equally likable and believable. His narrative is unique among Mazer's narrative voices because it contains more humor than do the narratives of female protagonists. (p. 40)

From Mazer's foray into a boy's perspective on what is a complicated story of secrets and politics in **Downtown,** she comes back to familiar ground in her recent novel, the triumphant **Three Sisters.** It is a story with familiar Mazer themes and situations, and exceptionally strong characterization featuring the kind of protagonist whom she portrays most vividly. (p. 41)

Mazer has never shown the thoughts and emotions of one of her characters so completely as she does in **Three Sisters.** She makes Karen a totally believable, passionate, vivid character. Her style reaches its peak in this novel. (pp. 41-2)

Three Sisters shares with **I, Trissy** and **Up in Seth's Room** one of the most passionate, believable heroines in Mazer's novels. This recent novel, then, combines the subject matter she writes of best, a protagonist she describes most vividly, and a style she has perfected. Mazer is a writer who can be counted on to stretch her artistic range and to experiment with ideas and with forms; she is a writer whose curiosity about life and whose care for her individual characters lead her to write intriguingly, convincingly, and entertainingly about the concerns of young adults. (p. 43)

Along with the sheer pleasure of reading that Norma Fox Mazer's books and stories provide, one of the most important aspects of her work is the message that she gives to her readers. This message is inspirational, but not didactic; it is a thought-provoking view presented through the lives of her characters. Mazer presents certain themes over and over again, basic ideas that intrigue her, that appeal to her intellect.

Similarly, Mazer often writes about characters who are reminiscent of characters in previous books and stories. Unconsciously or not, she will present a scene in a book or story that she has delineated before and show different characters reacting to the same situation. Though she is an experimenter, a writer who does not hesitate to produce a book that is stylistically unlike anything she's done before, her characters are often familiar, turning over in their minds the problems and hopes and choices experienced by a previous Mazer character. Character and theme are inseparable in her works: If we run across a very

independent young woman in two of her works, a theme in both works is liable to be independence. For this reason, a discussion of her characters is intrinsic to a discussion of her themes.

Mazer is interested in ethical dilemmas, such as the justification and consequences of a parent kidnapping his own child, or the problems and consequences of a politically active couple giving up their child and going underground when they are sought by the police. Mazer is also interested in ideas such as the existence of a matriarchal society, and the importance of the female in such a culture as compared with our own; yet the ideas and the dilemmas she explores are presented in the framework of stories about contemporary teenage protagonists who move in the settings and in the plots she devises, reacting in ways that instill hope in those who read about how characters overcome adversity, behave independently, cope with being an outsider, and react to hypocrisy. Mazer takes her characters'—and her readers'—problems seriously. She places her characters in situations that demand a great deal from them, and she does not let her characters down; they respond powerfully, underlining her themes.

The themes that Mazer explores are vital to her teenage readers. Strong themes are crucial to any affecting works of fiction, and Mazer's recurring themes, one of which may dominate one novel and put in a cameo appearance as a subtheme in another, are clear and important to her audience.

The most admirable message that Mazer delivers to her readers is: Although life isn't easy, "don't despair. There is strength inside you." Her professed ambition of instilling hope is realized in, for example, **Taking Terri Mueller,** in which her character draws upon her emotional strength and overcomes a difficult situation. Terri has been comfortable for years with her loving father, who, however, kidnapped her from her mother after he lost custody of the small child. (pp. 59-60)

The problem facing Terri Mueller is an exceptionally difficult one, but almost all of Mazer's characters face problems and difficult situations, whether they are unusual or whether they are common dilemmas of teenagers.

In **I, Trissy** Trissy must face a difficult and enormously upsetting situation, that of her parents separating. Her spirited, indignant reactions, if not socially correct, seem reasonable, given her character. Readers who vicariously enjoy Trissy's sometimes outrageous behavior are witnessing a human being reacting to and adjusting to her situation and one who is eventually strong enough to accept that her parents will not get together again. (pp. 60-1)

A veritable tower of strength is Finn in **Up in Seth's Room.** This forceful character demonstrates the theme of finding strength inside yourself. In the novel, everyone wants something from Finn, including her parents, who want her to drop Seth. Finn does one of the most difficult and courageous things any of Mazer's characters do: She tells her parents she is going to disobey them and she continues to see Seth. (p. 61)

Finn has won, but she lets her parents win, too, by setting the hour when she must return from seeing Seth. Finn overcomes both peer pressure and her parents' narrowmindedness. She confronts everyone, she makes a compromise with her parents, the only ones who really have a say in what she does, and she continues to see Seth. Readers are shown that none of this pressure need push them to do things they don't want to, that they may argue with their parents' ultimatums. (p. 62)

The emotional strength that Mazer's female characters learn to rely on is missing from many of her male characters. Rather than exemplifying Mazer's message themselves, her males serve as challenges that the females must stand up to. Mitch, in *Someone to Love,* tries Nina when he states, "A man's feelings aren't like a woman's." Seth, in *Up in Seth's Room,* speaks of "the male creed. . . . It means that the macho thing to do with a girl is never take no for an answer. Just keep trying. Wear her down. . . . " In *Three Sisters* most of the men are unpleasant characters. While the father is a weak, shadowy figure, Karen's boyfriend David drops her when she insists on keeping her virginity; Tobi's boyfriend Jason is a brutal drunk; and Liz's boyfriend Scott is untrue to her. Men and boys, thus, often make Mazer's protagonists confront life's difficulties. (p. 63)

The strength of Mazer's characters is often tested by their inability to change bad circumstances. Jenny in *A Figure of Speech* is a prime example of a girl with such a disturbing problem. She is powerless to keep her grandfather from being forced to give up his basement apartment, and she is powerless to keep him from being placed in a nursing home. She acts irresponsibly, to go with him when he takes the initiative to avoid the nursing home. She is a child in a family where the adults decide what is to be done, even if all the adults (including Jenny's brother and his bride) act unfairly. Unable to accept the situation, Jenny acts unwisely. (pp. 63-4)

Some protagonists must summon their inner resolve in order to make their own difficult decisions. As discussed above, Finn in *Up in Seth's Room* makes the crucial decision to see Seth against her parents' wishes, and Jenny chooses to see Rob in similar circumstances in *When We First Met.* As Rhoda says to Jenny in that novel, "You can't make decisions about your life based on what's going to make everyone else happy." Mazer's characters show her readers that some circumstances cannot be changed, and she shows how strong girls adapt to these circumstances. She also shows them that, with courage, there is hope for change in difficult situations and that girls like Mazer's readers can make decisions and changes to make things better.

Independence is a major theme that runs through Mazer's writing. Her characters are often seen breaking away from parents or guardians, outgrowing childhood. They make things happen, rather than letting things happen to them. In this way, they are making their own choices. They also take responsibility for their actions and become more responsible by starting to get along without the protection they've begun to resent having. (pp. 64-5)

Independence in Mazer's fiction sometimes means independence from the unwelcome influence of men upon her characters. . . . Fifteen-year-old Jessie Granatstein in **"Up on Fong Mountain"** is a prime example of Mazer's showing her readers how an independent protagonist rejects the domination of a boyfriend. Jessie and her boyfriend BD disagree about what to do one evening, and

when BD accuses her of being "picky," she gives in, only to think later, "I realized, just like that, he had talked me out of what I wanted to do and into what he wanted to do." Their disagreements mount until they have a serious fight about what to do one night, when BD wants to go to a movie. "I haven't made up my mind what I want to do tonight," Jessie tells him. "Nobody asked me what I wanted to do, only told me what they wanted to do." They break off the romance after another exchange in which Jessie complains,

> "We're going to do this, we're going to do that, we're going here, we're eating this—don't you think I have a mind of my own? You want your own way all the time. You never ask me anything. You just barrel on ahead. You want to lead me around by the nose!"

No reader can be in doubt about Jessie's sense of independence after this speech, and Mazer shows that girls can be independent. (pp. 65-6)

Fights with parents are dramatic examples of the difficult but necessary process of breaking away in order to grow up. Finn's mother, in *Up in Seth's Room,* seems utterly without understanding as she forbids Finn to see Seth. Jenny Pennoyer and her mother get along like oil and water, and this is not an unusual relationship between mother and daughter in Mazer's fiction. The fights underline the distance between parent and child as a child grows into an adolescent.

Relationships among women and girls are a crucial aspect of Mazer's work. From the slap Trissy receives from her mother after she finds Trissy's "Memo to My Mother," there is a train of incidents of mother-daughter antagonism. (p. 67)

Three Sisters is a book that examines not only the sisters' relationships but also the mother-daughter one. In one scene the daughter is the one who invades the mother's privacy, by reading a book review she has written.

Not all relationships between protagonists and a mother, or aunts, or other older women are antagonistic. Though Zoe in **"Peter in the Park"** needs to break free from her family, the women who live with her are loving, caring, and special to her. The most congenial women characters appear in *Saturday, the Twelfth of October,* the fantasy that features a matriarchal society. In this idealized, peaceful society Mazer's characters get along well, but when Mazer writes contemporary realism, they fight with each other.

As Mazer explores aspects of independence throughout her fiction, she often writes about a protagonist working or hunting for a job. Holding a job is seen as a mature and independent thing to do, and finding a job shows that the world outside of home and school is hard. Several of Mazer's characters, including Karen in *Three Sisters* and Seth in *Up in Seth's Room,* are demoralized after searching for a job, for example, and some who have found work are treated badly by their employers.

Mazer likes to show independent characters who make things happen, rather than let things happen to them, and she shows the difference between them. . . . Her independent-minded characters may make mistakes, but her readers see them making decisions and controlling what happens to them.

Taking responsibility for one's independent actions is an idea that Mazer writes about in many stories. In *Someone to Love* the professor who had sex with Nina incenses her when he tries to take responsibility for what happened. He tells her, "I wanted it to happen. . . . Did you know that?" She thinks, "Had it all happened, then, because *he* had made it happen? And where was she in that scene?" (pp. 68-9)

Another important message that Mazer communicates throughout her fiction is that it is difficult to be an outsider. Because of their inner strength, various outsiders are seen adapting to their situations. Joyce, of *Mrs. Fish, Ape, and Me, the Dump Queen,* is ostracized because her guardian, Old Dad, runs the town dump. A boy in school recites a ditty he has invented about her: "*Orange peel* in her ear . . . She—smells—queer!" (p. 69)

Sometimes characters feel like outsiders because they long for a boyfriend they don't have, especially when it seems that everyone else has one. Wanting someone to love is a notion that Mazer explores in several books. In *Up in Seth's Room* Finn feels "hollow" and "empty" after being physically close to a boy she does not care about. She is lonely and imagines that she might die before loving someone: She thinks of "never being in love, never having someone of her own. . . . I want someone, too," she says. (p. 70)

In addition to showing many characters coping with being outsiders, Mazer shows how her protagonists react against hypocrisy. The truth, Mazer shows, is preferable to euphemisms and lies. This major theme gets full treatment in several of her books. In *Taking Terri Mueller,* for example, Terri discovers that for almost all her life she has believed a lie that her father has told her: that her mother died when she was small. She must come to terms with this monstrous lie, which he has long since justified to himself. The lie is unacceptable to the woman Terri's father is becoming close to and she stops seeing him, but a girl cannot similarly dismiss her father; she must accept that the deceit has taken place and reform her relationship with her father.

Downtown is a novel that is essentially about secrets; Peter has his secret from the world, that his politically minded parents are fugitives and, unintentionally, murderers. His girlfriend, Cary, has a less dramatic secret: She keeps from people that she is a foster child, her mother is a dope addict, and her father an alcoholic bum. The need for secrecy is symbolized by the fact that even Pete's name is a false one. In *Downtown* readers see that the actions of Pete's and Cary's parents have forced them to live with deceit.

Mazer's crowning achievement in dealing with her major theme of hypocrisy, however, is *A Figure of Speech.* People "never said what they really meant," Jenny muses. The character sympathetic to Jenny, Grandpa, rejects the euphemisms offered by his son when he calls dying "passing away." Jenny thinks: "Pretty words for ugly things! Grandpa hated those cover-up words, those figures of speech, and now so did she!" (pp. 71-2)

An idea that is repeated in Mazer's books is the injustice and hypocrisy of having one set of rules for kids, another

for adults. When Jenny's parents are rude to Grandpa in *A Figure of Speech,* she complains that they are not respecting their elders, as she's told to do. They tell her to be quiet, and she thinks, "One law for *them,* another for kids." Finn, in *Up in Seth's Room,* receives a postcard from her father and doesn't want to let her mother see it. "You never let me see the letters he writes you!" says Finn. When her mother explains, "That's different," Finn says, "It's always different when it's you. . . . One set of rules for you. Right? And another for me." (p. 73)

Mazer's messages makes her books not just entertainments, but inspiring, thought-provoking works. Her ideas make readers see things in a new light, and she presents situations that readers can apply to their own lives. Besides being pleasurable to read, her books are informative, rare, and valuable in that they can instill hope in readers who may feel overwhelmed by their own circumstances. Mazer can be recommended to any readers who might need to find the "strength inside" of themselves. (p. 74)

She has a special talent for creating realistic teenage girl characters and is a tireless experimenter with forms and points of view. Her messages (that life is hard but that one has the strength to survive; that independence is necessary and positive; that one can cope with being an outsider; and that living the truth is far preferable to hypocrisy) are meaningful and heartening.

Her interests, her intellectual curiosity, and her talent make her a unique writer in the young adult field. (p. 83)

> *Sally Holmes Holtze, in her* Presenting Norma Fox Mazer, *Twayne Publishers, 1987, 92 p.*

TITLE COMMENTARY

I, Trissy (1971)

A facile, resolutely modern novel in the form of ramblings set down by 11-year-old Trissy on the typewriter her father gives her when he moves out of the house in the process of separating from her mother. Between the wish-fulfilling stories she makes up, the time-killing games ("I will now type all the words I can type using just my left hand"), the Mother's Quotient test, the sixth-grade humor (teen-age boys' "underarm perspiration odor is enough to knock you dead at 20 paces"), runs the story of a misunderstood child whose impulsive escapades invite rejection from the father she misses and the mother she resents. (Trissy's mother represents that new juvenile villain, the middle class mother: among her sins are wearing hair curlers and baking cakes from mixes.) Trissy also squabbles and makes up with her best friend, taking up in the meantime with a black girl who emerges from a vacuum to demonstrate Trissy's racial impartiality. It's all set forth in triple-spaced typed lines that girls can skim through in no time and forget as easily.

> *A review of "I, Trissy," in* Kirkus Reviews, *Vol. XXXIX, No. 20, October 15, 1971, p. 1121.*

In a semi-diary format, the 11-year-old narrator views the weeks after her parents have separated pending their divorce. Trissy's actions during this period seem severely disturbed—e.g., she destroys a cake her father has re-

Mazer working at the family camp in Canada.

ceived from a lady friend and smears the frosting all over the walls of his apartment; her attempt to burn her "baby junk" in a plastic wastebasket almost burns the house down, etc.; however, her final acceptance of the situation comes immediately after her father patly reassures her that she will still be Trissy Jane Beers even if her mother remarries. Interspersed are compositions that Trissy might have prepared for school and some of her imaginings are presented in play form, but the characters are one-dimensional and Trissy's journal jottings lack the humor and insights of those in Fitzhugh's *Harriet the Spy* (Harper, 1964).

> *Peggy Sullivan, in a review of "I, Trissy," in* School Library Journal, *Vol. 18, No. 5, January, 1972, p. 59.*

A Figure of Speech (1973)

Fine, strong affection based on a mutual need presents a plea for our reconsideration of today's old people. Jenny has felt an unwanted child all her thirteen years. When her "thoroughly middle-class" family starts a campaign along lines of what's best for eighty-three-year-old Grandpa, Jenny is personally wounded. She has shared most of her

hours with the old man, who was alert, interested in life, and no trouble to anyone.

Details of the story are unimportant here; the point driven home with tremendous force is a painful, but proven, one—when we feel we are no longer needed, we begin to atrophy, physically and emotionally—a theory shown to be fact, repeatedly, in institutions and "old folks homes." . . .

Very good—moving without becoming maudlin—and deserving of a place in non-fiction sections because it speaks the truth about our contemporary selfishness and ingratitude.

> *Mrs. John G. Gray, in a review of "A Figure of Speech," in* Best Sellers, *Vol. 33, No. 16, November 15, 1973, p. 382.*

The family is a potent web, linking the fortunes of one generation with another's. Of all the linkages in that web, the one between child and grandparent is often the strongest. In *A Figure of Speech* Jenny Pennoyer loves her Grandpa, and finds it tough to get along with the rest of her family. This is hardly surprising, considering what a selfish lot they are. Grandpa lives in the basement, which is damp, but at least it keeps him out of the way. . . .

The crisis comes when Jenny's brother drops out of college and comes home with a young wife, and the couple look covetously at Grandpa's basement apartment. A small fire on his cooking stove gives the family their chance, and they move him upstairs to share a bedroom with Jenny's teen-age brother—where Grandpa is even more in the way.

When the old man asserts himself by running away, back to his remembered past, Jenny goes with him to share the last days of his life. "Didn't suffer a bit," say her parents, talking about his death. "A real comfort to us that he went so easily." But then they have a cozy figure of speech to cover up the truth about anything. . . .

[Two books on this subject, *A Figure of Speech* and Gil Robin's *Changes*], written in a quiet, remorselessly realistic style, are infused with a deeply felt compassion and humanity. And yet neither quite rises to the importance of its subject. Death is always a mystery; when it comes it is a cataclysmic finality. Rightly perhaps, the authors concentrate on those aspects of aging that can be avoided. (Families don't have to be cruel. Old people's homes don't have to repel.) The authors tell us about dying rather than about death. "If we'd thought of it in time, we might have saved him," says Jenny's mother. But the truth is that no one can be saved from death—either his own, or another's. Children, too, must face this; it is one of the conditions of life.

Norma Mazer in *A Figure of Speech* comes closest to the heart of things. The death of Grandpa in *Changes* is merely a message on the telephone, a disembodied sort of death, while *A Figure of Speech* offers us an image of death itself: an old man lying in the attitude of sleep on the wet grass under an apple tree.

> *Jill Paton Walsh, in a review of "A Figure of Speech," in* The New York Times Book Review, *March 17, 1974, p. 8.*

In the story of thirteen-year-old Jenny Pennoyer and her octogenarian grandfather, the euphemisms which cloak the attitudes of the middle-aged and the young toward the elderly are presented as a series of shabby self-deceptions. . . . The denouement is tragic, not simply because the old man dies but because Jenny cannot reconcile her family's post-mortem commentaries with their actions toward the man who had once lived with them. The subordinate characters are seen primarily from Jenny's and the grandfather's points of view; they are one-dimensional types, hypocritical and unlikeable—except for the baby Ethel who is too young to play more than a crawl-on part. Yet, the tendency toward melodramatic oversimplification is offset by the significance of the situation and by the crusty personality of grandfather, who refuses to "go gentle into that good night." (pp. 152-53)

> *Mary M. Burns, in a review of "A Figure of Speech," in* The Horn Book Magazine, *Vol. L, No. 2, April, 1974, pp. 152-53.*

The fine definition of all characters, the plausibility of the situations and the variety of realistic insights into motivation make this book almost too good to be true. There is no point at which it passes into an area of depiction or explanation that would exceed the experience of a young adolescent. But there is also no point at which the psycholog-

ical perceptiveness and narrative control would disappoint an adult reader.

It is hard to say whether the story would be more poignant to a young or old reader. The child may read with a strong identification with Jenny as victim; the adult will probably read with appreciation of the exposure of the stupid, attritive family conflicts. The vindication of the old man, which entails Jenny's vindication also, is one of the most pleasing Justice Triumphs plots that could be devised. (p. 207)

> *Tom Heffernan, in a review of "A Figure of Speech," in* Children's Literature: Annual of the Modern Language Association, *Vol. 4, 1975, pp. 206-07.*

The language interchanges in [this] book are exciting. The old man always fights for what is real in language and life, rejecting the euphemisms applied to him. He refuses, for example, to be categorized as a "senior citizen" and as he writes in one note, he will not be "passing away" but will die. (pp. 68-9)

Unlike the institution described in *Grandma Didn't Wave Back*, the nursing home in this story has nothing to recommend it. More important than the lack of basic comforts which are carefully described is the clear implication that the old man will continue to receive the same insensitive treatment that he has received at home. Jenny reacts violently when she visits Castle Haven. "The back of Jenny's neck went cold. She felt sick, sick. She hated this place and pitied every old person here. . . . She didn't want to . . . hear Mrs. Burr McCarthy going on in her calm, sensible way about the 'lovely' residents".

Despite his acerbity, grandfather comes through as a real character—brave, stubborn, independent to the end, determining his own fate even to the point of succeeding in taking his life. Professionals and parents before recommending this book will have to decide whether the emotional resilience of this courageous "old codger" justified the grim, detailed representation of this very real situation. (p. 69)

> *Karel Rose, "The Young Learn about the Old: Aging and Children's Literature," in* The Lion and the Unicorn, *Vol. 3, No. 2, Winter, 1979-80, pp. 64-75.*

Saturday, the Twelfth of October (1975)

The author of the sensitively written *A Figure of Speech* turns to fantasy in this intriguing new novel. Fourteen-year-old Zan Ford becomes the victim of an unexplained time warp which removes her instantaneously from a park in New York to the same spot during the Stone Age, where she encounters a primitive tribe. Forced to remain with the small group of cave dwellers, Zan slowly and painfully assimilates, learning the language, adjusting to communal living, but never fully accepting her imprisonment in the past. Yet when she finally returns to the present nearly a year later, Zan acknowledges her attachment to and respect for the people she left behind. Mazer artfully withholds solution to the mystery of the time warp and handles the creation of a prehistoric people and environment with considerable skill. Zan's reactions to her experience are realistic, as are the attitudes of other characters toward her. In all, a well-placed, unusual fantasy.

> *A review of "Saturday, the Twelfth of October," in* The Booklist, *Vol. 72, No. 1, September 1, 1975, p. 44.*

This unpromising fantasy redeems itself at every turn: though Zan gets in the end the first period she'd longed for in the beginning, the wish fulfillment is tempered by the contrast between her mother's passing congratulations and the People's glorious celebration of such an event; though the theoretical background of the time trip is flimsy, the inadequacy (and eventual emotional betrayal) of the teacher who proposes it adds dimension to Zan's lonely accomplishment; and though the opposition of the two cultures, to our disadvantage, is a current cliche, Zan's interim companions and her relationships with them are realized with convincing ease.

> *A review of "Saturday, the Twelfth of October," in* Kirkus Reviews, *Vol. XLIII, No. 20, October 15, 1975, p. 1195.*

Consider for a moment this plot: a 14-year-old girl who lives in a crowded city is by accident swept back into the primeval past. A world of cave men. At first horrified, she gradually learns to become one of them, discovers the joys and sorrows of primitive life—and finds that she has bridged a metaphysical river where past, present and future are one. Suddenly she is returned to the modern world, but no one believes in her journey. In her own mind, she has been away for a year—in the mind of her family, for a day. She is sent to a psychologist and learns to behave like a "normal" person. But the memory of an earlier, more beautiful life haunts her, and she prays never to forget, never to become ordinary again. Her story ends on a note of pain.

In synopsis, I find this idea fascinating. But in Norma Fox Mazer's rendition something has gone wrong. It is not only that her book is too long (which it is), but that the mechanics which make it work are not dramatic. All science fiction and fantasy demand a crisis through which a human being can journey from one world to another. But our young heroine's dilemma is no more crucial than the fact that her brother and his friends have read her diary (a document fraught with the fear of menstruation). Enraged by this, she flees to a nearby park, leans against an ancient boulder—and is transported back to a world of innocence.

The premise does not succeed, and no one is sorrier than I, for Mrs. Mazer is a dazzling writer and brings to her work a literacy that would be admirable in any type of fiction. Her sense of character and place are expert, her use of suspense masterly and her descriptive powers superb. But one wonders why menstruation looms so largely in the plot, why it has been chosen as a device to show the innocence of the cave people and the frozen sophistication of the girl. One also wonders why—over and again—biological realism is forced upon stories that do not need it. Perhaps the fault is not Mrs. Mazer's, but merely that we are going through a strange transition in children's books—one in which many writers are unsure of both boundaries and horizon. (pp. 12, 14)

> *Barbara Wersba, in a review of "Saturday, the*

> *Twelfth of October," in* The New York Times Book Review, *October 19, 1975, pp. 12, 14.*

Most of [this] book is devoted to a convincing and dramatic account of Zan's life with "the People," of the tribal superstitions and living patterns, of the simple acceptance of bodily functions, and of the warmth and loyalty of the larger family. When Zan is—as suddenly as she left—returned to a New York park, she is stunned to find that her months away have taken a single day, disturbed by the realization that nobody believes any part of her story. She tries to bring into her life the simplicity and candor she had known with the People, wistfully vows never to forget them. This . . . is an effective handling of the time-shift device; although the first shift is abrupt, the second (back to today) successfully integrates the dual experience, and the portion of the book that describes the People has strong characterization and story line. (p. 68)

> *Zena Sutherland, in a review of "Saturday, the Twelfth of October," in* Bulletin of the Center for Children's Books, *Vol. 29, No. 4, December, 1975, pp. 67-8.*

Dear Bill, Remember Me? And Other Stories (1976)

Eight stories that turn on small moments of defiance or determination. Mazer is at her best dissecting all-female families—in **"Peter in the Park,"** an intense tale of breaking out of maternal bondage, or in the splendidly ironic **"Guess Whose Loving Hands,"** in which an uncosmeticized cancer victim is cheated of an honest acknowledgement of her impending death by her ministering mother and sister. The women are drawn with every nuance and even a smothering mother is not without sympathy. Unfortunately, the men have a limited range, tending to be jellyfish, skunks, or dark horses, e.g., the men in **"Chocolate Pudding"** are spineless wino Dad and a reverse snob who's turned on by the heroine's poverty; **"Mimi the Fish"** is menaced by her beefy butcher father and romanced by a dreamboat who is as much an unknown quantity to her as to readers. Death, alcoholism, divorce are unremarkable facts of life in these stories which defy the self-help problem-solution mold and, though boy-girl interest is always there, are anything but romantic confessionals. Quiet and unaffected, these are fiercely felt renderings of misplaced love and search for selfhood.

> *Pamela D. Pollack, in a review of " 'Dear Bill, Remember Me?' and Other Stories," in* School Library Journal, *Vol. 23, No. 2, October, 1976, p. 119.*

Short story collections at this level are scarce, and when a good one (such as Anne Moody's *Mr. Death,* 1975) does appear on a YA list it often seems to have wound up there by default. Mazer's more conventional stories have none of Moody's strength and sharpness, but they are clearly broadcast on a young teenager's wavelength, with the signal unobtrusively amplified as in good YA novels; and just as clearly, Mazer appreciates the short story form, with its narrow focus and spotlit moments, where others might do up the same material as diluted novels. Except for **"Zelzah,"** a resilient immigrant of "long ago," these are sympathetic views of ordinary, contemporary girls and their relationships with mothers and new boyfriends. In the funniest, and shrewdest, a socially insecure girl ends up carrying limburger cheese all through her first date—maneuvered by her once-popular mother who had seemed desperate for the same success for her daughter. Elsewhere a thirteen-year-old breaks free of the loving protection of her mother, aunt, and grandmother; a working class teenager discovers her bouncy, light-hearted mother's affair; a dying eighteen-year-old pleads with her smiling mother and sister to acknowledge the truth; and there are some happy pairings as when the loner who lives in a trailer with a drunken father and uncle finds a boy who shares her enthusiasm for chocolate pudding. The modesty of the characters' social backgrounds and intellectual horizons, not to mention the brevity of the pieces, adds to the stories' appeal as sturdy rungs on a gently sloping reading ladder. (pp. 1101-02)

> *A review of "Dear Bill, Remember Me? And Other Stories," in* Kirkus Reviews, *Vol. XLIV, No. 19, October 1, 1976, pp. 1101-02.*

Teens and adults will enjoy this readable collection of short stories by Mazer, the perceptive, stylish author of **Saturday The Twelfth of October.** Most of them concern the traumas of adolescence—love and losses—and one, **"Guess Whose Friendly Hands,"** is about a teenager dying of an incurable disease. Mazer depicts first dates as more pleasant than they actually are, but readers won't mind. Lighter and more fun than Anne Moody's very heavy recent story collection, *Mr. Death . . .* but as well-written. (pp. 38-9)

> *Joyce W. Smothers, in a review of "Dear Bill, Remember Me? and Other Stories," in* Children's Book Review Service, *Vol. 5, No. 4, December, 1976, pp. 38-9.*

In the eight short stories, the heroines are all young girls, each passing through a crisis in search of her own particular freedom. A certain similarity among the stories is noticeable; many of the mothers are rather protective and most of the girls are fatherless or have ineffectual or unfeeling fathers. Individually, however, each girl's struggle to reach her goal is realistic in the presentation of the options now open to young people. Zoe in **"Peter in the Park"** is almost suffocated by the excessive love and understanding of her grandmother, her mother, and her aunt; her mild rebellion in the form of a late-night walk in the park brings her a sense of satisfaction. "She is fourteen, she did what she meant to do, and to tell the truth, she feels, quite simply, splendid." Tart and amusing Jessie in **"Up on Fong Mountain"** strives to be accepted as a person rather than as the appendage of her overbearing boy friend. . . . And the admirable last story, **"Zelzah: A Tale from Long Ago,"** concerns a quiet and determined immigrant girl who breaks away from the conventional peasant role of wife and mother to become a teacher—alone and by her own efforts. A somewhat uneven, but varied and thought-provoking collection with a theme of timely and universal interest. (pp. 58-9)

> *Anne A. Flowers, in a review of "Dear Bill, Remember Me? and Other Stories," in* The Horn Book Magazine, *Vol. LIII, No. 1, February, 1977, pp. 58-9.*

The Solid Gold Kid (with Harry Mazer, 1977)

This first collaboration by the Mazers is less of a novel than we've come to expect from either, but it is a well-paced suspense story with a believably varied cast and enough close interaction to give the adventure a little more than plot interest. The central character is superrich Derek Chapman, and very early on he is kidnapped from near his prep school along with four relatively poor townies who just happen to be waiting at the same bus stop. The kidnappers, a man and a woman, are brutal and increasingly desperate, and the five teenagers—one black, two female—alternately bear up, bicker, scheme, despair, and even neck (if that's what you call it when your hands are tied behind your back) as they are beaten, imprisoned, shot at and shifted from a speeding van to an isolated cabin to a burning boathouse to a remote water tower. . . . Overall the other four are less bitter than they might be toward Derek, whose Dad in the end provides them with medical care and college trust funds at the snap of a finger; and though the experience gives Derek a sense of identity apart from his powerful father, his social consciousness doesn't develop much beyond the early conviction that his wealth is "not his fault." But if **The Solid Gold Kid** never reaches [Harry Mazer's] *The Dollar Man*'s level of humanity, the focus here is on the thrill of the ride and the tensions among the captives.

> *A review of "The Solid Gold Kid," in* Kirkus Reviews, *Vol. XLV, No. 7, April 1, 1977, p. 360.*

Separately, both members of this husband and wife team have produced books of uncommon interest. Harry Mazer's *The Dollar Man* was the tough, poetic story of a fat boy who fantasizes a rich, protective dad to take the place of the father who doesn't even know his son's alive. Norma Mazer's **Dear Bill, Remember Me?** managed to project adolescent naiveté without parodying it—a rare accomplishment. Together, alas, the Mazers seem to cancel out each other's virtues. The best that can be said about **The Solid Gold Kid** is that the authors have hit on a plot with 14-carat potential. The mass kidnapping of five teenagers, previously strangers, is a premise that's virtually guaranteed to keep youngsters turning pages. . . .

Unfortunately, the Mazers aren't content to spin a straight action adventure. They gum up the works trying to make serious statements. Often, these teenagers sound less like crime victims than self-conscious participants in a weekend encounter group. Especially annoying is the attempt to deal with Derek's guilt over being disgustingly rich. First, the other young people berate him for being the cause of the plight. Then, after they've been rescued and Derek's father has arranged to pay for their hospital bills, they seem to forgive him. "Being rich is just one of those miserable facts of life you have to live with—like my limp, maybe," says Pam. This is the kind of dialogue that passes for profundity here.

On another occasion, Derek muses lugubriously, "It was fate, I told myself, and I thought of fate like a giant hand scooping up the five of us, squeezing us together in this unbearable, hateful intimacy." Actually, young readers know as well as the Mazers do the difference between fate and contrivance. They may well be satisfied with the latter, and as a thriller this is passable fair. Too bad it tries so hard to be more.

Joyce Milton, "A Kid's Ransom," in Book World—The Washington Post, *July 10, 1977, p. 10.*

Two writers have combined their distinct talents to produce a skillfully written and credibly plotted suspense story with fascinating psychological overtones. . . . The teenagers, from diverse racial and social backgrounds, are incisively individualized characters; closely confined and under the pressure of constant terror, their attitudes toward one another alternate between genuine solicitude and snarling hostility. The appalling events reach a climax with a breathtaking police chase; but more significantly, the reader feels that the story is essentially concerned with the human capacity for survival and with the futility of violence and hatred. (pp. 451-52)

Ethel Heins, in a review of "The Solid Gold Kid," in The Horn Book Magazine, *Vol. LIII, No. 4, August, 1977, pp. 451-52.*

Up in Seth's Room: A Love Story   (1979)

In Finn's parents' eyes Seth has two strikes against him: he is 19, four years older than she, and he is the brother of the medical student Finn's older sister is living with despite her working-class parents' outrage at this sinful way of life. But Finn continues to snatch moments with Seth, and once he gets a room of his own those moments turn into heated under-the-covers sessions that end in the same old argument, as she refuses to go all the way. Finn's friend Vida doesn't help, with her praise for making love and her insistence that Finn take up with insinuating Jerry, whose very eyes speak incessantly of sex. Finn and Seth break up over the issue, then come back together, and the outcome (before he effectively ends the relationship by moving to a farm in Vermont) is this: despite his early protest ("Do you think it's right [for me] to shoot off into the wall?"), he finally agrees that "there are other things to do that will make us both feel good." A cliché situation, with some goopy descriptions of sexual bliss and what might well be seen as a ludicrous solution in these days when technical virginity has pretty much lost its cachet. But one can imagine other girls becoming involved in Finn's lonely battles (defying her parents, disagreeing with Vida, resisting Seth). And the fact that different readers can come out of this taking different sides—Finn's, Seth's, even the parents'—attests to Mazer's skill in giving the single-issue story some human contours.

A review of "Up in Seth's Room," in Kirkus Reviews, *Vol. XLVII, No. 23, December 1, 1979, p. 1380.*

A good book for young people, they say, is one that can be enjoyed by all ages. Norma Mazer has already proved that she is a writer of good books, particularly in **A Figure of Speech,** but this book is strictly for teenagers, although the under-12 Judy Blume crowd will probably sniff it out.

The questions we follow relentlessly from beginning to end are the perennial ones of adolescence: Will she or won't she? And what's it like? . . .

Well, to make a long story short, everyone should be pleased with the outcome. Finn sticks to her guns, although the fact that she "doesn't" is hardly more than a technicality. There are enough explicit scenes to give young readers who don't know a good idea of "what it's like."

Although Seth finally lets up on the pressure, he almost immediately moves away. A perfect ending for first love: no more temptation, parents relieved, girl's principles intact, and a good-bye forever scene that justifies a nice cry. If the characters are less fully developed than those Mrs. Mazer has given us before, young readers probably won't notice. They'll be too busy turning the pages.

Jean Fritz, "Up in Seth's Room," in The New York Times Book Review, *January 20, 1980, p. 30.*

[This] story will interest most teenage girls as they face their sexuality and parental conflict over boyfriends. Finn is a strong, interesting character. Seth and Finn's parents are not as well drawn (they are flatter characters), but they are adequate. This is a good story which provides a nice change from teenage girls desperately trying to lose their virginity. However, Finn's and Seth's love is not without sexual play. This title will be good for book discussion groups and programs dealing with sexuality.

Susan Levine, in a review of "Up in Seth's Room," in Voice of Youth Advocates, *Vol. 3, No. 1, April, 1980, p. 35.*

Mrs. Fish, Ape, and Me, the Dump Queen   (1980)

Mazer seems to have had in mind a "Marty"-like romance, set in a garbage dump. The tale is told from the point of view of Joyce, orphaned ward of her uncle Ape Man, the town trash collector. Mocked and ostracized by other children for her association with rubbish (they dub her the Cootie Queen), she lives a sheltered routine with her surly, diamond-in-the-rough guardian ("We don't need anyone but us. The rest of them jerks can go jump in the lake."). But when the sturdy isolationist has a stroke, the girl enlists the aid of fat Mrs. Fish, the cleaning lady at school, who has conversations with her bird Toot Sweet(!), complains of aching feet, sports black chin hairs, and serves tidy sunshine sermons with tea ("What we look like is only . . . the outside of the package. The real you is like a light shining through."). In the ailing giant's rude behavior, the lonely custodian sees buried gallantry. He, in turn, demonstrates his burgeoning love by hiding one of her butterfly barrettes under his pillow. The trio become an odd family in the end and the young heroine, with her overweight mentor's guiding voice in her ear ("I yam what I yam") is finally able to share her Swiss cheese sandwich with a new friend. The tone here is self-conscious and contrived. People fly into rages, sing manic songs, do dances, and fling taunts for no visible reason. And a tedious series of lists, e.g., the contents and infinitum of the junkyard, substitutes for true detail.

Laura Geringer, in a review of "Mrs. Fish, Ape, and Me, the Dump Queen," in School Library Journal, *Vol. 26, No. 8, April, 1980, p. 114.*

[After Mrs. Fish agrees to live with Joyce and her uncle,

Old Dad,] life promises to be happier for Joyce; there's even a hint, at the end of the story, that a girl at school, who had been friendly until she learned from other classmates that Joyce lived at a garbage dump, has come around and wants to be friends again. The anguish of the outsider is vividly and realistically portrayed in this story, simply structured and well written, but it's marred a bit by the dominance of the two strong, almost overdrawn characters of taciturn, hostile Old Dad and the gushing, ever-giving, ever-forgiving Mrs. Fish.

> *Zena Sutherland, in a review of "Mrs. Fish,*
> *Ape, and Me, the Dump Queen," in* Bulletin
> of the Center for Children's Books, *Vol. 34,*
> *No. 3, November, 1980, p. 58.*

Steadfastly maintaining self-respect in spite of their derogation by others, the three protagonists—Joyce, "Ole Dad" and Mrs. Fish—have a great deal to teach readers of any age.

Joyce, the central character who tells the story, lives with her uncle, Ole Dad, in a garbage dump, of which he is the caretaker. Together, they recycle old garbage into useful forms, critically eyeing the materialism and wastefulness of others. Ole Dad is a positive, nurturing single male parent, still a rarity in children's books.

Each of the three central characters must face the challenge of enduring the age-old sport of name-calling, and children who have experienced this indignity for any reason will find new strength from this story. . . .

What is remarkable about Joyce is her ability to remain proud and uncompromised, in spite of her loneliness. This loneliness is eased, however, with the arrival of Mrs. Fish, a temporary custodial worker at the school. This large, loving, somewhat eccentric woman creates a shelter for Joyce in her small basement office, and offers her both strength and humor.

Like the other two protagonists, Fish is stigmatized by classist and bigoted attitudes, enduring the shouts of "Crazy Fish!" as she wheels her cleaning cart through the halls. Her response to name-calling is a consistent one: "Tush on them all!" Joyce responds to her with great admiration, seeing her as "big, fat, strong and beautiful." . . .

The relationship that eventually develops between Ole Dad and Mrs. Fish constitutes a moving subplot; the struggle Ole Dad has in overcoming his insecurities and lack of trust in order to experience a growing love is especially touching.

The heart of the story lies in the process of these three individuals beginning to work as a unit, drawing deeply on each other's goodness and individuality, with the mutual understanding that their relationships are far more important than validation from an unsympathetic outer world. As Joyce describes them, they are "like three people who had bumped into each other and didn't know how to get untangled." The author tackles the problem of being different with tremendous success, and gives her characters the ego-strength and values to be invulnerable to others' judgements. The differences, in this case, are of appearance and class, but any child who has known what it is to be "different" will learn from this book a new possibility

of pride and a sense of encouragement that being "different" does not necessarily mean "alone."

> *Leonore Gordon, in a review of "Mrs. Fish,*
> *Ape, and Me, the Dump Queen," in* Interracial
> Books for Children Bulletin, *Vol. 12, Nos. 7*
> *& 8, October-November & November-December,*
> *1981, p. 17.*

Taking Terri Mueller (1981)

Considering all the recent publicity about divorced parents who kidnap their own children, there was certain to be a juvenile novel on the subject sooner or later. And this is a good one, not just capitalizing on that gimmick—in fact, readers don't learn until halfway through the book what has actually happened—but developing strong characters and a plot that involves the kidnapping angle as a basic element. Terri has always been told that her mother died when she was four years old, and since her father has effectively cut off all contact with most of their relatives (he does maintain a tenuous relationship with his sister), Terri has no sources of information on her family. Terri and her father apparently have a warm, loving, open relationship; he explains their frequent moves from one city to another by his "Restless Feet." But during her 13th year, Terri begins to wonder about the gaps in her knowledge of the past and, to her great distress, she learns the truth. She does manage to contact her mother, over her father's emotional objections, and eventually re-establishes a relationship with her and with the grandparents she has all but forgotten. All the characters are very human. Both parents are portrayed sympathetically; while the author does not excuse or approve of the father's actions, it is clear that he acted out of love.

> *Karen Ritter, in a review of "Taking Terri*
> *Mueller," in* School Library Journal, *Vol. 28,*
> *No. 4, December, 1981, p. 67.*

The ramifications of [Phil's disclosure that he kidnapped Terri] and Terri's eventual reunion with her mother comprise the [latter part] of this well-written, fast-paced story. For a book that begins so benignly, amazing emotional depths are reached. Strong characterizations on all sides make Terri's eventual decision about who she will live with realistically difficult.

> *Ilene Cooper, in a review of "Taking Terri*
> *Mueller," in* Booklist, *Vol. 78, No. 7, December 1, 1981, p. 500.*

Mazer does a fine job of taking Terri through the emotional ups and downs caused by her discovery [that her father kidnapped her]. She wants to contact her mother, but she's afraid her father will be jailed. She's mad at him for denying her a permanent home and an extended family, but she loves him for the sacrifices he's made to keep her. Against her father's wishes, Terri goes to visit her mother. Again, the awkwardness and the tension of the mother/daughter meeting is well done. Terri ultimately faces the decision of whether or not she lives with her mother or goes back to her father. The book is timely and well written. The subject of divorce and deciding which parent to live with will strike a familiar chord for many teens.

> *Dick Abrahamson, in a review of "Taking*

Terri Mueller," in The ALAN Review, *Vol. 9, No. 3, Spring, 1982, p. 15.*

The greater part of this book, dealing with Terri's doubts and discoveries, is successfully told in the third person from her viewpoint. As she moves towards her denouement the author slips into other modes: letters, Terri writing in the first person, a chapter presented through the eyes of the mother. The letters are acceptable, but otherwise these changes are disconcerting, disturbing the flow of what is otherwise a well plotted, clearly written story which arouses interest, compassion and understanding in the reader.

> *R. Baines, in a review of "Taking Terri Mueller," in* The Junior Bookshelf, *Vol. 52, No. 3, June, 1988, p. 159.*

When We First Met (1982)

Jenny and Rob: as Jenny's friend Rhoda points out, their initials are the same as Romeo and Juliet's. Their situation is similar too. Jenny Pennoyer and Rob Montana are drawn to each other on first sight, then realize that Rob's mother was the driver who hit and killed Jenny's sister Gail two years earlier. Knowing how her mother nurses her grief and her grudge against Mrs. Montana, and sends her tortured reminders through the mail, Jenny resists Rob's overtures. Eventually however they fall in love. At first Jenny keeps the relationship from her family, and she breaks with Rob later when it seems too much for the Pennoyers. But finally, after Mrs. Montana attempts suicide and Rob is seen with another girl, Jenny decides that she must live her own life, and that Rob is a part of it. Though the relationships and the characters are less contoured than those in *Up in Seth's Room,* Mazer's ability to take her teenage characters' relationships as seriously as they do themselves gives this something of that same soap-opera appeal.

> *A review of "When We First Met," in* Kirkus Reviews, *Vol. L, No. 22, November 15, 1982, p. 1241.*

Mazer's novel is plotted on a situation that a less sure hand would reduce to a soap opera. But the award-winning author invests the ordinary people in her story with realism and draws readers into lives tragically altered when Nell Montana is convicted of drunken driving and fatally injuring Gail Pennoyer. Two years later, Gail's sister Jenny, 16, and Rob Montana meet and fall in love. . . . Mazer adroitly handles ensuing developments and earns one's admiration for making each person's viewpoint understandable and the suffering of all deeply affecting.

> *A review of "When We First Met," in* Publishers Weekly, *Vol. 222, No. 24, December 17, 1982, p. 75.*

[The] snail's pace of the story's development could turn a potential reader off. Once into the book, we have a melodramatic love story complete with objecting parents, non-understanding older brother and "I'm-old-enough-to-make-decisions-for-my-own-life" scenes.

A bit disappointing compared to *The Solid Gold Kid* and

Up In Seth's Room which contained much more action and energy. *When We First Met* is totally harmless (a few kisses and hugs) yet totally lifeless.

> *Barbara Lenchitz Gottesman, in a review of "When We First Met," in* Voice of Youth Advocates, *Vol. 6, No. 1, April, 1983, p. 38.*

Summer Girls, Love Boys, and Other Short Stories (1982)

A single neighborhood is apparently the setting for nine short stories that are otherwise unrelated and are uneven in quality. Among the best of them is **"How I Run Away and Make My Mother Toe the Line,"** in which a young girl—big, mouthy, and prickly about her rights—runs away from her weary, bossy mother, only to realize on her return a grudging respect and love for Mom. In the story the author has successfully used the rhythms and cadences of street talk to reveal character and plot. Another good tale, **"Down Here on Greene Street,"** again shows the author using specific speech patterns and details of food, dress, and furniture with a sure hand, as a middle-aged widow reaches a decision to remain alone in her own home rather than move to Florida with a man she is genuinely fond of. Other stories, however, are not as successful because of a certain slickness in style and because the reader feels less concern for the central characters. All of the stories revolve around girls or women and deal with the discovery each one makes about herself or others, opening the way for growth or at least for an enlightened acceptance of life. Some of the narratives lack the dramatic impact of good short stories, but throughout the book the author skillfully articulates the speech and emotions of believable people. (pp. 660-61)

> *Ethel R. Twichell, in a review of "Summer Girls, Love Boys and Other Short Stories," in* The Horn Book Magazine, *Vol. LVIII, No. 6, December, 1982, pp. 660-61.*

The author of several young-adult novels and a short story collection, *Dear Bill, Remember Me?,* Norma Fox Mazer writes in a naturalistic, warm, conversational style that reminds one of Saroyan or early Carson McCullers. Her new collection, *Summer Girls, Love Boys,* like her previous one, was written specifically as a book, a fact which gives the stories an unusual unity and connectedness. . . . *Summer Girls* is accessible to teen-agers as well as adults. Most of the main characters are young people, but Mazer writes about them with an affectionate irony that older readers will appreciate. (p. 313)

One of Mazer's strong points, and one that makes her rare among contemporary writers, is the ease and skill with which she writes about poor people. Her characters hardly ever graduate from high school, and often work in bakeries or factories. Unlike, say, Raymond Carver, who observes lower-class people with sardonic detachment, Mazer gets into their world, rendering their speech and manners accurately and affectionately. In **"Carmella, Adelina, and Florry,"** set in 1949, a young woman takes a job as a punch-press operator in a mica insulating factory to please her handsome Marxist boyfriend. Remembering the experience years later—the bawdy talk among the women she befriends, the foiled attempt at reforming horrendous factory conditions—she realizes that it was this bond between the women that made a lasting difference in her life; the boyfriend has long been forgotten.

Mazer's characters are often eccentric, even bizarre, like crazy Aunt Clare, with whom one teen-age heroine spends a short vacation in **"Amelia Earhart, Where Are You When I Need You?"** Home from her job as a cleaning lady, Clare spends days on end playing Monopoly with her niece until the two of them are ready to drop. Once she is back home, the niece realizes that their relationship has no future, that her aunt is permanently and irrevocably removed from reality—and it is this unsparing tone that protects Mazer's stories from sentimentality. One waits throughout **"Carmella, Adelina, and Florry,"** for instance, for a *Norma Rae*-like climax in which the victorious factory workers triumph over their oppressors. But no, the women lose their jobs and move on. Life, either because of social forces or the habits of character, is less subject to alteration than one would like. (pp. 313-14)

> *Norma Klein, "Not for Teens Only," in* The Nation, *New York, Vol. 236, No. 10, March 12, 1983, pp. 312-14.*

Unified by its setting on "Greene Street," Norma Fox Mazer's collection of stories also has another unity: perceptions by young women, most of whom have some fault (too tall, overly romantic, mean), one of whom is seemingly perfect. Each story has a strength and a sharpness of vision that delights and surprises in its maturity.

The first story is the major disappointment of the book, because of the length of its epistolary exposition. One wants to tell the teen-ager Richie, "Get on with it, girl!" because her voice lacks distinctiveness. Despite a contrived solution, the ultimate realization of the mutual, bursting first love between her and Stevie, to whom she is writing, leaves a warm feeling.

If **"Avie Loves Ric Forever"** somehow fails, all but one of the other stories make up for it with a precise, tight, fast-paced style.

"Do You Really Think It's Fair?" is a particular marvel of revelation. We hear only Sara's voice telling about her younger sister's fatal accident, but we know what the psychologist says, and we also learn of Sara's love-hate feelings about her sister. Sara asks, "Does justice exist?" With her, we must arrive at our own responses.

Mrs. Mazer has the skill to reveal the human qualities in both ordinary and extraordinary situations as young people mature. The stories are marked by subtle character development and quiet action. It would be a shame to limit their reading to young people, since they can show an adult reader much about the sometimes painful rite of adolescent passage to adulthood. We may not be familiar with the blue-collar Greene Street neighborhood, but Mrs. Mazer's stories will help us to become acquainted with the people who live there.

> *Ruth I. Gordon, in a review of "Summer Girls, Love Boys and Other Short Stories," in* The New York Times Book Review, *March 13, 1983, p. 29.*

Someone to Love (1983)

Shy and lonely, Nina finds college life overwhelming compared to her small town; just as lonely, Mitch is a college drop-out because—although he had no academic problems—he had felt out of place. They fall ecstatically in love and decide to live together; Nina hates lying to her mother, but she wants to be with Mitch all the time. When the relationship begins to fray, both are restless, both afraid to lose the security of their mutual commitment. Each is unfaithful, they quarrel repeatedly, and it is Nina who finally decides to break it off. Written with perception and sympathy, this speaks eloquently of the young adult's conflicting needs and emotions as he or she strives for security and stability and independence; Mazer sees keenly the ambivalence of older adolescents as they grope painfully toward maturity.

> *Zena Sutherland, in a review of "Someone to Love," in* Bulletin of the Center for Children's Books, *Vol. 36, No. 8, April, 1983, p. 155.*

This is a typical Mazer novel, well written, with believable characters with whom young adult readers will empathize and understand. Sex is an essential part of the relationship between Nina and Mitch but it is not explicit. Altogether, this is an honest and touching look at a bittersweet youthful love affair which is sure to appeal as much as Mazer's *Up in Seth's Room.*

> *Audrey B. Eaglen, in a review of "Someone to Love," in* School Library Journal, *Vol. 30, No. 1, September, 1983, p. 137.*

[This] book marks a real first in adolescent literature in its realistic depictions of two immature people living together. It also provides an antidote to previous titles about pregnant wives supporting student husbands through college, and the ubiquitous unrealistic teen romances. The dialogue and characterizations are superb, without a wasted word. Nina's streetwise younger sister, Nancy, provides some needed perspective on the relationship during a Christmas visit, without the rotten sermonizing many YA novelists of lesser skill give in to. A useful book beyond casual reading for freshman orientations in colleges, values discussions in teen sexuality rap sessions, and high school guidance offices.

> *Mary K. Chelton, in a review of "Someone to Love," in* Voice of Youth Advocates, *Vol. 6, No. 4, October, 1983, p. 206.*

Downtown (1984)

Mazer has chosen a contemporary subject to explore in her latest novel: the impact of the actions of 1960s revolutionaries on their now-teenaged children. Pete (born Pax Martin Gandhi Connors) Greenwood lives with his uncle under an assumed name because his parents' political activities have forced them to live as fugitives for the past eight years. Mazer excels at capturing the thoughts and language of Pete, his friend Drew and his unhappy girlfriend Cary as well as their interactions with each other and with adults. Readers move back and forth from Pete's normal adolescent days to his nights of terror-filled dreams to documents and letters which piece together the story of his past. The premise that children pay a terrible price for the passions of their parents is effectively executed through the characterization of Pete and his uncle. There are, however, several flaws in the novel which may keep readers from understanding or enjoying it fully. The first is that the FBI didn't trace Pete in the course of the eight years; the introduction of two FBI men so late in the story is quite incredible. Secondly, although Pete's parents' letters are masterpieces of '60s rhetoric and obfuscation, it is likely that they are too philosophical for young adults who have not known '60s activists to understand. The ending is frustratingly unclear. Pete's mother surfaces, having separated from his father, and wants him to come to live near her while she is in prison. While there is some resolution in Pete's relationship with his uncle, his relationship with his parents remains unresolved. There is no glimpse of Pete's reunion with his mother, no clue as to whether or not the awful burden he has carried for eight years will be relieved. For collections where Mazer's books have been popular and where the impact of the '60s is included in the social studies curriculum. (pp. 134-35)

> *Barbara Chatton, in a review of "Downtown,"*
> *in* School Library Journal, *Vol. 31, No. 3, November 1984, pp. 134-35.*

Pete/Pax, seemingly well encapsulated in his new self, zooms in and out of memories and the liquid fears he nicknames the White Terror (which he hopes isn't too racist a term). Privately he pores over the press clippings that represent most of what he knows of his fugitive parents, nailed as they are to the high mast of history. Occasionally two tough agents tail him in cars and harass him, hoping to glean some information about his parents. Over the years he has had a few sudden meetings of a low-key but still scary nature with his parents at motels and drive-in movies. And there are some loving letters, laundered to remove any telltale signs of the senders' whereabouts. If the letters are full of the frumpy seriousness of the very committed, they also display nothing but good motives, floating on a sea of Kahlil Gibran philosophy.

However offstage the letters and clippings are, they represent part of the book's moral center and the crux of the novel's story, which is about the keeping and judicious revealing of secrets. Pete's confidante is the appealingly touchy Cary Longstreet, and she turns out to have a secret of her own hidden inside her aloof bubble. She is a foster child whose dead mother was a drug addict and whose living father is an alcoholic. . . .

Downtown is wonderfully compassionate about all its potentially extreme characters, so we believe that Pete/Pax, our sensitive hero, will manage to meet himself and his conflicts maturely.

> *Mopsy Strange Kennedy, in a review of "Downtown," in* The New York Times Book Review, *November 25, 1984, p. 28.*

Norma Fox Mazer has an uncanny gift for taking a topic as current as tomorrow's headlines and developing it into a first-rate novel. Her latest story, like *Taking Terri Mueller,* once begun is hard to put down; once finished is almost impossible to forget. . . . Unlike many contemporary confessional novels, the first-person narrative presents a number of finely wrought characters: all well-meaning, none completely unsympathetic, all believable. Probing, fast-moving, powerful, *Downtown* is one of those

rare books which explores an emotionally charged subject without becoming an essay in disguise. It is both readable and noncomplacent—a remarkable combination of suspense and social commentary.

> *Mary M. Burns, in a review of "Downtown,"*
> *in* The Horn Book Magazine, *Vol. LXI, No. 1, January-February, 1985, p. 61.*

Supergirl (1984)

This media tie-in has the campy humor and outrageous personalities true to the Superman tradition. The movie probably gets that across in a more entertaining way than the book; however, for teenagers who like to read about the movies they've seen, *Supergirl* is a natural YA choice.

> *A review of "Supergirl," in* Kliatt Young Adult Paperback Book Guide, *Vol. XIX, No. 1, January, 1985, p. 22.*

Three Sisters (1986)

Karen Freed, 15, is the youngest of three sisters, a position she finds particularly problematic. Her oldest sister, Liz, is a poet and the family beauty—in Karen's eyes, perfect. Tobi, the middle sister, is smart and in her own words, passionate. She's also outgoing, outspoken, and headstrong. Who am I? Karen wonders. What's special about me? "Well, you—you're our monkey," Tobi tells her.

Where her sisters are concerned, Karen feels she can never compete, let alone win. Liz and Tobi have boyfriends; Karen loses hers. Liz and Tobi are close and seem to include Karen only when it's convenient. Beyond that, she's just their little sister, needing protection, certainly, but left out of things—secrets, problems, activities. To top it off, they think Karen is much too sensitive.

Things begin to change, however, when Karen falls for an "older man," handsome, sensitive Scott—to whom Liz is engaged to be engaged. After all, Scott has kissed Karen. Did Karen read it wrong? She doesn't think so, and takes steps to see more of Scott. She feels guilty about what she's doing to Liz, and very grown up, too. Liz and Tobi soon discover what she's up to, and for a while, Karen's already fragile world is shattered. But with a new-found strength, Karen summons the courage to begin patching up her relationship with Liz.

Author of such well-received novels as *Taking Terri Mueller* and *When We First Met,* Mazer delivers a gentle, engaging story of sisterly feelings and family dynamics. There's no holding back on details or emotions here. The Freed sisters, Karen especially, are girls every reader might know. But while Karen's mother emerges as a caring, independent woman, no clear picture of her father evolves. He seems to sit just outside the family, more spectator than participant. And Karen, the character who changes most dramatically, is still perceived by Tobi and Liz at the end as their overly emotional little sister. Realistic, yes, but perhaps frustrating for the reader who is sure Karen deserves something more for all she's been through. Still, Mazer's story is a grabber, a fine piece of contemporary fiction.

A review of "Three Sisters," in Kirkus Reviews, *Vol. LIV, No. 1, January 1, 1986, p. 53.*

The story of 15-year-old Karen's crush on her older sister's boyfriend. This is not a Betty Cavanna crush, though. Karen actually tries to climb into bed with Scott. He's too sick with flu to take advantage of the situation; the showdown, where both of them must face facts, comes later. As side issues, Mazer also attempts to portray the changing nature of Karen's relationship with her sisters and Karen's own emotional development. After a promising opening, it becomes clear that Mazer is attempting too much, and that none of the plot lines is strong enough on its own. The novel deteriorates into a soap opera for teens: loosely connected scenes, occasionally intense, sometimes mildly titillating, peopled by shallow characters moving to an abrupt ending ("tune in tomorrow"). This impression is strengthened by the "Sweet Valley High" style dust jacket. Of course, soap operas have a ready audience, but Mazer has done better than this in the past and will do better again. Better to wait. (pp. 177-78)

Barbara Hutcheson, in a review of "Three Sisters," in School Library Journal, *Vol. 32, No. 7, March, 1986, pp. 177-78.*

Karen's sense of neglect and isolation is well drawn as are her feelings of injustice, her jealousy, and, above all, her self-deluded fantasy of attracting the love of Liz's boyfriend, Scott. Karen's self-justification, anguish, and, at times, irrational behavior as she pursues Scott are skillfully handled in a compelling portrait of a young girl dealing with emotions and physical reactions she barely understands and still less knows how to control. The frictions, pleasures, competitions, and irritations of family living have a strong reality and, as tension mounts in final confrontations, come boiling to the surface. Each sister, and Karen in particular, finds her love affair is not the perfect romance she had imagined, but each emerges with a greater understanding of the meaning of love and with a reaffirmation of affection for one another. (pp. 457-58)

Ethel R. Twichell, in a review of "Three Sisters," in The Horn Book Magazine, *Vol. LXII, No. 4, July-August, 1986, pp. 457-58.*

A, My Name Is Ami   (1986)

A satisfying novel about the ups and downs of 12-year-old Ami's relationship with her best friend, Mia. Ami's mother has recently separated from her father. Feeling disoriented and lonely without her mother, the situation worsens when Dad begins dating Ami's gym teacher. Mia is the only one who understands, and the safe, exclusive friendship the two share is Ami's strongest support system in her changing life. In this reassuring book, Ami and her mother come closer to understanding each other; Ami learns about her own self-worth and gains confidence. Mazer shows strong insight into the mind and moods of adolescent girls. The writing is light but consistently sensitive and realistic, as the joys and disasters of the characters flow towards a moving and memorable ending.

Karen Levi, in a review of "A, My Name Is Ami," in School Library Journal, *Vol. 33, No. 4, December, 1986, p. 106.*

Mazer has a deft touch for characters and her dialogue runs true. She has captured the essence of a young girl trying to cope with her changing emotions about her parents, her brother, her best friend, her father's "new friend," why her mother left them, and the boys at school. Most girls will . . . enjoy the story.

Janet R. Mura, in a review of "A, My Name Is Ami," in Voice of Youth Advocates, *Vol. 9, No. 5, December, 1986, p. 220.*

B, My Name Is Bunny   (1987)

The narrator is Bunny (her real name, and she hates it), who is thirteen but looks older; she is happy in the love of her family, the lively grandmother in Toronto she visits each year, and her close friend Emily. It's because Emily doesn't want to go to a concert that Bunny is alone when she meets James. He's eighteen and clearly thinks Bunny is older than thirteen. He also thinks she's named Emily (she's lied about it), which causes some confusion when she telephones. Eventually Bunny tells James her age—but she finds it just as hard to tell Emily she used her name. It's a plot development that's capably handled but that doesn't quite mesh with a second plot about Grandma's having a stroke and coming to live with the family, a change that Bunny adjusts to with difficulty. While not as strong structurally as some of Mazer's earlier books, this shows the same capability in firm character delineation and is written with a good flow and a good ear for dialogue.

Zena Sutherland, in a review of "B, My Name is Bunny," in Bulletin of the Center for Children's Books, *Vol. 40, No. 6, February, 1987, p. 114.*

An enjoyable book, even though it has two strikes against it: the cover and the title. The cover has photographs of two cute 18-year-old girls trying to look and act like 13 year olds. It doesn't work. The title—***B, My Name Is Bunny***—follows ***A, My Name Is Ami,*** making one wonder about ***Z, My Name Is Zebediah*** and everything in between. Bunny, however, is a likable, true-to-life character who hates her name and wants to be a professional clown. Her friendship with Emily is the source and depth of this simple story of two teenagers learning about life. Both have the usual amount of minor problems (babysitting and boys) and major problems (parental divorce and illness in the family), and they weather them well in a realistic school/family setting. Bunny is both hurt and angered at the effect that her grandmother's stroke has on her personally. Mazer takes Bunny through the stages of growth and acceptance with accurate and touching emotions. Her storytelling should capture young readers once again. (pp. 172-73)

Judie Porter, in a review of "B, My Name Is Bunny," in School Library Journal, *Vol. 33, No. 7, March, 1987, pp. 172-73.*

Bunny is a refreshingly honest and normal 13 year old. . . .

Emily is quiet and sensitive and Bunny is outgoing and comic. Bunny has a wonderful, active grandmother and when a crisis develops around the grandmother, Bunny and Emily come to understand that growing up may have

Mazer with husband Harry Mazer, 1982.

problems but if you have a best friend the pain lessens and there is room to grow and change.

> *Janet R. Mura, in a review of "B, My Name Is Bunny," in* Voice of Youth Advocates, *Vol. 10, No. 2, June, 1987, p. 80.*

After the Rain (1987)

Adolescent Rachel has always been a little afraid of Grandpa Izzy, her mother's father; sharp-tongued and irritable, the old man seems to have no kindness or softness in his nature. After the family learns that he has terminal cancer (which Izzy isn't told), Rachel begins to visit him and walk with him daily, and by the time he is near the end and hospitalized, she has come to love him. This is a story all the more moving because Mazer preserves Grandpa's dignity as a character, so that both during his life and after his death, as Rachel adjusts to loss, her grandfather is consistently taciturn and graceless—and the book speaks convincingly to the power of family love that is strong enough to accept this. Some of the text is exposition, some consists of entries in Rachel's journal, and the whole is smoothly fused, balanced in mood by some comic moments and in structure by Rachel's relationships with her peers, her parents, and a much older brother to whom she writes long, revealing letters that are never answered.

> *Zena Sutherland, in a review of "After the*

Rain," in Bulletin of the Center for Children's Books, *Vol. 40, No. 9, May, 1987, p. 174.*

Step by grudging step, Rachel and her ornery grandfather come together in the last months of his life. . . . Even surrounding characters are revealed with care, and rich visual imagery adds depth. Close to death, Grandpa Izzy takes Rachel on a fruitless quest to find the concrete handprint Izzy left on a bridge that he helped to build as a young man. After Izzy's death, Rachel finds the print, creating a symbol which binds the book together, past, present, and future. Mazer's uncomplicated prose, mostly dialogue, is effective and readable. In its portrayal of a family coalescing around an old tyrant, and of a young woman achieving adulthood, **After the Rain** sounds a resonant note.

> *Carolyn Noah, in a review of "After the Rain," in* School Library Journal, *Vol. 33, No. 8, May, 1987, p. 116.*

This story about a teen-ager coming to terms with her grandfather's death is beautifully and sensitively written, sounding the basic chords of the pleasures and pains of family relationships.

What distinguishes this book, making it linger in the heart, are the realistic portrayals of the tensions, guilt, and sudden, painfully moving moments involved in Rachel's and Izzy's situation. Further, Rachel's position in a family widely separated by generations gives a rich context to her experiences: she and Izzy are not alone—their struggles take place amongst others whose strengths and weaknesses lend depth to the story. At story's end, Izzy is gone, but Rachel goes on, taking, in her way, Izzy with her.

> *A review of "After the Rain," in* Kirkus Reviews, *Vol. LV, No. 9, May 1, 1987, p. 723.*

When [Rachel and her parents] learn that her grandfather Izzy has cancer, Rachel decides, probably correctly, that the only way her two working parents will be able to get this difficult old man through his final months is if she takes on the task of seeing to him once a day. It's surprising that she should make such a decision, but once the reader accepts her choice and begins to join her on her daily visits with the crotchety old man, the story becomes both moving and wise. And Rachel's rewards become clear, as she manages to break through the wall of years and illness and really learn to know and love Izzy before she loses him.

The lucky Rachel Cooper learns the value of her grandfather in time, and she also learns to deal with death and loss. But her parents learn, too. Once again, their learning comes from listening to their child. Rachel feels that, in her grandfather's last days, she must be by his side. Her parents fear she's a bit over the edge. But she explains her situation to her teachers, and they give her work to do at the hospital. Convinced of her commitment, her parents let her stay. They also, through their understanding, give her the gift of being with Izzy when he dies. She is able to accommodate both her new found love for the old man and her grief, because the adults around her allow her the freedom to do what she feels she must.

Though there is a symmetry to the plot that might annoy some, Mazer deals with death and loss in an original and sensitive way. Unsanitized, Izzy's death is very close to us. An adult reading the book might even feel shock that a child of 15 would be drawn or permitted to stay this close to death. It is a credit to Mazer that she respects her heroine, and her readers, enough to allow them both the choice of witnessing a moment of grief and loss. (p. 19)

> *Cynthia Samuels, "Books over Troubled Waters," in* Book World—The Washington Post, *May 10, 1987, pp. 19, 21.*

Silver (1988)

Mrs. Silver is very happy when she and Sarabeth get a chance to move to the other end of their trailer park; it means a different—richer—school district. Sarabeth isn't so sure, until she meets Grant, a beautiful rich girl who welcomes Sarabeth (anointing her "Silver") into her clique, a coup that Sarabeth pulls off under less than honest pretensions. Mazer doesn't ever resort to the easy or expected in this novel, and it's a particular pleasure to see some rich kids in YA fiction who aren't lonely, bored, and disaffected. Like all kids, however, they have problems, as Silver discovers when new friend Patty reveals she is being sexually abused by her uncle. Even here the novel doesn't become didactic, and Mazer allows the girls and Mrs. Silver to solve the problem themselves, wisely keeping herself out of the way. Neither the lives of the rich nor those of the trailer park residents are romanticized or stereotyped, but are seen honestly through Silver's perspective, which is realistically limited. We never get a full picture, for ex-

ample, of Mrs. Silver's romance with chimneysweep Leo, just as we never quite find out why Silver's new boyfriend unexpectedly drops her. It's a convincing viewpoint and perspective, more revealing than most so-called first-person YA novels.

> *Roger Sutton, in a review of "Silver," in* Bulletin of the Center for Children's Books, *Vol. 42, No. 3, November, 1988, p. 79.*

Fast paced, with realistic dialogue, this easy-to-read problem novel stuffs all of this plot (including boyfriend troubles for Sarabeth) into one book. The characters are undeveloped, and readers won't care that when Patty moves in with Sarabeth, Grant disappears from Sarabeth's life almost without a whimper. Convinced that the plot will revolve around Sarabeth and Grant, it's a real shock when two-thirds of the way through the book, the molestation aspect appears and is dramatically presented and easily resolved within the last third. In spite of the plot inconsistencies—the ease with which Sarabeth falls into the sophisticated, wealthy group and the easy, uncomplicated resolution of the molestation, this moves easily and interestingly enough along that confirmed Mazer fans will want to finish it. (pp. 127-28)

> *Kathryn Havris, in a review of "Silver," in* School Library Journal, *Vol. 35, No. 3, November, 1988, pp. 127-28.*

Mazer's story unfolds smoothly. She has an ear for dialogue that gives her scenes an easy credibility, and the story's central drama of a girl's physical abuse is handled without oversensationalizing the plot. There are plenty of noticeable lessons on snap judgments and preconceived notions of people, emphasized by the contrasting relationships Sarabeth observes around her. And of course, the message that help must be gotten for victims of sexual abuse is loud and clear in both plotting and characterization. Mazer is a practiced hand; her contemporary story should easily find an audience.

> *Denise M. Wilms, in a review of "Silver," in* Booklist, *Vol. 85, No. 5, November 1, 1988, p. 485.*

Heartbeat (with Harry Mazer, 1989)

In their second collaboration, two admirable novelists use a classic love triangle as the basis for a poignant, believable story.

Tod Ellerbee is a tall, handsome loner, bruised by his Vietnam vet Dad's opting out of his engineering career after Todd's mother's death and by his subsequent drifting from one job, and home, to another. Tod's best friend, Amos, is a cheerful wit to whom Tod owes his life (Amos heroically saved him after a foolhardy dive). Shy, short, and attending a different school, Amos begs Tod to get to know Hilary and then introduce him (her parents are pushing college, but she has a job as an auto mechanic—part rebellion, more genuine interest). Reluctantly, Tod obliges; the inevitable occurs.

This is a perfect example of a well-worn plot made new by its fully realized characters. All three protagonists here are nice, competent, conscientious kids; with the pasts and personalities the Mazers allot them, each step, each response they make or take seems inevitable. Tod and Amos have too deep a friendship to become enemies—in fact, when Amos becomes tragically ill, Tod tries to conceal his love for Hilary from him. Hilary, to whom love for a boy is a new experience, finds to her confusion that she loves both. A grand, beautifully crafted story. Readers will be lured by paperback-like, idealized jacket portraits, but they'll be well rewarded. (pp. 766-67)

A review of "Heartbeat," in Kirkus Reviews, *Vol. LVII, No. 10, May 15, 1989, pp. 766-67.*

A highly readable, above average young adult novel. . . . [The plot] would all be fairly cliché stuff were it not for the fact that Amos is stricken with a heart disease that ultimately causes his death. The strength of the story lies in the characters' relationships with each other, their feelings of obligation and commitment, and an understanding of when the needs of others take priority. This is a fast-paced novel that just avoids melodrama. It should prove popular with teens.

Trish Ebbatson, in a review of "Heartbeat," in School Library Journal, *Vol. 35, No. 10, June, 1989, p. 124.*

The Mazers borrow the plot outline from *Cyrano de Bergerac* or perhaps from Longfellow's *The Courtship of Miles Standish* for this disarming teenage romance about a star-crossed relationship between Tod Ellerbee; his best friend, Amos; and Hilary, the object of their individual desires. Strong, nonstereotypical characterizations of the major players in this drama and age-appropriate minor themes flesh out the familiar story. . . . Add to this dilemma for Tod the attentions of another girl, along with strained relations with his aloof Vietnam veteran father, and we have a yeasty brew developing—although there is no happy ending. The authors' strong narrative sense keeps the reader engaged, while short chapters move the story briskly along. Sure to please, this novel could serve as a popular introduction to classic works of the same theme.

Nancy Vasilakis, in a review of "Heartbeat," in The Horn Book Magazine, *Vol. LXV, No. 5, September-October, 1989, p. 630.*

Patricia (L'Ann) C(arwell) McKissack

1944-

(Also writes as L'Ann Carwell) Black American author of nonfiction and picture books, reteller, scriptwriter, and journalist.

Major works include *Martin Luther King, Jr.: A Man to Remember* (1984), *Flossie and the Fox* (1986), *Mirandy and Brother Wind* (1988), *A Long Hard Journey: The Story of the Pullman Porter* (1989).

The author of a variety of works for young readers in the early elementary grades through high school, McKissack characteristically focuses on black history and folklore in both her fiction and her nonfiction. She is perhaps best known for creating informational books, biographies and histories with both historical and contemporary settings about figures and movements that have influenced the development of the black experience. McKissack profiles such notable personalities as Martin Luther King, Jr., Mary McLeod Bethune, Paul Laurence Dunbar, Frederick Douglass, and Michael Jackson in her biographies, which are often praised for their candor and depth. In addition, she is the author of several books on the history of civil rights; perhaps her most well known work in this area is *A Long Hard Journey: The Story of the Pullman Porter,* in which she outlines how a small group of porters formed the first black union in America. *A Long Hard Journey,* which quotes from primary and secondary sources including personal interviews and includes labor and railroad song texts and poetry at the beginning of each chapter, is considered both an authoritative history of its subject and an exciting story. McKissack is also noted for her histories of the Aztec, Mayan, and Inca Indians for early graders, works praised for filling the need for works on this subject for this age level. As an author of nonfiction, McKissack often includes controversial topics such as racism in her works; however, she is acknowledged as an even-handed writer whose presents information on sensitive issues in a balanced and calm fashion.

McKissack is also noted for her fiction, especially for her lightly nostalgic picture books set in the rural South. Blending fantasy and reality and written in Southern dialect, the works feature young black female protagonists whom observers consider especially appealing. McKissack has contributed to several series, including the nonfiction series People of Distinction and New True Books; for the Start-Off Stories series, she adapted several traditional tales, including "Cinderella," "The Three Billy Goats Gruff," and "The Little Red Hen" into condensed versions for beginning readers. A junior high and college teacher who is also an editor of children's books and an educational consultant on minority literature, McKissack has often collaborated with her husband, writer Frederick L. McKissack. In addition to her biographies, histories, picture books, and retellings, she has written several books on religious subjects, an informational book on insects, radio and television scripts, and articles and short stories in magazines for both children and adults. The McKissacks received the Coretta Scott King Award for *A Long*

Hard Journey in 1990, and McKissack has also received several awards for her religious works.

(See also *Something about the Author,* Vol. 51 and *Contemporary Authors,* Vol. 118.)

TITLE COMMENTARY

Martin Luther King, Jr.: A Man to Remember (1984)

For slightly older readers than Harris' *Martin Luther King,* this biography of the slain civil rights leader has a pedestrian appearance but an adequately written text. King's childhood, schooling, and activities as an organizer come through clearly; McKissack also recalls the cracks in the movement when King's philosophy of nonviolence seemed to fail against conditions in the North. News photos provide much of the illustration, but they're darkly reproduced. Useful supplementary material.

A review of "Martin Luther King, Jr.: A Man to Remember," in Booklist, *Vol. 81, No. 1, September 1, 1984, p. 68.*

In a biography that has considerable depth for this grade level, McKissack addresses King's relationship with other black leaders, movements, politicians and the FBI as well as allegations of Communism. King's uncertainties and concerns, particularly with the rise of Black Power, are portrayed in a way that makes his character understandable. Chapters are introduced with poems from various black authors that set the tone for what follows. A time line at the end places King in the perspective of world affairs. The book is well indexed and, if McKissack is somewhat in awe of her subject, the treatment is nevertheless reasonably balanced. Plenty of background material is included for readers to whom King is an historical, rather than contemporary, figure. While the principle use of his biography will be for reports, it is readable enough for anyone who wants to know about Martin Luther King and is a good complement to Haskins' *The Life and Death of Martin Luther King* (Lothrop, 1977).

> *Carolyn Caywood, in a review of "Martin Luther King, Jr.: A Man to Remember," in* School Library Journal, *Vol. 31, No. 2, October, 1984, p. 160.*

This is the most imaginative of the books reviewed [here]. The Introduction begins with a pertinent quote from "Letter from a Birmingham Jail," and each chapter is prefaced by a relevant poem by a Black poet, a quote from King's speeches or, in one instance, a quote from an unidentified Black grandmother who walked during the Montgomery boycott. This book humanizes King more than the others and does not dodge the issue of racism. All of the influences on King—his strong father and grandfather, his strong mother and grandmother, Morehouse College and the works of Frederick Douglass—are presented. McKissack also identifies other Civil Rights workers and such organizations as CORE and SNCC. A serious fault, however, is the omission of Ella Baker and her role in the development of SNCC.

> *A review of "Martin Luther King, Jr.: A Man to Remember," in* Interracial Books for Children Bulletin, *Vol. 16, No. 8, 1985, p. 5.*

Michael Jackson, Superstar! (1984)

The problem with writing about Michael Jackson is acknowledged up front by McKissack, who states that she has gathered materials on this intensely private superstar from newspapers, magazines, and previously written books. "This is the story of the 'public' Michael with a few of the glimpses of his inner world he has chosen to share." Those parameters are outlined nicely in this profile, which is more complete than Mabery's *This Is Michael Jackson*. The picture is definitely positive, with scant mention of Jackson family strife and with Michael's too-good-to-be-true image fully intact. Perhaps it's too much to expect a more analytical, clear-eyed view of the Jackson phenomenon. Right now, this presents the best quick profile yet.

> *Denise M. Wilms, in a review of "Michael Jackson, Superstar!" in* Booklist, *Vol. 81, No. 12, February 15, 1985, p. 847.*

This presentation of the superstar tries to validate Jackson as school subject matter. The preface apologizes for the necessary reliance upon secondary material, and it is followed by the usual juvenile biography components: a

chronological account, a fact summary and an index. The inclusions of an astrological symbol and "colors" for each of the Jackson brothers emphasize peculiarly subjective data in contrast to McKissack's no-nonsense narrative. All inside photographs are black and white, generally of the publicity variety, and are reproduced with varying degrees of graininess. Fans want up-to-the-minute fan magazines. Non-fans can probably find enough in very basic reference sources. This title is in neither category and therefore will be of limited use.

> *Dana Whitney Pinizzotto, in a review of "Michael Jackson, Superstar!" in* School Library Journal, *Vol. 31, No. 9, May, 1985, p. 92.*

Paul Laurence Dunbar: A Poet to Remember (1984)

In both [*Louisa May Alcott: Author, Nurse, Suffragette* by Carol Greene and *Paul Laurence Dunbar*], the authors treat their complex subjects with authority, respect and considerable objectivity. . . . The Dunbar biography is particularly well done. Dunbar's place in American letters is far less secure than that of Alcott's. His poetry—particularly that about slave life on Southern plantations written in black dialect, to which he owes his fame—has been criticized as "Uncle Tom" and overly idyllic. By painting a strong portrait of Dunbar's mother, a former slave, and the cheerful, positive attitude toward her experiences which she shared with her son, McKissack does much to explain Paul's perceptions. The author also makes a good case for the enduring value of Dunbar's dialect poetry, illustrating with excerpts and her own commentary the sensitivity and appreciation which Dunbar expressed for the language and the people who spoke it. On the other hand, McKissack (and critics generally) consider Dunbar's standard-English poetry to be derivative in style. Dunbar was born shortly after the Civil War, and this account of his life reflects how rapidly the status of Afro-Americans deteriorated as the century neared its close.

> *Tess McKellen, in a review of "Paul Laurence Dunbar: A Poet to Remember," in* School Library Journal, *Vol. 31, No. 7, March, 1985, p. 166.*

Mary McLeod Bethune: A Great American Educator (1985)

The biography of Bethune, a great educator, black leader and advisor to many, including Franklin D. Roosevelt, is a warm story that gives a good view of a slave's life both before and after slaves were freed. Bethune's talents are well described, but her humanness shows through. *Mary McLeod Bethune* (Crowell, 1977) by Greenfield is a simpler but also excellent story for grades two to five.

> *Deanna J. McDaniel, in a review of "Mary McLeod Bethune: A Great American Educator," in* School Library Journal, *Vol. 32, No. 7, March, 1986, p. 167.*

A serviceable biography of black educator Mary McLeod Bethune, this describes her early life as the first free-born child of her parents, who had been slaves until they gained their freedom following the Civil War. It also covers her struggle for the education her parents realized she was meant to have. "My life is one series of miracles," Bethune once told an audience, a tone that McKissack picks up on as she describes the pivotal events that allowed this young black woman to educate herself and build a school, which survives today as Bethune-Cookman College. Black-and-white photographs are sprinkled throughout, and a detailed list of dates puts Bethune's experience in context with world affairs.

> *Denise M. Wilms, in a review of "Mary McLeod Bethune: A Great American Educator," in* Booklist, *Vol. 82, No. 15, April 1, 1986, p. 1224.*

Aztec Indians; The Maya; The Inca   (1985)

It is a credit to these three titles that one can read them in succession and finish with a sense of the distinctive characteristics of three separate civilizations. Because of their brevity, however, the format does not serve these complex topics as well as it does other subjects covered by the [New True Books] series; a number of complicated issues are mentioned without adequate explanation—human sacrifices in Aztec and Mayan religious rituals, or the deciphering of Mayan hieroglyphs, for example. The books cover the daily life, religion, government and present-day descendants of their respective peoples; well-chosen color photographs give life to the texts. *The Inca* is particularly well organized, providing a brief but interesting overview of Inca life, including the societal concern for the collective welfare of the people. Less successful is *The Maya,* which begins with an uninteresting survey of the location of Mayan cities. The books do not convey to young readers the extraordinary accomplishments of these peoples in relation to their contemporaries in Europe. A good bit of interesting information is collected here nonetheless, and there are no comparable books available for this age level; Sonia Bleeker's works on the Maya (1961), the Inca (1960) and the Aztec (1963, all Morrow; all o.p.) are more informative, but they are for a slightly older audience. (pp. 74-5)

> *Rita Auerbach, in a review of "Aztec Indians," in* School Library Journal, *Vol. 32, No. 8, April, 1986, pp. 74-5.*

Easy-to-read text [of *Aztec Indians*] discusses the history, religion, language, customs, and final days of the Aztecs. Compared to many other young children's books in English about the Aztecs, this one should be singled out for not emphasizing the Aztec practice of human sacrifice and for including important Aztec achievements. Excellent color illustrations, including reproductions of murals by artist Diego Rivera as well as Aztec picture writing and photographs of Aztec objects, add immensely to the narrative. Inexplicably, two photographs from the Teotihuacan culture are included.

> *Isabel Schon, in a review of "Aztec Indians," in* The Reading Teacher, *Vol. 40, No. 1, October, 1986, p. 107.*

Cinderella; Country Mouse and City Mouse; The Little Red Hen   (with Frederick McKissack, 1985)

In their attempt to adapt these stories for beginning readers, the authors have condensed much of the content of the original tales. However, only in *Country Mouse and City Mouse* have details been altered significantly. The setting is the present, the story is told by the country mouse, and a noisy garbage truck frightens him away from the city. Each page of text contains one or more short, simple sentences with limited vocabulary. Following each story is a word list containing between 30 and 90 words. . . . [Because] of the lack of detail, some of the excitement of the original stories has been lost. It is as if the meat is missing from the sandwich, leaving only the bland taste of bread. (p. 82)

> *Joan Hamilton Bowman, in a review of "Cinderella," "Country Mouse and City Mouse," and "The Little Red Hen," in* School Library Journal, *Vol. 32, No. 9, May, 1986, pp. 81-2.*

Flossie and the Fox   (1986)

McKissack tells "a story from my youth, retold in the same rich and colorful language that was my grandfather's," a delicious reversal of Red Riding Hood that serves as parable of black outwitting white.

Flossie Finley is to carry eggs through the Tennessee forest to Miz Viola, watching out for the "ol' slickster" fox, who loves eggs. Flossie isn't scared, but "disremembers" ever seeing a fox, so when the fox introduces himself she remains unconvinced—through several delightful exchanges as the fox becomes more and more distraught at her lack of recognition ("I am a fox, and you will act accordingly." ". . . Unless you can show you a fox, I'll not accord you nothing!" and "I may never recover my confidence." ". . .You just an ol' confidencer"). The fox uses big, pretentious words, but Flossie's sly good humor gets him every time.

[Rachel] Isadora's watercolor, ink and pencil illustrations fully realize the spirit of the text, with Flossie's sturdy, self-reliant stance and the fox growing progressively more tentative and defensive. Mellow green, lemon, rust and earth tones fill a safe, sun-dappled world. A perfect picture book.

> *A review of "Flossie and the Fox," in* Kirkus Reviews, *Vol. LIV, No. 14, July 15, 1986, p. 1120.*

The watercolor and ink illustrations, with realistic figures set on impressionistic backgrounds, enliven this humorous and well-structured story which is told in the black language of the rural south. The language is true, and the illustrations are marvelously complementary in their interpretation of the events. This spirited little girl will capture readers from the beginning, and they'll adore her by the end of this delightful story.

> *Helen E. Williams, in a review of "Flossie the Fox," in* School Library Journal, *Vol. 33, No. 2, October, 1986, p. 164.*

Based on a story remembered from the author's childhood, this tale of wit triumphant from the black tradition

McKissack with husband and collaborator Frederick McKissack.

of the rural South—with its lilting cadence and colorful, carefully phrased dialect—fairly sings on the page. Exactly the right note of suspense carries the reader from page to page, as small Flossie Finley outsmarts a wily fox determined to steal her eggs by refusing to be scared until he proves that he is indeed what he claims to be. As he pridefully points out the various aspects of himself—luxurious fur, long pointed nose, sharp claws and yellow eyes, bushy tail—she cleverly compares each characteristic to that of another animal: rabbit, rat, cat, or squirrel. Totally discombobulated by her boldness in withholding the respect he thinks is his due, the would-be trickster—never suspecting that the innocent Flossie knows exactly what she is doing—is lured into accompanying her to her destination, where his plans are suddenly disrupted by a menacing hound. Although the text can stand alone as a wonderful example of folk literature, Rachel Isadora's handsome, full-color, double-boxed illustrations enhance and extend the plot, underscoring Flossie's triumph, suggesting the sinuous slyness of the fox, and capturing the splendor of sunlight gleaming on a path through the woods. . . . Well suited for picture-book hours, the book is a real charmer, thoughtfully crafted and carefully designed. (pp. 48-9)

> *Mary M. Burns, in a review of "Flossie & the Fox," in* The Horn Book Magazine, *Vol.*

LXIII, No. 1, January-February, 1987, pp. 48-9.

The Civil Rights Movement in America from 1865 to the Present (with Frederick McKissack, 1987)

The McKissacks present an extensive history of the civil-rights struggle in America with attention not only to blacks but to other minorities, as well as to women and children. The report begins with the aftermath of the Civil War, describing the social conditions and political climate that resulted in the first rights for blacks but shortly thereafter shifted to permit repressive, rights-curtailing laws to be enacted in the South. As the McKissacks move into the twentieth century, issues of child labor, women's suffrage, and the great immigration movements receive coverage. And through each twentieth-century presidency, the gains, setbacks, and major social and political currents are described. In appearance, this looks like a textbook. But the writing is brisk and straightforward, and the pages are plentifully illustrated with photographs and reproductions of old prints. Also appearing periodically are boxed time lines that review the major events within a certain period, and cameos that briefly profile the famous and not-so-famous individuals who have made notable contributions to the cause of civil rights. A lengthy but unannotated bibliography is appended, and there is an index. This should find heavy use in school and public libraries; it offers a well-defined overview of a subject that is a frequent topic of classroom study.

> *Denise M. Wilms, in a review of "The Civil Rights Movement in America from 1865 to the Present," in* Booklist, *Vol. 83, No. 19, June 1, 1987, p. 1525.*

Despite its focus on blacks, [this] presentation is admirably balanced with discussions of other minority groups, the handicapped, and roles played by whites in the translation and implementation of the U. S. Constitution and its Amendments. Despite the omission of the exact wording of these basic documents, some careless editing, and the book's text-like format, this book provides a broadened perspective of civil rights history, which makes it more useful than Jackson's *Blacks in America* (Watts, 1980; o.p.), Spangler's *The Blacks in America* (Lerner, 1980), or Winslow's *Afro-Americans '76* (Afro-Am, 1975; o.p.). Because it can be read and enjoyed as a straight narrative, public and school libraries will find the book useful.

> *Helen E. Williams, in a review of "The Civil Rights Movement in America from 1865 to the Present," in* School Library Journal, *Vol. 33, No. 11, August, 1987, p. 86.*

Frederick Douglass: The Black Lion (with Frederick McKissack, 1987)

The McKissacks supply a sympathetic yet balanced portrait of the Black Lion, as Douglass was called, as they chart the man's life from his birth as a slave through his death as an accomplished writer, orator, and leader in the antislavery movement. Each chapter begins with a quote from *The Life and Times of Frederick Douglass,* setting the scene for the event in Douglass' life that the authors are addressing. They describe tragedies as well as high points and discuss the times in which Douglass' strategies differed from others within the black movement, for instance, his falling out with his former mentor, William Lloyd Garrison. Although the authors are careful to identify their material and quotations in the body of their text, they have not included any source notes or bibliography. Scattered black-and-white line drawings are included and a chronology is appended. (pp. 482-83)

> *Barbara Elleman, in a review of "Frederick Douglass: The Black Lion," in* Booklist, *Vol. 84, No. 5, November 1, 1987, pp. 482-83.*

The King's New Clothes; Three Billy Goats Gruff (with Frederick McKissack, 1987)

[These] two titles reduce classic tales to vocabulary controlled texts that have the bare form but none of the embellishments of successful retellings. Andersen's *The Emperor's New Clothes* has been reduced to stilted sentences and phrases. "Look! The King has new clothes. Look! Look! The King has more new clothes. Look! Look! The King loves new clothes." The sinister tailors are reduced to being "bad men." This is a bland retelling of a classic once filled with rich language. McKissack's retelling of *The Three Billy Goats Gruff* is somewhat more palatable

as a story, but the predictable clash between troll and Very Big Billy Goat Gruff does not provide the oomph of the retellings illustrated by Marcia Brown (HBJ, 1957; o.p.) or Paul Galdone (Clarion, 1973). The clear, sharp colors of the illustrations [by Gwen Connelly for *The King's New Clothes* and by Tom Dunnington for *Three Billy Goats Gruff*] far outshine the texts. The multi-flounces, layers, and colors combined in the kings' gorgeous robes bring an elegance that is lost completely in the text. These cursory retellings will be readable, but with little, if any, meaning for those children whose prior experience does not include the traditional retellings.

> *Sharron McElmeel, in a review of "The King's New Clothes" and "Three Billy Goats Gruff," in* School Library Journal, *Vol. 35, No. 8, May, 1988, p. 86.*

Mirandy and Brother Wind (1988)

As a prefatory note explains, this picture book was inspired by a photo of the author's grandparents winning a cakewalk—"a dance rooted in Afro-American culture"— and her grandfather's boast that, in her dancing, his wife had captured the wind. In the book, Mirandy determines to catch Brother Wind and have him for her partner in the upcoming junior cakewalk. She tries a number of tactics springing from folk wisdom, and finally succeeds in trapping her prey in the barn. At the contest, Mirandy chooses to dance with her friend Ezel—but, with Brother Wind to do her bidding, the two friends win the cakewalk in style. Told in spirited dialect and rendered in lavish, sweeping watercolors [by illustrator Jerry Pinkney], this provides an intriguing look at a time gone by. As a story, however, it proves somewhat disappointing. After the colorful description of cakewalking in the author's note and the anticipation created through Mirandy's own eagerness, the brief and rather static scenes portraying the dance itself are a letdown.

> *A review of "Mirandy and Brother Wind," in* Publishers Weekly, *Vol. 234, No. 16, October 14, 1988, p. 72.*

As she did in *Flossie and the Fox,* McKissack has created in Mirandy a character full of vigor, humor, and imagination. Pinkney captures the liveliness of the story in his expansive paintings, dappled with impressionistic hues; these are prosperous, happy country folk of a few years ago. . . . The half-imaginary wind is shown, top-hatted, in evanescent blues. An entertaining, unusual story.

> *A review of "Mirandy and Brother Wind," in* Kirkus Reviews, *Vol. LVI, No. 21, November 1, 1988, p. 1607.*

The inspiration for this delightful book by Patricia C. McKissack was a photograph of her grandparents when they were teenagers, taken in 1906 after they had won a cakewalk contest. "It's never been difficult for me to imagine my grandparents strutting around a square with their backs arched, their toes pointed, and their heads held high," Ms. McKissack writes in an author's note. "They were full of life's joy . . . Papa used to say he believed Mama had captured the Wind. I believed it too."

Ms. McKissack will make believers of her young readers

as well. Her story, a tender tale of a young girl's first dance and her first shy brush with puppy love, is as filled with "life's joy" as the photograph she treasures. Jerry Pinkney's rich, detailed illustrations beautifully capture her grandparents' youthful good spirits. . . .

Although this is not a history book, the past lives within these pages. Ms. McKissack and Mr. Pinkney's ebullient collaboration captures the texture of rural life and culture 40 years after the end of slavery. From Brother Wind "high steppin' " across the first page to Ezel and Mirandy in "Sunday best" cakewalking across the last, each page of *Mirandy and Brother Wind* sparkles with life.

> *Valerie Wilson Wesley, in a review of "Mirandy and Brother Wind," in* The New York Times Book Review, *November 20, 1988, p. 48.*

Monkey-Monkey's Trick: Based on an African Folk Tale (1988)

The easy-to-read style of controlled vocabulary is well-suited to this repetitive trickster tale based on an African story (although no source is indicated). Hyena offers to help Monkey-Monkey build his new house, but Monkey-Monkey refuses, knowing Hyena is "full of tricks." But when the Beautiful Creature offers, Monkey-Monkey is grateful, even though he knows "someone who sings that way." And when the Ugly Monster steals the stew, Monkey-Monkey "knows someone who eats that way" but can't quite make the connection. Eventually, Monkey-Monkey manages to turn the trick on the trickster, who builds the house while the monkey, disguised as a zebra, "sat in the sun and watched." Simple and rhythmic enough to encourage chanting along, and full of enough twists to keep older kids interested. . . .

> *Roger Sutton, in a review of "Monkey-Monkey's Trick: Based on An African Folk Tale," in* Bulletin of the Center for Children's Books, *Vol. 42, No. 5, January, 1989, p. 129.*

Monkey-Monkey's Trick, based on an African folk tale, will appeal to both readers and listeners. Disguising himself as an Ugly Monster, Hyena has the upper hand until Monkey-Monkey learns that he has been tricked. Because Meisel's illustrations give viewers a glimpse of who is in disguise, the refrain, " 'I know someone who sings [eats / dances / laughs] that way,' thought Monkey-Monkey. 'But who?' " will encourage audience participation. Watercolor-and-pen illustrations supply ample context clues for young readers, who will enjoy practicing their reading skills to find out which animal is the best trickster.

> *Gale W. Sherman, in a review of "Monkey-Monkey's Trick," in* School Library Journal, *Vol. 35, No. 11, July, 1989, p. 68.*

Nettie Jo's Friends (1989)

McKissack, known for *Flossie and the Fox* and the more recent *Mirandy and Brother Wind,* joins forces with [illustrator Scott] Cook, who debuted last year with a painterly version of *The Gingerbread Boy.* Their combined talents in this book create a folktale that, if convoluted, has many

valuable points. Nettie Jo's mother is sewing her a new dress for a wedding. But Nettie Jo wants to make sure her doll, Annie Mae, has a new dress, too. She has the fabric, but with all the women preparing for the wedding, a sewing needle is scarce. So Nettie Jo leaves home to find her own needle, enlisting the help of a rabbit, a fox and a panther. The story aptly shows the power of a little imagination in creating solutions, and there is a fine piece of dramatic tension when Nettie Jo gets up the courage to face Panther. But the rest of the story unwinds without a definite sense of cause and effect; the animals race around—predator and prey—but their sudden attack of good manners is inexplicable. As for Cook, he again employs a technique that leaves shimmering streaks of paint on the page. But Nettie Jo's face, capable of great expression on some pages, seems almost frozen in others. The potential for excellence is here, but readers' expectations will remain mostly unfulfilled.

> *A review of "Nettie Jo's Friends," in* Publishers Weekly, *Vol. 235, No. 2, January 13, 1989, p. 89.*

Once again, McKissack has created a warm, faintly nostalgic story with roots in the rural South. Like the heroine of *Flossie and the Fox,* Nettie Jo is appealingly forthright and self-confident. The story is nicely patterned and repetitive, with a few surprising twists that add humor and a touch of drama. McKissack gracefully incorporates elements of fantasy into her otherwise realistic setting, creating a very child-like world in which magic is expected and accepted. As in her previous books, she displays a real feel for language. Her authentic Southern vernacular is rich and rhythmic with a natural flow that reads well aloud. Cook's illustrations are a perfect match for McKissack's story. The fluid lines and natural postures of his figures provide each character with an animated individuality. Warm-skinned Nettie Jo is especially attractive, depicted as a bright, sunny black child without any trace of cloying sweetness. The fuzzy, out-of-focus look of Cook's pictures supports and reinforces the fantasy of the story. . . . (p. 90)

> *Linda Boyles, in a review of "Nettie Jo's Friends," in* School Library Journal, *Vol. 35, No. 9, May, 1989, pp. 88, 90.*

This is a wonderful blend of folk and fantasy elements, enhanced by the folksy Southern dialogue between the characters, and the portrayal of the sprightly woodland creatures and handsome humans, in sepia tones, by the artist. *Nettie Jo's Friends* will be a welcome addition to the picture book or young reader shelves.

> *Barbara Rollock, in a review of "Nettie Jo's Friends," in* The Five Owls, *Vol. III, No. 5, May-June, 1989, p. 74.*

A Long Hard Journey: The Story of the Pullman Porter (with Frederick McKissack, 1989)

Covering a 150-year period, this sympathetic account successfully focuses on the efforts of a small group who sought to gain recognition for the Brotherhood of Sleeping Car Porters, the first black American-controlled union. Led by Asa Philip Randolph, better known to recent generations as the organizer of the 1963 march on Washington, this revolt is profiled in an approach that emphasizes the men's commitment and sacrifices during their intensive 12-year struggle. Early, uneven chapters cover the development of the sleeping car, the contrast between the porters' societal and communal status, and (the most engaging) railroad folklore. Quotations from primary and secondary sources, including personal interviews, are used in a text that is generally clear and competently organized.

> *Julie Corsaro, in a review of "A Long Hard Journey," in* Booklist, *Vol. 86, No. 2, September 15, 1989, p. 187.*

Based on primary sources (including interviews) as well as on published materials, a detailed account of the rise of the first black union and the conditions that made it necessary.

Whatever his motives, after the Civil War George Pullman offered newly emancipated men steady jobs on his luxurious Pullman cars; at first the porters took pride in their new status and were grateful. But it was soon clear that the long hours, low pay, and threat of lost jobs for the meanest of reasons (e.g., any response to harassment by racist passengers) were neither fair nor tolerable. In 1894, Eugene Debs made an abortive attempt to unionize the railroad, excluding blacks; but it was left to A. Philip Randolph to lead the long fight for recognition. His efforts to organize the Brotherhood of Sleeping Car Porters, begun in 1925, finally bore fruit when its first contract with a corporation was signed in 1937.

This is not only a chapter in black history or labor history; it's also a stern reminder of the perennial struggle against arrogant power and unenlightened self-interest. The McKissacks' narrative, though not always smooth, is clear and dramatic. Bibliography of sources.

> *A review of "A Long Hard Journey: The Story of the Pullman Porter," in* Kirkus Reviews, *Vol. LVII, No. 20, October 15, 1989, p. 1532.*

[This] is a story of conflict—between wage earners and a corporate giant. (p. 303)

Although in-depth investigations into historical events such as this are important and provide a background for understanding later events, I doubt that many middle and junior high schoolers will find the topic of interest or worth their time. This is not so much the story of the Pullman porters as it is their legal struggle for fair wages and working conditions. (pp. 303-04)

> *Judy Druse, in a review of "A Long Hard Journey," in* Voice of Youth Advocates, *Vol. 12, No. 5, December, 1989, pp. 303-04.*

An exciting labor history, as well as a stirring narrative of a side of the civil rights movement that youngsters know little about. . . . The text is liberally peppered with personal reminiscences including those of the "Women's Auxiliaries," who kept the union alive when company spies kept tabs on their husbands and brothers. A nice added touch is the use of poetry and labor and railroad song texts as chapter headings. The book is illustrated with well-reproduced black-and-white historical photographs, and has an attractive cover. In all, an excellent introduction to the subject.

> *Rosanne Cerny, in a review of "A Long Hard Journey: The Story of the Pullman Porter," in* School Library Journal, *Vol. 36, No. 1, January, 1990, p. 125.*

A Troll in a Hole   (with Frederick McKissack, 1989)

In *A Troll in a Hole,* a boy tries to get help for a troll stuck in a hole. A message passed from character to character becomes more and more scrambled, until the final message has nothing to do with the troll or the hole. The book has severe problems. There are mixed-up phrases that will not be comprehensible to emerging readers; they will have difficulty with much of the vocabulary even in its conventional form and will not understand the intended humor. In fact, some of the sentences are so complex that even experienced readers may wonder what the author is trying to convey.

> *Sharron McElmeel, in a review of "A Troll in a Hole," in* School Library Journal, *Vol. 35, No. 15, November, 1989, p. 78.*

Jesse Jackson: A Biography   (1989)

Charismatic, energetic, and articulate, Jesse Jackson has also been accused of unscrupulous ambition, as in the case of his using Martin Luther King Jr.'s assassination to further his own career by appearing almost immediately afterwards on the Today Show. To her credit, McKissack mentions the controversies that have dogged Jackson's activities, including the financial scandal attached to Operation Breadbasket, but she champions him candidly: "while SLCL's high council refused to make a comment, Jesse was trying to stop the senseless death and destruction" after King's death. Occasionally the tone is adulatory, as in the implication that Jackson's advocacy is responsible for the drop in sickle cell anemia rates. However, the information is factually solid without becoming too detailed, and, in spite of a few stylistic flaws, the text is accessible and easy to read. Although it would have been helpful for students doing research to have source notes included, especially for quotes, there is a bibliography and index. Illustrated with black-and-white photographs, this a guaranteed choice for reports on U.S. political leaders.

> *Betsy Hearne, in a review of "Jesse Jackson: A Biography," in* Bulletin of the Center for Children's Books, *Vol. 43, No. 4, December, 1989, p. 89.*

While McKissack's respect for Jackson is evident in her writing, she is not afraid to deal with the less than pleasant episodes of Jackson's life. Both his alleged mishandling of organizational funds and his "Hymie-town" remark are discussed. On the other hand, McKissack points out that while a white person might be portrayed as being "promising, inspired and dilligent," this often translates into being "uppity, audacious and arrogant" when describing a black person. Amply illustrated with black-and-white photographs, the book nicely updates Dorothy Chaplik's *Up With Hope* (Dillon, 1986) and Ann Kosof's *Jesse Jackson* (Watts, 1987).

> *Tom S. Hurlburt, in a review of "Jesse Jack-*

son: A Biography," in School Library Journal, *Vol. 35, No. 16, December, 1989, p. 114.*

There may be no one in American public life who engenders deeper, more divergent feelings than the Rev. Jesse Jackson. Some dismiss him as an anti-Semite, unworthy of the high office he has sought. Some, though aware of the historic significance of his Presidential campaigns, see him as an opportunist. Others gauge the degree of anxiety he seems to generate among some whites—and figure he must be doing something right.

Patricia C. McKissack has done an admirable job of evoking these disparate views of a driven and compelling man in her book, *Jesse Jackson: A Biography.* The author of more than 20 books for children, Ms. McKissack knows how to capture the attention of young readers. Opening with an image of Mr. Jackson's stunning victory in the 1988 Michigan Presidential primary, she establishes him immediately as a man who is used to defying expectations: "Some political analysts . . . insist that he is 'unelectable.' " His primary win "is a victory for him and America. Jackson's win shows that inner city blacks and suburban whites can rise above racial prejudices."

In covering the crucial points of Mr. Jackson's life and career, Ms. McKissack paints a vivid picture of the combination of religious and political commitment that has always been key in African-American public life. She is especially adept in transmitting for young people the loneliness of the outsider, a feeling all too real for the young Jesse Jackson. And in tracing Mr. Jackson's move to Chicago from North Carolina, she depicts with insight and clarity the face of Northern racism.

Most of all, she is conscious of Mr. Jackson's status as a role model for young people, and writes of both his successes and his shortcomings with refreshing candor. The complex story she tells may seem at odds with the simplicity of the language she uses. At first glance, it may seem the book is meant for an intelligent student in the middle grades. But Patricia McKissack is excellent at conveying sophisticated themes and ideas, so that *Jesse Jackson: A Biography* can be read with pleasure by both children and young adults.

> *Rosemary L. Bray, in a review of "Jesse Jackson: A Biography," in* The New York Times Book Review, *February 25, 1990, p. 32.*

Taking a Stand against Racism and Racial Discrimination (with Frederick McKissack, 1990)

[*Taking a Stand against Human Rights Abuses* by Michael Kronenwetter and *Taking a Stand against Racism and Racial Discrimination* are two] fine titles in a new series [which] provide information on crucial issues of social responsibility. They give historical background with brief accounts of some important leaders, urge young people to "take a stand," and tell them how to get actively involved. . . .

[The] McKissacks have done several books that deal with civil rights. Like Kronenwetter, their tone is quiet, their approach informed, candid, and evenhanded. The best section is based on their interviews and group discussions with high school teens of various racial and socioeconomic backgrounds. In fact, this section calls out for expansion, especially the lists of "problem attitudes" in students and teachers, which raise complex issues of self-hatred, denial, euphemism, condescension, etc., as well as the more overt racism of name-calling and jokes. The authors argue persuasively that open discussion is positive and that different doesn't mean inferior or threatening.

Both books have a clear, readable design, with much white space and many subheads; they include photographs, source notes, a bibliography, a list of organizations, and an index.

> *Hazel Rochman, in a review of "Taking a Stand against Racism and Racial Discrimination," in* Booklist, *Vol. 86, No. 17, May 1, 1990, p. 1691.*

Posy Simmonds

19??-

English author and illustrator of picture books.

Major works include *Fred* (1987), *Lulu and the Flying Babies* (1988).

A satirist and newspaper cartoonist whose weekly strips for the *Manchester Guardian* and other papers and cartoon collections for adults such as *True Love* (1981) and *Pick of Posy* (1982) have made her recognized as an especially observant parodist of English middle class life, Simmonds is a recent contributor to the field of children's literature whose two humorous picture books, *Fred* and *Lulu and the Flying Babies,* are often praised for their cleverness and charm. Combinations of reality and fantasy which demonstrate Simmonds's flair for social commentary, both books are considered engaging spoofs with appeal for all ages. *Fred,* the story of a cat whose double life as a beloved house cat by day and a famous rock singer by night is discovered by his young owners, is praised for exploring the subject of death in a touching and amusing manner. In *Lulu and the Flying Babies,* small Lulu, forced into a museum against her will by her parents because of the needs of her baby brother, is taken into several paintings from a variety of periods by two cherubs, one of whom pops out of a painting and the other off of a pedestal. Considered an especially delightful introduction to art museums, *Lulu and the Flying Babies* is also noted for providing both a pointed look at High Art and a sympathetic view of sibling rivalry. Simmonds, whose art is often compared to Raymond Briggs, illustrates her books with colorful pictures in a cartoonlike style using line, crayon, and dialogue balloons. Her illustrations for both stories include details that show young observers how the fantasy experienced by her child characters has slipped into reality and is oblivious to the adults in her works; at the close of *Lulu,* for example, a butterfly that has escaped from a still life remains fluttering in the museum.

TITLE COMMENTARY

Fred (1987)

For her first children's book, Posy Simmonds has set herself a doubly difficult task: to make a cat the principal character without thereby becoming whimsical, Gothic or a soft number for pet-lovers; and to write about death, a topic on which most children's literature, as Empson would say, has been prepared to stay blank. Cats and death do not make the most obvious of combinations . . . It is a tribute to Posy Simmonds's originality that she makes a match of such strange bedfellows.

Fred himself—fat, furry, domesticated—is a more familiar bedfellow, asleep perpetually on wall, fridge-top and ironing board, "the laziest cat in the world" according to his child-owners Sophie and Nick. When he dies the children feel sad but are hard pressed to find words for his gravestone: as far as they know, he "did nuffing" all his life except the occasional "wees" in the flowerbed. It comes as a surprise, then, when, after Fred has been buried under the buddleia, Mrs Spedding's Ginger—togged out in digital watch, top hat and mourning garb—discloses the history of Fred's other existence once put out at night. The Tom Jones of tomcats . . . , he had been "the greatest singer in the world", wowing and miaowing them in alleys and backyards with his group The Heavy Saucers. Hence the packed-out, rock-star's funeral service over which Mrs Spedding's Ginger presides . . . , the lavish wreaths laid on Fred's grave, and the noisy wake (with sardine and fishbone delicacies) among the local dustbins.

Sophie and Nick observe all this wide-eyed: *Fred* belongs to the genre of the night-ride, the children escaping the known world in an adventure which overturns their tidy assumptions about animal (and human) behaviour. The book's format, largely comic strip but with occasional full-page drawings, is one which bears the hallmarks of Posy Simmonds's *Guardian* column, but readers of Raymond Briggs's work may also be struck by certain similarities: when the children creep downstairs past their sleeping parents there is an eerie echo of *The Snowman.* But the adventure stays close to home, the fantasy element is restrained, and the ending has no truck with the convention

243

that all might have been "just a dream": far from being returned to daylight normality, the house, the garden, even Fred's gravestone are transformed by what has happened during the night. It is a benevolent ending, but not a woozily ambiguous one.

Posy Simmonds has flourished for so long now, by the standard of most newspaper cartoonists, because of a capacity to go on defeating our expectations: where we, as readers, might clamour for more George Weber or Edmund Heep, she has gone on experimenting, and in the process has developed baroque and allegorical forms to offset or contain her social realism. There is no lack of the latter quality in *Fred:* the uncharming but charmingly observed children, horribly convincing in their mixture of companionship and squabbling ("Hey, you got more than me"); their gangling liberal parents; the gentrified urban setting. But it is in the funeral train and ceremonial cat-mourning that the book is most richly imaginative and best exploits an operatic tendency which is coming increasingly to figure in Posy Simmonds's work.

> *Blake Morrison, "Under the Buddleia," in* The Times Literary Supplement, *No. 4383, April 3, 1987, p. 357.*

[A. N. Wilson's] *Stray* is as much an adult's book as a children's book, like all the best 'children's literature'. Posy Simmonds' *Fred* is another such. My children pounced on this brilliantly accomplished picture book, my six-year-old son insisting on reading it aloud from cover to cover several times. . . . The story works perfectly, and the drawings are full of acute observation and spot-on humour. I loved it. (p. 39)

> *Nigel Andrew, "Raining Cats and Dogs," in*

From Lulu and the Flying Babies, *written and illustrated by Posy Simmonds.*

The Listener, *Vol. 118, No. 3038, November 19, 1987, pp. 39-40.*

Told in cartoon-like panels of line and crayon with dialogue (sometimes in bold print) in balloons, this is an off-beat tale which veers toward the macabre on occasion, and it is difficult to determine its focus. There is not enough depth of feelings to use it as a tool in comforting a grieving pet-owner, yet there isn't enough humor—except for highlighting the differences between cats and people—to justify that aspect as the premise for the story. In addition, Nick's lapses into baby talk are annoying, particularly as he appears to be well out of the toddler stage and has an otherwise adept vocabulary. Marginally amusing, but this is one you can put outside at night—with the cat. (pp. 76-7)

> *Kathleen Brachmann, in a review of "Fred,"* in School Library Journal, *Vol. 34, No. 4, December, 1987, pp. 76-7.*

Now this *is* a real book . . . a real book being one that is multi-layered, that offers something to any reader, child or adult, and that gives you far more than at first appears. *Fred* qualifies absolutely. . . . All I can say is rush out and buy it even if you haven't so much as a baby to give you an excuse. This strip cartoon format story of the demise of Fred the family moggie is an absolute delight. Full of pathos, wildly funny, touching and comforting, it will intrigue, entertain and amuse. The detail in the drawings and the absolutely right characterisation of both people and cats are matched by an original and thoughtful storyline. There are few comic books that could also help one to come to terms with death. This is one. Don't miss it.

> *Liz Waterland, in a review of "Fred," in* Books for Keeps, *No. 58, September, 1989, p. 9.*

Lulu and the Flying Babies (1988)

Lulu is angry: Dad is taking her on an outing, but baby Willy in his backpack gets all the attention and forces them out of the falling snow and into the museum. There, she goes on strike and shouts so obstreperously that Dad leaves her sitting under a painting, sniffing. A cherub in the painting advises against picking her nose, another (on a pedestal) chimes in, and the two join her on a tour: they play in the snow in a Dutch landscape, splash in an impressionist sea, growl at a Rousseau tiger, and nibble fruit from still lifes.

The old sibling-rivalry plot is mixed delightfully here with an inspired introduction to art museums. Simmonds' illustrations convey the domestic contretemps with sympathy and wit; her renditions of the works of art catch their essence nicely and incorporate the invasion of the toddlers with appropriate humor. The welcome that Lulu gets from her little brother and the final scene of the happy cherubs telling a guard all about their adventure make a satisfying conclusion to a charming story.

> *A review of "Lulu and the Flying Babies," in* Kirkus Reviews, *Vol. LVI, No. 20, October 15, 1988, p. 1534.*

In *Lulu and the Flying Babies* Posy Simmonds again demonstrates her clever journalistic flair for spotting a middle-class movement. Taken by her father to the museum, Lulu throws a tantrum ("NAOWH. Not coming in *here!*") because she would rather play in the snowy park. While she is happily fiddling with her nose, a putto suddenly pops out of a grandiose painting ("That's *filthy!*") and another marble putto climbs down from a pedestal. Together they swing Lulu up in the air (just as two adults swing a child up between them) and then fly her in and out of the paintings.

In this modern adaptation of the *Through the Looking Glass* theme Lulu and her putti friends play in the snow in a seventeenth-century Dutch winterscape, splash in the warm blue sea in a naive summery painting of the Breton school, eat the fruit in a still-life, creep up on a Douanier Rousseau tiger and climb into a formal equestrian portrait to offer the horse some crisps. Although pre-reading children may not yet have heard of Europa and the Bull, Bacchus or Neptune, they will laugh when Lulu describes the putti parents to an art gallery attendant: "Well . . . his mummy's wearing a pink nightie and she's riding a *cow* . . . and his daddy's got a big *fork* and *grapes* on his head . . ." With an eye for the ludicrousness of High Art worthy of Osbert Lancaster, Posy Simmonds will probably make readers of all ages putti in her hands.

Alexandra Artly, "Socializing Scenes," in The *Times Literary Supplement, No. 4469, November 25, 1988, p. 1321.*

This is Posy Simmonds's second comic-strip book published for children, but like her earlier *Fred,* it can appeal to any age. Three-year-old Oliver read it with me and relished Lulu's early whining as she is dragged to the art gallery. He was enchanted by the flying babies of the title, who 'come alive' and leave their respective works of art to escort Lulu through various famous paintings. He had no problem with the idea that you can steal cherries from a still life and spit the stones out down a craggy mountainside in the next painting along. Older children identify the sibling rivalry, the playful fantasy element and one or two of the paintings as well. What the new book shares with *Fred* is a taste of that invaluable reading experience where we, as readers, know something that the adult characters don't know. Here the butterfly, escaped from a still life, is still fluttering round the edges of the page as Lulu goes home through the snow with her unwitting father. The immense satisfaction is re-experienced at every reading. A book to put alongside Mike Dickinson's *Smudge.* . . .

Judith Graham, in a review of "Lulu and the Flying Babies," in The Signal Selection of Children's Books, 1988, *The Thimble Press, 1989, p. 8.*

CUMULATIVE INDEX TO AUTHORS

This index lists all author entries in *Children's Literature Review* and includes cross-references to them in other Gale sources. References in the index are identified as follows:

AAYA: *Authors & Artists for Young Adults* Volumes 1-4
CA: *Contemporary Authors* (original series), Volumes 1-131
CANR: *Contemporary Authors New Revision Series,* Volumes 1-30
CAP: *Contemporary Authors Permanent Series,* Volumes 1-2
CA-R: *Contemporary Authors* (revised editions), Volumes 1-44
CDALB: *Concise Dictionary of American Literary Biography,* Volumes 1-4
CLC: *Contemporary Literary Criticism,* Volumes 1-63
CLR: *Children's Literature Review,* Volumes 1-23
DLB: *Dictionary of Literary Biography,* Volumes 1-95
DLB-DS: *Dictionary of Literary Biography Documentary Series,* Volumes 1-7
DLB-Y: *Dictionary of Literary Biography Yearbook,* Volumes 1980-1988
LC: *Literature Criticism from 1400 to 1800,* Volumes 1-13
NCLC: *Nineteenth-Century Literature Criticism,* Volumes 1-29
SAAS: *Something about the Author Autobiography Series,* Volumes 1-8
SATA: *Something about the Author,* Volumes 1-60
TCLC: *Twentieth-Century Literary Criticism,* Volumes 1-39
YABC: *Yesterday's Authors of Books for Children,* Volumes 1-2

Author Index

CUMULATIVE INDEX TO NATIONALITIES

Nationality Index

ENGLISH
Adams, Richard **20**
Ahlberg, Allan **18**
Ahlberg, Janet **18**
Aiken, Joan **1, 19**
Ardizzone, Edward **3**
Ashley, Bernard **4**
Awdry, W. V. **23**
Base, Graeme **22**
Bawden, Nina **2**
Bianco, Margery Williams **19**
Bond, Michael **1**
Boston, L. M. **3**
Briggs, Raymond **10**
Brooke, L. Leslie **20**
Browne, Anthony **19**
Burningham, John **9**
Burton, Hester **1**
Caldecott, Randolph **14**
Carroll, Lewis **2, 18**
Chauncy, Nan **6**
Christopher, John **2**
Cooper, Susan **4**
Corbett, W. J. **19**
Cresswell, Helen **18**
Dahl, Roald **1, 7**
de la Mare, Walter **23**
Doherty, Berlie **21**
Farmer, Penelope **8**
Gardam, Jane **12**
Garfield, Leon **21**
Garner, Alan **20**
Gerrard, Roy **23**
Goble, Paul **21**
Godden, Rumer **20**
Grahame, Kenneth **5**
Greenaway, Kate **6**
Handford, Martin **22**
Hill, Eric **13**
Howker, Janni **14**
Hughes, Monica **9**
Hughes, Shirley **15**
Hughes, Ted **3**
Hutchins, Pat **20**
Jacques, Brian **21**
Jones, Diana Wynne **23**
Lear, Edward **1**
Lewis, C. S. **3**
Lively, Penelope **7**
Lofting, Hugh **19**
Macaulay, David **3, 14**
Mark, Jan **11**
Milne, A. A. **1**
Nesbit, E. **3**
Norton, Mary **6**
Oakley, Graham **7**
Ottley, Reginald **16**
Oxenbury, Helen **22**
Pearce, Philippa **9**
Peyton, K. M. **3**
Pienkowski, Jan **6**
Potter, Beatrix **1, 19**
Pullman, Philip **20**
Ransome, Arthur **8**
Serraillier, Ian **2**
Sewell, Anna **17**
Simmonds, Posy **23**
Streatfeild, Noel **17**
Sutcliff, Rosemary **1**
Tenniel, Sir John **18**
Townsend, John Rowe **2**
Travers, P. L. **2**

Treece, Henry **2**
Walsh, Jill Paton **2**
Westall, Robert **13**
Wildsmith, Brian **2**
Willard, Barbara **2**
Williams, Kit **4**

FILIPINO
Aruego, Jose **5**

FINNISH
Jansson, Tove **2**

FRENCH
Berna, Paul **19**
Brunhoff, Jean de **4**
Brunhoff, Laurent de **4**
Guillot, Rene **22**
Saint-Exupery, Antoine de **10**
Ungerer, Tomi **3**

GERMAN
Benary-Isbert, Margot **12**
d'Aulaire, Edgar Parin **21**
Ende, Michael **14**
Heine, Helme **18**
Kastner, Erich **4**
Kruss, James **9**
Rey, H. A. **5**
Rey, Margret **5**
Richter, Hans Peter **21**
Zimnik, Reiner **3**

GREEK
Aesop **14**
Zei, Alki **6**

HUNGARIAN
Galdone, Paul **16**
Seredy, Kate **10**

INDIAN
Mukerji, Dhan Gopal **10**

IRISH
O'Shea, Pat **18**

ISRAELI
Shulevitz, Uri **5**

ITALIAN
Collodi, Carlo **5**
Munari, Bruno **9**
Ventura, Piero **16**

JAMAICAN
Berry, James **22**

JAPANESE
Anno, Mitsumasa **2, 14**
Iwasaki, Chihiro **18**
Maruki, Toshi **19**
Say, Allen **22**
Tejima **20**
Watanabe, Shigeo **8**
Yashima, Taro **4**

NEW ZEALAND
Mahy, Margaret **7**

NIGERIAN
Achebe, Chinua **20**

NORWEGIAN
d'Aulaire, Ingri **21**

POLISH
Hautzig, Esther R. **22**
Pienkowski, Jan **6**
Shulevitz, Uri **5**
Singer, Isaac Bashevis **1**
Suhl, Yuri **2**
Wojciechowska, Maia **1**

RUSSIAN
Korinetz, Yuri **4**

SCOTTISH
Bannerman, Helen **21**
Barrie, J. M. **16**
Burnford, Sheila **2**
Stevenson, Robert Louis **10, 11**

SOUTH AFRICAN
Lewin, Hugh **9**

SPANISH
Sanchez-Silva, Jose Maria **12**

SWEDISH
Beskow, Elsa **17**
Bjork, Christina **22**
Gripe, Maria **5**
Lagerlof, Selma **7**
Lindgren, Astrid **1**
Lindgren, Barbro **20**

SWISS
d'Aulaire, Edgar Parin **21**
Duvoisin, Roger **23**
Spyri, Johanna **13**

WELSH
Dahl, Roald **1, 7**

WEST INDIAN
Guy, Rosa **13**

CUMULATIVE INDEX TO TITLES

Title Index

Title Index

Title Index